Mussolini and his Generals

This is the first authoritative study of the Italian armed forces and the relationship between the military and foreign policies of Fascist Italy from Mussolini's rise to power in 1922 to the catastrophic defeat of 1940. Using extensive new research, John Gooch explores the nature and development of the three armed forces; their relationships with Mussolini and the impact of his policies and command; the development of operational and strategic thought; and the deployment and use of force in Libya, Abyssinia and Spain. He emphasises Mussolini's long-term expansionist goals and explains how he responded to the structural pressures of the international system and the contingent pressures of events. This compelling account shows that while Mussolini bore ultimate responsibility for Italy's fateful entry into the Second World War, his generals and admirals bore a share of the blame for defeat through policies that all too often rested on irrationality and incompetence.

JOHN GOOCH is Professor of International History at the University of Leeds. His previous publications include *Army, State and Society in Italy*, 1870–1915 (1989) and, with Eliot A. Cohen, *Military Misfortunes: The Anatomy of Failure in War* (1990, 2006).

Cambridge Military Histories

Edited by

HEW STRACHAN, Chichele Professor of the History of War, University of Oxford and Fellow of All Souls College, Oxford

GEOFFREY WAWRO, Major General Olinto Mark Barsanti Professor of Military History, and Director, Center for the Study of Military History, University of North Texas

The aim of this new series is to publish outstanding works of research on warfare throughout the ages and throughout the world. Books in the series will take a broad approach to military history, examining war in all its military, strategic, political and economic aspects. The series is intended to complement *Studies in the Social and Cultural History of Modern Warfare* by focusing on the 'hard' military history of armies, tactics, strategy and warfare. Books in the series will consist mainly of single author works – academically vigorous and groundbreaking – which will be accessible to both academics and the interested general reader.

Titles in the series include:

Mussolini and his Generals

The Armed Forces and Fascist Foreign Policy, 1922–1940

John Gooch

University of Leeds

CAMBRIDGE
UNIVERSITY PRESS

CAMBRIDGE UNIVERSITY PRESS
Cambridge, New York, Melbourne, Madrid, Cape Town, Singapore, São Paulo

Cambridge University Press
The Edinburgh Building, Cambridge CB2 8RU, UK

Published in the United States of America by Cambridge University Press, New York

www.cambridge.org
Information on this title: www.cambridge.org/9780521856027

First published 2007

Printed in the United Kingdom at the University Press, Cambridge

A catalogue record for this publication is available from the British Library

ISBN   978-0-521-85602-7 hardback

Contents

Illustrations

Acknowledgements

The first of my many debts is to the Trustees of the Leverhulme Foundation, whose award of a major research grant made it possible to carry out the work which is the foundation of this book. Their generosity made it possible for me to employ Dr Robert Mallett as my research assistant and without his energetic labours in the archives in Rome I should not have undertaken and would never have been able to complete such an ambitious task. Additional financial support provided by the British Academy Small Grants Fund and by the School of History of the University of Leeds enabled me to complete the research and to purchase essential microfilms.

Working in Rome has always been the greatest of pleasures, thanks in large part to the kindness and hospitality of the officials in charge of the archives there. My first – and most long-standing – debt is to successive heads of the Archivio Storico dello Stato Maggiore dell'Esercito, most recently colonel Massimo Multari and colonel Matteo Paesano, for their unstinting help and support and to lieutenant-colonel Filippo Capellano, *dottore* Alessandro Gionfrida and the staff at Via Lepanto for their warm welcome and friendly assistance. Work at the Archivio Storico della Marina Militare was carried out with the encouragement and aid of admiral Renato Sicurezza and admiral Mario Buracchia, and *dottoressa* Ester Penella was an invaluable fount of advice, assistance and (at the most welcome moments) *caffè*. Colonel Euro Rossi, head of the Ufficio Storico dell'Aeronautica Militare, gave me the warmest of welcomes and I have greatly benefited from and much appreciated the help of lieutenant-colonel Carlo Cipriani and lieutenant-colonel Giancarlo Montinaro in guiding me through an archive which has suffered particularly heavily from the ravages of war. *Dottore* Andrea Visone graciously consented to my consulting the archive of the Ministero degli Affari Esteri, and *dottoressa* Stefania Ruggeri and *dottoressa* Laura Lamia helped me to grapple with the complexities of its bureaucracy. The staff of the Archivio Centrale dello Stato in EUR are models of patient assistance and the authorities who run it deserve the highest plaudits for their enlightened policy in respect of its opening hours.

In Florence the gods of fortune have smiled on me. My valued friendship with a fellow military historian, Count Niccolò Capponi, has allowed me not only to consult the archive of his grandfather but also to enjoy the hospitality of his generous and delightful family. To Count Neri and Countess Flavia Capponi I can only say a heartfelt thank you. In Vicenza, *dottore* Mauro Passerin's kind assistance helped me make the most of a visit to the Museo del Risorgimento e della Resistenza.

Every historian owes a debt to those who have preceded him, none more so perhaps than one who ventures into foreign fields. My first debt in this regard is to the doyen of Italian military historians, professor Giorgio Rochat, whose gentle and necessarily distant encouragement over many years has been more than matched by his personal generosity. Professor Lucio Ceva has been no less kind and supportive, and the friendship of professor Piero del Negro and professor Nicola Labanca has enabled me to participate in more than one gathering of the small but convivial band of Italian military historians. In Rome, *dottore* Ciro Paoletti has fulfilled the multiple roles of comrade, guide, advisor and chauffeur to perfection. In London, professor MacGregor Knox has unhesitatingly agreed to every request to support a grant application as well as sharing invaluable source materials with me, and in Washington Dr Brian Sullivan has provided me with a home from home, a library which I have been able to plunder at will, and an apparently bottomless fund of knowledge about the matters of professional interest which first brought the three of us together and now unite us as friends.

My last debts – but by no means my least – are to my editors, professor Hew Strachan and professor Geoff Wawro. Along with Michael Watson, Elizabeth Howard, Helen Waterhouse and Gwynneth Drabble at Cambridge University Press, their support, advice and help have contributed greatly to a final product whose imperfections are my responsibility alone. David Appleyard of the Graphic Support Unit at the University of Leeds drew the maps.

Grazie a tutti.

John Gooch

Abbreviations

AA. VV.	Various authors
ACS	Archivio Centrale di Stato
all.	allegato [attached]
ASAM	Archivio dell'Ufficio Storico dell'Aeronautica Militare
ASMAE	Archivio Storico del Ministero degli Affari Esteri
AMR	Archivio dei Musei del Risorgimento e di Storia Contemporanea del Comune di Milano, Civiche Raccolte Storiche
att.	attached
AUSSME	Archivio dell'Ufficio Storico dello Stato Maggiore dell'Esercito
AUSMM	Archivio dell'Ufficio Storico della Marina Militare
b	busta
c	cartella
CSMG	Capo di stato maggiore generale
DBFP	*Documents on British Foreign Policy*
DDI	*I Documenti Diplomatici Italiani*
DGFP	*Documents on German Foreign Policy*
f	folio
fasc.	fascicolo
fr	frame
HNA	Hungarian National Archives
MRR	Museo del Risorgimento e della Resistenza, Comune di Vicenza
N	*numero*/number
n	*numero*/number
OO	*Opera Omnia di Benito Mussolini*
racc.	raccoglitore
Rep.	repertorio
Scat.	scatola

sf.	Sottofascicolo
SHAT	Service historique de l'armée de terre, Vincennes
T.	telegram
To.	Telespresso
UKNA	National Archives (UK)

Frontispiece: Mussolini with marshal Pietro Badoglio

Able, ambitious and self-promoting, marshal Pietro Badoglio became
the leading military personality in Fascist Italy. A Piedmontese soldier
of the old school, loyal to the king above all else and therefore
something of a potential threat to Mussolini, he was made chief of the
armed forces' general staff in 1925, a post he held for the next fifteen
years whilst simultaneously serving for part of the time as
governor-general of Libya (1928–33). His task was to co-ordinate the
war preparations of the armed services, though after only two years
Mussolini reduced both his status and his powers. Regarding war
against Britain and France as potentially disastrous for Italy, Badoglio
oversaw fitful attempts at co-ordination in such a way as to make it
difficult still to know whether he was skilfully resisting Mussolini's
policies or cynically going through the motions of doing his job.

Map 1. Central Europe

Map 2. South East Europe and the Balkans

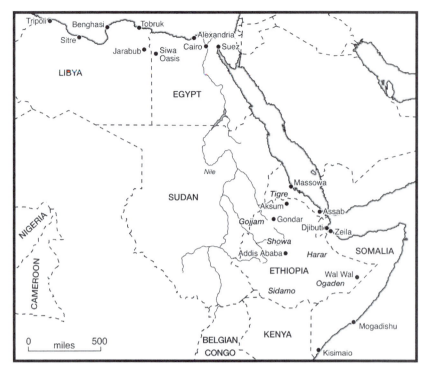

Map 3. Ethiopia and its neighbours

Introduction

Fascist foreign policy has been the object of intensive scrutiny by historians ever since the regime collapsed – and indeed before it did so – but no consensus has yet emerged as to its goals or its fundamental characteristics. Anglo-Saxon historians, led by Denis Mack Smith and Donald Watt, have until recently tended by and large to see it as a gigantic bluff carried out by a blustering and incompetent poseur, the keys to whose character and make-up are to be found in a propensity for violence which was apparent in his early years, in his choice of journalism as a *métier*, and in the twists and turns of a political career apparently bereft of any principle save the acquisition and maintenance of power. Renzo De Felice, Mussolini's foremost Italian biographer, and his pupils present a very different picture. In their eyes Mussolini was an industrious and politically adroit realist who sought for as long as possible to 'balance' between the rising power of Nazi Germany on the continent and the extant power of Great Britain to control the seas that surrounded it. War – outside the confines of Italy's colonies – was not central to his plans and war with England something not sought or even accepted as in due course inevitable, but forced upon him. When a European war broke out in September 1939 it was unexpected and at that moment unwelcome. For the next nine months or so he waited, calculating that he would not have to fight because the Germans were doing the job for him and hoping to expand his 'Roman Empire' on Hitler's coat-tails. In June 1940, believing that the collapse of the western democracies was imminent, Mussolini pounced.[1]

While the history of Italy's foreign policy between 1922 and 1939 is well known and strongly contested ground, that of her armed forces is, for most English-speaking readers at least, more or less unknown territory. The view that bluff was the defining feature of Fascism provides an explanation which unites the leading English historian of the older school with the doyen of Italian military history. For Denis Mack Smith, it was not a shortage of resources which was chiefly responsible for the military inadequacies of Fascism, but the fact that the money was spent on the wrong things: 'grandiose fascist buildings. . . sports stadiums, barracks and splendid parades'. In the hollow world of Fascist posturing, the Duce's need to manipulate the armed forces had deleterious consequences which magnified and even institutionalised their shortcomings. Particularly, the need to ensure that the high command caused him as little trouble as possible led him to appoint a series of lickspittles who offered no danger of opposition – and no hope of reform and regeneration – because they possessed little or no initiative.[2] Giorgio Rochat for his part sees an army not intended for war at all but one designed and maintained to suppress domestic political opposition. Because it was unfit for war – a charge which could certainly and with some justice be extended to cover the air force and perhaps the navy as well – Mussolini pursued a policy 'which backed imperialistic ambitions not with force, but with propaganda and bluff'.[3]

The full nature, extent and causes of the military 'bluff' – if indeed that is quite what it was – upon which Mussolini's aggressive ambitions relied have remained largely unplumbed. Some advances in our understanding have occurred. Latterly the less than dazzling performance of the three services during the Second World War has, not unsurprisingly, focused attention on their many shortcomings and led scholars to delve into the inter-war years in an attempt to identify both the nature and the causes of their deficiencies.[4] However, in many respects the picture remains skeletal. Nor has much been done to examine in detail the strands of foreign and military policy in Mussolini's Italy in order to explore their relationship and assess the extent and nature of the responsibility borne by those on both sides of the politico–military divide for the position in which Fascist Italy found itself in June 1940. Discarding bluff as an unnecessary and unconvincing explanation, MacGregor Knox has suggested that the answer is to be found in institutionalised military incompetence deriving primarily from the recruitment, traditions and training of the military. When set alongside the picture of an 'intentionalist' Mussolini who saw war as the means by which to achieve his long-term goals, the catalogue of failures and inadequacies which in 1940 condemned the armed forces to defeat answers some questions but raises others.[5]

What follows, then, is an attempt to marry two hitherto largely separate approaches to the history of Fascist Italy in order to see how they fit – or do not fit – together and to explain why things happened as they did and produced the outcomes they did. Since it would be impossible to attempt such a task without clearly coming down somewhere in the contested ground of Fascist foreign policy, I have perforce had to develop my own picture of what that policy was. Any claim it may have to originality perhaps lies in a strategic approach to the analysis of the international scene from Rome's point of view which puts more emphasis on the smaller Mediterranean and Balkan powers than is often the case. I have also paid more attention to the incoming intelligence on which Rome could draw in making policy than is commonly given to it. As far as Mussolini goes, I take the view that he was single-minded and brutal but also politically competent and certainly not a fool; had he been, he could not have maintained his domestic position so effectively for almost two decades. Like Stalin his calculations were rational, though their rationality was not that of a Chamberlain or an Eden. The armed forces over which he presided developed under many pressures. Each had its own character, purpose, strategic outlook and leadership – gifted or otherwise. All three services had to accommodate themselves to Fascism and to its leader, a task which they undertook with differing degrees of enthusiasm and one which was profoundly affected by their leader's conceptions of his role and theirs.

1   The beginning of the Fascist era, 1922–1925

Fig. 1 Mobilising the nation: female Fascist soldiers

As Italy entered the First World War, Mussolini identified the spiritual preparation of the population as one of the 'co-efficients' of victory. By the time that he came to power he was fully convinced that the psychological mobilisation of the nation was every bit as important as its physical mobilisation. The militarisation of society which he oversaw, and which was purveyed in images such as this, had two purposes. On the one hand it was an act of propaganda directed at Italians and foreigners alike to show them that Italy was ready for war. On the other, it was a practical act designed to ready the Italian people for the war he expected to come.

Mussolini, military power and the goals of foreign policy

As a young man, Benito Mussolini was by instinct, upbringing and inclination entirely out of sympathy with the Liberal state and with the army which served it. He was, however, far from being a pacifist, as his violent childhood and adolescence went to prove. A native of the 'red' Romagna and the son of a radical socialist, he combined as a youth the ideals of an anarchist with the enthusiasms of a militant nationalist; in 1898, at the time of the Greco–Turkish war and then aged fifteen, he dreamed of fighting with Amilcare Cipriani's legione garibaldina to free Crete from its oppressors. Having returned to temporary exile in Switzerland in December 1903 partly in order to avoid conscript service, he bowed to his mother's wishes eleven months later and came back to fulfil his military obligations under the terms of a general amnesty for military deserters proclaimed to celebrate the birth of prince Umberto. Between January 1905 and September 1906 he served with the 10th Bersaglieri stationed at Verona, participating with enthusiasm in the everyday life of the army and earning the accolade in his leaving certificate that he had always distinguished himself 'for capacity, zeal and excellent (*ottima*) conduct'.[1]

Passing from Marxist socialist to interventionist in 1914, Mussolini was called up with his class of reservists on 31 August 1915. For eighteen months he served in the front line, earning promotion to corporal but failing to pass officer candidate school, almost certainly because of his background of subversive socialism. The experience impressed upon him the 'mechanical' nature of industrial war (something of which he did not altogether approve), the courage of the rank and file and the importance of national discipline if the nazione armata was to triumph.[2] On the Carso in February 1917, he was seriously wounded when a mortar exploded during ranging fire, killing five of his companions. After five months in hospital, he was sent on convalescent leave which was to be extended until the end of the war.[3]

Mussolini's reading of Italy's experience in the world war in which he had participated – albeit to a limited extent – led him to conclude that the key to victory lay in the superiority of mass armies that were not mere inert instruments of the high command but were morally as well as physically mobilised for war – the *massa cosciente* ('conscious mass'). The nation standing behind them must be militarised to provide the maximum moral and material support. Weapons were by no means to be neglected – in August 1918 he called for 'more men and more fire' – but not all of them met the needs of the Italian front; 'elsewhere machines are enough,' he argued, 'here machines are needed but above all men'.

The 'mental fossilisation' of the general staff earned his disdain, particularly because it failed to recognise, as Napoleon had done, that speed of manoeuvre was the key to victory. Defeat at Caporetto had finally changed Italy's war for the better, leading to improvements in the morale and material conditions of the army which reflected an identity of outlook between army and nation that had not existed before. Once in power, however, he characteristically shifted his position and decided that the recovery of 1918 had not been due to the institution of a more liberal regime but to the imposition of 'the necessary discipline of war'.[4]

In both military matters and foreign affairs Mussolini was untrained and technically quite unprepared, learning as he went along in a process of self-education. His military education, such as it was, appears to have come largely from reading, from which he took the lessons he wanted. In 1933, he cited Marshal Gallieni's *Carnets* to justify taking over the war ministry for a second time when faced, like its author, with the absolute ignorance of a backward general staff; and he found in Joffre's *Memoirs* both evidence of a decisive 'Fascist style' and useful lessons on how to remedy the defects of a high command paralysed by peacetime routines and 'excessive scholasticism'.[5] After the Second World War, and in circumstances in which they had much to explain, his generals broadly agreed on his talents as a supreme commander. General Mario Roatta, head of SIM during the early 1930s and an adroit if unscrupulous operator in a world of manipulators, claimed that '(T)he substance, the true essence of military questions, escaped him completely'.[6] General Ubaldo Soddu, deputy chief of the army general staff and then under-secretary of state for war in the later 1930s and a convinced Fascist, had seen at first hand an intuitive genius at synthesis – 'or pseudo-synthesis' – who despised technical experts in general and soldiers in particular, who used military history as a source of anecdotes about great captains, and yet who despite all his defects had 'a genuine strategic mind'.[7] In foreign affairs, where his skills could make him an effective interlocutor on the international stage, Mussolini proved a rapid learner but one whose style was less appreciated abroad than at home.[8]

To his early domestic critics and to some historians, Mussolini's foreign policy in these years operated according to no discernible and considered plan; rather, it seemed 'more like a random and unco-ordinated striking-out in all directions in the hope of scoring points on the cheap'.[9] In fact, although he did not run it along the polished grooves of traditional diplomatic practice, Mussolini's foreign policy was neither as random nor as unfocused as it has sometimes been made out to be. The broad motive forces driving it were well established in his political credo by 1922. Aggressive nationalism deriving in part from the concurrence of an 'unfinished' Risorgimento and a 'mutilated peace' was joined to a reinvigorated imperialism which would surpass the very limited achievements of pre-war Liberal Italy. 'Imperialism', he declared on New Year's Day 1919, 'is the eternal and immutable law of life'.[10] Historical strategic, economic and commercial considerations on the one hand and the view that the Versailles settlement was a transitory state of affairs on the other pointed in two directions: to the Mediterranean and its eastern and southern shores, and to central and south-eastern Europe.

Behind this general façade, at least four strands can be identified which both shaped his foreign policy and inter-acted with military policy. In the first place, Mussolini came to power with a basket of specific territorial objectives which had included Trieste, Fiume and Dalmatia, as well as a more general intention to expand Italy's influence in the eastern Mediterranean and the Danubian basin. These goals were inter-meshed with a profound enmity for all Slavs which was shared by some of his diplomatic and military advisers and which was to be evident in both domestic and foreign policy in succeeding years.[11] Then, he found himself in office and in power – though in international terms Italy possessed little of the latter – at a time of considerable flux in international relations when the great powers were imposing territorial settlements on former enemies (Turkey), former allies (Greece) and newcomers to the international cast list (Yugoslavia) alike. Circumstances thus dictated a focus on the immediate which, though doubtless not uncongenial, was also unavoidable. The practical consequence was captured in a phrase of one of his diplomats which struck a chord with him: 'One makes policy in the circumstances of the present while taking account of the immediate future.'[12]

Since the Paris Peace Treaty had been imposed by the victorious Allied powers, the immediate goal in practising foreign policy was, as Mussolini told the chamber of deputies on 16 November 1922, parity of treatment for Italy with Great Britain and France. This was part of a third strand of foreign policy in these years: the maintenance of an international position that was, as he put it to the ministerial council in March 1923, 'as autonomous as possible'. Mussolini was therefore ready to use opportunities presented by the shifting chessboard of European diplomacy to co-operate with France in specific matters, even though in some respects her goals were antipathetical to his, but not to form an alliance with her.[13] Unsympathetic to the League of Nations from its inauguration as too democratic, he initially proffered pre-war coin in the shape of alliances and pacts. However, this reflected neither a belief in international balance nor a commitment to negotiation. Rather it was the selection of one diplomatic tool among many to be used for the purpose of strengthening

Italy's international standing and gaining preponderance in regions that were vital to her development as a major power. The uncertainties and readjustments of European politics in the post-war decade offered the opportunity to manipulate differences and divisions abroad in ways not unlike those Mussolini used at home.[14]

The final strand in Mussolini's early diplomacy was a willingness to contemplate, and on one occasion to use, naval and military force. In three of the four cases in which he did so during his earliest years in power, the possibility that France would be unable to help his intended victim was a central strategic consideration. In February 1923, he asked the heads of the navy and the army whether they could set up supply dumps to help Corsican separatists who he believed were about to rebel against France and form a legion of Corsican volunteers from the Italian army to lend a hand. After receiving a negative response from general Diaz, Mussolini was forced to suspend the idea 'at least for the moment'.[15] In the case of the occupation of Corfu in September 1923, traced below, there was not very much distance between Mussolini's preference for permanent occupation and the navy's readiness to hold the island 'as a pledge of reparations for current and anticipated Greek provocation'.[16] Here the Greek government's refusal to accept Italian ownership of the Dodecanese Islands, ceded to Rome by the Treaty of Lausanne in 1923, until May 1924 was probably the bridge linking the navy's strategic interest in the eastern Mediterranean with Mussolini's diplomatic appetite. Another factor in play which may have encouraged him to undertake his only overt use of force was the apparent instability and aggressiveness of the Greeks which might isolate them in the diplomatic community: on several occasions during the first half of 1923 he believed that they were about to go to war with Turkey again.[17]

France's near isolation as a result of her occupation of the Ruhr meant that she was in no position to support Yugoslavia when Mussolini effected what was to all intents and purposes the annexation of Fiume on 16 September 1923, three days after announcing the Italian evacuation of Corfu. This removed any significant risk of war – though Stresemann for one feared that Rome might be going to start one.[18] Had Mussolini been faced with the choice of war, and had he opted for it, then the navy's strategic stance – explored below – would in all likelihood have led it to follow him with a degree of enthusiasm, provided always that it did not have to face the Royal Navy. The fourth and final episode involving the real or apparent threat of Italian force in these years came in May–June 1924 when reports of Italian troop concentrations suggested that Mussolini might be contemplating war with Turkey. Italian interest in Turkey's defences persisted into the following year and tension in the region was not ended for a further eighteen months.[19] In this case, Mussolini was preparing to act on the coat-tails of a great power: having first mistakenly been led to believe that Italy might get the entire League of Nations mandate for Mesopotamia, he then waited to see whether a dispute between London and Ankara over the *vilayet* of Mosul would bring the two powers to blows.[20]

France was crucial to Mussolini's diplomatic calculations – and, as has been seen, to his military ones too. Before coming into office, Mussolini had hoped by offering either an alliance or a revived continental bloc based on the wartime alliance to take advantage of France's need for protection and support vis-à-vis Germany. Once in office he was acutely aware of the need to hold France and Germany apart so that Italy did not suffer exclusion or disadvantage in foreign affairs.[21] While there was no immediate danger on this front, France's military and diplomatic policy in eastern Europe presented him with potential obstacles that could frustrate his own policy goals. The voting of substantial credits and loans for war materials to Poland (400,000,000 francs) and to the 'Eastern alliance' of Czechoslovakia, Romania and Yugoslavia (300,000,000 francs) during 1923 strengthened a network of client powers, one of which was Slav.[22] The head of another, president Beneš, wanted to reunite Austria and Hungary under Czech sway – a policy which collided with Mussolini's ambition to build a Romanian–Bulgarian–Hungarian grouping on which to stand Italian domination of the Danube basin.[23]

During his first eighteen months in office Mussolini was able to take advantage of France's immediate need for international support in her campaign to force reparations from Germany. His support for president Poincaré's actions in occupying the Ruhr on 11 January 1923 in pursuit of German payments produced a valuable diplomatic return when France helped him extricate himself from the Corfu crisis in September 1923 by putting the matter to the conference of ambassadors, where she could exercise a strong influence, and not to the Council of the League of Nations. France's attitude was also crucial in persuading her junior partner, Yugoslavia, to accept Italy's permanent possession of Fiume under the terms of the Italo–Yugoslav pact of neutrality and friendship (the Pact of Rome) agreed on 27 January 1924. Although clothed in language which stressed the similar circumstances in which Rome and Belgrade found themselves and their need to ensure a free play to secure their respective interests, the Pact of Rome was in reality an attempt to break the Little Entente.[24] However, this was only a limited success and broader changes to Italy's advantage did not transpire. In particular, hopes that France was coming adrift from Great Britain as London oriented herself more closely towards Germany in pursuit of a secure route across the continent towards Asia – supposedly the result of the threat posed by French submarines and aircraft to Britain's passage through the Mediterranean and the calculation that a future French union with Italy 'however far distant' would cut off her route to the east – turned out to be a chimera.[25]

The advent of a radical left and socialist government in France in May 1924 brought to office a regime of whose immediate professions of continued friendship the Italian ambassador was somewhat sceptical, although he reported signs that France might be looking for military accords in case her relations with Germany grew worse.[26] By late June, relations were breaking down: as well as ongoing unresolved issues over the rights of Italian nationals living in Tunisia, Italy faced mounting public demonstrations of hostility as a result of the Matteotti murder which the government was unable to check. It appeared strange to ambassador Romano that Paris seemed unaware that this situation was more dangerous for France than for Italy, whose help she might need 'in decisive and historic circumstances'.[27] It was against this background that in late 1924 the Italian navy learned of the French naval statute and the Italian army discussed and rejected the Di Giorgio reforms.

Mussolini's advent to office coincided with a change of personnel at Italy's embassy in Berlin. Among the first despatches to land on his desk was a lengthy and extremely pessimistic report from the outgoing ambassador, Frassati. France, 'with an army highly experienced in war (*agguerritissimo*) and always ready to march', currently enjoyed a hegemony in Europe unequalled in history. Her goal was to divide Germany. If she then added to the Ruhr and the Saar the resources of west Germany and Upper Silesia, she would control almost all the coal and iron in Europe 'and will dictate her wishes to the entire continent'. The disappearance of Germany would then leave Italy with no room to manoeuvre in any other orbit. Frassati also stressed the economic costs to Italy of Germany's precipitous decline, which included loss of an agricultural market, an outlet for emigration, and a source of repatriated savings.[28] The upheavals in Bavaria during 1923 involving Kahr and Hitler, closely observed by Italian diplomats, served to confirm the state of indeterminate chaos in which Germany existed until Stresemann's three administrations at the end of the year helped crush Hitler's *putsch* and put an end to the runaway inflation which had so alarmed Frassati. The future might belong to the nationalists – and if it did there would be a frightful civil war and probably a French invasion – but the present appeared to Italian diplomatic observers to belong to the social democrats. However, Stresemann's violent attacks on the French proved only transitory, and neither of the ambassador's suppositions – that he would disappear as a failure or would be courageous enough to align himself with the nationalists who were 'the only hope for Germany' – was to transpire.[29]

Mussolini's interest in Germany as an active ingredient in his foreign policy was stirred by the Corfu crisis, and in mid-September 1923 he asked ambassador De Bosdari to sound out Stresemann on Germany's position in the event of an Italo–Yugoslav war in which France supported Belgrade. The reply was emphatic: given the need to solve the economic problems, there was no likelihood of Germany becoming involved in any way. The issue was not one of armaments, De Bosdari believed; Germany had enough aeroplanes and explosives left over from the war, and though she lacked guns and rifles her industrial capacity was almost intact and could without difficulty be reconstructed. Rather, the source of reticence was to be found in 'the moral and political state of the country'.[30] With no help to be expected from Stresemann's coalition either with regard to Yugoslavia or his schemes for the Danube basin, and encouraged by contacts from the nascent Stahlhelm, Mussolini now looked to the nationalist Right for tendencies which might be cultivated to his advantage.

An approach to general Hans von Seeckt, head of the Reichswehr, in November revealed the depth of anti-French feeling in the army. Von Seeckt declared that he regarded a war with France as inevitable and likely to happen soon, and expressed interest in reaching a concrete agreement with Italy. However, the Italian naval attaché who was serving as the ambassador's intermediary in the affair found 'a certain reservation' (*diffidenza*) in German military circles as to whether a common programme of action with Italy against a third power was practically possible.[31] The Italo–Yugoslav accord brokered by France in January 1924 removed the immediate need for German support and Mussolini broke off the talks.[32] The exact nature of the military power Germany might put on the table was in any case not quite what De Bosdari suggested, as the Italian military attaché reported at the end of 1923: although she had some six million men who had undergone wartime service, she was so short of weapons and equipment that she could only field at most thirty divisions and they would lack weapons of the quality needed for a modern army on a war footing.[33]

Despite his ambassador's reports, Mussolini was sufficiently encouraged by the direct approach from the Reichswehr to look further into the possibilities of military collaboration with Germany. In the spring of 1924, general Luigi Capello was despatched to Berlin, where he had conversations with leading military figures including general Ludendorff and general von Seeckt. Capello reported that the Germans still strongly wished for a war of revenge against France but were short of arms and hoped that the Italians might make up the gaps. However, he warned

Mussolini, in essence German national psychology had not changed despite their experiences in the war and its aftermath: 'at bottom they are still the pre-war Germans: self-infatuated and domineering'. It would be a good idea to remain aware of this fact if Italy had to deal with them.[34] When word of these discussions reached Stresemann's ears De Bosdari denied all knowledge of them, but in reporting the conversation to Mussolini he raised the question as to whether it was either advisable or prudent to continue to send such emissaries as long as the government in office was so opposed to the nationalist parties. The Duce backed off, scribbling on the despatch '*Si – non ne andranno piu*' ('Yes – no more of them will go').[35] With Stresemann heading for Locarno and amity with Britain and France, the German card would have to be laid aside for the foreseeable future.

While Italy's European policies did not overtly clash with those of Great Britain, her interests and adventures in the eastern Mediterranean raised the spectre of future naval rivalry. The worst case scenario was put succinctly in the autumn of 1922 by the Italian naval attaché at Constantinople, who distrusted Britain's preference for the neutralisation of the Straits and favoured a militarily strong Turkey as a check on Greece: 'The essential thing at this moment is to remove the danger that the Mediterranean is transformed into an English sea, which will one day face us with the dilemma either of starving or of following England unreservedly.'[36] In the aftermath of the Corfu episode England increased her naval strength in the Mediterranean by moving a division of the Atlantic fleet there, stationing the battle-cruisers *Hood, Repulse,* and *Renown* at Gibraltar and sending a floating dock to Malta so that the *Hood* would not have to return to Liverpool or Rosyth for careening.[37] Simultaneously Della Torretta – who like his fellow ambassadors in Paris and Berlin distrusted Great Britain – warned that it was unrealistic to think that London would disinterest herself in Greece which was one of the fundamental bases of her Mediterranean policy.[38] However, with Rome in collaborative mode over Franco–German hostility and reparations payments and London prepared to cede Jubaland to Italy in 1924 and to agree mutual delimitation of the Libyan–Egyptian border the following year, Anglo–Italian rivalry remained latent for the moment.

While Mussolini manoeuvred between the great powers and sought to manipulate or overawe the lesser ones, some of the configurations of later Fascist foreign policy began to settle into place. For the moment, however, ambition and appetite had both to be reined in. Fascist Italy, like the Liberal Italy which had preceded it and which was now being cast aside, was still 'the least of the Great Powers' – if indeed it was a great power at all. To raise it to the status he desired, and to achieve his goals, Mussolini needed force to press home whatever advantages he could conjure up on the international stage. This was the lesson of Corfu. In the early years, in different ways and for different reasons, none of his three armed services was in a sufficient state of readiness or efficiency to allow him to force the diplomatic pace.

Army, state and party politics

The legacies which the Italian army brought with it into the post-war years were powerful, complex and conflictual. Officially lauded as the instrument of the Risorgimento and the loyal standard-bearer of Italy's *re galantuomo*, king Vittorio Emanuele II, it carried a pre-war record that was in truth less than glittering. Defeated at Custoza in 1866 – a defeat which, as one of its most senior figures acknowledged, 'weighed upon it like a leaden cloak' – it had had to magnify the importance of the five hours of somewhat desultory military action which had led to the fall of Rome on 20 September 1870 and the final territorial unification of Italy. Its military record had been further undermined by the catastrophic débâcle which overtook it at the battle of Adua on 1 March 1896, the heaviest defeat ever suffered by a European army at the hands of non-white opponents during the age of imperialist expansion, and its conquest of Libya in 1911–12 had been only a limited success, extending not much beyond the Mediterranean littoral. The expansion of the Piedmontese kernel of the officer corps as other armies were amalgamated with it after 1861 produced bitter divisions at the higher levels between 'northerners' and 'southerners' which lasted for forty years. From the same moment, a contest began over the 'true' military legacy of the Risorgimento in which the Right's claims that the Piedmontese army had won the *guerra regia* ('royal war') were challenged by the Left's assertion that Garibaldi and his volunteers had triumphed in the *guerra di popolo* ('people's war').[39]

Both the course and the outcome of the world war added to the army's sense that its achievements and its virtues were not appreciated either by the politicians or the people at large, and that a growing gulf existed between itself and a society in which the industrial proletariat and the socialist party were becoming ever more powerful. Under the coercive command of general Luigi Cadorna, a ferocious disciplinarian who had more than one man in six in the army tried for military crimes and shot 750 soldiers, as well as sacking 217 generals and 225 colonels in 29 months, the army fought 11 gruelling battles on the Isonzo between 1915 and 1917 before being completely overwhelmed and almost broken at Caporetto on 24 October 1917. Cadorna went into retirement blaming the defeat on the indisciplined nature of the country at large – by which he meant the socialists – which had infected the army at the front. The echoes of the battle rumbled on into the next decade as a political debate about whether the defeat had been a military strike or a bid for a separate peace ran alongside a military one about what share of the blame fell on the shoulders of Cadorna's subordinates, Luigi Capello and Pietro Badoglio.[40] Under its new commander, Diaz, the army fought defensively until June 1918 before concluding the war with a successful battle at Vittorio Veneto in late October, a success many seemed inclined to under-rate in view of the contemporary collapse of Bulgaria and Austria–Hungary. Of the 5,500,000 men who served in the army during the war, official statistics indicated that 571,000 died and 451,645 were wounded.

Italy's army emerged from the world war swollen to more than twice its peacetime size: the pre-1915 army of twenty-five infantry divisions and three cavalry divisions had expanded to sixty-five infantry and four cavalry divisions, along with additional alpini battalions, assault units, artillery and air squadrons, and the permanent officer corps had increased from some 16,000 to 22,000, two thirds of whom were lieutenants and captains. Demobilisation, although slower than many wished, reduced the standing army from 3,760,000 in December 1918 to 1,578,000 in July 1919 and 552,000 by 1 December 1919.[41] Faced with economic depression and burdened by the costs of the war, parliament needed to economise. Accordingly, during 1919 it fixed the size of the peacetime army at thirty infantry divisions, suspended all promotions (a freeze that was not ended until 1924), and created a new 'special auxiliary' position for officers with lower pay rates and the requirement to serve for an additional four years before reaching pensionable age. In April 1920, needing to make yet further cuts in expenditure, parliament reduced each infantry regiment from three to two battalions, and cavalry regiments from five to three or four squadrons, and shrank the size of the officer corps from 18,900 to 15,000. The cuts hit the junior officers proportionately harder than majors, colonels and generals, and matters grew worse during the following year as officers' pay was reduced by 4 per cent, another 2,400 officers were transferred to 'special auxiliary service', and the length of time an officer could serve in that position was reduced to ten years. An officer corps accustomed to neglect or unnecessary bureaucratic interference before the war saw the pattern being repeated with a vengeance by the post-war Liberal governments and grew increasingly resentful and, at lower levels, disaffected.[42]

As well as feeling the frustrations of rule by a parliament whose liberalism was apparent when the Nitti government amnestied deserters in 1919 and whose determination to exercise civil control (only one pre-war minister of war had been a civilian) amidst parliamentary turbulence resulted in ten different war ministers serving in office between January 1919 and October 1922, the army also felt frustration at the foreign policy pursued by the Liberal administrations. After the war, its main ambitions were to hold on to Fiume, to maintain a presence in Albania and to gain access to the resources of the Caucasus and Asia Minor. Nitti's decision to accept the Allied demands to reduce the garrison of Fiume in August 1919, and Giolitti's withdrawal of all Italian troops from Albania in August 1920 in the face of a local insurgency and a mutiny among troops waiting at Ancona to go across the Adriatic to Valona, grated with a military leadership which had drawn up plans for the destruction of Yugoslavia in December 1918 and had proposed an Italo–Hungarian alliance against her to Horthy in November 1919. The decision at Rapallo to abandon claims to Fiume and desert a city which D'Annunzio had seized to great popular acclaim on 12 September 1919 generated a hatred of Great Britain, France and the United States, notably on the part of chief of the general staff, Pietro Badoglio; and Turkish aspirations evaporated when, as part of the preliminaries to the Treaty of Lausanne, the last Italians withdrew from Adalia in June 1921.[43]

Out of sympathy with the Liberals, and facing mounting social disorder as factory occupations and agricultural strikes broke out in the summer of 1920, the army increasingly aligned itself with the conservative Right. In the restoration of order which followed, the blackshirts of the recently formed Fasci di combattimento, some members of which had been part of the government's electoral lists in administrative elections in October 1920, were a useful tool for the government and for the army; but while their leader's declarations that the Italian people must be expansionist and that Italy was the power destined to direct all European politics from the Mediterranean were an agreeable contrast to the government's capitulation to the dictates of Italy's former allies, his domestic agenda was less reassuring. In May 1921, after having won thirty-five seats in the general election, Mussolini declared that while the Fascists did not intend to be a substitute for the republican party, 'nor do we have any intention of kneeling before the throne'.[44] When the Partito nazionale fascista was founded in Rome on 7–8 November 1921, its programme called for the permanent subordination of the army to the interests of the nation. Mussolini also promised to create a permanent party militia, and the following February the party executive transformed its squadristi into a paid paramilitary force. To an army steeped in loyalty to the kings of the house of Savoy and which believed that it alone had the right to bear arms in defence of the state, the nascent Fascist party represented a potential threat on two fronts.

While Fascist violence escalated, reaching its apogee during the first half of 1922, the army fought a political battle of its own against a government whose interference in military affairs was growing increasingly unacceptable. In November 1919 general Albricci presented proposals for an army of 210,000 men and a 12-month period of conscription.

The following year Ivanoe Bonomi, the first civilian war minister since 1908, proposed reducing the army to 175,000 men and imposing an 8-month term of conscript service, changes which would cut 300,000,000 lire off an annual military budget of 1,500,000,000 lire. Bonomi was then replaced by Luigi Gasparotto who brought with him yet another plan: the *forza bilanciata* ('budgetary force') would remain at 175,000 men a year, but military service would now be reduced to eight months. Gasparotto's plan hinged on providing extensive pre-military training, which parliament was not prepared to approve. In November 1921, the war minister proposed a further reduction of the army to 205,000 men in 20 divisions.

The parliamentarians were contributors to what was a widespread debate about the future of military Italy. The fact that in 1919 both the king, in his speech on the opening of parliament, and Mussolini in his Fascist party programme had endorsed the idea of the *nazione armata* revealed that very different meanings could be given to a term which appeared to embody the lessons of the world war. Military conservatives opposed a short-service militia type structure of the type favoured by left-wing civilian ministers for a mixture of professional, social and political reasons. Cadorna summed up their fears: 'I believe that a nation in arms will lead to a nation disarmed.'[45] Seeking to balance issues of quality versus quantity, some professional commentators favoured a small, technologically well-equipped force. Their best-known spokesman, general Roberto Bencivenga, came up with the concept of a *lancia e scudo* ('lance and shield') force: a small manoeuvre army of 150,000 men in 15 permanent divisions which would guard Italy's frontiers, providing the time needed to train recruits and manufacture equipment, while also able to strike outside Italy if needed.[46]

In January 1921, Bonomi had persuaded the senior generals to approve the abolition of the post of chief of the general staff, replacing it with an army council presided over by general Diaz, victor of the battle of Vittorio Veneto and the most prestigious figure in the active army.[47] Between November 1921 and June 1922, the newly created council debated the government's proposals. Starting from the premise that the period of military service *(leva)* could not 'for political and social needs' be more than twelve months, the army council decided that the entire annual contingent should be liable to call-up and that the only exceptions, other than a three-month period of service for those who were the main supporters of families, should be for people who had undergone appropriate pre-military training. Reserves should be called up for training for twenty days at least once during the first five years after they left the standing army. The resulting calculations produced a 'budgeted force' of 250,000 men a year, of whom 219,000 would be doing 12-month service,

24,000 would be doing only 3-months (equivalent to 6,000 full-time), and 25,000 would be permanent regulars. The latter group was 'absolutely indispensable with a *ferma* (period of regular military service) reduced to twelve months'.[48] The size of the peacetime army was ineluctably linked to that of the wartime one. The army council believed that sixty divisions were necessary 'to guarantee the national territory', of which thirty-six would be rapidly deployed along the land frontier; each wartime division would be formed from a peacetime brigade, of which there must be at least forty-two.[49]

Faced simultaneously with the need to retain parts of the class of 1901, due for release during 1922, as a result of the public order situation and to make economies by reducing the number of units detached from barracks, the army council stuck determinedly to its guns, telling the war minister that 'a smaller framework could perhaps respond equally well to the peacetime duties of the army, but it would not guarantee the training, mobilisation, or strength necessary (*sufficiente*) for war'.[50] When the minister announced in June that he intended to reduce the 'budgeted force' for 1922/3 to 210,000 men, the army and the government were on a collision course. The army council responded by informing the government that unless they got the 250,000 men they requested 'the army would be put in a situation where it could no longer meet requests for troops for non-military [i.e. policing] duties'.[51] While it recognised that certain elements of military organisation legitimately fell within the budgeting framework, it believed that the number of divisions necessary in wartime was 'independent' of it, being determined by 'the political and geographical conditions of Italy and by the composition of those large units'.[52] In other words, the army was claiming a degree of independent authority in political matters, and resting that claim on its special expertise and, implicitly, on its victories at Monte Grappa and Vittorio Veneto in 1918.

As the political crisis deepened and dissatisfaction with a government which, although it had authorised the start of the reconquest of Tripolitania in January, was in almost every respect proving unable or unwilling to satisfy the army's needs for budgetary sufficiency, and as social disorder mounted, the question of where Fascism stood in relation to its most dogmatic belief came to the fore. Mussolini had assured the army through the columns of his party newspaper, *Il Popolo d'Italia*, in March 1922 that he put a high priority on giving officers decent salaries, but on the much more important question of his attitude towards the crown his position remained unsatisfactory. On 22 August, the *Giornale d'Italia* published a letter from a group of officers writing in the army's name which expressed sympathy for Fascism but questioned the extent to which it embodied republican anti-monarchism. 'If the Fascists were, or were to put themselves, against the crown, 'they warned, 'our order would be: fire away (*fuoco fermo*)'. Mussolini replied next day in the columns of *Il Popolo d'Italia* with a double-edged reassurance: 'The crown is not at play because the crown does not wish to put itself in play.'[53]

As the Liberal era entered the last days of its existence, the army jousted with the government over what were ostensibly military details but in fact embodied fundamental points of political principle. Diaz wanted to legislate for the possibility of a *ferma* of more than twelve months, but war minister Marcello Soleri would go no farther than the current law allowing for the retention of an annual class beyond its term when necessary. General Giardino proposed a period of nine months' service if the army was limited strictly to preparing for war and eighteen months if it was required to undertake broader tasks such as the maintenance of public order, to which Soleri replied that parliament had already accepted a twelve-month term and that extending the *ferma* would soak up monies needed for fortifications, aeronautics, weapons and much else besides. While sticking to his position, he was prepared to acknowledge that the army could not reach its finished state until its outside activities had been reduced and its internal ones re-examined. About the possibilities of the former, Giardino was openly sceptical. General Vaccari pointed out that the government's proposed army would be smaller than the pre-war force.[54]

On 23 October 1922, the army council resolved that the twelve-month *ferma* was irreducible and depended upon 'proceeding without delay to radical and extensive reductions (if it is not possible totally to eradicate them) in the share that the army is called on to take in actions and detached duties foreign to the life, preparation and function of its commands, corps and services'.[55] Generals Grazioli and Giardino, both Fascist sympathisers, combined to make the final formula more explicit than it had originally been. By now, the soldiers were ostensibly arguing with Soleri over a difference in numbers of some 10,000 men, whom the minister believed would disappear from the lists as a result of the application of physical criteria to incoming recruits. However, lurking audibly in the wings was the question of the authority of the army in such matters, expressed in the person of general Diaz who, as Giardino reminded the war minister, was the man who would command the army in war and had the responsibility in peacetime of preparing the nation for war.[56]

While the generals debated, the final blow was about to fall on the Liberal era. So great was the flow of arms and explosives to the Fascists that in August Soleri had made corps commanders personally responsible for the contents of the army's magazines. 40,000 uniformed militia met Mussolini when he arrived at Naples on 24 October, and that night the decision was taken to launch the March on Rome on Saturday 28 October. In a situation that was obviously disintegrating, the army's stance was critical. In August general Pugliese, commander of the Rome garrison, who had 28,400 troops at his command, said that it would obey any order from the king and the government, whatever the circumstances. Badoglio told Diaz that in his opinion 'at the first shot the entire edifice of fascism will collapse', but characteristically when asked by Facta if the army would suppress the Fascist risings he declined to answer.[57] Diaz, whose son Marcello was an enthusiastic Fascist party member, knew that four members of the army council – Giardino, Grazioli, Pecori Giraldi and the duke of Aosta – supported the Fascists to varying degrees, and that the chief of the army general staff, Vaccari, was a *filofascista*. Given the evident differences in the attitude of the senior generals, intervention in support even of the crown was an option whose outcome was uncertain.

While Diaz's sense of the army's attitude pointed him towards inaction, Mussolini's awareness of its uncertain stance encouraged him to act. Once before, at the end of September 1920, he had contemplated armed action against Rome and had asked D'Annunzio to sound out general Enrico Caviglia, a former war minister with an exemplary record as a wartime army commander, as to whether the troops would support him. The answer then was no, but times had changed.[58] Grazioli sent colonel Emilio Canevari, a Fascist party member, to Naples on 23 October to tell Mussolini, whom he knew and with whom he had discussed the army's attitude towards Fascism in August, that the great majority were for it and that if they did not receive contrary orders they would remain neutral. Three days later, on the instructions of party secretary Michele Bianchi, an emissary was sent to Grazioli in Rome to tell him that the decision had been taken to march on the capital and to ask that the army not be ordered to move against the blackshirts as this would split it. Mussolini also had some contact at this time with Federico Baistrocchi, who would become one of his most trusted generals in the 1930s.[59]

Faced with the prospect of massive civil disorder in the capital and elsewhere, the king asked Diaz and Pecori Giraldi during the night of 27/28 October what the army's attitude would be if the government declared a state of siege and called on it to suppress Fascism. 'The army will do its duty', Diaz replied, 'however it would be good not to put it to the test.'[60] According to Italo Balbo's account of that night, Diaz already had in his pocket the portfolio of war minister in a government headed by Mussolini when he made his reponse.[61] Uncertain whether or not his cousin the duke of Aosta, who had moved to within thirty miles of the Fascist headquarters at Perugia, was plotting to side with the insurgents and displace him, and presented with the request from outgoing premier

Facta to sign a proclamation declaring a state of siege – which he reportedly locked in a box with the observation that 'after a state of siege there is nothing but civil war' – and aware also that Antonio Salandra would not form a ministry without Mussolini, the king chose not to depart from constitutional norms. On 30 October Mussolini was called to the Quirinale by Vittorio Emanuele and appointed prime minister. With four Fascist cabinet ministers beside him and 320,000 party members behind him, he was in legally in office but not yet indisputably in power. A few days later, the new premier offered Diaz the post of war minister and the duca della Vittoria accepted. At one stroke this shrewd move reassured the king and the Right that the army would maintain its role as a brake on social disorder and on the Fascist experiment, freed the army from the interference of civilian ministers and implicitly offered it autonomy, and protected the Fascist government against a move by the army to topple it.[62]

As much because of the turns of circumstance as through political calculation, Mussolini had effected a 'policy of the diagonal' which linked the army's *modernisti* ('modernisers') with its *conservatori* ('conservatives'). As a representative of the modernising element, Grazioli backed the Fascists for an inter-connecting set of reasons which others shared to varying degrees. Infuriated by the conflict between civilian ministers who were 'lost in democratic dreams with no substance' and the rigid and conservative *tecnicismo* of most of the army's hierarchy, he saw opportunities in a new political order to put younger officers at the top in peacetime as they had been in wartime, to bypass the confrontation between militarism and anti-militarism which had been a feature of Italian politics for some twenty years by fusing them within a nazione armata, and to remake the army on modern lines by moving away from the old obsession with infantry towards an integrated force which emphasised air power and mechanisation.[63] Diaz gave his explanation as to why he had accepted the invitation to join a Fascist-led administration to the newspaper *Il Giornale d'Italia* on 8 November:

Because I felt the sensation of the moment, because I felt that this was a patriotic duty, because I was entirely convinced that I should offer my services, as an associate and a leader, to a national government for the salvation of Italy at the most delicate hour of its internal crisis.[64]

Although this was not a judgement that any other officer in the Savoyard army was called upon to make, it was one which all could understand.

In January 1923, Diaz presented a new programme of military organisation for the king's approval. The term of conscription was raised to eighteen months, and the 'budgeted force' set at 180,000 men. Since the annual class of twenty-year-olds amounted to 240,000 only half could be taken into the army, which meant a return to the mass exemptions which had characterised the Liberal era. Alongside this, organisational reforms created a new Supreme Defence Commission which would consult both the army council and the admirals' committee, and a committee for the preparation of national mobilisation. While these reforms represented a freeing of some of the political controls on the army, and apparently pre-saged a more proactive role for it in the higher councils of government, the purse strings were tightened. In return for being allowed a good mea-sure of autonomy, Diaz had to accept what were to turn out to be the lowest military budgets of the Fascist era: 1.62 billion lire in 1922/3, and 1.39 billion lire in 1923/4.[65]

The army council settled down to the agreeable task of making detailed recommendations on narrower but by no means unimportant aspects of the new structures. Its first achievement was to propose that general Dallolio be offered the post of president of the committee for national mobilisation – a suggestion which it knew to be acceptable to Mussolini. Its broad deliberations were by no means wholly reassuring. In a dis-cussion on who exactly was responsible for correcting deficiencies in the artillery, Badoglio pointed out that a post-war plan to remedy shortness of range which had been apparent in 1914 remained a dead letter since the 1.5 billion lire it would require was not forthcoming. 'Presently, the field artillery is in very good condition,' he reported, '[but] the heavy and heavy field artillery is old and defective and requires the expenditure that was planned'.[66] A comparable lacuna emerged in the course of a discussion on the functions of generals designated to command armies in wartime. Pecori Giraldi, the vice-president of the council, observed that at present there were no plans for deployment either towards the French or the Yugoslav frontiers, and Badoglio confirmed that nothing further had been done with respect to an outline plan to deploy four armies against Yugoslavia which he had drawn up while serving as chief of staff. In the course of a discussion which revealed all too clearly that some of the corps which army commanders would need to defend their allocated areas were actually under the jurisdiction of other authorities, Giardino pointed out that, unlike before the war, conflict could now break out on the eastern and western flanks simultaneously and that although the position respecting the Adriatic had improved, the Tyrrhenian sea was so important to France as to encourage her to invade Sardinia and threaten Rome. In the end, Badoglio hammered out a rough and ready geograph-ical definition of the responsibilities of the four army commanders on the spot.[67]

The first broad survey of the needs of the armed forces in wartime was undertaken by the newly created Commissione suprema mista di difesa in June 1923. The commission took as its point of reference the rate of consumption of munitions and supplies in the last two years of the world war, although, as it pointed out, accurate detailed statistics were not available. Its calculations of the army's needs, based on materials drawn up by the army general staff and admittedly rough and ready, were staggering. A 'minimum' calculation of deficiencies required the expenditure of 1.6 billion lire on munitions and a further 1.25 billion lire on equipment, vehicles, uniforms and foodstuffs; a 'maximum' programme would entail spending 5.5 trillion lire on weapons and munitions (including 2,200 guns) and 3.5 trillion lire on other materials. A month's fighting under the 'minimum' hypothesis would consume weapons and munitions worth 381 million lire and materials worth 257 million lire; under the 'maximum' hypothesis, the numbers were respectively 804 million lire and 745 million lire.[68]

After pointing out that a large part of the war-specific machinery of the metal, chemical and mechanical industries had disappeared and that the labour force was rapidly losing its special expertise, the secretariat concluded that in a future war it was unlikely that Italy could count on entering immediately into the field with forces comparable to those fielded in the last one. Given the enormous demands that a war would impose, it seemed likely that Italy would seek to make use of surprise and carry its offensive to fulfilment before the enemy had adequate time to complete his mobilisation. Then 'either the war will move rapidly to a decisive phase or the forces [in the field] will gradually increase until they reach a size more or less comparable with the "maximum" hypothesis'.[69] While Mussolini's reactions to these statistics can only be guessed, their broad import was clear to all: Italy could not afford to fight another war like the last one in any foreseeable future. Almost immediately, the Corfu crisis focused attention on international politics and on the navy as the immediate instrument of policy.

In January 1924, his health deteriorating and his request for a 2 billion lire budget halved, Diaz decided to resign, although he was kept in office until after the elections in April. His first choice as a successor, general Ugo Cavallero, refused to take the position without an increase in the budget. Diaz then recommended general Antonino Di Giorgio. A declared pro-Fascist and as such an *uomo di fiducia* as far as Mussolini was concerned, but also a convinced proponent of independence for the army, Di Giorgio was prepared to try to live within the budgetary ceiling Mussolini had imposed and so got the job. Military costs were certainly escaping control: the 1923–4 budget set aside 1,292,000,000 lire for the army but applying the current conscription laws increased the actual cost to 1,508,000,000 lire. If the army carried on calling up the same

numbers of men, then even though it consumed some of its stocks a combination of increased prices and higher administrative costs produced a
projected army budget of 1,601,000,000 lire in 1925–6. However, the
incoming war minister assured the treasury encouragingly that under his
new scheme 'the costs will be contained within much more restricted
limits'.[70]

Di Giorgio's proposals to revise the *Ordinamento Diaz*, presented to the
army council on 10 November 1924, were based on the acceptance of
a smaller budget and a consequent economising on manpower in order
to maintain funds for supplies, fortifications and such like expenses. The
smaller part of the annual intake of recruits would serve eighteen months,
the larger part for between three and six months in 'skeleton' cadre formations. The exact proportions of the two portions were left to the minister
to determine year on year, and the size of the annual budget would decide
how many units would be maintained on a cadre basis and how many as
full-sized forces.[71] Although not immediately apparent to anyone outside
the ranks of the Savoyard high command, Di Giorgio's proposals were revolutionary. If carried through, they would refocus Italian military policy
away from its traditional preoccupation with manpower and its predilection for large numbers of semi-trained conscripts which absorbed most
of the monies available and towards one in which materiel and weaponry
would take a greater share of the budget.

In contemplating Di Giorgio's proposals, the army council had in mind
not only domestic concerns but also the contemporaneous debates in
France, where the length of conscript service had been reduced from
three years to eighteen months in 1923 and a further reduction to twelve
months was being considered, chiefly as a result of the diminishing size of
the annual classes of new recruits. The new *armée frontière* was designed
to protect the frontiers and cover a general mobilisation of the country
for what was expected to be a long war. A key feature of this war would be
the mass production of weapons and equipment, which would become
'a special struggle ... which will have a very great influence [on the out-
come]'.[72] The new organisation, which would produce a total force of
685,000 men, made evident 'the preponderant importance of infantry
in a modern army', and colonel Martin-Franklin judged that it would
leave France 'as before ... the number one (*primato*) military power in
the world'.[73] The main strategic preoccupation of the French, as Rome
knew, was the likelihood of a war with Germany, which would break
out suddenly 'when Germany feels itself less unprepared'.[74] In organisational terms, though, France was advancing down a path which, in Italian
eyes, would weaken her – and would weaken Italy, too, if she followed
suit.

The forza bilanciata was, as the chief of the central [army] general staff, lieutenant general Giuseppe Ferrari, acknowledged, the 'shirt of Nessus' because there was never enough money in the budget to keep fully manned the units that were believed to be at all times essential. Di Giorgio's proposal was an attempt to solve the hitherto unsolvable. The general staff was broadly in favour because the new arrangements would improve mobilisation and would allow the whole of the annual contingent to serve. It was also Di Giorgio's intention, Ferrari explained, to ask for a large 'extraordinary' budget to improve frontier defences, buy the necessary arms and munitions, and improve mobilisation supplies.[75] The council was disinclined to accept Ferrari's genial exegesis. Giardino pointed out that since an Inspector of the Army had never been appointed, since there was no chief of the army general staff old style, and since the vice-president, Pecori Giraldi, had been relieved of his job several months ago, no one who was technically and personally responsible for national defence was in a position to comment. He and others saw the proposals as an unwelcome return to the *scudo e lancia* ('shield and lance') design proposed immediately after the war by general Roberto Bencivenga as a compromise between the Left's wish for a 'nation in arms' and the Right's desire for a long service army.[76]

The discussion that followed revealed the army's concerns, and its priorities, with great clarity. Caviglia raised a central issue when he objected that the present arrangement put the future of the army into the hands of the executive power. Giardino believed that the proposals would make the army more vulnerable to financial cuts because the navy and the air force would certainly not agree to reductions in their budgets. Montuori observed that the proposed budget for 1924/5, roughly 1.9 billion lire, was one-ninth of the total state budget and that the army's share must never fall below this proportion. The generals were unanimous in their desire for firmer guarantees on future size and shape than Di Giorgio offered; at a minimum, they wanted 125 permanent battalions. Nor were they at all happy with the details; for one thing, basic training took 3 months and then the bulk of the men would be sent home before they and the permanent cadres could exercise together.

Dissatisfaction with both the present circumstances and the proposed changes was widespread. The council unanimously demanded that the old-style chief of the army general staff be restored and, sensitive to the fact that the general staff division of the war ministry had the power to modify staff plans according to their conception of practical exigencies, demanded that the chief of the general staff be given full authority over the staff so that he would not be a mere functionary of the ministry.[77] Everyone sprang to resist any reduction in the cavalry, the ensuing discussion revealing that the celeri units (mixed cavalry, cyclists and armoured cars) had not performed very well in the summer manoeuvres in 1923 and leading Caviglia to admit that during the war he had always refused them when offered, except during the pursuit after Vittorio Veneto when they were suddenly brought to a standstill.[78] However, the council accepted almost without demur Di Giorgio's proposal that tanks, of which the army then had one hundred, should not be distributed among the infantry but should form a separate entity after Ferrari explained that their function was as yet undetermined and that contemporary thinking envisaged not merely heavy tanks resembling land-bound versions of the ironclads of the American Civil War but also fast light tanks for the cavalry and for reconnaissance.[79]

In its concluding discussion, the army council reassembled its fundamental objections to Di Giorgio's proposals. No one, not even the civilian war ministers, had proposed such a radical reduction in the term of service. Economising on manpower to fund weapons, munitions and equipment was unacceptable; instead the regular annual budget should pay for training and materiel should be funded by special 'extraordinary' appropriations. The concept that for four months of each year there would be 90,000 recruits under arms and for the remaining eight months only 27,000 was a 'frighteningly small number'. Ferrari's unwise analogy with Switzerland, a nation that he claimed was technically well prepared, unleashed a tirade from general Giardino:

It is not possible that Italy be brought to the level of a neutral Switzerland. Italy is a great power and cannot forget her political, historical, geographical and demographic position. Nor, for another thing, does the Swiss army have the proven glories of the Carso, the Isonzo, the Piave and the Grappa.[80]

Without proof, he was unwilling to accept Ferrari's judgement on the Swiss army's technical capabilities. Giardino wanted the council to record its disapproval in principle with the whole project, but had to give way when three of the six members (including the president, the duke of Aosta) opposed this on the grounds that there was reason to believe that the minister would take account of their detailed recommendations – which, if their extemporised costings were correct, would add only another 180 million to a budgeted cost of 2 billion.

As the military opposition to Di Giorgio hardened, Mussolini was facing the most acute crisis of his political career. On 10 June 1924, the socialist deputy Giacomo Matteotti was abducted and murdered by blackshirt thugs of the so-called *ceka* who were following Mussolini's evident wishes if not his direct orders, and on 16 August his body was found. While the anti-Fascist deputies boycotted parliament until the militia and the other repressive organs of the Fascist party were dissolved, Mussolini took steps to mollify the military opposition and to strengthen his own somewhat shaky position in the face of a Fascist party many of whose leading members now wanted him to push the 'revolution' to its extreme. In November, Cadorna was rehabilitated and he and Diaz were given the new rank of Maresciallo d'Italia. The party militia, the MVSN, founded in 1922, was declared part of the armed forces by royal decree on 4 August and put under Mussolini's direct orders; subsequently, on 28 October 1924 it swore allegiance to the king. Its commander, general Emilio De Bono, a party loyalist, was forced out of office that month accused of suppressing evidence relating to the Matteotti case. After the *ras* of Ferrara, Italo Balbo, had briefly taken over and then resigned, the MVSN was put in the charge of general Gandolfi, who had all militia zone commanders replaced by army generals at the end of December. These moves only partially placated the army but enfuriated the party *ras* ('chiefs') who lost local control of the militia. On 31 December militia leaders burst into Mussolini's office to demand that either they and he consign themselves to the law like common criminals or that he liquidate the opposition and continue with the revolution. They also demanded the removal of the generals from the MVSN and its restoration to the party.[81]

On 3 January 1925, Mussolini appeared in parliament and took upon himself responsibility for all the violence that had marked Italian politics over the previous two years, adding that his government was strong enough to break up the seceding opposition completely and promising to give Italy the peace it needed with tenderness (*con l'amore*) if possible but with force if necessary. The militia, police and squadristi immediately set to, taking over the opposition's organisation and suppressing its newspapers. In these circumstances, Mussolini had to ensure that he kept the king and the army behind him while he directed a year-long programme which would end both parliamentary democracy and the activities of the Fascist left. Parliamentary scrutiny of Di Giorgio's plan, which threatened to unite opposition against him and deprive him of the qualified support of the king, came at an extremely awkward moment for Mussolini. The reverberations of a critical parliamentary report on the military budget produced in October 1924, which concluded by observing that the general agreement that modern armies needed the widespread employment of machines did not seem to extend to Italy's military supremos, still rumbled on. In the budget discussion two months later there was evident Fascist support for Di Giorgio's proposals, leading some soldiers to fear that if adopted it would reopen the door to a dominant Fascist militia. Many senior soldiers opposed Di Giorgio's ideas on technical grounds, but Liberal politicians supported them as a way of striking back at Mussolini.[82]

When the proposals were debated in the Senate between 30 March and 2 April 1925, Diaz, Cadorna and three of the five most senior generals (*generali d'esercito*) spoke against them. Mussolini, who had already made it clear that he would not put the matter to what would be a vote of confidence as long as the debate remained technical, closed the proceedings with a rambling speech lasting three and three-quarters hours in which he told the senate that national defence hinged on more than just the size of the army, pointed to the competing needs of the other services and the reminded it of the limits on finance. After praising bits of the plan, he carefully disassociated himself from what the military conservatives saw as its underlying and dangerous rationale, the nazione armata (citizenry in arms) – a policy which had been one of the planks of the radical Fascist party programme six years before. What was good for Switzerland was not necessarily good for Italy: 'The nazione armata in time of peace can be said to be spiritually armed, but it will never be able to overcome what is called a permanent army.'[83] After sketching a compromise in which Di Giorgio's forza massima of 325,000 men was kept in being for six months and not four, and a forza minima of 150,000 which split the difference between the Diaz and Di Giorgio plans for the remaining six months, Mussolini told the senate that time was needed to reflect and withdrew the bill.

One of the matters that had been raised, by Pecori Giraldi, was the value of unified direction at the top of the armed services. There were at this moment negative as well as positive reasons to advance down this path. Di Giorgio, who had resigned immediately after the debate, had to be replaced but Mussolini could entrust the war ministry neither to one of the generals surrounding Giardino, which would be to acknowledge political defeat, or to another outsider, which would be to risk its repetition. The advantages of taking the reins himself were that he could embed his control of the military at a delicate moment in his political life and institute reforms suited to his needs and ambitions. This he did on 4 April 1925. He could certainly not afford to entrust unified direction of the armed forces to anyone else, but fortunately neither the army nor the navy would accept anyone from another service. Admiral Thaon di Revel's unexpected resignation in May 1925 therefore enabled Mussolini to add the navy ministry to his portfolio and create a framework for civil–military relations which ostensibly provided for coordination of the three armed services. It was his intention, he announced in *Il Popolo d'Italia* on 25 May 1925, to hold both ministries 'for as long as possible'. The resulting arrangement, which contributed much to the final Fascist débâcle, would operate with one short interlude until the outbreak of the Second World War.

Naval policies, plans and ambitions

In the years before the Great War, Italian naval policy had been dominated largely by the recognition of threats. Anxious about the growth of the Austro–Hungarian fleet and therefore the security of Italy's position in the Adriatic, the chiefs of the Italian navy were no less concerned on the eve of war with the threat posed by France, one of the targets of the Triple Alliance which Rome had joined in 1882. Thus while the dominant position of the Austrian naval bases at Pola and Cattaro made war in the Adriatic a worrying prospect, the Tyrrhenian sea was an equal focus of concern, its naval dimensions being the need both to defend the Ligurian coast and to attack French convoys journeying to and from North Africa. However, an adverse strategic position also generated ambitions and appetites. Albania was a desirable acquisition since it would safeguard the Straits of Otranto, which must be in friendly hands if the Austrian fleet was to be kept out of the eastern Mediterranean. Naval ambitions also extended further east, sharpened by the seizure of the Turkish Aegean islands during the course of the Libyan war (1911–12). The ministry of marine wanted the island of Leros as a *base di appoggio*, while admiral Paolo Thaon di Revel, chief of naval staff, favoured holding on to the chain of islands between Cos and Patmos if a permanent military position in the Aegean was at stake, and the chain from Rhodes to Patmos if economic considerations were in play. Although bound by the Treaty of Lausanne (1912) to return the Aegean islands, Italy found herself at war with Turkey in 1915, making her future position in the area an open question.[84]

The Italian navy entered the war in 1915 oppressed by the weight of its defeat at the battle of Lissa forty-nine years earlier, a defeat explained to the contemporary Italian public as the result of lack of unity, discipline, patriotism and the highest sense of duty and subsequently put down to a want of aggression and of determination to impose his will on the enemy on the part of the fleet commander, admiral Persano.[85] The pressure on a youthful navy with no great tradition at its back to avoid passivity at all costs was reinforced by contemporary naval thought. Like all the major fleets of the day, the Italian navy was instructed to seek decisive battles from the outset because, as the clash between the Japanese and Russian at Tsushima in 1905 had demonstrated, it was by such engagements that the outcomes of wars were determined. The destruction of the enemy's mobile forces should be the central objective and should always be sought;

Lissa had been the fruit of a policy of avoiding that goal instead of pursuing it. As for the impact of recent technological developments on such a policy, the Italian navy was reassured by one of its leading theorists that it need have no apprehensions about the torpedo, which had not displaced the gun as the primary weapon of combat at sea.[86]

Events belied the prophecies of the experts and frustrated the ambitions of the practitioners, and instead of fighting a cataclysmic naval battle the fleets engaged in the naval war in the Mediterranean found themselves fighting 'a war of detail with ceaseless patrols, convoy and escort'.[87] Initial Italian naval plans looked to provoke the Austro–Hungarian fleet into a sortie and so bring about the anticipated clash of capital fleets. However, after one French battleship, the *Jean Bart*, was hit by a torpedo off Cattaro on 21 December 1914 and another, the *Leon Gambetta*, was sunk by torpedoes on 22–24 April 1915, Revel was unwilling to put his big ships at risk from enemy submarines or mines, both weapons which could be deployed most effectively along the enemy's broken coastline. Believing that Austria–Hungary would in turn seek to avoid a decisive naval encounter in order to preserve its fleet in being as an ongoing threat, and also that the war would be decided on land, Revel turned to light surface units, submarines and MAS torpedo boats as the instruments of a revised policy in which fleet units were based at Brindisi and Taranto to cut off the enemy if he sortied south from Cattaro.[88]

Italian battleships had a somewhat ignominious war. Untested in open combat, they suffered a number of humiliating losses: the *Benedetto Brin* blew up in 1915, and in 1916 the *Regina Margherita* was mined and the *Leonardo da Vinci* sank as a result of Austrian sabotage. They earned low opinions from their French and British allies, who felt that they showed the effects of lack of exercise and practice, especially as far as gunnery was concerned. Cruisers and destroyers were actively involved in the surface war in the Adriatic but had little opportunity to make a major mark on it, not least because the enemy fleet having sortied from its bases in May 1917 did not do so again until June 1918. Safeguarding the 'fleet in being' became the *leitmotif* for the war in the Adriatic on both sides. The best results were obtained by the MAS torpedo boats, in action after the first year of the war; the highpoint of their campaign came when captain Luigi Rizzo first penetrated Trieste harbour and sank the twenty-year-old battleship *Wien* on 9/10 December 1917, and then torpedoed and sank the modern Austrian battleship *Szent Istvan* on 9 June 1918.[89] As the war came to its end, a two-man human torpedo sank the *Viribus Unitis* in Pola Harbour on the night of 31 October–1 November 1918, a further demonstration of the virtuosity of at least some parts of the Italian navy.

For its senior members, the politics of the Italian navy's war were no less important than the ebb and flow of the fighting war in the Adriatic. Italy did not find it easy to fight as a member of an alliance, and emerged from the experience both sensitised and embittered. One powerful legacy of allied wrangling, evident later at the height of the Fascist era but identified as a fundamental strategic issue from the outset, was the view that the nation should rely on no other forces than its own, no matter what the sacrifices that were entailed in so doing.[90] Prolonged Allied squabbles over the rival merits of patrolling and escorting as the best means of convoy protection and over zoning the Mediterranean merely exercised the muscles, while even more extended disagreement over the proper form and nature of the Otranto barrage which lasted until it was finally completed – and then not entirely to Italy's satisfaction – in October 1918 tried the nerves. The introduction of inter-allied naval conferences in 1917 provided a theatre in which Revel fought tenaciously for the exclusive right of the Italian navy to conduct operations in the *mari nazionali* – which he interpreted as encompassing the Tyrrhenian and Ionian seas, the Adriatic and the Gulf of Sirte. Any naval incursion into the Adriatic by the United States he sternly resisted, chiefly on the grounds that she was not a signatory of the Treaty of London and would therefore not recognise its terms and support Italian interests there.[91]

Under the terms of the Paris Convention of May 1915 governing the Italian navy's entry into the war, Revel had been given full direction of all operations in the Adriatic conducted by the Allied fleets. When in 1918 the threat of a sortie by the Russian Black Sea fleet into the eastern Mediterranean caused the French to suggest that Italian warships might be transferred to that sector and substituted by French ships, he sallied forth once more to defend Italy's position as supreme naval authority in the Adriatic, telling the government to back him if it believed that the present and future prosperity of the country depended on its becoming a significant maritime nation.[92] Confronted at Versailles on 2 June 1918 with a proposal that admiral Jellicoe should become Supreme Naval Commander of the Allied fleets and that a French admiral be put in command of all naval forces in the Mediterranean, an affronted Revel walked out in disgust, accompanied by foreign minister Sidney Sonnino.

As the war ended and the victorious allied powers prepared for the Paris Peace Conference which would construct the post-war settlement, Revel, whose paramount concern led to claims that he was affected with *scabbia adriatica* ('Adriatic scabies'), acted to secure the navy's most important geopolitical objectives by *coups de main*. Between 22 October 1918 and 27 June 1919, the navy carried out the occupation of fifty-six ports, islands and inland sites along the length of the eastern

Adriatic coastline from Durazzo in the south – the first such action – to Monfalcone and Trieste in the north. Vice-admiral Millo, who became naval commander of the eastern Adriatic in November 1918 and to whom Dalmatia was 'as important as my country and my king', shared Revel's sense of the strategic importance of the region and also believed that the local Italian population deserved protection from the 'Slav hordes' (*marea slava*). Landing at Zara at the end of 1918, he immediately began a programme of Italianisation which caused the Nitti government to rap him over the knuckles a year later, and won the admiration of the newly formed Fasci di combattimento after promising not to leave Dalmatia for any reason.[93]

The creation of Yugoslavia under the terms of the Versailles settlement and the subsequent delineation of its north-western frontier at Rapallo on 12 November 1920, which gave Italy the former Austro–Hungarian province of Istria and therefore command of the northern Adriatic through the possession of Trieste and Pola, but which made Fiume into an independent state thirteen months after the poet and war hero Gabriele d'Annunzio had occupied it and gave away Dalmatia and the Curzolari islands, disgusted Revel and Millo as much as it did the nationalists. Having watched the promised gains for which Italy had entered and fought the war disintegrate at Paris under what he regarded as the weak hand of premier Vittorio Orlando, Revel resigned on 24 November 1919. Speaking in the senate shortly after the signing of the Rapallo Treaty, he warned that because Yugoslavia possessed Dalmatia and because Greece, thanks to its having gained part of the Albanian coast and its already owning Corfu, could now strategically dominate the Otranto channel, 'in the central Adriatic our security will be slight and in the lower Adriatic we shall be in a worse situation than we were during the last war'.[94]

While much had changed during and more especially as a consequence of the First World War, to the naval general staff Italy was still the prisoner of the same geographical and economic circumstances which had constrained her before that conflict had begun. An extensive coastline, along the length of which were strung out great cities and ports, required defence, as did a trading situation in which Italy was very heavily dependent upon imports. Strategically insecure in the northern Tyrrhenian sea because of France's possession of Corsica, which enabled her to threaten the naval base of La Maddalena, the ports of La Spezia and Livorno and the Ligurian coast, Italy needed to be able to prevent France, the power which most threatened her naval and maritime security, from linking up with and supporting Greece and Yugoslavia. Closing the Ionian and Adriatic basins off from her natural rival, in much the same way as

Germany had closed off the Baltic during the world war, required Italian control of the Sicilian channel, which was only partial, and of the Straits of Otranto.[95] Di Revel feared that French bases might be installed along the Dalmatian coast, which would once again make the country vulnerable on both flanks.[96] His successor as chief of naval staff, vice-admiral Alfredo Acton, shared his views about the strategic importance of the Dalmatian coast and the islands north and west of it that had been promised to Italy under article 5 of the Treaty of London. However, in tune with the political line of the government, navy minister rear-admiral Giovanni Sechi took up a more emollient stance.

In Italy's straitened circumstances, not least in respect of its merchant fleet which had lost two thirds of its tonnage during the war and which was now half the size it had been in 1914, restraint was the order of the day, notwithstanding the calls of the nationalists, the Right and heavy industry for a large fleet to support a policy of commercial expansion in the Balkans, the Levant and Africa. Sechi loyally followed premier Francesco Nitti's economical line of demobilisation and strict limits to arms manufactures. The navy was cut back in size from 120,000 to 34,000 men, construction of the only one of four wartime super dreadnoughts still on the slipway, the *Caracciolo*, was halted, and four old battleships and fifteen cruisers were condemned. The impression that the war in the Adriatic had made on the minister was evident in his first normal post-war budget, announced on 25 November 1920. Sums of 536,000,000 lire for ordinary expenditure and 311,000,000 lire for extraordinary expenditure were to be spent on eight minelayers, four destroyers, four submarines and eight MAS torpedo boats.[97]

Sechi's programme drew the fire of the conservative old guard among the admirals, whose faith in the power and primacy of the battleship had been reinforced by the argument of Italy's foremost young naval theorist, Romeo Bernotti, that its day was far from over and that the future lay in fast, 30-knot ships carrying eight or more very large guns.[98] Attracted by the emphasis on new weapons which suited both the purse and the character of a nation at once poor and audacious, the Fascists stayed out of the fray. Vice-admiral Umberto Cagni, a national hero as a result of his having snatched possession of Tripoli at the start of the Libyan war in October 1911, told the senate that capital ships were 'the foundation for the preparation of the certain defence of the *patria*, of its commerce, of its life'.[99] Revel reminded it that heavy warships were not defunct, pointing out that Great Britain, the United States and Japan were still building battleships and that they remained the backbone of major fleets notwithstanding the development of torpedoes and aeroplanes. 'The era of great warships is over only for states which, like today's Italy, do not have the financial means to build them', he thundered.[100] In the chamber of deputies, Sechi was attacked by vice-admiral Amero d'Aste for having reduced the fleet to a minimum when he could have reconditioned old battleships for the relatively modest sum of 50,000,000 lire each, one sixth the cost of a new one. Fuelled by a profound resentment of Italy's naval inferiority vis-à-vis France which other sailors shared and by a conviction that a battleship navy was 'a coefficient of success in all political, military and commercial undertakings', Cagni was instrumental in forcing a vote to rearm the antequated *Leonardo da Vinci* in February 1921. His victory was symbolic and temporary for Thaon di Revel subsequently cancelled the project, but his line of reasoning was to be central to admiral Cavagnari's dealings with Mussolini in the 1930s.[101]

On the central issue of the Adriatic, Sechi was no more successful in persuading a largely sceptical audience of the soundness of his position. His arguments that possession of Pola secured Italy's north-eastern provinces, that the wartime exploits of the MAS boats had shown that the east coast of the Adriatic was not inviolable, that holding it and having to defend coastal convoys from attack would be burdensome for an enemy, and that Austria–Hungary had never tried heavy bombardments or landings along the coastlines of the Romagna and Puglia all cut little or no ice. Nor did the point that Yugoslavia possessed no fleet of her own and had little prospect of getting one in the foreseeable future. Acton relinquished the post of chief of naval staff shortly after Rapallo, after having given an interview to the newspaper *Il Messaggero* in which he criticised both the minister and his strategic policy, but Sechi still confronted a hostile bloc of nationalists and a large part of the upper echelons of the navy. With Ivanoe Bonomi's accession to the premiership in June 1921, he was succeeded by two civilian ministers, both of whom acted simply as political figureheads and left the issue of what types of ship to build to their professional advisers.[102]

Scarcely had Sechi vacated his office before international politics intruded on Italian naval construction policy. On 8 July 1921, confronted with the prospect of a spiralling naval arms race with Great Britain, the United States government in the person of secretary of state Charles Evans Hughes telegraphed his ambassadors in Italy, France, Japan and Great Britain asking them to enquire of their accredited governments whether they would take part in 'a conference on limitation of armament ... to be held in Washington at a mutually convenient time'.[103] Bonomi accepted at once, and sent to Washington a group of delegates whose civilian leaders put priority on an outcome which would provide some relief for Italy's sagging finances at a moment when the economy was being rendered yet more fragile as a result of the strikes instigated by the Left in the *biennio rosso*, and social order was under attack by violent Fascist *squadre*. The Italian delegation hoped to trade support for America's aims against a reduction in Italy's war debts.[104]

Italian preparations for the conference were poorly co-ordinated. With only a fortnight to go before the delegation had to leave, vice-admiral Giuseppe de Lorenzi, chief of the naval staff, wrote to his minister asking that the 'line of conduct' that it would be required to follow be formulated in co-ordination with the Foreign Ministry and the War Ministry.[105] Nothing of the sort seems to have taken place. De Lorenzi recommended a stay of execution for the super dreadnought *Caracciolo* and an immediate start to the building of a group of 8,500 ton *esploratori* (destroyer escorts) and lighter craft. This advice reflected a perception of how the Washington conference would develop which turned out to be quite wrong. The naval general staff expected the British delegation to propose limitations or reductions in naval armaments based on the actual relative strengths of different national fleets. In the event of disagreement, it expected calculations to be based on the relative dependence of different states on the sea; this it interpreted as comprising the importance to the national economy of imported foodstuffs and raw materials and of maritime commerce in general, the requirement for maritime communications with colonies, the total tonnage of the merchant fleet, and 'other possible special circumstances'.[106]

Expecting that Great Britain, the United States and Japan would be allowed to maintain a fleet larger than such calculations suggested in order to be able to enforce the will of the League of Nations, the naval staff foresaw that Italy and France would tend to be relegated to 'the roster of small powers'. It was therefore suggested that agreement be reached with the French government as soon as possible on a common line of conduct. The Italian delegation should resist any proposals tending to create naval hegemonies; instead it should propose a division of the world into naval zones, in each of which 'the powers best situated and which have the greatest interests there' would have the mandate to ensure the execution of international obligations imposed by common action. As far as the Mediterranean was concerned, the two powers would have to be Italy and France *a parità di forze* ('in equal strength').[107]

Although the Italian naval staff wanted to maintain absolute equality with France in naval armaments, it recognised that this might be too large a pill to administer, and that 'perhaps reasons of high politics will prevent our delegates from maintaining a position which would put them in a bad light from the outset in respect to the intentions we would like to pursue and secure'. Accordingly, the head of the naval delegation, vice-admiral Alfredo Acton, was instructed to accept no more than 20 per cent inferiority.[108] The second main goal was to ensure that limitations should be determined by global tonnage and not by category, thereby allowing Italy to use her allocation to construct the type of ships that suited her needs best and not condemning her to permanent inferiority in all classes under regulation.

The strategic arguments to support Italy's ideal of naval parity with France, laid out in detail by vice-admiral Lorenzi, on the eve of the delegation's departure, were a mixture of traditional nineteenth-century concerns stretching back as far as the unification of Italy and new ones deriving from the circumstances of the day. Much less rich in foodstuffs and raw materials than her neighbour and therefore more heavily reliant on sea-borne commerce, a situation that was exacerbated by the fact that her population of some thirty-nine million was growing at a faster rate than that of France which it presently equalled, Italy also had to defend 7,245 kilometres of vulnerable coastline. Ships were essential to protect it:

light surface craft and submarines which, acting from prepared and provisioned bases, can extend their defensive action along neighbouring coasts; heavy ships to support the smaller craft, thereby allowing the latter to have the maximum tactical effect against the main enemy forces.

There remained the issue of colonies, a new factor in naval calculations which had appeared with the acquisition of Libya in 1911–12; as yet they provided the *madrepatria* with little or nothing, but they had to be nurtured through a critical period of growth.[109]

Hughes's proposals, unveiled at the opening session of the Washington Conference on 12 November 1921, came as a surprise to everyone: proportional limitations on the tonnage of capital ships possessed by the three major powers (the United States, Great Britain and Japan) in the ratio 5:5:3, a ten-year 'building holiday', and proportional ratios for cruisers, destroyers, submarines and aircraft carriers. Initially Italy and France were left for later consideration, but the civilian head of the Italian delegation, Senator Carlo Schanzer, succeeded in adding them into the main discussion. Disagreement then broke out within the Italian delegation. Hughes announced to the conference on 15 December 1921 that the United States, Great Britain and Japan had reached agreement on capital ship tonnage, with the former two allocated 500,000 tons each. Aware of the drift of discussions, Acton proposed on 13 November that Italy and France should seek battleship allocations of 200,000 tons each, with proportional amounts for smaller ships. The naval staff agreed, but added that if this was not attainable then he should adhere to the 80 per cent formula previously indicated and should secure Italy's right to use her allowance of other ships to build whatever she wished in every category including submarines. Schanzer strongly disagreed with Acton on the grounds that such a move ran against the spirit of the conference, ignored the government's concern with Italy's economic conditions, and threatened to create a very difficult position vis-à-vis France. When the news that Italy might accept an eight to ten inferiority was leaked to the *New York Times*, Schanzer found it opportune not to deny it, causing Acton to complain to Rome that it had made his task much more difficult.[110]

The final outcome of the discussions was the result partly of the calculations and wishes of powers greater than Italy and partly of her choice of a political line which enabled her to play a weak hand effectively. In consequence of their settling the issue of battleship allocations with Japan, Britain and the United States suggested a capital ship ratio of 1.75, equating to 175,000-tons of capital ships, for Italy and France, largely because Great Britain wanted to be superior to Japan and France in combination (5 to 3 + 1.75). Acton argued for a higher allocation of 200,000 tons, partly on the technical grounds that the lower figure would not allow Italy to build two divisions of three battleships each (the super-dreadnought *Caracciolo* had weighed 31,500 tons), and partly because a proportional allocation of cruisers, destroyers and submarines that he and others expected to follow would leave Italy too weak to meet her needs. Schanzer, who had already secured French acceptance of battleship parity in exchange for Italy's support in resisting proposals for land disarmament, urged Rome to accept, partly on the grounds that the Italian public was expecting a diminution and not an increase in naval armaments and partly because of the weight that such an allocation would impose on the public finances. In the absence of any instructions from Rome, he declared on 16 December that Italy would accept the 175,000-ton limit on the condition that France did so too.[111] Italy then watched while France made a fruitless attempt to overturn the carefully calculated ratios before finally acceding to the formula agreed by all the others.

Applying the agreed battleship proportions would give France and Italy 31,500 tons of submarines each. France's refusal to accept less than 90,000 tons of submarines, together with not less than 330,000 tons of light surface craft, destroyed attempts to regulate them. Apparently unconvinced by British claims that submarines were of no use for coastal defence or for the protection of lines of communication with colonies, Italy chose to side with France while expressing some concern at the possible economic and political consequences of her neighbour's naval programme. The five powers agreed to a limit of 10,000 tons and 8-inch guns for cruisers, although the Italian naval staff would have preferred 11-inch guns and 12,000-ton ships, and to allocations for aircraft carriers – a weapons platform which Italy did not possess then or there-after – which allotted 60,000 tons to Italy and to France.[112]

As Schanzer presented it to parliament, the Washington Treaty safe-guarded the interests of an Italy which, because it was entirely enclosed in the Mediterranean, needed a fleet second to none there 'not for reasons of old-fashioned imperialism, but for the undeniable needs of existence'.[113] For Italy, the outcome of the Washington conference was a notable suc-cess, though one which had its limitations.[114] France, to be sure, set no great store by battleships or aircraft carriers, building only one of each between the wars, but in 1922 this development could not have been foreseen. Also, no limits had been set on her ability to build the light craft she needed to control communications in the Mediterranean – craft which had proven their worth in the Adriatic during the war. Finally, in as much as the treaty was a setback for Paris it was a gain for Rome. France's pre-Washington building programme had focused 'principally on the actual composition of the Italian fleet', and in seeking equality with Japan at no less than two thirds the allocation of the greater powers, and limits of 350,000 tons on battleships and 330,000 tons on lighter craft, she was consciously going for figures which would be more than the Italian economy could bear.[115] Schanzer was thus justified in claiming to the senate during a debate on the ratification of the treaty in February 1923 that international recognition of Italy's naval parity with France was 'a notable advantage for our country, be it from the technical–military point of view and that of our security at sea, be it from that of our political prestige and our financial interests'.[116]

The likely consequences of the liberty which the Washington Treaty left France in building as many light surface craft and submarines as she wished became apparent immediately. While waiting to see whether or not France ratified the Washington treaty, the Italian naval staff learnt in May 1922 that her projected naval budget for 1923 would amount to 1,121 million francs, equivalent to two milliard lire, an increase of 324 million francs over the current year. In some alarm, de Lorenzi wrote to his minister pointing this out and contrasting it with his own budget of some 600 million lire. He pressed for more money in order to start at once on his own modest building programme which comprised three light cruisers, ten destroyers and ten submarines.[117]

In making this request, the chief of naval staff was acutely aware of the parlous nature of Italy's strategic position in the event of a war with France. Fighting the war at all depended first and foremost on securing supplies of food, fuel and raw materials, and the geographic–strategic conditions of the western Mediterranean made it impossible to protect traffic coming through the Straits of Gibraltar until such time as the balance of forces changed in Italy's favour. Italy therefore had no choice but to focus her naval resources on protecting trade entering the eastern Mediterranean via the Suez canal and the Dardanelles, which could provide coal from Heraklea (in Anatolia), petrol from Romania and grain from Bessarabia and Russia. France still posed a considerable threat in the shape both of her possession of Syria, which would enable her to construct a naval base at Alexandretta, and of her ability to make hostile use of the Greek Islands. In war, she could be expected to use submarines and light surface craft to attack Italian commerce from these locations, which would necessitate heavy surface protection by cruisers, destroyers, and minesweepers. Italy's naval bases at Taranto and Brindisi would be too far away to sustain the fleet at sea, so use would have to be made of Tobruk to protect traffic travelling between Crete and Africa. Defending traffic coming from the Suez canal and the Dardanelles would require the seizure of bases at Castelrosso and at Leros and Stampalia respectively. Over-optimistically, the navy thought that it could hang on to the two islands since it was no longer obliged to hand the Dodecanese back to Greece. It also hoped to establish its principal naval base at Marmaris, an ideal location if Greece were allied to France, as 'it is part of the territory over which our influence has been recognised'. Since no ships could be spared to defend traffic in the Red Sea and the Indian Ocean, the only solution to the threat in this theatre was to use troops to take possession of the French colonies of Djibuti and Obock.[118]

The diplomatic presuppositions upon which much of this planning rested quickly collapsed as Italy was forced to abandon her toe-hold in Anatolian Turkey and return the Dodecanese to Greece. In April, the Italian occupation corps in the eastern Mediterranean was withdrawn, and in December the Dodecanese Naval Command was disbanded. The consequent worsening of her strategic–geographic situation increased the burden on the fleet and thus tilted the naval balance further against Italy. Searching for partial solutions to what was becoming an intractable problem, Lorenzi demonstrated the navy's propensity to import its strategic weaknesses onto the foreign policy agenda by urging that Italy compensate for the vulnerability to enemy interception of its trade via Gibraltar and the western Mediterranean, which in 1919 was ten times the value of that passing through the Suez canal, and the improbability of finding compensating sources of raw materials in Russia, Yugoslavia or Anatolia in current diplomatic circumstances, by opening up trading links with Japan, Korea, China and the East Indies.[119]

As well as grappling with the international diplomacy of naval arms limitation and the seemingly perennial problem of Italy's strategic vulnerability, the navy also had to deal with a technical agenda on which the important issue of the role of air power and its relationship with the navy figured large. The admirals' committee met in May 1922 to consider the issue of aeronautics in general and the role of the aeroplane in naval activities in particular. Aware that the United States was moving towards laying down its first two aircraft carriers, the *Saratoga* and the *Lexington*, it was also equipped with a report from the air attaché in Washington discounting experiments in America in which torpedo-carrying aircraft had located three battleships after forty mile flights and been able to hit them. Guidoni pointed out that such strikes would need the assistance of long-distance reconnaissance and attack aircraft to have any effect, that the weight of explosive was too light to have much impact on modern battleships and that there was no evidence that attacks by torpedo planes were more to be feared than attacks by MAS torpedo boats. 'In case of real war', Guidoni concluded, 'an attack of this nature would not have had any result'.[120]

With no independent air force as yet in existence, the aircraft was a strong bone of contention. Thaon di Revel appeared to have an open mind on its future role, acknowledging that colonel Giulio Douhet had 'a big point': since they could go anywhere without obstruction, they could strike directly at the enemy's roots. Captain Valli, speaking for the Inspectorate of Aeronautics at the Navy Ministry, argued that the populace would not want to confide its defence to a force 'enclosed in such a fragile wrapping as today's aircraft', that it would take a long time to develop into a practical weapon, and that it was presently 'contrary to the ethical and aesthetical elements which we are accustomed to demand in our preparations for war'.[121] De Lorenzi concurred, believing that there was no evidence which presently justified the prevalence of air forces over the navy. Brigadier-general Siebert, Inspector of Aeronautics at the War Ministry, took a different view. The Americans were, he felt, correct in believing that aircraft could assume the defence of a country up to two hundred miles out to sea, and the navy beyond that distance. They could also defend land frontiers up to the same distance.[122]

Remarking on the shortcomings of aircraft as revealed in the American experiments, when they had found it difficult to score more than 2 or 3 per cent of hits on ships in motion, and on the experience of the world war, when no warship had been sunk from the air, the committee concluded that 'notwithstanding the many writings and opinions tending to exalt the value of aerial forces, they cannot yet be considered so important as to substitute, even in part, for the actions of naval and military forces in war'.[123] Nevertheless, Italy was a good target for nearby air bases – an obvious reference to the French, whose air force at this time numbered some 4,000 planes – and needed a force with which to hit the enemy. Aircraft could fulfil a number of tasks for the navy: observation and reconnaissance of enemy coasts, protection of supply convoys, the defence of naval bases and important coastal locations, and offence against the enemy at sea or in his bases. The committee therefore concluded that the navy needed 264 aircraft, and that they should be under the control of the chief of naval staff working through the inspector of aeronautics. In passing, it noted that there were few of the wartime aircraft factories left, and cast a vote in favour of airships.[124]

The general lines of naval construction policy that Italy would pursue during the middle of the 1920s were confirmed by the senior admirals at the beginning of October 1922, just as the Fascist disorders that culminated in the march on Rome and Mussolini's accession to power on 30 October were beginning. At a meeting of the admirals' committee presided over by Revel, the deputy chief of naval staff, vice-admiral Guido Chelotti, laid out de Lorenzi's plan to delay battleship building by fourteen years instead of ten for financial reasons, and to build three 10,000-ton cruisers to match those being built in France together with light esploratori, destroyers and submarines, the latter to form 'a group of units capable of carrying the underwater offensive into the Atlantic Ocean along the supply lanes of our probable enemy'.[125] Led by Acton, the admirals broadly concurred, though Cagni entered a dissenting note: delaying battleship building to accumulate funds to be spent in the future amounted to 'renouncing for ever the possession of big ships'.[126]

The committee was less enamoured of de Lorenzi's plans for the fleet in the case of war with France. The ideas of the naval staff now went little further than the distribution of the fleet in time of war, when the main concentration would be at La Spezia while smaller forces were stationed at Messina, Taranto, Pola and La Maddalena.[127] De Lorenzi's chief recommendation was that a new principal fleet base should be established in northern Sardinia. The chief of staff was accused by Cagni of dispersing defences in the manner of the pre-war *cordone* system, and by Revel of failing to start the planning process by considering what the enemy could do. Acton, after pointing out that in wartime the two principal tasks which the Italian navy must fulfil would be the destruction of the enemy's naval forces and the protection of sea-borne supplies, argued that since the main French base was located at Biserta, the major naval offences and the attacks on Italy's trade routes would come from the south, a *punto d'appoggio* on the lower Tyrrhenian sea between Gaeta and Naples was needed.[128]

If not of one mind about how and what to plan, the naval high command was united in its view about its relations with the cabinet. Having rejected at the outset *a grandissima maggioranza* ('by a large majority')

Revel's suggestion that they might want to invite the secretary general of the Foreign Ministry to attend and describe Italy's situation vis-à-vis foreign powers, they accepted without demur his proposal that, when their deliberations were concluded, they should invite the minister and the secretary general 'and explain our naval possibilities to them, so that the people directing our foreign policy may know what force they can count on in the future in carrying out their mandate'.[129]

The tide of national politics now briefly caught up the navy. On 30 October 1922, Mussolini took office as prime minister and next day he invited Revel to serve as navy minister in his new cabinet. Both parties could see utility in a political partnership. Prior to coming to power, the Fascists had shown a limited but positive interest in the role of the navy as an instrument of national policy and an interest in parts of the world which could only be reached or retained with the aid of a powerful fleet.[130] Revel, who had followed Mussolini's campaign in the newspaper *Il Popolo d'Italia* to regain Italian rights in the Adriatic and Mediterranean, was much in sympathy with them. Having been in Naples during the Fascist party congress on 24 October, at which Mussolini had announced that in a new government the Fascist party intended to have control of the war, navy and foreign ministries, and after which the decision to unleash the March on Rome was taken, he had also been favourably impressed by the strongly monarchical sentiments voiced by party leaders, writing shortly afterwards to the king's aide-de-camp 'Now we can do nothing but show fascism our back, either by running away from it or by preceding it.'[131] He chose to collaborate with the as yet untested new regime. Mussolini's choice was a shrewd one: a freemason and an ardent monarchist, Revel was a reassurance to the navy and the crown that Fascism in power did not intend to disturb or displace either party.

The post-Washington world presented Italy with the prospect of a naval competition with France in categories of unregulated ships, the immediacy of which became evident when the naval attaché in Paris reported in December that the French government was seeking an addition of sixty million francs to the naval estimate, to be spent on nine new submarines and fifty-four aircraft, the latter as a general reserve for the southern frontier. The official justification that these were means necessary to defend the coasts against Germany cut no ice with the attaché, who suggested that they might more probably be explained by 'the arrival in power in Italy of a strong government, firmly decided to guarantee its position in the Mediterranean', and by the belief that Revel, whose ideas were well known, would improve and develop the Italian navy.[132] The former supposition at least was correct: from 1921, French naval plans focused chiefly on single-handed wars against Italy or Germany, and by 1929 French planners were contemplating the possibility that both would combine in a war.[133] The Italian naval general staff continued thereafter to regard France with considerable distrust. In October 1924, Ducci reported that she seemed on the verge of building in disregard of the Washington treaty under the guise of colonial necessity. The vehicle for the deception she was already working towards was Indochina, for which the colonial press was pressing claims for its own fleet. The goal was supposedly to have this fleet completed by 1926, when the treaties on naval armament would expire.[134]

At the opposite end of the Mediterranean the uncertain situation in Turkey, where the Chanak crisis saw British troops defending the neutral zone on the bank of the Straits against Kemalist nationalists, prompted the Italian naval attaché at Constantinople to warn in October 1922 that the one nation which could easily block them was Great Britain. Complete disarmament of the Straits was the ideal solution, while a strong Turkey, capable of closing the Bosphorus and also of preventing the reinforcement of Greece, with whom Italy had permanently conflicting interests, would be welcome. What was necessary at all costs, the attaché advised Rome, was 'to avert the danger of transforming the Mediterranean into an English sea, which would one day present us with the dilemma either of being starved or of following England without reservation'.[135] This accorded exactly with Mussolini's view of the Mediterranean as *mare nostrum*. From London, Rome learned that the fall of the Lloyd George government as a consequence of the Chanak crisis offered no immediate prospect of any change in the hellenophile policy pursued by the First Sea Lord, Admiral Beatty, notwithstanding the presumed attractions of accords with Italy.[136]

Under the terms of the Washington treaty, Italy was allowed to retain ten existing battleships totalling 182,000 tons and France ten totalling 221,170 tons. Both powers had to 'build down' to their agreed tonnages, and could begin building new ships to replace vessels that had reached twenty years of age in 1927. As Italy had five dreadnoughts in service displacing 112,900 tons to France's seven displacing 164,500 tons, the opportunity was open to her to modernise her older ships or to scrap ships and thus permit new build. Difficult as this would be to sustain financially, by the end of 1922, before the Washington treaty had been ratified by the Italian parliament, some elements within the navy were looking forward ambitiously to the mid-1930s and beyond. If France and Italy built at the rate of two ships a year from 1927, and each ship took four years to complete, both powers would have five modern ships by the time that the treaty ran out. Both powers should denounce the treaty two years before it was due to lapse in 1936; in its place, each power should be allowed to build four divisions of battleships, Great Britain and the United States having four ships per division, Japan three, and Italy and France two. Everyone should be allowed to start building a new battleship division every five years, beginning in 1940, thus maintaining the replacement rate of twenty years laid down by the Washington treaty. Among the reasons put forward in support of the idea were that it would create homogeneous divisions in which ships would all be of the same type, that it would keep the dockyards in business whereas on the present terms they would be without work between 1937 and 1947, and that it would allow Great Britain to maintain its two-power standard vis-à-vis Italy and France.[137]

Such musings represented the flights of fancy to which the navy could all too easily become prone when it projected the balance of naval forces forward a decade into the future. More prosaically, the fleet was having considerable difficulties keeping itself afloat in a state of proper efficiency. To keep costs of refitting the five Italian battleships (*Dante, Doria, Duilio, Cavour,* and *Cesare*) down to affordable levels, the dockyard command had to be ordered to carry out only those improvements specifically agreed by the minister, and to use ship-board personnel as much as possible in order to reduce labour costs.[138] The *Doria* was operating at only 60 per cent efficiency by October 1922, a month before work was due to start on her, due to imperfect functioning of her 152-mm guns and defects in her engines and electrical services; among other problems, her main condensers were wearing out after eight years' service. The commander-in-chief of the Mediterranean fleet, vice-admiral Solari, put part of the blame for the difficulties he was going to have in putting right the defects on the shoulders of the system of conscription, which deprived him of trained sailors when the old class left and diverted the attentions of the permanent personnel from maintenance and repairs to training the new class when it arrived.[139]

In the early summer of 1923, as it was about to find itself caught up in the Corfu incident, the navy had an opportunity to participate in the deliberations of the new Commissione suprema mista di difesa and to put forward its calculations as to what it would require to be able to fight another war like the 1915–18 war. Unlike its military counterpart, the naval general staff did not put forward a 'minimum' and a 'maximum' programme. Nor did it include any provision for new build – possibly a calculated omission designed to make its requests more palatable. In order to mobilise, it claimed to need munitions and materials amounting to 2.8 billion lire, and to fight 288 million lire a month.[140] The figures were not far short of the army's 'minimum' programme, but when added to it they produced astronomic sums. As it happened, the turns of international politics were about to make these calculations even more academic than they already appeared to be.

With the Italian withdrawal from Turkey, the Levant division of the fleet based itself on Rhodes, although ships drawing more than three metres could not winter there and would have to retreat to Marmaris, where the Turks kept a coal supply for them. Naval thought focused on the future of the Dodecanese which, according to Giuseppe Fioravanzo, 'with wise organisation of ports, custom duties and shipping, must become our base of operations for the peaceful conquest of Asia Minor and the centre for the distribution (*irradiazione*) of Anatolia's riches in our export trade from that country'. Stampalia and Leros could serve as bases for the light surface and submarine units necessary to defend the islands, and friendship with Turkey would be welcome since the country was 'in complete misery because of the technical and administrative incapacity and dishonesty of those who run it and because its people are not adapted for progress'.[141] Shortly, a chance turn of events would allow Mussolini the first opportunity to unveil his preferred policy of aggressive international revisionism by moving into the selfsame region.

Relations between Italy and Greece grew tense during the summer of 1923 as the Treaty of Lausanne, signed on 24 July, ended the war with Turkey. Uncertainty about whether the Turkish Grand Assembly would ratify the treaty was not resolved until 23 August. As part of the final settlement, the treaty confirmed Italian possession of the Dodecanese islands. Greece immediately objected, as it had already objected to the provision in the Treaty of 9 November 1921 admitting an independent Albania to the League of Nations under Italian protection which assigned the region of Cacciavia to Albania when, to the Greek way of thinking, it was part of Epirus. Foreseeing the possibility that force might need to be applied, and eager to strengthen Italy's position in the Adriatic, Revel issued a set of instructions incorporating an escalatory ladder of operations culminating in the military occupation of Corfu, to be effected without using force and without infringing on the lives of the civil population. The island would be held as a gauge of Greek acquiescence over the Dodecanese, and light surface units would remain in its waters afterwards.[142] An intelligence report at the beginning of August noted that there were only some two hundred troops and two hundred policemen on the island, which had no fortifications worth the name. The French were reportedly cordially disliked and the Italians respected, even though they were feared and disliked as much as ever. The islanders were politically divided and economically straitened: the city had no electric light as the Belgian generating company had not been paid for eighteen months.[143]

On 27 August 1923, a group of unknown bandits murdered general Tellini and a group of Italian officers who were engaged in delimiting the Greek–Albanian frontier near Janina in Greece. Mussolini immediately sent an ultimatum to the Greek government demanding an enquiry under the authority of the Italian military attaché in Athens, an indemnity of 50 million lire, and various other humiliating recompenses and when only a part of his demands was met he ordered an expeditionary force to occupy the island of Corfu. The choice of means reflected the Duce's preference for action. The location, as the French ambassador François Charles-Roux pointed out to Paris, was a strategic position of primary importance.

The task of applying force was given to the Mediterranean fleet under vice-admiral Solari. At the end of July, he was ordered to interrupt the fleet's summer exercises and put in to Taranto. While waiting there, he carried out a study of 'a demonstrative exercise against Greece' at Salonika, Piraeus and Patras, and a successive action to occupy Corfu.[144] This was now put into action. At 9 a.m. on 31 August a force of two battleships, two cruisers, five destroyers, two torpedo boats, four MAS boats and two submarines appeared off the island, and when the Greek garrison refused to accept the terms of surrender quickly enough, the task force commander opened fire to protect the troops he had already landed – an action, he afterwards stated, which 'would not have been started or completed, and which would have been suspended, if the white flag had been raised'.[145] These *sette minuti di fuoco*, in the course of which an Italian shell hit part of a barracks sheltering Albanian refugees, killing seven and wounding ten, greatly exercised the international community which quickly demonstrated that it was not prepared to see the League of Nations flouted or sanction the use of force by one of its members.

Faced suddenly with the prospect of a naval confrontation with Great Britain, the navy reined in a Duce evidently unable to weigh his wishes against capabilities. Bernotti was hastily summoned to Rome by the chief of naval staff, admiral Gino Ducci, to reinforce data on the relative strengths of the two navies. The burden of the comparison was made plain to Mussolini when, at a meeting of the council of ministers on 12 September, he asked how long Italy could last out against Great Britain. Revel reportedly responded laconically, 'forty-eight hours'.[146] The following day, he sent Mussolini two memoranda calculated to dissuade him from the gamble he appeared inclined to take. In the first, he suggested that Italy could take on a 3-handed war against Yugoslavia, Greece and Great Britain provided that the air force could deploy at least 200 planes in Sicily, supplies of fuel and raw materials could be guaranteed from central Europe, and men and money be sent into Egypt to foment a revolt.

In the second, he pointed out that virtually the entire western coast of Italy, including the naval base at La Maddalena, was wide open to attack by France.[147] The same day, Ducci warned Mussolini that the fleet was too weak to detach units to defend the Dodecanese in the event of war with a power stronger at sea than Greece and therefore that the islands would have to be protected by artillery, submarines and seaplanes based on Rhodes, Leros and Stampalia.[148]

With every calculable factor counselling against going over the brink to war, Mussolini took one step forward and another one back. On 16 September, general Giardino was nominated governor of Fiume. On 17 September, Revel drafted detailed instructions to the governor of Corfu, vice-admiral Diego Simonetti, who had arrived on the island fifteen days earlier without any official guidance at all and who had therefore based his brief period of rule on Mussolini's pronouncements in the newspapers, for the Italian withdrawal from the island. Italian pride was salved with a funeral service for the dead in Athens cathedral, full military honours when the bodies were put on board the *San Marco* for transportation home, a twenty-one gun salute from the Greek navy, and a financial indemnity.

The Corfu incident showed Mussolini that the international community would not put up with the unilateral use of force to resolve disputes and make territorial adjustments. It also demonstrated that the navy, while a vital instrument of Italian overseas policy, was too weak to risk in a war with a major power such as Great Britain. The naval general staff used the opportunity to explore the lessons of the incident, and required the heads of the four naval commands at La Spezia, Naples, Taranto and Venice to report with a view to improving the mobilisation of the fleet for defence and offence. Vice-admiral Simonetti reported that the effects of the post-war demobilisation on Taranto were such that a month after the start of mobilisation 'it was very far from being in a state of efficient defence'. The artillery defending the port, particularly anti-aircraft guns, were not capable of effective action; complicated administrative arrangements had slowed down the provisioning and supply of warships; command authority had been overwhelmed with peripheral responsibilities; and the naval authorities had been kept in the dark about the army's plans.[149] Quite how much Mussolini knew in detail about the navy's weaknesses is uncertain, but the general outlines of the picture were clear enough.

During the crisis weeks at the beginning of September Rome lacked guidance on how the Royal Navy intended to act as the Italian naval attaché in London was unable to contact any of the senior naval authorities, all of whom were out of town or unavailable. By early October, the navy was more fully informed. Admiral Beatty's hellenophile inclinations were reportedly no less weak, and while the Royal Navy wanted Greece as 'a vassal rather than an ally', the Bank of England had advanced capital and financial support to her, so that from both quarters there was very little sympathy for Italy. Rome's actions had created a feeling of 'unease and disturbance' because Italy had acted too precipitately and in a way which could have unleashed a war. British public opinion, more opposed to war than any other, was not able to judge its own government accurately, captain Bianchi reported; 'here, more than anywhere else, national and individual egoism flourish, along with the desire to subordinate everyone else to their will, to avoid anything which can even distantly disturb their quiet life'. Thus the British government was able to present as disturbers of the peace a country which made others respect its rights and its dignity.[150]

For the navy, as for the army, ambitions and appetites had ultimately to be tempered by finance. In the opening years of the Fascist regime budgetary allocations were low, a situation which did not change until Italy's renegotiation of her war debt with Great Britain in January 1926 opened the way for foreign capital to fund expansion. In 1922–3, the armed forces consumed 22.4 per cent of state expenditure; over the period 1923–31 the proportion increased to 31 per cent. Revel faced a fight for funds not merely with the army, traditionally the senior service, but also with the newly created Regia Aeronautica, brought into being by Mussolini in March 1923. He scored a success in getting Mussolini to agree to a programme of ship replacements at a time when his interests were aroused by the new service. However, in the early years the navy still ran a long way behind the army: of 8,130,000,000 lire allocated to defence budgets between 1924 and 1926, the navy received 25.7 per cent against the army's share of 61.9 per cent and the air force's 12.4 per cent. Revel's first budget demonstrated that the new regime could be favourably disposed to the navy, however, as it received 52,000,000 lire instead of the preceding year's 32,000,000 lire.[151]

Revel repeatedly emphasised the central role of the navy both in national defence in time of war and in supporting the exercise of foreign policy. In the latter respect, he played on themes which resonated with Mussolini's most profound beliefs about race and nationality by emphasising the need to keep contact with the sizeable part of Italy's population – reportedly one-sixth – who lived overseas, as well as with her colonies. His priorities were reflected in the doubling of the proportion of the naval budget allocated for the construction and maintenance of ships from 2.3 per cent to 4.6 per cent over three years. The naval general staff, in battling for more funds, played on the established theme that Italy more than any other nation needed sea-borne supplies to live and to fight. After the Corfu incident, it was also able to point to the lack of sufficient naval power to enforce Italian rights in questions of international politics.[152] To back this up, French naval manoeuvres in the spring of 1924 appeared to be rooted in the belief that Italy would take advantage of any temporary international embarrassment to press her claims and designed to warn her against making any demands respecting Tunisia, Corsica or rectification of the joint land frontier.[153]

Revel accepted that naval appetites could not be fully met. The 1923/4 naval budget amounted to 768,638,000 lire. He twice demanded reductions in the draft budget for 1924/5, cutting it down from 1.365 milliard lire to 1 milliard lire. The naval general staff's response, apparently designed to demonstrate to the minister the unacceptable price of such a reduction, was to propose that after fixed costs had been met the construction programme for the year be cut by five sevenths in monetary terms. This would entail axing both 10,000-ton cruisers allowed under the Washington treaty and already included in the 1923/4 programme and two aircraft carriers, as well as six out of twelve destroyers and four of ten submarines from the 1924/5 programme.[154] Faced with last minute increases in pay and expenses and the possibility of a budget amounting to only 930,000,000 lire, the naval general staff proposed reducing the number of torpedoes on destroyers from twelve to eight and on board submarines from eighteen to twelve.[155]

Although constrained by the decision to allocate a global sum of 3,200,000,000 lire for national defence, of which he could claim no more than a third, Revel pointed out to Mussolini what the consequences were going to be. The monies for new build would rise from 120,000,000 lire in 1923/4 to 160,000,000 lire in 1924/5, while the sum available for coastal defence would be only 27 million. Both sums were 'evidently unequal even to the most basic needs of our maritime power'. In order to fit annual budgets to the four-year building programmes the navy had to design for the forward projection of force, and to produce by 1928 a fleet capable of 'fortifying us as far as possible against the surprises of the future', Revel asked Mussolini for a budget of 1,204,000,000 lire for 1924/5 which included an annual 'extraordinary credit' of 190 million for new build for each of the coming four years (1924/5–1927/8) in addition to the 160 million allocated in the ordinary annual budget. With 350 million a year for new build, Mussolini could have a fleet of four cruisers, eighteen destroyers, four 1300-ton submarines and fourteen 800-ton submarines, ten MAS boats, twelve minesweepers and a number of smaller craft. The aircraft carriers had disappeared from the navy's list.[156]

In the event, Revel got less than half what he asked for. An extra 35 million lire was added to the standing allocation of 120 million for new build for 1924/5, and the navy planned on a small increase in that figure to 40 million for each of the following three years, giving

a total for new build of 160 million a year. The two four-year programmes for 1923–7 and 1924–8 would thus produce two cruisers,
twelve destroyers, ten submarines, four MAS boats and six minesweepers. Now planning under Revel's direction in quinquennial and not qua-
drennial programmes, the navy looked forward to 1925–30 and a rise
in building funds to 200 million a year in the last two years. Adding
together its expected and projected new-build monies, it expected to
be able to build two more cruisers, four destroyers, one heavy and
four medium submarines as well as various light craft.[157] Even at this
rate, Italy was going to fall behind France. In December 1924, France
introduced a 'Statut naval' fixing the tonnage of the main categories of
warships for a period of twenty years. Projecting forward credits voted
hitherto, the Italian naval attaché advised that by 1928 France would
have six new cruisers (out of nine), eighteen new destroyers (out of
forty-six) and twenty-three new submarines (out of sixty-two). In ten
years, the fleet would settle down at eighteen 10,000-ton cruisers, thirty-
six 2,300-ton esploratori, seventy-two 1,250-ton destroyers and fifty-
eight submarines averaging 1,500 tons.[158] The aim behind the programme, not openly acknowledged in France, was to give a margin
of superiority of 100,000 tons over the combined fleets of Italy and
Germany.[159]

If the detail of the Italian plans was speculative, the framework was not.
Thanks to Revel's efforts, quinquennial budgeting replaced annual budgeting with the passage of the 1925/6 financial legislation.[160] However,
as his period of ministerial office drew to its close – he would resign on 7
May 1925 – there was much criticism in naval circles of the outcome of
the first years of Fascist rule. Admiral Sechi could see no visible improvement in the situation, while admiral d'Aste pointed out that since a cruiser
cost at least 130 million lire and a battleship 350 million, the sums forthcoming restricted Italy to building only light ships. Revel was forced to
acknowledge that given the fall in the value of the lire, the sum available
was not equal to pre-war budgets. Fascism seemed to be incapable of
formulating or funding the detailed naval programme necessary to back
its grandiose ambitions for freedom of action in the Mediterranean, and
in antagonising both the French and the British it was putting Italy in a
worse position than she had been in before 1914.[161]

The Italian navy had carried out no grand fleet manoeuvres since 1910,
and plans to resume them in 1923 were thrown awry by the Corfu incident. Vice-admiral Solari led his fleet on a cruise to Sicily and Tripolitania
and back, and carried out joint MAS boat – submarine exercises in the
Straits of Messina before being diverted to Taranto to prepare for action
against Greece. A planned exercise in which the four ships of the battleship division would anchor at La Maddelena, whose defences would then

be tested by MAS boats and submarines, to be followed by a second phase at Portoferraio in which aircraft and light surface craft would co-operate in the hunt for submarines, and a third at La Spezia to test the effectiveness of hydrophones gave clear evidence of the navy's preoccupation with defence. The battleship division was scheduled to practise defence against night attacks by MAS boats and daytime attacks by destroyers.[162] All this, too, was interrupted by the Corfu crisis.

General fleet exercises in the spring of 1924 followed similar lines, concentrating heavily on defence against submarines and on the use of hydrophones, MAS boats and aircraft to hunt them.[163] The first full strategic manoeuvres between contesting parties took place that August in the Sicilian channel. The scenario was the defence of a convoy of merchant ships travelling from Tobruk to mainland ports against attack by a thinly disguised French fleet. The neutrality of Greek ports placed an additional burden on the Italian fleet as it could not flee to them if followed. The defending 'red' fleet under rear-admiral Massimiliano Lovatelli was adjudged to have won, largely because the attacking 'blue' fleet under rear-admiral Ugo Conz found it difficult to find the convoy and then to concentrate forces against it because of poor radio-telegraph communications.[164] Afterwards, the manoeuvres were held to have shown the deficiencies in the air arm and to have confirmed the navy's need for its own aeroplanes and for at least one aircraft carrier, as well as the utility of heavy submarines (1,000–1,200 tons) and of 1,200-ton destroyers.[165]

The vexed question of the Italian navy's failure to construct aircraft carriers, which was to resonate long after the Fascist period ended, was closely bound up with the creation of an independent air force, as well as with the complex of unresolved ideas in the minds of the admirals about the future nature of sea power and the roles of different kinds of force, including aircraft. In June 1923 the admirals' committee pronounced in favour of building at least one aircraft carrier to accompany the fleet in order to defend it against air attacks and to launch them. In December, the *Giuseppe Miraglia* was adapted to launch seaplanes. In March 1924 the admirals' committee considered the question again. In answer to the objection that it presently took three hours to launch forty planes, it was pointed out that several carriers would overcome the problem. The admirals concluded by recommending the construction of at least two carriers.[166] Revel, who had argued to Sechi in 1921 that 'the development and use of aeroplanes in war on our seas and along our coasts is today the most essential element of national defence', only to be told by the minister, who was a 'battleship admiral', that aircraft carriers were unnecessary in an enclosed sea like the Mediterranean and that 'a well organised network of coastal air stations' was a perfectly good substitute, clearly regretted counter-signing the decree creating the Regia Aeronautica in March 1923 and now made it clear that in his view naval aviation should be given back to seamen and that the construction of aircraft carriers was of the highest importance.[167] However, no provision was made for one in the budgets he presented after December 1923.

The role of air power in future wars was but one element in the doctrinal contest which enfolded the navy as it sought to devise its first construction programmes. Faced with the varied experiences of the world war, in which battleships had not met in defining fleet actions of the kind envisioned before its outbreak and in which submarines had posed a sufficient threat to the ultimate victory of the Allies as to make it quite unclear whether they were weapons of potential strength at sea or evidence of actual weakness, defenders of the traditional supremacy of heavy ships and big guns such as Sechi and Alberto Da Zara warned against mistaking the modifications which technology had introduced into war for fundamental changes in its nature. Taking an evolutionary position alongside the traditionalists, Bernotti proposed the development of 30-knot warships armed with eight or more big guns and protected against the threat of torpedo attack. On an opposite tack, theorists such as Alfredo Baistrocchi (brother of the future under-secretary of state for war Federico Baistrocchi), Arturo Riccardi (under-secretary of state for the navy and chief of naval general staff 1940–3) and Guido Po focused on the central importance of protecting the sea lines of communication for Italy, a country which had had to import 51,000,000 tons of goods and raw materials in the world war and had lost 955,291 tons of merchant shipping.[168] Thus, while 'traditionalists' favoured heavy battleships which could challenge first-rank naval powers, 'innovators' propounded the merits of fast, heavily armed light cruisers which would only be effective against second-rank naval opponents.[169]

Air power was part and parcel of this debate in two respects. At a practical level, the influence and effect that aeroplanes would have on war at sea in the future had to be extrapolated on the basis of very limited experience during the world war. In the political arena, claims for the supremacy of air power in war and therefore for its complete independence had to be contested if the navy's budgets, power, autonomy and even existence were not to be seriously threatened. The target was colonel Giulio Douhet's popular work *Il dominio dell'aria*, first published in 1921, and its central tenet: *resistere sulla superficie per far massa nell'aria* ('resist on the surface to mass in the air'). Giulio Valli observed that resisting at sea meant more than simply standing on the defensive and that Douhet's promised destruction of the enemy could only work if it was immediate and complete, while Fioravanzo and Bernotti stressed the need to co-ordinate action at sea, on land and in the air and to think in terms of aero–naval warfare as an intermediary role lying between the use of air power in independent and auxiliary roles.[170]

Debates on these lines would expand and develop in subsequent years as the three services contested with one another for political favour. For the time being, the strength of the conservative 'battleship admirals' and the fact that Revel had successfully amended article 8 of the decree of 28 March 1923 to secure naval control over the employment of any aircraft assigned to the fleet meant that the case for constructing an aircraft carrier languished. The issue was symptomatic of the situation the service found itself in after the first three years of Fascist rule. Though the aspirations of the new regime were grandiose, precise details and clear political direction were absent. In these circumstances, the naval authorities found themselves in a situation in which there was no guidance to be had from theory because, as Bernotti afterwards remarked, 'naval strategy was in a period of change in which it was difficult to evaluate the significance of likely changes in the physical appearance of the fleet and in the possibilities of action'.[171]

Aeroplanes, air power and Fascism

In 1911, Italy became the first state to use aeroplanes in war when experiments in aerial bombardment (initially with hand grenades) and aerial photography were carried out during the Libyan war. In common with other European powers, Italy's stock of military aircraft was initially small: when war broke out in Europe in August 1914, twenty-eight combat-ready aircraft and eighteen reserves were put at the disposal of military headquarters. The role of aircraft in modern war was as yet uncertain but the question as to who would control and direct them arose almost immediately. The solution, adopted in January 1915, was to make the Corpo aeronautico an independent agency, but to put it under the command of the relevant military and naval authorities when deployed in war. The aerial war began on 24 May 1915 when Italy's only dirigible, the *Città di Ferrara*, was sent to bomb the Austrian port of Pola. This was the start of a more or less continuous campaign during which the Italians bombed Trieste, Pola, Fiume and other Austrian cities, while the Austrians struck particularly at Venice, Treviso, Mestre, Vicenza, Verona, and Padua, launching 343 bombing raids in all which, according to official figures, killed 984 people and wounded 1,193.[172]

Italian air power first began to make a contribution to the ground war during the third battle of the Isonzo (18 October–4 November 1915), though its employment thereafter was much inhibited during the winter by the high winds (*bora*), cloud, rain and snow that characterised the climate of the region in which the war was being fought. The efficiency of Italian fighter aeroplanes, and therefore defence against Austrian reconnaissance, was also hindered by the lack of synchronised machine-guns, a deficiency only remedied at the start of 1917. Like its military counterpart, the air component was taken by surprise by Caporetto and much of its equipment was lost in the retreat that followed, though it claimed to have shot down thirty-nine enemy aeroplanes in seventy fights by mid-November. A reorganisation of the air force the following spring, which saw the creation of the Comando superiore di aeronautica under general Luigi Bongiovanni at supreme headquarters and the concentration of both fighters and bombers in *masse*, improved the air force's efficiency. During the battle of Vittorio Veneto the Italians put 400 aeroplanes into the skies against at least 470 enemy planes.[173]

Considerable industrial effort was put into the new arm during the war, with 105 factories employed in manufacturing airframes, aero engines and propellers. At the war's end, the Italian air force had reached a strength of 2,725 aircraft. Out of a total of 11,986 planes manufactured during the four years of war, almost half had been built under licence and only 2,208 were entirely national products, a statistic which reflected Italy's problems in developing and manufacturing aero engines in particular, but also airframes.[174] These problems were to last throughout the Fascist era.

The chaos of post-war Italian politics was replicated in the chaotic nature of the arrangements made for the provision of air power in peacetime. Responsibility for supply was passed from a commissariat within the ministry for arms and munitions, which was abolished in December 1919, to the industry ministry, then the treasury, and next to the transport ministry before finally coming to rest in the war ministry. During the brief period in which the treasury was the responsible authority war surplus aircraft were sold off, much to the outrage of a parliamentary committee of enquiry which reported, under the auspices of Fascism, in 1923. The staff set out the needs of the nascent force in respect of the types of aircraft it wanted – fighters, strategic and tactical reconnaissance planes and heavy bombers – and settled on a peacetime strength of thirty-six squadrons, requiring a total of only seventy-two new aircraft a year to be kept functional.

While the state was allowing air power to settle into a lowly third place behind the other services, air power enthusiasts and Fascists began to develop the mutual attraction which would put the air force in a unique position in the fabric of national defence. Mussolini had made his first aeroplane flight as a passenger in August 1915, and began pilot training himself in July 1919, qualifying as a pilot on 13 May 1921.[175] The columns of his newspaper, *Il Popolo d'Italia*, were opened up to aviation enthusiasts, and he associated himself closely with the long distance *raid* in which Italian aircraft flew from Rome to Tokyo between 8 January and 30 May 1920, an event which led the chamber of deputies to institute a public enquiry into what it regarded as a scandalous waste of public money. On 27–8 March 1921, *Il Popolo d'Italia* co-sponsored a national conference in Milan to which Gabriele D'Annunzio, a wartime hero as a result of his air exploits which included a raid on Vienna, gave his seal of approval and at which Mussolini spoke on 'the press and the air force'. Calling for the establishment of an independent air ministry, the conference concluded that 'the air force is about to become the decisive arm in the future conflicts between peoples and therefore the means must be readied to safeguard the command of our skies'.[176] Industrialists and manufacturers, including Caproni, Breda and Macchi, gathered around Mussolini, and so did wartime pilots and others, attracted, as general Giuseppe Valle afterwards explained, 'by the upsurge of fascism since they saw it as the only means of saving the country from the shipwreck to which subversives were driving it'.[177]

Alongside Mussolini when he received the king's invitation to form a government on 29 October 1922 was Aldo Finzi, a wartime pilot who had taken part in D'Annunzio's celebrated raid on Vienna on 9 August 1918 and a Fascist of 'the first hour'. Finzi was made under-secretary of the interior ministry and given the task of setting up the administrative structure of an independent air force. Meanwhile, Mussolini set up a test of the efficiency of the air force in which all available aircraft were ordered to take off and fly for one hour. The results, trumpeted in the press on 24 January 1923, purported to show that only seventy-six aircraft were fit to fly. The service's own official statistics, by contrast, showed that the army had 237 aircraft in working order and the navy forty-eight. As was to become his wont, Mussolini was exaggerating the deficiencies for political purposes; on 31 October 1923, 420 aircraft passed another flying test, and a year later *Il Popolo d'Italia* reported that the figures for March 1923 were 286 aircraft in working order.[178] Mussolini's manifest misrepresentation of the facts to the cabinet served two political purposes. As well as being another 'demonstration' of the incompetence and ineptitude of the Liberal governments he had displaced, it offered striking evidence to support his scarcely veiled contention that air power was not safe in the hands of the army and the navy and his intention to create an independent air force.

On 24 January 1923, the Commissariato per l'Aeronautica was created with Mussolini as commissary and Finzi as his deputy, and funds amounting to 122.6 million lire were transferred from the budgets of the other two services to run the fledgling force. Two months later, on

28 March, the Regia Aeronautica was established by royal decree. Speaking at Centocelle aerodrome in November of that year, Mussolini explained the mixture of military and political calculations which had prompted him to set up what was, in the wake of the British example, only the second independent air force in the world:

As head of the government with the enormous responsibility of the existence, independence, freedom and well-being of the Italian people, I am obliged not to believe in universal peace, and still less in perpetual peace. No one knows whether the war of tomorrow will be exclusively an aerial or a land or a naval war. For me, it is enough to ponder on what others are doing. If others are arming in the skies, then we must arm in the skies.[179]

The only other continental power building a sizeable air force at that time was France, with an air division comprising 296 bombers and 300 fighters.

General Pier Ruggiero Piccio, Italy's third-highest scoring wartime fighter ace with twenty-four 'kills' and a *medaglia d'oro* (the Italian equivalent of the Victoria Cross or the Medal of Honor) to his credit, became first commandant general of the air force and as such the senior serving officer.[180] Its first full budget for 1923/4, was set at 256 million lire, climbing the following year to 450 million, and Finzi began the custom of advertising design competitions *(gare)* for new planes which was to be a feature of aircraft procurement under Fascism for the remaining years of peacetime. Finzi's methods as an administrator were rough and ready, and gained him enemies both inside and outside the new service: officials involved in the previous management of the air force and associated with the other two services were sacked in large numbers, to be replaced by discharged officers of the same political cast of mind as himself, and promotions were awarded without regard to regulations. In his favour, it can be said that there was a great deal to organise – or reorganise – and that among his achievements were the establishment of the air force academy at Livorno and of a corps of aeronautical engineers.[181]

On 24 June 1924, ten days after Matteotti's abduction and murder, Finzi was replaced as vice-commissar by lieutenant-general Alberto Bonzani, a Piedmontese artilleryman later destined to become chief of the army general staff (1929–34). As always, Mussolini's action in sacking his deputy is open to several interpretations. As well as being potentially implicated in the Matteotti murder by virtue of his position at the interior ministry, Finzi was also a member of that section of the party which was pushing Mussolini to extremes, and therefore in both respects a useful person to discard. From another point of view, Finzi's methods were not settling the new arm on an even keel and made him an obstacle to establishing good relations with the other two services which was now one of Mussolini's priorities, so his choice of an utterly conventional soldier suggests that his motives were as much to do with his conception of the politics of inter-service and intra-service relations as they were with his public and parliamentary troubles.

Bonzani inherited a force numbering 1,181 aircraft, of which 748 were ready for combat. Unsusceptible to the seductions of air power as much by instinct as by background – he reportedly never got into an aeroplane – he set about putting the new force on a sound organisational footing. Regulations passed in August and November 1924 settled enlistment, the hierarchy of ranks, promotions, lengths of service and pensions. In April 1925, the post of commandant general was converted into that of chief of the air staff and, after Piccio was despatched to Paris as air attache, left vacant for the time being. Finzi had depended on wartime Spad XII fighters to sustain the air force in being and had ordered Nieuport 29s – both French aircraft – as replacements. Bonzani defended the policy to parliament on 24 November 1924, pointing out that 'no Italian experimental engin[e] had passed the test which was required to be mass-produced', and that Italian manufacturers could only reproduce old-fashioned 200-horse power engines which were not as reliable as the foreign 300-horse power versions mounted in the Nieuports.[182]

The exercises carried out by the adolescent air force under Finzi and Bonzani demonstrated both the present shortcomings and the future potential of the new arm. In experimental air manoeuvres held in Friuli in May 1922, the servizio di collegamento, which was intended to co-ordinate troop movements on the ground by using aircraft to inform ground commanders of the movements of their own and enemy forces, was tested. It did not work as well as was desired, due to the lack of suitable means of communication and the deficient functioning of the signals posts. The following year, aircraft were incorporated into manoeuvres held in August south of Lake Garda to test the attributes of the celeri divisions. The air component of the exercise was designed to test air reconnaissance and to assess the potential contribution on the battlefield of formations of fighters attacking troops on the ground and of night bombing of bridges and communications. Neither reconnaissance nor the servizio di collegamento worked particularly well due to a combination of factors: column commanders did not ask for help from the air component and did not obey instructions to make their troops clearly identifiable from the air, fog and cloud affected activities, and the celeri units lacked the radio-telegraphy capacity to communicate effectively with the aeroplanes. The information that air reconnaissance could provide was, though, deemed 'indispensable'. The bombing and fighter exercises, in which two and thirty-two aircraft respectively took part, were notably more effective. In the latter case this was due to the troops taking little or no evasive or defensive action. Despite the limitations of various kinds, the effect of direct air intervention on the battlefield was deemed 'undeniable' and the potential of air power to enhance the chances of the attack was recognised as obvious.[183]

The degree to which things could become unstuck when the air force collaborated with another service became glaringly apparent the following year when in August it took part in the first naval grand manoeuvres to be held since 1910, in which the 'Blue' and 'Red' fleets, commanded respectively by admirals Lovatelli and Conz, manoeuvred against one another in the Ionian sea. The tasks of the air components, which were given a secondary role in the exercise, were to conduct aerial surveillance of coastal waters, to reconnoitre enemy bases, and to attack enemy ships which happened to come in range. A catalogue of errors and failures ensued – not all of them entirely the airmen's fault. The air force was accused in the press of not being able to tell the difference between MAS boats and destroyers; 'Red' aircraft attacked one of their own submarines by mistake; the airships which were supposed to carry out long-range reconnaissance (the aircraft allocated to the fleets had a range of only one hundred miles) were grounded for twenty-four hours by the weather; and communications between ships and planes worked poorly. To cap it all, when the 'Blue' fleet sailed into Augusta harbour at the end of the manoeuvres its flagship, the *Doria*, was torpedoed by 'Red' – because, said admiral Lovatelli, the air escort abandoned its proper formation to overfly the fleet in a celebratory *volo di festa*. The senior airman involved, Ernesto Coop, indignantly defended his force against most of the charges, pointing out among other things that Lovatelli's initial orders for the air force had been 'vague and imprecise' and that communications had failed because the fleet personnel in charge of radio-telegraphy lacked sufficient ability. He was left impotent and fuming when Lovatelli ended his public summary of the lessons of the exercise with the demand that all naval air units should belong to the Regia Marina.[184]

Bonzani now proved himself to be exactly the kind of man Mussolini needed to nurse the infant air force while keeping good relations with the other services. In September 1924, after the naval manoeuvres had concluded, admiral Thaon di Revel complained very strongly about the very poor contribution that air force had made. Its involvement had been very limited ('*scarsissimo*'), and the assistance it had rendered was 'almost nil' as a result of the few aircraft that had taken part, their poor quality, the inadequacy of the seaplane stations and the pilots' lack of training in sea searches. Revel demanded that aircraft be put on all ships ('today a warship without aircraft is incomplete'), that the navy be given a large number of seaplanes and dirigibles ('truly indispensable for reconnaissance'), and that it be given full control of all marine aviation without restrictions of any sort.[185] Bonzani's reply – two months later – was a model of bureaucratic competence and professional moderation. After pointing out that the S 16 seaplane had a range of only 150 kilometres, and that it was not the air force's fault that there were neither ships capable of carrying reconnaissance aircraft nor carriers – 'the only solution which will significantly widen the range of aircraft action' – he noted that in October the air force had only been given 6 days' notice of joint exercises and that of 143 naval aircraft only 36 were in a fully usable state, as the navy well knew. Up to 1923 it had spent only 9 million lire on seaplanes – a measure of how little interest it had in air power. On the central point of inter-service politics, the navy's need to own its own aviation, he was emollient, telling Mussolini that he 'broadly agreed'.[186]

Bonzani's evident readiness to compromise on the issue of which service controlled which aircraft, which significantly eased Mussolini's problems and must therefore have made him aware of the value of his subordinate, was the background to the production of the decree-law of 4 May 1925 which Mussolini presented as air commissary. The new legislation set the peacetime strength of the Regia Aeronautica at 182 squadrons, two and a half times the number Bonzani had inherited from Finzi, divided them up between the air force (seventy-eight squadrons), the army (sixty-nine squadrons) and the navy (thirty-five squadrons), and gave the army and the navy command over the units temporarily allotted to them for as long as necessary so that their training for war could be improved. It thus appeared to be a considerable step forward, but any thoughts it may have encouraged that inter-service rivalry could be overcome would prove to be premature.

The selection first of Finzi and then of Bonzani as heads of the new air force, and the concept of the use of air power inherent in Bonzani's tripartite division of it, represented a deliberate move to keep at arm's length the most eloquent proponent of independent air power in Europe, colonel Giulio Douhet. By the time that Mussolini came to power Douhet, whose first article on air warfare had been published in 1910, was extremely well known as a polemicist as a result of the publication in 1921 of his book *Il dominio dell'aria*, which trumpeted the supremacy of the bomber in future warfare. He was equally well known as a bitter critic of the wartime army high command in general and of Cadorna in particular. After the March on Rome, Mussolini opened the columns of *Il Popolo d'Italia* to him, and Douhet used them to argue that the army and navy were useless without a strong air force, and that the air force was presently so weak that the only alternatives were to abolish the other two services or 'to create an air element capable of defending our skies, be it even at the cost of proportionally reducing the forces of the other services'.[187] His appointment as director-general of military aviation was therefore brief, as the navy demanded that Mussolini annul it. Douhet responded with another book, *La difesa nazionale*, in 1923 in which he pressed the case for the creation of 'a real air force' and the institution of a ministry of national defence to formulate an organic military policy, and wrote twice to Mussolini in 1924 asking to be allowed to 'straighten out' aviation. Although Mussolini gave him an interview, his request was not met.[188]

While he greeted its appearance with qualified pleasure, Douhet recognised that the Regia Aeronautica was not founded on the lines that he had propagated in his many publications. Instead of being a homogeneous body with a single, clearly defined and unique scope, it was, he noted in *La difesa nazionale*, 'a bundle of all the most heterogeneous aeronautical elements of the nation, with no distinction made between them, and what their roles (*scopi*) may or can be'.[189] Behind his customary hyperbole lay a significant truth: the air force was being created according to no single strategic doctrine. In fact, the early years of the independent air force were to be characterised by an intense and unresolved debate about the correct use of aeroplanes which was just now beginning. Gradually during these first years the debate began to assume its shape; in the second half of the decade it would deepen, but it would never really be resolved.

Discussion and division over the 'true' role of the aeroplane in war began at once when Amadeo Mecozzi, who was to become Douhet's main antagonist in an increasingly bitter battle of ideas, challenged his theory of the bomber's capacity to attain and maintain mastery of the skies. Mecozzi noted that in the last war losses from high-level bombing had been less than those inflicted by fighter planes and anti-aircraft guns. Yet to develop what would become in time a sophisticated set of concepts of air war, he pointed out in 1922 that there were effective modes of defence against waves of bombers, such as dropping bombs on them – a technique which was incorporated into the provisional regulations for fighter training in 1925.[190] Others soon contributed to the debate over how to use Italy's nascent air power. Lieutenant colonel Natale Pentimalli, who sided broadly with Douhet, accepted the air as the first and decisive line of national defence and dilated on the virtues of gas as a weapon particularly suited for use by aeroplanes; general Roberto Bencivenga set out the role of air power as a force multiplier for the army with an important part to play in increasing the tempo of action; and colonel Angelo Gatti pointed out that what one side could do by way of pulverising a nation's capital cities from the air the other could do too, and portrayed air power as one among many components in the future 'war of machines'.[191] The ongoing debate of which these were the opening salvoes encapsulated the situation in which the newest of the three services now found itself. Doctrinally as well as politically, there was everything to play for under the new regime.

2   Domestic checks and international balances, 1925–1929

Fig. 2 Inspecting the Fascist air force

Created in March 1923, the Regia Aeronautica suffered from the start from unresolved and potentially conflicting goals. A propaganda weapon under Italo Balbo, it showed the Fascist flag around the globe with long-range air 'cruises' to Russia, South America and the United States. It was also a war-fighting instrument, and Mussolini put Balbo on notice in 1928 that he had ten years to prepare it for war. In the 1930s, under Balbo's successor Giuseppe Valle, its weaknesses became increasingly serious. A 'shop-window' force of increasingly obsolescent aircraft with no clear doctrine of air war to guide it, its capacity to contribute to Italy's European wars was much less than its image suggested.

Neither Mussolini nor his deputy at the foreign ministry, Dino Grandi, bothered to attend the signing of the Kellogg declaration outlawing war in 1928. Indeed, apart from signing the Locarno treaty in person in 1925, the Duce generally absented himself from international conferences for the next twelve years. His diplomacy during the latter part of the 1920s was chiefly directed at fashioning a springboard from which to launch the first stage of Italy's expansion overseas. The tools he needed to carry out the military actions which were the corollary of his foreign policy were not yet in a state to be able to use or to threaten war. To add to his frustration, the bureaucratic structures and processes by means of which the armed forces were to be chivvied towards readiness for war proved slow and cumbersome, a consequence not merely of his own shortcomings but also of the inadequacies of his chosen lieutenant whose readiness to share the Duce's ambitions and facilitate their achievement was rather less than wholehearted.

The pattern of foreign policy

In the aftermath of the Matteotti affair and the party crisis of December 1924, Mussolini developed the legal structures which enabled him to exert control on both the extremists within the Fascist party and the state at large. Domestic legislation occupied a central place in his political life between 1925 and 1927, during which time the grip of Fascism on parliament was enforced through such measures as the Acerbo electoral law and the suppression of the trade unions in October 1925. This process had a multiple purpose, for it sought to reinstitutionalise Italy, to cement Mussolini's powers and position and to provide a firm basis for his expansionist foreign policy. The reciprocal relationship between domestic and foreign policy was exemplified in the Lateran Pact of 1929. Another important example of the intermixing of the two arenas of power was the settlement of wartime debts with the United States in November 1925 and with Great Britain in January 1926 on highly favourable terms. This eased Italy's financial position temporarily, but an adverse balance of payments, resulting from the fact that Italian exports covered only one quarter of the import bill, led Mussolini to declare the opening of the 'battle for the lira' in August 1926, a struggle which was resolved eleven months later when the exchange rate was fixed at nineteen lire to the dollar and ninety-two lire to the pound sterling with the so-called *quota novanta*.[1] This had its effect on state financing, and particularly on defence budgets. Autarchy and nationalism were the pre-eminent themes of domestic policy, but foreign policy was by no means neglected.

On 1 December 1925, Italy became a co-signatory to the Locarno Pact guaranteeing the common borders of France, Germany and Belgium. Mussolini's decision to join as a signatory doubtless owed something to the propaganda value it had for domestic purposes, but the fact of his adherence shows that he did not quite regard it as a matter of no importance.[2] While membership demonstrated that Italy was perceived to be a major player on the international scene, and suggested that she was going to be a collaborative one, the terms of the pact ran counter to Italy's interests in that securing Germany's western borders might well funnel any expansionist tendencies southwards in the direction of Austria. Locarno was also an irrelevance in that it could not produce what Mussolini wanted, a guarantee of the Austro-Italian frontier on the Brenner and a commitment to oppose a union of Austria and Germany. Neither were forthcoming because Stresemann explicitly excluded any intention on Germany's part to seek such a union and because Great Britain would not go beyond guaranteeing the Rhine frontier, offering instead assurances that if the annexation question arose Italy could count on her 'full and entire' support. However, as his ambassadors in London and Paris pointed out to Mussolini, the pact would open up the possibility of closer collaboration between Britain and France and of a new grouping of powers. If Italy did not take part then she would find herself marginalised and likely under suspicion as an expansionist and warrior nation who had deliberately stood aside from it.[3]

Most of Mussolini's interests were either irrelevant to Locarno or of marginal and indirect relevance. Some of those interests were located in places where there were disputes in which he took a considerable interest, and which he chose to regard as important to Italy. One was Tangier, a port internationalised at the time of the Algeciras conference in 1911 but then closed to Italian ships by France in 1923. Although Spain seemed weak in the face of French pressure, Mussolini was determined that the port should remain in Spanish hands rather than French, and to this end signed an Italo–Spanish Treaty on 8 April 1926. His position was entirely in accord with his oft-struck public stance: 'an increase in French influence in Morocco would make the Mediterranean from Syria to Tangiers a French sea, with a window on the Atlantic'.[4] Another was Tunisia, where France proved continually evasive when faced with Italian hostility to her plans to 'de-nationalise' Italian citizens living there. This dispute rumbled on until January 1935 – Mussolini rejecting a French proposal en route in June 1929 – when an agreement to introduce changes over a twenty-year period from 1945 was incorporated into the Laval–Mussolini proposals, only to be denounced by Ciano in December 1938.[5]

At the other end of the Mediterranean, the uncertain position of a number of states offered Mussolini the opportunity to manoeuvre and manipulate to his own advantage. Ushering Ahmed Zogu to power in Albania in 1925, and signing the first pact of Tirana on 27 November 1926, giving Italy the right to intervene there at the Albanian government's request, destroyed the 1924 agreement between Rome and Belgrade and led to the two countries breaking off diplomatic relations the following summer. By no means the least important consequence of the pact was that it opened up new and potentially more rewarding possibilities if Italy went to war with Yugoslavia.[6] The conclusion of the second pact of Tirana, a twenty-year defensive alliance between Italy and Albania, on 22 November 1927, led Austen Chamberlain to observe that he could scent 'the smell of powder'.[7] Mussolini's visceral loathing of Yugoslavia appeared to be reciprocated by the Serbs as a result, the military attaché Visconti Prasca believed, of French machinations. The news of the Franco–Yugoslav Treaty of guarantee and security of 11 November 1927, to which the second Tirana pact was Mussolini's immediate response, was greeted as the pouring of 'boiling oil on the fire of hatred (*odio*) which is already spreading like wild fire against Italy'.[8]

Yugoslavian ambitions to gain a foothold in the Aegean in the shape of the port of Salonika aided good relations between Italy and Greece, whose support Mussolini wanted in order to put pressure on Turkey.[9] Turkey, weak as a result of internal troubles and facing the loss of the *vilayet* of Mosul, given by the League of Nations to Iraq in December 1925, seemed during 1926 to be about to become a victim of Italian aggression carried through on the back of very tense Anglo–Turkish relations and the possibility that they might deteriorate to the point of conflict. However, this was not to be. Militarily, secret preparations were thwarted when Tewfik Bey apparently signalled Ankara warning of naval preparations at Naples to launch an expedition against Anatolia, upon news of which Kemal mobilised four Turkish army corps.[10] For a while, though, Turkey remained a live issue. Italian military intelligence (SIM) intensified its activities during the summer and autumn of 1926, establishing new intelligence centres on Rhodes, at Cairo and at Piraeus to watch Turkey and carrying out a 'telephotographic' survey of the coasts of Syria and Asia Minor.[11] Diplomatically, Italian ambitions in this area were checked first when London and Ankara settled their differences over Mosul in June 1926, and then by Turkey's policy of keeping open links with Russia, with whom she signed a Treaty of friendship and neutrality on 17 December 1925, thereby ending any possibility that Rome could join Moscow in partitioning Asia Minor. Russia had good reason to be at odds with Italy when Mussolini's policy of building good relations with

Romania finally led him to ratify the Treaty of Paris (October 1920) on 8 March 1927 and recognise Romania's possession of Soviet Bessarabia. This in its turn opened up the prospect of Yugoslavia turning to 'the great mother and protectress of all Slavism', Russia, for diplomatic support against Italy.[12]

Turkey was one of the longer term targets of Fascist foreign and military policy, and in November 1926 a paper on a possible military operation in Anatolia was drawn up by the army general staff and passed up to higher authority for consideration.[13] However it was an objective the attainment of which, Austin Chamberlain told Mussolini on 30 September 1926 in the course of vetoing an Italian attack, was 'a question of waiting'.[14] Also, as Raffaele Guariglia, director general of the European and Levant section of the Foreign Ministry, pointed out, Italo–Russian tension 'precludes for a period of unforeseeable duration the possibility of preparing the foundations (*basi*) for the diplomatic action through which we could hope to realise our aspirations in Asia minor in future'. When eventually the Turkish problem was 'solved', it would require naval support from Great Britain, of which Italy might have only a relatively modest need, and military support from Russia on land, which would be essential.[15] These characteristically over-ambitious Fascist objectives – which Aldovrandi denied to Stresemann, telling him that Mussolini was pursuing a policy of friendship towards Turkey 'far from any adventure which obviously would not be worth the tremendous responsibility and the risk of a war' – were soon deflated. By the spring of 1927, the Turkish government had quelled revolts in its eastern provinces and army reform was sufficiently far advanced for it to be able 'if not to prevent, then certainly to hold in check for a long time any foreign force which in a two-handed war were to try its chances on her coasts'.[16]

Although were many troublespots where Mussolini could either look for opportunities or, by such actions as supporting Croat separatists against Yugoslavia, or backing the Macedonian IMRO agitators based in Bulgaria, stir them up, the main lines of Europe's political configuration were very clear and were not susceptible to significant modifications. As far as Germany was concerned, field marshal Hindenburg's election as president in April 1925 appeared immediately to offer some chance of following a policy of collaboration with her.[17] However, her re-entry into the community of European powers was guided by Great Britain, as an anti-Russian move, and under Stresemann's direction her foreign policy offered no obvious openings into which Mussolini could poke an oar. Stresemann repeatedly emphasised that anschluss was not and would not be on Germany's agenda, told Italian diplomats that Germany had only two interests – freeing the Saar, which he achieved in

an agreement with Briand at Thoiry on 17 September 1926, and Poland –
and warned Mussolini that his aggressive language in speech and in print
simply created what he implied but did not quite say were entirely reasonable fears. Unless and until Germany's political orientation and the tem-
per imparted to her foreign policy under Stresemann's direction changed,
the most Mussolini was able to hope for was that Germany's admission
to the League of Nations might make the 'crisis' of that body more acute
and might show people how fragile its foundations were.[18]

Relations with France ran the gamut from formal coolness to hot
choler; at one low point, Mussolini angrily accused her of being 'peren-
nially in conflict with Italy's entirely legitimate and modest aspirations'
from Abyssinia to Albania.[19] Rumours of war were periodically fanned
by the press of both countries. In France's case, the Italian ambassador
reported at the height of one such crisis in December 1926, they were the
result of a recognition by the French of 'the present and future strength
(*forza*) of the Fascist state', and the feeling that Italy nursed a 'profound
and incurable' animosity towards France.[20] On this occasion at least the
evidence went against Mussolini: Ricciotti Garibaldi had been arrested
in Nice the previous month fabricating a plot by Italian exiles to invade
Italy, with the result that France's military and naval defences were temporarily strengthened and there was talk in Paris of preparing for war
until tension declined at the end of December.[21]

Mussolini's temperature was kept high by periodic reminders that
French hostility to Italy was fomented by the anti-Fascist *fuorusciti* (exiles)
she insisted on harbouring and by masonic conspiracies. He did nothing
to rein in his newspapers or change his policies, convinced that right
was on his side. One fact he could not escape: over and over again his
ambassadors told him that Great Britain's preference was to work with
France and not with Italy, that London did not accept the hostile por-
trayal of France conveyed by Italian diplomats, and that if forced to choose
between Paris and Rome she would always choose the former.[22] The service ministries were likewise left in little doubt about the fundamental
shape of European politics. Shortly after the second pact of Tirana and
the Franco–Yugoslav Treaty of 1927, the military attaché in London,
lieutenant-colonel Amerigo Coppi, observed that 'although Italy enjoys
greater sympathy, the corner-stone of British policy is friendship with
France, which will not be sacrificed for any reason'. No one should therefore be under any illusions about what would transpire in the event of
conflict between Italy and France.[23]

The agreements reached between London and Rome – notably the
cession of Jubaland concluded in the summer of 1925, the abortive deal
in December 1925 which would have allowed Great Britain to build a

barrage on Lake Tsana while Italy was to be compensated with railway concessions and the joint Anglo–Italian stance against France over the latter's wish to open up Abyssinia to a free trade in arms – did not do very much to further Mussolini's ambitions or allow him to step closer to his goals. Indeed the latter almost immediately aroused Mussolini's suspicions when Great Britain agreed with alacrity to Ras Tafari's request to purchase arms which included two tanks, six mountain guns and six anti-aircraft guns. The news that the French minister in Addis Ababa, in collusion with his British counterpart, was simultaneously trying to break up the Anglo–Italian front caused the Duce 'a certain preoccupation'. The incident closed when Britain agreed to exclude artillery from the shopping list and Grandi agreed that the other arms could go to Ras Tafari even though he was not strictly entitled to them. It did nothing to deepen relations between the two powers since Mussolini wanted to use an entente in the region against France but Britain did not.[24] Perhaps Mussolini's greatest success as far as England went was to woo the British foreign secretary, Austen Chamberlain, who in October 1926 was 'confident that he [Mussolini] does not mean to embark on a policy of aggression which the resources of his country would be unable to sustain'.[25]

The aggressive stance Mussolini took in matters of foreign policy during the second half of the 1920s required new men with 'fascist' outlooks to promote and conduct it. Early evidence of the changes in hand came in January 1926, when the secretary-general of the *Consulta* (Foreign Ministry), Salvatore Contarini, was dismissed for being too sympathetic to Yugoslavia and France. After the brief reigns of two successors, the post was put into permanent suspension in March 1927. Meanwhile, Mussolini handed day-to-day control of the foreign ministry to Dino Grandi, who served as his under-secretary of state there from May 1925 until September 1929, when he was appointed minister. Grandi was unwilling to be encumbered by 'experts' of the old school, and the disappearance of the secretary-general's post helped him to monopolise foreign policy by removing the role of semi-independent co-ordinator played by Contarini and his successors.[26] He also embarked on a programme of reforming the diplomatic and consular service, all of whose officials were inscribed in the Fascist party in 1926, building new embassies and supporting the Fasci dell'estero organisations overseas, thereby adding an instrument of semi-formal diplomacy to the more conventional diplomatic tools at his disposal.[27] The new tones of Fascist foreign policy under the joint hands of Mussolini and Grandi became yet more evident when, in 1928, ex-party hierarchs – nicknamed the *ventottisti* by the old hands – were brought into the consular service in substantial numbers.

As his career during these years goes to prove, Grandi's outlook on foreign affairs accorded with Mussolini's temperament at the time. Strongly averse to France and Yugoslavia and hostile to the Little Entente, Grandi distrusted Germans but saw them, along with Russia, as one of the young 'proletarian' nations whose interests partially converged with Italy's. Locarno, and the Franco–German alliance which it embodied, he saw as sanctioning the *subalternità* (subordination) of Italy and therefore as something to be used only until its inevitable failure. Great Britain he partially respected and partially despised, regarding her as a second rank enemy. The League of Nations, which he disliked as the embodiment of liberal democracy and 'Wilsonianism', was nothing more than an implement to be used by Fascism in its expansionist course.[28]

In December 1927, Mussolini listed his 'minimal' aims as far as France was concerned. As well as rectifying the Tangiers situation, adjusting the southern and western frontiers of Tripolitania, dealing with the irritating issue of the activities of Italian exiles in France and revising the League of Nations mandates, he demanded a free hand in the Balkans and the eastern Mediterranean 'so that Italy's political and economic expansion does not encounter direct or indirect hindrances from France'.[29] For Grandi, as for Mussolini, the goal of Fascist foreign policy was the achievement of the *impero italiano* in the Mediterranean. The Balkans were to serve as Italy's launching pad, and the Italo–Albanian treaties of 1926 and 1927 were a crucial foundation of the programme which would first secure the Adriatic, the indispensable precondition to any such expansion. France therefore represented the greatest obstacle because of her backing of Yugoslavia. By 1929 Grandi believed her to be creating every kind of difficulty for Italy, 'pushing the Serbian military class (White Hand) to paroxysms and to dreaming the mad dream of a Greater Balkans, of the Adriatic, the Aegean, and the Black Sea'.[30] He along with many others was convinced – wrongly – that a secret military treaty existed between France and Yugoslavia. In reality, and unlike the case in respect of Romania, Czechoslovakia and Poland, France had neither a staff accord nor even an exchange of military letters with Yugoslavia and in 1930 rebuffed king Alexander's overtures for a military mission.

While Grandi focused his attentions on the eastern Mediterranean, his senior subordinate Raffaele Guariglia directed his gaze southwards in pursuit of the attainment of Mussolini's imperial dream. Early in 1928, at a time when Italian troops in Libya, having secured possession of the coastal strip a year before, were launching a simultaneous advance into Sirtica from Tripolitania and Cyrenaica against Senussi rebels, and some four months prior to Mussolini's agreeing in July to the occupation of the entire Sahara, Guariglia presented a grandiose design to extend Italy's empire in Africa.

> The rational programme of the future expansion of our mastery (*dominio*) of North Africa must logically tend to cross the barrier of the Great Desert and to plant us in the relatively fertile and populous regions on the 'other shore' of the Sahara. Once there we shall have to direct our aspirations, at least initially, towards the objective of least resistance and therefore, avoiding the very solid barrier of Britain's possessions of the Sudan, Uganda and Kenya, seek rather to open the way for ourselves to the Gulf of Guinea.[31]

Guariglia's programma massimo involved extending the southern frontier of Tripolitania as far as the northern border of Nigeria and then west via Lake Chad to the western frontier of the Sudan. Italy could then obtain the north-eastern corner of Nigeria by cessation from Britain. This would put her in a position to move on the former German mandate of the Cameroons, thus 'realising the territorial continuity of our African *dominio* from the MEDITERRANEAN to the ATLANTIC'.[32] Guariglia added proposals for a programma medio and a programma minimo which pushed the boundaries of Libya south but not as far as Nigeria, but recommended against their adoption since they neither put Italy in control of the southern caravan routes nor provided the springboard from which to attain 'our larger African programme'. Rather, if the programma massimo were not undertaken, Italy should for the time being leave things as they were, expressing her dissatisfaction and explicitly reserving her rights in the area.

Mussolini thought it 'opportune' to take action which would disabuse the French of the idea that Rome was only interested in the question of Greco–Turkish relations, and instructed his ambassador in Paris to raise with the Quai d'Orsay the question of Libya's southern and western boundaries and Italy's right to priority treatment in the event of a revision of the mandates. Since the programma massimo seemed for the moment to be very difficult to realise, he suggested starting with the median menu and if necessary falling back on the minimum.[33] Manzoni chose to raise Lake Chad and was met with the flat assertion that it was 'impossible'. France was willing to consider 'a simple rectification of the frontier involving a few square kilometres of land' but nothing more; ceding territory as far south as Chad would cut French Equatorial Africa off from French West Africa. Rebuffed over Tangiers and Tunisia in the same conversation, Manzoni was reduced to uttering the vague threat that unless something positive were to come out of the discussions 'our common adversary, who is waiting for nothing more than to wedge itself between us and separate us still further in order the better to be able to fight first one of us then the other, will profit from this for her own interests'.[34] Asked to say who he meant, Manzoni declined to do so on the record. For Mussolini, the attempt to play a weak diplomatic hand had ended in failure and frustration.

Mussolini's attempt to knit together a network of alliances in central Europe to undermine France's Little Entente did not get very far. Romania, which signed a friendship pact with Italy on 16 September 1926, three months after having signed an accord with France, was preoccupied by the dangers posed to her by Russian and Hungarian territorial ambitions so that the best that could be hoped from her was the neutralisation of anti-Italian hostility. Ambassador Durazzo warned Mussolini at the start of 1927 that as far as Bucharest was concerned strong-arm tactics (*metodo forte*) would not work, and he did not adopt them.[35] The treaty of friendship had a secret clause appended to it determining that accords were to be reached by the general staffs of the two powers over action in the case of unprovoked aggression on one of them – a fact which Grandi characteristically denied to his own ambassador.[36]

In March 1926, Hungary and Bulgaria indicated that they were willing to join an agreement to form a Danubian–Balkan region under Italy's aegis, and on 5 April 1927 Italy signed a ten-year pact of friendship and arbitration with Hungary. As with other countries arms were becoming an established lubricant of Fascist diplomacy and so the interception at the St Gotthard pass of a consignment of weapons destined for Budapest on 1 January 1928 had no effect on Mussolini, who showed no intention of acknowledging the international effects of his actions and abandoning Hungary. Eager for their part to have Italian weaponry, the Hungarians suggested using Poland, whom they had supplied with ammunition during the Russo–Polish war of 1920, as an intermediary.[37] They were keen to speed up their negotiations with Italy by getting access to Italo Balbo at the air ministry and Ugo Cavallero at the war ministry, but this process appears not to have yielded the fruits Rome might have expected: by spring 1929 the Italian military attaché in Budapest was reporting that Hungary was buying arms from Germany and urging the use of greater efforts to emplace Italian weaponry there.[38] The Soviet Union, which specifically disavowed any interest in the Balkans except insofar as events there affected their western neighbours but which did take a close interest in Italy's relations with Turkey, correctly identified Mussolini's emerging wish to knit together a Hungarian–Polish–Romanian grouping but characteristically misinterpreted it as being directed as much against the USSR as against France.[39]

Throughout 1928, Mussolini was preoccupied with stitching together three-way ties with Turkey and Greece as a prelude to dismembering

Yugoslavia. The generic content and purpose of his grand design was uncompromisingly revealed to Titulescu: 'It is necessary,' Mussolini told the former Romanian foreign minister in January, 'that the turbulent and megalomaniac Serbs be reduced to their proper proportions'.[40] The murder of the leader of the Yugoslav Peasant Party, Stefano Radic, in parliament in June 1928 and the military dictatorship which ensued created a situation simultaneously both alarming and promising. Mussolini maintained links with Croat separatists, using Fulvio Suvich in Trieste to keep in close contact with them, and as the pacts with Greece and Turkey progressed he checked with them to ensure that they would not be disadvantaged by his policy towards Yugoslavia.[41] As far as formal diplomacy was concerned, this entailed delaying for six months the renunciation or renewal of the Italo–Yugoslav Treaty of 1924, which fell due in January 1928, and then refusing to be hurried when the Yugoslav government enquired in December 1928 what his intentions were regarding renewal.

At the beginning of February 1928, Mussolini learned that the Greeks were discussing with Turkey the possibility of signing a five-year non-aggression pact. At the same time Turkey, sensing a Yugoslav threat to Constantinople and at odds with France over Syria and over what she would later describe as the latter's 'Napoleonic tendencies' since the end of the world war, suggested a non-aggression treaty with Italy. Mussolini at once seized on the possibility of converting the two proposals into a three-power pact which would permit Italy to create under his aegis what he termed, in a reference to Italy's pre-war diplomatic alignment with Germany and Austria–Hungary, a *triplice del Mediterraneo*.[42] The official Turkish proposal was made on 20 February and the Italo–Turkish pact was signed on 30 May 1928. The fact that it was not approved by the Turkish parliament until December and not signed into law until 19 July 1929 was an indication of the difficulties Mussolini would face in trying to shepherd Turkey into his flock.

Greece proved more overtly difficult to bring into the fold. She refused to join a three-power pact, or even to sign a treaty with Turkey which was Mussolini's second-best outcome, unless protocols were attached specifying that compensation would be paid to Greeks ejected from Turkey in 1922. Turkey would not agree to do so, and by June Mussolini, evidently at the end of his patience, was demanding a statement from Athens as to its exact intentions in regard to Italo–Greek relations.[43] Then, in August, Eleftheros Venizelos won a Greek election. As he was open to a bilateral agreement negotiations thereafter proceeded smoothly. A Treaty of neutrality and reconciliation between the two powers was signed in September 1928 and the Greek parliament ratified it on 11 February 1929.

Mussolini's diplomacy, designed to create a favourable environment in which to settle the Yugoslav question by force of arms if needs be, was only a very limited success. Turkey's goals – a Balkan Locarno under the slogan 'The Balkans for the Balkan people' – were very different from his. In moving towards them, she was determined to avoid either regional hegemony by any one power or partial blocs, which were his goals.[44] Thus no three-power pact transpired, and neither did Greece and Turkey settle their differences and sign the bilateral pact which he intended as an alternative third leg of his Mediterranean triple alliance. Instead, Venizelos reached an agreement with Yugoslavia over Salonika early in 1929 giving Belgrade the right to transit arms through the port in peacetime but not in wartime, an achievement which the French and Yugoslav military establishments regarded rightly as a victory for Yugoslavia and a setback for Italy.[45] By that time it was clear that, as far as Mussolini's diplomatic designs were concerned, nothing had gone quite right.

At the Locarno Conference Mussolini posed as a statesman who was ready to take on the role of guarantor of peace in Europe.[46] Less than three weeks later, speaking on Armistice Day, he took a different stance. Not only did he most certainly not believe in perpetual peace, but the era of wars was not over. To face it, Italy needed 'an army which is potent and respected, a powerful navy, [and] an air force which dominates the skies'.[47] In an international environment in which other powers were all too often proving either intractable or intransigent, Mussolini needed these weapons to make his diplomacy work.

Mussolini and the control and direction of the armed forces

Mussolini took personal control of the war ministry on 4 April 1925 in the wake of general Di Giorgio's resignation. Through his newspaper, *Cremona Nuova*, the secretary of the Party, Roberto Farinacci, immediately called for the 'Fascistisation' of the army. Mussolini was, however, moving in a different direction. In the course both of exerting centralised control over the semi-independent *ras* (local party bosses), and of heightening his own power and insulating himself entirely from any authority save that of the king – achieved by creating for himself the new post of *Capo del governo* to replace that of *Presidente del consiglio* (prime minister) and removing entirely any responsibility to parliament in a law passed on 24 December 1925 – he had no intention of letting the army slip from his control into party hands. To this end, he rejected a plan hatched by general Maurizio Gonzaga, Gandolfi's successor as head of the MVSN, and Luigi Federzoni in the spring of 1926 to amalgamate the army and the MVSN, sacking Gonzaga and taking personal control of the force that October.[48] In the moves he was now to make, he may also have had in mind remarks made by general Pecori Giraldi during the debate over the *Ordinamento Di Giorgio* about the need to integrate control of the armed forces, and Grazioli's suggestion in December 1922 that a single unified ministry of defence be created to run the armed forces. Finally, his increasingly aggressive foreign policy required much more out of the armed forces than they had been called upon to give hitherto – and would make demands which at the moment they were not ready to shoulder.

To serve his new purposes and meet his new demands, Mussolini created the position of Capo di stato maggiore generale (chief of the armed forces general staff) on 8 May 1925. Initially, the new office was intended to come under the direct control and authority (*dipendenza*) of the war minister, but in the final version drafted into law oversight was given to the *Capo del governo*. In peacetime, the chief of the armed forces general staff would preside over the defensive organisation of the state, drawing up the necessary studies and arrangements on the basis of the conclusions reached by the Commissione suprema di difesa, and would formulate the war plan, giving directives to the chiefs of staff of the navy and the air force to ensure that they contributed to the achievement of the common objectives. In wartime, the duties allotted to him were ill defined. In order to be able to fulfil the functions of his office, the Capo di stato maggiore generale was given the right to correspond directly with the army, navy and air force authorities. The new post, according to the first article of the law, could only be filled by someone with the rank of *Maresciallo d'Italia*, *Generale d'esercito* or generale d'armata (any general designated to be an army commander in wartime).[49]

Admiral Thaon di Revel was absolutely unwilling to accept the permanent subordination of the navy to the army which the new law embodied and immediately submitted his resignation. Mussolini, whose first thought was that his navy minister's resignation had something to do with the air force, refused to modify the essence of his proposals and the king, after trying to talk Revel out of leaving but failing, commented cynically '[He] always has his resignation in his pocket.' Revel retired for the third and final time on 9 May 1925, the day after the new post was written into law.[50] Mussolini explained a part of his thinking to the senate a few days later. The co-ordinator of the armed forces and of national defence must come from the army because 'it is the impressive force, it is the armed mass which is by a long way superior in men and in means to the others'. There were, he went on, three groupings beyond the Alps: the West (by which he meant the French), the Germans and the Slavs. One or other of them would invade Italy, and 'therefore . . . we must conceive of tomorrow's war as predominantly a land war'.[51]

Mussolini now decided to hold all three ministries – the commissariato aeronautica, of which he was already head, was converted into a ministry on 30 August 1925 – himself. His reason for doing so, he explained, was that reforms were necessary in the army and the navy, in both of which traditions and rivalries existed which hampered unity and improvement. 'A sailor would not be well accepted by the army, and the navy would not accept the supremacy of a general.' Therefore what was necessary was someone 'who has sufficient authority and prestige not to be debated with but to be obeyed'.[52] To help him at the war ministry, Mussolini picked out as under-secretary Ugo Cavallero. The youngest brigadier general in the army, Cavallero had retired in 1920 rather than grind his way up the ranks in the face of a post-war promotion block and had carved out a successful business career working for Pirelli. He now returned to help revive and improve an army he regarded as having begun to disintegrate under the post-war regime.[53] On Cavallero's recommendation Mussolini appointed Pietro Badoglio as chief of staff of the army on 4 May, and a month later, on 8 June, Mussolini gave Badoglio the new post of Capo di stato maggiore generale, thereby amalgamating the two positions into one. Among Badoglio's qualifications for office in Mussolini's eyes was the fact that, as ambassador in Brazil at the time, he was the only generale d'esercito who had not taken part in the destruction of Di Giorgio.

Although openly ambitious, Badoglio was not overtly unpopular. Marshal Caviglia regarded the appointment of a man who had fled when his army corps had collapsed at Caporetto in October 1917, 'abandoning first three divisions and then a fourth and carrying panic into the rear', as a joke, and warned Mussolini that it would be the ruin of the army, the monarchy and Italy. However, he had to allow that when it was announced no one broke the silence.[54] In an attempt to prevent Badoglio using his position as chief of the army general staff to tighten the grip of the camarilla of conservative Piedmontese generals on the army yet further, Mussolini disregarded his candidate for deputy chief of staff, Scipioni, whom Badoglio described as rather resembling a pharmacist, and instead appointed Grazioli, whom Badoglio had sought expressly to exclude on the grounds that he was 'very ambitious, a slippery character and not very frank'.[55] In January 1926, Mussolini removed 'techno–political' questions from the remit of the chief of army general staff and lodged them in the war ministry, further weakening Badoglio's power and increasing that of Cavallero.[56]

Mussolini's design is not difficult to discern. Backed by his own unchallengeable authority, Cavallero at the war ministry would reorganise and modernise the army while Badoglio, assisted by an army deputy who was both a moderniser and openly supportive of Fascism, would simultaneously revitalise military planning and co-ordinate all three services to create an integrated war machine which could then be used to back Fascism's challenges to the established order in Europe and beyond. Meanwhile, Mussolini would return to his favourite ground and foster the *disciplina nazionale* that was the most important element of Fascism and by raising national morale would multiply Italy's power, strengthening her against foreign attack and readying her people for military struggle.[57]

Mussolini's scheme foundered almost immediately. Cavallero, one of a number of generals who were – or who labelled one another – *ambiziosissimo*, worked to try to split up the combined post of chief of the army general staff and chief of the armed forces general staff, backed by the under-secretaries of state for the navy and the air force. Cavallero also kept Grazioli at arm's length from the organisational side of the army, and the deputy chief of the army general staff spent two uneasy years working on strategic case studies before leaving Rome on 1 February 1927 to take command of the Bologna army corps. While the navy, formally in the hands of admiral Giuseppe Sirianni as under-secretary between May 1925 and September 1929, was more or less left to its own devices, a new ingredient was thrown into the political *mêlée* that was Fascist civil-military relations with the appointment of Italo Balbo as under-secretary of state for the air force on 6 November 1926. An intransigent squadrista, founder of the blackshirts and first head of the Fascist militia, the *ras* of Ferrara was both a proven organiser and something of a political threat to Mussolini. Giving him charge of the development of the most Fascist of all the services would simultaneously harness his talents and channel his otherwise dangerous ambitions.[58]

The unstable mixture that Mussolini had created soon ignited. In December 1926, Badoglio learned through SIM that Balbo was plotting to oust the king if he blocked the further advance of Fascism. As one of the prime movers behind the March on Rome, Balbo was a focus of frequent rumours; however on this occasion he was blameless, the 'plot' apparently having been fabricated by Mussolini to impress the king.[59] Without waiting to secure authority from Mussolini, Badoglio at once mobilised units of the army and the *Carabinieri* to protect Villa Savoia. Mussolini already had reason to doubt that Badoglio would prove the reforming arm he wanted: in October 1925, he had received a memorandum on armoured warfare from Badoglio advising that large expenditure should be avoided and that study should be limited to a machine adaptable to the Alpine frontier. He also knew that Cavallero and Badoglio, bitterly jealous of one another, were no longer on speaking terms.[60] His designs to improve the co-ordination of the three services threatened, the *Capo del governo* now moved to strengthen his own powers and reduce Badoglio's. A decree law of 6 February 1927 opened up the office of Capo di stato maggiore generale to the navy and the air force as well as the army, split the posts of chief of the armed forces general staff and chief of the army general staff, and made the former a 'technical consultant' with the right only to give opinions to the Duce on the co-ordination of the defensive system of the state and to propose the appropriate arrangements and also the general lines of the overall war plan. Badoglio was obliged to consult with the chiefs of staff of the three armed forces, but instead of being empowered to write directly to them he had to go via their ministers, which meant in practice their under-secretaries. By contrast the chief of the army general staff could write directly to any higher authority. To emphasise the dilution of Badoglio's powers, his office staff was cut to six. Mussolini's first choice to succeed Badoglio as chief of the army general staff, general Mombelli, found convincing reasons to decline the appointment, occasioning an outburst by the Duce against all the senior generals in the army except Di Giorgio and Albricci and a lament at the anti-Fascist spirit dominating the military hierarchy.[61] The post went instead to a loyal Piedmontese subordinate of Badoglio, general Giuseppe Ferrari, which meant that the military remained in the hands of the conservative clique.[62]

In his role as co-ordinator of the armed forces, Badoglio failed to provide either the tempo or the aggressive direction that Mussolini wanted. In July 1925, Badoglio had told Mussolini that war plans against France and Yugoslavia aimed to 'deal a robust blow' at the latter from the outset. In October 1926, against the background of worsening Italo–Yugoslav relations, Mussolini was in the mood to cash that cheque. It was important – 'without losing a minute of time' – to prepare the twenty mobilisable divisions of the army and give its officers an offensive and aggressive mind-set: 'By good fortune, Italy is capable today on inflicting on Yugoslavia one of those lessons which are sufficient to correct the mental and political deformities of any people.' But, he warned Badoglio, there was not a minute to lose.[63] Though there were tensions inside Yugoslavia, notably between Montenegrins and Bosnians, Badoglio doubted that the Croats and Serbs could now be split up. He was also aware that the Yugoslav army had made 'very notable progress', thanks particularly to arms imports from France and Belgium and access to Czech weaponry, so that presently it was 'a weighty instrument of war'. In any war with Yugoslavia, Italy needed to beat her quickly. In order to do so, he told Mussolini, three pre-conditions would have to be met. First, all forty Italian divisions would have to be put into the field against Serbia's thirty, and Rome would therefore need to be sure that neither Germany nor France would intervene. Secondly, Italy would need to mobilise faster than her enemy, which she would be able to do in 1928 when the 1919 railway improvement programme was complete. Thirdly, the new tactical doctrine which was designed to 'give aggressive character to our action', would need time to bed down.[64] As would become increasingly obvious, caution was the watchword of the Piedmontese military caste that Mussolini had recruited to order and form his army.

Up to that point, Badoglio had held eight meetings of the service chiefs during 1925, at which they had discussed such matters as the division of the artillery budget, munitions supplies and which service was responsible for coastal defence in which localities, and had begun to consider preparatory planning studies for war against Austria. He called none at all during 1926.[65] In February 1927, prompted by Mussolini, he held the first of two meetings of the service chiefs summoned that year, sketching the military situation in the event of a war with Yugoslavia and allotting planning tasks to the respective heads of the armed forces. As far as the general position went, Badoglio believed that Italy had 'a good chance of success' against Yugoslavia alone, but if France were allied with her and Italy thus forced to conduct operations on two fronts 'the situation for Italy would be tragic, at sea, on land, and in the air'. Therefore the essential political preliminary to any war was to isolate Yugoslavia.

Determined to impart greater impetus – and no doubt greater aggressivity – to the planning process, Mussolini summoned another meeting in July 1927, and announced to those present that it was to be regarded as 'the first meeting for the systematic preparation for war'. He then listened while Badoglio told his generals and admirals that the political situation, according to Mussolini's own directives, was such that 'we can be almost certain that a conflict of this kind [war with Yugoslavia] will not break out in the immediate future'. Badoglio then outlined a planning process according to which the chiefs of staff would consecutively consider the three fixed elements in planning: *copertura* ('cover'), mobilisation, and deployment. Doing things Badoglio's way meant that Italy would not be militarily prepared for such a war until 1932 at the earliest.[66] Faced with the statement that map exercises would begin in December, Mussolini could do no more than instruct that the next meeting be held on the eve of these exercises. The pace picked up during 1928, when seven meetings were convened to discuss aspects of the Yugoslav planning, before declining again with only four meetings in 1929.

During these latter years Badoglio was much taken up with interservice politics, blaming Cavallero for 'torpedoing' him, and the two became bitter enemies. Badoglio witheld a high military decoration from

Cavallero and let it be known that he was willing to let bygones be bygones only as long as Cavallero, the younger man, made the first move.[67] The dispute was aired in public as well as in private: at the Armistice Day review in November 1928, the pair did not salute one another because each thought he should be the first to receive the honour. The king now made one of his rare interventions, remarking that this had to stop. Since the two men evidently could not work together, Mussolini reshuffled the pack. Cavallero's resignation as under-secretary of state was accepted on 2 November 1928, and he was replaced by a young Piedmontese major-general who belonged to Badoglio's clique, Pietro Gazzera. Mussolini had appreciated Cavallero's army reforms – and no doubt his open atti-tude to Fascism – and as compensation for being put on half-pay made him a count.[68] Badoglio was given the post of governor of Libya from 1 January 1929, but was allowed to stay on as chief of the armed forces general staff. Having asked Mussolini the previous autumn for a title he could pass on to his children, he was created marchese del Sabotino. The honours, far from being the rewards for success, were tissues masking the failure of Mussolini's first attempt to reshape the armed forces and ready them for the purposes he had in mind.

While Badoglio was supposed to devote himself to the detail of plans for national defence, Mussolini intended to provide general direction through the annual meetings of the Commissione suprema di difesa. Founded in 1923, and reorganised in 1925, the commission was supposed to function as a co-ordinating organ linking the political institutions of the state with the military in order to resolve questions of national defence and to estab-lish the norms which would govern all national activities directed towards preparing for war. As this body normally met over the course of three or four days once a year, and as its sessions generally lasted between two and three hours, it did not get very far. Giuseppe Bottai left a memorable description of it in his memoirs:

I have never seen so much paper in any other body: programmes, plans, estimates, graphs, diagrams, statistics. Mussolini moved about with aplomb in this wild forest; he seemed to know the most secret paths and track ways. He put his finger on the delicate point in every document and illustrated it effectively and forcefully. But one had the sensation of a dialectical or polemical ability, not of someone who was in gear with this great machine. No one reached any conclusions.[69]

Opening the fourth series of meetings on 30 June 1925, and betray-ing something of his current preoccupations, Mussolini told its mem-bers that its task was 'to provide in the least possible time the greatest amount possible of means for the defence of the country'.[70] They were not always able to adhere to his implicit demands that they be succinct and focus on the big issues: a discussion on the defence of dams in October 1924 descended into a debate about which service could make the best reinforced concrete, and another in June 1925 on the introduction of courses on military history into Italian universities got briefly entangled in the question of how much should be paid to the writers of the necessary textbooks. Among the plethora of issues upon which it briefly alighted, many revealed just how materially weak Italy was. A discussion on improving the country's stock of horses and mules, the latter a particular concern of Marshal Diaz, vice-president of the commission, because they pulled artillery, led general Dallolio to advise his fellow members that 'we should not put too much weight on mechanised traction (*traino meccanico*) because for some kinds of artillery its use is debatable, for others it is impossible, and finally because we are short of trucks'.[71] Earlier, in 1923, the commission decided to make provisions favouring arms exports and to encourage the manufacture of machine-guns, rifles, pistols and cartridges because they needed less labour and fewer raw materials.[72]

The decision taken by the Commissione suprema in October 1924 to propose that all adult men and women be liable to call up for national defence in time of war, which was enshrined in law on 8 June 1925, opened up an almost limitless vista of legislative and organisational requirements.[73] By June 1927, the commission was still discussing the general framework of laws that would be needed to effect a national mobilisation, the way in which the ministries of state must be incorporated into the process, and the organs necessary to make it function. Related issues included the mobilisation and employment of the labour force in wartime, for which in 1928 regulations still had to be drawn up, the normalisation of common patterns of goods such as cars, telephones and radios to aid mass production in war (for which the auguries were not good in as much as the army and navy had by this date made no progress whatever in agreeing common patterns for artillery despite having started on the issue in 1923), and the question of how to arrange for the insurance of shipping in wartime.[74] The not unimportant question of the role which the colonies would play in war, first raised in June 1923, had progressed only as far as the admission by the end of 1927 that in order to be able to assess their role and contribution, data was needed on their present production and its likely future development and also on the defensive needs they themselves absorbed. By that time, some 70,000 troops had been engaged in the still ongoing reconquest of Libya.[75]

The scrutiny given by the commission to the raw materials situation, although necessarily episodic because of the way in which it worked, produced both important information and worrying prospects. By the summer of 1925, censuses of the iron, machine, automobile and aircraft industries had been carried out. Steel production was deemed adequate for wartime needs if based on 1917–18 rates of consumption – at which Badoglio helpfully pointed out that things were that much the better in that consumption in the early stages of a war would not be so heavy – but the location of plants in north and western Italy made it dangerously vulnerable to enemy action. However, demand for cast iron outran supplies by 900,000 tons a year, and it was calculated that two or three years would be needed to achieve a notable reduction in this shortfall. Scrap-iron too was in short supply, not least because France had forbidden its export to Italy, and Russia was scouted as a possible source of stocks. Fuel oil was another problem. Admiral Sirianni, under-secretary of the navy, volunteered the information that the navy had reserves of 190,000 tons, enough for four months' war use, and Mussolini urged that petroleum needs be met by a combination of national extraction, searching for substitutes, and looking overseas to Mexico and Russia for supplies.[76] Experiments to extract oil from asphalt-bearing rock in Sicily and the Abruzzi got nowhere, and by 1928 it was acknowledged that oil stocks would run out after at most two or three months of war and that further supply by sea had to be guaranteed To make matters worse, oil plants were vulnerable to air attack and putting storage tanks underground, the only economic means of protecting them since anti-aircraft defences would require 'an enormous dispersal of means', was being blocked by AGIP as too expensive.[77] While oil was the most serious problem, there were also shortages of copper, aluminium and chemicals to manufacture explosives.

As far as arms manufacturing was concerned, the commission concentrated on three areas: aircraft, artillery and gas. By 1928, aircraft output was officially recorded at 150 planes per month, a figure which would quadruple after 6 months of wartime production. The Regia Aeronautica put its needs in war at 900 aircraft per month. The secretary-general of the commission could do no more than express the hope that it would be possible to resolve the deficiencies and arrive at a situation where demand and supply were in balance 'after a period of time which it is not possible now to determine'.[78] This would take at least a year. Meantime, the only obvious route to improvement was to expand peacetime domestic production by encouraging civil aviation. As far as artillery went, Italy had a park of five thousand guns in reserve but most of her artillery was obsolete. Replacing hundreds of guns of eight or nine old-fashioned types, each with twelve days' supply of ammunition, would take milliards of lire, Badoglio pointed out. In any case, he held that domestic industry was incapable of doing the job; during the world war, the new types of guns built entirely in Italy did badly, and the quality of the types reproduced from foreign designs was poor. When the commission proposed improving quality by developing a School for Artillery Construction, and gave the job to Cavallero, Badoglio suggested instead setting up a model factory – a small Krupp, Skoda or Schneider, as he put it – which would design new artillery suited to Italy's special needs ('our artillery must have as its primary characteristic its employment in mountains'), and then sustaining it by developing an arms market among the small countries who likewise would have to fight in mountainous theatres.[79] As far as gas – 'a weapon which will certainly find immediate employment in a future war' – was concerned, shortage of plant and materials meant that production was limited and reserves minimal.[80]

If, during these years, the Commissione suprema was making any ground then it was only doing so very slowly. Partly this was because it scanned the problems of defence from a lofty viewpoint – though, like any group of professional experts, it could descend from time to time into pointless detail. Partly it was the inevitable result of a bureaucracy collectively making recommendations its members were not then either aided or coerced into putting into effect. In June 1927, for example, the decision was taken to set up within three years detachments of personnel who did not belong to the armed forces to man territorial anti-aircraft defences, and the job was handed to the war ministry. 'It would be interesting now to be able to know what has been done and what there is in mind to do,' the secretary-general of the commission noted drily seven months later.[81] Mostly, however, its glacial pace and limited progress were the ineluctable consequences of Mussolini's way of employing it as a meandering gadfly. In 1925 it alighted on a characteristic piece of propagandistic nonsense, setting up a national competition with monetary prizes for twenty-five pictures on themes from the Italo–Austrian war of 1915–18. Of the sixty-three paintings submitted only seven were deemed worthy of prizes. The following year, after some time spent considering whether to offer larger prizes in order to be sure of filling in the gaps, Cavallero dropped the idea as a waste of time and effort.

Budgets, forces levels and military organisation

Financially, the years between 1925 and 1929 were better ones for the armed forces in Italy than those they had experienced in the first period of Fascist rule. Total defence spending rose from 3,558 million lire in 1925/6 to 4,507 million lire in 1928/9. Although its proportional allocation fell back slightly over this period, the army enjoyed the lion's share, rising from 2,129 million in 1925/6 to 2,777 million in 1927/8 before dropping by 122 million lire the following year. The navy's budget climbed during the same years from 980 million lire to 1,218 million lire before likewise falling in 1928/9 by 67 million lire. The air force budget rose from 449 million lire in 1925/6 to 632 million lire in 1926/7 and then settled at 700 million for each of the following two years.[82] However, Italy was still a relatively poor country compared to its great power rivals. Its national reserves in 1927 amounted to only 20 billion lire, and by 1930, Italian national income at 400 billion lire was less than one third the size of France's (1,350 billion) and Germany's (1,450 billion), and one quarter the size of Great Britain's (1,650 billion). As the poor relation among the services, the air force was especially well aware of the disparity in circumstances it faced and of the fact that both the British and French air forces were able to increase their budgets in 1928 and 1929. 'We are moving among giants: giants in wealth, in finance, in raw materials, in technical and mechanical plant and equipment,' Italo Balbo told the chamber of deputies in 1928.[83]

Finance, Mussolini told the senate on 9 March 1926, was the basis of the new military structure he intended to introduce to replace the failed design of Di Giorgio. The Ordinamento Mussolini, in fact the work of Cavallero and Badoglio, was to be a compromise between Bencivenga's *lancia e scudo* and the large peacetime 'framework' army the generals had favoured. Following the pattern of the 'triangular division' adopted by other European armies during the world war, the new Italian army would comprise thirty divisions in wartime, not sixty as previously, each made up of three regiments, not four as before.[84] Putting the proposals to the army council, Badoglio justified the reduction in the number of divisions partly on financial grounds, which made it impossible to secure the extraordinary budget of 11,000 million lire which would be required to maintain a force of fifty-two divisions, but also on the somewhat contradictory grounds that the changed political situation allowed Italy to maintain a standing force of smaller size but also made it preferable to have an army 'less numerous but more readily mobilisable rather than a stronger army which was less ready'.[85] The three-regiment division (*divisione ternaria*) provided, he argued, a more effective utilisation of Italy's demographic superiority in relation to her 'less fortunate' industrial situation since there already existed enough artillery to equip the divisions to the requisite standard, as well as offering better territorial protection in the event of war and the prospect of speedy and effective mobilisation and deployment. The members of the army council unanimously favoured the *divisione ternaria*, either as a result of their wartime experience of commanding both kinds of division or of their having observed its trial at the manoeuvres at Canavese earlier in the year. Marshal Cadorna added his support.[86]

As finally legislated, the budgeted force of 250,000 men would be split into two contingents: 150,000 men would serve 18 months, and 50,000 men would serve 6 months. However, since the budget was based on 190,000 men under arms it would be necessary to send men on licensed leave (*congedi*) and therefore gaps would open up in the ranks. This was not quite what Badoglio had proposed to the army council, which had been assured that the number would drop to 220,000 but only when 40,000 had completed pre-military training.[87] Finance had again restricted choice. The total size of the officer corps shrank from 14,000 to 11,850, a reduction achieved by virtually halving the number of lieutenants while increasing the numbers of officers in the higher ranks. This had the sole virtue of improving promotion opportunities so that all officers could expect to retire having reached at least the rank of lieutenant colonel, rather than captain as before.[88] Other than the *divisione ternaria*, though, the resulting force was a weak compromise between two contending schools of thought which produced an army two fifths of whom would be virtually untrained and which would depend for expansion in wartime on junior officers it did not have. Most critical of all, it was a design formed through a combination of professional preference and political expediency, not one conforming to a clear strategic concept.

When he became Capo di stato maggiore generale and army chief of staff in 1925, Badoglio paid special attention to the armament of the army in the light of budgetary constraints. Given the need to provide the mobilisation arrangements for the new thirty-division army and ensure its rapid deployment by rail, and to stay within the budget, the generals were told in a series of eight meetings between June and August 1925 that nothing new could be manufactured other than light machine guns, anti-aircraft guns and a few pieces of artillery. In any case, there was more than enough artillery of every type, either built before 1914 or captured during the war, to equip the army. After sorting out which guns should go into mobilisation equipment and the general reserve, the costs of providing the necessary ammunition and bringing the guns into an efficient state was calculated at 900 million lire, to be spread in equal instalments over ten years. Detailed consideration was given to the preparation and stocking of magazines, the amounts of ammunition to be held ready for use and in reserve dumps and the volume of explosives necessary.[89] The decisions were informed by only the most generic considerations as regarded the likelihood of war, such as the need for twelve days' supply of ammunition for some types of gun (e.g. frontier artillery) but only four days' for others (e.g. fixed anti-aircraft guns).

Badoglio's successor as chief of army general staff, general Giuseppe Ferrari, came into office on 1 February 1927 and lasted for exactly a year before resigning. Out of sympathy with Mussolini's decision to allow the newly created combat battalions of the MVSN to take part in annual army manoeuvres, Ferrari was deeply offended by the way that Cavallero was altering traditional infantry structures with scant regard to his views. Mussolini made clear his opinion that Ferrari belonged to the traditional school of soldiering that was stuck in the mentality of the world war. He wanted, he told the chief of staff, to get away from 'what I would call static conceptions of battle – that is battles [in] which [soldiers] leave one trench to take another one'.[90]

Ferrari refused Mussolini's invitation to stay on in office and in a parting shot laid out the army's deficiencies and weaknesses in the face of a two-handed war against France and Yugoslavia, now made possible as a result of the treaty between the two powers. In such a war, France could field twenty-five or twenty-six divisions against Italy after twenty days and another ten within three months, requiring at first twelve and then eighteen Italian divisions to defend the frontier. The Yugoslav army, which was improving apace thanks to French assistance, could put twelve divisions on the Venezia Giulia frontier. Although Italy had the manpower to raise sixty divisions – 'a force which would not be excessive' – she had only twenty-one at her disposal, sufficient only to defend the frontiers and then not for long enough to shield the mobilisation of Italian industry and of additional manpower. In the present international situation Italy needed at least thirty-one divisions in a state of complete efficiency to defend herself; if she aimed to take the offensive and inflict a decisive defeat on Yugoslavia she needed all sixty. To bring the twenty-one extant divisions up to full efficiency, which required weapons, ammunition, and training, to carry out the necessary improvements to such essential services as anti-aircraft defences and artillery, to provide the 935 tanks that were necessary, and to create another five divisions would cost 4,350 million lire. A second tranche of 1,380 million would be needed to create a further nine divisions, and a third of 4,770 million for twenty more divisions. As Ferrari remarked, these numbers amounted to 'a very grave financial problem' and the sums involved were 'very burdensome' (*molto gravosa*). To round things off, Ferrari demanded more authority for the Capo di stato maggiore generale, who should in wartime assume supreme command of all three armed services, and less interference from the war ministry which 'though it has neither competence nor technical responsibility in matters of training and employment [of troops], can intervene according to its own views', thereby rendering the entire general staff and its chief impotent.[91]

If Ferrari hoped to prise loose the purse strings and to enthrone Badoglio as military supremo, he miscalculated on both counts. Mussolini was unwilling to part with political power and unable to part with more money. Instead, after leaving the post of chief of the army general staff vacant for five months and then briefly appointing a nonentity, and having despatched Badoglio to the governorship of Libya, Mussolini appointed general Alberto Bonzani as chief of staff on 4 February 1929. Seven months later, on 12 September, he relieved himself of the position of war minister and gave it to general Pietro Gazzera. Both men were cut from Piedmontese military cloth, both were in Badoglio's camp, and both were staunch monarchists. However, Mussolini was not surrendering control – something it was not in his nature to do. Bonzani was an extremely capable staff officer with considerable organising ability, as his record in the world war and his time at the nascent air ministry went to prove.[92] He and Gazzera were put to work to improve the efficiency of the army within the limits Italy could afford. The army's budget stayed more or less exactly the same as it had been under Ferrari until 1930, when it rose slightly.

The ideals of Fascism made few obvious inroads into the army during these years. In January 1926, officers had to declare in writing if and when they had belonged to the freemasons, and in March 1927 Cavallero announced the introduction of lessons on Fascist legislation into the military courses for officers, prompting Mussolini to remark that 'Up till now, they [the army] have ignored the fact that there has been a revolution!'[93] The role which the army should play as exponent and exemplar of *cultura militare*, understood in Italy in the sense that the philosophers Benedetto Croce and Giovanni Gentile used the term 'culture' as embodying the complex of ideas and notions which influenced public actions and the collective and individual lives of citizens, was the subject of only modest debate. Not until the 1930s did the propagandistic needs of the state harness the military to its service. The *Scuola di Guerra* opened a cultural office in 1922 and held a series of public lectures, and from 1925 the universities offered courses in military history – the course at Turin that year attracting 487 students. Professional military debate, seriously hampered when the main military journal *Rivista Militare* was closed in 1918, revived when it reappeared in 1927, only to be suppressed again six years later. Picking up a pre-war concern, and building again on Gentile's idea that the nation was a project to be constructed, the pre-war concept of *pedagogia militare* was revisited in the light of the role the army could play in educating the nation. This seems not to have amounted to much more than improving conditions in the barracks and raising the educational and cultural level of junior officers, and until the 1930s little appears to have been achieved by way of developing principles and imparting instruction appropriate to a Fascist state.[94] To Mussolini, this state of affairs can only have suggested that the torpor of the pre-war 'barracks army' had not disappeared.

Unlike the air force, the army tended to value machines much less than men. The world war produced a view that machines, and particularly tanks, were worth no more than the moral force of the men who drove them and that the strength of the army resided in its main aggregation of manpower: 'what the infantry is worth is what the army is worth, because the infantry is always the agent of victory'.[95] In 1923, acknowledging Italy's inability to match other powers in mechanising her army and concerned that she did not also slide into inferiority in respect of manpower, Diaz described manpower as 'our unquestioned resource'.[96] In saying this, he was voicing an article of faith shared even by later advocates of motorisation such as general Ettore Bastico. The army's emphasis on the primacy of its human resource carried it along parallel lines with Fascist thought and propaganda, which put a premium on the spiritual forces of the nation as its first line of defence. In the following decade, Mussolini would put at the head of the military high command men who promised to make those lines converge.

The intellectual world of the army was pre-eminently influenced by its experiences during the world war, which was read by the leading authorities in the 1920s such as Bastico as teaching the virtues of caution and which had inoculated them against the aggressive tactics practised to such little effect by Cadorna. Numbers were seen as the most secure factor, and quantity would prevail over quality. War would be lengthy, but a large peacetime army capable of mobilising quickly and going into action before its enemy could do so was reckoned to be the best way of shortening it as much as possible. Attack would be even more difficult than it had been, and defence more solidified. The regulations for the employment of infantry divisions in combat (*Criteri d'impiego della divisione di fanteria nel combattimento*) published on 15 December 1926 embodied conservative traditionalism, declaring that enemy resistance would be reduced by artillery and defeated by infantry.[97]

Never having used tanks – in May 1918 there were only four on the Italian front and none were used in combat – and unable easily to see any use for them in the mountainous frontier zones they expected to defend or attack, the army found it difficult to conceptualise their role in war other than as supports for attacking infantry, a role for which they were tested by Badoglio in the 1926 manoeuvres.[98] Instead it fell back on the accepted principles such as mass and surprise. Machines could indeed be seen as much as a cause of the problems of war as a solution to them, and tanks as a phenomenon generated by the trench warfare of the western front and not relevant to other kinds of campaign in other theatres. The army's views were officially summed up by Cavallero in the *Normi generali per l'impiego delle grandi unità* ('General Regulations for the employment of major units') of 1928, according to which manpower provided the 'resolution of combat' and mechanical means were defined as 'a support for the actions of the combatant' whose effectiveness depended on the intrinsic value of the men who employed them. Thus, 'well-trained troops nourished by a strong combative spirit' could defeat an enemy even if he was equipped with much superior means, while tanks – 'where the terrain allowed' – were an auxiliary means which functioned 'not even as a partial substitute for infantry but to save them time and casualties'.[99] Together with Cavallero's *Norme per l'impiego tattico della divisione* ('Regulations for the tactical employment of the division'), also produced in 1928, they embodied a belief that the offensive was the only way in which to win a combat, and a conception of how to conduct it by a combination of fire and movement which, while still essentially conservative, did embody the most positive aspects of wartime experience.[100]

At the moment when these regulations were promulgated, evidence that there were new ways to conceive of mechanised and armoured warfare was being forwarded to Rome from London. The newly appointed military attaché, lieutenant-colonel Adolfo Infante, observed with growing enthusiasm the experiments with tanks being conducted by the British army. The views which were gaining currency there stressed the physical impotence of troops in the face of an enemy equipped with the new means, its moral influence, and the irresistible shock it could impart when employed en masse. Infante suggested that although continental armies could not move to complete mechanisation, 'they can no longer do less than equip themselves with a significant proportion of mechanised forces to serve as a manoeuvre nucleus capable of breaching the enemy front, preventing the stabilisation of the line, and giving weight to the strategic designs of the commander'.[101] Observing the 1928 manoeuvres confirmed to him that the conceptions behind them were fundamentally correct and revealed important lessons: that tanks could conceal themselves unless in absolutely open ground, that mechanised units were as mobile as cavalry, and that there was no reason to believe that tanks could not operate in mountain zones – in support of which he cited the British expert colonel J. F. C. Fuller. When the manoeuvres were misreported in Italy to suggest that they had reaffirmed the importance of cavalry, Infante at once corrected this misapprehension.[102]

Infante had arrived in London believing that war was more a clash of moral forces than of material ones. By 1931, his last year in London, he had become an enthusiastic proponent of mechanised warfare, pointing out that it had effected both a tactical revolution by virtue of its speed and its unpredictability and a strategic one in that it allowed a return to 'the classical Napoleonic art of manoeuvre'. His beliefs that the new mechanical weapons needed to be embedded in small, long-service armies and that their employment, tactically and especially technically, 'requires troops of advanced professional culture, attainable only after many years of service', directly conflicted with the preference of the Piedmontese traditionalists for large, manpower-heavy infantry armies.[103] In 1934, he summed up his views in the *Rivista di Artiglieria e Genio*: 'these new means will constitute the decisive element in future war'.[104] By that time a debate was under way, encouraged by Mussolini, in which the proponents of new weapons and new methods were encouraged to challenge the Piedmontese traditionalists.

A limited navy

Of the several forces determining the size and shape of Italy's fleet, the budget was the most immediate and the most inescapable. That in its turn was influenced by exchange rates and reserves. In June 1925 Mussolini refused admiral Acton's request for new funds for naval building until there was an improvement in the currency position. Foreign policy considerations were called up in support: the hypothesis of a conflict with France was unrealistic, it was impossible for Italy to contemplate entering into an arms race with her, and Yugoslavia was a weak naval power.[105] As a result of these and related considerations, naval budgets barely altered at all during the latter part of the 1920s: the overall budget for 1926/7 was 1,209,595,130 lire, for 1927/8 1,218,970,030 lire and for 1928/9 1,151,782,030 lire. The decline in the latter figure was due chiefly to the effects of the revaluation of the lire. In 1927–8, with improvements in supplies and munitions given priority, almost three million lire was cut from the allocation for new build; the following year the allocation – 409,000,000 lire – was not reduced.[106] The 1928 budget formed the first stage of a new quinquennial programme that was set in motion partly for political reasons, to prepare Italy in the event of likely international complications after 1933, and partly for technical reasons resulting from the pace of ship construction.[107]

In deciding what to build with its money, the navy kept both eyes on France. At the start of 1925 admiral Ducci, the chief of naval staff, pointed out that within a short space of time France would have twelve light cruisers to Italy's four, twenty-two 'Pantera' types to her four, sixty destroyers to her thirty-four, and seventy-four deep-sea submarines to her seventeen. By 1932, he estimated, the strength ratio between the two powers would be one to three. Merely to keep the same proportionate relationship, Italy would have to allocate 320,000,000 lire a year to new build. After being informed that the minister – Mussolini – did not want to publish an extensive programme which would stimulate building elsewhere, the admirals decided to build two more *Trento*-type cruisers costing 152,000,000 lire each, a fifth long-range submarine, four medium submarines and four fast 38-knot destroyers.[108] The preference for light cruisers conformed with the ideas of men such as vice-admiral Simonetti, commanding the Upper Tyrrhenian region, who foresaw a future war with France as chiefly likely to consist of fast incursions by enemy surface units on both flanks of the peninsula, supported by bombers and submarines in the west, to bombard the industrial establishments of the north-west, strike at national morale, draw the fleet into disadvantageous combat, attack maritime traffic and attempt to land in Sicily. Italy would need to respond fast, and would need more ships which might be weaker rather than fewer stronger ones.[109] In conformity with this scenario, naval grand manoeuvres in the summer of 1925 tested the fleet's capacity to counter an enemy invasion of Sicily by surprising the convoy under sail and attacking it at the moment when it began landings.[110]

To build one of the new 'Treaty'-class 35,000-ton battleships such as the *Nelson* or the *Rodney*, laid down in December 1922, would cost 850,000,000 lire – approximately 90 per cent of the entire 1925/6 naval budget.[111] For financial reasons alone, therefore, the prospect of replacing Italy's ageing battleships was for the moment dead, although Acton, a 'battleship admiral', persuaded the admirals' committee to reduce the crew of only one battleship and not two to 50 per cent manning in order to arm more light surface craft as he wanted five battleships in full commission.[112] There remained, however, the as yet undecided question of whether to build an aircraft carrier. To resolve it, Mussolini personally called a meeting of the admirals' committee in August 1925. After dangling before them alternatives which included two improved *Trento*-class cruisers (costing 152,000,000 lire each) or up to six lighter ships, he heard Acton pronounce against carriers on the grounds that seaplanes could provide the necessary reconnaissance and bombing capacity, that they were costly, defenceless and vulnerable because of all the aircraft fuel they carried, that it took an hour for them to get all their planes airborne, and that since Italy could only afford one there would be no reserve if it were sunk. Having listened to Acton, Mussolini concluded that a carrier was only useful for a country which foresaw the possibility of an oceanic war.

[B]ut this is not our situation because a sine qua non for appearing on the Ocean is first to have dominated the Mediterranean, which can only happen if, as a result of a decline in French power, we can take possession of her African colonies.[113]

None of the eight admirals who spoke after Acton thought an aircraft carrier necessary and only two thought it useful. Instead, they opted for four super-fast 5,000-ton *Di Giussano* light cruisers which did thirty-seven knots under trials but never reached that speed again.[114]

France was the reference point not merely for the navy's own internal calculations but also for its political manoeuvring for funds. At the end of 1926, the shift of three *Condorcet*-class French warships to the Mediterranean, where they formed a training squadron with a group of old battleships and joined a squadron of six battleships already there, excited Acton's anxiety. The 'intense activity' of the French Mediterranean squadron throughout the year, frequent French air flights along the coast towards the Italian frontier and over La Maddalena, 'systematic' night cruises by torpedo boats, acceleration of work on the carrier *Béarn* and the increasing frequency with which French visitors 'showing attitudes not always free of suspicion' were travelling or staying along the Ligurian coast were all brought to Mussolini's attention.[115] All this was a concentrated preamble to a bid for more funds which Acton laid before the Duce at the end of the year.

With respective tonnages of 267,000 and 347,000, Mussolini was informed, Italy had 76 per cent of the 'naval potential' of France. The French naval budget for 1927 had allocated 600,000,000 francs for new construction, and the build that resulted would probably be completed during 1930. By that time, France would have retired 83,000 tons and Italy 87,000 tons of old ships. However, while France had planned new construction totalling 182,000 tons, Italy had only 114,000 tons in the pipeline, of which the *Trento* cruiser, four 5,000-ton destroyer leaders and six 800-ton submarines had yet to be ordered. Following these calculations through, France would have 446,000 tons of warships in 1930 to Italy's 294,000 tons, reducing Italy's 'naval potential' to 66 per cent. The situation was 'precarious'. To remedy it, Acton asked for another 1,000 million lire spread to build another *Trento*, twelve destroyers and twelve submarines, totalling 43,600 tons, as well as 200 million to build appropriate support craft and improve the Tyrrhenian bases. This expenditure, spread over four years, would restore the 'naval potential' ratio to 76 per cent.[116]

The budget allocations showed that Mussolini, whose mind was turning to a land and air war with Yugoslavia, was not in a position to meet the navy's demands. For the time being, therefore, it could do little more than develop projections of the ships it would need to build in wartime in order to fill the gaps in its inventory that were becoming ever more apparent. In 1928, the naval staff calculated that it would need 39,400 tons of ships during the first year of a war, to include eight destroyers, fourteen submarines and twenty MAS boats, as well as 15,000 tons of other assorted craft. The following year its wish list for the first twenty months of war, assuming that no building took place in the first eight months, added up to 156,500 tons and included forty-eight destroyers, forty-eight submarines and ninety-six MAS boats.[117] These ambitious lists probably reflected both the increasingly aggressive line being taken by Mussolini towards Yugoslavia and the navy's awareness that it was making no ground in its competition with the other two services for money.

In 1927, confronting a situation in which the supporters and the opponents of battleships faced each other in equal numbers, the future admiral De Zara called for a series of experimental combined exercises involving battleships, escorts, auxiliary aviation and the air force as a means of avoiding the kind of fatal errors that had occurred during the world war as far as submarines were concerned. 'Everyone can see the damage resulting from the lack of a unified doctrine,' he declared.[118] De Zara's substantive criticism – that naval thought was languishing – would only begin to be resolved at the start of the 1930s when the theories of France's admiral Castex were introduced to Italian readers, lifting strategic theorising to a higher plane than the one it occupied during the 1920s. In the meantime, naval thinking dwelt on the lessons of the immediate past, on the inescapable dilemmas posed by Italy's geographical and economic vulnerability, and on what one commentator has termed 'the oppressive influence of the evolution of means'.[119]

Among the community of naval analysts many recognised that the chief lesson of the world war as far as Italy was concerned was the need to control the sea lines of communication in order to secure external supply, and saw this as more important than battling the enemy's fleet or preventing it from operating. By no means everyone shared this outlook, however, and in 1930 the navy was reminded that the fundamental axiom of strategy was to destroy the enemy's forces.[120] The construction choices made within the limits imposed by the Washington Treaty added another dimension to the problem of devising an all-embracing doctrine. The means being put into the navy's hands at this time – the fast, 10,000-ton *Trento* cruisers, the equally fast light cruisers of the *Di Giussano* class begun in 1928, and the heavy destroyers of the 'Jaguar' and 'Lion' classes – encouraged thoughts of aggressive action at sea. There was plenty of opportunity for competition as to how best to use them. Thus while Giuseppe Fioravanzo argued that light ships should be used to attack and protect traffic at sea and not to engage the enemy directly in a conflict of attrition, an activity which should be undertaken by aircraft when the enemy was in port and by submarines and mines when he was at sea, Oscar de Giamberardino declared destroyers to be the 'fulcrum' of naval action, with light cruisers intervening only when support was needed and submarines and seaplanes acting separately but in concordance.[121]

The question of the role of aeroplanes in naval war and the correct use of air power was even more vexed, since strategic questions were intimately bound up with the issue of how far air power was to be the monopoly of the Regia Aeronautica. In December 1927, Balbo called a meeting with the new chief of naval staff, admiral Burzagli, at which he demanded that the navy and the army give up its auxiliary aviation. Put up to respond by Burzagli, admiral Bernotti, deputy chief of naval staff, pointed out the important role of aircraft in locating and attacking submarines, reconnaissance, and tactical co-operation with surface units during fleet actions. Naval air power had to act immediately and required specialised personnel. It would be needed against battleships and for aircraft carriers; if Italy abandoned the latter platform, Bernotti pointed out, others including Italy's possible opponents in war would not. To his surprise Burzagli, perhaps more attuned to the politics of the situation and to Mussolini's personal interest in the air force, simply abandoned the navy's position.[122] At a meeting between Balbo and the under-secretary of the navy, admiral Sirianni, on 27 January 1928, Balbo conceded that the navy could retain seaplanes for long-distance reconnaissance.[123]

Douhet's formulation *resistere sulla superficia per far massa nell'aria* ('resist on the surface to mass in the air') was immediately challenged by the navy on a variety of grounds. Giulio Valli argued in 1928 that command of the air could be no more than an intention and that the numerous variables affecting its attainment meant that it was at best highly unlikely that it could be achieved immediately and completely, the only way in which it could work. Fioravanzo, who favoured co-ordinated action by all three services, pointed out the following year that 'resisting' at sea was not the same kind of activity as 'resisting' on land but was similar to 'resisting' in the air, entailing as it did sortying out against the enemy to the extent that qualitative, quantitative or operational superiority allowed.[124] The main proponent of 'aero–naval' war was Romeo Bernotti. In a lengthy memorandum on 'Foundations of Naval Policy', which he sent to the under-secretary of the navy, admiral Sirianni, in September 1927 and which Sirianni forwarded to Mussolini, Bernotti allowed that future war would be characterised by the large-scale employment of aircraft, but argued that as far as war at sea was concerned 'aeroplanes will be a very important means of reconnaissance and attack, but cannot be adequate substitutes for warships in respect of the bulk of the functions they carry out'.[125] Since battleships would be exposed to intense offensives from the air, the necessary air escort could only be assured beyond a certain distance from the coast if they had aircraft carriers at their disposal.

To the objection that ships operating in the Mediterranean would generally be in range of land-based air, Bernotti replied that its effectiveness was a function of the timeliness with which information and orders could be transmitted between ships, shore stations and planes, and more besides.

The high speed of ships and their unpredictable changes of course make the co-ordination of ships and planes anything but easy. Planes coming from the coast do not give sufficient certainty of timely and co-ordinated action in respect of reconnaissance, active defence against enemy aircraft, and tactical naval moves; it is also doubtful whether such aircraft can provide anti-submarine escort service with the necessary continuity and intensity.[126]

The argument did not convince Mussolini, who insisted on maintaining his reservations about building an aircraft carrier.[127]

Admiral Sirianni sought to take some of the sting out of the conflict between the navy and the air force, suggesting somewhat unconvincingly that the two services had much in common:

The air force is superior to the navy in speed, in freedom of movement and in the extensiveness of its horizons; it is inferior in its autonomy and its ability to stay put; but their objectives have this in common, that they act directly on an enemy's capacity to resist and his national life.[128]

However, a bitter polemical contest marked the closing years of the decade. Douhet, attacked by Bernotti for his exaggerated picture of a swift and cataclysmic aerial war and confronted with the case for a naval air element and the argument that an independent air force must co-operate with the fleet, responded by arguing that to divide up the air force and create auxiliary components would be to weaken its striking power and deprive it of the capacity to overwhelm the enemy. The navy's task he defined as simply to prevent any enemy movement in the Mediterranean without Italy's consent. Fioravanzo argued that the greater the conflict in terms of time and space the more important was the navy, but Douhet would not give an inch of ground. Other airmen took less extreme views but nevertheless backed their own service. Francesco Pricolo saw a role for auxiliary aviation including bombers, but argued that carriers were a useless and unnecessary luxury since the operational monitoring of enemy fleets could be done by radio interception and tactical monitoring by flying boats and light surface craft, and also because they could not carry heavy bombers. Amadeo Mecozzi at first favoured auxiliary aviation for the navy, but by the end of the decade only supported a reconnaissance capability. He did not openly pronounce on aircraft carriers, but saw no need for them in the *mari ristretti* ('restricted seas') in which Italy would operate.[129] With 'battleship admirals' at the head of the navy, and political advantage lying with the air force, younger proponents of aircraft carriers such as Valli and Maugeri could make no headway. Nor, without either a compelling strategic doctrine or an imminent war scenario, could the navy as a whole progress as far and as fast as it wished.

Among the various considerations influencing the nature of Italian naval policy not the least important was the international community's attempt to progress in the matter of disarmament in general and naval arms reduction in particular. On 25 September 1925, the League of Nations established a preparatory commission to prepare the ground for a future disarmament conference. The commission began its work on 18 May 1926, and completed it on 9 December 1930. The line taken by the Italian navy at the outset was that all armaments were indivisible and that naval arms should not be treated separately from land and air arms. Nor was any settlement based on the status quo acceptable, since this would advantage the most heavily armed powers: 'because the Washington Conference established a precedent in this sense, that is not a good reason to repeat the error and the injustice', the navy argued.[130]

The Italian navy backed a 'one power standard' in all categories of arms which would give it parity with the most heavily armed continental European state, although even this would not provide security since Italy's geographical situation and lack of raw materials made her vulnerable to other powers. In naval terms, this translated into the demand of parity as of right with France. In order not to be outmanoeuvred by France, and perhaps saddled with a global tonnage which was beyond her capacity, Italy would not specify a figure. The naval staff were also decidedly against any attempt to abolish submarines or to restrict their use in war, but were ready to consider extending the 'naval holiday' on battleship construction agreed in 1922.[131]

The proposals favoured by Great Britain, the United States and Japan involved quantitative limits by tonnage and qualitative limits by category of warship which would be determined by displacement and calibre of gun. The Italian delegation ranged itself firmly against these propositions, committing itself, along with France, to limitation by global tonnage and not by category of ship. As the Italian delegate, captain Ruspoli, pointed out, the 'standardisation of types' that would result from the proposal put forward by the largest powers would deny Italy the possibility of compensating for her overall weakness by building ships with different qualities. Italy was already in a difficult position as a result of the limit of 175,000 tons put on her battleship tonnage: five 35,000-ton battleships were insufficient for her needs as a great power, but if she built more smaller units they would not be powerful enough to challenge other powers' battleships. The latter consideration was one of the three key issues for Italy, along with the need to accommodate the financial restrictions she faced and to build enough ships of different types.[132] In the event, the preparatory commission was unable to come to a decision on the competing methods of determining naval arms during its third session (21 March–26 April 1927). As a result of the Italian navy's negative stance during the discussions the deputy secretary of the League of Nations, Paulucci di Calboli Barone, and the chief Italian delegate, general De Marinis, warned Mussolini about the bad publicity being generated and suggested that in future Italy should bring her own proposals to such meetings and seek to harmonise them with the interests of as many other states as possible.[133] This was not Mussolini's normal way of conducting foreign affairs.

On 10 February 1927, president Calvin Coolidge invited London, Paris, Rome and Tokyo to attend a further naval disarmament conference which was to be held in Geneva. Admiral Acton was reluctant to abandon the principle that arms limitation was indivisible and as well as reiterating the fundamentals of Italy's stance in respect of naval arms reduction – parity as of right with all continental European powers measured by global tonnage – he felt that it was necessary to resist any further reductions in naval power until the Mediterranean powers who were not signatories of the Washington Treaty were subject to the same limitations as those who had adhered to it.[134] This last was a significant consideration for Italy. Not only had Russia been added to the Mediterranean powers as a result of the opening of the Dardanelles under the terms of the Treaty of Lausanne, but there was nothing to stop the non-contracting lesser powers building ships beyond the agreed international limits of displacement and armament, even though the Washington signatories had bound themselves to build only to agreed limits on behalf of non-contracting parties and not to cede any of their own warships to them. Nor could they be stopped from buying or building ships in categories as yet not subject to international restriction.[135]

Italy could not afford to agree to the application of limits to presently unregulated surface craft and submarines when the smaller states such as Spain, Greece and Turkey – any or all of which might be her opponents alongside one or more great powers in a Mediterranean war – would not be affected. As one internal briefing note put it: 'As far as continental Europe is concerned, there exists an undeniable interdependence between every kind of armament of every single power and ultimately it is not possible to adopt measures of a partial kind applying only to the five great Naval Powers.'[136] In its official reply to Coolidge's invitation, the Italian government pointed out that whereas the United States enjoyed a 'favourable geographical position' it enjoyed an unfavourable one and could not expose itself to the risks deriving from its vulnerable lines of communications, its exposed coasts and islands, and the presence of other nations which were building or planning to build warships. For these reasons, Italy could not participate in the upcoming conference.[137]

The Geneva conference, which the Italians attended as observers and which opened on 20 June 1927, collapsed when the British and Americans were unable to agree on the displacement, armament or numbers of cruisers to be allowed under an extension of the Washington treaty to light craft, although they were able to agree limits on destroyers and submarines. Conscious of its inferiority in heavy surface craft, with only five pre-war dreadnoughts in service and four cruisers built or building, the Italian navy would accept no further limitations in armaments unless they were framed only in terms of global tonnage and incorporated the principle of parity with any other European power.[138] As far as the as yet unregulated cruiser class was concerned, Italy could see advantages in ships heavier even than the 10,000-ton 8-inch (203-mm) model proposed by the Americans at Geneva, and would have preferred 12,000- or even 15,000-ton ships.[139] She also faced considerable problems as regarded her battleship allocation. The 175,000-ton limit she had accepted allowed her to build five 35,000-ton ships, but she needed six to form two divisions of three ships each, which would mean smaller ships unable to take on opponents who would have built to treaty limits. Also if she laid down battleships between 1930/1 and 1936/7 then the statutory age limits which applied would mean that she could not begin to replace the oldest ship until 1947/8, thus losing the chance to build the latest types for more than a decade. If, however, she stretched out her building programme then she would have a group of disparate ships with fifteen or twenty years of technological differences between them. With allocations of fifteen ships each, these were not problems faced by Great Britain or the United States.[140] Starting on battleship construction was thus a delicate issue for technical reasons alone, leaving aside considerations of international politics or finance.

While publicly backing the navy's stance in the disarmament talks, Mussolini was privately willing to settle for less. If Italy could not get parity with France, he told admiral Siranni in August 1927, then she should build a fleet which represented for France what the German fleet had represented for Great Britain before 1914 and would do again: 'an incubus and a threat'.[141] Declaratory policy was more intransigent. Reviewing in the senate the failure of the fourth and fifth sessions of the preparatory commission (30 November – 3 December 1927 and 15–24 March

1928), the first marked by the conflict between France's determination to put security before disarmament and Germany's determination to regard disarmament as an obligation deriving from the Versailles Treaty and the second by disintegration after Germany backed Russia's unsuccessful bid for complete and general disarmament, Mussolini reiterated the main principles underlying Italy's position: interdependence of all types of arms, proportions not to be based on the status quo, and parity with the heaviest armed continental power. These, he suggested to applause, stood counter to the frequent talk of Italian militarism, 'the smallest mote compared to the many great beams of others'.[142]

The principles of naval parity with any other continental European power and of arms limitation by global tonnage were now established tenets of Italian foreign policy. Communicating them to the French ambassador in October 1928, Grandi suggested that the five signatories to the Washington Treaty might advantageously consider postponing until 1936 the building of battleships which could begin under the original terms in 1931.[143] The naval general staff, detecting French reluctance to accept the principle of parity, felt that the two fundamental principles Grandi had communicated to Beaumarchais were as far as they could go, and still represented a serious risk to national security. While Italy's lack of raw materials, long lines of communications and open coastlines made her vulnerable, France's two naval frontiers meant that she could not be blockaded and the terms of the Locarno treaty gave her British support against the German navy.

Even if we were to have effective parity of force with France we would still be in a condition of great inferiority in respect to her. We should not make the mistake of supposing that France's professionals (*tecnici*) and statesmen are unaware of the very elementary facts.[144]

The question of whether to build large battleships was discussed at a meeting of the council of ministers on 25 January 1929. Sirianni, Acton, Burzagli and Rocco – all 'battleship admirals' – argued for taking up the forthcoming opportunity. Thaon di Revel took the opposite tack, as he had always done, and supported limiting naval building to 10,000-ton cruisers and submarines on the grounds that they would be more useful in a war against France. Mussolini agreed with him.[145] The battleship question was for the moment dormant, but the state of Italy's relations with France, Mussolini's foreign policy initiatives and the progress of military planning meant that the issue of naval construction most certainly was not. At the same cabinet meeting it was agreed to increase the new-build allocation in the naval budgets for 1930/1 and 1931/2 from

407 million lire to 600 million lire, a decision which Mussolini ratified in August.

Teething troubles at the air ministry

In August 1925, Mussolini established an air ministry with himself as interim minister, and five months later he made his own position permanent. Relations between the under-secretary of state, general Bonzani, and the first chief of air staff, general Pier Ruggiero Piccio, were poor. Piccio, who had insisted on continuing as air attaché in Paris, was doing neither of his jobs properly and was irresponsibly making demands about what was required to prepare the country for war without taking any account whatever of budgetary limitations.[146] Bonzani was kept under more or less continuous attack from various quarters, accused of permitting Masonic infiltration into the air force, of presiding over an excessively large and expensive bureaucracy, of encouraging a high lifestyle in the Aeronautica, and of creating an air force many of whose planes were obsolescent and whose efficiency for war was half what was claimed for it. Bonzani defended himself vigorously against palpably inaccurate statements about the proportions of the budget he had spent on different items. He also admitted that no one in the air force, including himself, was satisfied with the material presently in service but pointed out that he had not wished to shout its defects to the four winds. Both he and Piccio had kept Mussolini personally informed about the shortcomings.[147] However – and judging by the consequence – Mussolini decided that Bonzani was becoming too much of a political if not a professional liability. On 5 November 1926 he was brusquely fired, and next day Mussolini appointed the *quadrumvir* and veteran of the March on Rome Italo Balbo in his place.

Ambitious, competent, restlessly active and with more than a touch of flamboyance, the thirty-year-old appeared a good choice to catapult the new service to the forefront of the public scene, to formulate the rules which would guide its development, and to sweep away the bureaucratic inertia which already infected the new ministry.[148] But if he was politically qualified for the job, Balbo was not obviously professionally qualified for it. A reserve captain who had served in the alpini during the world war, and been decorated for gallantry, his rank of general in the Fascist militia in no way prepared him for his transportation across the chasm from political soldiering to control of one of the three fighting forces and the rank of *generale di squadra aerea* to which he was appointed on 10 August 1928.[149]

Bonzani claimed, probably accurately, to have handed over to his successor 800 combat-ready aircraft and 800 reserves. This would have made the Regia Aeronautica the second-largest air force in the world at that time, behind France which had 1,350 combat-ready aircraft, and approximately equal to the Royal Air Force, which had 850 front-line aircraft in 1926 and 750 a year later.[150] Balbo, not without political motives for diminishing the size of his patrimony, contested the figures, first claiming that the true number of combat-ready aircraft was only 551 and then reducing it to 405 a few days later. Putting the air fleet to the test, he ordered all aircraft to take to the air on 28 November for continuous flights of two and a half and three hours; 335 aircraft took off, and 104 were not able to complete the exercise.[151] Mussolini was at once informed of the parlous situation. As was always to be the case with the vexed question of aircraft numbers, the figures he was given were manipulated to suit Balbo's ends: after the exercise, the under-secretary presided over a meeting which produced the statistic that the air force possessed 633 aircraft that were ready to fly.[152] Since the Yugoslav air force was estimated at 300 effective aircraft, the balance of forces in the air made the single-handed war against her which Mussolini seemed increasingly ready to contemplate appear possible. It clearly ruled out the war with the Franco–Yugoslavian alliance which his foreign policy seemed increasingly likely to bring about.[153]

Balbo had much to do. Everything was in short supply – fuel, lubricants, spare parts, ammunition and bombs – and in his first year of office the Italian aircraft industry produced 420 aircraft and 900 engines, little more than it had managed in 1915. His procurement policies were not entirely successful, but his personnel policies, inspired by the appropriately Fascist slogan *'largo ai giovani'* ('space for the young') were vigorous and effective. The force expanded in size from 2,340 officers in 1925 to 3,060 in 1931, and in the flying branch the proportion of middle-ranking and senior officers went up.[154] Tests for the 40 per cent who could expect to advance beyond the rank of captain were stiff, and age limits for generals low; 55 for the highest rank, *generale di squadra aerea*, 48 and 46 for the next two ranks.

Although he had himself joined the Fascist party in January 1921, the new minister did not aggressively politicise the air force from within, apparently making few recommendations for party membership and refusing to allow it to influence promotion. However, in a circular on the 'Moral and Political Education of Airmen', issued on 6 December 1927, Balbo did urge officers to speak out in favour of Fascism; to do so 'was not carrying out political intrigue in the barracks because Fascism today is identified with the nation'.[155] He was also more than willing to preside over an air force which was Fascist in image and appearance. In his first year in office he had every aeroplane marked with the *fascio littorio* symbol; in his second every airman entitled to the ribbon for participating in the March on Rome was allowed to mount it when in uniform and the saluto romano was introduced for airmen not wearing hats. He used his ministerial powers under a law on officer status and promotion of 23 July 1927 to admit 1,146 second-lieutenants, including some party officials and members, to the air force on the basis of little more than possession of Italian citizenship. This action reflected his fondness for executive power, and its effects were resented.[156] The office-bound were not immune from his attentions either. In the new air ministry building, opened in 1931, office hours ran from eight until three, and lunch was taken during a forty-minute break at noon and eaten standing up as no chairs were provided in the dining hall.[157] Neither of these practices were ones with which the employees of other government offices were familiar.

The independence of the air force was never seriously in question during Balbo's period of office. However, in July 1928 admiral Sirianni mischievously sent Mussolini a paper by a fellow admiral which suggested that the air force was unnecessary either as an offensive or a defensive force, that there were other no less effective means of air defence, and that the army and the navy needed all the aeroplanes going. The argument was not easily acceptable, Sirianni suggested, but needed thinking about. The air ministry crushed the argument. Rear-admiral Marsilia had got his numbers wrong: the French air force was at least two and a half times larger than he said it was. An enemy capable of carrying out an uncontested air offensive could inflict 'irreparable damage' on the country. In any case the creation of the armed forces was encouraging the collaboration and reciprocal awareness that was 'necessary in peace and more than indispensable in war'.[158]

In 1927, Balbo listed his objectives for a fellow flying student: 'First we must create a sporting air force, then a disciplined air force, and finally a militarily efficient air force.'[159] Much time, attention and money – perhaps too much – was lavished on the first of these objectives. Under Balbo's direction, Italy competed in the Schneider Trophy each year, winning it for the only time in 1926 at a cost of 3,860,000 lire. However, he did not look kindly on the *raids* – long-range flights by individual pilots chasing records – which had been a prominent feature of the early years of the air force and in March 1928 announced that they were to cease and be replaced by cruises (*crocieri*) by 'multiple squadrons of at least eighty aircraft flying together in order to enrich our flying personnel not only with precious experience of the skies, the climate and far distant countries, but also with the necessary practice at flying in mass formations'.[160] As well as testing equipment, personnel and organisation, the *crocieri*, which were designed to 'depersonalise' flying and thereby escape from the idolisation of individual 'aces', garnered world-wide publicity for Balbo, for his service and for his master. The first *crociere* saw sixty seaplanes fly across the western Mediterranean via Mallorca and return along the Spanish and French coasts between 26 May and 2 June 1928. The following month, Balbo flew on a 'Cruise of the European Capitals', calling at Paris, London, Berlin and Munich. In 1929, he led another cruise by thirty-five aircraft across the eastern Mediterranean to Athens, Istanbul, Varna, Costanza and Odessa. Later, in January 1931, he flew across the Atlantic from Morocco to Brazil and in July 1933 he made his last and most spectacular 'cruise', flying across the North Atlantic via Londonderry and Reykjavik to Chicago and returning via the Azores. The *crocieri* were not inexpensive – the North American cruise cost 7,000,000 lire in immediate expenses alone – and were criticised by a few people at the time and by more since. However, these spectacular flights served at least two practical purposes: they served as sales demonstrations for the Italian aircraft industry, and they also demonstrated the potential strategic reach of a modern air force.

The exact role of the air force in the event of war was unclear when Balbo came into office and remained so throughout his period of office, although he made some headway in organisational terms by gradually whittling down the air assets of the army and the navy. In spring 1927, the best he could do was to give parliament a broad statement to the effect that the air force increased the fighting power (*potere bellico*) of the other two services by weakening the enemy air force through the bombing of its bases and factories and by preventing it from attacking the other two services, particularly during the delicate process of mobilisation.[161] The following year, this sketchy outline was considerably expanded. At the meeting of the chiefs of staff of the armed services called by Mussolini on 18 July 1927 to discuss 'systematic preparation for war', in the course of which the Duce told his generals that 'war may be far off or perhaps not far off but it will certainly come', marshal Badoglio accepted that the first hostile action in such a war, whether or not it had formally been declared, would be an enemy air offensive against Italy. She should aim to counter by bombing enemy airfields immediately. Mussolini demanded offensive plans because, as he remarked, the more rapid offensive action was, the greater was the probability of success. Out of the meeting came a menu of air operations which included attacking enemy air bases, particularly when air fleets were gathering ready for take-off, bombing the population to depress morale, disrupting mobilisation, interrupting communications, and bombing fleet bases.[162]

Tactical experience was necessarily limited, despite Balbo's increasing the total flying time from 50,400 hours in 1926 to 81,000 hours in 1929. A joint exercise with the army in the summer of 1926 showed that ground–air communications still suffered from the same kind of problems identified in the celeri exercise in 1923 and the naval exercises in 1924 – exacerbated on this occasion by the fact that information from the umpires to the directors of the manoeuvres was given precedence over that coming from the airmen. The fighter squadron arrived late on the scene and showed the effects of 'very little training for flying in patrols and a lack of preparation for the work'.[163] The Aeronautica's role in the aero–naval exercise held in June 1927 to practise the defence of the Tyrrhenian basin was more limited and perhaps also more congenial to the airmen. They were tasked to bomb 'enemy' military and industrial plants in the Gulf of Naples and to 'mop up' any hostile light surface craft encountered en route.[164]

In September 1927, 218 aircraft took part in large-scale exercises held between Brescia and Pordenone designed chiefly to test the outcome of an encounter between two bomber masses with escorting fighters, but also to study a range of related problems including long-range aerial reconnaissance, fighter combat to 'police' the enemy's skies and low-level bombing. In the detailed scenario developed for the exercises, which incorporated a tangible dig at the army by referring indirectly but unmistakeably to Caporetto, the defending 'Blue' air force had also to cover its reorganisation 'in a period of grave crisis' while at the same time protecting northern Italy's industrial centres, railway communications and hydro-electric works.[165] Balbo sent Mussolini a series of excited telegrams describing the exercise in terms so generic that it was impossible to make anything of it save that all the aeroplanes were efficient, the personnel robust and hardy and 'the organisation absolutely perfect'.[166] Bad weather affected the main part of the exercise, though a characteristically optimistic Balbo reported that it gave absolute mastery to the offensive. In fact, it must have been difficult for the air staff to come to any hard and fast conclusions on many of the major tactical issues. Mobilisation had worked well, and so had aircraft maintenance – especially important when many of the aircraft were kept in the open during appalling weather. The airmen had exhibited dash, courage and self-denial but, as the chief of air staff remarked at the end of the exercises, they had sometimes shown 'an excessively bellicose and aggressive spirit' with the result that parts of the pre-planned actions had been disrupted.[167] For a variety of reasons communications were still very defective. The use of fighters as combat escorts for the bomber fleet was never tried out because of the bad weather, the final daylight bombing exercise had not been properly carried out because of inadequate preparation of crew and aircraft, and the low-level bombing had been too high and had lacked surprise.[168] The one element of the exercises that had been a demonstrable and unqualified success was bombing carried out as part of a surprise night attack that 'Blue' unleashed at the start of the exercises. General Armani was in no doubt as to the significance of the episode. 'This confirms to us', he remarked 'that the nation that succeeds in securing the initiative in operations will have a very important (*notevolissimo*) initial advantage'.[169]

The air exercises scheduled for 1928 reflected the growing preoccupation of all three services with a two-front war as Badoglio followed Mussolini's directives and began to co-ordinate planning for a possible war with Yugoslavia. They were designed to test the capacity of fighter defences to prevent or contain enemy air offensives which might otherwise degrade the efficiency of the land forces, to protect the major industrial and population centres, and to contribute to domestic bomber offensives.[170] Air intelligence from abroad suggested that defence was no easy matter. The Italian air and military attachés in London reported that groups of bombers had been able to get through to London during the air manoeuvres of July 1927 thanks to cloud cover, and that in the August 1928 exercises the defence had 'lost' 151 aircraft in the course of 'shooting down' 139 attacking bombers, leading the *Times* newspaper to conclude that it was impossible effectively to defend the capital.[171]

The depth of the reservations in the higher echelons of the air force about doctrine and about intellectual activity in general, and the degree of scepticism about the relationship between discussion and experimentation which Balbo had espoused, was evident in the guidance which general Armando Armani, chief of air staff, produced in April 1928 for the forthcoming grand summer manoeuvres. There were no safe lessons from the past, Armani told his officers, and the only competent and responsible body as far as the evolution of doctrine was concerned was the air staff; 'war doctrines are not the fruit of pure imagination, they are the result of experience'. The chief of air staff also aimed a scarcely concealed blow at the under-secretary's style and policies. 'The Aeronautica, like any military organisation, must prepare itself for war,' he pronounced, 'and therefore its every effort must be directed towards this without regard either to the demands or the approbation of the public'.[172] In the event the manoeuvres – the first of their kind – had to be cancelled because of lack of readiness (*limitata efficienza*) in units and could not be undertaken until 1931.

The actual and prospective state of the air force at this time was far from reassuring. Its total stock of available aircraft on 1 January 1928, including reparable ones, amounted to 1,345 planes – not enough to equip and back up even the 73 squadrons to which it had been reduced in 1926. The reliability of the bombers' engines was so poor that they could not be considered ready for employment in war. The air staff were worried by the lack of preparations so far made for chemical warfare.

Looking ahead to a war in which they expected to lose 55 per cent of their aircraft in the first three months, they calculated that at present production rates of 170 aircraft a month it would take four and a half months to replace war losses for the current force and five and a half if they had the 89 squadrons and 914 frontline aircraft they thought necessary. It was 'absolutely necessary', the air staff told Badoglio, that the Commissione suprema di difesa produce 'the executive directives necessary to increase the potential [capacity] of our air industry'.[173] As the activities of the commission increasingly made apparent, the idea that fundamental economic weaknesses could be remedied by executive fiat was a pipe-dream, though one from which its head and almost all of its members never escaped.

In September 1928, Mussolini told Balbo that there would be a war in 1938 and ordered him to prepare the Aeronautica accordingly. Calculating that a start would have to be made on all the preliminaries by 1930, Balbo called a meeting of his air force generals to come to some recommendations on the types of aeroplanes and bombs the air force would need. Their conclusions enraged him, as he duly informed Mussolini. The discussion had proceeded on the basis of a hypothetical and generic concept of war, applicable to any and every power, and had made no reference to Italy's probable adversaries. Concrete objectives in different war scenarios deriving from clear plans of action and leading to decisions on appropriate means had been entirely lacking. Among other things, the airmen had suggested reducing the range of aircraft from 3,000 to 2,000 kilometres since no European capital was more than 800 kilometres away. Balbo pointed out that London was 950 kilometres away, and that range had to take account of such matters as gaining height, headwinds and unexpected changes of route.[174]

Planning was not the only area in which the air force was deficient. In resolving the issue of how it would be deployed in the war which Mussolini foresaw, it had an even more fundamental problem, as Balbo openly acknowledged to the chamber of deputies on 23 March 1928. 'The air force does not yet have a true and proper doctrine of war, fixed according to rigid and immutable principles', he told parliament:

It is enriched by all the technical and tactical experiences which are continuously being perfected and it advances with the dizzying progress of the studies which are being fervently developed all over the world.[175]

At his best in making an organisation work, Balbo was either unable or unwilling to impose upon the air force a unitary strategic doctrine which would shape both aircraft procurement and operational planning. Ready to use the kind of terminology to which Giulio Douhet had given currency over the previous years – in November 1927, arguing to Mussolini for special budgetary treatment, he said that in the interests of national defence Italy should ready herself to take 'command of the air even at the cost of reducing the power of the army and the navy' – he was much less willing to embrace unreservedly the ideas it expressed.[176] Some Douhetian themes were convenient: the independent role of the air force in war, the need for a first-strike capability and the central role of mass aerial attacks in future war. The latter, however, was in part a matter of degree, and in the stress he continued to lay on the destructive power of aircraft Douhet went well beyond the technical capabilities of the day.[177] Thus, while opening up the columns of the official air force journal, *Rivista Aeronautica*, to him and allowing him to publish some twenty articles between 1927 and 1930 (the year of Douhet's death), Balbo also encouraged a rival theorist, Amadeo Mecozzi, to air his ideas.

In the late 1920s, Mecozzi began to refine his ideas and develop his critique of the shibboleths of Douhetian thought, acknowledging that the air arm would have a great influence in any future war but disputing the means and methods by which it would attain and exercise that influence. 'Command of the air' he thought unattainable in practice and therefore mistaken in theory. Rather, he proposed the goal of aerial 'supremacy', which would be only local and temporary and not universal. While agreeing that the air force must be autonomous, he did not accept Douhet's supremacist claims for it, which by 1927 involved rejecting any idea of siphoning planes away from the main force into 'auxiliary' functions, an action which he labelled 'useless, superfluous and dangerous'. Instead he argued that air force, navy and army must co-operate since all three arms pursued a single common end in war. The concept of inter-connected warfare, which he termed *guerra aerea concomitante*, would be further developed during the next decade.

Extending theory into practice, Mecozzi rejected Douhet's espousal of a single type of 'battle plane' and began campaigning the merits of the pursuit fighter (*supercaccia*), and of ground attack 'assault aviation' which would deliver many distributed attacks in preference to the small number of cataclysmic strikes by means of which Douhet proposed to attain and use command of the air. Mecozzi's ideas had many ramifications, and in proposing them he forced the nascent air force to consider issues such as the role of air bases and their defence, which would delay the breaking of the aerial equilibrium and so give the navy and the army the time to wage their wars, and the merits of dive-bombing which Douhetian theory simply sailed over.[178]

Mecozzi and Douhet took their posts at either ends of the theoretical spectrum, but within the Regia Aeronautica opinion ranged right along it.

Moderate Douhetists accepted the utility of auxiliary aviation and questioned whether command of the air could be achieved at the outset of a war. Pragmatists questioned whether the air was the only decisive theatre and pointed out that although the French had had absolute aerial superiority during the Riff war in Morocco this alone had not been a winning factor – a point Balbo would enlarge on later in the 1930s after the Abyssinian war to demonstrate that Douhetian ideas did not fit with colonial wars. Sympathisers with Mecozzi observed that aerial battle was the only way to attain aerial supremacy, and that this necessitated the use of pursuit aircraft. Confronted with the arguments of one of his adversaries whose critical observations about such issues as the importance of gas in future warfare, which he regarded as unquestioned, rested on the agnostic foundation that the future was essentially unknowable and that therefore many things were possible, Douhet replied with palpable irritation that theories of the *giusto mezzo* ('just mean'), while convenient, derived from indecision and uncertainty: 'They seek to resolve everything and in fact resolve nothing.'[179] In one sense, this can stand as a summary of the situation as far as air force doctrine was concerned at the time of his death in 1930. While Douhet's thoughts were clear, coherent and systematic, Mecozzi had still fully to develop his. Left in a state of indecision about the architectural design of a future air war, the Regia Aeronautica was therefore quite unable to resolve fundamental questions about the components from which it would be constructed – such as the types of planes to build or the balance between speed, manoeuvre and protection in a fighter. Italo Balbo stepped into the gap, equipping the air force with manoeuvrable CR 20 biplane fighters which pleased the crowds at his air shows, BR 3 and Ca 101 day-and-night bombers which had range but were slow (the former no faster than contemporary fighters and the latter slower), and the rugged and dependable Savoia Marchetti SM 55 seaplanes which he used for three of his aerial cruises.[180]

At the start of 1929, the Commissione suprema di difesa considered the question of the active anti-aircraft defence of Italy as one of thirteen major agenda items it discussed during fifteen hours spread over five days. Two years earlier, it had assigned the responsibility to the army, supported by the fascist militia (MVSN). The minister of public works, Giuriati, questioned that decision in the light particularly of the progress made in the metal construction of aeroplanes. When the new army chief of staff, Bonzani, defended the present arrangement on the grounds that the accuracy of bombing diminished when the height at which bombers had to operate was increased and therefore the size of the target shrank, and that anti-aircraft guns could be concentrated on major targets so as to prevent them flying at levels low enough to do serious damage, Balbo waded into the attack. The present system should be labelled 'passive' not 'active', he argued, and the money would be better spent on fighters. Gazzera backed Bonzani, pointing out that recent statistics suggested that a quarter of all planes shot down in the world war had been hit by anti-aircraft fire and that three complete batteries of anti-aircraft guns could be purchased for the cost of a squadron of twelve aeroplanes. The deputy chief of air staff, De Pinedo, supported his chief in terms that Balbo may have seen as insufficiently uncompromising, telling the commission:

The problem of air defence can only be resolved in an indirect way, that is by building a strong air force which will strike the enemy's air force and his centres of production at the start of hostilities, thereby making it impossible for him to conduct any further offensives.[181]

When general Dallolio, president of the committee for civilian mobilisation, backed the army on the grounds of civilian morale, and admiral Sirianni pointed out that improvements in artillery since 1918 would make it more difficult for bombers to fly at levels low enough to be accurate, Balbo was beaten. Summing up, Mussolini characteristically shared the responsibility for deciding the points to be defended and the weapons and subsidiary means by which they were to be protected between the four chiefs of staff (including the MVSN) and the president of the committee for civilian mobilisation.[182]

In accordance with Balbo's express wish for concrete plans, which in its turn derived at least in part from Mussolini's warnings about future war, De Pinedo produced the Regia Aeronautica's first operational plans in May 1929 – and sent them to the chiefs of staff of the army and the navy without Balbo's knowledge. It was not a document designed to give reassurance to an external audience or support to internal authority. Presently, the air force disposed of aeroplanes 'a good part of which can be considered out of date and of very little use in war'. It would take between three or four years to replace them, but because of the rapid changes in aircraft characteristics it was difficult to see what the new planes would be able to do. The Regia Aeronautica was 'in a very critical condition in regard to its efficiency for war': its bombers were of little value, squadrons had fewer aircraft than they should, and there was a general lack of reserves and mobilisation supplies. In the event of war against France alone (*Ipotesi Ouest*), Italy should use the air supremacy she could obtain against what was strictly an auxiliary air force to secure possession of Corsica, which could then serve as a base for attacks on Provence and the industries in the Rhone valley and operations in support of the army's advance along the Cornice. If the war lasted for any length of time, attacks on enemy sea traffic and defence of domestic shipping would become important. As far as a two-front war against France and Yugoslavia was concerned, defeat could only be avoided with 'a good preponderance [of air strength]'.[183]

Balbo's relations with his chiefs of staff had been poor: Piccio had been sacked in February 1927 as a result of spending too much time in Paris, where he had insisted on continuing as air attaché, having attracted accusations of treason as a result of his luxurious life-style and admitting to playing the stock exchange, and his successor, Armani, had been injured in an air accident in September 1928.[184] De Pinedo, acting chief of staff, believed that he had been promised the succession if Balbo's air cruise to the eastern Mediterranean went well, and when he was brushed aside by Balbo he went directly to Mussolini.[185] When he had taken office, he told the Duce, there had been no concept for the employment of the air force in war and no study of the specifications needed for war planes. The problem was to be found at the top. The air force needed to be directed by 'a thinking soldier, highly competent in matters of employment and in technical areas, profoundly logical and reflective'; such a person only matured after years of active service. After pointing out that French bombers could fly at heights that Italian fighters could not reach, though French fighters could, De Pinedo concluded that the condition of the Italian air force was such that he could foresee 'great disappointment at the moment of need'.[186] In an accompanying memorandum which spelt out the deficiencies in detail, De Pinedo estimated that an extra 650 million lire would be needed over four years to renew the air force, during which time 'it would be necessary that the general political conditions allowed us to exclude any likelihood of war' or otherwise Italy would have to resort to extreme measures such as buying aircraft from abroad.[187]

Presented with a choice between the two men, Mussolini made the only one which politics would allow. Balbo stayed, and De Pinedo was relieved as deputy chief of air staff and sent off as air attaché to Buenos Aires, retiring from the air force three years later. On 28 August 1929 Giuseppe Valle replaced him as deputy chief of staff. The episode and the situation it revealed taught Mussolini two things: that whatever his personal predilections war was not on the cards for a few years, and that there was still much to do before the air force was capable of playing its role in his aggressive designs.

War planning

Given its long-standing and explicit rivalry with France, the fact that the Italian navy was first into the lists in developing war plans is not to be wondered at. In 1924, a detailed consideration of the defensive and offensive circumstances that would shape a single-handed war between the two powers concluded that the proximity to the enemy of the ports of Savona, Genoa and Leghorn and the island of Elba in the upper Tyrrhenian sea meant that only defence was possible. Likewise, the Tuscan and Roman coastline would have to be protected against any invasion. The central position of Naples would make it the main base for heavy surface units in any war, and also a main recipient for neutral merchant shipping coming from both the eastern and western Mediterranean. Trapani and Cagliari would be important bases for light surface forces, as would La Maddalena.

At this time, the only air threat came in the central Tyrrhenian from planes based in Corsica, and in the stretch of water between Sardinia and Sicily which could be reached from Tunisia; 'elsewhere aerial offensives will be less intense and more rare'.[188] The rapid development of air power would soon change this planning parameter. Lines of communication across the western Mediterranean were 'paralysed' by enemy naval bases in metropolitan France, Algeria and Tunisia; however, as far as enemy air offensives were concerned there would always be a central zone 'of near tranquillity' where ship-borne planes would be able to act.[189] Tripoli and Tobruk would have to be defended, the latter as a port of refuge for warships and merchantmen. Beirut represented a possible threat to traffic between Port Said and Tobruk. On a wider front, while Italian ships could cross the Atlantic without threat other than from Martinique, the French would control the approaches to Gibraltar from Morocco and their naval base at Dakar.

Given these geographical realities, the Italian navy planned to close the Ionian sea and the eastern Mediterranean to the French by preventing their forces moving from Tunisia to the Levant, attacking strongly any enemy detachment which succeeded in penetrating the eastern basin, and continually contesting enemy submarine activity. The Tyrrhenian sea south of Elba would likewise be closed off to the enemy. The main zones of direct action against the French would be the gulf of Genoa, the Sicilian channel and the western Mediterranean. The object would be to immobilise the main part of the enemy's forces east of a line running from the Franco-Italian border via Corsica, Sardinia and Pantelleria to the frontier between Tripolitania and Tunisia. This was, as the naval staff recognised, a defensive plan and they acknowledged the need to act aggressively. Therefore, 'in order to pin the enemy down in the west, as well as to deprive him of an ideal air base and excellent bases for light craft', Italy would launch an invasion of Corsica at the most opportune moment.[190] If the enemy undertook offensives against Liguria, Elba,

Sardinia or Sicily, the distribution of forces proposed under the scheme would enable the navy to respond.

While this allowed the planners to paint a reassuring picture of the relative calm which would then prevail in the eastern Mediterranean, they recognised the threats which might be forthcoming in the Indian Ocean from French ships based at Djibuti and Madagascar. To solve this problem, an Italian naval detachment would be posted in Eritrean ports and auxiliary cruisers would operate from Kisimaio. The possibility of seizing French Somalia was also raised. In the Atlantic, long-range submarines, if not allowed by international law to attack isolated French ships, would attack military convoys and warships, bombard coastal points and carry out *colpi di mano*. All of this only met the 'uncertain conditions' which would exist at the outbreak of a conflict. Once the enemy's intentions were apparent, 'the plan of operations will have an orientation which corresponds to them, always however adhering to the concept of indirectly protecting our traffic by tying the enemy down in zones far from our lines of communication, and with actions animated by a high offensive spirit'.[191]

In its early foray into the realm of strategic planning the navy showed itself well aware that it could not afford to neglect the influence of international circumstances on its actions.[192] Britain would have to be benevolently neutral because she provided most of Italy's raw materials and in peacetime shipped 60 per cent of her overseas requirements; therefore the navy's plan did not even contemplate Britain joining France 'which would be absolutely disastrous for us'.[193] Spain's benevolent neutrality would open up the prospect of contraband sources of raw material and bases for submarines on the Atlantic coast. An alliance would be even better as it would give Italy a naval base in the Balearics, but although Spain enjoyed an excellent geographical position it had few ships and would bring with it defensive needs of its own. Its obvious geographical advantages would however produce a resuscitation of the idea of informal and formal links four years later.[194] The best to be hoped for from Yugoslavia was rigid neutrality; if she aligned herself with France, the Adriatic would have to be reinforced. A neutral Greece, if not one favourable to Italy, was essential for otherwise the eastern Mediterranean and the Ionian sea would become major theatres of operation. Turkey's stance would in all probability be determined by Greece: if hostile, she would cut off Italian access to the resources of the Black Sea and increase the vulnerability of the Dodecanese. The neutrality of both powers was therefore to be preferred. Acutely conscious of Italy's dependence on imported raw materials, which could be threatened by any open or concealed international hostility towards her and which could cause her to lose the war, the navy concluded with a planning requirement which showed how little it understood either the ways or the intentions of its new political master:

A solid diplomatic preparation is therefore necessary before war [occurs]; and then during the conflict it will be necessary cautiously to conduct a wise international policy, in order that intrigues, interferences and the lack of benevolence of certain states do not render ineffective even the most brilliant advantages that our arms obtain.[195]

When, in July 1927, Mussolini demanded a 'systematic preparation' for war the army had an array of deployment plans. In form, they resembled their pre-war predecessors, outlining the positions in which units would be deployed in various scenarios and indicating general lines of advance and strategic objectives. The self-imposed constraints under which the planners operated were evident in the preamble to Plan 1A for a war in which Italy faced Germany and Austria combined – a scenario which they admitted was unlikely in the international situation of the day:

A precautionary plan naturally does not go beyond the opening period of hostilities, partly because seeking to foresee the further development of events would lead onto ground which is absolutely hypothetical and arbitrary, and partly because the future availability of forces and means will change.[196]

The plan envisaged deploying eighteen divisions on the main Austro–German front while the remaining three guarded the Swiss border. No troops covered the French or Yugoslav borders, although an addendum to the plan spoke in terms of thirty divisions – more than Italy currently had – nine of which would be deployed against Yugoslavia. The planners expected Germany to violate Swiss neutrality, as she had done in Belgium in 1914, upon which Italian troops would also cross the Swiss frontier and advance rapidly to take up positions between 40 and 65 kilometres beyond it. While German forces could get quickly from Bavaria into the Tyrol, they could not get quickly into Carinthia. There, eighty-four Italian battalions could drive through twenty-seven Austrian battalions – half Austria's total force – to reach the line Ankogel – Lake Millstatter – Villach. Setting aside the lessons of the world war, which suggested that this region was likely to be a defender's dream and an attacker's nightmare, the planners counted on an initial superiority in manpower, a 'great preponderance of artillery', and 'above all the major contribution which aviation will make for us'. They also planned to use gas to interdict five zones including Innsbruck.[197]

The skeletal and highly schematic quality of Italian military planning was a feature of the other two major plans which were in force when Mussolini made his intervention. Plan 2A, for war against Yugoslavia, was drawn up in two variants. If France assumed a benevolent attitude, twenty-one divisions of infantry and two of cavalry would be deployed in a three-pronged attack along the line Fiume – Karlovac with Zagreb as the strategic objective. If Austria assumed a similar attitude, then Italy would hold a defensive position just beyond the frontier on the line Stol – Tuhovic with seventeen infantry and two cavalry divisions and await the availability of more troops before going on to the offensive. Plan 3 for war with France envisaged a two-pronged drive on Marseilles via the coastal Cornice and the col di Tenda by eleven divisions, while four more divisions stood on the defensive in the mountains to the north.[198]

Mussolini now ordered Badoglio to carry out the preparatory planning studies needed to fight a single-handed war against Yugoslavia.[199] As well as being decidedly unconvinced about Italy's readiness for such a war, his Capo di stato maggiore generale was not in tune with the kind of planning that Mussolini now wanted him to oversee. In 1923 he had criticised 'pre-ordained war plans *alla* von Schlieffen', holding that planning should be limited to the drawing up of forces and the forming of an order of battle, while the concept of operations 'should be fixed only after having made contact with the enemy and having then perceived his distribution of force'.[200] Faced with the Duce's command in July 1927 to make plans he smartly reversed his position, telling Mussolini that while many military writers had raised doubts about the utility of war plans 'since the unknowns are too many and the facts almost always develop in ways not foreseen' he did not share this opinion and citing in his support Plan XVII and 'the Moltke plan'.[201] He then initiated a painstaking and time-consuming process by beginning with the principal foundations of any plan: cover (*copertura*), mobilisation and deployment.

The Franco–Yugoslav and Italo–Albanian pacts signed in November 1927 both had implications for the single-front war which, in February 1927, Badoglio had believed likely to result in tragedy for Italy. The new diplomatic alignments had no discernable impact on his handling of the planning process. During an intensive six-day planning session to prepare for a staff exercise to test the mobilisation element of war plan Ipotesi Est against Yugoslavia in January 1928, the Capo di stato maggiore generale resolutely refused to consider a two-front war. When colonel Carlo Graziani, head of the operations staff of the Regia Aeronautica, switched the attention of one session from a one-front to a two-front war, Badoglio immediately reined him in:

We absolutely cannot consider mobilisation on two fronts because in our current circumstances this would be like seeking to commit suicide. We already have a lot to do to organise ourselves against the East ... we cannot think of doing so against East and West except as a useless sacrifice.[202]

The preparatory planning revealed a parlous situation if it came to war. To keep thirty divisions on the march would require bringing 15,000 mules up from the south and requisitioning 10,000 motor vehicles. Only six railway lines existed on which to move them up towards the frontier, though a programme of improvements incorporating some double-tracking, due for completion in eighteen months, would permit 140 trains a day to arrive on the Isonzo. Between Tarvisio and Gorizia there were no railway lines at all. The twelve roads leading to the Yugoslav frontier were in poor condition and their number diminished once the troops got beyond it: there were only six or seven roads between Lubljana and Zagreb and three beyond the latter town. The fact that the Isonzo had only two bridges, the Tagliamento two, and the Piave three seriously constrained all movement. In the course of the discussion on railway movements it became apparent that the army had as yet made no plans to allocate personnel to unload the trains as they arrived at their off-loading stations.[203]

If anything, the air force was in an even more parlous position. General Armani, after remarking that his office was scarcely two years old and that much remained to be done, announced baldly that 'The actual strength of seventy-three squadrons is absolutely insufficient for any needs whatever.'[204] Introducing France into the discussion by the backdoor, colonel Graziani pointed out that it would have 206 squadrons by 1929 and then unveiled the air force estimate that French aircraft production could increase from 200 to 5,000 aircraft a month as soon as a war began – a figure Badoglio was rightly disinclined to accept. The Yugoslav air force was reckoned to have 400 effective planes. The Italian air force therefore needed 170 squadrons by 1932. The Aeronautica was correct in its evident assumption that this was as much a bidding opportunity as it was a planning exercise: in closing the final session, Badoglio revealed that Mussolini had asked him to produce a schedule showing how much money was needed to accelerate preparations for war.[205]

Like the air force, the navy saw in the planning process a budgetary opening. Aware of the limited assistance which the army wanted from it in the event of war with Yugoslavia, which amounted to not much more than naval gunfire directed against coastal roads on the army's right flank, landings on the islands of Veglia and Arbe and assistance in defending Zara, it calculated that only a small proportion of the fleet would be needed for operations in the Adriatic in the event of war under Ipotesi Est.[206] However, the likelihood that France would take advantage of the inevitable incidents that would occur at sea led it to conclude that full mobilisation would be necessary in the event of war in the east. Given the state of the fleet, in addition to the current build (two 'Trento' cruisers, four destroyers and four submarines) it therefore required extra build in the shape of two destroyer leaders, sixteen destroyers, eight submarines and additional light craft and MAS boats by 1932. As far as heavier craft, delimited by the Washington treaty, were concerned, the navy wanted three 23,000 ton cruisers to match the four 17,500-ton ships for which the French had 'undoubtedly' for some time had plans ready. The bill for this list of naval necessities amounted to an additional 1,350 million lire. While the requirement for the cruisers depended on the turns of external policy, the lighter craft were indispensable; they would cost an extra 130 million lire a year over four years. Another 280 million were needed for urgent expenditure on arms and munitions, special craft and arms for merchant ships, and a further 440 million for such things as coastal defences and communications nets. In all, the navy needed 1,252 million lire. It did not think it necessary to state even in general terms what operational activities would be undertaken with the additional ships it so evidently felt it needed.[207]

The navy's own plans for war against Yugoslavia started from the assumption that their opponent's navy, whose component of submarines and torpedo boats was increasing daily, would be likely to attempt a few swift incursions against Italy's coast and maritime traffic and would defend against resupply operations carried out after Italian landings around Zara or on the Croatian or Albanian coastline. Given its over-whelming superiority, the Italian navy must go on the offensive from the outset to ensure that enemy operations did not go unpunished. Its other tasks would be to assist land operations '*within the limits of reasonable safety*', and to guarantee the movement of all naval traffic in the Adriatic. On the evidence of the world war, the difficulties of dealing with enemy submarines and mines could best be met by using older ships in the the-atre. Given the wide range of options available to the Yugoslav air force as a result of the small size of the Adriatic the Regia Aeronautica would need to make more aircraft available. The major part of the fleet could be stationed either in the Tyrrhenian or Ionian seas 'to ward off possible complications arising from the international situation'.[208]

Badoglio reported the results of the initial paper exercises to Mussolini at the end of March 1928. Noting that once started mobilisation could not be stopped, he pointed out that therefore the mobilisation order and a declaration of war 'must now be considered the same thing'. Even in the case of Ipotesi Est precautionary measures would have to be taken in the west and 'complications' which would require action in other sectors could not be ruled out.[209] The army and air force demands were shaved down. Badoglio did not think that the sixty divisions which general Ferrari had just pronounced indispensable were immediately necessary, nor was the reserve artillery and other parts of his shopping list. The air force could manage with a hundred squadrons, which Badoglio split almost exactly evenly between bombers, fighters and reconnaissance aircraft. The navy's demands he passed on unaltered on the grounds that it acted not only as a cover for the army's flank but as a ready reserve capable of meeting any contingency. The logic he used to justify this stance was one which rendered the navy relatively immune from the kinds of professional and political questioning to which the other two services were periodically subject:

Even in respect of Ipotesi Est, the navy's strength must be such as to make it a potential threat of such weight as to discourage other powers from intervening against us, and to give the country in any circumstances that vital reassurance (*respiro di vita*) which allows us immediately to face possible complications with an untroubled mind.[210]

Badoglio computed the bill as amounting to 6,668 million lire – less, he reminded Mussolini, than the 11,000 millions that Ferrari had just asked for. If the money was not forthcoming, he warned, then in future the cost would increase.

In the face of Mussolini's enthusiasm for military preparations, the army was if anything even more cautious than Badoglio about the prospects of war. The best scenario was also among the least likely: Plan 1, for war against Austria and Germany, and Plan 4, in which Switzerland also joined in against Italy. Starting from the assumption that the enemy would take between nine and twelve months to mobilise fully behind a protective shield of between 390,000 and 520,000 troops, the soldiers sketched two possible variants. In the first scenario, six divisions would attack north to take the line of the Inn river, while seven divisions attacked north-east to reach the line Aukogel–Villach. Since only light advanced cover would face the Italian army when it was fully mobilised on the fifteenth day of hostilities, its action must be 'rapid and decisive'. If Switzerland was also a combatant, three divisions would drive for the crest of the Ticino salient via the St Gotthard, Spluga and St Bernardino passes. As well as additional alpini and other regular troops, several battalions of Fascist militia were incorporated into each plan.[211]

A single-handed war against France (P 3) presented a much less agreeable picture about which the general staff were markedly less optimistic than they had been a year or two earlier. Since France could deploy twenty-five divisions against Italy's eighteen in the first week of hostilities, and another twenty divisions by the end of the third week, an offensive would only be possible at the first stage. Even then, the valleys of the Tinea and Vesubia down which the Italian attack would develop would offer very limited scope since there were at present no roads on the

Italian side. Otherwise, Italy would have to take the defensive and stand as close to the frontier as possible. Against Yugoslavia (P 2), the main theatre would be the Julian Alps. Since the balance of forces would probably be equal – two hundred battalions on each side – and since the steeply wooded slopes of the area created considerable obstacles, Italy would have to adopt a strategic defensive with limited local offensives to gain better positions on the ground. If an offensive were to be undertaken, it would take off from Piedicolle–Fiume and drive towards Metlika–Karlovac. In the worst case scenario of war with France and Yugoslavia combined (P 3+2), the planners acknowledged that a strategic defensive was the only possible option 'until particularly favourable politico-military conditions allow us to change our stance'. The greater threat lay in the west, where the desirable objectives of Turin, Genoa and Milan were within enemy reach; there only in the Val d'Aosta could resistance afford to fall back from the frontier. In the east, local offensives would be possible and if necessary the enemy could be held and worn down on the lines of the Isonzo and the Tagliamento.[212]

At this stage the army's planning appears either to have ignored or discounted the observations of its military attaché in Yugoslavia, lieutenant-colonel Visconti Prasca, about the strategic opportunities that beckoned in the Albanian theatre and the difficulties likely to be encountered on the Julian Alps. With an army 1,300,000 strong, the Yugoslav high command planned to 'saturate' the frontier with men and mount a prolonged defensive there while awaiting diplomatic or military intervention by third parties which it regarded as inevitable. The Italians were expected to try to 'turn' the mountain front either from the south by landings on the Croatian or Dalmatian coasts or from the north by breaking through via Austria to link up with Hungary, whose neutrality the Yugoslavs considered 'decisive'. Though the Italians were expected to stall on all three fronts, Visconti Prasca reported that the Pact of Tirana had upset the Yugoslav military's confidence that they could handle their opponent.[213] Despite this information, the Italian general staff stuck to its plans.

The central planning process continued slowly. After the burst of activity in January 1928, Badoglio held only two further meetings during the remainder of the year. At the first, in mid-October, after congratulating everyone on the work done on the pre-mobilisation phase, he requested the chiefs of staff of the three services to draw up lists of the provisions which would have to be made to facilitate general mobilisation in order of precedence. The high command would then move collectively into the next phase and would consider the questions of mobilisation and deployment. His intention was to arrive at a final conclusion on Ipotesi Est by the following spring. 'The political problem', he told the assembled generals and admirals, 'is based on the firm belief (*fiducia*) that the Yugoslav problem will be isolated so that, in the event of war, we shall only have to deal with the Yugoslavs.'[214] Evidently having read the army's plans, Badoglio pointed out that the enemy would undoubtedly be prepared for an Italian offensive directed towards Lubljana, the only part of the northern zone that offered any real opportunity to deploy large numbers of troops but also one which favoured the defence, and directed the planners' attention towards three other options – landings on the Dalmatian coast or at the mouth of the river Narenta (Neretva) aiming at Sarajevo, and an offensive from Albania. In a brief meeting at the very end of December, he suggested Scutari or Uskub as the targets of an Albanian offensive, and reminded the generals that the offensive in the north must have clearly offensive characteristics – thereby requiring them to disregard his own warnings about the enormous difficulties posed by the border landscape.[215] Unusually, foreign policy was closely in step with this military development: on 31 August 1928 the Italian military attaché in Albania, colonel Alberto Pariani, had negotiated military accords committing Zog to raising three divisions (60,000 men) in five years. The negotiations were deliberately designed to conceal from the Albanians one of Italy's principal aims, to secure the use of Albanian coasts and territory in wartime.[216] However, the Albanian department of the foreign ministry was unclear as to the role the country would play in military action, a situation which was more characteristic of the methods Mussolini adopted during these years and the systems he used to carry them forward.[217]

In mid-January 1929, Badoglio called two meetings of the chiefs of staff to review progress in making preparations for mobilisation and for the *periodo di sicurezza* during which the process had to be protected before deployment and then military mobilisation against Yugoslavia actually began. The Capo di stato maggiore generale found much still to be done. The army had yet to devise a system for protecting the railways in consultation with the *Carabinieri*, and needed to carry out practical studies for locating stocks of equipment near the frontiers and positioning artillery. Its policy of keeping the entire stock of gas masks at the laboratory of Scanzano came in for passing criticism. Local mobilisation centres lacked space in which to store stocks of necessary equipment, a deficiency which would have to be overcome by renting extra space. The problem of what to do with the alien population in the combat zones had still to be worked out. From all this, Badoglio concluded that further study was needed before he could assure Mussolini that as far as the army was concerned the *fase di sicurezza* could be activated as soon as it was needed.[218]

The navy reported that as far as the minor operations to occupy Zara and Veglia were concerned the arrangements for requisitioning, concentrating and readying transport had not yet been defined. For the expedition to Albania at least thirty-four ships would be needed, and studies were under way on how to echelon them. Study of the needs for an expedition to Dalmatia were at 'a very embryonic stage'. A major problem was that the navy's specialist landing troops, the Reggimento San Marco, numbered only 319 in peacetime; they would have to be made up with army officers, anti-aircraft units who were substituted by MVSN forces, or personnel from the naval school at Pola.[219] Although he felt that it was possible to be over cautious about the requirements for a successful landing and that the Dardanelles expedition had shown that it was possible to land troops elsewhere than in organised ports, Badoglio concluded that in the present state of the road network the possibility of major operations in Albania 'appears somewhat doubtful'. When they were complete it could be the zone for the most rewarding military operations.[220]

The air force stressed its aim of moving on to a war footing very quickly, to which end its squadrons had already been concentrated in two zones in northern Italy. In the course of reviewing its arrangements for the *fase di sicurezza*, it revealed that it needed 3,000 tons of bombs for a war with Yugoslavia but presently had only two thirds of that amount, and that although half its bombs were charged they were left over from the world war and not much to be relied upon. After the group had remarked on the shortage of motor vehicles, the need to requisition grounds for support services and the need to increase pilot training facilities, De Pinedo used the occasion to make a bid for more funds. Italy's budget of 700,000,000 lire sustained a force of 97 squadrons, while France's 2,000,000,000 lire supported 140 squadrons. The explanation of the difference lay in the fact that France also maintained a reserve of aircraft while Italy did not. Assuming a monthly wastage rate of 40 per cent in war, the air force needed a substantial reserve until such time as domestic industry was in a position to produce the equivalent volume of new aircraft. An extraordinary budget of 1,000,000,000 lire spread over three years would be required to create this reserve and the necessary support services. Badoglio promised to report this to the *Capo del governo*, adding that if such sums could not be found it might be necessary to revisit the organic figure of ninety-seven squadrons and reduce it. He closed the session with the announcement that study of the *fase di sicurezza* was complete, that mobilisation arrangements were matters for the individual chiefs of staff, and that he intended to move on to study operational arrangements, a process which should be completed within the current year.[221] The chiefs did not meet again until October, when two more sessions concluded their year of collective deliberations.

The slow progress which the chiefs of staff were making in providing Mussolini with a viable war was mirrored in the deliberations of the Commissione suprema di difesa, which held its annual session over five days at the end of January and the start of February 1929 – without the benefit of Badoglio's presence. It recorded that enquiries into the technical requirements for mobilisation were completed for forty-four provinces but were still to be done for seventy-two more. Fundamentals were once more at issue, and again jostled with matters of factual detail. Admiral Sirianni raised the question as to whether the state could actually estimate its production over five years, to which Balbo responded that it could. General Gazzera reported that Italian artillery was not inferior to that of Yugoslavia; when compared with French artillery, its range was a little shorter but its mobility was much greater than was required by Italy's mountain terrain. This drew from Dallolio the response that quantity was what mattered and that for this the contribution of private industry was needed. The navy wanted preparatory work done so that light surface craft could be built more quickly. A session on fuel supplies in which Mussolini demanded that the army and navy hold stocks of coal sufficient for six months of war led to a somewhat desultory discussion on the value of reductions in taxes and duties for companies producing fuel from Italian asphalt. About the only raw material Italy had in some abundance was manpower: Gazzera reported that 3,500,000 men aged between twenty and forty were fit for military service.[222]

The last day of the annual session provided evidence that the difficulties Mussolini faced in trying to create a war machine were not solely military in character. In a discussion on 'organs of civil mobilisation', which would be responsible in wartime for such matters as commercial operations and food supply, Giuriati, minister for public works, and Michele Bianchi, under-secretary of state for the interior, ganged up against the proposal to create regional committees on the grounds that organisation in war should be as much like peacetime as possible and that policy was to use the prefects. Martelli, minister for the national economy, pointed out that the new arrangements were not the same as those used in the world war, to which Dallolio responded by reminding the commission that in 1927 it had decided that the new arrangements should be the same as in the last war. Mussolini was forced to prorogue discussion of the matter with a characteristic half measure: the commission accepted the proposals for regional committees for commercial operations, but would review them in respect of food supplies 'in the light of the growing functional capacity of the provinces'.[223]

Mussolini's frustration, never far from the surface, burst out during the course of the commission's proceedings. The old Italy, he told Dino Grandi, had produced nothing but tenors, mandolin players and orators; he would give the Sistine Chapel, the Duomo in Florence and the entire contents of all the national museums for a single military victory. The cause of Italy's decadence and servitude was the classical humanist tradition. To end it he hoped that Providence would 'before very long allow Italy the possibility of a fortunate war, short and merciless'.[224] The immediate target of his hostility was still Serbia. Reports that Yugoslavia had introduced a new mobilisation plan and was constructing new fortifications on its Slovenian frontier doubtless reinforced his predilections. On 26 February he told the Fascist Grand Council that before long Serbia would be carried to war, that the spark would be provided by Albania and that it was necessary to accelerate the tempo of Italy's war preparations.[225]

The death of Stresemann – 'this genuine enemy of Italy', Grandi noted in his diary – offered an opportunity to break one lock on Italy by ending the close Franco-German relationship, and the advent of a Labour government in England would shortly likewise offer an opening for a move to sever Anglo–French ties and so break another. Grandi believed that Fascism was now entering its 'Bismarckian' phase. If so, the Bismarck Mussolini had in mind was not the German chancellor but the Prussian minister whose diplomatic manoeuvres had prepared the way for the military victories of 1866 and 1870–1. With opportunities about abroad, something new had to be tried at home to speed up the military renaissance he needed if he was to emulate the 'Iron Chancellor' and use armed force to put his schemes into effect.

3 Military constraints and diplomatic restraint, 1929–1932

Fig. 3 The guardians of *mare nostrum*

The navy occupied something of a privileged position in the Fascist defence establishment. To an Italy which had imported 51,000,000 tons of goods and raw materials in the First World War, the centrality of its role in keeping open the Mediterranean supply lines was self-evident. Naval rivalry with France – a country Mussolini loathed – gave it political as well as strategic cards to play. Allowed a considerable amount of autonomy, it projected an image of advanced technological efficiency which belied its inability to come up with answers to a Mediterranean naval war with Britain and France. Because he left it more or less to its own devices, Mussolini only learned this unwelcome truth on the eve of war.

On 12 September 1929 Mussolini relinquished his formal hold over the Italian foreign ministry, appointing as his successor his thirty-four year-old deputy Dino Grandi. Although an adoring disciple, Grandi had some doubts about his master's capacity for diplomatic deception: he was, the new minister noted in his diary exactly a year after he entered office, 'the least machiavellian of statesmen'.[1] It may well have been Grandi who was the less machiavellian of the two. In the three years before he was fired, he was allowed to act out a foreign policy of his own devising which presented Italy as a collaborative and not an obstructive member of the international community. At the same time, Mussolini developed a policy of supporting or assisting countries such as Hungary and Bulgaria with aims apparently so extraneous to Italy's real interests that the more traditional diplomats at Palazzo Chigi were both mystified and annoyed.[2] Also, within the budgetary constraints imposed by collapsing prices, contracting production and mounting unemployment, he encouraged his three service ministers to expand and develop his instruments of war.

Behind what appeared to be a disjointed and even a contradictory policy lay the belief that war would come when Germany was back on its feet and could resolve the issues at the top of its agenda – the Danzig corridor and anschluss.[3] Mussolini also calculated that there were a number of moments in the international calendar when tensions could mount perhaps to uncontainable levels: the French evacuation of the Rhineland on 1 July 1930, the disarmament question which Germany would raise in 1931, the French presidential elections in 1932 and the programmed renewal of the Young Plan in 1933.[4] Mussolini was already moving cautiously towards Berlin; Budapest and Vienna were the first two stages along this route. His immediate interests were directed towards France and Yugoslavia, states he both loathed and distrusted. A quick war against Yugoslavia was his ideal, but his generals told him repeatedly that they could not give him this and he suspected that if France saw a chance to deal him a crippling blow she would intervene at once. A longer game was therefore going to be played, he explained to his war minister, general Pietro Gazzera, in which diplomacy prepared the way for military force:

When in 33–34 the encirclement of Yugoslavia will be complete (with Austria, Hungary, Bulgaria, Greece benevolently neutral, Albania) and we are sure that Turkey will allow us to pass through the Straits, then we can finish the game with Yugoslavia.[5]

To carry out this scheme – and to be ready for a general war which might break out in 1935 or 1936 – Italy needed time. 'He will play the pacifist while we prepare', Gazzera noted after one of his private audiences with

Mussolini.[6] While the service ministers worked on the war machinery, Grandi was handed the mask of diplomacy.

Mussolini's foreign policy

On entering office as foreign minister, one of the very first acts of the former *ras* of Bologna was to order a bust of Francesco Crispi for his office. This summed up the paradoxical quality of his thirty-four months in office: while privately he echoed the tones of aggressive nationalism embodied in the Sicilian premier's ultimately disastrous career, his public policy was more akin to that of the conservative diplomats of the *Destra* (Right) who had controlled Italy's foreign policy in the immediate aftermath of the Risorgimento. In acting thus he was performing as Mussolini wanted him to perform, though the Duce did not envisage carrying on with what was essentially a diplomatic charade for as long as his deputy did and before long began publicly to demonstrate that he did not share his foreign minister's professed enthusiasm for a policy of international collaboration and peace.

Grandi believed that the European system worked on the 'immutable' laws of balance. However, until Germany was back on its feet Italy could not take full advantage of a system in which Berlin was not yet powerful enough to act as a counter-weight to Paris. In the short term, therefore, he had to make use of France. In the longer term he believed that it was 'the law of fate' that Italy would have to go along with Germany, but that was at least a decade away. He fully shared Mussolini's ambition to strengthen his armed forces ready for future use, to which end Mussolini surrendered all three service ministries to professionals. To be 'the determining power' from a military point of view – as Grandi believed she had been in 1914 – Italy had to arm herself. 'Until we have 60 divisions ready, we shall not count effectively in European diplomatic activity', he noted a month after taking office.[7] On this basis Grandi developed the diplomatic line he thought he should take:

It is necessary to give the sensation that Italy wants Peace, cries for Peace, and has a horror of war. This is the 'face' of Italy as I must present it abroad.[8]

Mussolini approved: this posture would make Italy's military preparations easier, preparations which were continuing and would gather pace once Italy's economic convalescence advanced. While Italy armed, Grandi would anaesthetise the powers by applying 'chloroform' and 'morphine' for five or ten years – he was not yet quite sure how long.

While loyally pursuing the public line he had agreed with his master, Grandi was not confident that Fascism had mastered the distinction between policy – 'the religion of great truths' – and diplomacy, which was simply the art of deceiving one's enemy so as to be in the best position to make war on him.[9] The exposition of Fascist foreign policy he presented to the Fascist Grand Council on 8 October 1930 can scarcely have enlightened the mystified. Nor can parts of it have pleased Mussolini. The nation's interests were not determined by its form of government, Grandi told the paladins of the party; it had permanent interests which came before the interests of political ideology. This preamble was intended to soften objections to both a general Italo–French accord 'which is and remains, notwithstanding everything, the principal objective of the policy we are following', and an agreement with the Soviet Union. Italy's presence at Geneva and the role she was playing in the deliberations of the League of Nations were justified by the concrete advantages such collaboration offered, which she had not always seen in the past. Here Grandi dangled Austrian independence and the possibility of colonial mandates in front of the *gerarchia*. Italy's policy was peace, they were told repeatedly. Her line was disarmament, a policy especially suited to a country that was rich in manpower but poor in raw materials and therefore unable to compete. Her lack of political, military and economic power meant that she could not be a protagonist in Europe, but she could be the *peso determinante* (decisive weight) for one or other of the protagonists.[10] Five months later Grandi treated the chamber of deputies to a much abbreviated but essentially similar exegesis of Italian foreign policy in which he emphasised the peaceable direction of Fascist foreign and domestic policy over the previous nine years, underlined the value of the League of Nations and the concept of international justice that lay behind it, and defined Italy's mission as one of 'balance [and] conciliation between people, races, different and conflicting ideas'.[11]

While Mussolini approved of Grandi's public position and conduct, he did not like either the conception of Fascist foreign policy or the observations about the policy of peace put forward by his foreign minister in these speeches. His own declaratory policy sounded very different. In a speech at Leghorn early in May 1930 he declared that Italy was not eager for 'precipitate adventures', but warned other powers not to 'try anything' against her independence and her future. A few days later, speaking to the blackshirts of Florence, he addressed Italy's priorities more directly: 'Words are a very beautiful thing, but rifles, machine-guns, ships, aeroplanes and cannon are more beautiful still', he told his adoring audience.[12] A fortnight after Grandi lectured the Fascist Grand Council on Italian foreign policy, Mussolini publicly distanced himself from fundamental parts of it. A state of 'moral war' against Italy existed and was being backed up by preparations for material war being made by unnamed powers along her frontiers. Italy was arming to meet these threats and to defend herself. He attacked the League of Nations as responsible for maintaining the existence of two categories of state – the armed and the disarmed – thereby indicating where his sympathies lay. Finally he contemptuously dismissed the phrase 'Fascism is not for export', used by Grandi, as banal and certainly not one of his. Fascism was universal, and one day he could foresee a Fascist Europe.[13]

France was Grandi's first target, and in one respect at least she initially seemed likely to be more amenable than before. The election of the Labour government in England in June 1929 deprived her of a reliable partner and instead produced a cabinet which, Manzoni hazarded from Paris, aimed first to collaborate with the United States and then to do more than its predecessor to bring France and Germany into balance.[14] However, although the geometry of international relations might seem to have changed, the possibilities of Italo–French convergence were still slim. Questions of disarmament and of naval arms limitation, which seemed to be possible meeting points when Grandi came into office, would both turn out to be areas in which the two powers had quite contradictory and unreconcilable views.[15] Grandi was in any case deeply suspicious of France. She was 'arming terribly' and was not only 'the most armed state in Europe' but also 'ready for war materially and spiritually'.[16] French policy seemed to confirm Grandi's – and Mussolini's – suspicions. Not only was she arming Yugoslavia – a policy Mussolini said must stop before Italy would consider reaching any agreement with her – but she also made what Italy regarded as hostile approaches to Austria and seemed intent on penetrating into the Danube basin and setting up an economic union there through the medium of the Little Entente which directly challenged Italian policy and interests in the region.[17]

Grandi accordingly adhered to the general line he felt best combined Fascist Italy's public face as international peace-maker, her role as *peso determinante* and her status as a force increasingly to be reckoned with. She would not refuse an accord with France, but France must come to her first. When that happened, Germany would follow. Then, one day, Italy would be the arbiters of whether or not there was war on the Rhine.[18] Worried that France was at the apogee of her European power and certain that Italy lacked the diplomatic, financial and military weapons to fight the 'battle of Italo–French relations' at this moment, Raffaele Guariglia advised Grandi to *cloroformizzare* Italo–French relations. His interpretation of the term – talking with France and solving the big problems such as agreeing trans-Saharian transport routes by agreement – accorded with the foreign minister's interpretation but not Mussolini's. The Duce had no real intention of reaching a broad agreement with France on the range of issues which divided the two powers.[19]

France showed no signs of any interest in dealing with Italy until the spring of 1931, when Paris began to signal that agreement over their respective Mediterranean interests might be possible. Pierre Laval came to power in January 1931 and quickly communicated his desire to reach agreement on a wide range of issues including naval armaments. Perhaps partly because Laval shared Mussolini's and Grandi's views on the Bolshevik peril – anxieties which were given a boost by the fall of the Spanish monarchy on 14 April 1931 – the Italian foreign minister conceived something of a liking for the Frenchman. Small, ugly, dishevelled in appearance and straightforward in manner and speech, he was 'the first Frenchman towards whom I have not felt that instinctive apathy that fills my spirit whenever I have contact with a Frog (*gallo*)'.[20]

On three separate occasions between July and September 1931, and again in February 1932, Laval and others gave broad hints that they would support giving Italy a 'free hand' to pursue her 'special interests' in Ethiopia. Despite enthusiasm for such a venture in the higher reaches of the Palazzo Chigi bureaucracy, Grandi chose not to venture down an avenue along which Mussolini was not willing to travel. Far from seeing her as benevolent, the Duce feared that France might be working herself up for a preventive war against Italy which she would unleash in 1933 if the Geneva disarmament conference did not produce the results she wanted.[21] He also knew that an armed intervention in Ethiopia, which would require lengthy preparations and a great deal of money, was impossible for the time being.[22] When put alongside Mussolini's suspicion that France might join Yugoslavia in a war against Italy, the French invitation looked like a trap to weaken and distract her. Believing that the 'incontrovertible divergence' between France and Italy resulted from the former being a satisfied power while the latter needed outlets for her surplus population and sources of raw materials, and that a revision of the African mandates was the way out of the dilemma, Grandi simply did not conceive either the problem of France or the solutions to it in the same way that Mussolini did.[23] Mussolini's refusal to allow him to respond to a French invitation to talks in mid-March 1932 signalled the distance between master and minister in regard both to policy and to method.

While Rome was glad to see the back of Stresemann in 1929, Mussolini believed that the colour of the current German government made friendly relations with her impossible for the time being. Adopting his default position, Grandi had Berlin informed indirectly that from his perspective Germany did everything possible not to help Italy and that she must change the general direction of her policy before she could expect much in the way of help.[24] His approach to Germany was not to approach her. Over time, Germany must be brought to realise that Italy did not want or need her and therefore Germany should not feel that she could count on Italy's support against France. With patience the proper atmosphere would ripen and ultimately the time would come for Italo–German friendship.[25]

In fact, there was little for Grandi to work with in the German political arena. Pan-German nationalists signalled their enthusiasm for an alliance with Italy, but they were on the fringes of politics. The National Socialists, who saw Italy as Germany's only natural ally, made similar noises and Hitler reassured Rome on several occasions during 1930 that he excluded any possibility of re-annexing the South Tyrol. He also made plain his fundamental mistrust of France – a fact noted by Mussolini.[26] In the first half of the year, with only 250,000 party members and estimating that they would take thirty to thirty-five seats in the coming elections, the Nazis did not appear to count for much: in June 1930 Orsini Barone forecast that they would never be able to govern because they lacked 'men who could lead' and a 'unitary programme'. However, their acquisition of 107 seats in the September elections, along with the success of Hugenberg's nationalists and the rise of a group of young and ambitious generals headed by Kurt von Schleicher, began to open up new prospects: the election 'signalled the defeat of democracy in Germany', the delighted consul-general of Bavaria told Grandi.[27] All of this made little difference to the course of diplomacy during 1930 and 1931 because the German foreign minister, Julius Curtius, continued the Stresemann line, not seeking common ground with Italy but working for what Grandi decried as the 'democratic illusion' of Franco–German reconciliation.[28]

During 1931 two events, one Berlin's doing and the other Rome's, cut the diplomatic ground from under Grandi. In March the proposal for an Austro-German customs union awakened fears of anschluss, which for Italy was both unacceptable and threatening. Grandi could only recommend continuing with his present 'Geneva policy', and was eventually rescued by an international veto of any such conjunction.[29] Then in June, without consulting anyone, Mussolini agreed to the Hoover proposal for a one-year moratorium of Germany's war-debt repayments. Grandi, who wanted to limit German and French power equally, felt that by severing the linkage between reduced reparations and limited German rearmament Italy had given a hostage to fortune. 'Arming a Germany free from the burden of reparations is a very different thing from arming a Germany burdened by them', he pointed out to Mussolini. The outcome of increasing German power at the expense of France would be that one day Italy would have to submit to German preponderance or link herself to France. Either would be the end of Italy's freedom.[30]

Although Mussolini did not believe that Italy could for the time being join herself with the present 'cowardly government' in Germany, he was consciously making friendly gestures of which the moratorium was only one. At the back of his actions lay two fundamental calculations. For the time being Germany was not powerful enough to help him in a war with France. Therefore she had to arm. He explained his stance to the war minister, general Pietro Gazzera, three weeks before the Geneva disarmament conference opened on 2 February 1932:

Either everyone disarms or Germany arms. We must support her. We must be extremists in this respect . . . France will not want to disarm. And the blame will be hers. Our historical–dialectical position is to oppose France.[31]

While Bruning's cabinet showed signs during the first half of 1932 of wanting to bring German policy more into line with Italy on a case by case basis, Mussolini was content to wait on events. The symptoms of 'malaise, discord and uncertainty' which his observers told him in September were growing ever greater boded well for the arrival in power of the kind of right wing nationalist and revisionist government he both wanted and needed.[32] Maxim Litvinov saw which way the wind was blowing. In January 1932 he asked whether if Hitler came to power Italo–German relations would get closer.

While France was a medium- to long-term concern to Mussolini, Yugoslavia was the immediate military thorn in his side. Hence a great deal of military energy went into planning for war against her during these years. The fundamental cause of his hostility, which Grandi shared, was simple: Yugoslavia had shown and continued to show herself ready to act as the anti-Italian instrument of France. The Italian naval attaché at Belgrade put it in a nutshell: Yugoslavia was at one and the same time 'an interested party for her own reasons and an effective and conscious instrument in the anti-Fascist struggle'.[33] A regional dispute further embittered relations: Italy claimed the right to intervene in Albania under the terms of the Pact of Tirana, something which Yugoslavia continually and resolutely refused to accept.[34] Strategic considerations to do with control of the Adriatic and the western rim of the Balkans, of which Mussolini was well aware, which influenced the attitude of the armed forces towards Yugoslavia and played their part in shaping Italian strategy, also contributed to the hostility between Rome and Belgrade.

At bottom, Grandi shared Mussolini's view that matters could only ultimately be settled between Italy and Yugoslavia by force of arms. After a straight talk with the Yugoslav foreign minister Jeftić in January 1930, he thought that 'War with Yugoslavia is inevitable.'[35] However, he believed that the time was not yet ripe – as did Badoglio. The foreign minister therefore looked to diplomacy to try to weaken Yugoslavia as much as possible. He was more than happy also to stand in the wings while a military competition developed between the two powers as this would force Belgrade to spend money on arms which would be out of date in seven or eight years and would at the same time impoverish her.[36] In fact, as Raffaele Guariglia pointed out to his chief, Italy's actions and reactions played a considerable part in pushing Yugoslavia to cement her union with France.[37]

Grandi's chance to solve the dispute by diplomatic means came in March 1930 when Marinkovitch approached him with the news that Yugoslavia was tired of being France's client and suggested a direct understanding between the two powers. Ambassador Galli immediately challenged any notion that Yugoslavia was about to change its pro-French policy – though two weeks later he was forced to acknowledge that such a move was indeed under consideration – and Mussolini set impossible conditions, requiring that Belgrade renounce all links with Paris. Grandi was forced to temporise, keeping Marinkovich waiting until the following January. In November Galli reported a further acceleration of the Yugoslav arms race with the arrival there of Czech artillery. By spring 1931 Italian diplomacy had descended to making economic threats.[38]

Circumstances conspired to defeat Grandi's attempt to put diplomacy in the driving seat, but more importantly so did people. Ambassador Galli, one of a number of *fascisti autentici* ('true fascists') among the diplomats, saw Masonic conspiracies at work everywhere in Yugoslavia and reported every sign that Belgrade wanted to improve her standing with Rome as evidence of hypocrisy and weakness.[39] The military attachés contributed mightily to the atmosphere of tension and hostility. From Tirana, colonel Alberto Pariani reported in November 1929 that Serbian military preparations would be complete by 1931. His ambassador confessed himself 'stupified' at Pariani's misrepresentations of the situation and later complained that the military attaché was encouraging Albania to draw up war plans 'more appropriate to the Prussia of Frederick the Great than to the Albania of king Zog'. Told to draw out preparations for war against Yugoslavia, Pariani had by July 1932 done exactly the opposite.[40] From Belgrade, colonel Sebastiano Visconti Prasca sent reports that Serbia was arming feverishly which Grandi passed along to

Mussolini. Although Visconti Prasca eventually left in April 1930 after being caught up in a spy scandal – Grandi believed French counter-intelligence had given him away – and driving the ambassador to distraction with his insolent and undiplomatic behaviour, worrying reports continued to arrive for several years to come. Most importantly of all, Mussolini was deeply hostile to Yugoslavia. In September 1930 he believed that she was seeking to gain time to ready herself for war with Italy, and two months later he was afraid that she might try a move against Albania. As he saw it, a Yugoslavian attack on Albania which would force Italy to honour her defensive alliance with Tirana might be the spark which ignited into a war with France. In1931 he needed 'five or six years of tranquillity' before Italy would be militarily prepared for that.[41]

Elsewhere in the Balkans and south-eastern Europe Grandi was unable to make the progress Mussolini sought and produce a diplomatic platform for expansion. Attempts to stitch together a body led by Turkey and including at one point Greece, Bulgaria and Egypt as a counterpoise to a hostile Danubian grouping failed because they did not accord with Turkey's goal of a Balkan pact that included Yugoslavia, something she succeeded in bringing into being in April 1934. Indeed Ankara moved in entirely the wrong direction, showing signs of interest in a pact with France and accepting an interest-free credit from the Soviet Union in April 1932 in preference to a smaller interest-bearing Italian loan.[42] Greece too evaded Italy's reach. In May 1929 confirmation that she had signed a pact of friendship with Czechoslovakia suggested that she might be drifting towards the Little Entente. Italo Balbo's aerial exploits, described below, may not have helped Rome's cause. When in June 1929, at the start of his first 'cruise' to Odessa, Italian seaplanes stopped off in Greece ambassador Arlotta incautiously remarked at a public dinner that seeing an Italian squadron fly over Athens made him feel the presence of the *patria* even more strongly than if a squadron of warships had arrived.[43] By the beginning of 1931 Grandi admitted that the chance of Greece forming part of a Mediterranean pact had gone and that the best to hope for was to keep her out of hostile combinations.[44] Romania simply resisted Italian attempts to loosen her ties with France and to penetrate the Balkans.

Austria, a complex political battle ground for Mussolini in terms both of its internal politics, which often displeased him, and its external function as a potential component of a Danubian federation, produced no gains over this period. In an attempt to foster a political regime of a suitable complexion, that is one that would renounce any interest in the South Tyrol, quell domestic Marxists and socialists and keep Austria out of the embrace either of Germany or of a Hungary nursing ambitions for a revival of the dual monarchy, he first gave money to prince Starhemberg and the right wing Heimwehr, then abandoned him for chancellor Dollfuss before asking for his support against the Nazis and the Marxists in June 1932. As for anschluss, by mid-1931 Grandi thought that the best that could be done would be to retard it for a generation while Italy resolved the Alto Adige question, resolved her economic problems, and built the Danube provinces into a counter-weight.[45] By the beginning of 1933 both Mussolini and general Gazzera appeared to regard it as something that could one day be tolerated.[46]

The only recruit to the Italian cause was Hungary. Fearful of French attempts to revive the Little Entente and nursing revisionist ambitions in respect of Czechoslovakia and Yugoslavia, she approached Rome about the possibility of military collaboration in October 1929. Mussolini's encouraging response in ordering the setting up of an exploratory military–technical committee was the start of an expanding relationship lubricated by arms sales during the coming decade. Both Grandi and Mussolini took it for granted that recruiting minor European states increased Italy's power. Marshal Badoglio disagreed: 'militarily they are worth less than a box of beans', he told Grandi in March 1931.[47]

In seeking to make Italy the *peso determinante*, Grandi may subconsciously – or consciously – have wanted to usurp England's role in shaping the European balance of power. He certainly wished to rid Italy of one of the strongest legacies of the Risorgimento, wanting to see Anglophilia go the way of Germanophilia, gone with the world war, and Francophilia, which had declined as tensions with France mounted.[48] The Labour government which came into office in July 1929 was not a very good prospect: hostile by nature to Fascism, it showed early signs of being sympathetic to Germany but also of aligning itself with France.[49] Grandi regarded its pacifism, its support of the League of Nations and its commitment to disarmament as manifest signs of cultural decadence. He soon fell out with the Labour foreign secretary, Arthur Henderson, who he decided was not to be trusted. For its part the Labour government suspected – rightly as we have seen – that Grandi's attitude towards Geneva and the League was not genuine and that Italy was trying to create an anti-French alliance. This had the effect of causing London to rebuild its links with France.[50] International naval disarmament, examined below, was the central theme of Anglo–Italian diplomacy during the Grandi era. From Rome's point of view, perhaps its most encouraging features were that with two million unemployed by 1930, troubles in Palestine and hard issues about the future of Egypt and India to resolve, London had other things beside Fascism to preoccupy her mind.

While Italy maintained a strong interest in Ethiopia, there was little she could do during these years to extend her footprint in East Africa beyond Eritrea and Italian Somalia. Militarily she had her hands full in Libya, where general Rodolfo Graziani began the last phase of the pacification of Cyrenaica in June 1930, clearing the Djebel and moving the entire population down to concentration camps on the coast. Not until 24 January 1932 was Badoglio able to announce that the rebellion had been defeated. News in June 1930 that the French were supplying the emperor with aircraft was unsettling. In January 1931 Grandi, worried about a possible French attack on Ethiopia, complained at Mussolini's lack of interest and Italy's inability to fight a war there.[51] The head of Grandi's personal office, Pellegrino Ghigi, advised a forward policy:

It is certain that Abyssinia is the only demographic and economic outlet still left open to us. To penetrate it requires money – to take it, probably war.[52]

The foreign minister agreed that economic penetration of Ethiopia was of 'primordial importance', but there was not much he could do.

It was left to another of Grandi's senior advisers, Raffaele Guariglia, to press the case with Mussolini a month after he had relieved his foreign minister of office. Italy would have 'no real colonies' in East Africa until most of Ethiopia was taken and the 'simulacra', Eritrea and Somalia, were joined together. If Italy really wanted an empire then this was the only place left. Guariglia expected Italy would have to fight for it but passed lightly over the problems this might throw up. A military expedition would not present 'the difficulties and dangers of our past wars', he forecast confidently, because modern European military techniques made it possible to win quick victories against the major centres of resistance, although naturally a great deal of time would be required to pacify such a large country. Air power was the weapon by means of which fundamental resistance could be overcome 'but it will have to be employed without reserve [and] on the largest scale'. The one indispensable precondition for such action was an accord with Great Britain and France.[53] In Grandi's time, however, Mussolini had neither the military instrument nor the diplomatic space to take such a gamble.

Deliberating the needs of war

The chief issues on the agenda of the Commissione suprema di difesa when it met between 31 January and 22 February 1929 were to do with industrial mobilisation and supply. General Alfredo Dallolio, head of armaments manufacturing, was able to report that data had been gathered which would for the first time allow the calculation to be made of what industry could provide in the event of sudden mobilisation. The enquiry into food supplies had been completed for forty-four provinces and would incorporate another twenty-two during the present year. Admiral Sirianni, who had completed a survey of shipyard capacity, told the commission that ships might be built in only eight months. The following December he reported that in the event of war the shipyards thought it was 'not absolutely impossible' to get units ready in that time provided they had the specialist labour, and forecast that forty-eight destroyers, forty-eight 700-ton *torpedinieri*, forty-eight submarines, forty-eight submarine chasers and ninety-six MAS boats would be completed within twenty months.[54] Dallolio and Balbo wanted quinquennial programmes of orders but Sirianni did not, and differences emerged over whether and to what degree to protect private industry in the competition for orders. Mussolini resolved the issue by setting up an inter-ministerial committee. Gazzera raised the question of whether private industry had the qualitative skills to manufacture artillery, to which Dallolio responded that the problem was more centrally a quantitative one. Dallolio then reported deficiencies in the aero industry in respect of 'volume and opportuneness', drawing from Balbo the riposte that while military aviation was already selling abroad, civil aviation was still buying from Germany and Holland.[55]

On the question of raw materials, the commission decided that government ministries must build up a stock of 5,000,000 tons of coal sufficient for six months of wartime consumption, that private companies would be required always to keep liquid fuel tanks at least one-third full, and that mineral oil deposits in Sicily should be developed to produce at least 25,000 tons a year.[56]

Questions of organisation and administration were perennial, and the commission's annual deliberations suggested that progress in some areas was glacially slow. Likewise, concerns to hold sufficient stocks of coal and liquid fuels, and to develop national resources rather than buy overseas were ongoing, and slow but incremental progress was reported in 1930.[57] One issue which came to a clear head in 1930 was the question of the civil organisation and military function of the colonies in wartime. Three years after he had first been tasked with doing so, the minister for the colonies, general Emilio De Bono, was able to bring to the commission data on the production of individual colonies, the amount by which it exceeded local needs, and its deficiencies. At that point no more could be done because there existed no definition of the functions which the colonies were to fulfil in wartime.[58]

De Bono took the view that the colonies should be able to look after their own needs as regarded the civil population and the mobilisation of troops, and that the little the colony could offer the *madrepatria* by way of supplies was not worth running the risks associated with transporting it. Troop levels were being reduced in Tripolitania, but although France kept several divisions under arms in Tunisia he did not regard them as posing any real threat because 'it will never suit France to gamble on the undertaking of invading Tripolitania'.[59] In fact, as De Bono acknowledged when pressed on the point, it was highly doubtful whether the colonies could defend themselves because their stocks of munitions had been run down and they had no domestic arms production capability.

Gazzera took issue with De Bono, pointing out that France had seven divisions in Tunisia, Algeria and Morocco which were conjoined by good road and rail links. To his way of thinking the difficulties of transporting troops to metropolitan France might of themselves encourage an action against Tripolitania. Further inducements to attack could be found in the possibility of depriving Italy of the colonies' productive output 'which it seems must be notable in the future', and of naval and air bases controlling the central Mediterranean. Finally, the more Italian troops there were in Tripolitania the more French troops would have to be stationed there, with advantageous effects on the balance of force on the western Alpine frontier.[60] The chief of the army general staff, general Bonzani, concurred: reducing troop strength in Tripolitania, which De Bono appeared to favour, might simply encourage a French attack, and Eritrea needed to be strong enough to take the French base at Djibuti which split it off from Italian Somalia and threatened traffic in the Red Sea.[61]

It was not until 10 June that Badoglio took up the question, asking the services what in their view the colonies must be organised to face. The war ministry proposed increasing local output of wheat and other grains, oil and livestock for domestic needs and intensifying research into the production of aluminium, phosphates, potassium, magnesium, manganese, zinc and other minerals, as well as increasing production of tobacco, for the *madrepatria*.[62] The army general staff, reiterating earlier arguments, stressed the importance of Tripolitania for air and sea control of communications in the western and central Mediterranean and the fact that it, and not Cyrenaica, would be the immediate target of French operations in war. The port of Tripoli must therefore be fortified as a top priority, with other border points to follow. Eritrea was more vulnerable to a French attack with Abyssinia as her ally than to a single-handed attack from Djibuti. However, major questions remained to be answered before such matters as the forces to be mobilised in the colonies could be decided. Certainly the munitions stocks laid down in the summer of 1928 were too low.[63]

When the Commissione suprema di difesa considered the colonial question in February 1930, the navy put forward an extensive 'wish list' to enable it to defend Tripoli, Tobruk, Massaua and Assab comprising seventeen batteries of medium and light artillery and assorted searchlight batteries, booms, and aircraft.[64] Couching its response in terms of a two-front war, it now emphasised the certainty that traffic with Tripoli and Benghasi would be attacked along with the likelihood of supportive or diversionary enemy naval operations along the Libyan coast. Tobruk also functioned as a protective base for traffic going to and from Port Said and would therefore need submarines and light surface craft as well as guns. The vulnerability of traffic in the Red Sea to French interception from Djibuti made it the theatre likely to see most enemy activity, and therefore both Assab and Massaua needed surface craft as well as coastal defence works, in this case including a pair of cruisers. The lengthy list of wants, which was neither concisely summarised nor costed, concluded by throwing in the possibility of engaging in commerce warfare in the Indian Ocean from Kisimaio.[65]

Badoglio presented a concise summary of the issues to Mussolini in late August. Tripoli and Tobruk would function in war as bases from which to launch air and naval actions in the central and western Mediterranean and protect sea traffic; the function of land forces there was a defensive one. Much the same held true of Eritrea. Somalia's needs were defensive only, though he signalled the navy's interest in Kisimaio and commerce warfare. The colonies must provide for their own defence, other than where the war plans dictated the detachment of air and naval units to bases within them, and for the military forces that might be deployed there.[66] In its way, the memorandum was a bureaucratic masterpiece: general, imprecise and yet simultaneously carrying an authoritative air, it included no numbers or costs and can have given the Duce only the vaguest idea of what the armed forces were discussing.[67]

While long-running issues such as developing national resources and economising on purchases from overseas were still very much a part of its agenda, the meeting of the supreme defence commission in February 1931 paid closer attention than usual to the state of the weapons programmes and armament of the three services. Since Mussolini decided the agenda, this can only have been a reflection of his personal concern. Gazzera presented a detailed report on new artillery, experimental models of which had been commissioned both from state and private industry in line with a decision taken the previous year. Contracts were being given to small companies as well as large ones to spread expertise and manufacturing capability, to which end the export of arms also contributed.[68] In all, the war ministry planned to construct 800 new guns at a cost of 250,000,000 lire, of which 600 should be available by 1935. Progress was being slowed down, as Dallolio acknowledged, by a shortage of specialist skills – to remedy which four special schools were to be set up – and by a shortage particularly of steelworks.[69]

That there were problems with the navy's proposal to programme for the production of a mass of light craft and submarines within twenty months of the outbreak of war, which had been accepted the previous year, was evident from any but the most superficial reading of Sirianni's submission to the commission. It had presumed that the building of heavy warships and merchantmen would continue unaffected. It also depended on the shipyards not losing any specialised labour, having the necessary supplies of raw and semi-finished materials available as needed, having guaranteed electricity supplies, and being able to make available all the heavy plant the navy said it wanted. This was an ambitious scenario, but behind Sirianni's verbiage lay the admission that only the electrical supplies were reasonably certain. The necessary draft orders and the thousands of detailed and general designs had yet to be done. There were other problems too: the sole periscope factory could only produce equipment for twenty-four submarines and not forty-eight in twenty months; Italy could not manufacture gyro-compasses; all the underwater acoustic apparatus came from abroad; and the two torpedo manufacturing plants could produce only 800 of the requisite 1,200 533-mm torpedoes in the time envisaged, a figure that would decline as soon as stocks of the 450-mm torpedo had run out and they had to be replaced.[70]

In his presentation to the commission, Sirianni made a further crucial admission. While his plan had involved the production of 156,000 tons of shipping in twenty months, the industry was presently able to manufacture only 60–65,000 tons in that time. Studies into the necessary raw materials and labour supplies were under way, and the navy minister felt able to assure the commission that as regarded the ships and machinery 'no great difficulties are foreseen'. Passing lightly over the other problems with panglossian optimism, Sirianni concluded that 'altogether good results are being obtained', a judgement apparently confirmed by the fact that the hereditary prince of Persia and numerous of his officers were attending courses at Italian naval schools.[71] Characteristically, Mussolini first alluded tangentially to the serious problems that had been uncovered, pointing out that for the programme to be realisable when required everything must be done that was necessary to make this possible, including limiting the reliance on foreign products 'which the navy will look at with particular care'. He then homed in on the fact that the torpedo plant at Fiume was dangerously close to the frontier. This allowed the commission to spend the rest of the time devoted to the navy discussing the no doubt absorbing but essentially minor question of whether a third torpedo manufacturing plant was needed in addition to the ones at Fiume and Naples.[72]

As Balbo had not yet returned from his trans-Atlantic flight to Brazil he was not present to put forward his own service's case and his under-secretary, Riccardi, stood in for him. On the face of it, matters appeared better as far as the air force was concerned. Italy had plenty of aluminium and magnesium from which to make light alloys, and the only foreign-designed aircraft (Ro 1) was about to be replaced. By the sixth or seventh month of war, the industry could manufacture some 700 planes and 600 engines a month; however, these were theoretical calculations 'leaving out of account the availability of raw materials and labour both quantitatively and qualitatively'.[73] Budget restrictions had not allowed the air force to build up reserves of either materiel or manpower as had been hoped the previous year, but Balbo had left the outline of a three year plan which would permit a partial fulfilment of this objective including a 33 per cent reserve for the frontline squadrons. At Badoglio's suggestion, put on the basis of German practice, Mussolini proposed that new routes be given to civil airlines only on condition that they undertook to use aircraft which could rapidly be converted for military use and were of national manufacture.[74]

If further confirmation was necessary to convince Mussolini that the lacunae in Italy's industrial capacity were such as to make war unthinkable on any rational grounds for the foreseeable future, it came when the secretary of the commission, colonel Ivaldi, reported on materials acquired abroad in the last financial year. They had risen in value by 122,000,000 lire over the previous year and had amounted to 682,000,000 lire. While a large part of this went on primary materials, especially coal and tobacco, much also went on manufactured goods. The immediate solutions to the problem were to avoid buying abroad goods that the country could provide, to encourage domestic industry to manufacture goods the government needed, and to increase production in Italy and her colonies of raw materials that were presently imported. Ministers fell over one another to give examples of what was deemed politically bad practice. Sirianni pointed out that Italian companies produced bronze propellers which could only be used on light craft but bought propellers for cruisers from abroad, even though they could manufacture them, because they could be made more quickly, to higher technological standards, and more cheaply; Ciano contributed the information that the railways bought from abroad, particularly sprocket wheels; Riccardi added that Italian silk was not manufactured at a high enough quality to be used for parachutes; and Dallolio pointed out that Marelli, which made magnetos for the air force and the army, was going through a crisis because other ministries were fitting motor vehicles with Bosch magnetos. Everyone agreed that the purchase of raw materials and manufactured goods from abroad must be diminished, and Mussolini proposed that the Committee for Civil Mobilisation keep an eye on it.[75]

In 1932, the Commissione suprema di difesa picked up the story on the issues it had raised the previous year, learning that the problem of manufacturing optical glass had yet to be solved, that a third torpedo manufacturing plant was no longer considered necessary, that good results were being obtained in encouraging civil airlines to adopt aircraft which could be readily adapted to wartime use, and that for the first time the cost of goods purchased abroad had gone down to 598,000,000 lire. At this De Bono and Badoglio seem to have decided to throw the whole purchasing policy into reverse, pointing out that domestic industry frequently took advantage of the priority accorded to domestic sourcing to charge exaggerated prices and that budgets could often be stretched further by buying overseas despite the 10 per cent surcharge levelled on such goods.

When the commission turned to the seemingly straightforward issue of anti-aircraft defence the potential inter-service discord which bubbled below the surface suddenly erupted. Taking the two-front-war scenario as his starting point and admitting that it would be impossible to defend all or most of the major centres of importance in the country, Balbo proposed a system of fighter defence in which squadrons would be deployed on likely lines of attack in such a way as to be able to concentrate sufficient force on threatened points quickly enough to defend them. With thirty-one squadrons of ground-based fighters and three of seaplane fighters, not all the identifiable zones of importance could be defended. Balbo therefore proposed to allocate nine squadrons to the eastern front, one of which would defend Pola, fifteen to the western front, three of which would defend Turin, Genoa and Milan, two to defend Rome, three to defend La Spezia and two to defend Brindisi before possibly moving to Albania, while the three seaplane squadrons defended Cagliari, Trapani and Ancona. Finally, quoting a remark of Mussolini's to the commission the previous year that 'the queen of the defence is reprisal', Balbo argued that bombers must be given priority over fighters in future developments.[76]

Assuming attack to be the best method of defence in argument – though he was about to presume almost the exact opposite in the substance of the matter – Gazzera sought to demonstrate the fatuity of the air force's implicit argument that money spent on ground defence was money wasted. The aim of ground-based air defence was not to shoot down enemy planes but to defend vital points against bombing, which it did by interdicting air routes, by shooting down low-level bombers, therefore forcing them to operate at heights which made them inaccurate, and by breaking up formations and thus aiding defence fighters. Large-scale targets such as great cities could not be defended by artillery, but smaller ones could by concentrated fire. Practice demonstrated what artillery could do, and the war minister invited the commission to come to Nettuno and see for itself. Italy's closest neighbours were held up as an example in deploying ultra modern artillery – not always a good argument to use in a regime which for political and patriotic reasons was prone to discount lessons from abroad.[77]

Gazzera then questioned some of the basic operational propositions propounded by Balbo and the Regia Aeronautica. Aerial defence against surprise daytime incursions by masses of bombers aiming at targets near the frontiers or coasts would often be ineffective because late; against the large-scale attacks that were expected, fighters would suffer because they would be too few in number and because bombers flying in formation would have more effective firepower. In a word, the larger the mass of incoming bombers the less likely aeroplanes were to be able to do it much damage but the more likely anti-aircraft guns would be to hit it. Balbo proposed to use seventeen of his fighter squadrons to defend seven different locations, leaving only fourteen to protect 400 kilometres of frontier. Fighters were more important than bombers, whose numbers should be reduced and not augmented. To support his argument Gazzera presented the spectre of 'shuttle bombing' in which French planes flew across the Italian peninsula from Corsica to Yugoslavia and back. He then threw down the gauntlet as far as Douhetian ideas were concerned: 'it is very dangerous for us to promote the idea of offensive aerial warfare against enemy population centres because we have much more to lose than to gain, being exposed to damage which would be incomparably greater than that which we could inflict on the enemy'.[78]

Balbo rose vigorously to the defence of his own service against what was an attack on one of the most important foundations of its independence. After noting that his own bomber experts had never thought enemy artillery very effective, he drew to his colleagues' attention the fact that the Royal Air Force had but one preoccupation, bombing, and that only 19 per cent of their air force were fighters while 56 per cent were bombers. Italian figures were respectively 35 per cent and 25 per cent. It would, he argued, be a grave error for Italy to shut herself inside her frontiers and renounce the offensive, 'above all when taking into account a characteristic element of Italian aviation: aggressivity'.[79]

Giuseppe Valle weighed in to support his minister, remarking that Gazzera was defending the army against an attack that no one was making. Using a slightly self-contradictory logic, the chief of air staff argued that exercises testing what anti-aircraft guns and bombers could do were to varying degrees unrealistic and that the air force's own bombing contests had returned an average off-target error of no more than ten to twenty-five metres. He then bombarded the committee with statistics about the relative speeds of prototype French bombers and Italian fighters, the time taken for an artillery round to reach five thousand metres (seventeen seconds) and the distance a prototype fighter could fly in that time (one and a half kilometres), and relative costs before pointing out that in asking the air force to increase the number of fighters as against bombers the commission was asking his service alone to give up the offensive, the basis of all military action. The only people who would profit from this would be the French.[80]

In the heat of the moment Balbo had given several hostages to fortune. Gazzera seized on them. In April 1930 it had been agreed that 25 per cent of the air force should be bombers but in discussion Balbo had given a figure of 40 per cent. The Regia Aeronautica had by it own admission exceeded the agreed proportion and should return to it. Using the airmen's logic against themselves, the war minister also suggested that if masses of bombers were as potent as they believed then since France had 400 and Italy only 260 she would be exceedingly unwise to start a war designed, as Balbo and Valle had put it, 'to sow death and ruin in the heart of the enemy' since she would surely be beaten first.[81] Badoglio clearly deplored the opening up of first principles which had unexpectedly occurred and which could be read as a commentary on his success or otherwise in harmonising the activities of the armed forces. For him, two questions only were at issue. On the first, notwithstanding Balbo's plea to the contrary, responsibility for anti-aircraft defence should remain with the army not simply because it had a more developed territorial organisation but because if the Aeronautica became more tied to the ground it could lose some of its character, particularly its ardour. On the second, it was not the business of the commission to vary the agreed proportions of fighters and bombers.[82]

Tempers must by now have been running high, for this did not stop Bonzani from rehearsing in detail some of the army's arguments and throwing in the fact that the French were evidently planning to decide a war on the ground and had subordinated their aviation to the army. Gazzera and Sirianni backed Badoglio. Balbo asked where the army's figures on the proportions of fighter and bomber aircraft had come from, and on being told that they were his own (confirmed by the secretary) he declared that they were either a slip of the tongue or a stenographic error.[83] The air minister then went into a lengthy diatribe on the numbers to show that the proportion of bombers was only 30 per cent, throwing in such assorted and irrelevant points as the close contact he had maintained with Mussolini because the Duce was a master of materiel and the fact that 3 per cent of air force personnel died every year. The air force had never been attacked when it was small, and was being attacked now 'because the eyes of the world were upon it'.[84] Gazzera did not let matters lie, and his remark that what mattered were facts and figures and not feelings (*sentimento*) of the kind Balbo had made such play with doubtless raised the temperature of the meeting still higher.

There is nothing to suggest that Mussolini had ever before witnessed such an open and ferocious argument between the services, and certainly the commission never witnessed another one about such a fundamental strategic issue. His own intervention was unsurprising, though perversely it may have encouraged the servicemen by demonstrating his readiness to leave things more or less as they were. Reaffirming Badoglio's reading of the two main points at issue, he handed back the problem of the proportion of bombers and fighters to his Capo di stato maggiore generale and confirmed the army's predominant role in anti-aircraft defence before adding a few general observations of his own: in terms of vulnerable centres of population, France and Italy were on a par; the best means of defence for cities would be the evacuation of parts of their population; and all systems of defence could be useful.[85] The very evident failure of the three service ministers and the Capo di stato maggiore generale to reach any kind of commonality over what was a fundamental question of national defence very probably encouraged Mussolini to end the experiment he had begun in 1929 and to take back personal control of the army, navy and air force in 1933.

Naval policy, Fascist politics and the London Naval Conference of 1930

The invitation to attend the London Naval Conference which the Labour foreign secretary sent to Dino Grandi on 7 October 1929 was far from unexpected in the higher reaches of the Italian navy. The failure of the 1927 Geneva conference to reach agreement led the chief Italian technical delegate, captain Fabrizio Ruspoli, to warn of the difficulties which the question of cruiser limitation had engendered and to alert Rome to the likelihood that the conference planned for August 1931 would probably be advanced.[86] Sketching out the geopolitical ground on which the navy would base its stand, Ruspoli reiterated such well-established points as Italy's enclosed position in the Mediterranean, her dependence on overseas sources for four fifths of her foodstuffs and raw materials, and her 8,000 kilometre coastline with its exposed commercial centres, shipyards, industries and railways. To them he added another factor: Italy's merchant marine now occupied fourth place in the world behind Great Britain, the United States and Japan (third place if only ocean-going merchant ships were included). At the time of the tripartite conference in 1927, therefore, her navy was insufficient for the needs of national defence, 'especially when other great and small nations, favourably situated to interdict our vital maritime lines of communication, stayed outside the conference'. Hence Italy could only accept an agreement on naval arms limitation which was based on global tonnage, with the freedom to build whatever types of ships best met her needs within that limit subject only to a maximum gun size for all types, and on 'global' parity with any other European power. If this last condition were met, there would be no difficulty in reducing, even radically, the overall 'global' tonnage limit.[87]

Ruspoli, who as the leading expert in the naval general staff's *Ufficio Trattati* (Treaty Office) had attended the major international disarmament conferences as a member of the Italian delegation and whom Dino Grandi took with him to London as 'the only sensible and expert man' he had met in the navy, was a convinced proponent of the principle of continental parity. Among other things, he took account of the fact that the opening of the Straits meant that Russia now had the potential to be a Mediterranean power, while Spain had a 'Mediterranean battleship potential' of fifteen thousand tons.[88] More broadly, France had accepted the principle of parity with Italy with regard to light surface craft during the Washington Conference, and even though 'economically it will be difficult today to compete with France in respect of naval armaments, it is necessary to maintain the principle of parity unadulterated (*integro*) so as not to put the future at risk and to safeguard ourselves against any eventuality'.[89]

The second major issue which would confront Italy at the forthcoming conference was whether limitation would be by global tonnage or by standardisation of type. Ruspoli expected the particular circumstances of each navy to play a major role in its attitude to this issue and forecast that while Great Britain would go for standardisation of type, the United States would opt for the global tonnage model, leaving itself free to build the types of ship best suited to its needs and circumstances. For Italy, standardization of types would mean that it could no longer opt for what he called the 'risk' option of building asymmetrically – 'a fleet which allows the weak a good chance of holding off the strong' – and would instead have to match potential opponents in numbers of specific types of ship, which would accelerate and intensify naval construction if national security was to be maintained.[90] The position that Mussolini staked out publicly in June 1928 accorded closely with naval thinking: Italy would accept nothing less than parity with the strongest Continental power, and the status quo could not be the starting point for any agreement.[91]

Although no public announcements had indicated as much, the navy had by the start of 1929 formulated a secret quinquennial programme for the years 1930–5 – a period which it expected would see 'very delicate international situations' – which reflected its concerns and embodied its solutions to its problems. The programme would be its professional touchstone in the forthcoming conference. Limitations in relation to another navy either by numbers of ships or amounts of tonnage would not be acceptable 'because the conceptualisation of future maritime war can no longer be based on an ordered battle between equals, as was the case in the past'.[92] Italy had her own needs, and to meet them she must construct her own types of ship. The five-year programme, which was designed to replace the oldest ships and produce squadrons and flotillas of desirable sizes, required Italy to build 18,500 tons of surface craft and 3,600 tons of submarines a year as against figures of 25,000 tons and 9,000 tons respectively for France.[93] Battleships were not included as Italy could not be the first to build them, but consideration was being given to the possibility of using the 70,000 tons of build allocated to Italy for 1927 and 1929 by the Washington treaty to construct three 25,000-ton battleships armed with six 381 mm guns and capable of 28 or 29 knots, though the naval staff were evidently less than keen on these mastodons of the sea. The wherewithal to carry out the programme would come from an unpublicised and agreed increase in the naval budget which would raise the construction budget to 600,000,000 lire a year during the quinquennial period.[94]

Mussolini examined the Hoover–McDonald note with Grandi and admiral Sirianni on 10 October and agreed that Italy should participate in the upcoming conference. The decision was taken, Grandi explained to the chamber of deputies seven months later, partly because the cause of international disarmament was a vital question, partly because the success of the Hague Conference of 1929 in devising the Young Plan for German reparations gave every reason to believe that the disarmament question could also be resolved amid international amity, and partly because Fascist Italy had to attend if she was to defend her vital national interests and take her proper place in the international hierarchy of powers according to what he called the 'law of *moral prestige*'.[95] Other reasons to take part were also found: the possibility by so doing of indirectly manoeuvring France into reducing the building programme embodied in the *Statut naval* 'which we could not be in a position to match', the opportunity to manipulate the agenda during the preliminary exchanges, and the difficulty of refusing in the face of the 'wave of international optimism' created by Hoover and MacDonald.[96]

Grandi's statement to parliament embodied only a partial truth. While he believed that a war had to be delayed for five or ten years, he nursed a deep if sometimes emotionally ambivalent enmity for France: 'France wants, would like Italy as her vassal and will never again tolerate an Italy that is her equal', he confided to his diary in the midst of the preparatory discussions for the London Conference.[97] Mussolini, as his discussions with his war minister Gazzera would show, nourished an enmity for France that was at least equally as bitter, and a readiness for war which was much more pronounced. From slightly different viewpoints, and with different though congruent goals, the Duce and his foreign minister saw in the upcoming conference the opportunity to deceive France as to the depth of Italy's desire for arms reduction, to lull her into a false sense of security while Italian military preparations went ahead at the best attainable speed, and perhaps even to drive a wedge between Paris and London and so break one of the shackles that had hitherto contained Italian foreign policy.

The death of Stresemann and the election of a Labour government in England whose manifesto included a commitment to reach agreement on further naval disarmament and which, in pursuit of that goal, was already evidently turning away from Europe and towards the United States, opened up a new international landscape in which Briand's position was weakened by the departure of Austen Chamberlain and of his now defunct German partner. The entente cordiale was over, and the new 'mobility' that this imparted to the international situation was a great advantage to Italy's policy 'necessarily dynamic and necessarily changeable'.[98] Grandi's sense of the new direction in which things were heading was evident in his remark to the new German foreign minister, von Neurath, that Fascist Italy had never run behind Germany under Stresemann and it was not going to do so now. One of the levers he intended to use to split France off from her former partner was unwrapped when he told the British ambassador, Sir Ronald Graham, that Italy would align with Great Britain and the United States – and therefore against France – on the abolition of submarines. Italy's attitude on this question, he told Mussolini, would depend entirely on what France's was.[99]

A report from the Italian naval attaché in Paris that if Italy were to adhere to the Anglo-American position on abolishing or limiting submarines this would end any future naval negotiations with France scarcely came as a surprise, indeed it confirmed that France could be manoeuvred out onto a limb.[100]

An offer to Paris to exchange views on naval questions of mutual interest before the conference, suggested by Ramsay MacDonald, which drew the predictable reply that France would first like to know Italy's views after which it would divulge its own was also deliberately designed to wrong-foot the Briand government.[101] The reply – that Italy would accept any figure as the global limit on tonnage as long as it was not surpassed by any other continental European power – was accompanied by the offer to set the issue in the larger framework of a Franco-Italian understanding for which, Grandi calculated, France was not ready.[102] Everything was being done and would be done to make France appear the obstacle to further naval disarmament.

Grandi prepared for the London Conference at a time when tension with Yugoslavia was becoming ever more acute. Evidence of mounting pressure on Albania was reported to Rome early in December, the Italian military attaché in Belgrade, Visconti Prasca, was caught engaging in espionage immediately afterwards, and in early January the Italian ambassador in Belgrade reported the arrival of French submarines.[103] If Yugoslavia started a war with Italy, Grandi believed, '*France will jump on our back* and we shall have a two front war', something Italy was not yet ready for.[104] The 'tone' that Grandi and Mussolini now agreed to adopt abroad as the powers prepared to discuss naval arms reductions concealed the true political dimensions of Italian policy.[105]

Although there was no question about the demand for parity with France, Grandi had no easy task in convincing the navy of his line on submarines. Sirianni was at first far from certain whether it would be better for Italy to have absolute freedom to construct as many of them as possible or to set limits on them, but gradually came down in favour of limitation. Mussolini then had to be won over to their joint position, and proved none too easy to convince. A speech by Herbert Hoover on the freedom of the seas enabled Grandi to set the technical question in its wider context, wherein free lines of supply would largely solve the problem of Italy's being imprisoned in the Mediterranean. It would also, Ruspoli pointed out, remove the argument of those nations pressing for the continual reinforcement of their navies – their fear of starvation.[106] Sirianni was won over, and after a month of hard work Mussolini finally authorised his foreign minister to go as far as the complete abolition of submarines if necessary.[107] Dealing with the naval staff – 'wooden, unrealistic, unprepared, inflexible, [and] unintelligent' – and with Siri-anni, and persuading the latter to see sense over submarines had, Grandi recorded in his diary afterwards, driven him mad.[108]

Political exchanges in December gave both accurate and misleading indications of how negotiations might be expected to proceed. The Ital-ian embassy in London told Sir Robert Craigie, the Foreign Office's chief naval negotiator, that just as Britain would have to take account of Amer-ica's demands, so Italy would have to regulate her demands in relation to the French naval programme. Craigie then advised Rogeri that Italy should state the programme she wished to follow without taking into consideration France's demands.[109] Rogeri learned that, responding to an initiative from Washington, London would welcome an exchange of views on 'freedom of the seas' even though the subject was not on the agenda – which did not transpire.[110] And René Massigli told Arthur Hen-derson that France could not accept any extension of the Washington agreement on battleships to other categories of warship, or agree to abol-ish submarines.[111]

The naval line to be pursued at the London Conference was defined at the end of December. The principal of a 'one power standard' relative to continental European powers came at the head of the list, although even strict parity would leave Italy in a condition of 'unstable inferiority' given that other powers controlled the Mediterranean exits. This meant that the technical stipulations of any treaty assumed great importance, and that therefore Italy could not give a definite response until agreement had been reached on relativities and on numbers of ships. The British proposal to lower battleship displacement from 35,000 tons to 25,000 tons, reduce the maximum calibre of guns from 14 inches (406 mm) to 12 inches (305 mm) and increase the age for replacement from twenty to twenty-six years would make it possible for Italy, which was not at the moment building battleships, to build heavily gunned battle-cruisers. However, extending the years in service would mean stretching out the building of the few ships she was allowed or else going without any new construc-tion for a considerable period. Accordingly this proposal could only be accepted on a number of quite complicated conditions. France must also agree to it; battleships in service which exceeded the new limits must be scrapped or Italy must be allowed to lay down the two 35,000-ton warships which the Washington treaty had given her the right to build between 1927 and 1929; France and Italy must still have the right to build 175,000 tons of warships; and Italy must be able to use her total allocation of tonnage to build as many ships as she wanted provided that none exceeded the new maximum.[112]

The naval staff were ready to link battleships to the submarine ques-tion 'because it would be suicide to renounce the latter without prior destruction of the former', and propose the universal scrapping of all warships over 10,000 tons. Such a proposal must have 'an enormous repercussion, especially in England and America', and if accepted would notably reduce the disadvantages to Italy of giving up submarines. It would also discourage the otherwise inevitable arms race which would begin when one great power began building large warships.[113] Otherwise Italy could accept the proposal to delay building battleships from 1931 to 1936. As regarded submarines themselves – 'an excellent weapon for the weakest powers' – Italy could accept a limitation in numbers but not one which, when set in conjunction with the capability to keep only one submarine in three on patrol, left it too weak in boats at sea. Nor could it accept one which excluded submarines under 600 tons 'because even the smallest submarines are efficient in the neighbourhood of their bases and in restricted seas like the Mediterranean and especially the Adriatic'.[114] This was not exactly in line with the pronouncement by the council of ministers on 18 November that Italy would not accept limitations or reductions in submarines.[115] Nor, self-evidently, did it correspond with the line Mussolini and Grandi had decided to take – a fact which suggests either that the navy was kept in the dark about the political strategy which was to be applied in London or that it was not persuaded by it.

On the question of whether cruiser limits should be raised to 10,000 tons and 8-inch (203-mm) guns, Italy was prepared to agree on four conditions. France must do so too; there must be no limit on numbers but only on global tonnage; enough tonnage must be allocated to her to allow her to build six cruisers (as against England's fifteen); and agreement must also be reached on light surface craft and submarines. The other major proposal on the table was to reduce total tonnage of aircraft carriers from 135,000 to 125,000 for Britain and the United States and to extend their life from twenty to twenty-six years. Again, Italy could accept if France did so too, if she was allowed at least 60,000 tons, and if she could build ships of 15,000 tons rather than the maximum 25,000 tons. As regarded the method of limitation, Italy could only accept global tonnage and not standardisation of types. Even with the legal right to parity conceded, unless substantial arms reduction occurred she would always be far from parity in reality. Until such a time she must be able to build 'differently' from her likely adversaries – either a smaller number of superior types or a larger number of weaker units 'with which contemporaneously to attack or defend a larger number of objectives than an adversary with stronger [individual] units could defend or attack'.[116] Other issues which the Regia Marina regarded as important were light surface craft 'which will undoubtedly constitute the greatest and most discussed of the many problems at the Conference', armed merchantmen, naval bases, lesser navies and the freedom of the seas.[117] It is a measure of how differently naval issues were perceived in Rome and London that most were not considered at the conference.

When Grandi arrived at the London Conference, which began on 21 January 1930, the French had been informed that Italy demanded naval parity with any other continental power, which meant her, and that Rome would accept any tonnage figure France felt necessary for herself, and the British had been informed that Italy could not accept the present state of naval armaments as the starting point for calculating any future balance.[118] Whether he had perceived that France could never accept parity with Italy for reasons she could not make public, namely that in a war she would have to fight Italy and Germany combined for which she calculated she needed 800,000 tons of warships, is a matter for guesswork. Certainly the figures gave him some support, for they showed that France possessed 77,000 tons more than Italy – the result of building to the *Statut naval* between 1922 and 1929 – a 'surplus' which was emplaced in her larger fleet of submarines (ninety-two to Italy's fifty-seven) and in her heavier destroyers (of which both parties possessed sixty).[119]

During the first week of talks – which began, Sirianni remarked, on a plane more culinary than political or technical – a gap opened up between Italy on the one hand and France and Great Britain on the other which ended any chance of dividing the two latter powers. London and Paris agreed that the first step should be to establish the methodology to be used to reduce naval armaments while Grandi held out for decisions of principle on the coefficients of relativity and ratios of strength between the five navies and the maximum levels of their respective tonnage. Inept diplomacy had missed an opportunity to split London from Paris, for French prime minister Tardieu had taken the line at the outset that there were no applicable mathematical formulae and that the starting point must be the needs of each individual nation, which was not the approach favoured by America or Britain. The explanation is to be found in the priorities laid down by Mussolini, whose parting instructions to Grandi were that renouncing parity with France, already established in principle at the Washington conference, would be 'a politico–moral *catastrophe*' and that it was not to be countenanced even if the cost was the collapse of the London Conference.[120]

In its second week of deliberations, the conference debated the American preference for using global tonnage figures, the British proposal for limitation by categories of ships with a measure of transference allowable between them, and the French proposal for a transitional method in which each power would be given a global tonnage which it would not surpass during the period of the convention and would then indicate how it intended to divide the total tonnage between classes. Admiral Sirianni suspected that this last was a cover from behind which France intended to raise once more the issue of parity with Italy in battleships and aircraft carriers that had been established at Washington, and was pleased when this failed.[121]

The multi-track nature of the deliberations, in which Britain was on the one hand trying to maintain a favourable balance among the 'oceanic' powers whilst on the other simultaneously seeking to depress France's allocation, created difficulties which admiral Burzagli quickly identified. Since London wanted a maximum global allocation of 1,200,000 tons for herself and America, she could not maintain a two-power standard in Europe and concede France more than 600,000 tons whereas France wanted to build the 800,000-ton programme of the *Statut naval*. He saw this as a problem since it required London to force down the French figure given Italy's demand for parity and raised the possibility that she might therefore not support the Italian request.[122] In fact, it was another opportunity to weaken France which Grandi's diplomacy allowed to go begging.

To support her position that the current base-line was a good place to start from, France tabled figures on 12 February purporting to show that her current fleet amounted to 682,000 tons and that by 31 December 1936, on current plans, it would total 724,000 tons. Burzagli saw this as opening 'the most delicate phase' of the discussions since the figures were too high to be accepted by England, and France would only consider lowering them if compensated with political guarantees.[123] Sirianni pointed out that the first figure included ships whose construction had been authorised but not yet begun, auxiliary ships which were not normally counted, and over-age ships which should not have been counted. When they were recalculated, France possessed 527,000 tons of warships to set against Italy's 347,000 tons. In terms of cruisers, destroyers and submarines – the ships at issue – France's 320,000 tons presently stood against Italy's 260,000 tons, and in 1936 she would have 430,000 tons against Italy's 294,000 tons. The figures had been 'massaged' to hide the real increase planned by the French, and also to give them a stronger position vis-à-vis the Royal Navy than was actually the case by using only numbers actually in service for 1936 but including ships under construction or for which parliamentary approval had been given for 1930.[124]

The fall of the Tardieu government on 18 February led to a three-week pause in the main negotiations, but by now there were increasingly clear signs that Italy would not be a co-signatory to any agreement. Twice MacDonald asked Italy to formulate a programme incorporating a lower total tonnage than France's which would help him negotiate with Paris to reduce its numbers, and twice Grandi refused on the grounds that this would fatally compromise the principle of parity – a right to which the French would never agree, the British premier acknowledged.[125] Comforted by the Duce's assurance that he had been following his instructions faithfully – 'better alone than weakened' – Grandi enumerated for Mussolini the outcomes Italy could be sure of attaining if no agreement were signed: unmasking France, propagandising Fascism abroad and giving the Italian people an immediate sense of the necessity for new sacrifices 'in order to complete our naval, land and air armament'.[126] Tardieu offered Italy parity in the Mediterranean – and was predictably turned down. MacDonald indicated that Great Britain would not accede to a Mediterranean Locarno, the only thing which might persuade Italy to accept less than parity with her Latin neighbour. Offer was met by counter-offer. Grandi proposed parity only in under-age ships on the premise that over-age ships would fall out of the equation naturally and not be replaced – which would implicitly acknowledge overall parity. Briand proposed putting off agreement on tonnage levels until 1935 and building according to their respective programmes which would ensure French superiority. Each was rejected.

Grandi's proposal was designed to give him a tactical advantage over Briand, and was one he knew would be unacceptable. He stuck limpet-like to Italy's initial position partly to obey the Duce's wishes and partly on the basis of a miscalculation of Italy's position. On the one hand, he believed that solving the Italo–French dispute was the key which would unlock the door to a five-power agreement 'and therefore without Italy a general accord cannot be reached'. On the other a four-power agreement without Italy could give her an advantage by fixing France's maximum tonnage without limiting Italy's.[127] Sirianni, who recognised that a four-power pact would mean that the others could make Italy appear responsible for any subsequent changes in their arrangements, was not so sure and confessed that he was perplexed because he could not weigh up the possible damage to Italy's prestige that would result from accepting the French offer of parity of programmes in relation to 'what seems to me a practical advantage for the Nation'. Outside a five-power pact, Italy would have to reach parity with France by 1936 and would thus have to embark on an expensive and arduous naval arms race.[128] Grandi got Mussolini's backing: 'Do not swerve from our position and do not make any further conciliatory proposals of any kind, either directly or indirectly', the Duce told him on 21 March in the second of two similar telegrams. Both were deciphered by the British within the week.[129]

At the last, with the conference breaking into two and the United States, Great Britain and Japan ready to reach agreement on cruisers and submarines, France offered what the Italians described as a vague formula

– which was also a scarcely veiled threat – that in a five-power agreement they would build 35,000 tons of warships a year and outside one 45,000 tons a year. Working through the implications of this proposal, the Italians calculated that agreeing to it would leave them 200,000 tons behind France and allow them to build a maximum of 24,000 tons a year.[130] This in its turn was declined. With the final plenary session on 12 April signalling the close of the London Conference, Grandi, who had been infuriated in January by the failure of Italian newspapers to give proper emphasis to the independent Fascist viewpoint which he and his delegation had propounded, turned to what he regarded as the far from insignificant matter of the press treatment of his work. The newspapers should explicitly state that the conference had been a success for the Fascist regime: for the first time Italy had been treated on an equal footing with the four world powers, 'and Italian action, ever consistent from the first day to the last, has constituted one, if not the greatest, of the forces guiding the whole course of the Conference'.[131] Combining self-inflation, flattery and obsequiousness, the foreign minister told Mussolini that in standing up for herself – and standing 'splendidly alone' – Fascist Italy had at last shed the bounds of the *antico liberalismo italiano*, had broken the circle of global anti-Fascism, and was leaving London 'amid the sympathy, the respect and, let us even say, the admiration of the world'.[132]

The London Treaty was signed on 22 April 1930. Its most significant part related to the agreement on limiting cruisers and submarines reached between the United States, Great Britain and Japan, but all five powers bound themselves to extend the 'holiday' in battleship building to 1936, with France and Italy keeping the right allowed them at Washington to replace 70,000 tons which had reached the age limits between 1927 and 1929. A maximum displacement of 2,000 tons and a maximum armament of 5-inch (130-mm) guns for submarines was agreed, and a sub-commission's recommendation that submarines must operate like surface warships and could not sink merchantmen without warning was adopted.[133] Neither Italy nor France was bound even by these limitations since neither power ratified the treaty. Admiral Burzagli, in tune with Sirianni's thinking, recommended that Italy not respond to the conference by starting a programme aimed at reaching parity with France since it was a race Italy could only lose given the economic disparity between the two countries.[134] However, on 30 April Italy announced that her building programme for 1930-1 would include one 8-inch cruiser (*Pola*), two 6-inch cruisers (*Montecuccolo* and *Attendolo*), four destroyers and twenty-two submarines, amounting in total to 47,000 tons – five thousand tons in excess of the French programme for the year.

This aggressive announcement may well have had more than a degree of political calculation behind it, for attempts to reach a naval agreement with France that would benefit Italy were not yet done. On 3 June Grandi reassured the senate that if the London Conference had failed then it was not Italy's fault. He also offered to defer getting started on the 1930 programme if the French would do the same.[135] A partial French acceptance opened the way for conversations, and on 1 March 1931 the two parties produced the draft of an agreement. A somewhat complicated formula applying to the 1931–6 programmes froze the building of heavy cruisers after the end of the year, limited the build of light cruisers and destroyers to replacements, and limited submarine build to the completion of the 1930 programmes and replacements up to the end of 1931. By fixing the maximum end tonnage and agreeing to an annual build that was more or less identical, Italy had in fact tacitly abandoned her adherence to the parity principle and signalled her readiness to accept the status quo and with it a substantial naval inferiority. The agreement collapsed within three weeks when the French claimed that it applied only to build completed during the quinquennium and excluded ships that were overage in 1936. This interpretation would allow them to lay down 67,000 tons of extra shipping between 1934 and 1936 to replace vessels that would reach their age limits between 1937 and 1939. Attempts to bridge the gap, to which Great Britain was party, failed and the issue of further naval arms limitations was left to wait upon the opening of the Geneva Disarmament Conference in February 1932.[136]

The war plans and preparations of the Regia Marina

As the naval staff turned its mind to the forthcoming London Naval Conference, collaborative planning for operations against Yugoslavia began to get down to detail, albeit in a somewhat leisurely way. In March 1929, after pondering the matter for two months, the naval general staff responded to enquiries from the army general staff about naval assistance for the landings which would cover the right wing of an attack with a series of queries of its own. The help that the Reggimento San Marco (Italy's small force of marines) could give the army in occupying the islands necessary to cover traffic to Zara depended on how much help the army wanted from the selfsame unit in occupying Veglia, and such matters as the size and points of departure of the forces which would have to be transported to the islands of Veglia, Lussino, Cherso and elsewhere were as yet unknown. Burzagli suggested that representatives of the two staffs should meet to clarify matters, adding that decisions about the precedence to be given to different landings were nothing to worry about 'given the exiguousness of the enemy's naval means'.[137]

In a war with France, the question of reinforcements from North Africa loomed large. The navy calculated that Toulon, Biserta, Bône and Philippeville were within range of aircraft based respectively at La Spezia, Cagliari and Trapani, and southern Sardinia, while under current conditions Oran, Algiers and Bougie were unreachable by coast-based Italian aircraft. The staff concluded that transport of black troops from Casablanca, Oran and Algiers would be effectively immune from attack save by submarine. The nucleus of the French navy was expected to gravitate towards North Africa, basing itself on Biserta but if necessary shifting to Bône, Bougie or Algiers. Its strategic goals would be to assure dominance of the western Mediterranean, interrupt Italian traffic from Gibraltar and communications with Spain, protect troop transports, aid Yugoslavia, take the offensive against Italian mobile forces and coasts and impede Italian maritime traffic in the eastern Mediterranean as much as possible. French battleships would be based on Algiers and possibly Oran.[138] Though no general conclusions were drawn from this data, the difficulty of impeding French troop movements was very evident. As part of its consideration of this aspect of a war against France, the naval general staff worked out a plan to 'bottle up' the port of Biserta at the outset of hostilities. Such an operation would require five old merchant ships, eight destroyers (none of which might be available given the demands of other sectors) and four submarines, and would depend on complete surprise, a moonless night, and putting enemy gun batteries and searchlights out of action. As an alternative, ordinary merchantmen might be sailed into the port in broad daylight and then scuttled. No one weighed up the odds of success or failure.[139]

By September 1929, responding to a directive issued by Badoglio on 2 April, the naval staff had prepared an outline of its perception of a two-front war against France and Yugoslavia. The immediate enemy objectives would be the protection of troop convoys from North Africa and assistance to the Yugoslav navy in the Adriatic. France would certainly try to cut Italy's maritime communications from the start, though the effect of such operations would take some time to be felt. Attempts by the French to occupy Sicily or Sardinia were thought improbable, but operations to occupy Elba and block the channel at La Maddelena appeared more likely. It was also conceivable that the enemy would try from the outset to tempt the Italian navy to give battle so as to use its superiority to win command of the sea; the most likely route to such an eventuality would be an attempt to penetrate the Adriatic and obstruct the transport of Italian troops to Albania. Since Badoglio had made the strategic defensive the order of the day at the start of hostilities 'to harmonise the employment of the armed forces', large-scale landings on the enemy's coast were ruled out. This left the navy with limited options: attacking enemy transports with submarines and light surface craft as well as aircraft, carrying out the Biserta operation, and taking possession of Djibuti (an operation which had yet to be studied). In any case the Otranto Channel would have to be blocked, the Aegean watched, the coasts of Sicily, Sardinia, and Elba guarded and naval traffic in the eastern Mediterranean protected.[140]

The war book, produced a fortnight later, developed an even more pessimistic scenario. An attempt to bring the Italian navy – which might be in 'a state of crisis' at the start of hostilities because of the difference between its peacetime and wartime establishments, its dependence on conscripts and its need to recall untrained reservists – to battle by penetrating the Ionian Sea and the lower Adriatic was on the cards, but so too now was a landing on Sicily or Sardinia to tempt the fleet out. While Italy could expect to block sea supply routes to Yugoslavia via Cattaro, Salonica and the Straits, her Balkan enemy could expect to keep going 'because while she does not have large resources neither has she great requirements'. Evidently wishing to escape from Badoglio's strictures about the primacy of the defensive, the naval staff warned against lapsing into passivity: protecting traffic alone would give the enemy complete freedom of action and create 'a situation unsustainable in both political and military terms'. The opportunities for offensive action were however limited, amounting to attacking enemy transports in the western Mediterranean, blocking the Otranto Channel, watching the Aegean, seizing Djibuti, and attacking unspecified Yugoslav bases.[141]

While the operations being proposed required some fairly straightforward co-ordination with the army, they raised more fundamental questions about the use of air power. The navy proposed to re-examine the question of its allocation of auxiliary aircraft in the light of the number of actions now under the spotlight. It also wanted to know exactly how many aircraft would be made available in the initial period of hostilities to act against enemy bases, embarkation points in North Africa and enemy naval forces which might be embroiled in counter-offensive operations in the Upper Tyrrhenian sea. The final item on its list was the distribution of aircraft to protect naval bases and naval forces in action at sea within the limits of their range.[142] None of this was likely to be greeted enthusiastically by Balbo and his airmen. However, when the chiefs of staff met to consider the navy's war plan on 4 October 1929 rear-admiral Valli did not raise these issues and so the question of air cover was not discussed.

Badoglio had detected much more fundamental defects in the navy's plans. It was over-emphasising the defensive, which had to be interpreted with reason; it had 'an absolute strategic value' but should be more broadly interpreted at a tactical level, especially in naval warfare. It was not likely that the French would try to penetrate into the Adriatic at the start of a war, so the navy should not be over-preoccupied with this improbable eventuality. The immediate problem in this theatre was likely to be attempts by the Yugoslav navy, for all its lack of size, to interrupt Italian troop transports. Protecting domestic naval traffic mattered less in the first stage of a war than in the succeeding period, and during it the Italian navy should concentrate on attacking the enemy's North African troop transports. The Djibuti operation could only work with absolute guarantees about the attitude of the Ethiopian empire; it should therefore be studied but no weight given to it. Finally, Badoglio did not think the enemy would try major landings simply to draw out the fleet since his freedom of manoeuvre would be seriously hampered by the need to cover his own troop convoys and the supply routes that would have to be developed.[143] The whole thing can only have seemed a humiliation to the navy for almost every part of their plans had been subjected to a withering criticism.

The navy's examination of detailed elements of its task was no more encouraging. Tripoli was so important to any campaign in the eastern Mediterranean, and the moral and material repercussions of its loss would be so great, that this could not be contemplated; however, its protection would absorb all the modern naval forces Italy possessed. The conclusion was that it must be able to defend itself, with assistance from aircraft transferred as and when needed from the metropole.[144] A major exercise was carried out in April 1930 to test Italy's capacity to interdict French troop convoys crossing the western Mediterranean in the shelter of the Balearics using aircraft, submarines and night attacks by surface craft. It was found that the distance between Algiers and Oran and the Italian naval bases on Sardinia meant that decisive results could not be expected from such attacks, although they were the only way to oblige France to locate most of her naval forces in that sector.[145] Admiral Bernotti, commanding the attacking force, found himself hampered by a lack of aircraft in the most important phase of his action, and admiral Melina, commanding the convoy, concluded afterwards that the daylight engagement by surface craft which had ended the two-day exercise had shown that an inferior naval force faced annihilation.

As far as defending Italian traffic in the eastern Mediterranean was concerned, the outlook was more optimistic. There was always the possibility that the French might persuade Greece to join them, or seize a base such as Suda Bay or Navarino Bay, or else might attack Italian bases in North Africa or the Aegean. However, French attempts to control shipping leaving the Suez canal at Port Said could be contested by Italian sub-marines and surface craft operating from Tobruk, and if Egyptian neutrality was maintained merchantmen could travel through her territorial waters as far as Sollum, ninety miles from Tobruk. Goods in neutral bottoms could be trans-shipped into national craft at Alexandria. Traffic exiting the Dardanelles might face limited opposition from French sub-marines whose nearest base would be at Beirut, whereas Italian units were well placed at Leros, but would have only a seventy-mile dash between the neutral waters of Turkey and Greece.[146] All in all, the navy calculated that it could probably hold its own in this theatre.

Temporarily confident that it could defend sea traffic in the eastern Mediterranean and also the routes between North Africa and Sicily, the navy began to turn its attention to a more distant theatre. Admiral Valli had included the occupation of Djibuti in his presentation to the chiefs of staff on 4 October 1929, prompting Badoglio to remark that it could only be done with an absolute guarantee about the attitude of the Ethiopian empire. The navy now sought to evade that restriction and also to use the new theatre as a springboard to the open ocean. It was in the Red Sea, and not in front of Port Said, that supplies coming from the East would have to be defended 'because it is there that France will intercept our maritime communications, while in the Mediterranean it will only maintain an intermittant control made difficult by our watchfulness'.[147] France would send her own supplies via the Cape of Good Hope, out of reach of Italian naval interception in the Red Sea or Mediterranean, while controlling Italian traffic from Djibuti, seventy miles from the Straits of Perim. It was 'certain', Burzagli told Badoglio, that France would look to acquire 'absolute predominance in this basin, be it by detaching a significant naval force there, be it by using to our disadvantage the privileged position it enjoys in Abyssinia'.[148] The idea of attacking French lines of communications not just in the Red Sea but also in and to the Gulf of Guinea, Senegal and the South China Sea rather than defending Italian ones, which could be done with a new type of ship resembling a tramp steamer, did not appeal to the naval staff and was not taken up by it.[149]

Instructed by Mussolini to assure himself about the state of readiness of the plans for a two-front war, Badoglio called the chiefs of staff together on 22–23 October 1930. Burzagli reported that apart from the Adriatic bases only La Spezia, La Maddalena and Taranto were ready for war. The more western deployment which Mussolini wanted could not be effected until Trapani and Cagliari were improved. In a war the initial naval operations would be landings on the eastern Adriatic coastline, for which additional air cover was necessary, protection of the Ligurian and Tuscan coasts and interdiction of French traffic in the western Mediterranean, for which tactical and strategic air reconnaissance and direct offensive intervention by aircraft would be of great value. French oceanic convoys from Morocco to her Atlantic coast would be checked by 'a few long-range submarines'. Protection of the Aegean islands and traffic in the eastern Mediterranean did not figure in the schedule of initial operations because the theatre was more favourable to Italy. Burzagli added that recent exercises had given yet more support to the value of aircraft carriers. Recognising the appearance of a very obvious Trojan horse, Valle intervened at once to note the contribution that the new Do X seaplanes were making, upon which everyone congratulated everyone else on the satisfactory progress in air–sea and air–land co-operation.[150]

Badoglio's sessions never penetrated very far into naval thinking. Beneath the accommodating surface it presented, its interests were wider than they appeared. As instructed, it duly explored the details of landing military forces at Durazzo.[151] However, it also began to look to the Red Sea and the Indian Ocean as likely theatres of action. In expansionist mode, it soon had one eye on Kisimaio in Somalia as a base from which to conduct commerce warfare in the Indian Ocean. As so often, it couched its ideas initially in defensive terms: French forces could attack Italian shipping from Diego Suarez and Djibuti, and might seize Assab. Improving the naval defences of Massaua and Assab would also bring economic and security benefits to the colony, and might help to speed up the building of a road from Assab into the interior for which Rome was pressing. From a political point of view, the possibility that France would in wartime supply arms and munitions to the Ethiopian empire via Djibuti in order to initiate possible military action against Italy was not to be excluded, not least because in a war France would seek to create difficulties for Italy anywhere she could. The naval general staff had no doubt that Djibuti must be seized; if it were, the Ethiopian empire would have no reason to protest as long as rail and coastal traffic was assured and it was offered a possible share in control of the port.[152]

After a thirteen-month gap, Badoglio summoned the chiefs of staff to a five-day rolling meeting between 5 and 10 November 1931. Since Mussolini was reported to have accepted the Capo di stato maggiore generale's warning about the difficulties of a two-front war on being reassured that a defensive in the west would hold, the planners examined only the case of a single-front war against Yugoslavia. Admiral Ducci, chief of naval staff, bore out Badoglio's warning. After listing in detail the artillery and anti-aircraft defences of the major bases he concluded that given the state of the ports of Trapani and Cagliari, the navy 'does not have available either in Sicily or in Sardinia the bases (*punti di appoggio*) it would need to act effectively in the western Mediterranean'.[153] Brindisi, Venice and Pola were in a satisfactory state, though in many of the *piazze* only a single battery was ready to go into action at once. As far as a one-front war was concerned, the bulk of the fleet would be stationed at Augusta, Taranto and Brindisi, with detachments at Ancona and Pola and a squadron of destroyers at Leros. Mobilising former conscripts to fill out the crews would take ten days. Overall, he estimated that the navy was 70 per cent ready to go into action at once. The naval balance showed France to be superior in battleships, both sides more or less equal as regarded cruisers, a one-third French superiority in destroyers and light surface craft and a marked superiority in submarines. Ducci put in a strong word for aircraft carriers, two of which were under consideration, and countered robustly when Valle said that they would be lead weights for the navy.[154]

A discussion on reconnaissance aircraft later in the proceedings showed how much had been glossed over the previous year and how ill co-ordinated the services actually were. Ducci and Valle clashed over new types, the airman thinking they did not need the capacity to launch tor-pedoes and required no more than a single machine-gun and the sailor disagreeing on both counts. Valle did not want sailors or soldiers on the technical committees which finalised aircraft design and procurement, at which Badoglio declared that there must be exchanges of ideas between the services when defining types of aircraft and that the other two services should take part in the experiments which produced the final specifica-tions. Later, in response to Ducci's observation that the navy had only a single long-range reconnaissance squadron of four aeroplanes, Valle told him that another squadron would arrive in 1932 and two more in 1933. Ducci pointed out that to carry out its part of the war plan it needed to push its aerial reconnaissance as far as the western ports of Algeria, and that fleet units operating north of the Balearics would need aerial sup-port if they were not to find themselves in a decidedly inferior situation to the French, whose air bases would be close at hand.[155] Since Badoglio refrained either from summing up the lengthy sessions or from asking the chiefs individually to do so, no one can have been much the wiser at the end as to what the navy could actually achieve in a war other than doing its best.

Although the navy was not to know it, thirty months would pass before Badoglio summoned the chiefs of staff again in May 1934. In the mean-time, and doubtless expecting to face another such examination of its abilities and intentions, it turned to some of the questions thrown up in the five-day meeting. Badoglio had decided at the close of the last session that the defence of the Aegean islands of Leros, Rhodes, Stampalia and Castelrosso would become the navy's responsibility in war. Arrangements were made to send additional personnel to Leros, where through lack of manpower only one anti-aircraft battery could go into action immediately.[156] At the same time, it questioned its own strategic supposition that Leros and Tobruk gave it an advantage in the eastern Mediterranean basin. Looked at close up this disappeared in the face of the grave risks facing Italian commercial traffic exiting the Suez canal due to the proximity of Beirut. Captain Wladimiro Pini, head of the operations department, accordingly put the somewhat far-fetched suggestion to Ducci that when the mandates ended it would be politically convenient to detach France from Syria.[157] More realistically, Pini threw a dash of cold water over the project to bottle up Biserta, a '*desperate operation*' for which modern ships were not available and in which older ships would need protection and thus might draw most of the fleet into an unwanted engagement.[158]

With its eye on the eastern Mediterranean basin, the navy revisited the question of the relationship between the Red Sea and the Suez canal. A general survey of the economic considerations which were brought into play led it to reverse its position on the necessity of seizing Djibuti. In wartime, India, Japan and China would provide coal, Australia, Argentina and Brazil would respectively supply meat, cereals and wood, and cotton would come from India, South Africa and South America. Since these materials would reach Italy via the Cape of Good Hope and the Indian Ocean, the strategic function of the Red Sea linked with that of the Indian Ocean. The political problems inherent in an occupation of Djibuti – particularly if, as seemed likely, the French had made arrangements to cede it to Abyssinia during a period of hostilities – led the navy to consider abandoning the idea. France could protect its own trans-Atlantic traffic which was out of range of the Italian navy, but could only directly intervene from Diego Suarez against Italian traffic coming round the Cape of Good Hope. All this meant that France would find it easier to operate against Italy in the eastern Mediterranean, and that Djibuti, because of its distance from Diego Suarez and its proximity to Massaua and Assab, represented no threat.[159] Ducci endorsed this view in its entirety, and it accordingly became official policy.[160] After examining the position in the Far East, he concluded that the four Italian ships stationed there were so weak relative to the French squadron that the only sensible course of action was to sell two of them, intern the third at Shanghai, and try to get the fourth back to Massaua.[161]

Balbo and the 'disciplined air force'

'Our air force', Balbo was accustomed to saying during his years as air minister, 'is no more than a propaganda office, though this was indispensable; now we must begin building a military air force for which not even the weapons have been studied'.[162] His efforts to bring about the reconfiguration and redirection of his service – which his own fondness for spectacular aerial *coups de théâtre* did much to make necessary – were for a variety of reasons unsuccessful, and he left office in November 1933 a frustrated and an angry man. Much of his frustration was generated by his absolute failure to secure the funds he believed necessary to turn his visionary schemes into reality. If, as has been suggested, Balbo managed 'on a beer budget . . . to give Italy's Aeronautica a champagne reputation', then that was in part a reflection of the fact that champagne was never on offer.[163]

Between 1929 and 1933, the air force budget amounted to approximately 770,000,000 lire a year. This share of the available funds represented about 15 per cent of the total defence budget, and amounted to half what the navy received and less than a quarter of the army's portion of the monies Mussolini was prepared to disburse to the three services. In his speeches to parliament, Balbo asked for more money whilst simultaneously giving the impression that all was going well under his far-sighted direction. Thus in his budget presentation on 14 March 1930 he reassured the chamber that, far from being inferior to the planes of other powers, Italian bombers had characteristics that were distinctly superior to them 'if we are given the funds to reproduce them'.[164] Later in his speech he expounded at some length on the dangers Italy was running in not increasing the air force budget, the impossibility of making up with good will for heavy financial deficiencies and the cause of the insufficiency in funds, which he put down to 'lack of aerial awareness' (*coscienza aeronautica*). To ram the point home he dwelt on the French air force budget, which had gone up 144 per cent in 1929 and amounted to 22 per cent of the total defence budget, half what the army received and more than that allocated to the navy. The fact that twenty-two members of parliament took part in the four-day debate over it suggested, he hinted broadly, that *la coscienza aeronautica* was alive and well – and living in France.[165]

The chamber was presented with another collection of French statistics in the budget debate on 27 April 1932, showing that the total sum made available to its air force in 1931/2 was 3,252,000,000 francs as compared to Italy's 745,000,000 lire. The eloquence of the numbers, Balbo added, saved him from further oratory. Here lay one of his weak points: his delivery of his 1927 budget speech had been so tedious that Galeazzo Ciano described it as flying with the engine switched off. In the senate debate on the budget, during which aerial doctrine got an airing, senator Romeo, sustaining his viewpoint by reference to Douhet's theories, called for more money for the air force and suggested abolishing the cavalry to find it. This provoked a predictable protest from general Gazzera and led the parliamentary commentator (*relatore*) on the air budget to contest Douhet's ideas and to point out the need too for a strong army and navy. Balbo's response was that his service firmly believed in 'the fatal supremacy of the air force in the first moments of hostilities and its autonomy as a combat arm during the development of the war, as well as the decisive tasks that will fall to it at its conclusion'.[166]

The essentials of Balbo's case, which never changed, were enumerated when in May 1933 he faced a reduction of 58 million lire in his budget:

the vulnerability of the peninsula from the aerial point of view, the possibility of organising via the air force the only effective defence, that is to say lightning and probably decisive reprisals against the enemy, and the relatively small economic exertion which the air force required from the country in return for its great efficiency relative to the other armed forces.[167]

In a final flourish, he informed the audience that while it was an Italian – Douhet – who had invented modern air power theory, France was now forging ahead in putting it into practice. This was doubly misleading, for while the French air force was not and would not come to be in the grip of Douhetism, neither – thanks in part to Balbo's support of Mecozzi – was the Italian air force.[168]

With military aircraft costing between 200,000 and 500,000 lire each, Balbo's budget would not stretch to a large air force. Partly for this reason, his investment in new aircraft was less than that of his two predecessors: in seven years he ordered approximately 2,000 planes where Finzi and Bonzani had ordered 2,300 in four years.[169] Achievements consistently failed to reach planning targets: in July 1929 the air force target was ninety-five squadrons, but on 1 January 1930 the Regia Aeronautica comprised only eighty-seven squadrons, each of six aircraft with no reserves. A year later the figure had only increased to eighty-nine squadrons, and two years on to 101 squadrons. The July 1932 plan aimed at 100 squadrons, the fighter squadrons each comprising nine aircraft plus three in reserve and the remainder six planes plus one to three reserves, and the July 1933 plan aimed at 112 squadrons amounting to 990 aircraft in line and 300 reserves.[170]

Behind these relatively restrained scenarios, Balbo nurtured extravagant designs for what he could achieve if given enough money. In 1932, he estimated that in wartime Italy could produce 700 aircraft a month after six months, rising eventually to a maximum of 1,000 aircraft a month. Aircraft engine output would mount from 120 units to 1,300–1,400 a month after eighteen months. The figures were extrapolations based on the exertions of three aircraft manufacturers who, preparing for the 1931 summer manoeuvres, had produced and repaired 600 aircraft, delivered

600 new engines and repaired 550 in three months.[171] A year later, in his final flourish, he produced a comprehensive rearmament programme which would allocate 3,000,000,000 lire a year to the air force, as well as 30,000,000,000 lire in extraordinary funding over ten years, and claimed that he could prepare the aircraft industry to produce 30,000 aircraft a year.[172] His own remark about his failure to achieve his target of 3,600 aircraft and the 3,000,000,000 lire it would cost to build – that the absurdity of the sum saved the chamber from taking it into consideration – may also be applied to his rearmament scheme.

Like the other two services, the air force was now obliged, under the reluctant direction of Badoglio, to develop plans for a two-front war. De Pinedo, deputy chief of staff, began a consideration of the problem with an observation that suggested the uncertain ground on which his force stood: no other arm was subject to comparable oscillations in the relative powers of offence and defence as a consequence of technological progress. The fact that, as he acknowledged, most of today's aircraft were antiquated and that the appearance of new types in three or four years would radically change the ways in which they could be deployed gave his ideas an air of transitoriness which was perhaps unavoidable. His rehearsal of the limitations of the air force – the shortage of aircraft and the lack of reserves – and his remark that even if the present-day air force were put into the fullest state of efficiency 'it would still be insufficient for the most limited needs which a war will present' imparted a sense of unreality to the planning process, though the heads of the other services would surely have taken it as a conventional preamble to the request for more money which they were accustomed to make themselves.[173]

French air doctrine, which foresaw using aeroplanes as auxiliaries of the army and navy, suggested that daylight bombing would not penetrate more than a few kilometres over the frontier. However, De Pinedo argued, this was the result of the experiences of the world war. In an Alpine war, which offered much greater opportunities than those on which French doctrine was presently based, the French air force might seek to turn the Alpine chain by sea or make use of bases in Corsica and Tunisia. From the mainland the French could bomb as far as Venice, Bologna and Florence with fighter escorts as far as Milan and Genoa, but climatological conditions would hinder continuity of action; from Tunis they could use all types of bombers against Sicily and Sardinia; from Corsica, the source of the greatest threat to the peninsula, they could hit all of central Italy. The island's air bases must therefore be rendered unusable by the enemy and if possible it should be captured. As far as Italian air action was concerned, good targets existed at Lyons, Marseilles, Toulon and in the valley of the Rhone but they were dangerously far distant and mostly out of range of fighter cover. Marseilles and Toulon could be hit from Tuscan bases, and Tunisia from the islands. Given the impossibility of being confident of reaching Paris and attacking 'the sources of enemy air power', the small extent of enemy territory the Regia Aeronautica could hit and the large and vulnerable area of national territory open to the enemy's air force, De Pinedo thought it would be sensible 'to avoid chemical warfare, which would be more dangerous for us than for the enemy'.[174]

As far as a war on the eastern front was concerned, Italian aircraft could reach all of western and southern Yugoslavia as far as Sarajevo, but not Belgrade. The Yugoslav air force for its part could reach Modena, Florence, Naples and Taranto but not Rome. There was not much Yugoslavia could do against Italy in the air. Her air strength derived mainly from the countries which supplied her with aircraft: Czechoslovakia, Germany and France. Diplomatic action should prevent resupply, and could prepare the way for air operations to break her communications with outside sources of aircraft. Other than this, there seemed to be no independent strategic contribution the air force could easily make in a war. The lack of large population centres and big industrial sites made Yugoslavia largely insensitive to air attack, and there were good political reasons not to attack Muslims, Bulgarians and Montenegrins who might well want to detach themselves from Serbia. Having Albania on Italy's side would be 'of incalculable importance': De Pinedo compared it to the threat France could pose from Corsica. If Zara and the Dalmatian coast were occupied that would provide bases from which the whole of Yugoslavia, including Belgrade, would be vulnerable to Italian air action.[175]

In the event of a two-front war, in which the army and navy would 'probably have to adopt a predominantly defensive posture' and avoid being worn down, the air force would have to switch its resources from side to side as circumstances dictated whilst doing its best to minimise attrition rates. Only with 'a good preponderance of air power over both adversaries' would it be possible to avoid defeat. If Italy's air forces were 'very much more powerful than those of their combined adversaries', then it might be possible to compensate for the necessary defensives on land and at sea with 'an intense and victorious air offensive'. The defence of maritime traffic would be more important than ever, but given the multiplicity of tasks facing it and the limited resources it possessed the air force could only give limited support to such operations.[176]

Balbo's provisions for the air force and its role in the event of war against Yugoslavia and France were explored in some detail when the chiefs of staff met in October 1929 to review collective and individual progress in making preparations for conflict. General Valle, deputy chief of air staff, revealed that the air force expected to deploy 160 land-based fighters on the western front to protect it against enemy incursions, 60 on the eastern front and the remaining 100 aircraft in defence of the *patria*, a deployment which, as Badoglio observed, did not seem to fit with the army's intentions to fight a defensive action in the west and an offensive one in the east. The 200 land bombers available would be concentrated in a central position around Parma and Ferrara; since they could not cross the western Alps, they would concentrate on the eastern front and on operations against Corsica. Ten squadrons of sea bombers would, in accordance with the navy, act against France's lines of communication with the colonies and her naval bases. The eastern airfields were almost ready, and the western fields would be completed during 1930. Temporary airfields were being prepared at three sites in Albania, but any air element sent there would have to be detached from the forces deployed in Italy. No mention was made during the discussion of the likely size, locations and use of the enemy's air forces, and Valle was not asked to give a view as to how a war might develop.[177]

In his battle to gain hegemony over the other two services in the air, Balbo had some success but had to accept one major setback. One element of his plan to whittle down the numbers of aircraft allowed to the army and the navy involved arguing that this diversion of air strength weakened his power to confront an attacking enemy. The Consiglio suprema di difesa had already accepted the principle of aerial defence through aerial attack, but the army did not give up easily and in February 1930 it confronted the Regia Aeronautica on the contested ground of anti-aircraft defence when the defence council sought to complete the work begun on this in 1927 by identifying the important points on the mainland and in the colonies which must be protected.[178]

Bonzani, who spoke with extra authority as chief of the army general staff because of his previous service as under-secretary of state for air, pointed out that the French – and therefore the Yugoslavians – were not presently organising their air force around the idea of destroying the enemy air force on the ground; their first priority was reconnaissance aircraft and the fighters to defend them, while their bomber force existed mainly to prevent an opponent from bombing for fear of reprisals. He then noted that for the price of a squadron of twelve fighters the government could purchase three fully equipped anti-aircraft batteries, which did not wear out so quickly and which were immediately available to defend targets such as Italy's hydro-electric plants, all of which were within twenty-five kilometres of the borders, because they were on the spot. They could also defend the Regia Aeronautica's airfields, he added craftily.[179] Balbo complained that Bonzani had not said what was in the written record, for otherwise he would have protested, but he had already lost the contest to give fighter aircraft pride of place in the scheme for national anti-aircraft defence.

In April 1930 Badoglio, in unhurried pursuit of Mussolini's goal of a combined plan for war against Yugoslavia and France, laid down the law on matters of air force structure and organisation some of which trespassed onto what Balbo might reasonably consider his ministerial competence. Squadrons were to consist either of nine aeroplanes (fighters, day bombers, land reconnaissance and tactical naval reconnaissance), six (strategic naval reconnaissance) or four (night bombers), as well as reserves the numbers of which were to be determined by the air force in consultation with the other two services. The armata aerea was to control 60 per cent of squadrons, divided into 35 per cent fighters and 25 per cent bombers; the army would control 25 per cent and the navy the remaining 15 per cent. A clumsy arrangement whereby the air force decided on the characteristics and technical norms for employment of all aircraft while the other two services issued norms for their employment which defined their tasks and modes of action encapsulated the combination of wilful separation and enforced co-operation which characterised the relationship between the armed services.[180]

Dissatisfaction and ill-temper bubbled just below the surface. Bonzani complained that the air force was paying too much attention to 'defensive' fighters and not enough to 'combat' fighters which would protect reconnaissance and bombing missions. Admiral Valli complained that if the numbers of aircraft embarked on ships were included in the navy's share it would diminish efficiency because new ships were being built to carry their own reconnaissance planes and the navy was looking to build an aircraft carrier, so that the number of land- or sea-based squadrons would have to be reduced. When Giuseppe Valle told him that the navy should not expect long-range reconnaissance aircraft to have the capacity to deliver bombs or torpedoes as this activity belonged to the armata aerea, admiral Valli served notice that the navy might in future build its own ship-borne planes as they were an integral part of the ship's armament.[181]

Fresh from this imbroglio, Balbo learned in June 1930 that Mussolini had not put on the agenda for the cabinet a new organisational statute for the air force to replace the 1925 law, which had assigned forty-six squadrons of aircraft to the army and thirty-five to the navy, because he wanted the ministers involved to reach prior accord on its content. Four years of fruitless wrangling had shown that only the Duce's direct intervention could overcome the differences, Balbo argued, chiefly because 'the independence and the maturity of the R. Aeronautica does not get the recognition it is due from all the ministries', a criticism levelled directly at the war ministry and the finance ministry.[182] Intervention of this kind was not Mussolini's way of doing things, and when Balbo got his legislation on the statute book in January 1931 it merely left the details of the auxiliary aviation that was in the hands of the army and the navy to be worked out by all three ministries while confirming that defence against enemy air attacks was the responsibility of anti-aircraft units. This was at best only a limited victory for Balbo and cemented the air force's intention to pursue its own goals at the expense of co-operation with the other two services.[183]

In October 1930 Valle, now chief of air staff, was summoned to a two-day meeting of the chiefs of staff to review progress on the preparations and plans for a two-front war. Having followed the criteria laid down the previous year, the air force had not increased the number of squadrons, of which the armata aerea had fifty-eight, the army twenty and the navy thirteen. Quantitatively, the air force had grown from 850 planes the previous year to 1,365, or from 650 to 1,000 if one counted only the planes in the front line and in the flying schools. Qualitatively it was improving with the actual or prospective introduction of new types. However, although the situation 'could appear satisfactory' Valle pointed out that it was necessary to acknowledge regretfully 'the absolute absence of a reserve of planes and engines'.[184] Without more money, it would be impossible either to create a reserve or to increase the number of squadrons which was insufficient; there were, he told the chiefs by way of example, only twelve fighter squadrons to protect the whole of the western front, eight for the eastern front, two in Albania, and eight for the defence of rest of Italy.

The relative weakness of the air force was in part a reflection of the industrial weakness of Italy, and the air force's statistics did not make for comfortable reading. The extent of her inferiority in the opening stages of a war could be gauged from the fact that the aircraft industry would not be in a position to produce 600 aircraft a month, equal to projected consumption, until the sixth month of hostilities. One month's supply of bombs existed and it was hoped to increase stocks to a three-month supply by 1932. Gas munitions would be complete in 1931. The air force calculated that it needed 15,000 tons of aircraft fuel to last four months, but since there existed no storage facilities whatever commercial companies were being required to hold a ready stock of 3,600 tons. There were no stocks of lubricants. As far as timing went, the air force expected to begin operations twelve hours into a war and to be fully committed by the fifth day.

Badoglio registered the need for the army to say what it wanted the air force to do, particularly to retard Yugoslav mobilisation and deployment, which led Bonzani to note that gas would be particularly useful in the zone of land combat but not behind the lines or in attacks on cities, and that explosives would be better for fixed targets such as bridges, railway plant and communications nodes. Badoglio closed the discussion by remarking that the decision whether or not to use gas from the start of a war would be taken by Mussolini.[185]

Probably deliberately, Valle focused on the material shortcomings of the air force. It also faced considerable operational difficulties in a two-front war, particularly in respect of bases, which he did not go into in front of his fellow service chiefs. The air bases in Lombardy were too close to the French, and large airfields could not be created in proximity to the eastern frontier because they would then be in the army's zone of concentration. Bombers would therefore have to be based on the Emilian plain and in the Parma–Ferrara area. Given the French air threat from Corsica and Tunisia, Sardinia and Sicily ought both to be proper air bases, but Valle did not have enough aircraft to station bombers there permanently and could only provide them with a nucleus of maritime bombers. He was also short of fighters. With eight squadrons on the eastern front, fourteen on the western front and two in Albania, only two were left to cover Rome. Some important population centres would have to be left undefended and forces arrayed where the likely offensives were most to be feared.[186]

The manoeuvres and exercises by means of which the air force sought to develop doctrine and test the capabilities of air power naturally mirrored the war scenarios being discussed by the planners. In March 1930 the Aeronautica took part in an exercise run by the navy to test its ability to prevent French troop convoys getting from Algeria to Provence after a very brief period of tension. Although the bombers on both sides 'sank' a battleship and a pair of destroyers, 'bombed' bases, confirmed the convoy's movements and 'spotted' submarines, the convoy reached port though with heavy losses. The air observer taking part in the exercise drew two main lessons from it. First, reconnaissance aircraft and bombers needed longer range. Secondly, if technology could not provide the requisite means or if there was reason to believe that the air units allocated to assist the navy might be taken away for other duties, then it was necessary to begin to think about mounting more aircraft on warships and about aircraft carriers. Italy did not need big carriers like Britain, the United States or Japan: 'For us ships of medium tonnage, but very fast and possibly in substantial numbers (numerose), could represent a formidable means to maintain supremacy in Our Sea, that is the Mediterranean.'[187] Service rivalries and the predilections of the senior airmen meant that this was one lesson that was not going to be learned.

The authorities had some difficulty persuading airmen of the value of exercises in which large numbers of aircraft flew in formation, thanks to a widespread conviction that such manoeuvres were 'more or less useless as far as war is concerned' and were no more than 'demonstrations of the virtuosity of some detachment' or were carried out merely for the purposes of parades, reviews and flying exhibitions. Experience in the closing stages of the world war and contemporary developments in the other major air forces both suggested otherwise, and it was 'obvious to believe that in future conflicts air units will normally act en masse'.[188] In 1930 there was, it seemed, quite a bit to do to get air force personnel to acquire the skills and behave in the ways that their commanders required. Pilots lacked the technical ability to fly in close formation and the experience to be able to perform collective manoeuvres; tasks were not spread around so that all aircrew got experience but were given to the best pilots and crews; there was an excessive sense of *personalismo*; and airmen were obeying neither the flying rules nor superior orders. *Spirito di corpo* was held partly to blame because it tended to suffocate that *spirito di arma* which required that people recognise the necessity sometimes to sacrifice the needs and interests of their own particular detachment or speciality to a greater good.[189]

The air force was self-evidently far from ready to contribute to a two-front war with any hopes of success, and indeed not until 1931 was it in a good enough state of efficiency to allow it to undertake large-scale air manoeuvres. The first grand manoeuvres, which took place between 27 and 31 August, were consciously designed to be a practical experiment which, Balbo told the chamber of deputies in April, would allow the formulation of clearer ideas than those produced by numerous writers over the years and thus permit the formulation of a doctrine, something which he acknowledged that the air force currently lacked.[190] They were not, however, quite as open-ended as his remarks suggested. Balbo had clear goals in mind. First, he wanted to demonstrate that the group of airmen he had taken across the Atlantic to Brazil on his 'aerial cruise' at the start of the year were not a select elite and that every one of the three thousand Italian pilots was capable of the same kind of disciplined flying. Then he also wanted to shake up the thinking of everyone who, failing to take on board Douhetian thinking, still believed in wars of position and victory through the occupation of territory:

Many even today still consider as utopian the idea of a future war [that is] cruel, pitiless, [and] exterminating – and therefore short – in which forward defensive barriers are destined fatally to give way when factories are no longer able to produce, men and arms do not arrive and defenceless sons are hit with aero-chemical war.[191]

These 'backwoodsmen' would be in for a shock, the air staff believed, if war broke out tomorrow.

The manoeuvres took as their war scenario the initiation of hostilities by an un-named western power (France) a few days after a war had begun against an eastern opponent (Yugoslavia). The task of the home air force ('Blue') with 398 aircraft was to protect the military, industrial and population centres against attacks by the 490 aircraft deployed by 'Red', thereby allowing the army and the fleet to face the new situation. Detailed tasks included testing fighter protection of bombers, attacking and defending naval and air bases and disrupting lines of communication, but the main purpose of the exercise was to test and demonstrate the effect of the mass deployment of air power. 'Red' launched various night bombing attacks, low-level attacks at dawn and daylight bombing attacks using gas on La Spezia, Bologna, Milan, Florence, Ancona and Genoa from its headquarters in Pisa, and on the fourth day 'Blue' headquarters in Milan gave up.

This result, with its evident confirmation of Douhet's ideas, prompted Badoglio to remark at a press conference on 'the need to think seriously about the organisation of a potent air arm to defend ourselves against a method of war which has such decisive power'.[192] Privately though, Badoglio said that Douhet was mad. In his budget speech on 27 April 1932, Balbo told the chamber of deputies that the manoeuvres had 'given Italy a first summary vision of what future war will be' and had provided the data on which a doctrine of air war could be constructed, one which would have to take account of the mobilisation of manpower and industry, the employment of large fleets of planes, and the movement of men, machines and services from airfield to airfield.[193] Behind his self-congratulatory façade, it was easy to detect the fact that there was still a good deal to learn and to prove.

In August 1932, one hundred aircraft took part in air manoeuvres held concurrently with naval manoeuvres in the Tyrrhenian sea. The defending side had to get a convoy from Libya to the Gulf of Taranto, and the success of the attacking side in locating it with submarines and aircraft and then attacking it led former navy minister admiral Giovanni Sechi to conclude that aircraft carriers were not essential for *mari interni* and that it would be better to put the money into increasing the air force and its coastal bases.[194] The 1933 manoeuvres, a staff exercise carried out between February and April on the basis of a scenario in which France and Yugoslavia fought Italy and Germany, showed that the Regia Aeronautica had at least as much to decide about doctrine as it did to learn about practice: the defending team, tasked with launching an offensive against the enemy and his land, sea and air military organisation, excluded attacks on cities as *azioni terroristiche* ('terrorist actions') while the directing staff included them as *guerra integrale* ('integrated war').[195]

This uncertainty was a reflection of a doctrinal conflict in which the air force was immersed during Balbo's term of office and which he was either unable or unwilling to resolve. Giulio Douhet, who died on 14 February 1930, spent the last two years of his life rebutting the arguments of those airmen such as lieutenant-colonel Ernesto Coop who argued that auxiliary aviation had a place, albeit at the minimum level necessary, on the grounds that once its existence was admitted to be necessary it would be well nigh impossible to limit its size. He also took issue with Coop when the latter adopted his own long-standing position that any air operations directed against the vital centres of the enemy should be subordinated to those aimed first at the conquest of the air. 'The absolute application of this could be dangerous' because to arrive at victory required being absolute in principle but adaptable in practice, he argued confusingly and somewhat self-contradictorily in 1928.[196] Disbelieving either in the possibility of preventing enemy air forces from penetrating Italian air space or in the efficacy of fighter protection for the many vulnerable targets, he also argued for a multi-purpose self-defending 'combat' or 'battle' plane rather than specialised bombers or fighters and robustly rejected the view current in some quarters of the air force that the aerial offensive could only work once fighters had established aerial supremacy. To do this, he had to deny that rate of climb or manoeuvrability gave a fighter any advantage over a battle plane, which could fire at twice the rate of a fighter and not only frontally but in any direction.[197]

All this was very unhelpful to the air force because it did not translate easily or convincingly into a single tangible operational doctrine. However, as his very last polemical salvo showed, Douhet had his uses in the political battle Balbo was waging. He had, he remarked, always opposed the theory of the 'just mean':

A little land force, a little naval force, a little aerial force. This theory derives from the premise that the land theatre, the sea theatre and the aerial theatre can be equally decisive. Everything is possible in this world. And the *giusto mezzo* allows all possibilities . . . It is a convenient theory and compromises nothing, but it arises out of indecision and uncertainty.[198]

Robust, forthright and combative in pursuit of the central role for his own arm, Balbo fully shared this viewpoint.

After Douhet's death, his rival came into his own. In July 1929, Amadeo Mecozzi was given permission by Balbo to experiment with low-level bombing, which he was allowed to include as part of the 1931 grand manoeuvres, and in the latter year he wrote the first of two books in which he propagated his new tactical-operational scheme, *Aviazione d'assalto.* Assault aviation, he suggested, was not a substitute for bomber offensives *alla* Douhet but a complement to them, contributing to the operations of all three armed forces. It would not operate within the range of medium calibre land artillery or naval guns but would initially be used on appropriate targets alongside the bomber force, after which it could be used against the enemy's rear, against landings or along with further air operations to 'intensify the crisis in the moral and material forces which sustain the enemy's armed forces'.[199] Its singular merit was its capacity to hit small, precisely identified targets: troops, magazines, depots, artillery parks, railway plant, command headquarters, and above all rail, road, canal and river transport. As yet, Mecozzi was simply proposing a new speciality. Nothing in his early writings directly challenged Douhetian ideas, nor did he intend the new weapon to fall under the control of the other two services. However if, as has been suggested, Balbo's support for Mecozzi derived from a desire to attenuate Douhetism and to lull the other two services into a more tranquil frame of mind about the air force, then by doing so he also contributed to the aura of doctrinal confusion which enveloped the armata aerea during his reign.[200]

The five-day inquest into war preparations over which Badoglio presided between 5 and 10 November 1931 was the last in the series which had begun in 1927. Valle did not have encouraging news. The necessary airfields had been constructed and so had the tanks for fuel stocks, but there was no fuel in them and there were no munitions on hand since there were no magazines to hold them. To put this right would take six years at the current rate of expenditure of 10,000,000 lire a year. Badoglio regarded this state of affairs as 'a grave hindrance to the requisite intervention of the air force' for which remedial funds must be found.[201] Given the scenario of a single front war, the air force proposed to put eighteen squadrons on the eastern front and six along the Adriatic, while three protected Lombardy and Piedmont and the three squadrons of naval fighters went to Pola-Varano and Brindisi. Admiral Ducci drew from Valle the confirmation that specialist types of naval fighters were being phased out and replaced by land fighters, whose better engines would enable them to operate out to sea, and then asked whether they would be able to protect the navy when, as was foreseeable, it would be operating against the French navy and air force north of the Balearics. Valle acknowledged that only sea-borne aircraft could do this. He was also forced to admit that the air force did not currently possess bombs which could penetrate 12 centimetres of deck armour. A lengthy enumeration of the technical characteristics of the main types of aircraft in service among the major powers included an acknowledgement that the

British had a fighter which could climb to 6,000 metres in nine minutes, 'but these are machines specially adapted for the defence of London, and have very limited flying time'. Next year, experiments would begin on an Italian 'superfighter' which would be able to climb to 5,000 metres in seven minutes and fly at 375 kilometres an hour at that height.[202]

Bonzani's request that the army's situation with regard to reconnaissance aircraft be examined produced the response that the twenty squadrons allocated to it amounted to 193 aircraft and that every squadron save one comprised between 9 and 12 aircraft. The war minister noted dryly that three months earlier there had been only three squadrons available to support exercises by six divisions instead of six, a total of fourteen planes. At this point things must have grown rather tense as Valle responded by pointing out that the army had lost 97 aircraft during the year 1930–1, equating to 35 per cent of its total and costing 20,000,000 lire. Badoglio smoothed things over with the bureaucrat's solution which came so naturally to him: reconnaissance squadron commanders would send army corps commanders monthly lists of aircraft available and their state of efficiency.[203]

Evidently deciding that a combination of admission and attack was the best method of defence, Valle acknowledged that the navy's reconnaissance squadrons varied in size between four and seven planes but pointed out that in the previous year it had lost forty planes, which was proportionately not much less than the army. After noting that he only had one four-plane squadron of long-range reconnaissance aircraft, Ducci pointed out that a major naval exercise the following summer designed to test the possibility of disrupting French convoys from North Africa would require aircraft which could reach Tripoli. Co-operation was certainly not in the air: Valle said that September would be better, offered a single squadron of the armata aerea if the navy was determined to stick to June, and questioned whether Mediterranean troop convoys were in any case very important to the French now that they had linked their North African railway to the Atlantic ports. Badoglio decreed that for the time being they were. He also had to intervene on the side of the air force when Valle and Ducci reprised a well-established argument over whether long-range reconnaissance aircraft should have the capability to launch torpedoes, as Ducci wanted, or whether as Valle believed they should not. After another ill-tempered exchange over the army's bombing objectives, Valle revealed what the Regia Aeronautica would be up against. France had declared 3,076 planes at Geneva but probably had another 2,000 to 2,500 in stock; Yugoslavia had twenty-eight active squadrons and would have sixty-three by the sixth day of mobilisation.[204]

Not only was Italy's air force by its own account too weak to go to war, but the debates had revealed unresolved issues in respect of the military and naval air components which threatened to exact a heavy price in wartime. The state of the air force raised questions about Balbo's tenure of the war ministry, and particularly about the wisdom of spending monies which were in short supply on long distance 'cruises'. By now, however, the air minister's attention was increasingly focused on bigger political horizons. In 1931 he complained that he was not being made a *Maresciallo dell'aria* – a consolatory reward bestowed on him by Mussolini on 13 August 1933 not long before sacking him – and revealed his desire to become minister of defence or else to replace Badoglio as Capo di stato maggiore generale.[205] Fascist party politics now came into play: a police report forwarded to Mussolini noted that Roberto Farinacci was publicly supporting Balbo's claim that his presence on the trans-Atlantic 'cruise' increased its value by 70 per cent, and had said in the chamber of deputies that undeniably 'Balbo has created a Fascist air force while Gazzera has created an anti-Fascist army'.[206] In February 1932, to Dino Grandi's astonishment, Balbo revealed to the foreign minister that he and the other *quadrumvirs* regarded Mussolini as finished, that the party was no longer behind him, and that they intended to go to the king who would make De Bono – 'the old imbecile' – head of government.[207]

When it finally matured, his plan, which was supported by Farinacci and Giuriati, and possibly also by general Grazioli and marshal Caviglia, and was in effect a party-oriented coup to take over direction of the armed forces under the banner of efficiency, was that Mussolini should serve as a figurehead minister of defence while Balbo took over Badoglio's job. His design, which he took to the Duce in September 1933, involved cutting the army back to twenty divisions, of which five would be armoured, ten motorised and five alpini, increasing the navy and air budgets to 3,000,000,000 lire a year each, and spending a further 60,000,000,000 lire over ten years in extraordinary allocations, half of which would go to the air force.[208]

On 6 October Mussolini told the king that it was time for Balbo and Sirianni, the navy minister, to resign and that he intended to take over 'at least for some time', and on 5 November he told Balbo he was going to Libya to replace Badoglio as governor. A week later, he wrote to Balbo to tell him that although the air minister had reported that he was handing over a force amounting to 3,125 planes, a check had revealed that only 911 were ready for war, adding 'I consider the situation satisfactory.'[209] Balbo bristled. He had always included planes in production during the current year in his reports to parliament, he told the Duce, and while readiness for war was definable according to a variety of criteria, the 1,824 war planes in the inventory were in his opinion ready for war 'relative to the potential of the adversary'.[210] A more detailed explanation of the situation revealed that 259 of the 'missing' war planes were still being built, 341 were undergoing repairs, and the remaining 300 or so were spread around experimental units and specialised schools. Tourist planes, Balbo explained unnecessarily but at some length, might be used against a colonial opponent but not against a continental one such as France.[211]

There were many reasons for Mussolini to sack Balbo and move him overseas. Politically he represented an obvious and threatening challenge to the Duce's leadership, whereas to fall in with his ideas and make him Capo di stato maggiore generale would be effectively to single him out as his heir – a position Mussolini always held vacant. Jettisoning him has therefore commonly been interpreted in these terms. However, the military dimensions of the case were surely not without significance. Aside from the financial extravagance of his plans – 16 milliard lire a year would swallow two thirds of the entire state budget – Balbo's scheme would not reach fruition before 1942. Mussolini expected a European war before then. Nor, if he put Balbo into the co-ordinating role in defence planning, could he expect much less than had happened in 1925, when admiral Thaon di Revel had resigned over Badoglio's appointment. Gazzera would certainly resign, the upper reaches of the army were mostly loyal to Badoglio and to the Piedmontese traditions he represented, and given the feud between Balbo and in the navy most of the admirals would probably take a similar line. Finally, while the air force was representing Fascism on the international scene in an agreeably showy way, everything else suggested that it was not making as much progress as the other two services. The announcement on 6 November that general Giuseppe Valle, while continuing in post as chief of the air staff, would simultaneously serve as Mussolini's under-secretary at the air ministry signalled the end of an experiment. The flamboyant *ras* of Ferrara was replaced by a dour, hard-working professional administrator who, although a convinced supporter of Fascism, was in some ways more like Gazzera and Bonzani.

Gazzera and the preparation of the army

In January 1929 general Pietro Gazzera, as yet still under-secretary of state for war, compiled a survey of the army to date and a summary of its needs for Mussolini. France could mobilise twelve divisions against Italy in a week and twenty-five in two weeks, and Yugoslavia could mobilise twenty-two divisions. Of the thirty Italian divisions nominally available at once, shortages of clothes and equipment meant that only twenty-one could be mobilised, along with alpini and bersaglieri units and twenty battalions of blackshirts. Since three divisions would be needed to defend Sardinia and Sicily, two more would be sent to Albania and one to Zara, only fifteen or sixteen divisions were available on both land frontiers. In overall terms, Italy would be outnumbered two to one after two weeks. As well as another 411,500,000 lire on the ordinary budget, most of it to fund an increase of 40,000 in the size of the army, Gazzera asked for 8,000,000,000 lire which would be spent on improving the existing artillery, buildings, roads and railways. The monies did not include any provision for the army air force. In order not to overload the war ministries budget, he suggested helpfully, some of the costs could be off-loaded onto the budgets of the ministries of public works and communications. Gazzera also told Mussolini that although a number of studies for the deployment of the army existed there was as yet no complete plan for a two-front war, though one was now in the course of preparation.[212]

Although Gazzera had ordered Bonzani to start planning for a two-front war, Badoglio, demonstrably unwilling to lend any support to planning for such an unwelcome scenario, instructed the army chief of staff in March to begin planning for a war against Yugoslavia. Bonzani demurred on the grounds that in December 1928 Mussolini had instructed him to plan for simultaneous operations on both frontiers and sought direction from Gazzera and Mussolini. Even in the most favourable hypothesis, with half the Yugoslav army deployed against Bulgaria and Hungary and no French intervention, Italy could only put a force of 180 battalions on the Julian front, three quarters the size of the Yugoslav one. France would not wait for Italy to win her battles, and the four divisions posted on the Alps would not be enough to stop the twelve French divisions likely to be deployed there in the event of war. A war on both fronts could not be contemplated, he believed, until the thirty-six divisions of the second and third stages of expansion were ready – and that would take years.[213]

Mussolini clarified matters. It would be imprudent to assume that a conflict with one of Italy's neighbours could be liquidated before the other developed a serious threat, but it could also be assumed that war might occur in a more favourable situation for Italy than the present or that action by central European or Balkan states might require the employment of Yugoslav or French troops on other frontiers. A 'calm vision' of the European situation in the coming years allowed him to foresee that with judicious employment of the extraordinary budget of 8,000,000,000 lire which was to be given to the army over the next ten years, it would be ready in time to confront the possible outbreak of a war.[214] For the time being he was not willing to give Gazzera the money for extra manpower. Nor did he think Yugoslavia would attack Italy as she was short of money.[215]

In early June Gazzera reported that the relative balance of forces had worsened as a result of the speeding up of both Yugoslavian and French mobilisation, and that even in the most favourable circumstances the twenty-five infantry divisions that Italy would possess in 1931 would face an enemy two and a half times as large, without taking into account the island garrisons and forces to be sent to Zara and Albania.[216] Mussolini thought that the army staff was counting territorial troops as well as the standing army. Although France's pacifism was 'verbal', there was for the time being no point in trying to come to any agreement with a disarmed Germany for future co-operation against her.[217]

In August Gazzera reported that Yugoslavian war preparations had reached 'feverish intensity': 2,000 kilometres of railway had been built close to the Albanian frontier, and the Yugoslavs could now mobilise a force of 840,000 men in eight days backed by an air force of some 600 planes. Demographics would allow them to increase their army by half as much again. Yugoslavia was presently spending 40 per cent of her state budget on military expenditure, mostly for the army. As her armed forces increased, and encouraged by her French ally, she would gradually move from defensive to offensive plans. On the basis of his reading of the international situation, Mussolini resisted Gazzera's pressure for more money. Yugoslavia was trying to insinuate herself with Italy in order to try to get a permanent seat on the Council of the League of Nations, and France would never let her start a war. He did not believe that there would be a war before 1935–6.[218]

The army saw in Italo–Yugoslav tension and Mussolini's restive aggressivity an opportunity to bid for an even larger share of the defence budget and create a powerful if conventionally organised force like that which had emerged triumphant from the world war. In 1929, Bonzani presented a programme for 15,317 new guns and 58 million rounds of ammunition costing 17,000,000,000 lire – the equivalent of seven years of ordinary army budgets – which would take twenty years to complete. Although it was criticised for its 'Alpine character', meaning that it contained neither tanks nor anti-tank guns, Mussolini first approved of it but then, warned of the consequences by his finance minister, reduced the amount to 8 billion lire of which 1,600,000,000 was conceded over the next four years.[219] With this sum, and the limitations on Italian industrial capacity, Gazzera was able to make limited improvements, replacing worn-out equipment, developing new types of guns and building up a limited reserve of artillery to cope with the fact that the manufacturers could not meet an estimated wartime replacement rate of 6 per cent a month.[220]

It was not only in respect of artillery that the army considered itself unready for war. The working of the Ordinamento Mussolini of 1926 meant that because new classes were not called up until the end of April and old classes sent home on leave at the start of September, the majority actually serving only sixteen months and not eighteen as provided in law, the army was only at full strength for four months. Since it took two and a half months to get recruits into a state of sufficient readiness to fight, the army was only at maximum efficiency between 15 July and 1 September each year. The possibility of a war breaking out at any other time was, as Gazzera put it, 'truly worrying'. To remedy this and keep the two classes together longer, an increase in size was necessary. Though Mussolini told him in October that he 'hadn't a penny' Gazzera kept up the pressure, asking for 40,000 more men costing an extra 190,000,000 lire a year.[221]

By the end of 1929, the army possessed a group of plans to cover the Italian frontiers in the event of two-front war, in which it was assumed that the invaders from both directions would aim at invading the Po valley. Against Yugoslavia (Plan 5B), ten infantry divisions and assorted other troops would adopt a defensive position, while an expeditionary force of one – later two – divisions in Albania would draw off as many enemy divisions as possible from the main front. Against France (Plan 5L), which was expected to be able to deploy six metropolitan divisions and possibly three North African divisions within a week, some seven divisions and assorted additional forces would adopt defensive positions such as to force the enemy to fight a stationary war (*guerra stabilizzata*) in positions selected by Italy on her own or if possible the enemy's territory.[222] Since the French might choose to violate Swiss neutrality the northern frontier had also to be watched, although Bonzani thought it reasonable to presume in present circumstances that both Switzerland and Austria would remain neutral. The primary role of watching the frontier fell to the *Carabinieri*, machine-gun sections of the *Guardia di Finanza* and units of the frontier and forestry militia.[223] The other possible deployment the army might have to undertake would be to cross into Austria. The scenario Gazzera had particularly in mind was one in which Czechoslovakia seized a corridor linking herself up with Yugoslavia and cutting off Hungary. To block such a move one or two Italian divisions would be sent to occupy the province of Burgenland on Austria's eastern border.[224]

The army's progress in moving from the phase of *copertura* and mobilisation the previous year to operational war planning under the new scenario of a two-front war was examined by the chiefs of staff on 3 and 4 October 1929, along with that of the other services. It was, Badoglio remarked at the outset, an easy hypothesis to enunciate but a difficult one to determine in any detail. Bonzani reported that the army would mobilise twenty-five divisions and would initially adopt a defensive stance on both fronts before developing an offensive in the east. To assist in protecting the frontiers it proposed to emplace a number of artillery batteries, machine-gun companies and alpini battalions. Despite France's current preoccupation with fortification, an expenditure he had counselled Mussolini against in 1925, Badoglio believed that money was better spent on getting mobile forces ready for action. After being assured that the plans to assemble troops according to the proposed deployments would be ready on 1 January 1930, he told Bonzani to study a single-front war against Yugoslavia and received in reply an assurance that the matter was already in hand. Later, closing the two-day session, he instructed all three chiefs to study mass operations on the eastern front with light cover in the west and mass operations in the west with light cover in the east in that order.[225]

By the start of 1930, the diplomacy Mussolini was pursuing had not yet produced the results the soldiers hoped for or required. Even if parts of the French and Yugoslav armies were deployed elsewhere, Gazzera pointed out, a war against them would always be an arduous task. An alliance which would contain France was particularly important, not least because Hungarian co-operation and Austrian facilitation of it were 'very uncertain, and in the best hypothesis of limited material effectiveness'.[226] France could now mobilise seventy-three divisions in three weeks, and it was expected that the twelve likely to be deployed initially against Italy would undertake an immediate offensive. The Yugoslav army could field twenty-seven infantry divisions and three cavalry divisions in the same time. Italy could now expect to put twenty-nine infantry divisions into the field against them in two weeks, of which eight or nine would have to guard the Austrian frontier, the Tuscan coast, Elba, Sardinia and Sicily, and reinforce Zara and Albania, where an additional division could be mobilised. The odds against Italy were now roughly one to two and a quarter. To meet them, Italy must be able to mobilise forty divisions immediately and a further twenty as a war progressed.

There was some good news for Mussolini, though not much. As a result of improving promotion prospects morale among junior officers was good, though many generals were being held in suspense by the system of promotion through merit. The incoming conscripts were 'spiritually very much better than a few years ago'.[227] This was due partly simply to Fascism, but partly also to pre-military training which improved the spiritual and physical quality of recruits, though it had as yet had little impact as far as actual training for war was concerned. The infantry had 500 million rounds of ammunition but needed 700 million. The range of existing artillery was being increased as there was no money to do more than order prototypes; it had the 13 million rounds it needed for two weeks' firing. The army had one third of the 1,500,000 gas masks it needed, most of the phosgene (600 tons) but only one eleventh of the yprite (200 tons). It possessed only 8,000 of the 24,500 motor vehicles needed to mobilise thirty-one divisions, and would have to rely on requisitioning the rest. Tanks were conspicuous by their absence. According to Gazzera's calculations, the army needed an increase on the ordinary budget of 305,500,000 lire in 1930–1, after which it must be consolidated for at least five years. To get up to forty divisions and to carry out the necessary road, rail and construction work required an extraordinary budget of 8,000,000,000 lire; the one billion which had so far been allocated over the period 1931-6 would suffice to mobilise another five divisions.[228]

Italy's military situation had not improved when Gazzera reported again to Mussolini in June 1930. Indeed, his report made gloomy reading. In the event of war eleven Italian divisions in the west and sixteen in the east would each face thirty enemy divisions.

On the western frontier, the French army can deploy large quantities of weapons and modern technical equipment against the defensive terrain. In the east, the large wooded areas favour the Yugoslav soldier's propensity for individual combat and render our artillery and aircraft ineffective. Both frontiers are devoid on our side of modern fortifications.[229]

The army had very high levels of moral preparation and military spirit 'thanks to the regenerative action of the Regime', but it needed more men, supplies and equipment for at least forty divisions, and modern replacements for its antiquated weapons, artillery and technical arms. All this needed an extra 300,000,000 lire a year on the ordinary budget and an extraordinary allocation of 8,000,000,000 lire. Mussolini had increased the budgets for 1931–6 by 1,000 million lire and had indicated that there might be another 1,600 million lire. This would be enough, Gazzera believed, to expand the size of the army, improve its training and provide supplies but would do little or nothing to remedy the situation as regarded roads, railways, fortifications or weaponry. The latter need offered Mussolini the chance to kill two birds with one stone: in the light of disturbing reports from the *Carabinieri* in Turin he was now looking for a programme of military public works to employ a substantial part of the labour force.[230]

Badoglio allowed a year to pass before calling the chiefs of staff together in October 1930 at Mussolini's prompting to ascertain the state of readiness of the plans for a two-front war. Bonzani reported on details of the mobilisation and assembly plans for the twenty-eight divisions currently available in war and – perhaps deliberately in view of Badoglio's support for De Pinedo's proposal the previous year to abstain from using gas in an air war – remarked on 'the great advantage which would be obtained, in terms of economy of force, by barring certain pre-determined zones of the frontier with persistent toxic substances'. Apparently shifting his ground, as he not infrequently did on matters of detail, Badoglio observed that in principle no limitation need be observed on the employment of any weapon in war given that the future of nations was at stake but added that since the question was essentially a political one he would refer it to the *Capo del governo*.[231] A glimpse of the practical consequences of the serious problems of national resources and their distribution with which the Commissione suprema di difesa was supposed to be dealing came when Bonzani called attention to the fact that some two thirds of the annual import requirement of 23,000,000 tons of supplies presently came overland via maximum use of the Alpine railways. This was a situation which would not pertain in war. He also pointed to a shortfall of 500,000,000 lire in the monies promised for the railways by the ministry of communications. After hearing that France was spending roughly 10,000,000 lire a kilometre on defensive fortifications, Badoglio changed his position on yet another issue and said that where such fortifications would aid manoeuvre by the mobile forces the expense of constructing them must be met, though he accepted Bonzani's position that communications must have priority.[232]

At the close of the two-day meeting, Badoglio told the chiefs that the diplomatic situation on which the two-front war studies were based could be described as 'catastrophic', that it would be 'tragic' for Italy to find itself in such a war since a considerable amount of force would be needed to beat Yugoslavia alone, and that he would repeat the point to Mussolini so that he 'would be fully enlightened'.[233] The report cannot have gone down well at Palazzo Venezia. Shortly afterwards Mussolini complained to Gazzera that Badoglio seemed to be making little progress in co-ordinating war planning and adhering to his directive 'not to attack France, [which is] stronger, but Yugoslavia[which is] weaker'. He wanted to start a war in September or October, but acknowledged Gazzera's point that a war might start with a Serbian invasion of Albania and Italian intervention and that France might wait until Italy was heavily involved before herself attacking. Gazzera's programme would give him 'an army', but until then Italy was too weak to fight.[234]

In February 1931 the secretary of the Fascist party, Giovanni Giuriati, delivered a stinging attack on every part of the military bureaucracy. The Commissione suprema di difesa, which did no more than discuss issues and which scattered secret matters far and wide in its papers and reports, need not meet at all 'given the singular and fortunate privilege of the Fascist Regime that it is the Duce who decides'. With Badoglio absent in Libya the armed forces general staff was no more than a bureaucratic organ which did not exercise decisive and effective influence on the preparations being made by the three services. The army general staff was even

worse. A caste apart in an age of 'people's war', it was spiritually separate from the regime it served and in failing to study the developments
of other societies, the mentality of other peoples and their points of least
resistance it was preparing for the last war and not the next one. The
time and money spent on preparing men for military action through conscription was a waste of meagre resources given the role now played by
Fascist youth organisations, and money would be better spent on materiel
than on raw manpower. Finally, in giving the army such a large proportion of the defence budget, the state was guilty of crude and thoughtless
imitation; rather than risking entering a war in which all three of Italy's
armed services would be inferior to their opponents, money should go on
maintaining naval parity and building a powerful air force. 'Two thousand
aeroplanes are worth more than one Dreadnought. They can bring about
victory before the country feels the effects of the closure of the Straits of
Gibraltar.'[235]

Gazzera responded in carefully measured tones. The Commissione
suprema di difesa was a useful organ, though its membership could perhaps be reduced. In Badoglio's absence, Mussolini had provided the army
with all the guidance necessary for war preparation and co-ordination
with the other two services. The general staff was a professionally trained
body which all could enter; neither it nor the ranks of generals in the
army were disproportionately filled with artillerymen, as Giuriati alleged.
Contrary to the thrust of Giuriati's argument, the army was bound by
regulation and by Mussolini's own instruction to stand outside politics.
Moreover, it was the Fascist regime which had broken with the practice of
its Liberal predecessors and lengthened the period of service to eighteen
months, a recognition that the professional preparation of the army was
at least as important as its moral preparation. Gazzera brushed aside the
accusation of 'mimicry' on the grounds that the term had never passed the
lips of any soldier attending the Commissione. As for the idea of reducing
the army in order to increase the size of the air force, 'it would be folly
to think that we could attain and maintain a numerical and qualitative
superiority when we have to compete with a nation as formidably rich as
France, which has the means to arm herself and all her satellites'.[236]

Giuriati's outburst focused a challenge to Gazzera's vision of a reviv-
ified Piedmontese army of World War One vintage from a more vibrant
party. There was envy in the army, where promotions were stagnating, for
officers of the Fascist militia (MVSN), where they were rapid. Moreover,
the paramilitary activities of the party were expanding. In 1925 they were
given permission to form *Gruppi universitari fascisti* in all institutions of
higher education, and in 1929 they were allowed to run officer candidate
courses in universities, from which since 1927 all graduates had had to

enter the armed forces as potential officers. GUF members and others thus went off via these schools to be commissioned into the militia at a rate approaching three to four thousand a year. With the army commissioning some five thousand junior officers a year, a serious rivalry was beginning to develop.[237] Almost immediately Gazzera faced another challenge, but this time one emanating from within the higher reaches of the army itself.

In 1930, marshal Giardino published the first volume of a study in which he argued that the lesson of the world war was that modern defences were inviolable. Mussolini lauded the book in print. Grazioli, who regarded its thrust as dangerous, made a bid for Mussolini's favour by sending him a draft article in which he argued that technical and tactical developments had shifted the balance on the battlefield so that it now favoured the offensive and not the defensive and that what really prevented attacks from succeeding was the inability of the logistical machinery properly to support and sustain them. Behind it all lay the real reason for the decline in the art of manoeuvre, which was not the existence of trenches but the 'monstrosities' that were the over-sized armies of the day. In his accompanying letter, Grazioli shrewdly pointed out that to support his broad vision of foreign policy Mussolini needed to be able to count at any moment on an offensive instrument.[238] Mussolini showed evident signs of interest, hinting that publication of the piece might be useful so that the other side of the argument could be heard and adding that he had the impression that 'we are retracing the old footsteps of yesterday's war instead of taking account of the lessons of the last, decisive phase of that war'.[239]

Encouraged by this response, Grazioli sent the Duce the draft of a speech he had intended to make in the senate in which he aligned himself with Douhet in believing that a 'sudden and unexpected heavy blow, by air and by land, to surprise and jolt the enemy' was the best path to victory, described Italy's present army as 'pre-war', and proclaimed the virtues of a 'small army, perfected and ready for war in every feature, vibrant with combative vigour in every fibre, oriented towards the practical needs of modern war and animated with the impatient desire to fight it using the dynamic character of decisive manoeuvre warfare'.[240] In practical terms, the core of this new style army would comprise an army group of fifteen infantry divisions and two celeri (fast mobile) divisions ready to go into action at any moment.[241] Grazioli then published his views in the widely read journal *Nuova Antologia*, rehearsing his ideas in general terms and concluding with a call to 'courageously undertake the examination of our actual military apparatus, ready to change its shape (*orientamento*) radically if that is what is necessary to achieve the ends we have laid out'.[242]

Badoglio's generals were incensed. Bonzani saw the remarks as a complete and public statement of disapproval of everything he had done to prepare the army for war.[243] Gazzera supported him: the new ideas were not, as they professed to be, consonant with the spirit of the Fascist regime but antithetical to it since they sought 'to confide the fate of the country not to the spiritual and numerical superiority of our mass army . . . but to a handful of permanent mercenaries'. They were, the war minister held with evident dislike, the ideas of von Seeckt masquerading as an original Italian solution.[244] Mussolini was not prepared to support the request by two of his most senior army officials for disciplinary action, reminding Gazzera that Grazioli was a senator and therefore entitled to make political observations and finding only a few lines of his article to have been *incriminabile* ('actionable'). The piece should not be withdrawn, but Grazioli should be asked to formulate his thoughts better and not in the public arena.[245] The affair rumbled on for a couple of months, during which articles commissioned by Gazzera argued that it was numbers that counted in war and that mechanised warfare was impracticable, before Mussolini put a stop to it with an article in *Il Popolo d'Italia* on 15 October in which De Bono stated that recent attacks on the army had been exaggerated. Six weeks later, on 31 December 1931, Giuriati was sacked as secretary of the Fascist party and replaced by Achille Starace.

The Grazioli affair, which was probably not unconnected with the changing of the guard in the party, had an influence on the direction Mussolini would impart to the army as the new decade developed. For the time being, he decided to leave its rebuilding in the hands of the conservative military bureaucrats. However, ideas had been put into the public and professional arenas which would be shortly picked up and developed by others. Both Giuriati and Grazioli had in different ways raised the issue of the interconnection between Fascism and the debate on military reform, a link Gazzera had sought to play down by arguing (through an amanuensis) that since patriotic nationalism already existed in the mass army there was no need specifically to tie it in with Fascism. If reformists were to displace the old World War One model army – as they would – then they would have to tie their doctrinal and organisational proposals to the supposed characteristics of Fascism in order to succeed. If such a formula appeared, it would allow Mussolini to square an awkward circle by replacing an army which was increasingly an encumbrance to his foreign policy designs with one much more suited to them and at the same time appease those elements in the party which had been temporarily silenced with Giuriati's departure but which were always at the Duce's back.[246]

Meanwhile in 1931 the balance of forces looked no better than before. France could now mobilise twenty-six divisions in five days, thirteen of which would be ready for immediate employment., and seventy-three divisions in three weeks. Yugoslavia could mobilise seventeen infantry divisions within ten days and another sixteen after twenty days. By contrast, Italy could mobilise thirty-two infantry divisions in twenty days.[247] For the first time Gazzera hinted at potential problems within the officer corps. The generals and colonels were good, but the senior officers were 'somewhat mixed in quality' because not all had reached the pass level in promotion examinations, and the captains more so because of irregular patterns of wartime recruitment. The effect of the 1926 promotions law had been to reduce the number of subalterns, and the reserve lieutenants called in to make up the gaps had shown that 'they still have much to learn'. There were also problems with training, which tended to be 'schematic' because of a preference for using cadres or map exercises rather than getting on the ground with troops; and a combination of cost and brevity of the training period meant that there were no grand manoeuvres in which the higher staffs could be exercised.[248] Mussolini expressed himself content with the situation, and having already given Gazzera 500,000,000 lire in extra funds indicated that he was willing to find more when the economy picked up – not openly in the budget because of the disarmament conference which would then be under way, but by 'internal provisions'.[249]

By the summer of 1931, Gazzera was under pressure to speed up the pace of military preparations. The international political situation made it necessary to have preparations as ready as possible by 1933. Italy now had to add the Austrian and Swiss frontiers to her list of areas to be covered. The 'very delicate' situation in which Italy was likely to find herself required a programme of fortifications along the French and Yugoslav borders 'very much larger' than that hitherto envisaged. Nor was this all. Simply to speed up mobilisation was not enough when the French and especially the Yugoslavs had modernised their weapons inventories. Money was needed in particular for more powerful artillery, some of which would have to be brought from abroad if it was to be available in time. Mussolini had made 2,500,000,000 lire available in extraordinary funds over a five-year period between 1931–6; if the necessary work was to be done, Gazzera needed it all by 1934 and another 730,000,000 lire a year on top of that.[250]

Badoglio, who had warned Mussolini in the spring about the dangers of a two-front war and who believed that as a consequence of his description of its difficulties he had the Duce's permission not to put the plan into operation, directed the chiefs of staff to focus their attention on plans for a war against Yugoslavia alone (Ipotesi Est) when he convened them in November. It did not correspond to 'the actual situation', he admitted, but it should be studied nevertheless 'because political situations can change and make possible this eventuality, which appears improbable (*poco probabile*)'.[251] The two-front war now being deliberated upon was anathema to him; in March 1931 he told Dino Grandi that Italy should follow 'a strong policy of national dignity' and reach an accord with France and that he believed that to do what was being contemplated would be to commit 'national suicide'.[252]

Unusually, a direct difference of opinion rapidly emerged between the Capo di stato maggiore generale and the army chief of staff. When Bonzani reported that Italy and Yugoslavia would mobilise thirty-four and twenty-six divisions respectively (the Yugoslav divisions being larger), Badoglio suggested that this was an over-valuation of the enemy. In reply Bonzani reported that the Yugoslavs had received 2,000 railway wagon loads of materiel in the last year alone, including 250 modern Skoda guns. Badoglio thought Italy should assume the offensive, but Bonzani demurred: Italy lacked the necessary superiority of force and must wait until the second and third waves were mobilised. This would take some months, whereas since the Yugoslavs could mobilise their potential strength more quickly they would undoubtedly attack. This was too much even for Badoglio, who suggested that Italy ought not to stay on the defensive and that offensives should not be improvised. Bonzani retorted that the general lines of a plan already existed and that the actual manner in which it would be put into operation would be determined by the circumstances of the moment.[253]

After a brief moment of amity in which Bonzani and Valle announced that they had agreed a number of targets which the air force would strike to impede Yugoslav mobilisation and deployment, Bonzani and Badoglio clashed again on the measures to be taken to defend the western frontier during a war in the east. Bonzani had allocated seven divisions to watch France, a number the Capo di stato maggiore generale thought excessive. A compromise emerged in which an unspecified number of the 'western' divisions would form a reserve which could be used on the eastern front when the circumstances allowed. Bonzani then sketched out the lines of successive offensives which would target the western edge of the Lubljana basin before driving towards Zagreb, while secondary attacks from Dalmatia and Albania could push towards Bihac and the Serb 'industrial redoubt' around Kragujevac. Conditions were not yet such as to be able to launch anything other than limited offensives from Albania in favourable circumstances. Pariani had reported that the Albanians were very unreliable: if the Italians landed quickly they could put up a good resistance, but if the landings were delayed not much faith could be placed in them.[254]

While Bonzani put a positive face on the situation with respect to munitions and supplies, the situation he revealed was in truth far from ideal. The Yugoslav guns had longer ranges, but the Italians had more pack artillery which could be deployed so as to counter the enemy's advantage. Several models of gun were in the process of being replaced, but others were being provided with new ammunition in order to increase their range. The army expected to be able to get three quarters of the 40,000 lorries it needed by requisitioning 40 per cent of the civil stock of vehicles. 25 to 30 per cent of the necessary frontier defences were under construction or planned. Among the mass of detailed statistics that tumbled out were those on toxic chemicals: the army had all but 184 tons of its planned 1,100 tons of yprite, all the phosgene it needed, 60 per cent of the arsine, was not short of chloropicrine, and would soon have half the 1,600,000 gas masks it required.[255]

By the beginning of 1932, Gazzera was disinclined to believe that much was likely to come by way of aid or relief to the military from Mussolini's diplomacy. Neither Germany nor Britain appeared likely to provide the necessary distraction to France, the one being scarcely armed while the other had grave political and financial difficulties which were having their repercussions on its army. Albania was a useful support 'if also very burdensome'. Hungarian co-operation would be willing but not very effective, and Bulgarian aid both less certain and less in worth. The benevolent neutrality of Greece and Turkey and the support of the USSR could certainly be helpful, but possible Soviet aid would be too far off to be useful. If at the moment of conflict 'the political situation were to improve for us, our military problem would be less serious but still very arduous'.[256]

As far as the enemies' capabilities and intentions went, France could now mobilise sixty-one infantry divisions in six days at the commencement of a war and another ten in a further twelve days. The programme of railway, road and fortification building on the frontier which had begun in 1927–8 was being carried on with mounting intensity which seemed to confirm that in a war France would take the offensive. Yugoslavia, which was speedily re-equipping her infantry and rearming her artillery with new weapons, could field twenty-two infantry divisions in six days and another eleven by the thirtieth day of mobilisation. Italy could mobilise thirty-four infantry divisions and assorted celeri, alpini, bersaglieri and camicie nere at once, and another six divisions in three months. The military balance had shifted yet further against Italy and in favour of her adversaries, and now stood at 1 to 2.8.[257] In the light of the forthcoming Geneva arms conference, Gazzera suggested, it was in Italy's interests to try to reach force levels more or less equal to those of France and Yugoslavia, to disarm France and the Little Entente bloc as much as possible, and to let Germany rearm: 'The predictable future German danger becomes a second-order problem, to be left to the distant future.'[258] In one of the last communications he can have received before he was fired, Grandi was urged by an evidently concerned war minister to hold out at Geneva for parity at whatever level. At all costs, Gazzera believed, Italy must not terminate the modest rearmament plan which had begun in 1930 and would not conclude until 1936.[259]

4   Moving towards aggression, 1932–1934

Fig. 4 The image of power: massed ranks of the Italian army and air force

The public face of Italy's armed forces was shown in parades and ceremonies. Behind the scenes, bitter wrangling went on between three services who shared only one thing in common – their reluctance to collaborate with each other. The air force complained about shortage of funds – with some reason, as during the 1930s it received one fifth of the money spent on the services while the army took a half. The navy was able to stand largely outside this contest, making use among other things of a propaganda advantage neither of its rivals could match – the picturesque sight of modern Italian warships lying in the Bay of Naples.

In the years between 1932 and 1934 Mussolini began to put into effect the project for which he had been preparing during the previous decade but which he had been forced to delay – the expansion of Italy and the assertion of her right to be numbered as one of the great powers. The tidal currents of international politics helped him as the western democracies sought to contain forces which could otherwise lead to turbulence and aggression while Germany accepted a new regime which set about the task of unleashing them. Of the military instruments at his command, the air force while bellicose in tone and style was as yet still in its adolescence and the navy's lip-service to Fascism and the Duce barely masked its traditional defensive-minded caution. Both were essentially supporting players to the army, which Mussolini saw as the sword of conquest. Before that weapon could be used, as he now intended that it would be, it had to be tempered. In one service at least things would have to change if they were not to stay frustratingly the same.

Political fluctuations and the rise of Nazi Germany

On 2 February 1932 the Disarmament Conference opened at Geneva. Italy at once lined up alongside Germany to propose that all weapons forbidden to conquered countries by the post-war peace treaties should be considered as aggressive and therefore outlawed. In doing so, Mussolini had much more in mind than simply securing naval parity with France and revising the Versailles Peace Treaties to secure Albania and a slice of Yugoslavia.[1] He aimed to isolate France, severing her from Great Britain by making her demands for security guarantees at Geneva appear unreasonable, and to facilitate German rearmament. His policy had wider ramifications, for in weakening France's European position he would improve the possibilities for a single-handed Italian war against Yugoslavia. Grandi, who was increasingly unhappy at the pro-German line Mussolini was pursuing and was seeking an accord with France which might open up the avenue to gains in Abyssinia, was alarmed when in March 1932 the captive Italian press took a stridently anti-Hindenburg and pro-Hitler line in the German elections.

Mussolini declares himself an ally of the newly reviving German nationalism that seeks to reverse the results of its war against the whole of Europe. Fascist Italy reappears in its subversive, revolutionary, isolationist face. Is this in our interest?[2]

In pursuit of Mussolini's policy, on 23 July 1932 Italy withheld her support for a resolution put forward at Geneva by president Beneš paving the way for a substantial reduction of all armaments and especially those deemed to be 'aggressive'. French 'sensitivity and nervousness', already mounting after the collapse of the von Papen government and the advent of von Schleicher's administration, were heightened by what Paris interpreted correctly as Italian sabotaging of disarmament.[3] Mussolini then put forward a set of proposals of his own for disarmament which included outlawing the bombing of centres of population but which allowed exceptions where bombing was carried out in colonial territories – something he had in mind for his forthcoming war in Abyssinia. In doing so, he was already assuming that Germany would rearm. At best she would tailor moderate rearmament to the actions of other states, and at worst she would simply disregard international conferences and go ahead at her own pace and in her own way.[4]

In September 1932, Mussolini supported Germany's claim to equal status in armaments made by Rudolf Nadolny at Geneva in the face of the Beneš resolution. He did so in the knowledge, gleaned by Italo Balbo from conversations with a heated general von Hammerstein and a more prudent Kurt von Schleicher, that Germany under their aegis was looking for revenge and would at some unspecified time in the future turn to war first for the Polish corridor, then for anschluss and finally for Alsace Lorraine. If, after the conference ended, the other western powers did not reduce to Germany's level of armaments then she would build up to their levels over a period Mussolini expected to last for between eight and ten years. The time span was crucial given the pace and nature of Italian rearmament, for it would enable Italy to keep on at least equal terms with her former enemy 'even if it has a military apparatus like that of the pre-war period'.[5]

The diplomatic face of pre-Hitlerian Germany as presented by the officials of the Wilhelmstrasse was a little different from that of the soldiers. Von Bulow reassured Cerruti towards the close of 1932 that the 'right to arms' was only a question of principle given the state of Germany's budget, that she was not thinking of adopting tanks and would happily see submarines abolished, and that she would only seek to increase her own armaments and mechanise her army after five to ten years if by then other states were not on an effective road to disarmament.[6] Thanks to support from others – most notably the British – the first plank of Mussolini's policy was laid when the Geneva Conference reconvened on 4 December 1932 and seven days later granted Germany equality of rights.

At that moment Germany was demonstrably in political crisis. Quite how it would turn out was by no means self-evident. The Italian military attaché, lieutenant-colonel Giuseppe Mancinelli, noted that while junior army officers were strongly spiritually attracted to the National Socialist party their seniors doubted its constructive capabilities. The newly arrived ambassador, Vittorio Cerruti, thought that the Nazis were losing ground.

Hitler's hour had not yet come but 'one fine day' they might be able to manoeuvre themselves into power, without a revolutionary movement but with the sympathy of the Reichswehr.[7] Germany's future probably lay in a combination of the Reichswehr and 'the national anti-democratic and anti-parliamentary forces' but Cerruti pointed out that the national socialists were suffering from a number of problems including evident internal dissension and the fact that they were in the process of becoming more of a party and less of a movement.[8]

Hitler's appointment as chancellor of Germany on 30 January 1933, which came at a moment when the entire staff of the Italian embassy in Berlin was ill with 'flu', produced an evident change in the diplomatic complexion of Europe but one whose import was not easy to judge. The event had not been forecast by Italian diplomats – reasonably enough since Hitler's share of the vote had declined in the second election of 1932 – and indeed they had foreseen that he might lose ground, though whether the decline of his party would continue appeared debatable.[9] However, the new chancellor himself was by no means entirely an unknown quantity. Mussolini had used a private business contact, major Giuseppe Renzetti, to keep abreast of his political manoeuvres between October 1931 and January 1933.[10] He also received lengthy and informative reports from the Italian consul-general in Munich, Francesco Pittalis, who in June 1932 noted Hitler's public statement to the effect that it was in Germany's interests to come to an understanding on the South Tyrol rather than try to change things by the use of menaces. What was needed, Hitler said, was a 'new and far-sighted political orientation'.[11] The Duce was attracted to Hitler both by the specific promise of an uncontested future for the Alto Adige and by the much broader notion that Hitler might be his partner in manufacturing the 'new order' Mussolini wished to impose on Europe. The apparent ideological affinity between the two explained, Grandi believed, why Mussolini was 'so taken with Hitler'.[12]

Hitler initially sent Mussolini a series of warm messages, announcing that they would 'march [together] towards the attainment of fascism', reassuring the Duce of his determination to stand alongside Italy to prevent French hegemony and signalling his willingness to work with her and with Great Britain.[13] However it soon became apparent that he would be less malleable than Mussolini wished. Germany indicated that she sought an economic understanding which would divide the Balkans, Berlin dominating heavy industry while Rome took textiles and light industry, a dangerous prospect from Rome's viewpoint. In May Hitler made it quite plain that he would not budge an inch on Germany's freedom to rearm.[14] It also rapidly became clear that Hitler wanted to throw out chancellor Dollfuss and carry out elections which would allow the Austrian Nazis to shoulder their way to power in Vienna. His continued unwillingness to rein in Theodor Habicht was clear evidence that he and Mussolini did not see eye to eye over the future of Austria.[15]

Italo–French relations were poor on the eve of Hitler's accession to power and his advent did not do much to change them. French politicians appeared to believe that a 'Germanised' Italy was hostile to them and feared in the autumn of 1932 that she could start an undeclared war. In December general Weygand was reported to be in favour of a preventive war against Italy.[16] In the immediate aftermath of Hitler's arrival in power French diplomats uttered contradictory statements about the role Paris considered that Rome might play in keeping him in check. While ambassador Jouvenel was looking for a 'constructive' Italo–French policy, Paul Boncour believed that Italy would be no use to France in a war with Germany and favoured reaching an agreement with the USSR.[17] Laying out for the ambassador the many issues over which he differed with France, Mussolini made it clear that the only point on which their views coincided was Austrian independence. Even here there was disagreement on method as he opposed French suggestions that the country be neutralised.[18]

As Hitler settled into power, France was reported to be on the verge of aggression. Weygand, the Italian military attaché and the Paris correspondent of *Il Popolo d'Italia*, Antonio Pirazzoli, both said, did not to want to lose the chance to attack Italy and eliminate the menace she represented. The date had apparently been set for the beginning of April and the French expected to have the job done within three months. Ambassador Pignatti interpreted matters a little differently. France feared Germany and hence her war preparations, but she did not want a war and was looking for an agreement with Berlin.[19] The Italian military attaché read the political signs correctly in forecasting that war minister Daladier would not be able to persuade the chamber to increase the period of conscript service, currently one year, and also reported considerable doubts as to whether the reserve units which made up the bulk of the wartime army and which had never been called up together would be able to meet the increased pace of war.[20] Pralormo also saw the ongoing reform of French military and security policy as directed primarily against the German threat:

The new powerful defensive system [the Maginot Line] in the course of completion is not only, as French military critics are at pains to demonstrate, a bulwark against an enemy offensive but seems to represent . . . a notable facilitation of and protection for the outpouring of fast units collected together permanently behind it.[21]

The pattern of French rearmament, and particularly signs of feverish activity by the Schneider and Creusot arms works, led general Gazzera to believe in May 1933 that war might break out some time soon. However Mussolini calculated that the French did not want war and would only fight if Germany started a war by attacking the Danzig corridor.[22]

To reduce France's military and diplomatic power, Mussolini needed a rearmed Germany. The mechanism by which he proposed to bring this about, circumventing both the Geneva disarmament negotiations and the League of Nations, was the Four Power Pact which he drafted on 4 March 1933 and which was initialled at Palazzo Venezia on 6 June. Presented to the great powers as an instrument for revising Versailles, discussing disarmament and renegotiating colonial divisions under the auspices of the League, it was in fact intended as a means to secure measured German rearmament and to develop a controlling mechanism for European affairs. Rome's diplomats calculated that the Fascists' voice would more than equal that of the liberal democracies because France could not count on the undiluted support of a Great Britain which was 'semi-detached' as far as European questions were concerned. Mussolini also presented the Four Power Pact as the best route to the pacification of Europe since it would secure German support which was an essential precondition. As a means of managing German rearmament, however, it was undermined by German incomprehension and French intransigence.[23]

The pact was opposed by all three members of the Little Entente, by Poland and by Turkey and had not a little to do with Ankara's subsequent policy in the Balkans. More importantly as far as Mussolini was concerned, Hitler failed to grasp what from the Italian point of view were its potential advantages, particularly the fact that it enshrined the two basic goals of treaty revision and *gleichberichtung*, and insisted on conditions, which made Mussolini cross.[24] Goering pointed out that under the pact Germany committed herself to being treated as a second-class power for years whereas without it she could consider herself freed from Versailles, but was prepared to sign it, and Hitler too came round by early July. Mussolini presented the pact to Germany as a means by which to provide her with the time to create a solid internal structure as the necessary basis upon which to build her power. Cerruti explained the underlying logic of the idea to Hitler: 'the more that a regime shows itself to be strong and based on stable foundations, the more respected and feared it is abroad'.[25] However, it was plain from the outset that Germany did not want disarmament discussed by the four powers simply because of the presence of France.[26] For its part, Paris too wanted something that the pact could not offer. Asked why, given the strength of her frontier defences, France resisted German demands for 'modest rearmament',

Paul-Boncour responded that France might perhaps agree but only if strict controls were in place and a 'test period' was agreed.[27]

Neither Germany nor France was prepared to play the role Mussolini wanted. France would only consider disarmament talks if there was simultaneously a better understanding on central European questions, which translated as giving Czechoslovakia a place in the Duce's 'Danubian bloc', to which the Italian diplomatic response was that any such understanding would only fuel German suspicions and therefore make her unlikely to adhere to any acceptable plan.[28] Germany's withdrawal from both the League of Nations and the Geneva disarmament conference on 14 October 1933 removed the cover beneath which the pact might have effected its virus-like operation. Suvich, acting under the instructions of an evidently cross master, admitted as much when he told the German ambassador von Hassell that it had closed off the Four Power Pact.[29] The goal of the pact and the flaw which now condemned it to sterility were both displayed when Paul-Boncour asked Aloisi whether there was not a third way besides accepting German rearmament or taking preventive measures. The Four Power Pact was the way to get the necessary agreement between the powers, was the reply. Asked whether France might not try to attract Germany within its orbit, Paul-Boncour replied bluntly that France would object.[30] On 17 April 1934, France rejected Hitler's formal proposal for German parity in armaments, and with that Mussolini gave up his scheme. The French were told that he had no intention of taking any initiative at the moment or of undertaking any work of mediation, and also that, under continuous pressure from Berlin to meet Hitler, he would see the Germans before he saw the French.[31]

German rearmament, around which so much revolved, initially appeared to be slow in conformity with Hitler's pronouncement that Germany was not going to improvise an army but would found it properly.[32] In July 1933, the German military attaché in Paris told his Italian opposite number 'We can do nothing for two or three years', and in September colonel Mancinelli advised Rome not to be misled by Nazi propaganda as Germany was not feverishly preparing for revenge and was not presently strong enough to resist an attack by France and her allies.[33] German naval rearmament also seemed unlikely to threaten either the international scene or Italy's position in the near future. Although the German navy was still at heart a 'battleship navy', Rome learned in July 1933 that Hitler and Blomberg had decided not to build the 27,000-ton battleships the sailors wanted but instead to construct three 10,000-ton cruisers 'without excessive haste', their objective being only to control the North Sea.[34] Mussolini knew the German navy's medium-term intentions directly from admiral Raeder who saw a transition period lasting until the end of 1936 at the latest, during which time Germany would respect the general limits laid down at Versailles. She would take part in the forthcoming London Naval Conference only on condition of having full quantitative equality. Since she could not afford to build the battleships she was entitled to under Versailles, she would stick to the *Deutschland*-class. Rome was also informed that Germany was building submarines but had denied any intention of doing so to the French naval attaché.[35]

As the Four Power Pact slid towards the diplomatic dustbin, France appeared to be moving in the right direction anyway. Hitler's electoral successes and the inexorable drift of the tides at Geneva against her in respect of her wish to keep Germany disarmed or to have international guarantees of her security as recompense for changing her position forced her closer to Italy. By early October, evidently preoccupied with the state of Italo–German relations, the French were seeking an exchange of ideas with Palazzo Chigi; the fact that premier Eduard Herriot was talking of an Italo–German military alliance was seen as a diplomatic manipulation intended to prepare the way for some form of Italo–French understanding by highlighting the threat against which it would be counter-posed.[36] Another impetus pushing Paris towards Rome was her apparent belief that Italy could be the route to an understanding with Germany.[37] In thinking that Mussolini was 'the most moderate figure in the Italian government on questions concerning Franco–Italian relations' and that he believed in the League of Nations as both the appropriate and the necessary institution under the aegis of which an entente should be achieved, the French were falling victims to a combination of deception and wish-fulfilment.[38]

During 1934 Mussolini's calculations about German rearmament came to pieces. Just before the new year Hitler made it plain that he was not prepared to go along with Italian ideas of a graduated and staged programme of rearmament.[39] Over the turn of the year and with the intention in mind of marrying the international and military dimensions of German rearmament, Suvich suggested to von Neurath a policy of *gradualità,* starting with minor rearmament over the first year to avoid the impression of 'excessive armament' but building up to the German goal of a 300,000-man army. Mussolini proposed a six year convention based on the same principle to ambassador de Chambrun, though without revealing the intention behind it.[40] However during 1934 the pace of German rearmament greatly speeded up, thereby affecting both Italian diplomatic and strategic policy. In March the foreign military attachés in Berlin were agreed that Germany would be in a state of military inferiority for between five and ten years, but by June Cerruti believed that his previous year's estimate of a five-year period – and Mancinelli's estimate of seven or eight years – were well wide of the mark. 'One can . . . now be certain,' he advised Mussolini, 'that by 1938 at the latest, if nothing happens to prevent it, Germany will be able to put into the field a powerful army perfectly equipped with the most modern weapons'.[41]

Cerruti's belief that Germany could raise an army of 300,000 was soon leapfrogged. In September, Mancinelli estimated that she could already put 588,600 men into the field and calculated that before long that number would increase to 1,200,000.[42] By the end of 1934 Rome knew that the German air industry was on the point of starting full war production, that the German navy intended to build a fourth and fifth battle-cruiser which might be complete by the autumn of 1936, and that the German army was experiencing the pangs of expansion as industry struggled to meet its needs for heavy and field artillery and light and medium tanks.[43]

Alexis Léger, secretary-general of the French foreign ministry, had told the Italian ambassador in the summer of 1933 that in the present circumstances France had no choice but to rearm.[44] However, her actions during the early summer of 1934 were not such as to suggest that she had anything other than diplomacy in mind to deal with the mounting German problem. The Italian military attaché reported no signs of abnormal activity and believed that the French military saw no possibility of a preventive war and did not think that conflict was close, and the naval attaché explained the fact that the Hotchkiss and Creusot armaments plants were working three shifts a day as due to their having orders to fill from Japan, Poland, Brazil, Turkey and Argentina.[45] Ambassador Pignatti, a typical Fascist diplomat who regarded his hosts with a combination of paranoiac suspicion and ideological hubris, could only explain this in one way: if the military and naval attachés were correct, then 'France has inflated [the scale of] German armaments and does not fear them'.[46]

The apparent instability of the Nazi regime was displayed almost immediately in the 'Night of the Long Knives' on 30 June 1934, producing a reaction among Italian observers in which considerable distaste was mixed with puzzlement and speculation. The Italian consul in Munich congratulated Italy on not having a word for *Lustknaben*. The naval attaché, remarking on the 'moral lapses' which characterised the SA's most eminent figures and the dissipation of public monies by them and their cronies, was inclined like his military opposite number to take the official explanation of a plot seriously. The role of the Reichswehr in the events leading up to the purge, its bitter hostility to Roehm's proposals to subsume it within his own party organisation as part of his goal of forming 'an SA state', and von Blomberg's effusive thanks to Hitler appeared to show that the armed forces 'wished to underline their attitude of complete loyalty and adhesion towards the ideas and the actions of the Führer'. The lack of obvious public support either for the 'plotters' or for the government was evidence that the new regime had not yet been able 'to induce a profound change of spirit such as to induce direct and active popular participation in events so important to the life of the nation'.[47] Mussolini took particular note of the belief that the defeat of 'leftist' tendencies and the reinforced position of the German army had a wider significance:

The recent non-aggression pact with Poland would thus represent not so much a truce in the problem of [German] demands on her eastern frontier but the start of a new and lasting direction in German policy.[48]

The notion that conservative and nationalist forces were now more firmly in the saddle and that Nazi party adventurism had been squashed gave added weight to the German general staff's view that anschluss would be an error. Two weeks after this reinterpretation of the distribution of power inside Germany chancellor Dollfuss was assassinated.

Discerning what was going to happen next inside Nazi Germany was no more straightforward after 20 July than it had been before. The Italian consul in Dresden reported the view that for France the German danger was over for some time as the Reichswehr was now in charge.[49] Cerruti, who was already proving a shrewd and far-sighted observer of Nazi Germany, smelt a number of rats in the official version of events and also foresaw the possibility of future conflict between the SS and the Reichswehr but maintained, partly as a result of what he saw at the Nuremberg party rally in September, that the popular adulation of Hitler had increased and that for the moment at least the Nazi party had not lost any of its strength.[50] The fact that Hitler, on succeeding marshal von Hindenburg as chancellor in August 1934, did not choose Blomberg as his vice-chancellor suggested that the army was less likely to act as a brake on the Führer than optimists believed.

The abortive Nazi coup in Vienna on 25 July and the assassination of Dollfuss – a personal friend of Mussolini whose family was staying with the Duce at the time – which followed swiftly on the heels of the so-called Roehm *putsch* caused Mussolini intense momentary anger and led him to move troops up to the Austrian border. Goering had declared a year before that anschluss could only come in the distant future and with Italian agreement, at the same time asking for absolute Italian neutrality in the event of a German–Austrian conflict – an action which triggered Italian military planning for such a contingency.[51] However, evidence of his duplicitous nature was to hand in the months immediately prior to the abortive Nazi *putsch*. At the end of May, only a matter of days before the signing of the Yugoslav–German commercial treaty, he denied saying in Belgrade that Germany would favour closer relations with Yugoslavia and he also asked Gömbös 'Why are you against anschluss? It would allow us to collaborate militarily so well.'[52] At their Venice meeting in June, Mussolini and Hitler clashed when the Führer indicated that although anschluss was not an item for discussion there must be elections in Austria, the Nazis must participate in the government according to the result, and future questions about Austria should be decided by agreement between Germany and Italy. Mussolini opposed elections and argued that Dollfuss could not be expected to accept under pressure.[53]

Although Nazi involvement in the *putsch* was evident, it was far from clear whether and how far Hitler was directly responsible. Italian military intelligence, which had been monitoring events inside Austria for four months, warned the regional Italian army commanders on 5 June that a large-scale national socialist outbreak directed from Munich was imminent, but its reading of preparations which were designed not to compromise the German government did not directly implicate either Hitler or his administration.[54] The events could be explained, Cerruti suggested, as the action of individuals such as Habicht who regarded themselves as empowered by the punitive action of 30 June to punish Dollfuss for opposing Nazi annexationists, as a manifestation of the fears of the Nazi 'left' at the increasing dominance of the 'right', and as the inevitable consequence of the impact of the racist ideas of Hitler, Goebbels and Rosenberg on a group of individuals who wanted the triumph of 'integral Germanism'.[55] The speed with which Reichswehr and SS units cleared the Austrian Legion away from the frontier the day afterwards supported the image of a Hitler desperate to avoid unleashing it and causing serious international complications.[56] Hitler might thus have learnt the lesson, though taken together the events of June and July suggested to Cerruti that a man as impulsive as he was might try an adventure which would lead to war if there were fresh upheavals within the Nazi party or if the German economic situation became desperate.[57]

Although the Austrian *putsch* rang alarm bells in Rome, it presented the opportunity to gain some diplomatic advantages. Most important was the sudden increase in the leverage Italy could exert over France. The assassination and the evidence it gave of the German threat brought the French closer to Italy, both in terms of the general European balance of power and of the maintenance of Austria's independence – and led them to say so to Italian diplomats.[58] Barthou, who was looking for an invitation to Rome in the early autumn, saw a danger in an Italo–French understanding as it might move Yugoslavia closer to Germany. Depriving Belgrade of her long-standing ally would, however, considerably ameliorate one of the Duce's long-standing preoccupations and reconfigure a problem which, as will be seen, he could not solve militarily.

In March 1932 Mussolini rejected an approach by king Alexander of Yugoslavia which included an offer of favourable trading arrangements and a modification of the 1927 Franco–Yugoslav Treaty. He claimed to be willing to come to a comprehensive accord with her, but the Yugoslav price for helping maintain Austrian independence and preventing German expansion in the Balkans was too high: Belgrade demanded that Italy abandon its claims to rights over Albania and its support for Hungarian revisionism. Mussolini ignored indications coming from Belgrade in August that the Yugoslavs were interested in renewing contacts with Italy and reaching an agreement and instead backed Croatian Ustashi in an attempted insurrection in September. This signalled the start of a period of a mounting tension between the two countries. At its height the Serbians greatly inflamed Italian feelings by lopping off the heads of the 'Lions of Trau' which symbolised the rule over the Adriatic once exercised by Venice.[59]

In January 1933 Mussolini wanted to fight Yugoslavia. Although this was a moment of great diplomatic uncertainty, which had its advantages, the ground was far from prepared: the previous month France had rejected an offer to recognise her predominance in North Africa in return for a free hand in Yugoslavia. King Vittorio Emanuele was convinced that if Rome did go to war with Belgrade the French would attack at once. Gazzera did not think Yugoslavia would attack Italy during the current year, prompting Mussolini to ask why then were they themselves waiting? Chiefly, the war minister explained, because Italy had to fear French intervention either at once or when Italy was deeply committed in the east. 'France could give us a lesson that would last us for half a century', he told the Duce. If Italy had to fight Yugoslavia, then it must be in the context of a general war in which France was distracted by Germany.[60]

To deal with the situation, Mussolini proposed to increase his subvention to the Croats – 'the only people worth anything' – from 70 million lire a month to 120 million lire, to reach a military convention with Hungary for military action against Yugoslavia, and to arm the Bulgarians during the year. War must be avoided before 1934, when France would be nearing her impending demographic crisis.[61] After a month during which he received repeated assurances that the Yugoslavs did not want to attack anyone, that their military movements were purely defensive, and that they were afraid of an Italian attack, Mussolini cut off aid to the Ustashi in February 1933 and ordered that revolutionary action cease.[62]

The crisis was not yet over however, and at the beginning of March Mussolini was afraid that the Yugoslavs might attack him. Gazzera calmed him down: they had cover and if they stayed awake a sudden attack could not succeed.[63]

The rise of Hitlerian Germany, the failure of the Geneva disarmament conference and the unstable situation in Austria combined to change Yugoslavia's attitude to Italy. Over a period of three months starting in September 1933, Belgrade put out a series of feelers to ascertain whether Rome was open to some kind of diplomatic accord. There were now strong reasons for Rome to respond. For one thing, Turkish moves in the Balkans threatened Italy's position and could best be checkmated by taking the Yugoslav piece off the board. For another, such an agreement would weaken France's hold on the region and over time empty the Franco–Yugoslav Treaty of all meaning. Finally, Pompeo Aloisi told Mussolini, it would give Italian foreign policy greater freedom by neutralising a Yugoslavia whose actions in respect of disarmament and the League of Nations had hitherto been negative.[64]

The danger of two-front war gradually lessened, and in early September Mussolini signalled that he was looking for a better relationship with Yugoslavia.[65] Three issues stood in the way of improved relations – Italy's support of expatriate Croats, her support for Austria, and a press war which caused Rome to stop a visit to Belgrade by an Italian parliamentary delegation and consider suspending relations with Yugoslavia. By late September, with Italy willing to retract some of its public criticisms and Yugoslavia eager to reach a 'press détente', the fuss died down.[66] The murder of Alexander I on 9 October 1934, in which SIM played a part, did not cause Yugoslavia to disintegrate as Mussolini expected, but neither did it lead Belgrade to change direction again and swing away from Rome. Instead, Belgrade focused on hunting for the guilty parties in Hungary.

The Yugoslav policy demonstrates that Mussolini's actions were not shaped only by his actual and preferred relations with the European great powers. Turkey was pursuing its own goals, which were not those of Italy. In March 1933 Ankara briefly raised the idea that the demilitarisation of the Straits might be ended – something which threatened to change the naval balance in the eastern Mediterranean to the disadvantage of Rome. Although she dropped it when no international support was forthcoming, it was plainly a state of affairs she did not intend to let go. It would be revived, angering Mussolini, three years later.[67] The Turkish attempt to build a Balkan pact incorporating Greece, Bulgaria, Romania and Yugoslavia was a more immediately serious matter. Italian diplomats first interpreted this as a move into France's orbit. Then

Mussolini perceived Turkish pressure on Bulgaria to join the pact as likely to drive her into the arms of Yugoslavia, creating a Slav bloc.[68] One of his motives in responding to Yugoslav feelers was to avoid such an outcome, a prospect he both detested and feared.

About Great Britain, the third party that was dancing in his European *quadrille*, Mussolini felt no great concern. In security terms only her navy had the power and reach to affect the continental balance of power in any significant way and it now appeared to view France as the main threat, declining to accept that the French had laid down the *Dunkerque* in response to the German naval programme. During 1932, in the process of building up the Home fleet, London cut back the Mediterranean fleet from six to five battleships (actually four because the *Royal Sovereign* was in dock at Portsmouth) and stripped it of an aircraft carrier and a flotilla of destroyers.[69] Economic constraints slowed the pace of her building schedules, considerably delaying the start of both her 1931 and 1932 programmes, and reductions in the 1933–4 budget cut back her cruiser programme from four to three.[70] In respect both of its size and its location, the Royal Navy looked less of a threat than it had been.

Diplomatically, Rome was increasingly in London's good books. Aloisi cemented a policy of presenting Italy as a reasonable and moderate member of the community of great powers, telling the British that France was trying to avoid the burden of responsibility for the impending failure of the Geneva conference by shifting the burden onto others.[71] Mussolini's subsequent 'annoyance and disgust' at Germany's exit from the League of Nations – which reflected no more than a temporary ill humour – went down well in London. So did his stand during the Dollfuss crisis.[72] By the end of 1934 it was clear that London's dislike of Mussolini's German policy had been overcome, that the British government wanted to exchange ideas with Rome and Paris about how to proceed in the face of German rearmament, and that it appeared to believe that the solution to the European problem lay more than ever in Italo–British collaboration.[73]

As 1934 ended, Mussolini faced increasing problems which both constrained and threatened to confine him – problems entirely related to the growth of German power and the possible reactions this might provoke. The threat to Austria, far from diminishing, appeared to have increased with the reported expansion in the number of German troops stationed on the Austrian frontier, although there was perhaps some comfort to be taken from the fact that the Reichswehr had apparently blocked an attempt by Goebbels to relaunch the annexation of Austria by triggering a coup while Europe was preoccupied with the Saar plebiscite in the coming January.[74] Alongside the signs that Germany might be looking for agreements with France and Great Britain there was the possibility that the Reich might use Poland to pressurise Hungary into closer links with Germany, draw Yugoslavia firmly into her orbit as she grew into a front rank military power, and also forge links with Bulgaria and Turkey.[75] A year earlier, Mussolini had regarded these states as four of the five 'cards' he held (the fifth was Greece) in the event of having to hold Germany in check.[76] However, the Duce's inclinations were always to use democracies but to align with Fascism's natural partner. Unsympathetic to the worries of anti-Germans such as Cerruti and Grandi, who were aware that Nazi Germany might become too big a problem to be controlled or managed at all, Mussolini characteristically saw a short-term opportunity in the flux of European politics in which he could use the military instrument created for him by his military chiefs to best advantage in pursuit of one of his long-term goals by a method he longed to use – force of arms.

The war machine

In the run-up to the annual session of the Commissione suprema di difesa scheduled for February 1933 all three services gave evidence of a serious concern as regarded the provision of raw materials. While Italy would need to import 2 million tons of iron in the first year of a war, Bonzani estimated that Germany, Austria and Switzerland could probably provide only 800,000 tons; the remainder would have to come from the United States and Great Britain under neutral flags or by very long sea journeys. Much the same problem existed as far as mineral oils were concerned: here roughly 2,600,000 tons could be imported from the USSR and Romania, leaving approximately 1,500,000 tons to be provided from the United States, Latin America, Persia and the Dutch East Indies under much the same constraints.[77]

The ministry of corporations suggested that cornering overseas deposits of petroleum, either in South America or Albania, would be costly and politically difficult and preferred to explore the possibilities of developing deposits in national territory. To make a somewhat dubious case politically agreeable it used the parallel of the 'battle for grain', arguing that only Fascism could develop 'an organic programme of research in our sub-soil'.[78] By the end of 1932, a five-year programme of domestic exploration was producing 26,786 tons of crude oil a year. This was, as the ministry elliptically admitted, a drop in the bucket. Nevertheless, it looked forward to producing a 'panoramic vision' of the availability of oil in which the sacrifices to be made would be fully justified 'because if there is petrol it must be found, and if there isn't we can at least say for certain that there is none'.[79] At a more practical level, with three oil cracking plants and five refineries Italy was able to produce 157,000 tons of refined oil in 1932, while importing a further 324,941 tons.[80] Stripped of their surrounding verbiage, these facts made Italy's fundamentally parlous position eminently clear.

The navy currently imported a million tons of oil a year from Batum, partly because of favourable financial terms and partly because of the relative proximity of Black Sea ports compared to Atlantic ports. Its storage tanks could hold 349,000 tons of fuel, a figure which was expected to increase to 752,000 tons by spring of 1934. This represented six months' wartime consumption, half the target storage capacity. Its immediate problem was to increase storage capacity, and its solution was to offer favourable terms to private companies building storage facilities on the coasts.[81] The air force, which at this time had no mobilisation stocks of fuel of its own, could only draw on 5,000 tons of fuel held by three private companies which was enough to last one week. To make matters worse, transportation difficulties meant that it would only reach the airfields on the fourth or fifth day of mobilisation. To remedy this entirely unsatisfactory situation, it planned to build five new fuel storage facilities so that by 1935 it would have 35,000 tons of fuel of its own, sufficient for forty days' fighting.[82]

The shortage of fuel was but one part of the much larger problem of Italy's heavy reliance on imports. As the navy pointed out, given that in war only 8,000,000 of the 22,000,000 tons which would be required could be brought in overland, Italy's capacity to resist would depend on the sea. It calculated that in wartime 33 per cent of imports would come via the Straits of Gibraltar (compared to 78 per cent in peacetime), while approximately 26 per cent arrived via the Suez canal and 41 per cent via the eastern Mediterranean and the Dardanelles. A heavy reliance was going to have to be placed on neutral ships to get past Gibraltar and through the western Mediterranean. Aware of the likelihood that an enemy would seek to cripple the Italian merchant fleet by slowing or preventing the departure of ships during a period of diplomatic tension so as to be able to seize them as soon as war broke out – a scenario Mussolini inexcusably ignored seven years later – the navy was already preparing instructions to be given to merchant skippers by local traffic officers in order 'to safeguard that precious naval commercial patrimony which for us constitutes one of the most indispensable means of struggle (*lotta*)'.[83] Working on slightly different proportions of imports, and passing so lightly over the problems as not to notice their existence at all, the ministry of communications pronounced that as far as railway and port capacity and merchant marine carrying capacity was concerned, 'the problem [of importation] is to be considered as solved in an affirmative sense'.[84]

The commission's discussions of the thirty-four items on its agenda in February 1933 were as usual brief and only superficially conclusive. Sirianni's recommendation that since naval construction works could not be moved from the more vulnerable north to the safer south of Italy they would have to be protected with anti-aircraft defences was solemnly accepted, as was Balbo's declaration that within two years no foreign aircraft would be in service with national civil airlines. The commission confirmed that the national production of explosives must be maintained and that a new establishment should be built in central Italy after Mussolini had declared the problem to be 'of fundamental importance', but left the various armed forces to work out any and all details.[85] The following year this decision was reversed. The commission spent a while considering anti-aircraft protection through the provision of warning sirens, shelters and trial exercises and the need for anti-incendiary measures, drawing from Balbo the interesting observation that the Aeronautica regarded anti-aircraft protection as central to defence against air attack and that he did not have faith 'either in anti-aircraft artillery or in fighters (*caccia*)'.[86]

Following Mussolini's lead the commission accepted that the situation had improved as far as petroleum was concerned, partly because of hopes of getting supplies from Albania and from national soil. Against Balbo's opposition to any foreign involvement, it was agreed that concessions would be given to foreign companies in areas which AGIP did not want to explore. During a discussion on the transportation of supplies in war, admiral count Costanzo Ciano, minister for communications, questioned the navy's assumption that losses could be held at ten per cent given that 18 per cent of ship-voyages in the world war had been lost, but after an exchange between him, Balbo, Badoglio and Sirianni the figure was confirmed. Apparently on the basis of no evidence whatever, an optimistic Duce opined that the figure of 22,000,000 tons of imports 'could today be considered notably reduced thanks to rationing and the productive potential of the country, and thanks to all the efforts which must combine to reduce imports to a minimum'.[87] Apparently annoyed by such genial views, or at least uneasy about them, Balbo said that he did not think that the Mediterranean would be navigable by surface traffic in war because of the action of the (presumably enemy) air force on traffic nodes. A major strategic debate threatened to blow up when Ciano flatly disagreed, but Mussolini immediately squashed it by concluding that the data must be kept up to date to give the responsible authorities the most up-to-date information on the problem.

During the 1933 session, the commission had established that the services needed to have sufficient fuel stocks to fight for six months. By the following year, the situation as far as fuel stocks were concerned had not significantly improved. While the navy had 574,610 tons of diesel and lubricants, enough to last for four months of fighting, the air force had two months' supply of petrol and oil (22,306 tons) and the army only three days' worth (3,105 tons).[88] Working to different figures, the army estimated its stocks by the coming spring as sufficient for fifteen days' fighting, during which time it would be possible to arrange for supplies from civil stocks. In all, the latter reserves were calculated at 120,000 tons, enough to meet the army's needs for three months.[89] Six months' fuel for the navy amounted to 750,000 tons, but it had only 350,000 tons of storage capacity and could build up to that capacity by the financial year 1936–7.[90]

Mussolini believed by 1934 that considerable progress had been made in many aspects of supply. Increases in production of wheat, maize, rice and potatoes meant that Italy was no longer prevented from being able to make war for want of sufficient bread. Lack of iron was no longer so much of a handicap because of the presence of deposits at Cogne and elsewhere and because iron was giving way to other metals. As far as oil was concerned, Italy would know within five years whether it had its own reserves and in the meantime Albania and Iraq would produce supplies, and Romanian production was increasing. Coal was the most difficult problem because Italy's own supply was limited and the main source had a relatively high sulphur content. Given that coal was a main means of resolving trade balances, he wondered whether the navy could use the 'smoky' Turkish coal or Polish coal. Cavagnari was certain that it could.[91]

Like the western democracies, Italy was growing increasingly sensitive to the threat posed by air power. Asked by Valle whether he believed in the efficacy of anti-aircraft fire by machine guns and cannon, Baistrocchi replied with what was by now the army's stock response. Aeroplanes alone were not sufficient defence as Italy would need an immense air fleet able to intervene everywhere at any moment. Anti-aircraft fire would not hit every plane, but would force attackers to fly high and thus make their bombing less accurate. Given the dangers of chemical war in particular, the population must be educated, prepared and helped to protect itself as far as possible. As was often his wont, Mussolini bestrode the incipient argument between Valle and Baistrocchi by backing both sides, declaring that 'the best protection is our air force' but simultaneously acknowledging the value of cannon, machine-guns and organised protection. Baistrocchi suggested a new provincial authority to co-ordinate air protection, but Badoglio countered that it would be enough to nominate a general who would go on periodic inspections and make sure things were being done properly, an idea Mussolini liked. Bonzani thought that because of lack of funds all that could be done for the moment was to engage in some propaganda work since the public did not really believe there was an air threat.[92]

After announcing the fact that the air force would during the course of the current year switch from five different types of aviation fuel to a single type thanks to the use of lead tetraethyl – currently made in America – Valle unveiled an ingenious scheme for maintaining stocks. Three new fuel storage facilities were being built during the course of the year, but since the budget did not allow the maintenance of the volume of fuel needed for three months' fighting commercial companies would revolve stocks through them and make them available to the air force if needed.[93]

As far as the shipping of wartime supplies was concerned, Cavagnari painted a picture of a weekly flow of two dozen Italian ships to and from Black Sea ports, half-a-dozen between national ports and from the Indian Ocean, and four or five neutral ships coming from England and America via Gibraltar. The key to protection of traffic in the eastern Mediterranean was Tripoli, which must be held or Italian traffic would become precarious. The navy's interest in Kisimaio and the Indian Ocean was briefly mentioned. Evidently unwilling to disregard what were unpleasant facts, Cavagnari pointed out that plans for wartime supply revolved to a considerable degree around purchases from Romania which formed part of the group of states hostile to Italy. To carry the imports Italy had 123,000 railway wagons and 1,274 merchant ships which Ciano thought sufficient, though she would need to hire 29 tankers.[94]

The Commissione suprema now no longer discussed details of rearmament plans and weapons programmes of the three services – indeed, Cavagnari did not mention the likelihood that Italy was about to embark on a capital ship programme in 1934, the first since the world war. Nor did it now deal with fundamental questions of air defence, as these had been resolved by 1932. New on the agenda were the complex issues of the control of imports and consumption and of wartime supply, which was ongoing, and of the transport of supplies in wartime, a problem which the sessions of 1933 and 1934 were held to suggest was technically solvable.[95] The commission was also now occupying itself with the problems of fossil fuel supplies. Issues of maximising use, economising and the use of national substitute fuels pointed to the extent of the problems but did not yet offer much more than optimistic aspirations that it might be solved. One example of the lengths to which the regime felt compelled to go was that of lubricants; after the air force had begun using castor oil as an economy measure its use was extended to other motors and by 1934 the problems it presented (which included unpleasant-smelling exhaust gases) were reported to have been solved. The air force was by now also experimenting with a lubricant mixture of castor oil and olive oil.[96]

The pattern of discussions in the commission suggest that it – and therefore Mussolini who controlled it – believed that much of the work necessary to organise the state for war had now been done. A wartime 'core staff' (*ufficio nucleo*) system and co-ordinating bodies had been set up for a wide variety of activities including the control of foodstuffs, labour and fuel, propaganda, and anti-aircraft protection. By 1933 all the ministries of state had completed their individual designs for war mobilisation. In that year also 5,200 draft production orders had been prepared which would be converted into actual orders for industry on the outbreak of war.[97] From a bureaucratic point of view, the commission could appear to have carried out the labours of Hercules: vast amounts of statistical information had been gathered and inventories prepared, new structures had been created on paper and sheaves of regulations printed. However, behind this façade there were serious structural problems which threatened to debilitate any war effort. The commission's enquiries had highlighted but had not really been able to resolve the fundamental problem of the lack of natural resources. Nor had it done anything to resolve the strategic conflicts within and between the armed services beyond making *obiter dicta* pronouncements about where authority lay in one or two of the contested areas. Taken together, the nature of its discussions and the outcome of its labours leave the impression that in directing its activities Mussolini was not doing much more than building a Potemkin village made of paper.

Army plans and organisation

Under Pietro Gazzera's direction, the Italian army was developed and consolidated along traditional Piedmontese lines, modified by the experience of the world war. In April 1932 he defended it against general Federico Baistrocchi, whom Mussolini would select as deputy war minister when he personally took over the reins fifteen months later, on the grounds that it conformed to 'the geographical reality of Italy with respect to her frontiers, the shape (*forma*) of her territory and the distribution of the population', and to national finances. As evidence of its 'plasticity' and 'elasticity', he cited its having absorbed changes in the organisation of the cavalry, the introduction of celeri units and a new division of troops between the Po valley and the rest of Italy 'without losing its

Table 4.1   *Italian and French army budgets 1926–34*

Italy	lire	France	lire
1926–7	2,093,348,746	1926	3,272,312,000
1927–8	2,078,209,045	1927	3,806,159,100
1928–9	1,997,628,000	1928	4,522,925,100
1929–30	2,060,478,045	1929	4,309,425,000
1930–1	2,181,936,015	1930–1	4,708,875,000
1931–2	2,307,715,554	1931–2	4,800,760,500
1932–3	2,320,870,547	1932–3	4,081,121,100
1933–4	2,009,367,747	1933–4	4,543,703,100

characteristic physiognomy'.[98] This was the stance of a conservative, and probably also a calculated staking-out of that position against reformists such as Grazioli and Canevari who were arguing for an offensive army resting on quality and not a defensive one founded on quantity. While it suited Mussolini to leave the army in the hands of an incremental reformer for the moment, the question which hung over it was whether it could – and would – do what he decided was necessary when the moment came.

Despite his successes in winning extra money, Gazzera presided over an army which was steadily losing ground to its Latin neighbour. France had reduced its term of conscript service to twelve months in 1928, and a core of 178,306 career soldiers and non-commissioned officers – of whom there were 67,038 as compared with Italy's 13,550 – increased her costs marginally, as did the higher salaries she paid her officer corps.[99] Nevertheless, the annual budgets told their own story.[100]

Things were worse even than the raw figures suggested. Both countries actually spent more each year than the budgeted sums, but French spending was proportionally greater than Italy's. Colonial military expenditure (a separate budget heading) was an overall drain on Italy's budget and her expenditure overseas was greater than France's in each of these years save for 1931–2 and 1933–4, taking resources from the army at home. Finally, France spent almost four times as much as Italy on weapons, materiel and fortifications between 1926 and 1931/2.[101]

For the time being, the army had to meet the not-inconsiderable demands of a defensive–offensive one- or two-front war on Italy's frontiers. By the beginning of 1932, the army calculated that it would have thirty-four mobilisable divisions plus supporting troops to put into the field against twenty-seven Yugoslav divisions. The need to guard the western frontier, the mainland coasts and the islands would leave only fourteen Italian divisions on the Julian alps to face a Yugoslav army which, because of similar needs to protect the Albanian, Bulgarian and Hungarian frontiers, would amount to sixteen divisions there. Once again, the balance of forces was in fact worse than these bald figures suggested: in all 190 Italian divisions would face 261 Yugoslav divisions which were larger than their Italian equivalents. The Italian army planned a limited offensive during the opening stage of a campaign in preparation for enemy counter-offensives, and then an attack on the enemy main line which was forecast to be along the line of the Littai river. Action would begin on the tenth day of mobilisation, with the main forces starting off three days later. In the second phase of the operation, assuming that France and the Little Entente remained strictly neutral, nine divisions initially guarding the west and the islands and six new divisions would be available for the attack on the Littai towards Zagabria. The aim was to raise Croatia and aid Hungary who would probably take the field. Supporting operations would be launched from Dalmatia and Albania across Croatia, Bosnia (which was too mountainous for much to be done) and towards the Aegean.

Of the three preconditions essential for success, naval and maritime superiority were more or less secure, though there was no guarantee that enough shipping would be available to transport three divisions across the Adriatic for operations in Albania or Dalmatia. The third precondition, superiority of force on the common frontier, could not be guaranteed in the opening stage and was unpredictable thereafter since all would depend on how the first phase developed. The scenario was far from promising, and an evident undertone of pessimism was reinforced with the observation that Italian bombing was likely to have little effect on enemy population centres and that both sides' capacity to bomb each other's communications was likely to balance out.[102]

Military planning still offered little more than a reasonable prospect of defending Italy in the event of war and a half-hearted and incomplete sketch of how to deploy available force if offensive action was required. This was not much use to Mussolini when the Franco–Yugoslav treaty was renewed in October 1932. Tension mounted during the following five months both with Yugoslavia because of military measures on the frontier and with France. Mussolini became alarmed at news of Yugoslav troops movements along the frontier at the end of November, but was temporarily quietened by Gazzera's response that there was nothing to worry about at any point along it. At the beginning of January 1933, believing that Yugoslavia had lost its equilibrium and that Alexander I wanted a war with Italy win or lose, Mussolini asked Gazzera if he thought Yugoslavia would launch a war during the year. The war minister thought not.

[MUSSOLINI]: Why not?
[GAZZERA]: Because she is not ready.
[MUSSOLINI]: Then why do we wait?
[GAZZERA]: Because we shall gain more than she will. But above all we [should] fear the intervention of France, either at once or when we are deeply committed. France could give us a lesson which will last us half a century. If we have to fight Yugoslavia, it must be as part of a general action with France distracted by Germany, etc.[103]

Reporting on the state of the army at the start of 1933, Gazzera found little or nothing in the way of solid external support for Italy if war came. Hungarian co-operation should be more precisely defined through the conclusion of a precise military convention, and the benevolent neutrality of Greece, Turkey and the USSR would be helpful in the provision of supplies, but otherwise there was no real sign of any power coming to Italy's aid by offering distractions elsewhere. For the first time, Gazzera was concerned that the enemy might open hostilities before Italy did. There were those, he told Mussolini, 'who assert that France believes that it would be an easy task to gain the Po valley and thinks to employ her superabundance of forces in operations against Tripolitania and our main islands'.[104] French railway, road and fortification building were seen as clear evidence of an intention not only to halt any Italian advance but to support an attack across the frontier by French troops covering it. There were likewise signs such as the transformation of infantry regiments into mountain troops and the establishment of magazines near the frontier indicating that the Yugoslavs had modified their previous defensive stance in the event of war and now intended to take Fiume and advance towards Postumia and Trieste.

Against France's sixty-one metropolitan and thirteen North African infantry divisions, and Yugoslavia's thirty-three divisions, Italy could mobilise thirty-seven infantry divisions plus assorted celeri, alpini, bersaglieri and other troops, rising to forty divisions in six months' time. In all, 485 Italian battalions and 858 mobile batteries would face 1,276 French and Yugoslav battalions and 4,270 mobile batteries, slightly better odds than the previous year.[105] French covering units could deploy faster than the Italians, but Italian units could just beat Yugoslav ones. The disproportion between the two sides did not allow 'the formulation of daring plans which could logically lead to a rapid decision of the conflict'.[106] Accordingly, Gazzera did not offer Mussolini any – which would have been entirely out of character – or indeed refer to military plans at all. Instead, he moved into political territory to argue that the forthcoming Geneva disarmament conference must not consolidate Italy's numerical inferiority in relation to France and Yugoslavia, but must disarm France and the Little Entente as much as possible – 'their strength is above all material, our possibilities lie rather in manpower'. Finally, he pointed out the convenience, from the military point of view, of arming Germany, Hungary, Bulgaria and Austria, or allowing them to arm. An armed Germany could become dangerous for us as a result; for now it seems useful to us.[107]

Gazzera put forward a very positive picture of the army's state of being, but there were grounds for Mussolini to conclude that things were not going as he might want. A higher priority was being put on defence than on offence: 'once the doors are closed to prevent surprise', then the war minister allowed 'it is good to dedicate the available monies to increasing the offensive efficiency of the mobile army'.[108] Armoured brigades and divisions on the English model were low on the list of priorities because of terrain and budgetary limitations; though the problem of motorisation was being studied 'with real passion', it was the obstacles that were stressed and not the possibilities; 200 fast Ansaldo tanks had been ordered but no 9–10-ton tanks had yet been produced because of construction difficulties.[109] Complaining directly about the 140,000,000 lire cut Mussolini intended to apply to the army's budget in 1933–4 and asking not merely for its restoration but for an additional 210,000,000 lire, Gazzera pointed out that it had done something by way of quantitative improvement but emphasised how much remained to be done in respect to qualitative strength. The structure emplaced in the Ordinamento Mussolini of 1926 was susceptible to modest evolutionary change but not to 'radical transformations which would put the army back into a period of crisis from which it is only now emerging after the armistice'.[110] The reference to the Grazioli case, which obviously still rankled, was barely concealed at all.

Gazzera had reported to Mussolini that 141 fortifications were under construction on the western border and 87 on the eastern border, but that more would be necessary to add depth to the system. The army, acting according to a long-established inclination, put a priority on defensive operations primarily in order to neutralise an enemy's quantitative or qualitative superiority and to gain the time needed to put Italy's war potential into effect. However, lack of money meant that only the principal invasion routes had been fortified and then only with small and cheap works, leaving the main burden to be shouldered by mobile troops taking advantage of the mountainous terrain with the aid of field works which had yet to be constructed. In the circumstances, the main goal of neutralising enemy power could not be achieved yet; all that would be possible in the immediate future would be to hold the frontiers long enough to cover the mobilisation and deployment of the army. Given the value and importance of Piedmont and Liguria, and the narrow depth of the Alpine chain, the western frontier must be held on the watershed, and the northern frontier likewise. The eastern frontier, partly because of extensive afforestation, lacked positions of evident tactical value and so would be held by an elastic defence consisting of strong road barriers backed by a second line of defences designed to assist the manoeuvre of mobile troops. The technical solution derived from the experience of the great war, which had shown the value of the machine-gun in stopping and breaking up attacks; networks of small, heavily protected and mutually supporting posts would be set up, along with anti-tank defences in the few parts of the frontier zones suitable for tanks.[111]

In July 1933, Mussolini decided to sack Gazzera and take over the reins of the war ministry himself. Although Gazzera's spectacular ascent through the higher reaches of the Annuario Militare, which had seen him rise from a major-general in thirty-fifth place in 1930 to fifth-placed general designated to command an army in 1934, doubtless created professional jealousies his removal was a reflection of Mussolini's complicated foreign policy designs which now included the intention to fight a war against Abyssinia in1935, and the possibility of war against Yugoslavia and France to which both Gazzera and Bonzani were opposed.

General Federico Baistrocchi, nicknamed 'Frederick the mad', whom Mussolini chose as his under-secretary of war and to whom he gave the same prerogatives previously enjoyed by Gazzera, was made of quite different mettle. On entering the War Ministry, he reportedly announced 'Fascism enters here with me.'[112] Evidence that the Fascistisation of the army was now about to occur was not long in coming. In August 1933 Baistrocchi issued a circular ordering that the Fascist hymn 'Giovinezza' be played at military ceremonies after the Royal March, and immediately afterwards he permitted officers to join the Fascist party, something that Gazzera had resisted and Mussolini had forbidden since April 1930.

Thanks to the open pronouncements of Goering and others about anschluss Mussolini was well aware of Nazi Germany's designs on Austria, and under Baistrocchi the army soon set about preparing for that unwelcome contingency. On 9 October 1933, he ordered Bonzani to prepare plans to send an army corps into Austria to act alongside Austrian forces to prevent anschluss and maintain public order. By the end of November, the army had a plan to use the Verona and Bologna army corps to protect its own territory against infiltration by Austrian expatriates, to repress irredentist riots and to collaborate with regular Austrian troops in maintaining public order in the Tyrol and Carinthia while other powers did likewise in provinces bordering on their own territory.[113] Reporting the following February, the chief of army general staff pointed out that the plan explicitly excluded Italy alone working with Austria and pointed to the desirability of the Czechs occupying the Passau-Salzburg area of Lower Austria. While Yugoslav intervention was not indispensable it could be useful to have their intervention in the Graz basin, though it would be necessary to clarify their intentions 'so as not to be surprised on the Giulian frontier'. To occupy the Tyrol and Carinthia, and the zone either side of the Klagenfurt–Vienna railway which Bonzani deemed essential, more forces would be required than were stipulated in Plan 34, but since France would not be a putative enemy this did not present any problems.[114] What did present potential problems was the speed with which planning for a war against Abyssinia was gathering pace. It would be very imprudent, Bonzani believed, to strip divisions away from the northern frontier because even if Europe were peaceful at the start of operations in Eritrea nothing guaranteed that this situation would last more than a few weeks. 'Look at the outbreak of the great war and the consequences for Italy of the Libyan war [of 1911–12], which was begun in peaceful circumstances,' he warned Badoglio.[115]

In passing, Bonzani remarked that Switzerland did not seem uninterested in the situation that would arise were other states to intervene in Austria and appeared to want to add the canton of Vorarlberg to the Swiss Confederation. SIM believed that Switzerland had made little military progress during 1933, aware of the incapacity of its forces to undertake the defensive duties required of them but having done no more than draw up preliminary studies for reform.[116] In its view Switzerland was decidedly more of a defensive cast of mind, fearing that the suppression of the social-democrat riots in Austria in the spring would push unwanted elements including Nazis across its frontier, and also that the possible collapse of the Dollfuss government might provoke the armed intervention of neighbouring powers. As far as actively intervening itself in Austria was concerned, military intelligence suggested that Switzerland believed it had neither the 'legal, material or spiritual' basis for such action.[117] There was thus nothing other than a highly tuned sensitivity to 'worst case' scenarios to justify Bonzani's fears. Indeed, at the time of Dollfuss's assassination the Swiss army was preoccupied with the need to build defensive fortifications along the Rhine frontier and the Jura and around Schaffhausen, Basle and Geneva in order better to prepare itself for a world war which, according to one respected military writer, was possible during the current year and probable during the coming one.[118]

Looking further into the military dimensions of a possible anschluss, the general staff considered the possibilities of Italian offensives against Munich and Vienna in the event of war against Germany and Austria. Both scenarios were premised on an alliance with France; the former would require France to cross the Rhine while Yugoslavia and Switzerland stayed neutral, the latter merely that France enter a war while Czechoslovakia remained neutral and Yugoslavia and Hungary maintained benevolent neutrality. Without some certainty as to the latter, an Italian advance on Vienna would risk catastrophe if the two states 'believed to be neutral, were to reveal themselves as enemies when our army was close to reaching its objective'.[119] The terrain was more difficult, and the weather posed more problems, in moving against Munich than against Vienna, as did the local population. Politically, the capture of Munich was not likely of itself to produce the separation of Austria from Germany: aside from the fact that Hitler's centrist tendencies would make it unlikely that Bavaria would be allowed to split off from the Reich, an attack would have to reach Regensburg to stand a chance of securing this, and that would be moving in a different direction from a French attack in the north-east towards Wurzburg. Vienna, although possessing great moral importance, was of little military significance and to reach it would involve a dangerous flank march to push out into a void.[120] On the eve of the Austrian crisis, the army was effectively ruling out a war to defend Austria as politically complicated and practically infeasible.

By the beginning of March, SIM was reporting that the danger of a destabilised Austria, resulting initially from social democratic challenge to the government which could then trigger an intervention by Austrian Nazis from Bavaria backed by the German National Socialist Party, seemed to be diminishing and that the German authorities had given orders to prevent any such move.[121] The movement of Yugoslav forces from Zagreb to Maribor indicated that an Italian move into Austria would trigger a similar Yugoslav move, and an admittedly suspect (because Yugoslavian) source suggested that if Italy moved then Prague would send in a full army corps in order to resist either a restoration of the monarchy or a move by Hitler.[122] The seriousness of the crisis, and the fact that the Germans were reportedly in Cortina d'Ampezzo gathering intelligence, led Bonzani to call the corps and divisional commanders together on 2 March to clarify details of Plan 34 and recommend reconnaissance over the frontier.[123] The Austrian situation was the more unsettling for Italy because in the Austrian Tyrol the Heimwehr and the national socialists were reported to be encouraging hostility to Italy as much as to the Dollfuss cabinet.[124]

In April, as king Alexander was swinging from a pro-French to a pro-German line and to favouring the anschluss, SIM got wind of the discussions which would lead to the signing of the Yugoslav–German commercial treaty on 1 June. This probably made it easier to believe Austrian intelligence that Berlin and Belgrade were discussing a share-out of territory after anschluss, with Yugoslavia receiving Klagenfurt and Fiume in return for ceding Germany an access corridor to Trieste.[125] Since Plan K envisaged emplacing an Italian division in Klagenfurt, Bonzani foresaw 'a convergence and perhaps a conflict of interest' there.[126] Early in May SIM reported rumours that the German National Socialists intended to try a coup de force against Vienna, using the Austrian Legion in Bavaria as its instrument and triggering pseudo-communist riots in order to force the dispersal of the Austrian army.[127]

The fact that Hitler's first meeting with Mussolini in Venice in June 1934 went badly was unsettling, the assassination of chancellor Dollfuss the following month much more so. Mussolini at once moved troops to the frontier. The immediate danger soon passed, with reassuring reports that the Austrians were repressing Nazis in Styria and east Tyrol, that Hitler had flown to the frontier near Salzburg to prevent attempts by Austrian Nazis to cross the frontier, and that there were no untoward troop movements on the Yugoslav or Czech frontiers. By the start of August the situation was progressively returning to normal.[128] Nevertheless, orders were issued that if Italian troops crossed the Austrian frontier under the terms of Plan K and if they came into contact with Czech or Yugoslav troops, they were to consider them friendly as long as they were not subject to hostile action or obliged to act differently.[129] Although the movement of Italian troops to the frontier had apparently helped to maintain Austria's independent status, in other respects it did not help: in the predominantly Nazi province of Carinthia, and also in the Tyrol, Italy's military measures increased local antipathies towards her.[130]

Although the immediate threat to Austria had blown over, the danger was obviously not past. Plan 34 was updated in November 1934 – as Plan 'Z' – with minor variations: as well as possibly operating in Carinthia, the Bologna army corps was now ordered to prepare for employment at Salzburg or Vienna. As before, the scenario was intervention on behalf of an Austrian government which might well have declared a state of siege, and the emphasis was on acting with speed and decisiveness. No mention was made of the political circumstances in which the operation might or should take place.[131] The plan was reissued in May 1935, and was still 'live' eleven months later.

Preoccupied with the Austrian problem for much of the year, the general staff made only limited progress as far as planning for a war against France and Yugoslavia was concerned. Abandoning any thoughts of taking the offensive, the planners now proposed an initial defensive on both fronts which would force the enemy to fight a *guerra stabilizzata* on ground chosen by Italy. The French were expected to launch particularly aggressive offensives, possibly supported by mechanised units, along the Upper Tanaro, Dora and Chisone rivers, across the rest of the land frontier and along the Ligurian coast. They might also violate Swiss neutrality to make use of the Great St Bernard Pass. A detailed list of locations which Italian troops must occupy to provide defensive cover to meet this threat was duly drawn up.[132] How the Little Entente might act in the event of such a war was something of an unknown quantity. German sources had suggested the previous year that the Czechs would hold the bulk of their troops along the Austrian frontier for use against the Germans if necessary, the Romanians would concentrate on the Russian threat, and the Yugoslavs would stand on the defensive in both cases and would not attack beyond their frontiers because of their economic and financial situation.[133] Now the planners expected a Yugoslav attack directed on Nauporto with a possible secondary attack through Austria aiming at Tarvisio. As before, a list of positions to be held was provided, along with the injunction to undertake small operations beyond the frontier where this would produce economies of defence. While defensive, the stance should be aggressive and not passive, with attacks between and beyond the framework of defences so as to keep the enemy in a state of constant alarm.[134]

Badoglio held no meetings of the chiefs of staff at all during 1932 or 1933, so that it was not until early September 1934, after three meetings devoted to the plans for the impending operation in Abyssinia, that the high command again turned its collective attention to European war plans. By now a new dimension had entered into the politics of defence planning – the possibility of German intervention in Austria leading to war. Mussolini regarded the European situation as 'so uncertain' as a result of recent events there that he instructed the three service ministries early in August to keep the armed forces on a state of alert 'in case they are called upon to respond to sudden crises'. They were also told to clamp down on any idle talk about 'our aggressive intentions in Abyssinia'.[135]

Badoglio shared his master's immediate concerns. He thought that the Austrian question was the pivot both of Hitler's existence and of Italian policy, and believed that 'given the German character the question is moving inevitably towards a solution by force of arms'.[136] Because Yugoslavia was shifting her orientation from France to Germany, it was now necessary to consider military action both in the north and in the east. There was no need to worry about France or England, Mussolini had told him: France would be with Italy, England favourably neutral. Badoglio's instruction to the army to continue normal surveillance of France and Switzerland and swing all forces to the north and east presented Baistrocchi with no problems since, he declared, he had studied the problem from his first day in office. He had already issued orders for a possible mobilisation and could replicate the situation of the previous July in three days. Baistrocchi was optimistic that troops could be moved towards the Austrian frontier during the winter so as to remove the sensation of a void there before the spring. In a fluid and necessarily somewhat superficial discussion in which almost everything was uncertain, even the degree of urgency which Mussolini felt should govern preparations, Badoglio suggested that Italy was not likely again to have a nine-month period in which to mobilise as she had in 1914–15.

By the time the military authorities next met, on 17 November, Badoglio had clearer political directions from Mussolini. The crucial moment for European peace would come on 13 January 1935, the date of the Saar plebiscite. The internal situation in Germany could lead the people to some desperate act 'notwithstanding the pacifist ideas of Hitler'. Plans must therefore be ready by 1 January 1935. The 'northern problem' could absorb all available Italian strength, so that although study should continue respecting the sending of Italian troops to Albania and the islands around Zara actual operations would depend on circumstances. As far as the eastern front was concerned, a dozen divisions would be allocated to fend off a possible Yugoslav attack. To reduce the immense uncertainties – 'today one cannot say where things will end up' – Badoglio had already asked Mussolini for a military convention with France according to which each army would have its own commander and operate on its own territory, France aiming at Berlin and Italy at Munich.[137] A shared sense of the German threat – though in Rome's case a temporary one – would be one of the considerations underpinning the agreement between Mussolini and Laval in January 1935.

Under instructions from Mussolini to bring the army to the maximum possible level of efficiency by the following spring, Baistrocchi listed the progress that had been made and outlined what still needed to be done. The eastern frontier defences, which were being intensively worked on under 'directives sent <u>by me</u> personally and checked on the spot', had to be completed, as did the necessary road works; more infantry weapons, including assault tanks and anti-tank guns for close-support action, anti-aircraft guns, munitions and chemical materials were needed; and the motorised celeri divisions 'which allow us to give to a war, <u>right at the outset</u>, the rapid character which can assure us of immediate successes' had to be properly constituted. Securing the most active co-operation between army and air force was also on the agenda; while the army's own squadrons were 'working intensively' to improve air-ground collaboration, the province of the armata aerea was 'to facilitate the rapid and effective intervention of the army by means of heavy, sudden and well co-ordinated advance action'. As will be seen, this was not quite the way the Regia Aeronautica viewed things. All of this needed more money since the extraordinary funds secured by Gazzera in 1929 were already over-committed. Accordingly Baistrocchi asked for a two-year 'exceptional provision' for 1934-6 'like that for Eritrea'.[138] All this went to confirm the fact that if Mussolini could afford to fight a war at all, he could only afford one war at a time.

Naval armaments and intentions

In 1931–2, the 15,000 tons allocated to new naval build had gone chiefly to build two new 6,700-ton cruisers (*Eugenio di Savoia* and *Emanuele Filiberto Duca d'Aosta*) In 1932, presenting a budget of identical cost (1,574,923,277 lire), admiral Sirianni admitted to the chamber of deputies that the navy was not yet an organic entity – though it soon would be. Its 'intense spiritual life and profound and intimate adhesion to the common ideals', which were 'the spontaneous gift of the [Fascist] Regime' were, he assured his audience, the chief source of its strength.[139] Whether he would have maintained in private, as he did in the chamber, that collaboration between the navy and the air force had developed widely may perhaps be doubted. Certainly its members were left in no doubt that wide-ranging and intense naval exercises were testing and improving every part of the navy, though the details were left rather vague. Rather more detail was forthcoming on the performance of the four new 5,000-ton *Condottieri* class cruisers, two of which had carried out 4,000-mile cruises at average speeds of twenty and twenty-five knots. Three 10,000-ton *Zara*-class cruisers would be in service by the end of the year with a fourth on the way, along with a *Trento*-class cruiser and a couple more *Condottieri*-class cruisers. Sirianni's philosophical credo that the navy's essential task was to adapt machines to men's will and not vice versa, and that 'our power comes not from mechanising man but from spiritualising machines' no doubt went down well with the Fascist chamber and at the Palazzo Venezia.[140]

The naval programme of 1932–3 allocated 29,000 tons to new build which was used to build two new cruisers (*Giuseppe Garibaldi* and *Duca degli Abruzzi*) and two 600-ton torpedo boats. In 1933, the navy faced a reduction in its budget for the coming year of 180,000,000 lire, more than two thirds of which was due to come off the allocation for new construction. For ten years the navy had focused on renewing outdated mobile naval forces, unable through shortage of funds to solve the problem of bases as well. The new navy was, Sirianni acknowledged, different from

Table 4.2 *Italian and French naval budgets 1926–34*

Italy	lire	France	lire
1926–7	1,131,385,130	1926	1,074,754,500
1927–8	1,133,360,000	1927	1,344,150,000
1928–9	1,065,712,000	1928	1,838,400,000
1929–30	1,116,363,630	1929	1,863,975,000
1930–1	1,335,396,000	1930–1	2,042,025,000
1931–2	1,430,802,800	1931–2	2,099,872,736
1932–3	1,435,873,277	1932	1,830,947,700
1933–4	1,258,122,277	1933	2,037,376,188

its pre-war predecessor in that it was designed to operate at higher speeds and was mainly composed of cruisers, destroyers and lighter surface craft. The stress which he laid on the potential of torpedoes, the upsetting effect of technological surprise and the place of the submarine which, despite its vulnerability to high speed action, repressive means and acoustic detection, was still difficult to locate and able to act in unforeseen ways gave clear indications of both the concerns and the orientation of the navy.[141]

By this time, the navy was getting substantial amounts of comparative data from the proceedings of the international disarmament conference at Geneva. They did not make for comforting reading. In 1933, the Italian navy recorded a global tonnage of 404,005 and the French a global figure of 628,603 tons at respective costs of 1,427,431,338 lire and 2,240,000,000 lire.[142] The average cost per ton was therefore 3,534 lire and 3,563 lire respectively. Despite the fact that almost half French shipbuilding was done in the five government arsenals whereas Italy, which had only two, employed private companies to do most of her work, Italy was therefore holding her own with her rival in this respect. However, although the Italian navy was getting more or less as much for its money overall budgeted expenditure in recent years was rather less comforting.[143]

In November 1933, the new chief of the naval staff put forward a plan to spend the 855,000,000 lire he expected to have for new build up to July 1938. Some 300 million lire would have to be set aside either for modernising the old battleships *Doria* and *Duilio* or as the basis for funding new battleships if that problem had to be confronted. As well as lacking battleships, the navy also lacked enough ships to carry out traffic escort duties; accordingly Cavagnari proposed building eight more 600-ton escorts to add to four already under construction. Since they would have to act 'intensively' in the eastern Mediterranean, 'less actively'

in the central Mediterranean and only 'intermittently' in the western
Mediterranean anti-aircraft guns were not necessary for their defence and
machine-guns would suffice.[144] Cavagnari's programme was designed to
meet three different objectives, deriving largely from the fact that the
enemy controlled or threatened most of the coastline around the western
Mediterranean but only Syria in the eastern Mediterranean:

> The objective we must therefore seek to realise in the western Mediterranean is
> to challenge the enemy's mastery (*dominio*) of the surface of the sea, while in the
> central Mediterranean we must exercise a continuous and active surveillance and
> in the eastern Mediterranean we defend as intensively as possible the traffic lanes
> which run there.[145]

The latter activity, though less brilliant, was the more rewarding,
Cavagnari thought. Avoiding 'the mirage of a naval battle whose consequences, if they went against us, could be decisively damaging to us', the
navy would engage in occasional night-time incursions into the western
Mediterranean by light cruisers and destroyers to attack enemy lines of
communication north of the Balearics, leaving continuous action against
them to submarines and aircraft.

As well as meeting this need, Cavagnari calculated that he would have to
face thirty-one fast French destroyer-leaders of the *Jaguar* and *Mogador*
classes which would attack Italian traffic and seek to draw defending
ships onto its main fleet units. The *Condottieri* were not fast enough to
match them, and not enough were available. From this scenario, the rest
of Cavagnari's programme emerged: another 8,000 ton cruiser of the
Garibaldi class, four 40-knot 3,000-ton destroyer leaders, three mine-
laying submarines – the naval staff dismissed using long-range submarines
in the Atlantic to attack enemy traffic from Senegal, Morocco and ports
in western France as 'diversionary action from which we could not expect
decisive results' – and half-a-dozen MAS boats.[146]

Although the French navy appeared to be concentrating on building
light surface craft, the possibility that it might build a new battleship had
been noted in the summer of 1930. Then, at the end of 1932, France
announced the decision to build the 26,500-ton battleship *Dunkerque* to
match the three 10,000-ton *Deutschland*-class German pocket battleships
started between 1928 and 1932. At that moment it seemed unnecessary to
do more than modernise the four old Italian battleships, given the uncertainties surrounding the forthcoming 1935 naval conference and the
apparent unlikelihood that France would build another *Dunkerque*-class
ship. However, the matter suddenly became urgent during the autumn of
1933 when France faced the prospect of four *Deutschland*-class German
battleships, three of which would be at sea by 1935.[147] On 2 March

1934, the French naval attaché in Rome formally informed admiral Cavagnari, under-secretary for the navy, that France intended to lay down a second *Dunkerque*-class battleship which would be completed in 1937, a year after its predecessor. The new build planned for 1934 (31,450 tons) would equal the total build voted between 1924 and 1932. Cavagnari was suspicious of the ostensible justification for the new ship, explained as a response to the four *Deutschland* class German ships, which he thought had an unnecessary margin of size and gun power over its putative rival.[148]

In considering how to react to this move, the navy noted that the French move had blocked the British wish to agree a 25,000-ton battleship limit at the next international conference in 1935 and that the United States had never agreed to go below limits of 30,000-tons displacement and 356-mm guns. Everyone was now building up to the agreed limits 'inspired by a complete scepticism about attaining a reduction in naval forces'. Even by following suit, the calculations showed that Italy would go through a very dangerous period of marked inferiority before things improved. During 1936 and 1937 she would face a rival who would possess nine and then eight remodernised battleships and one and then two new ones against which she could only deploy two old and two remodernising battleships of her own. The odds would improve slightly in 1938 when five modernised and two modern French battleships would face two unmodernised, two modernised and one modern Italian equivalents. In 1939 the odds would get better yet when France would have four modernised and four modern battleships to Italy's two unmodernised, two modernised and two modern ships.[149] All this arithmetic presupposed that there would be no departures from the international schedules laid down in 1922.

Not only was there an obvious strategic need to balance French construction, but politically it seemed to the Italian authorities that doing this ought not to trigger a dangerous reaction. This calculation appears to have been based partly on the fact that while Italy guaranteed France's frontiers under the Locarno Pact she had no reciprocal French guarantee against a German attack, and partly on the presumption that no one would query that right was on her side in the form of the provisions of the Washington Treaty.[150] Under the Washington 'tariff' Italy undoubtedly had room to build: if she were to remodernise all four of her older battleships and build two new 35,000 ton warships she would still be 18,468 tons under the agreed limit. In this optimal scenario, all six warships would be in service by 1939.[151]

Admiral Domenico Cavagnari, appointed under-secretary of state by Mussolini on 7 November 1933 by Mussolini after the Duce decided to sack Sirianni and take over the position of navy minister himself, made no mention of battleships in his first speech to the chamber of deputies on 5 January 1934, but six days later told the senate that Italy reserved the right to build up to her permitted limits in this category. He quickly gained Mussolini's approval to build a battleship of maximum tonnage and gun power allowed under international agreement if it came to that.[152] The Duce also considered the possibility of making political use of the circumstances to reinvigorate naval arms limitation talks with France, encouraged by the French decision to suspend the second *Dunkerque*. Cavagnari warned against postponing the building necessary to keep up with France or accepting any proposal to limit battleships to 27,000 tons unless accompanied by 'a real political understanding' between the two countries which must include equality of programmes over a number of years pitched at a level which matched Italy's financial position, as well as agreement on reduction and limitation of land and air armaments. For many reasons, including the fact that Great Britain already had two of them, Cavagnari favoured getting on with building a pair of 35,000 ton battleships.[153]

The news that Italy intended to build two new battleships, announced by the Havas agency on 14 June, produced a request from the Admiralty in London that she suspend any decision on their size and join in preliminary discussion for the forthcoming London naval conference, and a clear indication from the French navy that they expected both to be able to complete the two *Dunkerques* and to start on a 35,000-ton battleship in 1935. Ambassador Chambrun both confirmed and multiplied the incipient French challenge by declaring that at the London conference Paris would seek the right to build two new battleships.[154] Assailed by a series of more moderate requests from the Foreign Office in London to enter into bilateral discussions on naval questions, Mussolini was advised by Cavagnari to delay doing so and to separate questions relating to the forthcoming conference from the building of the two warships which should 'advance without delay'. Cavagnari's list of the occasions on which France had sought to manipulate the naval question in her favour, and his demonstration of how Italy by contrast had only stayed within her rights and had always shown good faith, must surely have resonated with the francophobe Duce.[155] A last attempt in July by the British Foreign Office, after accepting the 35,000-ton requirement, to limit the gun size to 356 mm (14 inches) and not 381 mm (15 inches) in order to counter an expected move by the United States to insist on a 406-mm limit at the upcoming conference failed, partly because the Italians were aware of American intentions.[156] The *Vittorio Veneto* and the *Littorio* were laid down on 28 October 1934 and entered service respectively in April and June 1940, a time period determined largely by the need to spread the price of the ships, estimated at 700,000,000 lire each, over a period of six financial years chiefly in order to support the cost of importing the necessary non-ferrous metals which had to be paid for in hard currency.[157]

War planning proceeded under new conditions, for the staff were now supposed to prepare *Libri di guerra* for each possible conflict which, while giving 'great weight to aero–naval correlation', were supposed only to cover the initial period of war since 'no human mind is capable of defining the events deriving from the outcome of the first operations in war, events which will suggest and perhaps even impose variations in the operational plans'.[158] As regarded the problem of a two-front war, the navy followed Badoglio's prescription of an initially defensive posture, defending the frontiers, Tuscany and the islands and preparing to reinforce Zara and carry troops to Albania, but had also to face the prospect of supporting a landing at Veglia which raised the question of which of the latter should have priority. After this, the demands of the western Mediterranean, which involved defence of traffic, attacking enemy commerce and mine warfare, had to be resolved and also traffic protection in the eastern Mediterranean. The list of questions to be answered in detail was lengthy.[159] As far as interrupting the transport of troops from North Africa to metropolitan France was concerned, the staff expected the enemy to ship three infantry divisions from Algeria and one from Morocco, along with a brigade of cavalry from each. The various crossings could be done in times varying between twelve and forty-five hours depending on route and speed. If the convoys left in daylight the Italian navy would have warning of their departure and would be able to counteract their numerical inferiority by undertaking night actions with destroyers in the seas around the Balearics; a night departure would mean Italian forces could only act the following day when the convoys would be near southern France, though submarines could impede their progress.[160]

Trade protection loomed large in the navy's mind, and by the middle of 1933 it had worked out a design for traffic protection in both halves of the Mediterranean. In the west, traffic would be protected by submarine action east of Gibraltar and around the Balearics and by intense activity by light surface forces aiming to bottle up the enemy in Biserta. This represented something of a change of heart, as eighteen months earlier the staff had been inclined to counsel against any attempt to bottle up Biserta as an act of desperation which would require ships which would be employed on other and more important duties.[161] In the eastern Mediterranean the enemy could make some use of submarines but could only make intermittent sorties with surface craft from Biserta and Beirut, which they were most likely to do if Italian shipping travelled in convoys.

Accordingly the navy favoured having ships travel separately other than coastal traffic and perhaps convoying shipping from Tobruk to Cape Matapan. The navy did not favour convoying as long as torpedoing on sight was not being practised, partly because it used up valuable shipping as escorts, and felt that aeroplanes and ships together could deal with enemy submarines in front of the Suez canal.[162] The Red Sea loomed large in naval planning because the larger part of the overseas supplies Italy would need in wartime came via the Suez canal, and could be interrupted by French forces there. In a two front war, Massaua should become the logistic base for the protection of traffic going into the Mediterranean, for attacking French traffic in the Indian Ocean and the southern Atlantic, and as a base for long-range submarines operating off the coasts of Morocco and Senegal. Assab would become both a port of refuge and an air base from which to render Djibuti unusable by the French navy.[163] By the end of 1934, *Ipotesi Alpha* had been dropped and the theatre was being considered only in relation to war with France or Germany. It was calculated that 2,100,000 tons of goods a year went to France via Madagascar and the Cape of Good Hope, and 1,700,00 tons to Germany via the latter. The navy planned to employ four surface warships, along with two or three auxiliary cruisers and four armed merchantmen, two medium range and two long-range submarines and a seaplane detachment in the Gulf of Aden and the Indian Ocean. A main base at Massaua and an advanced base (*punto d'appoggio*) at Assab would support the operations, while Kisimaio and Port Durnford would make ideal advanced support bases in the Indian Ocean. Massaua and Kisimaio, the two essential bases, must be readied first.[164]

In regard to the main theatre of war, the navy received an unexpected and irritating request from the army to help it out on the western frontier, where it was exposed to bombardment from the sea and disruptive landings along the Ligurian coast. It would be particularly helpful, Bonzani thought, if the navy could interdict the French coastal railway and thereby interrupt enemy deployment.[165] The navy studied small-scale landings at four locations on the French coast using MAS boats based at San Remo in order to blow up railway and road bridges, a more difficult task than it first appeared given the weight of explosives necessary to blow up stone bridges, the ease with which metal bridges could be repaired, and the population density of the area which would make detection likely.[166] Ducci's formal reply to Bonzani was not very encouraging. Given the enemy's capacity to take the initiative whenever he chose and to carry out disruptive actions quickly, the only ways to stop him were by standing patrols of surface ships or by laying traps with submarines or MAS boats. Neither of the first two resources could be spared in sufficient numbers, so the army must make do with passive defences (guns, armoured trains, torpedoes) and minor disruptive actions by MAS boats. Bombardment to interrupt the railways 'could be done more *economically* and perhaps also more *effectively* by the air force'. In case Bonzani had not quite got the point, Ducci added that the relative balance of naval strength 'demands the greatest caution in the employment of our naval forces and <u>absolutely counsels against</u> diverting a part of it to other parts of the theatre of operations where it cannot quickly be supported by the rest of the force'.[167] Badoglio had made no progress in inter-service co-operation, for the navy was no more inclined to help the army now than it had been in 1915.

By the beginning of 1934, the naval staff had worked out their general directive for a two-front war based on Badoglio's postulation of an initially defensive stance. France's defensive action would likely be limited to protecting troop transports across the Mediterranean. Her predictable offensive options to improve the strategic situation in the east were, in descending order of returns, the occupation of all or part of Sicily and the capture of Tripoli, Tobruk or Leros, none of which would be easy. In the middle and upper Tyrrhenian seas she could try to take Sardinia or occupy parts of it, capture Elba or attempt landings on the left wing of the Italian army, though none of these actions would have a decisive effect on the war. In the Red Sea she might occupy Assab and Massaua to interdict Italian shipping. Finally, she might try naval offensives in the western Mediterranean to annihilate Italian traffic coming via Gibraltar, and in the eastern Mediterranean to disrupt traffic there. The geographical–strategical situation, least favourable to Italy in the western Mediterranean, suggested offensive operations there and in the central Mediterranean aimed at restricting the enemy's freedom of movement and defensive operations in the central and eastern Mediterranean to safeguard traffic. The bulk of Italy's naval forces would operate in either direction from a central position based on Naples and Augusta, though it might have temporarily to go to the upper Tyrrhenian or the southern Adriatic.[168]

On a different front, Cavagnari and the naval staff were now starting to contemplate wars against new opponents. In May 1934, in the face of the worsening Austrian crisis, the navy minister approved a study for war with Germany and called for a similar one on war with England to be completed and presented to him as soon as possible.[169] At the first meeting convened by Badoglio to review European war plans for almost three years, held in early September 1934, and now required to consider action against Germany and Yugoslavia, Cavagnari asked who Italy's allies might be – a further indication of how poorly Mussolini co-ordinated political and military factors in his designs. The answer he got was that France would be actively supportive and England passive but favourably inclined. Badoglio thought that in naval terms Italy would be back in the same situation as she had been in 1915, but with the advantage of possessing Istria and Pola. Cavagnari next wanted to know whether France would prevent the exit of the German navy from the North Sea. The reply was that the accord which presently existed between the two powers was based only on convergent statements. 'Today we must study our options and our needs; then we shall adapt them to those of others', Badoglio told him by way of guidance. His observation that it was necessary to define the political line for the conduct of such a war well reflected the extent to which Mussolini kept his military leaders in the dark about vital issues of war-making.[170]

The Austrian crisis gave a new twist to the two-front war, for the navy also had now to presume that Yugoslavia would join Germany against Italy, Austria and Albania (both of whom would be unreliable allies), and France. The use of French bases would be highly advantageous to Italy, for while neither Germany nor France could get directly at one another, they would permit the combined navies to exert pressure on Germany in the North Sea, Atlantic, Indian Ocean and China Sea. Germany was estimated to import twenty million tons of goods a year by sea, mostly by way of the Indian Ocean and the Atlantic. Yugoslav traffic, apart from that in the Adriatic, would certainly travel under neutral flags. To defend this traffic, she would abandon shipping routes in the Red Sea and Mediterranean, and re-route Atlantic shipping through the North Sea instead of the English Channel. Without either aircraft or submarines (though the naval staff noted that Germans were working in Dutch yards and believed they could rapidly produce submarines if the war was lengthy), she would likely use her five modern cruisers to attack Italian shipping in the approaches to the Channel and Gibraltar, and might also make rapid incursions into the Mediterranean 'to sow confusion in our traffic and carry out coastal bombardments chiefly for moral effect'.[171] In these circumstances, the Italian navy planned to use the bulk of its fleet to defend the Mediterranean and act offensively in the Adriatic, using a nucleus of armed merchantmen and long-range submarines in the Atlantic. France's intervention would be welcome, since she would presumably take over the burden in the Atlantic and North Sea while the Italian navy took on the task of blocking the Otranto Channel, occupying Zara and Valona and supporting the right wing of an army offensive. This was what had been at the top of the navy's agenda for half a decade, and the plan amounted to a tacit admission that there was not much the navy could do to Germany in war.

Badoglio sought to concentrate the military chiefs' minds on the primacy of operations against Germany in Austria and on the need to adopt a purely defensive stance in the east, which meant leaving Albania out of consideration.[172] If this was directed at Cavagnari, it did not entirely succeed, for at the next meeting of the military chiefs the naval chief of staff wanted to talk about the detailed issue of the occupation of Valona. He was squashed by Badoglio who reminded him where the priority presently lay, reminded him also that it was now calculated that this would take an army corps of 100,000 men, and told him that not provoking Yugoslavia was now a priority.[173]

By the end of December, the navy had defined its position. It was evidently not disposed to accept much of what Badoglio had laid down as law. Its first task was to secure maritime communications across the Mediterranean and it took as its starting point a 'worst case' scenario in which France was in the enemy camp. If the appropriate political accords were reached this would lighten the navy's task, but even so Cavagnari was not disposed to diminish the defensive provision for the upper and central Tyrrhenian sea. As far as the Adriatic was concerned, naval calculations required that the situation be improved by occupation of its eastern shore regardless of whether or not the army landings took place and of whether or not France was an ally. Thaon Di Revel's view of the Adriatic evidently continued to hold sway in the higher counsels of the navy almost a decade after his departure. As far as offensive operations were concerned, the navy enumerated possible options which included cruises by long-range submarines in the North Sea, operations by submarines and auxiliary craft with cruisers in support up to 400 miles off Gibraltar, defence of the western entrance to the Mediterranean, and the seizure of Valona and at least four other islands off the Yugoslav coast.[174] Shortly after Cavagnari had settled on this position, the accelerated process of planning for the Abyssinian War rendered the whole question redundant.

Air force insufficiencies

Although Giuseppe Valle was named under-secretary of state for air on 6 November 1933, as a consequence of an air accident he suffered at Valencia flying back home to organise Balbo's reception he was unable to meet the physical fitness standards of a pilot which were a requirement to hold the post until 22 March 1934 and had temporarily to hand over the reins as chief of air staff to general Antonio Bosio. With Mussolini as minister, Valle, who was a card-carrying member of the Fascist party, lacked any kind of political or bureaucratic independence. He also had his hands full, being responsible for civil as well as military aviation, arms

Table 4.3 *Italian and French air force budgets 1926–34*

Italy	lire	France	lire
1926–7	668,880,000	1926	–
1927–8	659,520,000	1927	–
1928–9	646,220,000	1928	–
1929–30	629,850,000	1929	1,182,013,500
1930–1	635,180,000	1930–1	1,349,450,000
1931–2	673,920,000	1931–2	1,478,210,000
1932–3	673,320,000	1932	1,232,538,000
1933–4	615,068,000	1933	1,319,432,000

exports, and industrial policy. As far as his critics were concerned, Valle did not rise to the main challenge facing him, which was to move from the spectacular activities of his predecessor to concentrating on using all resources available to improve the combat potential of the air force. Instead, similar policies were continued with the result that while the air force felt it was at the cutting edge of technological progress, it was in fact increasingly falling behind.[175]

In 1933 the Italian air force possessed 1,507 aircraft and numbered 22,193 personnel as compared to France's 2,375 aircraft and 42,554 personnel. Calculations made in connection with the Geneva Disarmament Conference indicated that Italy had spent 946,069,236 lire on its air force to date and France 1,470,000,000 lire, producing a unit cost per aeroplane of 627,000 lire for Italy and 618,000 lire for France.[176] The comparative budget figures – which Italy exceeded in 1929–30 and 1930–1 and France exceeded in 1931–2 – showed how far the Regia Aeronautica was trailing behind the force it would have to face in the event of a two-front war.[177]

Balbo had warned in his budget speech to the chamber of deputies in 1932 that shortage of funds meant that the strength of the air force must decline in the future, and that he had to economise on materiel by using it to the utmost, thereby exposing air force personnel to ever-mounting risks. The budget for the following year, which Valle had to operate, announced that shortage of money meant an unavoidable reduction in size in order to maintain qualitative levels.[178] However, in July 1934 Mussolini gave Valle an extraordinary budget of 1,200,000,000 lire, which he used to develop a comprehensive organisation for pre-military training, to mount special courses in gliding, flying and *cultura aeronautica*, and to set up a college at Forlì for would-be young airmen. The first of these, which was something of a Fascist obsession in the 1930s, may well have been an unproductive use of the money.

In fact, Valle's personnel policies left more than a little to be desired. The law dating from Balbo's day according to which the minister could nominate as a reserve-lieutenant anyone he wanted to regardless of qualifications remained in force with minor amendments until the war; through it 1,093 people became officers between 1934 and 1940, when Pricolo abrogated it. The quality of the officer corps was also affected by the institution of 'Squadriglia P', set up in 1928 to allow major and minor party officials to get a civil pilot's licence. Young men who had failed the entry examinations for the Accademia Aeronautica used it as a stepping stone to a reserve commission and then, after volunteering later for service in Ethiopia or Spain, to a regular commission, with deleterious effects on both the morale and the levels of technical competence of the air force officer corps.[179]

The air exercises held in the spring of 1933 were designed to explore what the air force could do in the face of a two-front war in which Germany, Hungary and Albania were all involved on Italy's side. Although the air staff believed that the air force could and should make a decisive contribution in any future war through a combination of physical destruction and the erosion of morale – which it termed 'war of integral destruction' – it recognised that this was only possible when the Italian air force was at least as large as that of any other European power. Since that was not presently the case, the directing staff abandoned the Douhetian concept of *guerra integrale* and instead tested different modes of air warfare. In doing so they were careful to emphasise that such forms were 'of secondary importance ... and only imposed [on the air force] by the actual state of limited efficiency of the air arms'.[180]

The exercises showed that there was still much to do in the way of working out a comprehensive and appropriate air doctrine. Bombers tended to forget the fundamental principle of mass and spread their efforts in an attempt to hit lots of targets rather than concentrating on a small number and repeating their attacks until they were destroyed. Considerable differences of view emerged during the exercises about how to deploy and use fighters both between and within the two sides. Some forms of fighter action – particularly air watches (*crocieri di vigilanza*) and 'blocking' patrols (*crocieri di sbarramento*) – proved to be particularly unrewarding ways to use aircraft. Assault aviation – 'a delicate arm which must be prepared spiritually and materially for actions of great daring (*arditismo*) of an essentially episodic character' – proved particularly effective against 'French' air bases in Corsica but was unlikely to do so in the region between the frontier and the Rhone valley where targets were too large and too well-defended. The competing forces had organised their brigades and divisions in different ways. The directing staff concluded that combining the same kind of planes rather than mixing them up according to logistic rather than operational criteria was the better option for brigades, whereas divisions could be mixed according to the circumstances of the moment and the mission.[181]

The war scenarios being examined by the planners proved something of an incentive to inter-service co-operation. In the spring of 1934, the Aeronautica took part in joint air–naval exercises to locate and track French troop convoys en route from Algeria to Provence and to defend merchant traffic in the eastern Mediterranean basin.[182] In August it took part in the annual army manoeuvres held along the Tuscan–Emilian Apennines and designed to test the capacities of attack and defence in mountainous regions – a scenario not very far removed from that which would confront the Italian armed forces in a war with Yugoslavia. The 'Blue' air component was tasked initially with supporting the attack, particularly by striking at the enemy's rear and at the rail hub of Bologna, and then with checking the advance of a 'Red' division which had local air superiority by using assault aviation in particular. Several problems were thrown up. It proved difficult for the fighters to protect the army's auxiliary aviation since the latter's orders were changed at short notice according to the ground commanders' needs and because the fighters lacked any information about the enemy. Nor was it effective for air commanders to correlate the numbers of fighters they employed with the number of army aircraft to be protected if they wanted to win local dominance of the air for substantial periods. The experiments with assault aviation were deemed a very limited success: only the lead planes surprised the enemy columns, it then had to operate under heavy artillery and machine-gun fire, and it was vulnerable to enemy fighters both during attacks and while returning to base. Francesco Pricolo, who was directing the air exercises, therefore concluded that Mecozzi's assault units could usefully be employed 'only in very special circumstances of place and time which are not likely to occur on the tactical land battlefield'. On the other hand, a simulated night attack by bombers on Bologna and Florence was deemed a complete success.[183]

The contretemps between De Pinedo and Valle in 1929, and the former's unauthorised revelation of the air force's early plans, had raised alarms in the navy about the extent to which the air men aimed at domination in war. In one respect, the dominance of the 'battleship admirals' in the early 1930s made for improved relations: the joint manoeuvres in the Tyrrhenian sea in 1932 allowed them to make common cause with the airmen by using the timeliness of aerial intervention from land bases as evidence that aircraft carriers were unnecessary and that any extra monies should be spent not on them but on aeroplanes and landing fields.[184] However, this kind of political accord was not replicated in the day-to-day business of hammering out operating practices. For example, Valle and admiral Ducci reached an agreement in spring 1933 that the air force would develop torpedo bombs to be paid for by the navy; two years later Valle denounced it when the navy refused to meet the bills and Cavagnari responded by refusing to accept the air force's legally established responsibility for the training and deployment of torpedo bombing aircraft.[185] Later, when he was out of office, Valle claimed that he had created the aerial torpedo school at Cadimare in 1934, that he had perfected the aerial torpedo despite the resistance of many senior air force officers, and that by the time of the air show in Milan in 1937 both the S 79 and S 81 aircraft were armed with it.[186] His successor, general Francesco Pricolo, described the claim as 'a masterpiece of superficialities and lies' – a foretaste of the bitter post-war disputes over the air force.[187]

The Italian air staff maintained a healthy respect for the French air force, which had the capacity to 'mount a powerful [night] offensive action on objectives situated even at notable distances from its bases'.[188] In its planning for war, one of its concerns was France's possession of Corsica. This was something Mussolini shared: in July 1930, fearing that the French would use air bases on the island to bomb Rome, he ordered general Gazzera to prepare plans to conquer it and exactly two years later he reiterated his demand.[189] The air staff agreed that the island presented a grave menace; from it the French could launch surprise attacks along the whole of the Italian coast from Genoa to Naples. Possession of the island would be the best solution, but in present circumstances that was deemed impossible. Neutralisation of enemy air bases there was the next best thing, but given the large array of general tasks facing the air force in war and the shortage of aircraft with which to carry them out this was currently impossible. To do it the air force needed two extra squadrons of bombers and two fighter squadrons which, together with basing costs, would require 200,000,000 lire in extraordinary funds and an extra 25,000,000 lire a year on the ordinary air budget.[190] Mussolini does not seem to have been sufficiently persuaded to part with the money. In February 1934 Valle told the Commissione suprema di difesa that over past two years France had intensified work on air bases in Corsica which threatened Sardinia. The air force was spending 30,000,000 lire over three years to build an air base at Elmas to hold an entire air division, but lacked the funds to develop Stagnoni in Sicily.[191]

Valle took only a minor role in the chiefs' of staff contingency planning sessions for operations in Austria in September 1934. His chief concern was the availability of airfields which, as his contributions revealed, threatened seriously to restrict operations. There was only one Italian airfield close to the northern front, at Bolzano, and three more at Verona, Casarsa and Udine for operations against Yugoslavia. On the other side of the frontier a network of small airfields existed in the Inn valley but none were capable of taking heavy aircraft; only at Linz was a major airfield to be found. There were also problems with materiel. If the air force had to be ready for a war in 1935, Valle declared that it would have to sacrifice both quality and quantity as the bombers dated from 1925–7. The night bombing force could not be ready before the following spring.[192]

The air force looked further into the scenario of war with Germany alone or in alliance with Yugoslavia three months later. The hypothesis of war in the north and east was in some ways less serious than that of war in the east and west, though it presented 'conditions of great delicacy' because of Italy's geography and the situation with regard to air bases. Aerial reach presented the planners with what they regarded as serious problems. Against Germany Italian aircraft could only hit targets in southern Bavaria, a task which the terrain made difficult and Yugoslavian intervention would render more difficult still. Yugoslavia's main agricultural and industrial resources were in the north-east of the country and equally difficult to get to. While the main population centres and vital industries of both potential opponents were out of Italy's range, her own on the Paduan plain and as far west as Milan and Genoa were reachable by German and Yugoslavian aircraft. A major drawback to any Italian offensive – besides the height of the mountains, the distances involved and the lack of targets – was the lack of suitable airfields in the centre of the peninsula: only one, at Bolzano, could take heavy bombers, most of which would have to be based at Brescia, Verona and Vicenza.[193]

The operational conclusions that Valle drew from all this were scarcely encouraging. He could not give a priori significance to any specific air objectives. There were no demographic and industrial objectives which, if destroyed, could have immediate effects on the development of the war on land, at sea and in the air 'of the kind which, in the difficult and uncertain conditions which this conflict presents [us with], are the only ones of fundamental interest'. Therefore the air force would concentrate in the initial phases of such a war on air bases, lines and centres of land and sea communication, and frontier actions to support the army.[194]

The air force's conception of a two-front war caused evident concern in the navy, which regarded them as providing insufficient protection for the cardinal strategic points of Italy's position in the central Mediterranean, Sardinia and Sicily and wanted at least sixty bombers available to attack the French naval bases in north Africa, chief among them Biserta.[195] As well as having evident reservations about the strategic contribution the air force proposed to make in war, the navy was also conscious that it was itself equipped with aircraft which were obsolescent, which had only half the five-hundred-mile range they needed for reconnaissance at sea, and which in peacetime were restricted to operating no more than thirty miles from the coast. Finally, it regarded the theoretical studies for air force co-operation in wartime as no substitute for more concrete and practical agreement and as liable to leave the form of air intervention in war to undesirable decisions of the moment by the supreme command.[196]

Doctrines of war

In the early 1930s, Italian naval thinking naturally concerned itself with ideas current in France. Raffaele de Courten, who would become chief of naval staff in 1943, presented to Italian readers the writings of admiral Castex, the leading naval theorist of the day, who was defining command of the sea in a way which Italian sailors could both readily understand and see as an indication of the threat they faced: as the control of essential maritime communications. Castex also preached the pursuit of the naval battle against the bulk of the enemy's forces as the highest aim in war, and the offensive as the only correct attitude. De Courten also translated the work of the German naval theorist captain Otto Groos, who believed in the strategic defensive in war and in the right of sailors to exercise some influence on the making of national strategy by being able to present their strategic views to the political authority 'in a clear and convincing form'.[197]

The leading Italian naval theorist of the early 1930s, *comandante* Guiseppe Fioravanzo, argued that strategy had two principles: the first, which he labelled 'essential', was to destroy the enemy's will to fight, and the second, which was 'operational', was to meet the enemy in conditions of relative advantage. In a Clausewitzian formulation, the art of naval war was to impose one's will by means of offensive shock achieved by manoeuvring one's forces so as to surprise the enemy. Fioravanzo took a wide Mahanian view of naval power, which consisted of the navy, the merchant marine and naval bases, and saw its role as ensuring that the nation had the means to resist by safeguarding its seaborne supply, preventing the enemy from getting overseas supplies, guaranteeing 'the inviolability of the naval frontier' and maintaining links with the colonies. This was a formalisation in theoretical terms of the strategic tasks the Italian navy had confronted since the world war, and Fioravanzo's central tenet, the defence of communications, chimed with both its outlook and its planning. However, Fioravanzo went farther than many sailors in stressing the significance of air power as a crucial component of naval war, modifying Douhet's controversial dictum to read '*resistere sul terra per far massa nel mare e nell'aria'* ('defend on land to mass forces at sea and in the air').[198]

The basic precepts of naval strategy – defence of the sea-lanes and the command of the sea – were put into the public domain by propagandistic authors who propounded the virtues of the decisive naval battle as against commerce war and the central role played in such engagements by battle-ships.[199] However, as was the case to varying degrees with the other two services, the navy faced potential conflicts of interest with the regime over the relationship between strategy, politics and Fascist culture. Admiral Sirianni, at the moment of his enforced departure as secretary of state for the navy, sounded a decisively negative note by declaring that that there was no point in examining the tactical and strategic nature of future con-flict because since there was no knowledge of the political circumstances in which it would take place the conclusions could only be abstract.[200] He put a premium on political vision, which had allowed the English to beat the Germans in the world war even though the Germans were better at fighting, and on a rational organisation to express it. In Fascist Italy, where the political situation was deeply rooted in a new conception of the state, the head of government must have supreme direction of the armed forces in peace and war. Ministers, exercising a technical–administrative function, acted as interpreters of his thought, while the chiefs of staff rep-resented professional continuity and stood above 'political vicissitudes'. Sirianni's formula privileged the Duce and turned the professional heads of the service into no more than a subordinate functional elite:

[T]he political head must permanently follow and orientate his mind towards the problems of a general character inherent in war. His thoughts must be made known to his immediate collaborators who, through the executive structures they control, must translate them into actuality by preparing the requisite means.[201]

The model was Mussolini's ideal, and from 1934 he endeavoured to follow it. Its drawback was that for the navy, as for the other services, it opened the door to wars which professional considerations might well – and indeed would – counsel against.

In the army, the ideas of a mechanised force that Grazioli had expounded came into conflict with the concept of motorisation which gained a rapid hold in the army. Conservatives saw the transition from the pre-1914 army as being only a gradual one: Gazzera told the chamber of deputies on 16 March 1933 that

in our territories the horse will be widely employed again and for some time in the future, although its use will be reduced little by little as engines improve and motor vehicles become cheaper and more widespread.[202]

Motorisation had been pursued between 1918 and 1930, with tanks cast in the role of infantry supports. During the early 1930s it became wedded with the unique Italian concept of celeri units which mixed bersaglieri bicyclists and cavalry, opening the way to the light motorised divisions which would be the dominant feature of the army in the later 1930s.

The new idea was the brainchild of general Ottavio Zoppi, who after commanding an arditi division became inspector of Alpine troops between 1928 and 1930 and inspector of infantry from 1933 to 1935. Zoppi's ideas, tested in 1932 and embedded in official doctrine two years later, were predicated on the belief that the impasse of the world war could be overcome where the moral will existed to do so, and that manoeuvre and penetration could be brought back to the battlefield. To achieve this, he added light tanks as a third ingredient of the celeri cocktail. Zoppi's ideas put him in the 'modernist' school and gained the praise of general De Bono, among the most politically active and most politically favoured of Fascist generals. De Bono contributed a foreword to Zoppi's book *I Celeri* (1935) in which he compared the celeri spirit with that of the Fascist movement, based as it was on *dinamismo* and *arditismo*, the offensive spirit and rapid decisive action. In fact, Zoppi's formations were weak and his ideas backward since they looked to resolving the problem of mountain warfare on Italy's northern frontier by drawing on one part of the experiences on the Russian front.[203]

The idea of a war of manoeuvre was also at the heart of the work of the other major 'moderniser' of the early 1930s, colonel Sebastiano Visconti Prasca. Like Zoppi, he believed that the superiority of the defensive over the offensive was transitory and could be overcome. The aim of war was the *offensiva a fondo* to penetrate an enemy's defences, paralyse his logistic activity and ransack his resources. Unlike Zoppi, he believed that the cause of the stalemate in the world war had been technical and not moral. The infantry's problem lay in the last three hundred to five hundred metres of the attack – which he termed 'the blue ribbon zone' after Italy's highest decoration for valour, the *medaglia d'oro*. The solution lay not in increased artillery co-operation or in more machine-guns, which were a good defensive arm but a poor offensive one, but in portable firepower in the shape of light, mobile guns.[204] Visconti Prasca's belief that the three-regiment *divisione ternaria* was too big and too slow to manoeuvre effectively, and his conception of the role of tanks as one element in smaller and more powerfully armed *nuclei di battaglia* ('battle groups'), pointed towards the light motorised *divisione binaria* which would form the basis of the army's organisation in the later 1930s.[205]

Although Grazioli had not managed to prise the army from the grip of the traditionalists, he had shown that there was now a market for military ideas which combined modernisation, economy and elements of Fascist philosophy. Visconti Prasca fulfilled all three requirements. His definition of war as 'a struggle intended to defend and to win one's rightful position in international life' stood squarely within the confines of Mussolini's rhetoric, and his observation that political requirements must determine offensive and defensive military preparations directly challenged the Piedmontese conception of professional autonomy.[206] His work was well received by both the political and the military authorities. Mussolini liked it, as he had liked Zoppi's work, finding it 'strong, organic and *integralmente fascista*' ('wholly Fascist'), and Baistrocchi, whose objective was to slim down the size of the army and give it offensive mobility and greater hitting-power, indicated that it was entirely in conformity with the views of the war ministry. Visconti Prasca's critics were less impressed, remarking that everyone had had the same ideas, that the army only needed 'generic direction' to create structures able to do anything, and that to say that the army was the servant of foreign policy was 'dangerously impassioned'.[207]

In June 1934 colonel Adolfo Infante, perhaps the most knowledgeable commentator on mechanised war, entered the lists, publishing a study of mechanisation and motorisation in Italy. The circumstances were now more favourable insofar as the Geneva Disarmament Conference, at which Italy had suggested that tanks be abolished, had now evidently collapsed. Infante partly shared Visconti Prasca's opinion that attacking infantry needed more firepower, but differed in believing that his proposed solution – mobile light artillery – would slow down and encumber it and instead preferred the use of mortars. More importantly, to produce a war of movement required tanks and a greater stake in both mechanisation and motorisation. Answering the conservative critics who pointed out that tanks were useless in the mountains, Infante said that wars had never been won there and that Italy needed an autonomous armoured, mechanised and motorised force which she could use in other European theatres of operation and in the colonies. The armoured brigades he proposed would be the main instruments in a revived war of manoeuvre:

While the air force carries out the first great bombing actions against the vital centres of enemy war potential, an armoured brigade composed of some 200 tanks and capable of covering three hundred kilometres in twenty-four hours will be able to execute surprise penetrations, reach some of these centres and complete the destruction begun by the air force.[208]

The kind of war that Infante envisioned evidently owed more than a little to the ideas of Fuller and Liddell Hart. The kinds of tanks he recommended – 2-ton 'mountain' tanks, 4-ton light tanks and 9- or 10-ton medium tanks armed with a 37-mm gun on the chassis – were in line with others of the time.[209] Unfortunately as far as Italy was concerned, a combination of events would mean that the Italian army never advanced beyond the light armour concept Infante propounded, in considerable measure because light tanks were quicker and cheaper to produce than heavy ones.

Probably thanks to Baistrocchi's wish to modernise the army, Grazioli was given charge of the summer manoeuvres in 1934. His choice of Zoppi as one of the two opposing corps commanders and the employment of one of the celeri divisions were clear evidence that the high command's intention was now to test the new form of organisation, and the employment of Mecozzi's assault aviation for the first time made it clear that new thinking was being given its chance.[210] The manoeuvres were counted a success, though French military observers, who chose to praise the functioning of the logistic services and the marching powers of the infantry, made no mention of the celeri.[211] At their conclusion Mussolini invited Grazioli to observe the annual Soviet manoeuvres in the Ukraine the following month. He was much impressed, he told the Duce on his return, by the degree of mechanisation achieved in the army as a result of the first five-year plan and no less so by the manoeuvres themselves, during which celeri forces, both mechanised and unmechanised, had carried out *coups de main* and surprise penetrations into 'enemy' territory in dynamic and wide-ranging operations. He drew special attention to the employment of large mechanised formations as autonomous columns.[212] After the war, marshal Messe claimed that no one at the time took the slightest notice of the report.

The demise of general Douhet and the departure of Balbo cleared the way for air theory to concentrate less on 'grand theory' and more on practical tactical issues as Mecozzi's ideas, which were in tune with the mounting focus of motor-mechanised ground warfare, gained hold. In 1933, Mecozzi's *Aviazione d'assalto* depicted his methods of air action as a complement to aerial bombardment: while the *aviazione di bombardamento* sought from the start of hostilities to bring about the moral, economic and industrial collapse of the enemy nation, assault aviation did likewise by contributing to the operations of all three military arms. However, it was not to be seen as simply an auxiliary arm of the other services and should not be employed within the effective range of medium artillery or naval guns. Rather, it would be best employed in the earliest stages of a war, particularly against the enemy's communication lines, as a form of advance guard. After this it could be used against the enemy's rear or his retreating forces, against enemy landings, or as a supplement to heavy bombing 'to intensify, by low-level bombing, the crisis which the moral and material forces that sustain the enemy's armed forces will be suffering'.[213]

The unique quality of assault aviation was its capacity to hit small, precisely defined targets. It was not therefore intended normally for use in tactical actions and not at all when opposing ground forces were in contact with one another. Therefore, Mecozzi argued, in wartime requests by the army and navy must be resolutely resisted. Its proper targets were bodies of troops, their support services, magazines, supply dumps, weapons parks, railway plant, command structures, and transport nets. In cities, it might strike at stations, barracks, gas manufacturing works, municipal and government offices and the like. To ensure its proper use, it must have its own organic command under the direction of the central air force authority and be employed according to the decisions of the wartime Comando supremo which would be best qualified to deploy it to proper effect.[214]

In the spring of 1935, before the Abyssinian war, Mecozzi pushed his doctrine further to the centre of air war and began to propound the idea of 'the totalitarian conception of assault aviation' as both complementary and integral to the new ideas of mobile decisive war being fathered by Baistrocchi. Given Italy's vulnerable position in the face of the air attacks that her two likely enemies, France and Germany, could launch against her, the likelihood was that after three days' combat her cities would have suffered worse damage then theirs. From this Mecozzi identified the two essentials for Italian military action:

To impose combat on the enemy bombers in order to defend our territory, including especially our cities and air bases; [and] to ensure that the army aids the air force, not by putting up a strong resistance but rather by manoeuvring so that it penetrates into enemy territory and allows us to push forward our air bases.[215]

In practical terms the occupation of the Rhone valley and lower Bavaria, while it might not be decisive in terms of land warfare, would be so in terms of air warfare because of the increased security and protection their possession would afford to Italy's northern industrial cities. In the course of castigating France's defensive strategic attitude, Mecozzi painted a remarkably prescient thumb-nail sketch of 'the German army, which has not forgotten von Seeckt's teachings, pushing one of two wedges of ground forces [into France] with a penetrative power deriving from machines, men, dash, and will, but increased tenfold by the intervention of aviation'.[216]

Mercozzi's ideas were now cast in the form of a direct challenge to Douhet's comprehensive theories and to his privileging of massive bombing strikes on enemy industrial and population centres; if Italy propounded such ideas, not only would it be accused of inhumanity by others but because of its exposed position it would be the first to suffer from their application. Douhet's supporters, who saw Mecozzi's methods as disaggregating formations to a point at which decisive action was impossible and only 'aerial guerilla warfare' could obtain and who adhered to his basic propositions about the significance of long-range aerial bombardment of cities, opposed them. 'Pure' Douhetians viewed them as discarding the primary objective in war, the enemy's demographical centres, and as 'an unnatural deformation of the spirit, the development and the linear progression of the air arm'. The fundamental political objection to his ideas was that they opened the way to the loss of sovereign independence in the conduct of the air war.[217]

Military commentators on air power tended to take an anti-Douhetian stance partly for this same reason, and looked for air support in land operations. From 1934 onwards, the progress of the new ideas of land warfare and the allusions to air–ground co-operation made by Grazioli, Zoppi and perhaps most importantly by Baistrocchi led to talk of 'fusion' as the way of the future. For these commentators, the 1934 manoeuvres showed what might be done by way of ground–air co-operation. However for many airmen, including the future chief of air staff Francesco Pricolo, they represented an interesting but exceptional experiment which chiefly underlined the flexibility of air power but did not undermine the Douhetian principles which lay at its heart. The separation between the two arms was also formally embodied in the *Direttive per l'impiego delle Grandi Unità* ('Regulations for the employment of major units') published in 1935, which looked to the air force to carry out independent operations in the initial phase of a war while simultaneously contributing to the success of land operations 'with violent and intensive bombardments intended to paralyse the sources from which the enemy's army draws life'. The decision as to when and how a part of the air force could contribute to decisive victory by co-operating with the ground forces was left to the supreme commander of the armed forces, and the regulations further maintained the autonomy of air forces by putting their direction in wartime in the hands of the central Comando supremo. Although tanks were becoming important no mention whatever was made of tank–air co-operation, and indeed it would not be until 1941.[218]

Preparing the Abyssinian War

The idea of fighting a war to conquer Abyssinia began to come into focus during 1932. It was the product of diplomatic and political calculations to which were added computations of present and future military capability and a dash of 'forward' pressure by local commanders on the spot. Economic and political expansion in Africa was at or near the top of the agenda for many Italian diplomats. Not long before he was jettisoned Dino Grandi considered the problem to be 'of primordial importance', though his mind seems to have been set on finding an outlet for Italy's excess population and a source of raw materials through a reapportionment of African mandates.[219] In February 1932 Raffaele Guariglia made a forceful case for a more active policy in regard to Abyssinia and in August he again picked up on the twin themes of excess population and lack of raw materials, asking Mussolini whether it was not time to give Italy's Ethiopian policy 'a more dynamic and active character'. Ethiopia was getting stronger as it moved from being a feudalised to a centralised state, was now a larger obstacle than it had been a few years ago and could shortly become an imminent danger for Eritrea. Italy had the military means to win a quick war in the form of air power. The diplomatic ground was partially prepared in that France was showing a willingness to give Italy a free hand over the greater part of Abyssinia, but in this respect more was needed. An agreement with Great Britain as well as France was, he told Mussolini, 'the single indispensable point of departure'.[220]

Local initiatives for forward policies were evident in the expansionist ambitions of the governors of Somalia which, begun when Cesare De Vecchi took on the post in 1923, continued under his successor from 1928, Corni, who pushed bands of Somali irregulars into Ethiopia. In the spring and early autumn of 1931 the Ethiopians pushed them back, reaching the line of Somali outposts before first halting and then withdrawing. However, Italian sponsored guerrilla activity remained ongoing for several years to come.[221] After going on an inspection tour in the spring of 1932, general Emilio De Bono was pressed by the governor of Eritrea, Riccardo Astuto, to consider a war with Ethiopia. Although he shared the governor's sentiments, De Bono thought that the time was not yet ripe. Armed Italian intervention and a military success would stabilise the situation for many years but would require, he told Mussolini, a lengthy preparation and the expenditure of hundreds of millions of lire 'which would certainly be better employed elsewhere'.[222] In keeping with the forward ambitions of his nineteenth-century predecessors, the commander of the Eritrean garrison drew up a plan in September to use six metropolitan divisions to advance into Tigray and then await an Abyssinian counterattack.[223]

Early in November, De Bono summoned a number of senior officials including Fulvio Suvich and Pompeo Aloisi to a meeting which took Abyssinian policy a stage further. The military threat was virtually non-existent: the emperor could not raise more than five thousand men in twelve days, De Bono reported. Everyone registered their support for a *politica periferica* ('peripheral policy'). Raising the issue which Guariglia had regarded as fundamental to any expansionist policy, Alessandro Lessona asked whether Great Britain and France would allow 'a definitive solution' in the not-too-distant future. Evidently without an answer, De Bono announced that Italian policy would proceed by degrees. It 'could not have anything other than an offensive character', but would consist in the first instance of bribing tribes in the Ogaden and potential rebels on the northern border of Abyssinia.[224]

On 29 November 1932, De Bono produced the first Abyssinian war plan. An offensive war would require clear and binding prior political accords with France and Great Britain if the former were not to trap Italy into weakening herself in order to settle unsolved political questions with her. It would pit some 400–500,000 Abyssinians against an initial force of 85,000 Italians. The enemy would mobilise only slowly, would be seriously inhibited by lack of resources, and would present rewarding targets for the Italian air force while gathering and when on the move. De Bono expected to win the early encounters against local Tigrean forces two-thirds the size of the Italians with two divisions and a regiment of alpini (35,000 men) from the *madrepatria* and an air brigade consisting of six squadrons of bombers, four of tactical reconnaissance aircraft and a single fighter squadron. After this further troops would be necessary to develop operations.[225]

Mussolini expressed pleasure at De Bono's somewhat sketchy plans when presented with them in mid-December, and indicated that in the event of a war De Bono would be given command. For the meantime governor Vinci was instructed to avoid complications with Abyssinia and execute a policy of friendship. Despite all the talk, there was no possibility of Italy occupying the provinces of Gojjam and Tigray just now. For the moment three things held Mussolini back. First, the army was not prepared – 'we could fight them now, but the game is not worth the candle'. Secondly, the complications of the international situation at the start of 1933 could lead to a European war and Italy could not afford to be tied up elsewhere if that happened. Thirdly, the financial effort involved would have disastrous consequences for the state's finances.[226]

When serious military scrutiny was given to De Bono's plan in the latter part of 1933, the soldiers soon began to pick it apart. Bonzani undermined the idea that one month would suffice to prepare the operation, emphasised the imprudence of De Bono's scheme to send two separate columns on an initial drive against targets between 200 and 500 kilometres from the Eritrean and Somalian borders, and doubted whether the

air force could do much of use since there was only one target of any
political significance, Addis Ababa. His disparagement of air power was
adroit but somewhat tendentious: either it would dilute its effects, creating a general impression of lack of effectiveness 'when we need instead to
preserve its legendary effectiveness', or if it succeeded in breaking apart
Abyssinian formations it could create conditions favourable to guerrilla
war.[227] Badoglio disagreed both with De Bono's incautiously optimistic
scenario and with Bonzani's preference for an eighty-kilometre advance
and then awaiting the enemy's offensive. He preferred to wait on the
defensive on the Eritrean border while the air force took the offensive
against the gathering masses of the Ethiopian army.[228]

Mussolini decided nevertheless to put De Bono in charge of the campaign, which he now intended to put into operation during 1936. While
Badoglio thought that war with Ethiopia was inevitable and did not in
principle oppose it, he believed that much greater preparation was necessary and thought that the enterprise would be sufficiently difficult in itself
for it to be necessary to avoid any danger of international complications.
His preferred strategy was initially to adopt the defensive and wear down
the Ethiopian army before moving to a limited counter-offensive as a precursor to dividing the country up with France and England. Baistrocchi
and Bonzani shared his concerns about the primacy of European considerations and the French threat. They also worried about the deleterious
effects of such a campaign on the state of the army's supplies and equipment after Gazzera's careful husbanding of resources had built them up.
Both men shared a scarcely concealed anger that the party was trespassing on the general staff's business.[229] Two contrasting philosophies were
now in play. While the Fascists thought of 'colonial wars' and counted
on moral superiority, mobility and command powers to win, the soldiers
thought of a properly co-ordinated European-style campaign involving
large quantities of vehicles, guns and planes. The soldiers had some support from the king who was against a war after a personal visit to Eritrea
had shown him that the necessary infrastructure was lacking.[230]

The soldiers' reactions seem to have had an effect on Mussolini. First,
he prodded De Bono about the military preparations his scheme required,
producing the response that logistic preparations were needed, including the construction of roads.[231] Then he handed the dossier containing
De Bono's ideas and plans over to marshal Badoglio, newly returned to
Rome from his five-year stint as governor of Libya, for comment. Every
aspect of the plans so far adumbrated caused the Capo di stato maggiore
generale concern. Given the size of the task, international complications
had to be avoided; there was more than one European power, Badoglio
warned, that would like to see Italy get tangled up there. The power and

authority of emperor Haile Selassie over the tribal *ras* was now such that
the 'peripheral' policies of suborning local chieftains would not work,
and 'we would have all Abyssinia against us if we went to war with her'.
Badoglio's preferred scenario for a war he thought inevitable was one in
which Italy first stood on the defensive against attack and then moved
to the counter-offensive. A great deal needed to be readied – fortifications, intelligence, supply bases and communications, and airfields with
all their appropriate paraphernalia. De Bono's schematic plans left a lot
to be desired – 'in some areas they take as already completed works which
are still only projects'. In the face of all this Badoglio proposed that he go
on an inspection tour to find out exactly what the situation on the ground
looked like, and also delicately suggested that De Bono was not the right
person to take command of a military campaign.[232]

Mussolini called Badoglio, De Bono and Suvich to Palazzo Venezia
to examine his advisers' differing conceptions of a war at the start of
February. The minister for the colonies recorded the outcome in his
diary:

> Conclusion: it will be necessary to act. Badoglio will go there in March; but he
> will not be able to change anything. I will still be in charge of the operation. If
> things are quiet in Europe, Mussolini would like to carry out the operation in
> 1935.[233]

The meeting agreed on a scenario – an initial defensive with the intention
of following it up with an offensive in depth – and settled on August–
September 1935 as a possible start date for military operations. In a
move evidently designed to demonstrate his fitness to direct preparations
for the campaign and therefore also to command it, De Bono listed its
requirements, which included a metropolitan army division, a group of
alpini, seventy-two bombers and a squadron of fighters as well as munitions, artillery and motor vehicles, and asked for the money to start work
on the necessary roads as soon as possible. In an attempt to pre-empt
an inevitable conflict with Baistrocchi and Bonzani, he claimed that the
exceptionality of the case justified his being given everything that was
necessary by the war ministry for free, perhaps on loan.[234]

The concept of starting with systematic defensive preparations met
Mussolini's concerns about the international scene. If there was peace
in Europe during the next few years then they could serve as the basis
from which to launch an offensive or a counter-offensive; if, on the other
hand, the state of affairs in Europe was not such as to permit Italy to send
troops out to Africa then they would permit local forces to break up any
Abyssinian attack.[235] He rejected Badoglio's request to make a personal
visit of inspection to check on what he described as 'our very precarious

situation' but provided the funds his chief military adviser wanted for essential road building and permitted Badoglio to send his chief staff officer, colonel Visconti Prasca, in his stead.[236]

Meanwhile the extemporised machinery yawed. De Bono urged that Italy must be fully ready for a defensive by November 1934, the start of the six-month dry-weather fighting season; if the Abyssinians did not attack then, she should continue preparations to provoke them into an attack.[237] Bonzani, who had serious doubts about the picture of a unified attack by a single mass of Abyssinians which the colonial minister forecast, regarded the European situation as far from tranquil, and was opposed to 'any colonial adventure', was increasingly sidelined – a deliberate marginalisation of specialist military advice reminiscent of Crispi's neglect of his chief of general staff, Domenico Primerano, before the disaster at Adua in 1896 which worried Badoglio's own staff.[238] Badoglio stuck to his guns both on the proper strategic shape the campaign should assume and on the force levels it would need – three divisions from metropolitan Italy and one in reserve. A war with Abyssinia would be a serious problem for the other nations bordering on the country, he told Mussolini, but 'for us it is exceptionally serious (*gravissimo*) because we absolutely cannot run the risk of a serious setback'.[239]

Badoglio jousted with De Bono over the authority of the chief of army staff to prepare war plans for colonial operations, but although the legal and constitutional niceties of the latter's position were debatable Mussolini controlled the situation through his position as war minister. However he could not ignore the very substantial differences that had emerged between the contending parties. Matters had to be resolved and accordingly Mussolini called Badoglio, Bonzani, Baistrocchi, Valle and De Bono to Palazzo Venezia on 7 May 1934 to examine the question of military operations in Eritrea. The Duce decided that the logistical planning for the preparation and transportation of the three divisions that would be shipped out from metropolitan Italy would be given to the army general staff. The sub-text was evident: Mussolini had decided on a compromise under which the planning and co-ordination of the campaign remained in the hands of the 'colonials'. Valle supported De Bono's ideas for the employment of air power and argued that long-range bombers should be deployed to Eritrea in order to attack Addis Ababa. His ideas were opposed by Badoglio, who believed that such attacks would turn international opinion against Italy.[240]

Badoglio was seriously disturbed by the turn events had taken and following the meeting he took the unusual step of counselling against it in blunt terms. It would cost some six milliard lire, a third of the country's gold reserves, which would mean that equipment and munitions lost during the campaign could only be replaced slowly. This was a particularly dangerous prospect given the unstable situation of European politics which could alter at any moment, requiring every state to have its maximum force available. Sending substantial forces to Ethiopia 'will have the immediate consequence of making us less effective in Europe for some considerable time'. Given the inevitable extension of colonial responsibilities which would result from the war, another question arose: was the game worth the candle?[241] He did not rule out war with Ethiopia and acknowledged that provocations would have to be confected to make the Negus attack Eritrea.

Visconti Prasca, back in Rome after a five-week tour of the future theatre of war, provided a wealth of ammunition with which Badoglio could attack De Bono. The defences of Eritrea were entirely deficient, the road net was completely inadequate, as were water supplies, support services and accommodation, and intelligence on the ground was *nullo*. The existing organisation offered no guarantee of effectiveness and indeed presented a number of dangers: 'One cannot foresee the outcome of a defensive campaign against Abyssinia', Prasca's summary account concluded, 'and the less so in an offensive campaign unless radical and timely provisions are made'.[242] Examining the situation with Badoglio, De Bono and Suvich on the basis of Visconti Prasca's report, Mussolini ordered that 'defensive preparations' be completed as quickly as possible, after which the problem would exist of 'indirectly provoking action on the part of Abyssinia'. Meanwhile Italy was to behave towards Abyssinia as if acting on the basis of her Treaty of friendship. No word of the policy now being adopted must reach either the French or the British governments.[243]

The planning which followed showed the Italian system at its most confused. Bonzani thought military preparations should be made on the basis that the Negus might start a war before Italy was fully prepared, but Badoglio thought the Ethiopian army would need longer than the three months which would transpire between the start of Italian mobilisation and the appearance of the expeditionary force on the *altopiano* and so ruled out the possibility of a full-scale surprise attack. The two also disagreed on the size of the defensive perimeter in Eritrea. De Bono disregarded them both on this issue – though pretending to be in agreement – and determined to defend the whole of the colony, but took Badoglio's line against Bonzani over the likelihood of a surprise enemy attack and therefore the need to strengthen local defences.[244] It was typical of De Bono's superficial and contradictory approach that less than two weeks after rejecting Bonzani's cautionary suggestion he asked Valle for three bomber squadrons and a reconnaissance squadron, at least part to be available in Eritrea by the coming October when the rainy season would end, in order to strengthen the resistance the colony's troops must put up against a surprise attack the likelihood of which he was forcefully discounting to the army.[245] The minister for colonies was now becoming entangled in the careless and contradictory logic of his ill-considered plans, requiring 5,400 men as reinforcements from Italy to bring the colonial forces up to a state of readiness but reluctant to ask for them in case they triggered the very attack they were supposed to help resist.[246] De Bono also left Somalia to its own devices against the advice of Bonzani, Baistrocchi and Badoglio, informing the army chief of staff on the same day both that he did not believe the Abyssinians would attack it and still less that they would launch a diversionary attack on it in the event that they attacked Eritrea, and that he did not exclude the possibility of such a diversionary attack.[247]

As preparations gathered pace, the degree of confusion and disorganisation became ever more apparent. Visconti Prasca pointed out that, aside from the fact that the degree of alarm in De Bono's letters varied according to what he was trying to obtain, fundamental questions about the costs of roads, shipping and airfields and decisions about where the money was coming from had not been answered, and the details of the defensive line of the colony were still the subject of dispute.[248] The air force pointed out that its aircraft were not adapted to cope with the local conditions, rejected De Bono's request to send out single squadrons, and would only send out a group of forty aircraft in two echelons once all the necessary infrastructure was in place.[249] The navy had not studied the sending of reinforcements to Eritrea in advance of the main expeditionary force and did not regard itself as responsible for the task. Carrying out the expedition presented complex problems requiring herculean labours. Requisitioning the 120 ships required would completely disrupt national and international traffic and making the necessary adaptations to five sixths of them would take seventeen days if the yards dropped everything else; it would take eight months to order and construct the rafts, pontoons and towing vessels needed to disembark the expedition at Massaua; and the navy alone would need 400 tons of water a day for drinking and for its ships' boilers whereas the local supply amounted to only twenty tons a day. The list went on – diesel fuel, coal, rations – and the navy estimated the total cost at 251,990,000 lire.[250]

Badoglio called the chiefs of staff together in late July to discuss the situation. He was evidently unhappy: after relaying De Bono's forecast of a possible Abyssinian attack, he noted that the exact number of battalions that would be needed was yet to be specified, as was the covering line the troops would adopt. Sending out three regiments of advanced troops, which De Bono wanted, soon proved to be a more complicated matter than the colonial minister had imagined. Baistrocchi pointed out that after the conscripts were sent home from the metropolitan army on 24 August so few troops would remain that he could offer at most a single platoon from each infantry regiment. Badoglio suggested sending out a regiment of camicie nere ('blackshirt' Fascist militia), which De Bono accepted 'as long as they are well commanded' and which Baistrocchi backed. Roads would have to be built for which the army would have to advance the money. De Bono assured the meeting that the minister of finance had guaranteed the necessary funds.[251]

Valle confirmed that eighty planes would be available but pointed out that they would need to be of suitable types. Contracts for the machines he favoured, with a 1,000-kilometre range and a 1,000-kilogramme bomb load, would be issued in August and the planes would be ready in a year. If the Abyssinians took the initiative during the coming autumn machines from the metropolitan air force would have to be used; they would need twelve stages to reach Eritrea and would require over-flying rights from France, Egypt and England. In the circumstances, it might be better to transport them by sea. Valle thought he could get twenty-seven bombers to Eritrea by December. As far as air action was concerned, Badoglio thought that it would be necessary to be 'very cautious' about using gas, partly because it could lead to recriminations on the part of other powers and partly because no one knew quite how gas munitions would behave in high temperatures and on sandy ground. He wanted mass air action withheld until the enemy had massed his ground forces. 'From that moment no truce will be conceded and the full weight of the air offensive must be thrown on to the scales so as to obtain the maximum effect.'[252]

Admiral Vanutelli, deputy chief of naval staff, added to the mounting heap of difficulties to be overcome if Mussolini's design was to be turned into reality. The merchant fleet, from which vessels would have to be taken up to transport the expeditionary force, was necessarily spread all over the world and consisted mostly of cargo vessels now that the transportation of emigrants was no longer a significant activity, while the ocean-going liners which could transport large numbers of men could not get in to the port of Massaua. However, enquiries would be made on the assumption that shipping might be required on 15 September. Transporting preliminary reinforcements in peacetime meant hiring ships not requisitioning them; this, Vanutelli believed, was a job for the army. Trespassing on to the field of international politics, Vanutelli also pointed out that since Abyssinia was a member of the League of Nations and since Italy was a signatory of the Kellogg–Briand pact it would be necessary to ensure that Abyssinia was seen as the aggressor if difficulties were not to arise at sea.[253]

In saying this, Vanutelli was following the lead given by admiral Cavagnari a few days earlier. Exploring the impediments in international law which might obstruct Italy if she wished to fight the Abyssinians, the navy minister was able to find two possible avenues of escape: Italy could claim to be fighting in self-defence, a recognised right under all the international pacts and covenants, and she could claim that the dispute was not of such a nature as to lead to a war, as Japan had done over Manchuria. However, there was one apparently insuperable legal problem. If Italy did not legally declare war she could not intercept contraband of war going to Abyssinia, but if she did stop it she would be admitting the existence of a war and would therefore be in violation of the League of Nations covenant. There was also another potential international problem on the horizon. Even if accords were reached with Great Britain and France, the United States was certain to invoke the doctrine of 'non-recognition' which she had applied to Japan as a consequence of her unprovoked aggression against China. Cavagnari could not see a way to avoid either of these undesirable outcomes.[254]

The navy's capacity to ship an expeditionary force to Eritrea remained somewhat uncertain throughout the spring and early summer. In May, Ducci told Bonzani that it would need thirty days' warning to have the necessary shipping ready and that it could land a division and a half at Massaua within twenty days and another two divisions within a further twenty days. In all, the entire expeditionary corps could be disembarked in a period of between sixty and seventy days.[255] In July, with the mobilisation tables indicating that 120 ships would be needed, Bonzani asked the navy for more detailed information.

Admiral Cavagnari was concerned about the international dimensions of a war, given that troops would have to pass through the Suez canal and that the navy would be required to stop contraband reaching the Ethiopians. An expedition could be justified as a legitimate defence of the colony, but Italy must 'at all costs avoid assuming the legal appearance of the aggressor'. The procedures of the League of Nations which would precede a legal declaration of war could take nine months. Italy could disregard the League, as Japan had done in Manchuria, but the consequences could be very different. Although Cavagnari thought that formal sanctions would probably not be applied against Italy, the passage of ships through the Suez canal, the use of ports in the hands of League members for supply purposes, and the interruption of arms supplies to the enemy could all be impeded. Given all this, the navy chief thought it advisable to inject reinforcements into the colony gradually using ordinary transport, thereby reducing the size of the expeditionary force which would ultimately have to be mobilised and transported.[256]

Much evidently remained to be done before a campaign could be started in Abyssinia, but in any case the uncertain situation in Europe which was a consequence of the failure of the Geneva disarmament conference and of the situation in the Far East and which had just produced the Austrian crisis made Mussolini unwilling to risk reducing the efficiency of the metropolitan armed forces. 'Any undertaking which at this moment subtracts important military forces from the European scene must be regarded as very damaging and as producing a highly dangerous diminution in our capacity for war,' he told his military chiefs. Accordingly a façade of friendship with Abyssinia should be kept up. Meanwhile, De Bono was to accelerate defensive preparations and to consolidate Eritrea's defences on the defensive line Badoglio suggested. Badoglio's defensive strategy was also endorsed as the one to adopt in the event of an Ethiopian attack. Finally, Mussolini announced that three battalions of camicie nere were being readied to rush to Eritrea if needed.[257] He showed no particular sign of alarm when informed at the beginning of September that the cost of putting the four metropolitan divisions into Abyssinia for a year – the force level now being embedded in the planning – would amount to 4,850,000,000 lire.[258]

The build up of forces in Eritrea began slowly during September and October, accompanied by a chorus of doubts from the military about De Bono's over-optimistic assumptions on mobilisation and transportation times and criticisms of his vague operational designs based on the mobility of indigenous troops and on semi-improvised organisations. The doubts were confirmed in early November when brigadier-general Fidenzio Dall'Ora, appointed to head the intendance services for the campaign, reported that little or nothing had been done to improve the base facilities at Massaua, the railway or the roads and therefore that the task of sending out the expeditionary force 'must be considered if not impossible then certainly very difficult – a very onerous undertaking and one full of unknowns'.[259] Badoglio's reaction was now to down-play the difficulties, and he brought history into play to back himself up: during the 1896 campaign, in which both he and De Bono had taken part, two divisions had been pushed out into the Ethiopian *altopiano* with fewer supplies and less support.

The reason for Badoglio's surprisingly passive reaction to information which went to confirm his earlier doubts, and his quiescence in the face of de Bono's demonstrably deficient military plans, is probably that he realised that Mussolini was determined to conquer Abyssinia and intended to try to secure a bigger hand in the coming war for the

military professionals – and for himself.[260] Mussolini laid out his thinking in detail in a top secret memorandum at the end of December. He
was deeply concerned by two developments in Abyssinia. The first was
the increasing centralisation of power and authority in the hands of Haile
Selassie, a political development which would end in success if not interrupted from outside and one which increased the military capacity and
efficiency of the Ethiopian empire. The second was the transformation
of the Ethiopian army into a European style force in respect not only
of its organisation but more importantly of its weaponry. 'I regard the
Abyssinian military preparations as a most grave potential danger to the
safety of our colonies, especially if we were to be involved in Europe,'
he noted. From this analysis he drew two conclusions: time was working
against Italy, and the problem had to be solved by force of arms as soon
as Italy's military preparations made her sure of victory.[261]

The opportunity to settle this issue was provided by European politics,
which to Mussolini presented a two-year window of tranquillity. France's
willingness to declare her disinterest in Abyssinia save for the economic
concessions she enjoyed by virtue of running the Djibuti–Addis Ababa
railway, first unveiled by Pierre Laval at the end of November, removed a
considerable obstacle.[262] Together with the lessening of Italian pressure
on Yugoslavia, it would also improve relations with Belgrade. Yugoslavia
was in any case mired in domestic problems. French collaboration also
raised the prospect of a three- or four-power guarantee of Austrian independence, thereby reinsuring Italy against a threat of which she had very
recent experience.[263] Germany was in any case constrained from any
military adventurism by the state of her military machine, by domestic
considerations and by Poland's move towards France. Swift action would
minimise the likelihood of diplomatic complications:

No one will raise difficulties for us in Europe if the conduct of military operations quickly produces a *fatto compiuto*. It will be sufficient to tell England and
France that their interests will be recognised.[264]

The objective would be the destruction of the Abyssinian armed forces
and the total conquest of the country – 'the empire does not do otherwise' – and in order that the victory should be swift and decisive 'it will be
necessary to employ on a large scale the mechanical means which we have
and which the Abyssinians do not have, or not in significant amounts –
but which they could have within a few years'.[265]

Mussolini wanted at least 250 aircraft and 150 tanks in Eritrea and
50 aircraft and 50 tanks in Somalia (an indication that he was going
to take that theatre more seriously than De Bono), together with 'an
absolute superiority in artillery and gas'. The 60,000 soldiers to be sent

from Italy to join an equal number of local troops – 'better yet if they were 100 thousand' – must be ready in Eritrea by October 1935. The supplies used in the campaign would be gradually replaced so that the army did not lose its overall efficiency. Finally, Mussolini was sure that the Fascist masses would back the war, and so would the young. The only people who feared 'the adventure' were the remnants of 'the old world', but they were deceiving themselves and anyway politically and socially they counted for nothing.

The die was now cast. Mussolini had taken hold of the war, defining its aims and shaping its timetable. This was now much shorter than Badoglio's preferred schedule which would have extended the preparatory period to 1937 if he had had his way, partly on the grounds that the air force needed two years to construct the planes and build the bases that would be necessary. However, he too believed that 'the Abyssinian problem must one day be resolved by us'.[266] It was to be a war to express international power, not to win domestic popularity which Mussolini believed was already his.[267] It was also a further and decisive step in Mussolini's long-term objective of making the armed forces in general, and the army in particular, the instrument of an aggressive foreign policy. In only one respect were Mussolini's military and diplomatic preparations threatening to go awry. Diplomats and soldiers had alike emphasised the importance of having at least the tacit consent of both Great Britain and France before starting a war against Abyssinia. In order to win British goodwill, Fascist diplomacy was resorting to its customary deception. In London, the Italian charge d'affaires Leonardo Vitetti, told the permanent under-secretary at the Foreign Office, Sir Robert Vansittart, at the end of December that Italy had no desire to carry out an aggressive action in Ethiopia, 'with whom we wish to live in good neighbourly relations'.[268]

5   The trial of force: Abyssinia, 1935

Fig. 5 Ethiopia: Italian troops on the march

The Italian war in Ethiopia (Abyssinia) began on 3 October 1935.
Initially Mussolini put it in the hands of his most loyal Fascist general,
Emilio De Bono, but when it showed signs of stalling in November he
was replaced. Under the much more methodical direction of Pietro
Badoglio, the campaign was carried out with the blend of brutality and
efficiency which characterised Fascism's colonial wars. Gas warfare,
which the Italians fully expected to be a feature of any future European
war, played a significant part in securing victory. Italian troops entered
the Abyssinian capital, Addis Ababa, on 4 May 1936. Two weeks later
Badoglio left for Rome to claim his reward – which reportedly
included half the contents of the Bank of Ethiopia.

Fig. 6 Ethiopians admiring a poster of Mussolini

Once conquered, Abyssinia was supposed to become a model of
Fascist colonialism in which the white races ruled as a result of their
demonstrable superiority and based their relations with the natives on
'differentiation'. The policy foundered on two rocks: Mussolini's
insistence on the most violent measures in dealing with the 'rebels',
and his absolute refusal to allow his viceroy, marshal Graziani, to take
advantage of the splits in the feudal-tribal society to recruit allies and
partners. Among the native races, only the Muslims were singled out
for favourable treatment. The attempted pacification of Abyssinia
which cost the Italians 9,555 dead and some 140,000 sick and
wounded, ended on the eve of the Second World War in military
stalemate.

The military conquest of Abyssinia stood centre stage in Mussolini's
foreign policy designs in 1935. However, he had not 'abandoned all
hope of Italian expansion in Europe' in order to follow a policy of naval
expansion in the Mediterranean and military expansion in Africa.[1] As well
as seeking to take advantage of the shifting pattern of European politics
to manipulate international relations so as to create a diplomatic space
in which he could carry out his immediate plans, he had to consider the
medium-term threats and opportunities those same fluctuations might

present in relation to designs, ambitions and objectives on the continent which he had certainly not abandoned and, in some cases at least, simply could not discard. The African adventure had its own innate logic in the corpus of Fascist foreign policy, but it also had a European dimension in that it had to be effected before developments which might threaten it became realities. Mussolini more or less admitted as much to the senate on 14 May 1935: it was, he told them, 'precisely in order to be confident in Europe that we intend to secure our back in Africa'.[2]

Diplomatic preparations for war

Mussolini's goals remained basically unchanged throughout the twists and turns of international diplomacy during the first nine months of the year. It was his intention, he told Dino Grandi on 25 January, to resolve the Ethiopian problem 'in a radical manner', either by imposing direct Italian rule or by whatever other means events might suggest. Active military measures were being taken to this end which would be complete by October.[3] Instructed not to reveal any of this to the British foreign secretary, Grandi duly lied with aplomb. The Duce, he told Sir John Simon, 'absolutely does not have in mind attacking the integrity of Ethiopia and even less of making war on Abyssinia'.[4] After first abandoning the 'peripheral' policy in regard to Abyssinia, Mussolini next modified the policy of negation in respect of Great Britain. Grandi was firmly rapped over the knuckles in April for failing to get across to London Mussolini's determination to get a 'definitive solution' to the Ethiopian problem, and in the following two months Italy's goals were unambiguously communicated to the British, French and Germans. Italy sought direct control of the peripheral provinces making up the kingdom of Abyssinia, a protectorate over the Amharic 'core' (the provinces of Tigray, Gojjam and Showa), and the elimination of Abyssinia as a military power. She was not prepared to work through the League of Nations in Geneva, and if she was not given what she wanted then the alternative was war and 'the removal of Ethiopia from the map'.[5] As international tension mounted in late July, Mussolini made his position public in the regime's official newspaper, *Il Popolo d'Italia*. The bases of Italy's claims were 'the vital needs' of her people and her military security in East Africa. Put in military terms, 'the problem only admits of one solution, with Geneva, without Geneva, or against Geneva, that is, a military occupation of the African empire'.[6]

In Europe, Mussolini had to respond first and foremost to Germany, as did France and Great Britain. Buoyed up by her victory in the Saar plebiscite in January, which seemed to Italian diplomats to increase her inclination to go her own way in Europe, she seemed likely to grow ever more intractable as a result of the British policy of approaching her directly. Journeys by British diplomats to Berlin alarmed the French, thereby making them more desirous of Italian goodwill in Europe and therefore more willing to support Italy in Africa. One of the chief subjects of discussion was the prospective Anglo–German air pact which, if concluded, would split Great Britain from France and increase the latter's isolation. The apparently passive reaction of the Italian foreign ministry to the announcement of the reintroduction of conscription in Germany on 16 March and the news that despite this the British intended to go to Berlin may well have been the result, in part, of a tacit recognition that with Berlin's co-operation London might do for Mussolini what he had failed to do for himself during much of the previous decade and drive a wedge between France and Britain.[7]

If Germany's somewhat unpredictable diplomacy might in some respects be advantageous to Italy, her rearmament was another matter. In December 1934, Mussolini came by 'reliable evidence' that air bases were being prepared in Bavaria for an attack on Italy. Milch admitted their existence but denied that they reflected any aggressive intention towards Italy and explained them as being for regional training, and both von Blomberg and Fritsch passed strenuous denials via the German ambassador in Rome, Ulrich von Hassell, that Germany was making military preparations against Italy. The Italian air attaché gave credence to Berlin's version of events, believing that the activities in question were one end of a deployment directed against France.[8] The obvious connection between German rearmament, force deployments and the possibility of an attempt at anschluss with Austria reappeared three months later when the Italian consul at Innsbruck reported that the Reichswehr, SA and SS were massing in Bavaria, light artillery was appearing there, and 400 German fighters and 1,200 bombers were destined for the southern German frontier.[9] Goering's angry observation to Laval the following month that Germany could not tolerate Italy's taking part in non-interference treaties when she interfered in Austria to sustain a government there which would otherwise fall contained both an implicit military threat and a diplomatic warning not to participate in a multi-lateral guarantee. Since Laval was in close communication with Rome, Goering could be confident that both warnings would at once be passed on to Rome – as indeed they were.[10]

With the twin announcements in March of the existence of the Luftwaffe and the reintroduction of conscription, Germany now began to look like a cross between 'a gigantic barracks' and a 'fevered workshop'. The aircraft industry was reported to be fully mobilised, factories were working three shifts a day, and the officer corps shared a widespread certainty that war was near.[11] Hitler announced that Germany would create a thirty-six division army, but the Italian military attaché in Berlin was initially unable to say any more about when that might happen except that the necessary framework for it had not yet been created.[12]

Conflicting intelligence assessments of the likely employment of the new arms circulated in Rome. In December 1934 Cerruti suggested that Germany could attack Austria within 'less than two years'.[13] A month after the German announcements general Aracic, head of Yugoslav military intelligence, estimated that it would be four to five years before Germany would be ready for war. At the same time he signalled that Belgrade did not want Germany on her frontiers and would be ready to join a Franco–Italian bloc to protect Austria.[14] The French were reported to believe that Germany proposed to attack Czechoslovakia the following spring and that she planned to trigger an insurrection in Austria as soon as she invaded Czechoslovakia. In the war which would result, France planned to launch a 'violent offensive' against southern Germany and hoped for Italian assistance in the shape of an attack on Munich.[15] The air and military pacts which France concluded with Italy in May and July 1935 were both reflections of these strategic concerns and expressions of the diplomatic anxieties which lay behind them.

After attending the German army's summer manoeuvres, colonel Mancinelli was in a better position to comment on the first stage of German military rearmament. His news was reassuring. The programme of expansion was 'notably in arrears', especially as far as the supply of armaments was concerned: heavy divisional artillery was all of old types, there was little heavy field artillery, the infantry was armed almost entirely with old heavy and light machine-guns, and there existed only two companies of fast tanks. The 'marvellous individual freedom of action' of the infantry in past years had disappeared; now infantry squads were 'carried' by their non-commissioned officers. There was no evidence at all to support an impression of hurried preparation for imminent military undertakings. Rather everything was proceeding steadily but gradually according to a plan which evidently incorporated the factor of time.[16] Further comfort could be found in the distribution of the German army which, with ten infantry divisions on the Polish frontier, eight on the Franco–Belgian frontier, ten on the Czech frontier and three on the Austrian, showed an increase in the troop densities facing Lithuania and Czechoslovakia and 'minimal densities' on the Austrian and Swiss frontiers.[17] The military configurations appeared to bear out Hitler's declaration in late May that Germany would not interfere in Austria's internal affairs and did not intend to annex the country.

Italy's most accurate information about German rearmament came in respect of the navy. Despite French scepticism, the Italian naval attaché in Berlin, captain De Courten, shared the opinion of his British opposite number at the start of the year that no secret submarine building was going on in Germany. In late February he discovered that the Germans had slowed down construction of their fourth *Deutschland*-type pocket battleship in the expectation that an international agreement would be reached during the course of the year which would free them from the qualitative and quantitative restrictions imposed by the Versailles treaty and allow them to build more powerful battleships. If, however, no international agreement was reached due to French intransigence then they expected to regain sufficient freedom of action to be able to build ships larger than 10,000 tons, catching up for lost time by building rapidly thanks to the 'weighty construction capacity of German industry'.[18] Two weeks later, ambassador Cerruti reported that Hitler aimed to build a German navy of 400,000 tons or 34 per cent of the size of the Royal Navy. De Courten, who had picked up signs of the navy's intention to seek an agreement of this type the previous September, was initially unable to confirm a specific ratio (now 33 per cent) but offered well-informed speculation that Germany might use the additional tonnage to build five 28,000-ton battleships with 280-mm guns, three 15,000-ton aircraft carriers, a dozen new 6,500-ton cruisers, a total of fifty 1,000-ton destroyers, and twenty-five to thirty submarines of between 600 and 800 tons. He calculated that the programme would take ten years to complete, and believed it reflected increasing anxiety in the German navy about Russian naval armament which was reportedly shared by the British Admiralty.[19]

Rome was well informed about the subsequent moves leading up to the signing of the Anglo–German naval agreement on 18 June 1935. From Berlin, Cerruti reported the British invitation to Germany to send representatives for talks on 28 March, while De Courten relayed the content of Sir John Simon's initial talk with Hitler thanks to the indiscretion of his British colleague, and also reported Raeder's thinking on such technical issues as the number, displacement and armament of the different classes of ships Germany wished to construct. The German demand for naval parity with France which went along with the request for a German fleet 35 per cent the size of the Royal Navy was explained somewhat disingenuously by Raeder as being no more than 'a polemical affirmation by Hitler, made analogously with what was sought in respect of land and air armaments, but without any correspondence to reality'.[20] The manner in which the news of German submarine building that preceded the London talks was released to the French was a calculated insult, and the prospect that Germany would become a major naval power again provided a diplomatic impetus to France to tighten its relations with Italy – and therefore not to risk irretrievably losing the possibility of Italian support in Europe by siding against her over Abyssinia.[21] Great Britain's readiness to do a naval deal with Hitler, which was interpreted as a sign that her policy towards Germany was being 'readjusted', added military leverage to Rome's arsenal of diplomatic forces acting on France since it increased the pressure on Paris to reach naval agreement with her Latin partner in the Mediterranean. Although no joint Italo–French naval understanding was forthcoming, Cavagnari was able to report by mid-August 1935 that the French navy was co-operating to a hitherto unexampled degree.[22]

While German rearmament pointed to the advent of a stronger Germany, other reports reaching Rome gave reason to believe that Hitler was not yet politically secure. Although von Hassell asserted in January that Germany appeared finally to have understood that the state must have command over the party, Cerruti reported in June that Hitler was facing widespread discontent in the Gaus and might have to take refuge 'in a safe place'.[23] In mid-July Mussolini learned from his ambassador in Berlin – who would leave for the Paris embassy the following month, to be replaced by the pro-German Bernardo Attolico – that there was talk of a second 30 June against the SS, that the Reichswehr was making its anti-party sentiments apparent by such measures as not playing the Horst Wessel song, that in the smaller German towns the Nazi administration was increasingly unpopular, and that in the event of a showdown between the two sides Hitler was likely to go with the Reichswehr – all of which led him to expect an army coup d'état in Germany at any moment.[24] The evident tensions continued into September, when the army showed by its reactions to the imposition of a new flag and the news that the party would have the post of honour at the Nuremberg rally that it was clearly unhappy at the priority that Hitler was giving to the Nazi party. With a regime 'still in a state of evident formation and transformation, and . . . an army whose rearmament has scarcely begun', Attolico reported, 'Hitler's Germany cannot carry out a real foreign policy'.[25]

Although Germany emphasised her neutrality when the Abyssinian crisis began to blow up in the spring, her exact diplomatic stance was unclear. The Gauleiters were told that French and German involvement in the crisis had led to Italy's looking for closer relations with Germany, inaccurately since Mussolini had indicated that he was interested in a rapprochement as a consequence of the nascent Franco–Russian alliance and not of events elsewhere.[26] Berlin displayed evident anxiety at the military contacts between Italy and France and made it clear that she would regard a definite accord or alliance between the two powers as 'a catastrophe'.[27] Talking to Cerruti about Abyssinia, Hitler limited himself to remarking that these were the sort of problems that came along for peoples that were 'in full development' and that they were 'of capital importance for nations but are very difficult to resolve'.[28] Covert diplomacy was another matter. While repeatedly denying in public that Germany was arming the Ethiopians, Hitler provided money for Abyssinia to buy weapons in mid-July but ceased this policy two months later.

The point of greatest tension in Italo–German relations was Austria. Mussolini's inability to force Italian patronage on chancellor Schuschnigg, and the transparent refusals of both Britain and France to join Italy in guaranteeing Austrian independence may well have confirmed in the Duce's mind a view that he had been voicing since 1933 – that anschluss was inevitable sooner or later.[29] Mussolini first sought to shore up his position in Europe by reconstituting a British–French–Italian front and possibly adding Germany to it. The crucial point was Austria, he told the military high command in early February, but 'it can be presumed that we can expect a period of some three years of tranquillity in Europe'.[30] When the Stresa meeting, which was evidently an attempt to resuscitate the Four Power Pact of 1933 under a different guise, failed to produce anything concrete to underpin a general commitment to maintain Austrian independence and integrity, Mussolini turned to a second option in the shape of a Danubian pact. This was perhaps nothing more than a temporary expedient to stave off the inevitable, for in apprising von Hassell of his plan Mussolini remarked that 'a National Socialist regime was inopportune in Austria *at present*'.[31] The attempt to set up an Italian–Austrian–Hungarian pact of non-aggression and non-interference, secure the rearmament of the other two powers, bring Yugoslavia into the group and then underpin it with military accords showed immediate signs of faltering because of the internal hostilities between the intended partners and because their aims with respect to states outside the proposed grouping conflicted.[32] Increasingly isolated in Europe after he unleashed the war in Abyssinia in October, and more dependent on Germany as a result, Mussolini responded to a back-channel invitation to 'eliminate' the Austrian question, assuring von Ribbentrop early in November that it should no longer be 'a cause for disunity'. In return he got another undertaking of German neutrality and the promise of supplies of raw materials if sanctions left Italy economically isolated. He would ditch Austria before the campaign was over.

On the eve of the Abyssinian invasion Germany was distinctly cool over the Italian army's summer manoeuvres in the Alto Adige, which were regarded as 'a gratuitous demonstration directed against Berlin'.[33] On the day that the invasion was announced, von Hassell warned Mussolini that for Germany it was much too soon to engage in a struggle between the 'static' and the 'dynamic' nations.[34] However Mussolini was not looking for direct support in the war he had just begun, and in any case very shortly more encouraging expressions of German amity were forthcoming. Goering presented himself as keen to 'refresh' the old Italo–German friendship, of which he regarded himself as a pillar, but professed to be unable to move very far or fast because of the friendship between Italy and France which affected German public opinion. Nevertheless he indicated that Germany was prepared to co-operate with Italy outside the 'diplomatic bureaucracy'.[35] Not long afterwards, in von Ribbentrop's presence, Rudolf Hess referred repeatedly to the 'affinity of ideals' between Fascism and National Socialism and singled out anti-bolshevism as one of the natural bases for understanding and co-operation between the two powers – a remark seized upon by Mussolini.[36] The path which led to the Rome–Berlin Axis that Mussolini would announce twelve months later had begun to open up.

The advent of Flandin and Laval to the premiership and foreign secretaryship in France in October 1934 held out the promise of good things for Italy. Three years before when, in the course of an earlier attempt to improve Franco–Italian relations, Dino Grandi had raised the issue of compensation for the promised gains lost to Italy at the Paris Peace Conference, Laval had replied 'Ethiopia, for example'.[37] Flandin, approached at the same time by the air attaché in Paris, general Piero Piccio, whom Mussolini would use again as a back-channel in 1934, suggested that if agreements could be reached which protected French rights in Tunisia and French possessions in central Africa, France might undertake to leave Italy 'a free hand in Abyssinia'.[38] With both men again in office, the prospects for an agreement which would partially clear the diplomatic ground for war looked promising.

The international situation made them the more so in that Laval needed international support in the face of the rising military strength of Germany. Italy was a worthwhile ally on its own account as long as the tension between Italy and Yugoslavia could be resolved, and Laval also saw her as facilitating the Franco–German accord which was his other main objective.[39] Laval was the first to raise the issue of Abyssinia, and the Italian ambassador understood him to have in mind 'a partial disinterest by France in our favour in regard to economic–commercial issues'. Ambassador de Chambrun made the point to Mussolini in Rome the same day, and the Duce showed 'great interest' in it.[40] Several weeks before the Rome meeting which produced the secret agreement on Abyssinia, the French government had made it clear that while they could not cede the port of Djibuti to Italy, they were only interested in safeguarding their economic rights pertaining to the Djibuti–Addis Ababa railway and the narrow strip of land alongside it.[41]

Laval was the weaker party in the upcoming negotiations, not least because as a result of listening in to his telephone conversations with the French ambassador, Rome knew his negotiating positions. The discussions overheard by the Italian eavesdroppers suggested that Paris put the questions of Italians in Tunisia and the exact delimitation of the Tripolitanian frontier higher up its list than Abyssinia. In Europe, Laval wanted to draw Rome into system of mutual guarantees between Austria on the one hand and Yugoslavia and Czechoslovakia on the other by extracting from Mussolini a declaration maintaining Yugoslav integrity. This scheme hit a major obstacle when Romania pressed to be a party to a guarantee between the Little Entente and Austria so that everyone's frontiers would be protected, leaving Laval to conclude that it would be better to delay an accord on Austria 'until later'.[42] As regarding Abyssinia, Laval was ready to give Mussolini the two things he was insisting on: shares in the Djibuti railway and an economic 'waiver' (*désistement*). De Chambrun even hinted that there might be more to come, telling Suvich that what France was doing for Italy in Ethiopia 'is the most that we can do *at this moment*'.[43]

At the first meeting between Mussolini and Laval, on 5 January 1935, a range of issues including a non-interference pact to safeguard Austrian independence, the rearmament of Germany within the framework of the League of Nations, and Italian claims with respect to citizenship in Tunisia and the borders of Libya were all touched upon. Mussolini followed up the diplomatic signals already presented to him and pointed out that for him the main question was 'that of having a free hand in Ethiopia, the so-called "*désistement*"'. Agreeing, Laval said that he was 'only looking for a formula that will present the French position as proper even in the eventuality that it might become public knowledge in the future'.[44] At their second meeting two days later Mussolini reiterated the point and Laval replied that he 'understood the Italian concept' and that, aside from the economic interests it wished to protect, France had no intention of interfering with Italian penetration in Abyssinia.[45] Although neither the agreement which the two men signed nor the *procès-verbale* of their meetings made reference to Abyssinia, Mussolini's unpublished letter to Laval did refer to the specificities of French railway rights regarding the Djibuti–Addis Ababa line.[46] There was little room for doubt: Laval had signed away Abyssinia, in effect promising Mussolini 'a free hand' there as the Duce afterwards asserted.[47] In so doing he had added an important plank to the platform from which the Duce could launch the war he had in his sights.

Marshal Badoglio, whose sights were set on central Europe not Africa, moved swiftly to follow up the Mussolini–Laval agreement, listing the four scenarios in which the Italian and French armies might look to co-operate with one another: German mobilisation for any reason, German aggression against France in which Italy intervened, internal upheavals in Austria and German intervention in Austria following such distur-bances.[48] The Italian concerns were passed to Gamelin within a week of the conclusion of the Rome accords and shortly afterwards, at Badoglio's orders, colonel Mario Roatta arrived at the French embassy to establish arrangements for exchanging intelligence on the German army.[49] The French general staff agreed to examine the four hypotheses since they were of a military character and separate from political considerations. In the first case, the Italian general staff proposed the transfer of a battalion from each country to the other to affirm their solidarity. In the second, three Italian army corps would operate on the French right or three celeri divisions and nine alpini regiments would attack Bavaria via Salzburg – the option which the French military attaché, general Parisot, who was conducting the talks for Paris, preferred.

To the French way of thinking, the third and fourth cases elided into one another. In the event of a joint intervention with the concurrence of the Austrian government a single French division would be sent to the Udine–Tarvisio region as quickly as possible. If it was a question of fighting the Germans in Austria, two French divisions would be located on the northern Slovenian border along the Drava river between Villach and Judenberg-Volkermarkt west of Klagenfurt, separating the Italian and Yugoslav troops. The Italians were hopeful that Hungary could be kept neutral with a few promises, the exact nature of which they did not specify. If she did intervene alongside Germany she could easily be crushed by a combination of Czechs, Romanians and Yugoslavs.[50]

The rapid development of Franco–Italian military relations owed as much to Gamelin as it did to Badoglio, to whom it was certainly very welcome both professionally and also personally since the marshal was *francofilo*. Gamelin believed that the German army would be in a fully effi-cient state and able to undertake offensive operations by the end of 1935; its use could be provoked before then, and given the 'obscurity' of events it was not possible to foresee in which direction the weight of German mil-itary power might be applied.[51] In pursuit of closer relations he invited the Italians to attend the September manoeuvres at which motorised units would be put through their paces and reassured Rome that troop movements which would soon take place did not represent a strength-ening of frontier garrisons. He also specified the two divisions which would be co-operating with Italian troops in Austria, reassuring Rome that no coloured troops would be involved. Rome was also informed that the Haut Comité Militaire had authorised the French general staff to maintain direct relations with the Italian staff in order to study war scenarios. Gamelin expressed his gratitude for the assurance that SIM would no longer be actively operating against France, a move which he intended to reciprocate.[52] The planning agreements followed almost immediately. By the end of March the Italian general staff had worked out a design to send Armata 'F' comprising nine divisions to the Belfort–Lure–Montbeliard region of France in fifteen days.[53]

The French betrayed signs of military nervousness on the eve of the Stresa meeting, retaining 60,000 conscripts under arms for an additional three months and transferring units from southern France to the northeastern frontier to work on completing the fortification system. While not the 'vast movement of protective troops' trumpeted by the Paris correspondent of the *Corriere della Sera*, the moves were seen as a significant reaction to the German threat.[54] At the start of August, Gamelin went out of his way to emphasise the importance of Italy and France remaining militarily strong and closely linked to one another. British opposition to Italy's policy in East Africa could, he believed, generate serious repercussions in the Muslim world which might create difficulties for herself and for France. Speaking indirectly but plainly to Badoglio, Gamelin told the Italian military attaché that the French military authorities were following Italian action in Ethiopia 'with every sympathy'.[55]

At the end of August the French war minister, colonel Fabry, expressed a 'perfect understanding' of Mussolini's policy in East Africa, which he expected the Duce to take 'all the way'. His fears were that Hitler might one day decide to fortify and garrison the demilitarised zone of the Rhineland, in which case neither Laval nor any other French premier could do more than protest since France would not actively go to war. If a war transpired nothing was to be expected from England by way of military assistance for eight or ten months. Fabry was himself convinced that the first fortnight of the next war would be extremely important and perhaps even decisive. The war minister feared that, given her lack of military preparation and faced with an Italian military action in Ethiopia, Great Britain might declare that Italy's military efficacy in Europe was greatly diminished and abandon the Locarno treaties, prompting an immediate move by Hitler to remilitarise the Rhineland. While there was much in this conversation to reinforce Italian expectations of French backing at Geneva as the League crisis over Abyssinia reached its height, there were also grounds to support swift action: Fabry estimated that the Laval ministry could not last more than another two or three months.[56]

Playing on evident French fears about the aerial threat from Germany, Rome warned Paris in the spring of the danger that ongoing discussions between Great Britain and Germany about a western air pact might produce a recognition in principle that Germany could have an air force before broader questions of arms limitations and security pacts had been satisfactorily concluded. The latter and not the former was in France's best interests.[57] Italy and France concluded air accords on 12–13 May under which in the event of a German war against the signatories single-handedly or together, French airfields would be put at Italy's disposition a squadron of French fighters would go to the Italian sector of the front and between fifty and one hundred Italian bombers would go to France.[58] Next day, denying rumours of an air agreement between Italy, France and Austria, Mussolini told the Germans that only a civil-aviation agreement was being concluded along with preliminary discussions in case a western air pact did eventually transpire.[59] He doubtless took some pleasure from the fact that a similar deception had been cooked up by Balbo and Goering to conceal the true nature of their discussions about Italo–German air collaboration the previous year. It was agreed that plans would be jointly established to decide what actions the two powers' air elements would undertake, but conversations between the Italian and French air staffs in mid-September made only limited progress, naming the airfields each side would put at the other's disposal and concluding that the numbers of aircraft each party would provide could not be fixed but would be decided at the periodic meetings which were to take place in May and November each year.[60]

As a result partly of Gamelin's visit to Rome 25–28 June, the military plans for Franco–Italian co-operation made more progress than the airmen managed. If Germany attacked France or Belgium, Italy would send three army corps (comprising six divisions plus support troops) which would fight on the French right wing; if, on the other hand, Germany attacked Italy through Austria, France would send one army corps which would fight on the Italian right and link up with Yugoslav forces. The French high command undertook to do all it could to ensure that Yugoslav and Czech forces co-operated with the Italians and covered the right flank of the joint Franco-Italian force.[61] Shortly afterwards Pariani suggested that the two Latin countries should establish a common military policy and sought to persuade the French that Italy was the better prospect as an ally by demoting Great Britain in the league table of military powers on the grounds that air warfare rendered her former mastery of the seas 'illusory'.[62]

Naval relations between Italy and France never advanced as far as joint planning during the months leading up to the Abyssinian war, but there were intermittent signs of a modest thaw in relations. In March, Laval sounded out Rome on whether it would be possible to come to a mutual accord to slow down the building of the two 35,000-ton battleships to which each power was committed, but got little in the way of encour-agement for the idea from Suvich.[63] The new French battleships were announced in the 1935 naval programme, but after the Rome accords the accompanying propaganda orchestrated by the French naval general staff abandoned the theme that they were the response to Fascist Italy's having upset the balance of force in the Mediterranean and instead emphasised the need to be ready to parry the German menace, the requirement to replace over-age warships, and the continuing power battleships embod-ied. The Italian naval attaché estimated that both ships could be ready by the end of 1938, more or less at the same time that the Italian battleships were due to be completed.[64]

Because she wished Italy to avoid a war in Abyssinia at all costs, France took a diplomatic stance during the summer of 1935 which was of con-siderable assistance to Italy, working within the League of Nations to try to help Italy achieve its aims peacefully. In practice this meant resisting the pressure for sanctions (and resisting absolutely the idea of military sanctions), collaborating with Italy in a tactical plan to try to remove Abyssinia from the protection of the League by declaring her 'unfit' to be a member, and working on the British to try to ensure that their determi-nation to enforce the League Covenant against Rome did not aggravate the Mediterranean situation to dangerous levels.[65] By doing him this service the French provided Mussolini with time for the completion of his military preparations, offered the possibility of a diplomatic solution which might be acceptable to him (although such an outcome was highly unlikely), and most importantly perhaps acted as a restraint on Great Britain. Mussolini used this last facility in late August, warning Laval that Italy could not be an effective power on three fronts – Eritrea, the Brenner Pass and the Mediterranean – and that if there was a collision between Rome and London the consequences would be first anschluss and then a reduction in Czech capacity to resist Germany to virtually nil. France was also informed that the Italian armed forces faced the prospect of an Italo–British conflict calmly 'given our superiority in aeroplanes and submarines and our geographical position'.[66] The assertion was a consid-erable misrepresentation of the views of two of the three armed forces and of Badoglio, but it appears to have worked: at a cabinet meeting three days later, Laval was obdurate in his stance against sanctions.[67] In September, when economic sanctions appeared unavoidable, Laval worked to reduce them to a minimum.

After having been rapped across the knuckles by Mussolini in April for failing to get across to London the Duce's determination to reach a 'definitive solution' in regard to Abyssinia, Dino Grandi and his staff at the embassy took pains to remedy their error. Grandi's reading of the fundamentals of British politics produced advice to Mussolini that he copy the strong-arm methods of Japan and Germany in their dealings with the League of Nations as the best way to win the British over, and that Great Britain was likely to abandon her intimidatory actions in the face of the possibility that Italy might leave the League. In Rome, Aloisi shared his view that the League was a veil concealing Britain's true interests as a colonial power, which centred on Lake Tana. Asked by Mussolini on 5 August whether Great Britain was disposed to make war on Italy in order to stop her doing likewise on Abyssinia, Grandi reported no evidence of any serious consideration so far that London would act outside League procedure.[68] Asked again three days later whether Great Britain seriously intended to wage war on Italy, Grandi replied on 16 August that to the best of his knowledge no 'special measures' had been authorised. Four days later the Italian naval staff learned that Britain did intend to strengthen her Mediterranean fleet.[69] Still up-beat notwithstanding this information, Grandi assured his master at the end of August that the Duce's African policy had engendered sympathy and support which Italy did not have before, and that sanctions were unlikely because the Royal Navy would be too exposed to risk if it did apply them. As late as 19 September Grandi thought war was improbable but he did at last acknowledge that hostility towards Italy was mounting.[70]

While Grandi transmitted confident assurances of the unlikelihood that Britain would go to war, rumours of British reinforcements abounded in Africa and ricocheted around Rome. The arrival of nine fighter aircraft in Alexandria and eighteen crated aircraft in Aden, together with the transit of four seaplanes there, in late June and early July could be read in several ways.[71] Unconfirmed rumours flowered in May, June and July – that British troops were on their way to Egypt and Somaliland, that preparations were being made to double the size of the British bases at Aden, Port Said and Cairo, and that recruitment of the King's African Rifles in Kenya was being stepped up. Stories that up to ten battalions of troops were on their way from India to take up position on the Sudanese–Ethiopian border were however scotched when the Italian consul at Calcutta reported at the end of July that up to that moment no Indian army units had left the country. Confirmation that nothing untoward was yet happening came from his opposite number in Cairo who reported on 3 August that 'the picture of English military activity in the Canal zone and Sudan is restricted to light reinforcement of materiel and cadres and the study of plans for what would be necessary in the case of complications'.[72]

Although British military activity in Africa could undoubtedly affect an Italian military venture there, the most serious threat to Rome's imperial ambitions came from the presence of the Royal Navy in the

Mediterranean. On 22 May, admiral Cavagnari sought information on the Admiralty's attitude towards the Ethiopian question from the Italian naval attaché in London, captain count Ferrante Capponi. Capponi, whose flawless English and family connections helped to make him a particularly effective reporter of the British scene, learned that the Admiralty was principally concerned with the repercussions on the European situation and felt that the Lake Tana question could be solved by negotiation. He also detected political considerations in play: facing a general election in the autumn and under attack from the Labour Party for the failure of the Geneva disarmament conference, the National Government would look for as many successes as possible there in the cause of peace.[73]

The naval review in mid-July provided a useful opportunity for Capponi to check the actual state of the British fleet. Rome was informed that while most of the Mediterranean fleet was presently in home waters it would all be back in Malta by the end of the month, when its main units would consist of five battleships, three battle-cruisers and one aircraft carrier. More importantly, Capponi detected a tendency to want to shift the centre of gravity of the fleet to the eastern Mediterranean because of the extreme vulnerability of the Malta base.[74] The contradictory currents of British public opinion, which were hardening in favour of Abyssinia during the summer, made it difficult for him to judge in mid-August whether England would come out in favour of an Italian-controlled Abyssinia or against it. By the end of the month it was apparent that while opinion in the Admiralty was divided, the government-controlled and conservative–imperialist press, the City of London and the mass of public opinion was hostile to Italy – the latter 'not out of personal enmity but on grounds of principle'. The Admiralty appeared to be playing a key part in the British cabinet's decisions, counselling moderation because of the risk factor represented by the Italian navy and air force and the irreparable blow to prestige resulting from losses whatever the outcome of a war.[75] At the start of September Capponi learned that the assistant chief of naval staff, admiral Kennedy Purvis, particularly deplored the idea of imposing sanctions on Italy. He was left with the impression that the Admiralty was fully aware of the dangers it would face if it was decided to enforce sanctions against Italy, and also that its preparations were more a general precaution given current tension than preparations for action against Italy.[76]

As well as diplomatic and naval reports, Mussolini had other intelligence on which to base his judgements in the run-up to war for SIM was able to pass on highly confidential British documents thanks to their having recruited the servant of the British ambassador in Rome, Francesco Costantini, sixteen years before. In 1924 Costantini began passing on documents and then, probably in July 1932, he handed over a set of twenty-four British code-books. Costantini also worked for the NKVD – possibly with SIM's connivance – and during 1935 supplied Moscow with the British accounts of the Simon–Hitler–Eden meeting in Berlin on 25–6 March and the Eden–Mussolini meeting in Rome on 24–5 June amongst other documents.[77] It seems highly likely that Mussolini saw them all too. Although important, such pieces of intelligence probably played only a contributory part in Mussolini's decision-making on the Abyssinian War; the international diplomatic network functioned sufficiently well that much of the content of such talks was soon widely known. Three copies of the Maffey report, in which the British government concluded that no vital national interests would be at stake were Abyssinia to pass under Italian control, fell into Mussolini's hands during the summer, one stolen from the British embassy safe 'on the eve of the war', another decrypted by SIM and handed to him by Mario Roatta, and the third passed to Dino Grandi in London by the Soviet ambassador Ivan Maisky along with several other secret Foreign Office despatches.[78] Given all the information available to him, then, it is safe to conclude that Mussolini felt able to overcome his fear of sanctions and to continue on his chosen path to the complete submission of Abyssinia 'not so much through *intuition* as by reason of documented knowledge'.[79]

While the diplomats fenced during September, intelligence reaching Rome suggested that the military preparations being made by the British in Egypt were not such as to offer any direct threat to Italy. In the judgement of the Italian air attaché in London, even if the squadrons available in Aden and Iraq were added to Middle East Command it would still be insufficient to do more than police the interior and guard the borders of Egypt. To do anything more would necessitate sending reinforcements from the United Kingdom, which was currently engaged in reconstructing its air force and reorganising and improving metropolitan air defences.[80] At the beginning of the month British air exercises in the canal zone and at Ismailia were reported to be 'intensifying' and hangers at Abu Sueir were being converted into major repair facilities, but in mid-September no exceptional air activity was evident.[81] Local reports of the arrival of large numbers of aircraft, repeated in the Italian press, were revealed to be considerably exaggerated.[82] Military preparations, which included the arrival of quantities of munitions, the construction of radio stations and the movement of troops from one city to another 'to make the population think that reinforcements have arrived from outside', appeared to be defensive measures taken against the possibility of an Italian attack and internal disturbances. The military materials reaching Egypt by the end of the third week in September appeared to be arriving in 'relatively modest amounts such as to increase the efficiency of the occupation forces but not substantially to modify their organic composition'.[83] Since Mussolini had no intention of attacking Egypt, it was entirely reasonable for him to suppose that the dangers to his Abyssinian enterprise posed in this quarter of the Mediterranean world could be discounted, though 120 more aircraft arrived in Alexandria shortly before the Italian campaign began.[84]

On the eve of the declaration of war, the news arriving from London suggested that an important shift was taking place in the foundations of British policy. Grandi, who in August had several times urged Mussolini to attack Abyssinia at once, detected a decisive change of mind in British public opinion which now favoured collective action in defence of the League of Nations. In the face of this, he argued, Italy needed an early success in the coming campaign on which to construct 'an honourable compromise'.[85] The Italian military attaché, colonel Mondadori, found himself engaging in conversations which no longer excluded the probability of serious conflict between England and Italy, and noted increasing public pressure for rearmament.[86] On 27 September, with the Italian declaration of war only days away, Capponi offered his interpretation of the motives behind the movement of large parts of the Home fleet to the Mediterranean. It was reasonable to suppose that

the reinforcement of the Mediterranean fleet is not just an act of direct intimidation towards Italy, nor also an act intended to reinforce British prestige ... but appears to be a more serious matter, since it shows a readiness on the part of the Admiralty, which is the executive power of the British empire, to hold itself in readiness for any eventuality which could transpire as a result of an armed conflict between Italy and Abyssinia.[87]

While the Royal Navy was as much an incipient threat as an actual one, perhaps more so, a shift in public mood was not the same thing as a shift in government will, though the one might well lead to the other. Information of this sort may therefore have encouraged Mussolini to act swiftly before such a transformation progressed very far.

While much attention and energy was focused on matters to do with Abyssinia, Italian diplomacy both sought to act on and reacted with the broader currents of European diplomacy. Closer relations between Italy and France produced anxieties among the Danubian powers towards whom Rome had been sympathetic for some time. Hungary in particular worried that in closing up to France Italy would cease to be a revisionist power.[88] Gömbös asked for arms in November 1934 in the context of a possible attack by Yugoslavia and a hypothetical conflict between France and the Little Entente on the one hand and Hungary and Italy on the other.[89] A single-handed war against either Hungary or Bulgaria was indeed something Yugoslavia could consider undertaking without the aid of France, unlike a war against Italy, according to the Italian ambassador in Belgrade.[90] Mussolini now played two hands of declaratory diplomacy simultaneously, whilst characteristically pursuing a third covertly.

The Rome accords of January 1935 deprived the Little Entente of the hope of French support in the event of clashes with the Danubian powers, thus creating favourable ground on which Mussolini could reopen discussions with Yugoslavia, suspended after the autumn of 1933, for a pact of friendship and non-aggression perhaps leading to a military alliance. Mussolini encouraged the Yugoslavs to move in the direction he wanted by suggesting that the future union of Germany and Austria might have to transpire 'either as the result of a spontaneous [internal] movement or as the consequence of a violent action'.[91] As the international crisis mounted during August and September, Yugoslavia signalled that she wanted closer relations not with France or Germany but with Italy and that she hoped that a diplomatic understanding would be followed by a military alliance. At the end of November Mussolini responded: he was ready to move to a deeper accord and liquidate Croat emigration if Belgrade would suspend the trial of king Alexander's assassins currently under way in France.[92] Manipulating a favourable situation in European politics, he was able simultaneously to remove a threat which had preoccupied him since the late 1920s and strengthen his position in south-east Europe. Secondly, armed with an argument for parity of rights by virtue of Germany's unilateral announcement of rearmament on 16 March but moving cautiously in the run-up to the Stresa conference, he indicated that he would support the right of Austria, Hungary and Bulgaria, disarmed under article 19 of the Versailles Treaty, to rearm but would not support unilateral action by them.[93] After the Stresa meeting Bulgaria was demoted by Mussolini, who now decided to prioritise the question of parity of rights and rearmament only for Austria and Hungary.[94]

Military equipment, which had for some time been a tool of Italian diplomacy, now became the principal implement in Mussolini's covert diplomacy. Asked what she wanted, Austria requested a dozen 149-mm Skoda heavy field guns, a dozen 7.65-mm field guns, at least 25,000 rifles, fourteen fast tanks and ground radios. Mussolini had agreed with the Austrian foreign minister, baron von Berger-Waldenegg, that payment would be deferred until 1936. No Skoda guns were in fact available and only fifteen 7.65-mm field guns in a poor state. The tanks, now reduced to twelve and which the Austrian chancellor believed Mussolini had promised for nothing, could not be provided from stock coming on-line until July.[95] The question of payment posed bureaucratic problems as the Austrians wanted to pay the 840,000 lire for the tanks in two tranches in January 1936 and January 1937, to which Baistrocchi was prepared to agree, but this required an advance from the treasury since a debt could not be carried forward to the next financial year.[96]

Austria was one of three countries to which Mussolini promised arms. Bulgaria had been promised 60,000 rifles and 500 machine-guns, but these had never been passed over, and now sought 400 machine-guns. Hungary was being sent 25,000 rifles and 32 77-mm guns as a free gift, and on the strength of a promised loan of 70 million lire had ordered sixty fast tanks as well as clothing, equipment and gas masks. Austria's tanks – now increased to fifteen – would be provided at a cost of 1,050,000 lire interest-free.[97] Pariani was only prepared to dole out tanks at a rate of ten a month, of which seven or eight should go to Hungary, and pointed out that since both countries were forbidden to possess tanks under the terms of the post-war peace treaties they would have to be sent secretly. Sending regular batches of tanks to Hungary via Austria, a state which he thought 'entirely untrustworthy', posed obvious problems.[98] So too, though this was not apparently remarked upon, did Austria's desire to have at least three or four tanks to test in August manoeuvres. Because of domestic needs, the army wished to put back the first deliveries of tanks to October, but after Mussolini promised them to Austria in August the schedules were rearranged so that the Austrian order would be delivered by November 1935, and the Hungarian order by January 1936. The first four tanks were sent at the end of September in closed railway wagons labelled 'agricultural tractors'.[99]

When Mussolini and Schuschnigg met in Florence early in May, the Duce questioned his guest closely on the state of the Austrian army. On being told that it presently amounted to some six or seven divisions but lacked artillery and some infantry battalions he pronounced it 'already a significant force'. Schuschnigg asked for tanks, aircraft and howitzers, and passed on the information that the Hungarian general staff had approached Vienna about support in the event of an attack by Yugoslavia. The fact that Rome was beginning to move closer to Belgrade promised to improve Austria's military value as she would be able to focus her military energies on the German threat.[100] Mussolini agreed in principle to further transfers of war materiel to Austria, comprising fifteen more tanks, four Caproni 133 and five Caproni CR 20 aircraft.[101] Secret collaboration extended beyond supplying weapons to chemical warfare and in July the head of the Italian military chemical service paid a secret visit to Austria and Hungary to share knowledge on protective measures and on Germany's capabilities.[102]

In August the head of what was in effect the Austrian general staff, major-general Jansa, newly arrived in post after a period as military attaché in Berlin and armed with a clear idea of German feelings about Austria ('quite otherwise than friendly and fraternal'), indicated that he would be happy to open up secret military discussions with the Italian general staff on questions of mutual interest. Mussolini personally approved the establishing of contact.[103] The Austrians followed up with a request for assistance in organising their artillery. The head of SIM, Mario Roatta, was prepared to agree in principle but thought it useless to discuss material aid since Italy was not in a position to provide anything.[104]

Italy's imminent involvement in war in Abyssinia interfered with the supply of rifles to Danubian allies. At first it also caused the Hungarian general staff alarm at the possibility that the deployment of her troops there might distract Rome's attention from Europe, but by the end of September this had changed to a fear that Italy might not push her action there to the limit, in which case her prestige as a great power would suffer.[105] By early October Austria was pressing for its tanks in the light of the 'very aggravated' political situation and the serious position she would be in if conflict occurred. In exchange, she offered larch and fir wood for which the Italian air force had no use but which the artillery and the engineers were willing to take.[106]

Military collaboration with the Danubian powers produced a reward of sorts when the Hungarians offered to supply experts in mine warfare who would travel to Italy – and if required to Abyssinia, possibly disguised as Red Cross operatives – to help organise arrangements on the ground for defensive battles to halt the Ethiopian forces. Mussolini accepted the offer and the necessary arrangements were made to host three officers and receive some 120,000 mines.[107] De Bono then brusquely declined the Hungarian specialists and their supplies as not necessary.[108] The officers went to Civitavecchia nevertheless, and the materials arrived first in a sealed railway wagon and later in boxes labelled as machine parts for manufacturing oil.

Baistrocchi and army reform

On 1 October 1934 Federico Baistrocchi added the portfolio of chief of the army general staff to his responsibilities as under-secretary of state at the war ministry. Since his hands were full with ministerial business the deputy chief of staff, Alberto Pariani, effectively took over the day-to-day running of the new office. To an extent Baistrocchi was an outsider: an artilleryman who had attended the military academy at Modena, he had not been to the staff college and had not served on the general staff. However, his appointment was welcome in some quarters. Zoppi was friendly towards him and Badoglio, for whom Baistrocchi had served as artillery commander of II army corps during the world war, apparently so too. The Capo di stato maggiore generale promised to do all he could to help Mussolini's newly installed deputy and advised him that the most pressing question was that of officers' careers.[109]

Baistrocchi was determined to rejuvenate the officer corps under the slogan of *giovinezza* ('youth'), which both sounded like and was an expression of the value most prized by the Fascist party. A programme of mandatory early retirement for senior officers was approved by the chamber of deputies in May 1934; officers were sent on 'compulsory leave' without regard to their personal qualities; senior officers were required to involve themselves more closely with the work of junior officers; and the numbers of courses were reduced. Excess officers from the junior and middle grades were siphoned off into the Fascist militia, now responsible for anti-aircraft and coastal defence, where they occupied staff and command posts, and into the newly formed frontier guard command.[110] There was certainly much to be done: French observers saw weaknesses in the morale and effectiveness of the officer corps (although the civic education of the young under the Fascist regime was thought to be likely to have a positive effect), and after observing the 1935 manoeuvres the French assistant military attaché, colonel Catoire, thought that although Italian subalterns were excellent the colonels were no more mature in spirit than his own captains and the higher commanders were 'very superficial'.[111]

In pursuit of a much more mobile and offensive-minded army Baistrocchi had tested the new celeri units in the summer manoeuvres of 1934, with Badoglio's approval.[112] The thirty-one army divisions were given names instead of numbers in imitation of the ancient Roman tradition, and in December the length of conscript service was reduced from eighteen months to twelve. Pariani began to think about creating fully motorised divisions to reinforce the celeri divisions or to be used for other purposes, and in May 1935 he indicated that he wished to create two such divisions – with new and appropriately aggressive names.[113] By May 1936 they had come successively into being in the shape of the Trento and Po divisions. The deputy chief of staff also began a development which was gravely to weaken the Italian army by the eve of the Second World War – the creation of the two-regiment *divisione binaria* which in due course replaced the heavier three-regiment *divisione ternaria*. Initially the change owed quite a lot to practical exigencies. Two *divisioni binarie* were created on Sardinia; three divisions sent to Libya in September 1935 (two of which subsequently went to Abyssinia) were *binaria*; and some of the replacement divisions created in metropolitan Italy were *binaria*, as was the Po division.[114] The task of replacing divisions sent overseas (ultimately six metropolitan infantry divisions were used in Eritrea and one in Somalia), keeping the home units up to maximum strength and carrying out the annual major training exercises put the army under some strain. Pariani was concerned not to reduce the number of divisions in Italy. Thus he preferred to have thirty two-regiment divisions rather then twenty three-regiment ones. Beyond his immediate needs was a longer-term aim to transform the entire army, as his objective was a force of three celeri divisions, four motorised divisions and sixty *binaria* divisions which would normally be *ternaria* divisions in peacetime.[115] If this was indeed his intention, in the short term it came to nought: after the Abyssinian war was over the army reverted for a while to its former shape with only two *divisioni binarie* and two motorised divisions.

In 1935 Baistrocchi proposed to drive his programme forward with a range of new measures of which the foremost was a new set of regulations – *Directives for the employment of large units* – based on what he saw as a few fundamental principles. The new ideal was a rapid war of movement because that was more suited to the material conditions of the nation and to its new spirit 'created by the Victory [in 1918] and by the Regime'. Preparation for such a war would impart increased flexibility to the army since it implied 'the possibility and the capability of adapting ourselves to whatever other form of war may be imposed on us by *forza maggiore* and contingent needs; any preparation oriented towards another form of war would not find us ready for one of movement'.[116] New military regions would speed up mobilisation, while the three celeri divisions and one or two infantry divisions would form a force ready for immediate employment. The *divisione terneria* composed of nine infantry battalions and one machine-gun battalion, adopted in 1926, was to be retained and given more artillery; 'small, light, and adaptable to any terrain and situation', these formations best suited 'not only our frontier territories, which are harsh and difficult, but the ground we shall find beyond them'.[117] Horses were very much still a part of this new army, in which cavalry would contribute both to reconnaissance and to the assault. The infantry's firepower would be strengthened with assault mortars, light and heavy machine-guns and semi-automatic weapons. New artillery was on the way, as were trucks and tanks. The same light tanks (*carri veloci*) used by the celeri would be given to the infantry divisions as assault tanks on the grounds that this was a practical and economic solution 'in as much as their mobility, light weight and vulnerability [*sic*] ensures their use on any ground and in any circumstances'.[118] This last was to prove a major and costly piece of self-deception in five years' time.

Mussolini chose to chair the sessions of the army council which convened to discuss Baistrocchi's plan himself, a rare occurrence. Characteristically, he led the council into an analysis of detailed aspects of the new
military regions, asking a series of questions – why were the commanders
of military regions being given authority in matters of military discipline?
and why were their commanders being called 'inspectors'? – which illustrated his capacity simultaneously to delve into minutiae and to turn up
an unresolved and not totally unimportant issue of detail. After flexing
their intellectual muscles, the members of the committee agreed to accept
the proposal. The subsequent discussion about arrangements for guarding the frontiers was similarly disorganised and rambling.[119] Baistrocchi's
proposal to designate the celeri divisions and at least one infantry division
as ready for immediate employment drew strong support from Grazioli.
Bonzani countered with a conservative view: there were too few troops
in the other units to run the risk of weakening them still further in the
event of having to reinforce the stronger frontier units, and France's dis-
heartening experience mobilising a division made up solely of reserves
was a warning of the dangers of excessive dilution. Badoglio, a master of
this kind of debate, expressed approval in principle but pointed out that
during the period of the year when fewest recruits were in the ranks (the
so-called *forza minima* which resulted from conscripts being sent home
early for reasons of economy) units were so weak as to raise questions as to
whether the scheme could work given the state of the entire army. Everyone present probably understood that what he was really questioning was
whether it should work.

After reminding the council that he planned to use the entire annual
contingent rather than sending 60,000 on immediate leave as happened
presently, Baistrocchi threw down the reformists' glove: if the army, with
the means at its disposal, was to carry out the tasks confided to it, 'it must
forget the principle that all units must be composed in exactly the same
way in time of peace'.[120] Faced with the quintessential argument of the
ultra-conservative Piedmontese military that because of the way things
were they could not change, he threw in a shrewd political point: the pre-
military training provided by the Fascist regime made the basic situation
better, regardless of other factors. Expressly influenced by the experience
of the Dollfuss assassination, when he had been able to mobilise the
Brenner division at full efficiency only because it was at *forza massima* in
the middle of summer, Mussolini came down on Baistrocchi's side with
the rider that the bulk of the army should not be reduced below a given
strength.[121]

Baistrocchi's proposal to introduce two overlapping periods of conscription of twelve and eight or nine months and to take the whole

annual contingent, which elicited immediate support from the Duce and a lengthy disquisition on the function of Fascist pre-military training, gave Badoglio the opportunity to wriggle free of the possibility of appearing to be on the wrong side. Had this discussion happened before the one on the rapid-employment units he would not have raised the issue of the strength of the ordinary units, he said – indeed, he hoped the new ones would be as strong as possible.[122] After a fragmentary discussion on elements of the armaments programme Baistrocchi proposed to introduce, in the course of which the under-secretary announced that the war ministry had nearly settled on a 4-ton infantry tank armed with a 37-mm gun (it never arrived), the last session of the army council dissolved into an inconclusive discussion on a reform of the general staff system which Badoglio and Bonzani opposed.[123]

Baistrocchi's *Direttive* represented an attempt to impart general conceptions, rather than precise directions, to an army which was in the midst of an unresolved debate about the respective roles and merits of mechanisation and motorisation. The two terms, which at the start of the 1930s began to be seen as competing rather than complementary ideas, were respectively defined in the *Enciclopedia Militare* in 1933 as a revolutionary design which replaced traditional military organisations with a new type of army moving and fighting in machines and a means of improving the capacity of movement of a traditionally structured force logistically, tactically and strategically. The tangled nature of the debate was embodied in the ideas of Emilio Canevari, a probing military commentator but one whose personal links with Roberto Farinacci raised suspicions about how far he was actually pushing a party line. Canevari argued that to use vulnerable tanks to support infantry was a mistake when their characteristics made them pre-eminently an arm with which to achieve surprise, and only advocated assigning a battalion of tanks to every army corps, together with an unspecified number of groups of tanks and motorised artillery.[124]

The *Direttive* began with a Clausewitzian declaration that war was a continuation of foreign policy, the principle lines of which were determined by the international situation. Rich in men but lacking raw materials and almost isolated by the sea, Italy had to avoid a war of attrition and seek decisive victory through rapidity of movement by using manoeuvre to deliver timely, powerful and potent blows. While manoeuvre warfare was not always possible, and positional warfare might have to be undertaken, it was always the aim. Reserves were crucially important, as were logistical services which could not be improvised. Firepower was the indispensable means and artillery the most efficacious way to deliver it. At the point where he descended from general premises to detailed criteria,

Baistrocchi grew vague. Too much artillery weighed down the infantry and hindered its advance, but the correct balance must be decided by the commander's intuition on a case by case basis. While the accent was on the celeri, operating with direct air support, the door to more full-blooded tank warfare was not entirely closed:

Tanks – which because of our terrain and our war must be very light and fast – are not to be considered just as a means of combat, operating amongst and followed by infantry and celeri; they must also be seen as a mass which surprises, overturns and passes beyond [the enemy] in a decisive manner.[125]

While the Italian army was not yet in a position to be able convincingly to act according to these directives, there is clear evidence that Baistrocchi understood what he had to do to make this possible – improve the equipment and organisation of the army and change its mentality –and that, given time and resources, he intended to do just that.

This was reform from the top down rather than from the bottom up, and as such readily open to criticism.[126] Badoglio welcomed Baistrocchi's *Direttive*, but was seemingly not wholly persuaded of the doctrine they embodied and greeted them with qualified praise. 'If circumstances do not allow us [to fight] a war of movement, having created the manoeuvre mentality in our commanders will be something favouring a resumption of such a war as soon as a favourable opportunity comes along,' he told Baistrocchi before pointing out that organisation and logistics were the fundamentals without which there could be no movement and manoeuvre.[127]

While concentrating on the preparations for the Abyssinian War, Baistrocchi and his deputy kept the European war plans updated. Pariani, who had served as military attaché in Albania, had no doubt whatever as to where the greatest threat lay: 'Our true enemy is the slav who presses [on us] from the east'.[128] As far as he was concerned only two war scenarios needed to be catered for: Yugoslavia in alliance with France or with Germany. The planning process itself could be greatly simplified if the planners stopped multiplying all the different hypotheses and simply established the objectives, studied the ground to establish routes of advance and produced studies designed only to provide the basis for possible manoeuvres. This meant concentrating on two possible war theatres, the Tyrol and Carinthia, a focus which Baistrocchi approved at the end of 1934.[129] There was still concern among the planners about a possible move by Germany into Austria : a 'recent alarm' in late March 1935 led to instructions to SIM to watch possible German jumping-off points around Friederichshafen which might signal a move into the Vorarlberg or around Garmisch which could indicate an attack on the Austrian Tyrol.[130] In part, the planners were motivated by a measure of anxiety which had its basis in material inferiority. With better roads and more motor vehicles at their disposal, the Germans could arrive on the river Inn and at Villach before the Italians. If they did, not only would this pre-empt an Italian offensive but it would also threaten a defensive since the Alpine sector, especially around the Brenner pass, had no depth. Thus troops, supplies and munitions had to be stationed forward so that action could be taken quickly, the Bolzano–Trento railway had to be double-tracked and the roads east of Bolzano improved.[131]

Plan Z for Italian military intervention in Austria in order to maintain order there, or more directly to fight a war, was updated in May 1935. The staff envisaged two lines of advance, the Verona army corps moving on Landeck and Innsbruck in the west while the Bologna army corps drove towards Lienz and Villach in the east. In all, seven infantry divisions, three celeri divisions and three alpini divisions were slated to take part in the operation. The keynote features were to be fast, decisive actions. Evidently the planners did not know quite what to expect – nor did Pariani wish to specify any of the hypothetical scenarios he expressly disdained. Since the situation could change from a policing operation into a 'hot' war, forces were to operate in blocs which could carry out local operations but be rapidly concentrated – scarcely an easy task in the terrain in which they would be operating. The civilian population was to be treated correctly but watchfully and signs of insurgency or hostile acts were to be 'repressed with maximum energy'.[132] Finally, the troops were warned that in certain unspecified circumstances they could be started towards the Bavarian frontier in the Tyrol or at Salzburg, though no specific arrangements were outlined.

As Franco–Italian relations cooled in the autumn of 1935, the plan for war against France and Yugoslavia was updated and reissued. Initially operations would develop from Tolmino with the objective of seizing Lubljana within the first three weeks after which French pressure was expected to begin to make itself felt in the west. Tarvisio would be important either in the event of Yugoslavia breaking Austrian neutrality to try a turning movement from the north or, if the political situation allowed it, if Italy did likewise aiming at the Drava valley. Otherwise it would be the jumping-off point for a supporting action in which a fast column would push down the Sava valley. Italy calculated on a two-to-one numerical advantage on the fifth day of mobilisation, when she would have 117 battalions ready to face 85 Yugoslav battalions, but three days later the enemy would be numerically superior. The planners counted on surprise, superior artillery and aviation, and the celeri divisions as factors in their favour. Things would improve if states allied with Italy carried out military operations on other fronts – a guarded reference to the possibility that Hungary and Austria might become involved in a war, a likelihood which as yet had no solid foundation.[133]

Naval policy, planning and the Mediterranean crisis

On 15 January 1935, Cavagnari gave his qualified support to Mussolini's programme for the conquest of Abyssinia. It was, he urged, a case of 'now or never', and once political control of the country had been secured it must remain firmly and without qualification in Italy's hands. However, the preconditions for carrying out the programme were to secure both French and British agreement. In the latter case Britain's control of the Suez canal and her substantial interests in that part of the world were such that no risk of confronting London over them should be run.[134] While the responsibility for securing the necessary international conditions was Mussolini's, Cavagnari more than any other force commander had to take the international balance into account and attempt to forecast possible moves. The Royal Navy was evidently not prepared to weaken the Mediterranean fleet, though the naval attaché in London was told that the presence of a British battleship and destroyer in the eastern Mediterranean 'had nothing whatsoever to do with the Abyssinian question, but was simply connected to British interests in the region, such as those at Cyprus, Palestine, Egypt, etc'.[135]

Cavagnari's reading of the politics of the situation was convoluted. If Great Britain was hostile to Italy, France would probably line up alongside her, thereby breaking up the Italo–Franco–British bloc which acted as the only counter-balance to Germany. Unless dominion aid was forthcoming, London would probably find Germany installed at the channel ports, and rather than see this she would prefer to see Italy installed in Addis Ababa. On the other hand, the recent Rome accords gave reason to think that France might help Italy. The politics of the situation were critical since there was little the navy could directly do: Alexandria and Gibraltar were beyond its operational range, and Malta was not Britain's Achilles' heel in the Mediterranean. On the other hand, once installed in Ethiopia Italy could establish air bases there which would threaten British communications in the Red Sea.[136]

The diplomatic realignment being shaped by Mussolini and Laval, and the possibility of an Italo–French naval convention to match those being constructed by the army and the air force, offered the prospect of a change in the geometry of a war against Yugoslavia. In March the navy redrew its designs to encompass a four-handed war in which France and Italy fought Germany and Yugoslavia. The main theatre of war was presumed to be the North Atlantic, where combined French and Italian units would cruise in force in the channel and the North Sea with the aim of preventing German access to the Atlantic and thereby cutting off German sea-borne commerce – about which the navy had only the haziest ideas, assuming that roughly half of Germany's annual 60 million tons of imports came by sea and that the figure would reduce to some 23 million tons in wartime. French units based at Brest would also be able to cover Italy's vulnerable traffic from North America. Minor operations in the Red Sea and Indian Ocean, based on Massaua and Djibuti, would watch for German traffic or contraband seeking to round the Cape of Good Hope. The almost preternatural caution so often apparent in naval planning was evident in the assumption that German submarines would probably try to interrupt traffic in the Mediterranean and German surface units might try to enter it via Gibraltar – an action which would likely be beyond Germany's means for some years to come. The limitations imposed on Italy by her fleet structure became evident when consideration turned to what she could offer and what she would need in such a war. For action in the North Sea she could provide only submarines. Her *Condottieri*-class ships, which should not go too far from the Mediterranean, could be employed immediately outside Gibraltar but for this they would need a base at Casablanca. To meet German cruisers in the Atlantic she would need ships with a 6,000-mile range and suitable guns – of which she had none.[137]

Cavagnari, who had supported Mussolini's Ethiopian designs since the previous summer, enjoyed the Duce's continuing favour.[138] Although the meeting at Stresa in mid-April produced a measure of agreement between Italy, France and Great Britain about matters of common interest, behind-the-scenes discussions made it unmistakably apparent that London would oppose any Italian act of aggression against Ethiopia. On 14 April, the last day of the Stresa Conference, Cavagnari ordered the naval war staff to examine both the plans for a war against Yugoslavia and Germany and a war scenario in which Italy and France faced Great Britain.[139] In two days he had his answer. The hypothesis of a war against Yugoslavia and Germany had already been considered. As far as a conflict with Great Britain was concerned, the Royal Navy's likely strength in the Mediterranean – normally five battleships, eight cruisers and one aircraft carrier but possibly almost double that in wartime – dictated a 'state of active resistance and threat' until the French came in. Despite the enormous imbalance of forces, the naval staff could see possible lines of action. In a first stage, when fighting alone, Italy could use the control it exercised from bases in southern Sardinia and western Sicily over access routes to Malta to render the island base untenable and to maintain control of the central and eastern Mediterranean; British forces in the Red Sea and the Gulf of Aden could be contained and neutralised from Massaua and Assab; and in the Indian Ocean the British advantage could be reduced by using Kisimaio as a base from which to conduct sorties. The problems of traffic protection in the eastern Mediterranean were ones with which the staff were already familiar and which they thought could be managed. The main Italian naval forces, including the two available battleships, would be concentrated in the area between Augusta, Messina, Trapani, Cagliari, Palermo and Tripoli, and the navy would need 'the full collaboration of the air force in maximum strength for direct support of naval actions and for continuous attacks against Malta'.[140] In a second stage, when the French entered the war, 'aggressive operations could be developed to restrict the adversary in the western Mediterranean and undertake offensive activities in the western Indian Ocean'.[141] Apart from indicating the likely size of the opposition, the naval staff attached no force levels to this genial sketch.

Very conscious of the still extant diplomatic tension between Italy and Germany over Austria and of the improving military and diplomatic relations between Rome and Paris, Cavagnari next asked his staff to consider a scenario in which German troops crossed the Austrian border, leading to a war in which France was an eventual participant on Italy's side and Yugoslavia likewise on Germany's side. The actions to be carried out by the Italian fleet in such a war were much the same as already outlined – destruction of German commercial traffic in the Red Sea and Indian Ocean, submarine action in the Atlantic and barring enemy access to the Mediterranean – though a pre-war tone re-emerged when Cavagnari indicated that one of the actions to be guarded against was a German bombardment of the Italian coastline. He felt generally happy that the outline plan for war with Great Britain had fulfilled his directive, but asked for it to be deepened (*approfondito*) to consider the detailed provisions which would need to be taken 'when the conflict looms with alarming seriousness'.[142] In particular, Cavagnari wanted plans to be developed for combined air and submarine operations if British forces abandoned Malta and retreated to Gibraltar.

The naval staff developed a plan for war against Germany in more detail, pre-supposing that after initial neutrality France would be allied to Italy, identifying the parts of the Mediterranean which would have to be closely watched and producing a plan for the appropriate location of ships.[143] The war plan against England supposed that there would in due course be a politico–military–naval agreement between Italy and France but since that was only a potentiality and not an actuality the operational design rested on a presumption that France would be benevolently neutral and no more. England's strategic position in the Mediterranean presented 'a number of weak points, and Malta is one of them'.[144] Its approach routes to the west and the east were vulnerable to attack by surface craft from bases in Italy, north Africa and the Aegean, while strong air attacks could be launched against it from Sicily and southern Sardinia. Therefore it could be presumed that England might abandon the island, losing control of the central Mediterranean in consequence. The Royal Navy could avoid daylight attacks by Italian submarines and aircraft by slipping away from Malta and retreating to Gibraltar at night, when only Italian torpedo boats would be operative. If it retired there, the prospects were rosy. Italy would have

complete freedom of action in the eastern Mediterranean and the Red Sea as far as the Gulf of Aden, save for the provisions which will be made locally by the English to prevent passage of the Suez canal. However, Italy will be able to increase its traffic with the Black Sea and maintain communication with all the principal colonies.[145]

If the army was not engaged on the Alpine frontier, it could profit from Italian dominance of the central Mediterranean to undertake overseas operations such as the occupation of the eastern bank of the Suez canal 'to chase English troops away from it'. However, a retreat by the Royal Navy to Gibraltar did offer the chance to unite the Mediterranean fleet with units of the Home Fleet, something which would produce 'successive complications'. If the fleet retreated east from Malta to Alexandria or into the Red Sea, its path could be contested by aircraft and submarines; in any case, the port facilities at Alexandria, Port Said, Haifa and Akaba were not extensive and the zone was isolated from the rest of the Mediterranean. However, strategically this was not a welcome scenario:

If the English squadron retreats east, occupying the zone of the Suez canal and Alexandria, our general situation would be worsened, because this would remove any chance of our communicating with the Red Sea, and would also render traffic with the Black Sea dangerous. Finally, operations against the English fleet and its new bases would be very complicated.[146]

The tasks facing the Italian navy in the eventuality of such a war were for the most part already well rehearsed, consisting as they did of traffic protection, the defence of the metropolitan ports and coastline and colonial points, particularly Tobruk, Leros and Massaua, attacks on British naval traffic which would likely be most rewarding in the very early days of a war, and watching the Adriatic. Gibraltar could not be attacked either by sea or air, and so would have to be watched by both sea and air. A retreat eastwards by the Royal Navy would be impeded successively by air, submarine and surface attacks. British positions in Alexandria and the Suez canal would be subject to air attacks, while surface units were watched by aeroplanes and submarines.

Little was said about the role of the heavy Italian surface units, where the British had a battleship superiority of five to two, other than that their location would depend on whether other English forces reached Gibraltar and whether the British attempted to send units into the Adriatic. The navy presumed its lighter surface craft would have some success against the British since it had more cruisers (fourteen against eight) and its destroyer leaders (*navigatori*) were more powerful than British destroyers Moreover British Atlantic manoeuvres in 1935 suggested that the Royal Navy would operate against enemy traffic with individual units backed by a strong supporting force. If approached by enemy battleships, Italian light craft would use their superior speed and a relative abundance of bases to avoid an encounter. Since submarines could not be kept constantly at sea and would have a large area to watch, they would require very good intelligence service to permit timely action.

Although the tone of the planners was guardedly optimistic, there was much that was overlooked in their scheme. The closure of the Suez canal was considered only in relation to its effect on the passage of commercial traffic, and not on the forthcoming Abyssinian operation. Co-operation with the air force was poor, and the Regia Aeronautica's contribution to the operation was taken very much for granted. Even the navy's own capabilities were in key respects doubtful: all 115 of its reconnaissance aircraft were obsolescent, its submarines were slow to submerge and not very mobile, and it had given little attention to mine warfare, though minefields were one of the instruments to be used against Malta and Gibraltar.[147] Evidence of shortcomings in the actual or expected performance of some of the weapons systems to be used in such a war mounted. In June, Bernotti reported on an aero–naval exercise at La Spezia in which not one of the bombs dropped had hit its target; in August the Regia Aeronautica admitted that its BR 3 single motor biplanes could not operate at sea or against Alexandria; and during the summer the army's experiments with a 381-mm gun designed to bombard Malta ended in ignominy when the barrel failed after three rounds.[148] Nevertheless, Cavagnari and the naval staff were apparently ready to take on a war against Great Britain if required to do so.

Cavagnari now began to alert the other services to his needs and requirements. In late May the air force was requested to provide maximum support for operations against Malta, the army was asked to carry out a preliminary reinforcement and partial increase in efficiency of the harbour and fort defences for which it was responsible, and the colonial ministry was urged to arrange for the rapid attainment of a state of self-defence at Tripoli, Tobruk, Massaua and Assab. At a meeting between the deputy chiefs of staff of the air force and the navy in early June, Pinna told admiral Vanutelli that Gibraltar was beyond the range of the bomber squadrons – something the navy had already presumed to be the case – and added that though air strips were being or would be built at Rhodes and Tobruk, 'given the distances involved it is highly unlikely that either Alexandria or the Suez canal can be subjected to sustained and effective aerial bombardment'.[149] Such action would be possible, Pinna thought, when bombers with longer range began entering into service from the coming October. The colonies were alerted by Lessona to the need to ready their defences, which in the case of Tripoli meant bringing the supplies and munitions for the coastal artillery up to establishment tables and completing the anti-aircraft defences, for which only part of the necessary materials were in the colony.[150]

The position with respect to Malta looked much better. In mid-June, Pinna reported that the air force was studying the urgent need to put the airfields in Sicily and southern Sardinia in a state of readiness, that this would be done with great speed, and that some 150 aircraft would be available to bombard Malta day and night from the start of hostilities, concentrating not on airfields but on ships. His service's ideas were, he believed 'in perfect accord with the Navy's plan'. The Aeronautica was now evincing every sign of being ready to co-operate closely with the navy, readily acceding to Vanutelli's request that torpedo-carrying seaplanes be concentrated alongside the naval forces in the central Mediterranean zone.[151] Cavagnari asked for more fighter cover for the naval bases on Sicily and Sardinia and for additional aircraft for the coast reconnaissance and escort squadrons. Valle responded at the end of June that all the auxiliary naval aviation at the naval bases was or would shortly be fully equipped with long-range aircraft, that Tobruk 'which just now is completely devoid of everything' was being rapidly stocked with fuel and munitions, and that Leros which had already been improved to take an additional squadron of long-range aircraft was being further upgraded.

The air force's plan was being developed to link with the navy's, focusing on attacking naval and air targets on Malta and at Alexandria, attacking enemy shipping in the central Mediterranean and the Red Sea, watching Gibraltar, attacking the Suez canal zone and protecting naval and air bases from enemy attack. While attacks on Malta would have maximum effect, it would be possible to attack Alexandria from Tobruk either by land-based aircraft or seaplanes whose base should be ready in August. However, there were some acknowledged shortcomings: only one group of S 55-X aircraft could reach the Suez canal from Leros, and the use of torpedo-carrying seaplanes in actions at sea was presently being delayed because it had not yet been decided which type of aerial torpedo to use.[152]

With the crisis in the Mediterranean mounting, Cavagnari assured Mussolini in mid-June that the navy was ready, with only a brief warning, to undertake the effort required of it, being fully efficient in terms of materials and manpower. The task would be onerous, and while it would be possible to win some early successes if the air force was effective, they would be difficult to consolidate. Thereafter 'the navy will seek to resist to the utmost the enemy's pressure, which will grow day by day in a very grave manner'.[153] The war would not end within a few weeks, and thereafter the navy's main task would be to protect merchant traffic supplying Italy with raw materials.

All this was a preamble not to a warning about the strategic consequences of Italy's naval inferiority but to a bid for more funds. Pointing out that the Royal Navy was superior in battleships, that both the Regia Aeronautica and the Regio Esercito were or would shortly be building up their war materiel, and that the navy's ordinary and extraordinary building budgets were already largely committed up to 1939–40, the undersecretary made a bid for some new build. His grounds were that it would get ever more difficult to obtain the necessary supplies of raw materials once the war started, that the enemy's enormous superiority was not offset by what Italy had available, and that the character of the probable naval conflict would require extensive employment of what the Italian navy termed *mezzi insidiosi*. He therefore requested that Mussolini grant the funding to build ten submarines, twelve MAS boats, two destroyers, two escorts and two high-seas torpedo boats which could be ready to enter service within twelve to eighteen months.[154] If this was an attempt to warn Mussolini off a war with Great Britain, it was a very indirect one which pulled all its potentially big punches. Mussolini agreed to the submarines, which he wanted to be built en bloc and launched during 1936 with the cost spread over three years.[155]

Italian naval calculations were now affected by the Anglo–German naval agreement signed on 18 June 1935. Advanced notice of the impending deal had been picked up by the diplomats and the naval attachés: in London, captain Capponi learnt of the impending talks at the end of April from his German naval opposite number, Wassner, from whom he later gathered that Germany would not complete the new programme before 1942 and also that the German goal was naval parity with France.[156] Mussolini almost certainly knew of them from purloined documents and doubtless factored them into his calculations. At the end of May Cavagnari saw a positive benefit for Italy in an expansion of the size of the German navy, for it meant that she could 'now achieve victory in

Ethiopia'.[157] The strategical calculations were easy to make: a larger German navy simultaneously represented a potential diminution in British naval power and a threat to France which would likely reinforce the pro-Italian orientation of Laval's foreign policy, not least because Paris could not afford to see an Italo–German partnership as long as London remained cool to her increasing security dilemma and desirous of reaching agreements with Berlin.

As far as the naval balance went, Cavagnari pointed out to the Italian Foreign Ministry that 35 per cent of the British fleet amounted to 420,000 tons, a figure practically equal to the amount Italy would possess when the ships currently under construction were completed, and that therefore her principle of possessing a navy equal to that of the strongest continental power was not undermined by the agreement.[158] The agreement certainly challenged, if it did not undermine, Mussolini's belief that questions such as German naval rearmament should be resolved by general agreement, without doubt a means by which he intended to safeguard the position of 'medium-sized' maritime nations such as his own in relation to others such as France.[159] Cavagnari alerted the Duce to the fact that the agreement included a provision for Germany to build up to parity with the British empire in submarines, which indicated that she had now abandoned the view she had hitherto propounded in international gatherings that submarines should be abolished. In reacting to the development Mussolini thought it most important, while safeguarding Italy's fundamental interests, not to upset the friendly relations which had recently been established with France.[160] French hostility to the Anglo–German naval agreement, and her dissatisfaction with the future naval construction programmes towards which England was gravitating in pursuit of further limitations on naval armaments, can only have given comfort to Rome.[161]

The improvement in relations with France which had impacted favourably on military planning now began to percolate ever more strongly into naval planning. The news that Gamelin intended to ask the chief of the French naval staff to come to Rome to conclude a naval agreement which would complete those between the respective armies and air forces, and the prospect of Yugoslavia and Czechoslovakia joining France and Italy in an anti-German front in the event of a war in Austria, considerably improved the naval prospects in such a war as it removed the need to guard the Adriatic. The naval planners envisaged a division of the Mediterranean into an eastern Italian and a western French sector, and the location of Italian units at Oran and Algiers to share in watching the Straits of Gibraltar. The Atlantic should be a French responsibility, to which Italian cruisers and armed merchantmen might contribute, while

the Indian Ocean would be in Italy's charge. Looking beyond the immediate issue of war with Germany, the planners also wanted any future
naval agreement to cover hostilities with Spain, Greece and 'above all'
Turkey. This could be achieved through a security pact which guaranteed free passage through the Straits of Gibraltar, the Dardanelles, the
Suez canal and the straits of Bab-el-Mandab.[162] Other scenarios in which
all these potential allies might aid Italy included a war against England,
perhaps allied with Greece and Turkey, which would present problems
in the eastern Mediterranean and possibly too the Atlantic but also possibilities of gaining access to the necessary supplies of raw materials via
land frontiers and neutrals.[163]

As far as the navy was concerned the happy prospect of French aid had
not yet transmuted into anything concrete however, and in the meantime relations with London were worsening as Italian intransigence over
Abyssinia confronted British obduracy. Cavagnari began to grow concerned about at least some facets of an Italo–British war, telling the
colonial ministry at the start of July that lines of communication with
Libya and East Africa would certainly be contested by the British and
that therefore supplies would only reach them sporadically and at great
risk.[164] So, apparently, did Mussolini, for he instructed Cerruti, newly
arrived as ambassador to Paris, to use every opportunity to convince the
French of the value Italy set on the military accords – but also not to talk
as though Italy wanted mediation.[165] The king thought that in the event
of a war between England and Italy, France would side against Rome.

Mussolini now forced the pace, confirming a naval plan to transport
two divisions to Libya by warship in September which would put them
in a position to defend themselves.[166] As it stared a war with England
in the face, the navy began to express anxieties which previously it had
either not perceived or had suppressed. The naval bases at Augusta and
Siracusa were exposed to bombardment by an enemy with heavier guns,
and neither Naples nor Cagliari were safe. Moreover, if the British fleet
abandoned Malta it might set up a base in the Balearic Islands, increasing
the danger in the northern Tyrrhenian. Therefore the main Italian naval
forces would have to be based at La Maddelena.[167] This was a rather more
conservative deployment than had been proposed hitherto, suggesting a
distinct cooling of naval ardour – if it had ever been very hot.

With French support uncertain and Britain's attitude evidently
unyielding, Mussolini ordered Badoglio to examine the options facing
Italy in the event of a war with England. When the three under-secretaries
of the service ministries and their deputy chiefs of staff met on 13 August,
they heard Cavagnari announce that the fleet would be ready for action
from 30 August. This was the preamble to a lengthy factual statement on

the situation of the naval defences, to which the deputy chief of naval staff admiral Wladimiro Pini also contributed, which covered everything from coastal defences, where the navy noted that fixed anti-aircraft defences were weak along the entire coastline save for La Spezia, to the location and formation of armoured trains. The resumé of the state of naval defences was seasoned with passing observations which indicated that the outlook in the event of such a war was far from optimistic. Only three months' stocks of fuel existed. The two old battleships *Doria* and *Duilio* were very vulnerable to submarine attack. The defences of Tobruk and Leros were 'very modest' when confronted with the naval and air capabilities possessed by the British, particularly if they took a Greek island such as Stampalia; if these *punti d'appoggio* fell the navy's ability to protect vital traffic with the Black Sea would be compromised. Of Italy's fifty submarines only some twenty could be at sea at any one time and they would have to cover a very wide area; even in waters close to home they would need the co-operation of the air force, but naval aviation was not in a very efficient state.

Admiral Pini concluded with a side-swipe at the air force: 'This state of affairs increases the situation of decided inferiority of our naval forces in the face of the enemy we are considering, because little faith can be put in the capacity of air reconnaissance to aid the fleet at sea.'[168] Badoglio drew the inescapable conclusions: Italy was weak in the Aegean and also at Tobruk, and if the situation of 'extreme tension' developed before the campaign in East Africa had begun reinforcement of Libya would be 'sporadic' and in East Africa non-existent.

Cavagnari's summary of the naval balance of forces made for even gloomier listening. Against England's fifteen battleships Italy had none, as the ageing *Doria* and *Duilio* could not be put in line; thirteen Italian cruisers faced some sixty English cruisers; fifty modern Italian destroyers faced double that number of enemy ships; and the Royal Navy possessed six aircraft carriers capable of transporting 240 aircraft while Italy had none. Only in respect of submarines was there an equal balance. As far as the strategic situation went, England could block both ends of the Mediterranean with ease and create battle groups which would always be superior to Italian forces because of the presence of enemy battleships among them. Even if Italy won initial successes, and Cavagnari expected Malta to be evacuated at an early stage in a war, time would be ineluctably against her:

[W]e lack reserves, while Great Britain, putting in motion her huge war machine, can count on resources which are inexhaustible. Italy's merchant navy traffic will be reduced to the few national craft that can elude the enemy's surveillance and to returning ships. Whether we can count for very long on supplies from the Black

Sea is also problematic. In sum, the struggle will be extremely hard for Italy and even harder [*durissima*] for the navy.[169]

Cavagnari could find only one bright spot amidst the maritime gloom: England might hesitate in the face of a war with Italy given the possible imperial and global complications that might result from it.

Everything about this assessment of the likely strategic circumstances of a war with England was so strikingly different from what the navy had said and done before as to raise serious questions about its planning capabilities, and beyond this about Cavagnari's political objectives as executive head of the service. This was the first time that the naval balance of forces had been laid out in detail and the unpalatable but inescapable conclusions drawn from it. It was also the first time that the navy's hitherto modestly optimistic plans and scenarios descended from a series of abstractions to a concrete analysis which took serious account of what the enemy could do, rather than sketching what the Italian navy might do. In a characteristic finale which spoke as much to the navy's sense of its own shortcomings as to the appalling state of inter-service relations over which Mussolini presided, Cavagnari blamed the air force. The plan of operations which had been outlined reflected the deficiencies of the air force even more than the lack of battleships. If Italy had been able to count on 'the existence of a real and proper air arm', comprising at least a thousand modern planes, a war could have started with an intense surprise action by air and naval forces against Malta, or the blocking of the entrance to the Suez canal, after which 'energetic aero–naval pressure' could have been exerted on English bases from Gibraltar to Haifa or against the enemy's naval forces themselves while they were in motion. Other than replying to Baistrocchi's observation that everyone seemed to be limiting their plans to 'an absolute defensive' with the assertion that the air force's plans were 'fully offensive', Valle said nothing.[170]

Although the question of reinforcing the British fleet was under discussion from 6 August, the Italian navy was unaware of this. From London the naval attaché reported that he could detect no abnormal movements of warships, personnel or war materials, though he warned Rome that the attitude in some official circles of sympathy towards the occupation of Abyssinia by a friendly Italy was being eroded by the state of tension existing between the two powers.[171] Armed also with information from the Italian air attaché that there were no signs either of unusual movements or increases in the Middle East Air Force, itself insufficient for war unless reinforced from England where the metropolitan air defences were being reorganised and increased, ambassador Dino Grandi reported on 16 August that he knew of no special measures being undertaken in respect of the Italo–Abyssinian dispute.[172] The likelihood that the Royal Naval presence in the Mediterranean would be increased in the near future was evident, however, and the navy redrew its plans on the likelihood that rather than concentrating on Malta the Mediterranean fleet would rest on its eastern bases while the Home Fleet stood at Gibraltar. In the west, the enemy was expected to attempt naval bombardments and aero–naval attacks against the Ligurian coast, coastal merchant traffic, and La Maddelena, Naples, Palermo, Cagliari and Trapani; in the east, he would seek to penetrate the Aegean in order to attack Italian traffic coming from the Black Sea and also attempt to seize Italian islands in the Dodecanese. Against this, the Italian navy would deploy submarines and light and medium surface craft to screen the waters north-east of the Balearics, off Tunisia and between Sardinia and Sicily with the aim of launching night attacks, while in the Aegean old warships whose loss would not be serious would be deployed to Leros.[173] Directives for the deployment of air reconnaissance and submarines were prepared at the same time.

Fleet deployment plans were drawn up to cover both the possibility that the British fleet would stay at Malta, in which case the main Italian bases would be at Augusta, Taranto and Messina, or that it would abandon the island, in which case Taranto became the main anchorage. Both bases could expect to be attacked by carrier-borne aircraft and possibly bombarded by surface ships (Augusta was also open to air attack from Malta), against which the anti-aircraft defences of Taranto were better equipped than those at Augusta. Neither base could hold off ships armed with guns heavier than 305 mm, and neither could put down defensive minefields.[174]

The navy evidently needed the co-operation of the air force in the event of a war against England, both in generalities and in specificities: one of the first things it asked for after the reassessment of *Piano B* in August was more aircraft on Leros.[175] On 26 August Cavagnari and Valle met to go over the role the air force would be able to play if hostilities began. The results were not very encouraging, as Valle himself acknowledged. Only 150 planes were available for action up to 10 September, and they were so antiquated that they could only carry out night bombing; thereafter a squadron of seven long-range planes was expected to come into service each week. Asked what he could do if the British fleet were based in the eastern Mediterranean, Valle replied that in such circumstances the air force could do nothing. Forced to acknowledge that Italian bombers could reach Navarino, 300 miles from the Italian coast, he was then invited to consider whether they could not also reach Alexandria from Tobruk, a distance of 310 miles. No Italian aircraft could reach Gibraltar until the S 81, which had a 2,500-kilometre range, began to arrive in service at the rate of one a week from 10 September. As far as East Africa was concerned, since no agreement had been reached for formations of aircraft to overfly Egypt, as many as possible were being sent by sea. Valle was not disposed to send a long-range squadron to Leros unless there was evident need of it. Valle's dispositions generated a well-modulated feeling of discontent: there was only one squadron of fighters on the mainland nearer than Brindisi to protect Taranto, and the under-secretary for air was unwilling to relocate the squadrons at Catania and Augusta, which could be rapidly moved west if required.

The rather random nature of the discussion and the nature of the exchanges of information which took place – Valle had to ask if the Sicilian channel was thought untransitable, and in answer to an observation that torpedo bombers would be very useful he revealed that the planes would be ready before the torpedoes without giving away any dates – demonstrated how little Badoglio had done to co-ordinate the planning of the armed forces and led admiral Ducci to remark that the two services spoke different languages and used different figures. Valle reiterated that the new long-range squadrons which would be coming on stream at the rate of one a week could reach distant objectives such as Gibraltar and Alexandria, and when Ducci pointed out that they would not have the range to reach Gibraltar he was told that they would be flown by hand-picked pilots and would therefore take off over-loaded.[176] It is hard to see how the participants in this meeting can have ended it much the wiser or much better informed about the nebulous ideas Valle appeared to nurture.

Some matters of detail were cleared up when the deputy chiefs of staff met two days later: the S 55 *Atlantici* seaplanes would be kept in metropolitan waters ready to act in the Tyrrhenian sea or against Navarino, and if required to do so had the range to reach Leros without passing through Greek territorial waters; both parties would use bombs designed for land targets because there were no anti-ship bombs; and the navy would pass over information on the location of Italian and British shipping in the Mediterranean.[177]

The three admirals commanding naval districts took stock of their respective commands and concluded at the start of September that while morale was high and things were entirely satisfactory 'from a strictly naval point of view', deficiencies in coastal anti-aircraft defences and more particularly the deficiencies of the air force and the geographical position of Italy's bases meant that the longer the conflict lasted the worse would Italy's situation become relative to that of her opponent.[178] To get the best out of the air force a list of eleven specific targets on Malta, eight at

Aden and two at Berbera which the navy wanted bombed was passed to the Aeronautica.[179] General orders for the designated fleet commander in the event of war were issued on 12 September. His task was to intercept the enemy fleet coming from either its western or its eastern bases during the night after the first day of hostilities and prevent it reaching its objectives, and then to attack enemy forces which were not decidedly superior during their retreat.[180] A week later, reviewing the situation, the naval staff concluded that although Italy's geographical location at the centre of the Mediterranean conferred on her an optimum strategic position, her relative naval weakness vis-à-vis Great Britain meant that she could never profit from it to win control of the sea there.[181]

With the Mediterranean fleet abandoning Malta for Alexandria, where its flagship *Resolution* arrived last on 24 September, and with a detachment of the Home fleet comprising two battle-cruisers, three cruisers and six destroyers arriving at Gibraltar on 17 September, what were in fact precautionary naval measures assumed even greater significance in the mind of the Italian navy. Analysing the rapidly changing situation in the Mediterranean and the Red Sea at the end of the third week in September, the Italian naval staff concluded that England was not preparing a simple demonstration of force designed to intimidate Italy but had taken actions preparatory to war. She could be expected to prevent Italian ships from approaching the Suez canal or from exiting the Mediterranean via Gibraltar, to impede the arrival of supplies coming through the Dardanelles or the Suez canal, to bombard the coasts of mainland Italy, Libya, Eritrea and Somalia from the sea and the air, and to prevent supplies reaching East Africa from the Indian ocean. She would undoubtedly seek to destroy the naval forces opposing her in the knowledge that they would take ten years to rebuild, and to destroy the two new *Littorio*-class battleships under construction and the two older battleships undergoing conversion, as well as having designs on Leros, Tobruk, the Dodecanese, Saseno and the Italian position in Albania. Given the balance of forces and the enemy's strategic advantages, there was no apparent possibility of any decisive action against English naval and air forces or even of securing any initial success other than the bombing of Malta, which in the overall scheme of the war was a 'limited objective'. The conclusion, although not put quite so directly, was inescapable: Italy had no hope of fighting a short war let alone winning one, and in a long war the effect of normal attrition alone condemned her to defeat.[182]

Cavagnari, who may well have been the author of this lugubrious document, may not have been quite so pessimistic when conferring with the Duce: Mussolini held in September that the navy thought it could take on the British fleet in the Mediterranean and was 'impatient' to fight.[183] If Cavagnari was practising a deception, he was about to be rescued by diplomacy. While the British foreign secretary, Sir Samuel Hoare, gave what appeared to be a ringing British pledge to go to war in support of the covenant of the League of Nations on 11 September, he and Laval had ruled out the adoption of military sanctions in secret talks the previous night and had agreed that if economic sanctions were to be applied then this must be done with caution. Informed at once of this and calculating on the basis of a considerable amount of political and diplomatic evidence that the British 'naval parade' would therefore not become outright aggression because the British population was too pacifist and because no direct threat was posed to British interests, Mussolini adopted a plan devised by Raffaele Guariglia under which Rome would accept the explicit condemnation of the League of Nations and the limited imposition of economic sanctions in return for what amounted to qualified acquiescence in his colonial adventure. On 23 September the British ambassador conveyed to the Duce the news that the plan had been agreed.[184]

Although the immediate pressures were limited Cavagnari was concerned about the possibility that England might seek to transform economic sanctions into military ones and create incidents designed to provoke armed conflict. Accordingly he warned his naval commanders to avoid any action which might play into the hands of the enemy.[185] If sanctions did shift from economic to military, the vice-chief of staff suggested that this would come about via the declaration of a 'peaceful blockade' in which the Royal Navy would not assume the initiative with aggressive actions against Italy but would leave the responsibility for doing so to her. In the eastern Mediterranean, the enemy would be unlikely to occupy the Aegean islands and Tobruk at least at the outset, but would probably deploy submarines to direct steamships towards groups of surface ships for search; in the western Mediterranean they could not maintain blockade lines without the use of French bases and would probably rely on flying incursions against Italian traffic and population and industrial centres.[186]

The air force looked to be able in due course to undertake long-range operations in Abyssinia which would strike the enemy's armed masses and the most important territorial objectives, while at the same time participating in the defence of access routes to the colony. As far as colonial war proper was concerned, once full efficiency was reached Aimone Cat, the theatre air commander, expected to be able to hit the enemy's organs of resistance repeatedly and at will, weakening and dissolving his military power and reducing the occupation of enemy territory to 'a problem which is almost wholly logistical'.[187] Since this was not yet possible, immediate tasks would be tactical co-operation with advancing columns and troops in position or manoeuvring for counter-offensive operations, distant reconnaissance and strategic co-operation, as well as the defence of Asmara, Massaua and Assab against possible air incursions. In addition to securing lines of operations and getting information to assist ground troops, the air force would pursue a defeated enemy without pause and attack the enemy who would certainly mass as he had done in the past.

As far as aero–naval war was concerned, the lack of co-operation between the services in the past began rapidly to catch up with them. Experiments using a land bomber to carry torpedoes were only being begun as the war started, and regulations were being compiled for bombers acting against ships at anchor.[188] Coastal aviation squadrons were half the strength the navy thought they should be and were capable of putting into the sky only about forty-two aircraft a day, half the number required.[189] Valle's response was not entirely encouraging. The 168 coastal aircraft the navy wanted would be attained in April 1936; in the meantime reserve engines were being supplied to increase the activity of the extant aircraft though the intensive use the navy made of the squadrons under its control meant that they were quickly consumed.[190] The use of civil aviation aircraft to supplement naval reconnaissance, briefly held out to the navy, was rescinded when it was realised that in the event of war they would have to be used to supplement or replace maritime communications between mainland Italy, the islands and Libya.[191]

With the immediate threat of war dying away as the League of Nations excluded oil from the programme of economic sanctions and delayed their imposition until November, and while the naval staff put their minds to such problems as the protection of Sicily in war and the defence of Pantelleria and Lampedusa, Cavagnari turned to larger matters. The immediate stimulus which prompted him to formulate an ambitious new naval building programme was a directive from Mussolini requiring that the strictest economy be exercised in respect of imports of machinery, semi-finished and finished products and raw materials.[192] The directive put the navy in serious difficulties since there were no substitutes for imports of copper, tin and nickel which were essential, or for certain specialised products such as periscope tubes, gyro-compasses, thermionic valves and tungsten filaments which could not be produced at home. Without more nickel – and more coal, which the Terni works would run out of in mid-December – the *Vittorio Veneto* could only be equipped with six heavy guns instead of the nine planned.[193] In using the Duce's memorandum as a springboard for his ideas, Cavagnari doubtless also had in mind both the intensified inter-service competition for resources which was likely to be its immediate outcome and the political advantage the army might take from a successful military campaign in Abyssinia, as well as his own longer term ambitions for naval expansion.

The political opposition put up by Great Britain in the face of the African undertaking clearly showed how important maritime power was and how it functioned in overseas operations, Cavagnari argued. Had the war which had begun in the colonies and against a power with no naval frontier expanded to become a Mediterranean war, the navy would have become the force upon which the nation's destinies depended most heavily. In the 'latent' conflict between Italy and Great Britain, the greatest disparity was that of battleship numbers: if the *Littorio*, *Vittorio Veneto*, *Cesare* and *Cavour* had been ready to sail 'British arrogance would have assumed a lesser tone and French co-operation would have been more decided and more effective'.[194] Given that Italy could only expand overseas and that Great Britain had shown herself determined to oppose Rome's aspirations, and revealed her 'inflexible egoism', the likelihood that any future expansion would find Italy facing not just England but possibly also other first rank naval powers made a reinforcement of the navy unavoidable. Bundling together the division of Germany by the Polish corridor, the Japanese invasion of China, the troubles in India and the fact that Italy was enclosed in a sea whose exits were in the hands of others, Cavagnari argued that as long as these problems existed peace could not be assured. To face that situation Italy needed one thing more than all else – battleships. Moreover, the London Naval Conference was upcoming and the French had already signalled their belief that battleship construction could not be further renounced, another reason to press ahead with battleship construction 'for to be strong is always good, whatever may be the swings between rivalry and friendship'. With a customary Fascist flourish, Cavagnari assured Mussolini that the navy, whose 'material and moral' preparation had been acknowledged by the British when they had had to ask to use French ports in the event of possible action against Italy, was fully in tune with the rhythm which the Duce had impressed on the entire nation.[195]

The Mediterranean crisis freed Cavagnari to indulge his ambitions on a global stage. In May, he had been thinking of building nothing bigger than 8,000-ton cruisers and 2,500-ton destroyer leaders.[196] The two-part plan he handed to Mussolini in January 1936 was far more ambitious. 'Fleet A', to be constructed in the space of six years, would comprise 6 battleships, 22 cruisers, 116 destroyers and 75 submarines. 'Fleet B' or the 'escape fleet' (*flotta d'evasione*), designed to break out of the Mediterranean and to operate in the Atlantic, the Persian Gulf and the Indian Ocean, would comprise 9 battleships, 3 aircraft carriers and 36 cruisers. If it was to be constructed in the same time scale as 'Fleet A' then the shipbuilding industry would have to be expanded in order to be able to build an additional 445,000 tons of shipping; otherwise the programme would take at least 24 years.[197] The *programma massimo*, which demonstrated how readily the navy could lose all touch with reality in the Alice-in-Wonderland world of Fascist politics, had already hit an immediate obstruction when at the end of 1935 Mussolini told an admirals' committee that insufficient funds and the fact that they were of no use in the Mediterranean meant that the navy would have no aircraft carriers.[198]

Planning the land war

The Regia Aeronautica began the planning cycles for a land campaign in Abyssinia at the start of January 1935. Discarding earlier plans by De Bono for a pair of main air bases on the Ethiopian *altopiano* on grounds of practicalities, Valle suggested a network of five main air bases along the coastline from which the air force could sweep the zone of operations and carry out whatever operations were required, which might include '*the destruction of Addis Ababa, Gondar, and Harar and the systematic burning of the entire Somali moorlands*'.[199] The loss of forward air bases threatened to deprive the army of co-ordinated air support, but other considerations trumped this one. At the first meeting of the chiefs of staff convened to consider preparations, Badoglio accepted the scheme and with it Valle's declaration that the bases for 250 aircraft in Eritrea and 50 in Somalia could be ready by mid-July and the planes themselves in September. After some hesitation, De Bono accepted the new plan in March. At the initial planning meeting Baistrocchi was concerned about stripping Italy of the few tanks she had, but Badoglio reassured him that Mussolini had promised that materiel sent to East Africa would all be replaced. Admiral Vanutelli provided the information that the 60,000-man metropolitan contingent could be disembarked in six to seven months' time. Logistic difficulties began to loom large as the meeting heard that a major programme of road-building would still only create a single road suitable for motor vehicles linking Massaua on the coast with the main logistical base on the *altopiano*, and the question of the provision of water was raised. Along with the tanks and aircraft which would confer a 'crushing superiority' on the Italians would go other accoutrements such as flame-throwers and gas.[200]

The logistical needs of the army were far greater than those of either of the other two services, and in mid-January they led Badoglio to challenge Mussolini's timetable for war. He calculated that the Negus could concentrate some 250,000 troops on the frontier by December 1935, two months after the rainy season ended, whereas the Italian expeditionary corps, comprising 69,000 local and 70,500 metropolitan troops, could not have its supply networks in place before the rainy season began and could not therefore be on the *altopiano* before February 1936. After reminding Mussolini that he had said the war would be very hard, Badoglio uttered a warning in characteristic style: 'We cannot contemplate, I will not say a failure but even an incomplete success.' His conclusion was that it would require the whole of 1935 and the first eight months of 1936 'to be in a position to face such a difficult problem with the certainty of success'.[201] Valle fully agreed, but pointed out that the Abyssinians might make a move in December 1935 in order to chase the Italians to the sea and win a prestigious victory. In that case the air force was ready 'to halt and even break any offensive fancies, generating a salutary terror in the enemy from which we shall be able to profit in 1936'.[202] Accepting Mussolini's timetable and reconfirming his own troops requirements and preparatory schedule, De Bono pointed out that despite the difficulties under which he was labouring, notably the lack of labour and materials, work on the roads was proceeding 'with singular speed'. He was immediately more concerned about being attacked before the rainy season when 'the enemy would find us in a disagreeable state of crisis'.[203]

The disordered and disorganised way in which De Bono, now freed of any financial shackles by Mussolini, was producing orders for men and supplies worried both Pariani and Baistrocchi, and at the end of January the under-secretary for war urged that an organic plan be established as a template and that the responsibility for supervising the whole exercise be removed from the colonial ministry and given to the war ministry and the army general staff under the supervision of Mussolini, Badoglio and himself.[204] Baistrocchi had reason to be concerned: the air force was sending out ships that were only partly loaded, the colonial ministry was unilaterally hiring ships without telling the co-ordinating commission set up by Mussolini, and the railway authorities were complaining about the flood of wagons being ordered and sent to ports when no account was taken of the timing of the arrival of the ships that were supposed to transport the goods they carried.[205] Mussolini did allow Baistrocchi to take charge of the transport of troops and materials from Italy from the moment when the first metropolitan troops left – a concession which was not calculated to solve the larger problems of co-ordination that were emerging – but told De Bono in mid-February that 'he does not want me to correspond directly with Badoglio any longer, and has told him so too'.[206]

Although the colonial ministry, of which De Bono was the head, was nominally in charge of the arrangements for the war, Mussolini was well aware of the opportunities for wasting resources which would follow if it communicated individually with the three service ministries. Accordingly Badoglio was given the job of 'harmonising' its requests and passing them on to the armed forces. Since direct correspondence between him and De Bono was immediately vetoed, he would have to go through Lessona, under-secretary at the colonial ministry, as intermediary. The officials were already starting to run into financial problems: despite Mussolini's extravagant promises of virtually unlimited funds, the colonial ministry was very short of money and had not yet been given the 500,000,000 lire it had requested, the war ministry had used up or committed its ordinary and extraordinary funds and had seen none of the extra 172,000,000 lire it had been promised over three years, the air force was ordering on credit, and the navy was already 46,000,000 lire over budget on ordinary expenditure. Baistrocchi was concerned at how to stretch his budget to replace immediately the supplies being sent overseas with 10 per cent extra margin, as Mussolini had ordered, and Valle pointed out that he would not be able to replace the aeroplanes sent overseas until the autumn of 1936. Everyone agreed on the problems, such as factories already overloaded with orders and industrial companies which would increase their prices if having to operate on credit. It was presumed that the solutions would be found through the structures Mussolini had set up to oversee questions of supply and manufacture.[207]

The services did succeed in hammering out agreements on practicalities quickly, though De Bono's lack of a regular general staff hindered the establishment of an 'organic rhythm' in organising supplies and logistics.[208] Pariani scheduled transports to Somalia starting on 20 February but complained that De Bono seemed to know nothing about them, that he was being deluged with a disordered mass of requests and that excessive interference meant that there was little co-ordination of transportation. By the end of the month he concluded that the vagueness of the requests demonstrated that De Bono had no operational plan and no logistical one either. He was increasingly persuaded that the authorities in Eritrea 'do not grasp the extent of the pre-arrangements which are needed for operations of the kind proposed by Mussolini'.[209]

There was something to Pariani's suspicions, for De Bono was thinking vaguely that he could attack the Ethiopians if they did not attack him first, in which case the presence of large numbers of Ethiopians on the Somali front would be a help. Mussolini pointed out that if the Negus did not attack then the Italians would have to take the initiative, a task which would require 100,000 white troops in September increasing to 200,000 by the end of the year. De Bono would be sent these troops so that the offensive 'will have enough force to push right through and obtain the essential successes from the start'.[210] The Duce himself now added a new dimension to the planning. He was concerned lest the Abyssinians attempt to achieve a 'not impossible' success in Somalia which would have its effect on the Eritrean front, even if operations were going well there, 'since these operations would in any case last a long time'. He therefore wished reinforcements sent to Somalia, which De Bono had ignored. As the military swiftly agreed, increasing the size of the Somali garrison raised questions about the necessary supporting paraphernalia, including a high-command organisation.[211] Baistrocchi wanted men of action and character with a knowledge of the technical means which would be employed – that is, someone more up-to-date than De Bono. At the meeting, Badoglio proposed Rodolfo Graziani's name. Baistrocchi immediately sounded out the five designated army commanders, four of whom agreed that Graziani was the first choice.[212]

De Bono regarded Italian Somalia as a secondary theatre which needed primarily to defend itself and possibly to aid the main front with offensive thrusts if the enemy forces there were not too large. Alerted to the possibility that it might not be in a position to resist an enemy attack, and disregarding De Bono's belief that white divisions could not operate there, Mussolini first sent fifteen tanks, fifty aircraft and four Eritrean battalions and then diverted the first of the three metropolitan infantry divisions to the colony. He also sent Graziani there as governor and commander of the expeditionary corps. Reinforcing Somalia in this way affected the overall timetable, for it meant that the first Italian division could not reach De Bono in Eritrea before the latter half of July unless the navy was given wider powers to hire and requisition shipping.[213] The new commander was told to ask for more aeroplanes, tanks and white troops if he needed them, so that he could in due course undertake an offensive towards Harrar in concert with the northern operations.[214] This he did with a will, drawing a stinging rebuke from Baistrocchi who was running out of junior officers, having to stretch materiel, and by late March was evidently under some stress as a result of having to juggle the needs of frontier defence at home, De Bono's troop allocations and Graziani's treatment of his ministry as if it were a bottomless well.[215]

Badoglio inclined to the view that the two theatres were effectively separate because of the distance between them which meant that it would take the Abyssinian hordes some three months to transfer from one to the other. He also concurred with De Bono in thinking Somalia an unsuitable climate for white troops. Estimating the enemy at 200–250,000 in the north and 80–100,000 in the south, and believing that they could be arrayed along the Eritrean frontier between mid-November and mid-December, Badoglio calculated that by 1 December the second and third metropolitan divisions could be in place in Eritrea, along with 150 tanks and 250 aircraft – 'an element of enormous importance and absolute superiority over the enemy' – as well as more artillery and machine-guns than the enemy.[216] Initially Italy would have to stand on the defensive, for which a fourth metropolitan division would be both necessary and sufficient. How many troops would be necessary for a counter-offensive in depth followed by a fully fledged offensive, he could not (or would not) say:

> This will depend essentially on the results of the defensive period. If for example a major battle takes place with results clearly favourable to us, this could produce disorganisation of the Abyssinian forces and the consequent defection of chiefs who are luke-warm about the Negus's policy. However, it could be that the Negus does not attack us.[217]

Air power would play a major role in any defensive battle, particularly in reconnaissance; not surprisingly Badoglio, who was something of a sceptic about the airmen's claims for their bombers, coupled this acknowledgement with a warning against premature bombing attacks to which the enemy might then grow accustomed. It could also break up large masses of enemy troops beyond the frontier and thus force the Abyssinians either to attack or retreat. If they did not attack then the expeditionary force would have to advance in a series of cautious steps, preceded by a bombing campaign directed against all the principal population centres between the frontier and Addis Ababa, 700 kilometres from the border. In these circumstances air power would have a major role to play: 'it is with aviation that we shall have to break Abyssinian resistance'.[218]

Badoglio's cautious analysis was generally shrewd and well founded. Mussolini however needed a much more vigorous campaign, partly because he feared that given more time more arms would flow into the enemy camp and partly because if he adhered to Badoglio's leisurely timetable then the window of opportunity presented by the state of European politics might well close against him. Badoglio's massive army was a slow-moving animal which would need massive logistic support, whereas air power offered the chance to clear the skies of enemy planes and bomb troops, population, materiel and the resources of livelihood. Graziani, with 40–50,000 troops, 100 fast tanks and 50 to 100 aeroplanes, could launch a penetration in depth into Abyssinia. De Bono would be given five regular army divisions and five divisions of camicie nere, adding 200,000 white troops to the 100,000 native troops available, as well as 300 to 500 aircraft and 300 fast tanks. The Duce was determined not to repeat the mistakes of the past:

For want of a few thousand men we lost Adua. I shall never commit the same mistake. I wish to sin through *excess* and not *deficiency*.[219]

The timetable remained unchanged.[220]

Faced with what was now a rather different task, launching a decisive offensive from the outset, De Bono estimated that he could absorb five metropolitan divisions by October and that, alongside the two native divisions, this would be enough for the first stage. If this did not defeat the Ethiopians more divisions could be sent between December 1935 and February 1936, since the advance which would have to follow would be slow and cautious. Badoglio was insistent, maintaining that according to the men on the spot the logistical system was incapable of absorbing the numbers of men Mussolini intended to send within the time limits he proposed and rejecting Somalia as a principal theatre of operations on the grounds that Mogadishu had no port and that a force five times larger than that presently available would be necessary to face 100,000 Abyssinians. He also pointed out that the camicie nere were organised in battalions and that brigade and divisional structures would have to be built up from scratch and married to supporting artillery and engineer units.[221] In the face of a report by general Dall'Ora after a visit to the theatre that the air force would be ready by the end of October and that the roads would be able to support the needs of an entire army of eight divisions operating on the *altopiano*, backed up by De Bono, Badoglio took refuge in dissent and assertions that progress on the spot was in fact much less encouraging.[222]

On 28 March De Bono was formally appointed to overall military command in *Africa Orientale* and lieutenant-general Melchiade Gabba and brigadier-general Fidenzio Dall'Ora were respectively nominated as his chief of staff and head of intendance. Since both men were highly experienced regulars with good reputations in Rome, and since Gabba's appointment was the result of outmanoeuvring De Bono, who had wanted a different chief of staff, the war ministry began to feel more confident about the preparations for war. Baistrocchi took the opportunity to urge Mussolini to turn aside from his other roles and focus on his position as minister of the armed forces, to allow the army general staff to carry out the preparations for the war without interference and to reduce the military office of the colonial ministry – which was officially in charge of the venture – to a liaison role.[223] The Duce, whose heavy involvement in foreign affairs alone prevented him from contemplating Baistrocchi's suggestion, chose to disregard the proposals. Nor, more wisely perhaps, did he accept Lessona's suggestion that a frontier incident should be provoked which would allow Italy to act immediately, a premature action which, given the current state of preparations, neither De Bono nor Graziani supported. For the same reason, De Bono counselled against Mussolini's wish to denounce the Italo–Ethiopian Treaty of friendship of 1928 until the rainy season. Frustrated in this wish, Mussolini announced the mobilisation of three new Italian divisions on 31 May, a move he thought necessary in the light of the discussions at Geneva and their repercussions at Addis Ababa 'in order to make it clear that our will is unshakeable'.[224]

When the authorities in Rome reviewed progress in early May, they learned that the port of Massaua was clogging up with shipping due to failures to manage the unloading facilities and stagger the arrival times of incoming vessels. De Bono was instructed to set up a disembarkation office there with links to colonial and navy ministries. His arrangements to provide shelter for the two incoming Italian divisions were also incomplete and not yet obviously adequate. This led to a reconsideration of the whole schedule for troop movements, as a result of which it was decided to get two Italian divisions to Eritrea before the rains began, and two more along with five blackshirt divisions and 8,000 mules between the beginning of September and mid-December, by which time De Bono wanted his expeditionary corps to be complete. Impatience with De Bono's lack of method was evident. Cavagnari complained that the timetables were being upset by additional requests for 17,500 labourers, tanks, railway wagons and the like, while Baistrocchi suggested that rather than be governed by De Bono's requests it would be easier to work out how to send the means which would be required to carry out the plans which it was desired to put into action. Lessona admitted that there was no detailed information on the rate of progress of road construction. Everyone agreed that De Bono was misusing the shipping schedules by not being willing to receive divisions during the rainy season of July and August, something which should be overcome by making better preparations to shelter incoming troops.[225] They had no further opportunities to make collective assessments of their progress as Badoglio did not recall the military chiefs until long after the war was over.

While Badoglio remained implacably opposed to viewing Somalia as anything other than a secondary theatre of war which should limit itself to defensive operations, the choice of Graziani as commander there indicated that Mussolini expected something more. Tough, ambitious and ruthless, Graziani was highly experienced at colonial soldiering after ten years' service in Libya. Coming from an unconventional background (he had not attended one of the military academies or served on the general staff), he saw himself as something of an outsider and unlike the majority of senior officers gave his allegiance to the Duce rather than to the king and the *tradizione sabauda* which formed the bedrock for the professional lives of most of his fellows. He was still, however, a regular soldier unlike De Bono. To diminish the latter's authority, Badoglio proposed separate army commands for Graziani in Somalia and for Eritrea with De Bono exercising 'politico–military jurisdiction' over them. Mussolini turned him down on the grounds that too many High Commands were being set up.[226]

When he arrived at Mogadishu on 7 March, Graziani had at his disposal some 17,500 native soldiers and 200 motor vehicles; by August he would receive a white division of 17,000 men and some 700 trucks. His predecessor, brigadier-general Luigi Frusci, tasked with organising the colony to defend itself and to be ready to operate across the frontier, had characterised a defensive war as 'full of unknown dangers' because of the consequences of a setback on Abyssinian morale and more practically because the 900-kilometre frontier which lacked fortifications presented an enemy with a 'multiplicity' of possible invasion routes.[227] As soon as he arrived, Graziani ordered Frusci to prepare plans to concentrate a 30,000-man force on the frontier ready to take the offensive.[228] De Bono and Lessona allowed Graziani to make his preparations – and his peremptory requests for, among other things, 100 short-wave radios and 1,300 trucks – without remonstrance. Their opinions were hardly relevant when the Somali commander had the backing of the Duce, who explicitly approved his concept of an attack aimed at Harrar.[229] In Rome, Graziani's imperious demands, especially for regular and not reserve officers, angered Baistrocchi. However, the under-secretary of state knew that Mussolini supported Graziani's scheme and therefore his requests had to be given their due.

Graziani's requirements now mounted as his improvised campaign plans came up against the problems of moving troops on the ground: to get the 2,500 trucks he required by September 1935, Mussolini gave him permission to buy directly from Ford, who furnished four fifths of them. His demands were disruptive to the schedules for supplying Eritrea, and his arguments for making them were uncongenial to the soldiers in Rome. After learning from the Italian military attaché in Addis Ababa that the Abyssinians intended to adopt a defensive posture on the Eritrean front and attack Somalia, Graziani translated this into an attack by 150,000 Abyssinians before the summer.[230] Badoglio discounted these projections as exaggerated, and attempted once more to have the Eritrean theatre designated as the location of an Italian offensive while Somalia operated as a defensive theatre. Pariani, to whom the logistical difficulties of moving 150,000 Abyssinians were so evident as to discount the likelihood of such an attack, hazarded that Graziani's report 'suggests a fear that the Somali sector will be considered *secondary* ... and is thus not entirely objective'.[231] Baistrocchi agreed, but in the face of Mussolini's support there was nothing to be done. Mussolini subsequently ordered that Graziani be allowed to increase the number of native troops to 50,000 on the basis of the forecasts and to send in his requests for the necessary materiel and white personnel.

When Graziani sought to mend his fences with Baistrocchi by offering an emollient but none the less insistent explanation of his demands for urgent shipments of arms and munitions, a row blew up which exposed the conflicts of personality that exacerbated the shortcomings of the chaotic system for managing the preparations for war in Abyssinia which Mussolini had nurtured. Lessona insisted that all communications with the war ministry pass through his office at the colonial ministry since it was responsible for the military organisation of the colony. Having just received Baistrocchi's letter ticking him off for making extravagant demands, Graziani chose to placate Lessona and to explain himself at length to Baistrocchi. However, he was more than a little irritated by what he saw as the antics of the war ministry and complained to De Bono on 27 April, 'On the equator wasting energy is not possible in the way that perhaps it is in via Venti Settembre [the war ministry] in Rome.'[232] The affair, in which Graziani felt that as a result of the arrival of one of Baistrocchi's colonels carrying the letter of reproof 'for the first time in my life as a man of action doubts were raised about me in front of my subordinates', still rankled some weeks later.[233] Intricately related because of their positions, the rivalries of their respective ministries and the tactical alliances they needed to make in order to try to make their authority felt in an anarchic system, Graziani, De Bono, Lessona and Baistrocchi were competitors and combatants as much as they were colleagues.

By mid-June, with the danger of an Abyssinian attack apparently passed, Graziani felt that the situation in Somalia was such that De Bono could be confident 'not only of the possibility of the *integral defence* of the colony but also of an offensive contribution in the whole Eritrean–Somali theatre'.[234] In keeping with his decision now to run Graziani on a looser rein, De Bono asked him to compile outline plans for a defence of Somalia and for an offensive which would fit in with his own actions. He himself planned either to await an enemy attack in a fortified zone and then counter-attack, or to push an attack as far as Axum where logistical considerations would necessitate a halt and the offensive would be continued in the air. If the enemy attacked him, Graziani should act to prevent his concentrating on one front. If, however, the enemy waited, then offensive operations should begin from Eritrea while Graziani launched air attacks followed by feints and ground attacks in whichever direction he thought best, bearing in mind Harrar as the final objective.[235]

De Bono produced his plan at the end of June. It envisaged taking the offensive at the end of September with a force of 128,000 infantry and 348 guns and advancing some 50 kilometres along a line Adua–Adigrat–Axum in three columns. Publicly determined, he was privately more timorous: 'to move without being solidly ready would be a crime', he confided to his diary. 'As long as they are persuaded of that in Italy'.[236] The design met with the Duce's general approval and was passed to Badoglio for his comments. The devil, as always for Badoglio and the regular army, was in the detail. De Bono was determined to act quickly and to surprise the enemy but said nothing about the state and capabilities of the air force on whose contribution a great deal rested, and the sketchy logistical arrangements which depended heavily on pack animals seemed insufficient to support the kind of attack he planned. Badoglio raised carefully thought-out and pertinent objections. Given the importance of air action, as Mussolini himself had declared, was it safe to contemplate beginning the war before being sure that the air force – 'the only arm which gives us the possibility of operating with surprise' – was ready? De Bono's belief that a lucky blow could lead to the enemy's surrender was a dangerous illusion: 'the war will be long and very hard'. Big results would only come from a great battle and time and patience were needed to amass the numbers of men (four metropolitan divisions and at least three divisions of camicie nere) and the amounts of materiel needed to be sure of winning it.[237] Baistrocchi added further professional criticisms: the plan took too much account of the terrain and too little of the enemy, and in proposing to advance deep into enemy territory in three separate columns which were too far apart to give each other mutual support if the enemy infiltrated between them it was exactly like the scheme that had led Baratieri to disaster in 1896.[238]

Graziani responded positively to De Bono's invitation to produce a plan for Somalia. His forces were in a condition to be able to carry out defensive, counter-offensive and offensive tasks according to how operations developed – something about which it was premature to hypothesise and determine. The operational concept was for 'resolute and decisive manoeuvre at full range', for which the necessary corollary was plenty of motor transport 'to give us superiority of movement which will allow us, at least in part, to counter-balance our numerical inferiority'.[239] Native troops would defend the three sectors of the front and then operate as attacking columns, while the metropolitan division would form two motorised columns acting in support of the central column or reinforcing one of the other columns. Air power was an integral part of the concept, supporting and protecting the columns and carrying out strategic and tactical reconnaissance. Logistical support would be provided by heavy caterpillar tractors capable of towing heavy loads and working off the roads, allowing the columns to carry only one day's supply of food, water and munitions after the opening period of operations. Movement and firepower, the two advantages in Italy's hands, could be employed on a much larger scale beyond the Somali frontier than was the case in Eritrea, or so Graziani maintained.[240]

The operational concept derived from Graziani's successful use of smaller versions of it during the reconquest of Libya. It rested on his ability to drive his forces forward by acting as conductor, choreographer and wagon-master all rolled into one. Graziani had no doubts that he could do it, and no intention of being tied down to any hard and fast scheme. Accordingly he told De Bono that his intention was 'to leave myself the maximum freedom of action to manoeuvre and to act according to the contingency of events'.[241]

The design for the Abyssinian war now seemed decided, and Baistrocchi told the ever-demanding Graziani so:

The fundamental plan confirmed to me by the Duce. Offensive from Eritrea with the means indispensable to assure triumph there. Dynamic defensive Somalia with eventual counter-offensive outpouring.[242]

Everything at once went straight back into the melting pot when Lessona tried to persuade Mussolini to launch a major offensive from Somalia into the Ogaden, whose inhabitants were held to be hostile to the Abyssinians and well disposed towards the Italians. From the foreign ministry, Suvich backed the idea. The scheme was passed to Badoglio for comment on Mussolini's orders. The reply embodied the customary line of the Capo di stato maggiore generale: only native troops could serve in Somalia, the consequent force imbalance of one to four made it impossible to undertake an offensive there, and motor vehicles could not make an appreciable impact given the lack of roads.[243] The flow of complaints and demands from Graziani continued despite explanatory and ameliorating letters from Baistrocchi and Pariani explaining that they were doing the best they could for him.

Having told De Bono in mid-May that he must plan to strike some time during October – and the earlier the better – Mussolini now decided to accelerate his own timetable. On 2 August he warned De Bono that he should be ready at twenty-four hours' notice to start military operations at any time from 10 September, and on 6 August he expounded his plans to the king. Vittorio Emanuele gave them his consent but expressed the wish that the Duce would find a way of avoiding a conflict with England. This now became a concern, and three days later Mussolini instructed Badoglio to study the problem 'of our defence' as a matter of urgency. At the meeting of the under-secretaries held on 13 August Cavagnari and

Valle were decidedly pessimistic. The air force was caught at 'a moment of crisis', Valle reported: its planes, presently amounting to 346 aircraft, were ten years old and it was short of pilots, bases, stores and the like. Things were going to improve as 200 more planes would be available by mid-December, and by June 1936 the air force would have 1,500 planes.[244] As far as operations went, Valle simply remarked that his forces would have to spread their efforts across several thousand kilometres while the English could concentrate their 200 planes wherever they chose. Baistrocchi was bullish, pointing out that there were enough supplies in East Africa to last the troops which had already arrived until January. He suggested that the aid which the ground forces could give in the event of a war with England by attacking her colonies should be examined, and Pariani enquired as to exactly what operational plan was to be adopted in the event of a war. Both were blocked by Badoglio on the grounds that for the time being it was not possible to make operational forecasts: 'Our action will be the consequence of events.'[245] Baistrocchi subsided in ill-concealed dissent, remarking that *Piano B* (the predominantly naval war plan against England) had never been communicated to him.

Badoglio's report to Mussolini was veined with pessimism. The best the navy could do, given the inferiority of the fleet, was to wage a form of maritime guerrilla war; in any encounter with the heavy units of the British fleet 'the outcome, notwithstanding the valour of our men, cannot be in any doubt'. The situation of the air force was no better: its aircraft had years of flying on their clocks and had been heavily used training 2,000 pilots for the coming war. The best it could hope to do was to maintain its present size, not increase it. Moreover, Britain's 6 aircraft carriers and the 220 planes they carried gave her a well-protected mobile striking force which could attack anywhere. With her mastery of the seas, Britain could cut off Italy's supplies and strangle her. After the customary dash of pro-Fascist rhetoric, Badoglio concluded uncompromisingly:

It is my strict duty to tell your excellency that I believe the situation in which we shall find ourselves [in the event of war with England] is by a very long way the gravest that our country has ever faced in its fortunate history of national construction and consolidation.[246]

Baistrocchi, who laid great emphasis on the *spirito fascista* and who was advising the divisional commanders about to depart for Eritrea that what was required of them was 'geniality, elasticity in the employment of fire and movement, perfect logistical preparation, calculated audacity, [and] faith', took a more aggressive line.[247] Evidently irritated and disappointed by what he had heard on 13 August, he urged that 'audacious' naval action in the Straits of Gibraltar, the Sicilian channel and off Suez would be rewarding even 'at the greatest sacrifice'. Two divisions should be sent to Cyrenaica, Tobruk reinforced on land and at sea, possible colonial operations studied, there should be maximum co-operation between sea and air 'inspired by an aggressive attitude', the rate of production of arms and munitions should be increased, and supplies of raw materials secured. 'In case of a war with England', Baistrocchi concluded, 'a passive stance – inspired by the determination to take few or no chances – would be very dangerous and contrary to the spirit of the Regime which today has penetrated throughout the Italian people'.[248] Enthusiastic, wholly unconsidered and careless of the material facts established in session after session of the Consiglio suprema di difesa, this advice was doubtless more or less what Mussolini expected – and indeed hoped for – from his under-secretary for war.

The specific issue which led Baistrocchi to raise the possibility of military operations in North Africa was the possibility that the Suez canal might be closed. The diplomats thought this unlikely. The soldiers, however, could not afford the luxury of relying on 'soft' calculations which might go wrong. Pariani believed that if the canal were closed then the Italians would have to open it by attacking from Cyrenaica while probably having to adopt a defensive stance in Abyssinia. To do this the four available metropolitan divisions and four camicie nere divisions would have to be sent over, and for this prior arrangements would have to be made.[249] During the remainder of August and September he studied information provided by SIM on the country between Sollum and Alexandria, on caravan routes to and beyond Siva, on the Nile and the Atbara rivers and on Kassala and Port Sudan. All this suggests that he was contemplating a two-pronged attack on Egypt and the Sudan from the west and from the south via Agordat or Kassala.[250] The contingency never arose, but the idea was one to which Pariani would return two years later.

Mussolini's eagerness for war matched Baistrocchi's. On 26 June, the day after his meeting with Eden had demonstrated that British concessions were unacceptable, he had fixed the starting date for the operation as 24 October. After the tripartite meeting of 16–18 August also failed to produce the outcome he wanted, he told De Bono that at any time after 10 September he would receive the order to start the war within twenty-four hours.[251] De Bono reacted by seeking a month's delay and presenting a plan for a rapid but limited advance on Adigrat and Entiscio to present the powers with a *fatto compiuto*, but warned that with the troops at his disposal (two white divisions, two native divisions and two groups of Fascist militia) he could not securely occupy the territory he intended to invade. 'The *colpo di mano*, I have said, will certainly succeed, but afterwards?' he wondered to his diary.[252] Mussolini accepted a revised starting date of 18–20 September, which allowed for the arrival of more troops, partly because he wished to synchronise military movements with 'the general political situation', by which he meant the expected failure of the upcoming meeting of the League at Geneva to discuss sanctions, and partly because he distrusted the *colpo di mano*. Operations of this kind, he told De Bono, 'generally do not have my sympathy'.[253]

Early in September, after conferring again with the admirals and with Valle, Badoglio told Mussolini that the 'crushing superiority' of the British fleet in the Mediterranean meant that there was no chance of winning a battle or even of carrying out successfully the kind of 'guerrilla war' Baistrocchi had proposed. The air force, according to Valle, was in a state of crisis. In a war the Italian forces in East Africa, now more than 200,000 strong, could be cut off, and the impracticable terrain in Libya made it fruitless to think of an attack on Egypt mounted from the colony. His advice, though couched in the customary rhetoric of military obedience, was unambiguous: Mussolini could not 'expose the country to a disaster which would bear us down to a Balkan level'.[254]

Short of resigning – which he would never have contemplated – there was nothing Badoglio could do but offer advice which was ignored. With others offering different wares in the market place for strategic advice over which Mussolini was presiding, his attempts to delay the start of the campaign fell on deaf ears. In mid-August general Dall'Ora assured Mussolini that the logistical services would be ready by the time that the rainy season ended. Baistrocchi's reports suggested that preparations were proceeding efficiently. Neither he nor Pariani believed that Italy could retreat in the face of the League's attempt to impose a solution on her with England alongside it:

In my modest opinion, it is better to perish – and we shall not perish, we shall triumph – than to withdraw in the face of the bolshevik–masonic–anti-fascist league which so concerns you.[255]

In framing his views, Baistrocchi may have drawn support from (and Mussolini as war minister may have read) a report by the Italian military attaché in London relaying lamentations that Egypt had still not taken measures to reinforce its frontiers and that its troops were still in peacetime mode, and reporting the feeling that large Italian troop movements from Cyrenaica towards the Suez canal would represent a serious menace to imperial communications 'such as to make those statesmen who want to take the responsibility for applying sanctions to Italy think again'.[256] Badoglio's response was to point out that he looked at things solely from the military point of view. Cavagnari, Burzagli and Cantù all agreed with him, but now the matter was one for the Duce with his 'powerful mind' to decide; as soldiers, he and Baistrocchi would both carry out their orders.[257]

At the final hour it was De Bono, the ageing *condottiero*, who felt anxious about his force's readiness for battle. Although by the end of September he would have six divisions in Eritrea, two in the Red Sea and four more leaving Italy, he asked for two more on 17 September, raising once again the spectre of Adua. Badoglio advised Mussolini the same day that De Bono could begin operations as soon as he had six metropolitan divisions to add to his two native ones, thereby tacitly endorsing Mussolini's preferred timetable. On 29 September, using Haile Selassie's official declaration of mobilisation at Geneva as his excuse for acting at once without a prior declaration of war, Mussolini ordered De Bono to start his attack at 2 a.m. on 3 October.[258] After requesting Mussolini not to make too much of the first advance in the press – a vain hope – and remarking that he could be in a critical position if the enemy attacked while he was settling into the occupied positions – and thus indirectly allowing Badoglio a measure of foresight greater than his own – De Bono confided his concerns in his diary:

In Rome they have no idea of our difficulties! Intendance lacks a baggage train; there are mules but neither drivers nor saddles; we lack casks for water and we don't even have all the munitions on hand.[259]

Events were soon to show that he was as much out of his depth fighting a colonial war as he was planning one.

While supporting immediate action, Baistrocchi warned Mussolini of the major defect of De Bono's plan two days before it was put into operation: it was a scheme anchored to topography which disregarded the enemy, about whom the only available piece of information – that they had retreated thirty kilometres – had been provided by the Abyssinians and the League of Nations. More information was needed in order properly to co-ordinate the use of the means available on the ground, especially if the enemy chose to fight a war of position 'for which it is impossible to make adequate provision at the last moment, especially where the terrain is not favourable to easy movement'.[260] To hold back from using air power for reconnaissance in order to conceal his intentions and surprise the enemy would be a serious mistake on De Bono's part. Intelligence was certainly inadequate, and SIM was unable to say whether the Abyssinian preparations which it reported signalled an intention to operate on the offensive or the defensive.[261] However – and ominously for the future – Baistrocchi, Pariani and De Bono had in common the fact that, despite their different positions in and attitudes towards the professional military hierarchy, all three were generals who shared a willingness to enter into wars on the basis of incomplete plans which merely outlined the initial situation and left the rest up to improvisation.

Beginning the war

On 3 October 1935, general De Bono launched Italy's invasion of Abyssinia. In Eritrea he had at his disposal 179,161 men, 580 guns, 112 tanks, 3,683 motor vehicles and 130 aircraft; in Somalia general Graziani commanded another 50,000 men along with 117 guns, 45 tanks, 21 armoured cars, 2,000 motor vehicles and 38 aircraft. Facing them was an Abyssinian army composed of 5,000 imperial guard, 50,000 irregular imperial troops and some 300,000 irregular provincial troops. Three Italian columns advanced on a front 40 to 50 kilometres wide towards the towns of Adua, Axum and Adigrat 70 kilometres to the south. They reached their main objective on 6 October and two days later De Bono settled down to organise a temporary defensive line from which, in due course, he proposed to launch a counter-offensive 'in whichever direction or directions then appear appropriate'.[262] Plagued by logistical problems – the roads behind him were still being built and the landing facilities at the port of Massaua could not handle the volume of supplies now arriving – he asked Mussolini for a month's pause before making the next move forward to Macalle. At the same time he started a programme to suppress slavery in the region, behaving in some eyes 'more like a coloniser than a conqueror'.[263]

Time was militarily a luxury for Mussolini. As Fulvio Suvich pointed out on the day that De Bono ground to a halt, the initial military objectives were not enough to provide a satisfactory basis on which to develop negotiations; more territory needed to be taken in order to give a chance to exert more political and diplomatic pressure.[264] Time was no less of an economic luxury. On 7 October a League of Nations committee concluded that the covenant had been broken and that economic sanctions could be applied against Italy under article 16, and eleven days later the decision was approved. The sanctions, which forbade the export to Italy of key minerals, the importation of Italian goods and the concession of loans or subscription to shares, came into force one month later on 18 November. Italian gold reserves had fallen from 5.5 billion lire in June to 4 billion lire a week after the start of the war, and Italy had enough sterling and convertible securities to cover six months' import costs.[265] Faced with this situation, Mussolini tightened the economic screws in what was his first venture into wartime autarchy. The services were forbidden to order imported machine tools, machinery and finished goods and instructed to reduce orders for imported raw materials to 'the indispensable minimum'.[266] Over his head hung the threat of petroleum sanctions, on which the League was due to pronounce on 12 December.

Germany's neutral stance and her policy of deciding sanctions on a case by case basis were of little or no help to Mussolini on the diplomatic front.[267] Laval, however, worked on Mussolini's behalf from the outset of the war to ensure that sanctions were only economic and not military, that they were graduated, and that they were applied in a 'partial and bland' manner. Mussolini was assured by the French premier in late October that military sanctions were not under consideration, and at the beginning of November the British ambassador assured him that the same thing applied as far as London was concerned. He was also reassured that the president of the Suez Canal Company excluded its closure as a sanction. However, Laval also warned Rome that in no circumstances could France assume a stance which put her in conflict with England.[268] After learning this, Mussolini became increasingly convinced that the French premier was not pressing Italy's aims hard enough and in particular was failing to oppose the petrol embargo. De Bono's lethargy added to his worries on this score: the pause in military operations carried with it the danger that starting them again could cause the League powers to ratchet up sanctions in response.[269]

Although both Great Britain and France had formally excluded military sanctions, Mussolini did not trust either power very much. His fear was that if economic sanctions failed they could travel up an escalatory ladder which would end in war. Although he had put on the table his minimum demands, which included a mandate over the non-Amharic parts of Abyssinia and its controlled disarmament, he expected them to be rejected. However, nothing of vital significance was likely to happen until after the British general election on 14 November. By that time, and on the premise that 'we shall only surely have what we shall have occupied', Mussolini wanted the whole of Tigray up to and beyond Macalle to be in Italian hands. On 20 October, he told De Bono that he had the month he had asked for. Orders would arrive at the start of November. In the meantime De Bono was to push the Italian occupied zone forward by 'oil spot' techniques so that the final advance would not be over an excessive distance.[270] Mussolini intended that Macalle should be captured in the first week of November, after which he would announce the suspension of hostilities. This might lead to negotiations with the Negus; if it did not there would be time to improve the position both at the front and behind the lines.[271]

As Rome awaited De Bono's next advance – which after pressure from Mussolini he somewhat reluctantly agreed to start on 5 November – a new spectre loomed: that of an Anglo–French military alliance. During the first week of October the news broke that London had approached Paris about naval, land and air co-operation in enforcing article 16 of the League covenant. On 21 October the French naval minister confirmed that an agreement did now exist between the two powers but explained that it would only come into operation if Italy provoked an incident by reacting to the economic sanctions that were shortly to be enforced or if she carried out an act of deliberate aggression.[272] A formal pact of military assistance between the two powers, under the terms of which the British would have the use of French ports in the Mediterranean and military assistance if they were attacked by Italy, was agreed on 26 October.

Mussolini, who already had documentary evidence of it (probably thanks to Francesco Costantini), had no doubt that it showed what Britain's real objective was: war against Italy. France and England had entered a military alliance with the intention of 'sliding from economic to military sanctions and forcing Italy to cede in the face of the two fleets, armies and air forces'.[273] Dino Grandi, whose ability to misrepresent the policies of the power to which he was accredited was only surpassed by his capacity for oleaginous fawning on the Duce, confirmed Mussolini's suspicions. The Foreign Office, he reported, had been working for years to lay down the basis for an Anglo–French military alliance. Its immediate intention was to break the January 1935 Italo–French agreement and isolate Italy in the Mediterranean.[274] Later, ambassador François-Poncet added fuel to the fire by admitting to Attolico that the Quai d'Orsay was not as enthusiastic about Italy as Laval and that it regarded a close and intimate understanding with England as 'the best if not the only guarantee against Germany'.[275]

Mussolini needed rapid military successes in Abyssinia but the prospects were poor. Marshal Badoglio visited the theatre between 19 and 27 October and his report, written two days before De Bono was due to start his second offensive, was damning. De Bono was not making his command felt among the troops, which was scarcely surprising given that his exercise of it was 'substantially static both in spirit and in function'. He was not visiting the front and his senior supply officer, general Dall'Ora, was not visiting the commanders whose needs he was supposed to meet.[276] Badoglio's observations were confirmed by Alessandro Lessona, who accompanied him. In Rome, general Baistrocchi added his voice to the critical chorus. De Bono was advancing too slowly because obsessed by a need to mass forces which were increasingly weighing him and his logistic apparatus down. In circumstances in which England was pressing ahead with its 'perfidious policy' of isolating Italy and making war preparations, political and economic considerations both demanded swift action. Instead De Bono was moving slowly, governed by ponderous logistical preparations and seemingly preoccupied with avoiding the smallest setback.[277] De Bono duly got going on 3 November and with the aid of supplies parachuted to the advancing columns his forces reached Tembien five days later. Here he settled down once again, explaining to

Mussolini on 17 November that the logistical difficulties he faced 'are immense and require the time necessary in order to be overcome'.[278] Mussolini sacked him that same day, putting Badoglio in command of his Abyssinian gamble.

The Hoare–Laval proposals, which closed the year diplomatically, were never likely to succeed. The terms Mussolini was prepared to discuss differed little from those he had advanced two months earlier. Those on offer required Italy to retreat back to the line Axum–Adua, abandoning the half of Tigray conquered by De Bono in his second advance, and to allow Abyssinia access to the sea via Assab in return for minor frontier rectifications in Eritrea and the Ogaden. Mussolini, who postponed any formal reply until after the Fascist Grand Council meeting scheduled for 18 December, thought the proposed terms offered little satisfaction and Suvich thought they could not be accepted.[279] In a speech that day at Pontinia, Mussolini told the crowd and the public that Italy was in the African war for the long haul and would certainly emerge from it victorious: 'It will take time, but when one is committed to a struggle, comrades, it is not so much time that counts but victory.'[280] By the end of the day Hoare had resigned, forced out of office as a result of the public outcry following the leaking of the terms of the agreement in a French newspaper nine days earlier.

Surveying the political debris, Grandi found convincing evidence for a comprehensive conspiracy thesis. The alliance that had been realised in the recent accords with France, cooked up by Hoare and Vansittart during their visit to Paris at the start of the month, was a permanent one and not something tied to the present dispute. The 'League fanaticism' that had sunk the Hoare–Laval proposals was mostly artificial and had been got up by the Foreign Office. London and Paris were now sounding out Turkey and Greece with a view to knitting together a Mediterranean pact of mutual assistance. And the French had got what they had been after for fourteen years as the principal objective of their foreign policy – a concrete basis of military assistance to underpin Locarno.[281] A somewhat different perspective on the Anglo–French accords emerged from Paris, where the deputy chief of the French general staff, general Schweisguth, took pains to assure the Italian military attaché that the military pact would only be operative under the terms of article 16 of the League covenant and could be triggered only by Italian aggression against England.[282] General Gamelin went further, assuring colonel Barbasetti that France was doing everything it could to make sure that sanctions were not made any more burdensome and expressing the wish that 'before the rainy season there will be a military resolution in Abyssinia favourable to us'.[283] It was now Badoglio's task to lay this victory at Mussolini's feet.

Wars, arms and the Axis, 1936–1937

Fig. 7 Mussolini's massed armour on manoeuvres, 1936

Between 1934 and 1939 two Fascist 'young Turk' generals, Federico
Baistrocchi and Alberto Pariani, were given Mussolini's blessing to
recast the infantry-heavy Italian army on new lines. Their new model
army would be composed of a mix of mechanised units and light
lorry-borne infantry operating according to a doctrine of manoeuvre
warfare and inspired by a philosophy of boldness and action. Although
Mussolini found support for it in some of the later battles of the
Spanish Civil War, the experiment was in the end a humiliating failure.
Italian industry produced light, under-armed tanks and far too few
lorries, and the new 'binary' infantry divisions which were intended to
provide battlefield mobility lacked sufficient fire-power. Manoeuvres in
August 1939 to test the new ideas turned into a fiasco, exposing the
fact that the imaginative new design was in every respect beyond Italy's
capacity.

For Mussolini and the Fascist armed forces, the second half of the 1930s was dominated by wars both actual and likely. The slow start to the conquest of Abyssinia put Mussolini in a decidedly difficult position as international hostility towards Italy mounted and she came under increasing economic and diplomatic pressure. Badoglio took his time to consolidate the Italian position, but after smashing the Ethiopian front at the second battle of Tembien (27–29 February 1936) and the battle of Scire (29 February–3 March 1936) he launched his drive on the Ethiopian capital. Italian forces reached it on 4 May, winning the climactic battle of Mai Ceu (31 March 1936) on the way. Italian success made its mark in French military circles and contributed to a perception among French politicians at the start of 1937 that Italy's military, naval and air power would decide the outcome of a future war.[1]

No sooner was that war over than another began in Spain and within six months Italian forces were committed to it. Shortly, that commitment became irreversible as Italy's military prestige and Mussolini's *figura* were bruised by a much-publicised military setback. The wars in Abyssinia and Spain were episodes in the larger contest for Italian domination of the Mediterranean, and the main obstacle to that was Great Britain. England was now identified as Italy's most probable opponent in a future war. To prepare for this likelihood Mussolini and his new foreign minister, Galeazzo Ciano, 'chloroformed' London while the three armed services prepared in their different ways – and with differing degrees of enthusiasm – to fight her.

The creation of the Rome–Berlin Axis in October 1936 linked two powers which had in common overtly revisionist international agendas, a visceral suspicion of bolshevism, and the prioritisation of military preparations.[2] Its value to Rome was more symbolic than practical. Forecasting German policy required that Italian diplomats look into a kaleidoscope in which Hitler, the Nazi party, the Foreign Office and the German armed forces all exercised degrees of power and influence that were often hard to assess. The reoccupation of the Rhineland showed that they could guess wrongly about an unpredictable Führer. For Mussolini, German policy presented two unknowns. Diplomatically he feared being sidelined by a combination of Germany, Great Britain and France – a fear sharpened by Germany's hints that she might re-enter the League of Nations and by no means dispelled by assurances that if Italy left it she would not rejoin.[3] Militarily, the issues which had increasingly to be assessed were when would Germany be ready for the war which Hitler described as inevitable, and exactly what war would it be? In an unstable world in which his as yet unfulfilled ambitions were laced with diplomatic anxieties about small powers as well as great ones, Mussolini had two uses for military power. While he put it into action in Abyssinia and

Spain, he also employed it (with German encouragement) as a threat to bring Britain and France round to policies which would not obstruct his progress.[4] As the division between the Axis and the democracies deepened, the military balance, and Italy's position within it, grew increasingly important.

Foreign policy in troublesome times

Although Mussolini forecast in January 1936 that Germany and Italy shared 'a common fate' and that one day 'we shall meet whether we want to or not', the process of moving further into a common orbit was not without its bumpy episodes.[5] The German reoccupation of the Rhineland on 7 March 1936 was preceded by extensive diplomatic speculation during the preceding three months about such a possibility, though the actual timing took the Italian ambassador in Berlin by surprise. Mussolini was in any case ready to accommodate it: on 22 February he told ambassador von Hassell that he would not oppose a German reoccupation of the Rhineland.[6] The episode did show for the first time that Hitler was prepared to make adventurous moves in foreign policy. Since this one was undertaken in the face of a decidedly contrary attitude by the German military, it may have encouraged Mussolini to treat his own armed forces in the same way later on.[7] Mussolini's reassurance that Italy would not take part in any sanctions that might be imposed on Germany was another indication of the trajectory to which he was now committing Italy. Hitler's move also put up an obstacle to the further extension of sanctions against him: because the League made it plain that they were not going to act against Germany, the moral ground on which Great Britain might argue for doing so in Italy's case shrank.

There were, however, reasons to be chary of Germany. Hitler had suggested that she would return to the League of Nations, and while Attolico thought that if she did so it would be to co-operate with Italy, Cerruti believed this proved his contention that Germany really wanted an agreement with England and that a high price for such a return might already have been agreed – partly at Italy's expense.[8] Von Ribbentrop's appointment to the London embassy in September 1936 signalled the start of a policy which caused Rome concern for many months. Von Ribbentrop, who became foreign minister in 1938 and whom Ciano cordially disliked, showed a disquieting inclination to put Great Britain ahead of Italy.[9] The trend persisted: Hitler's apparent overtures to London at the start of 1937 over a colonial settlement, von Blomberg's visit to London to attend the coronation of king George VI, and von Neurath's acceptance of an invitation to go to England in June (subsequently cancelled) all aroused concerns in Rome. Ciano was particularly suspicious of

Germany's intentions in the latter instance, but Attolico blamed it all on English manipulation.[10] To counterbalance the flirtation with England, there were plenty of signals from the highest echelons of the Nazi regime that closer partnership was the broad goal. Himmler and Milch returned from a visit to Rome in the autumn of 1936 convinced that 'this time Italy must march with Germany', and after a visit in the early summer of 1937 von Blomberg reported to Hitler in 'absolutely positive' terms on all he had seen and reassured the Italian ambassador that Germany had no intention of abandoning '[our] interdependence and fundamental unity'.[11]

Although Germany and Italy were partners in the Spanish Civil War, the pursuit of a shared goal did not make the experience go smoothly. After hearing appeals for help by Spanish Nationalists on 20 and 24 July 1936, Mussolini decided a month later to send an Italian military mission to Spain alongside a German one to make proposals about aid to be given to Franco. When on 6 December 1936 Mussolini decided to intervene, ordering troops to be readied and a submarine war to be prepared, there were already grounds to suspect that German involvement would be limited. Although Goering was in favour of large-scale intervention the German army and navy were not, fearing that if complications ensued they would have the entire Red Army at their back. Rather than send reinforcements to Spain and increase losses, the Italian military attaché in Berlin supposed that Hitler would prefer to cut off Russian supplies across the Mediterranean by using the international non-intervention committee or the British government.[12] Marras's hunch was confirmed a matter of days after the Duce had made his decision when first von Blomberg and then Goering confirmed that German troops would not be going to Spain.[13] Things got no easier thereafter. In January 1937 Goering made it plain that Germany regarded Italy as most directly threatened by the spectre of bolshevism in Spain and therefore the lead combatant. Rome was able to persuade Goering to reverse a policy proposal recommending that all volunteers be withdrawn from Spain, but in April it failed to reverse his decision to send no more aircraft and July he made the proposal to withdraw volunteers again.[14]

Germany's growing military power and its inter-relationship with her foreign policy was a major factor in international relations during the mid-1930s and one which made an increasing impression on Mussolini. General Giuseppe Valle visited Germany in June 1936, and reported that the dominating current in foreign policy was hate and fear of bolshevism. While there was an evident hatred for Czechoslovakia, Russia was perceived as the future field of conquest; Milch and Goering told him explicitly that it took precedence over both Germany's colonial ambitions and anschluss. Germany intended to march on Russia in 1938 with Polish support and the tacit consent of England. The Balkans and Hungary were deemed to be of no particular importance but already to be within the German sphere of influence. Germany's attitude of ill-concealed hatred for London was subordinated to the need for her benevolent neutrality and for her money, which Valle supposed must be funding the massive aerial expansion he observed. France was despised and held incapable of any offensive military action. As far as Italy was concerned, there was 'unconfined admiration' for the Duce and great cordiality but the German authorities did not conceal their dislike of Italy's industrial co-operation with Russia and her military pacts with France.[15]

The pace of German rearmament reinforced the evident signs of bellicosity which were audible in Hitler's speeches and visible in everyday German life. Ambassador Attolico noted that 400 aeroplanes had taken part in a fly-past at the Nuremberg rally in September 1936. Later that same month, in a report read by Mussolini, the Italian military attaché noted that the bulk of the German army (7 divisions) was located along the French frontier, a deployment which was in part at least a reflection of the Austro–German accord and of improved relations with Italy. Although the German army had not yet reached its forecast efficiency, by the end of 1937 the country would have 'a very powerful means of war' which combined traditional imperial elements with the new living forces of National Socialism.[16] In August, lieutenant-colonel Mancinelli judged that the planned increase in the army from 600,000 to 1,000,000 men could not take place quickly because of a shortage of officers and barracks, but two months later Attolico reported that the German barracks were full, 800,000 rations were being issued every day, the output of the military schools had doubled to meet the demand for officers, and the Air Ministry had accelerated aircraft production and would have produced 4,000 aircraft by the following spring.[17]

Along with growing German strength went rumours of war. Early in September 1936 Hitler told admiral Horthy that he shared the Hungarian's view that Europe was already divided into authoritarian states and those with weak, socialistic and bolshevising governments, and that war between the two groups was inevitable.[18] In mid-September, Attolico reported that there were people in Germany who believed in 'wars of initiative'. In his opinion they could not for the moment prevail because the German army was too weak and lacked trained cadres.[19] However, that situation was rapidly changing. In December 1936 a report emanating from the Polish General Staff suggested that Germany would probably undertake military action against the Soviet Union the following spring, the evidence being the feverish rearmament of the two states and the

German fortification of the Rhineland.[20] Later that same month Attolico got hold of a secret report for Hitler in which von Ribbentrop emphasised the likelihood of a European war between the Fascist bloc and the Franco–Soviet bloc in the fairly near future.[21]

The role that armaments were going to play in Italo–German policy – and when they were likely to play it – was made more explicit during the early months of 1937. Visiting Rome in January, Goering emphasised the importance of sea power and told Mussolini that although Germany was sufficiently well armed on land and in the air it would be three years before she was sufficiently well armed at sea to stand beside Italy in a conflict. The Duce was warned not to over-rate the combat value of the air force against naval forces and not to spend battleship monies on aircraft. After Mussolini had inflated the current Italian battleship programme from six to eight, Goering declared that the twenty-eight battleships that Germany, Italy and Japan would possess when they had completed their building programmes would be 'a very considerable naval force in relation to [those of] other countries'. In March Goering indicated that Germany would have the warships she needed in five years time.[22] At the year's end he assured Rome that the *Scharnhorst* and *Gneisenau* would be ready for 1938, the first two 35,000-ton battleships would be with the fleet for 1940 and that two aircraft carriers would be ready 'before very long'.[23]

While Germany's naval rearmament progressed at a relatively slow pace, her army and air force were palpably increasing in strength. By the summer, according to Ciano, Mussolini was becoming 'inflamed' by Germany's military organisation. His visit to Berlin 25–29 September 1937 confirmed the impressions of Valle and others about the growth of German military power. He returned committed to a partnership with Germany in which he imagined that he would direct 'policy' while leaving the direction of war to Berlin.[24] Evidence that he failed to internalise the import of Goering's earlier observations and that he did not have any real understanding of sea power came when in December 1937 he told the Japanese ambassador that Italy was superior to Great Britain both in the size of her air force and the strength of her submarine fleet.[25]

During 1936 and 1937 Austria inexorably slipped to the edge of Mussolini's political vision as he moved gradually towards accepting anschluss as an inevitability that he would not oppose. On 6 January 1936 he told the German ambassador, Ulrich von Hassell, that if Austria should become 'a German satellite' he would have no objection, and some six weeks later said that he wished to see Germany and Austria reach a direct understanding.[26] Austria was German after all, he told the Hungarian military attaché colonel Laszlo Szabo, and had 'the opportunity to become

the second great German state of Europe, if they both find the way to
co-existence, while defending their own dignity ... And if they find a
modus vivendi, nothing is going to prevent an Italian–German rapprochement.' He was also convinced that the Germans would use the opportunity to threaten the Czechs.[27] The fact that Prague had supplied the
Abyssinians with two hundred heavy machine-guns in the spring – something Mussolini warned would not be forgotten – was but one reason
why he found nothing much to object to in such a move. He was well
aware that the Austro–German accords of 11 July 1936, which removed
'the last point of friction' between Germany and Italy, did not mean that
Berlin had renounced her aspirations towards Austria, which were being
left to the play of natural forces.[28]

During his visit to Rome in January 1937 Goering declared that
Germany could never renounce Austria and must one day have it 'at any
cost' even if she had to fight for it. German reassurances that there was
no 'south Tyrol problem' and that the Brenner frontier was not a matter
for discussion were transparent hints that Italy's interests did not extend
further north.[29] Three months later, when the reichsmarschall came to
Rome again, Germany's aim was unambiguously plain. Austria's position in Italian military–diplomatic calculations was in any case changing.
For one thing, she was the only secure corridor through which Italy and
Germany could carry on the exchange of goods which both now wished
to develop.[30] For another, as will be seen, she was proving an obstruction
to Italy's military designs. In May 1937 Mussolini declared Austria to be
'a German state' and by November he was happy to let events 'take their
natural course'.[31] In this instance, Italian diplomacy eased the task of the
military planners.

Mussolini's denunciation of the Laval accords at the end of December
1935 signalled his distrust of a Latin neighbour whom he increasingly
came to discount. The naval and military attachés in Paris speculated
at the start of the New Year that there probably had been and would
be Anglo–French staff conversations and that the British were discussing
making use of Ajaccio in Corsica. Navy minister Durand-Viel's denial
that there were any new contacts between the French and British naval
staffs cut little ice in a Rome prey to suspicion.[32] During the early months
of 1936 it seemed that there might be more to the agreements of 10
December 1935 than their being limited only to the period of war and to
the action France might take if Italy attacked Great Britain – something
Laval and the Quai d'Orsay denied.[33] Attolico and Grandi both advised
Rome that the accords were incompatible with Locarno and therefore
freed Italy from her obligations under the treaty.

Germany's reoccupation of the Rhineland on 7 March 1936 generated a fear that France might entice Britain into joint staff conversations as a consequence, though Grandi's reports suggested that London was not going to fall in with French wishes for a coercive policy directed against Germany.[34] When tentative naval and military conversations were held between Britain and France in April 1936 the French naval staff took great pains to brief the Italians on their content, which was limited to discussions about the security of the channel and the North Sea and the protection of a British expeditionary force going to France.[35] The army general staff did likewise, assuring the Italian military attaché that the discussions went no further than considering transportation arrangements for joint operations in Belgium or France, that in the event of an Anglo–Italian conflict the French army would never march against Italy, and that in its view such a war would be a disaster for all of Europe.[36] Put alongside the friendly noises being made by a patently anglophobic marshal Petain and the evident dislike felt by the French general staff for the Franco–Soviet alliance, this suggested that there was at least one political player at the Parisian table who was not in England's pocket.[37]

However, it was not the army but the government which ran French politics. The election of Leon Blum's Popular Front on 3 May 1936 and its installation in office a month later produced an administration whose complexion was disagreeable. However France now mattered less: Abyssinia was in Italy's hands, and on 19 June the French cabinet approved the abolition of sanctions against her. With that, Paris announced, the Mediterranean accords ceased to apply. The outbreak of the Spanish Civil War a month later, and France's appeal for international non-intervention, gave Mussolini the chance to deepen the domestic splits in a riven Third Republic by getting Paris to nail its colours to the mast of neutrality. In early September, detecting an 'anti-Italian trend' in what he presented as a series of provocative British gestures ranging from king Edward VIII's failure to visit Italy during a recent tour of the Mediterranean to British plans to create a new naval base in the Adriatic, Mussolini instructed Grandi not to co-operate in any way with the Non-Intervention Committee which had been set up to prevent outside intervention in Spain.[38] In the months that followed Italy was able, partly through her own cynical diplomacy and partly through the contradictory attitudes of the western democracies, to tie the committee in knots.

The outbreak of the civil war caused the French general staff to worry that Germany might try to interfere in Tangier and Spanish Morocco, that Britain would detach herself from France because of the different attitudes of the two governments to the war, and that the

Austro–German accord was evidence of an Italo–German understanding – worries that could only be to Italy's benefit.[39] Italian adherence to the 'direct non-intervention' formula, around which she manoeuvred in the months to come, certainly duped the French ambassador in Rome, Charles de Chambrun, who professed himself 'well-satisfied' with it.[40] Shortly afterwards de Chambrun was recalled and rather than contemplate having to issue a new ambassador with letters of accreditation which would have to acknowledge the king of Italy as emperor of Ethiopia, France left the post vacant for the next two years.

By the end of 1936 France's position appeared much more fragile than it had been at the start of the year. The Belgian declaration of neutrality in October which weakened France's defences against Germany was 'useful' for Rome's purposes.[41] Because of the problem of Germany France was now simultaneously reliant on the Soviet Union and tied to England's coat-tails, dependent for her security on the Royal Navy and the Red Army. Cerruti read her policy as one of 'passive defence'. She was not ready to shoulder the burden of a long war unless it was absolutely unavoidable, but whether on the Rhine or in the Mediterranean 'France will never dare to sustain for long a line of conduct different from that followed by England or which England counsels her to follow'.[42] Despite strong representations from Paris, France was excluded by England from the Gentlemen's Agreement signed with Italy on 2 January 1937. The Quai d'Orsay made its hostility towards the pro-German trend of Italian policy plain, and from London Grandi fanned the embers of conflict by reporting in April that confidential conversations were under way for an Anglo–French Mediterranean naval agreement.[43] In May 1937 Boris Stein, the Soviet ambassador to Italy, informed the Quai d'Orsay that in Rome France was simultaneously detested because of its left-wing government and scorned as a satellite of England. 'We shall arrange our affairs with Great Britain, one hears in these milieux, and France will follow. We don't have to concern ourselves with her.'[44]

For a Rome deeply hostile to Paris, the military information coming from France by the middle of 1937 was a mixture of the reassuring and the potentially alarming. Renewing contact with the French army after a period of two years, colonel Visconti Prasca's first impressions were of 'excellent commanders at the higher levels, intense professional work, generally excellent discipline, and [an army generally] improved in form'.[45] Gamelin told the newly arrived military attaché of his admiration for the Duce and Badoglio, and the attitude and conduct of the regime in the Abyssinian War. Visconti Prasca also learned that the army had never had so much money as under the Blum government; that the fortifications along the German frontier were well on their way to completion and those along the Belgian border were progressing at an accelerated pace; and that the materiel coming from the French arms industry was producing the tanks and other weapons which would allow him to prepare an army capable of operating offensively.[46]

Italy's involvement in the Spanish Civil War increased tensions with France. Mussolini's telegram congratulating Franco on the fall of Santander on 27 August 1937, the presence of Italian soldiers in Spain under the guise of 'volunteers', and Italy's attitude towards the Nyon meeting all made for contained tension in the diplomatic relations between the two countries.[47] Italian military moves added to it. In Berlin, ambassador François-Poncet dwelt on the accelerating pace with which the fortifications of Majorca were proceeding and the continuing transfer of Italian divisions to Libya.[48] The policies being pursued by Italy and Germany drove Daladier to a public declaration early in November 1937 in which he highlighted German and Italian aggressive intentions and the measures France was taking to rearm.

Because Rome was in the process of successfully stalking London she had little reason to care about France's reaction. The view in Berlin, Attolico reported after consultations with colonel Marras, was that although France's war preparations had much improved her operational situation in the event of war was actually less favourable than it had been in 1914. The reasons were fivefold: the Italo–German friendship, the way in which the Spanish situation was developing, the occupation of the Balearics, the presence of substantial Italian forces in Libya which would tie up many troops in French North Africa, and the reduced military efficiency of Russia as a consequence of the Purges.[49] Had she known about it, Rome would have taken no little pleasure in her calculation of the military balance from a report by the French military attaché at the end of November which, after surveying the development of the three Italian armed services, concluded that 'Italy possessed substantial military power which constituted a real danger for France'.[50]

Mussolini's decision to intervene in the Spanish Civil War which broke out on 17 July 1936 seemed to his critics difficult to understand, since he appeared to have little more than a vague idea of securing an Italo–Spanish understanding which would 'upset the Mediterranean balance, threaten Gibraltar, and create the problem of a third front for the French general staff'.[51] In fact his aims, rational enough in their own terms, were strategic, political and ideological. Among the reasons to intervene was the strategic gain to be made from a Nationalist victory, which might provide the Italian navy with bases in the Balearics – though Ciano denied this. The war also had an ideological imperative. Both Mussolini and

Ciano were viscerally anti-Bolshevik and anti-Communist.[52] Reading a report of Hitler's speech in January 1937 on the occasion of the fourth anniversary of the Nazi seizure of power, Mussolini underlined the passage in which the Führer described bolshevism as 'a real and tangible danger for Germany' whose manifestation was visible in Spain.[53] A few days earlier, in discussions with Goering, Mussolini had forecast that the next big surprise for England would be the growth of communism there.[54]

The Spanish venture, which has been described as Ciano's first big foreign policy error, was an even greater one for Mussolini for he miscalculated the war on at least two different levels. First, neither he nor Ciano understood that Franco did not want to win the war quickly, although Roatta observed this early on and ambassador Roberto Cantalupo was told so clearly and reported this to Rome.[55] Secondly, his involvement in the war involuntarily deepened and widened when Roatta suffered a visibly dramatic defeat at the battle of Guadalajara between 12 and 23 March 1937. Roatta's explanation cast serious doubt on the expectations Mussolini may likely have nursed as to his army's military capabilities after the Abyssinian triumph – and those of its commanders. Six weeks earlier Roatta had attributed the capture of Malaga to 'the dash, passion and valour of the column commanders, their officers and their troops', adding unwisely that '[w]e can look forward with the greatest confidence [*fiducia*]'.[56] Now he had to report inept officers who were unprepared or unfit for the posts they occupied, troops who had 'the defects of their qualities' being passive, credulous and impressionable, and unit commanders who found themselves in the position of 'men driving a fine car who found that they had a steering wheel made of rubber'.[57] Mussolini acknowledged that he was now militarily and politically embedded in Spain:

First) I do not intend to send and I shall not send any more men to Spain ... Second) I shall not withdraw [any] men from Spain until the setback of Guadalajara, which is more political than military, is avenged.[58]

Paradoxically, Italy's involvement in the Spanish Civil War was the critical factor in the thawing of Anglo–Italian relations in 1937. At the start of 1936, discounting Vansittart's assertion that the aim of British foreign policy was to resurrect and enlarge the Stresa Front, Dino Grandi sent Mussolini a string of reports claiming that British policy aimed to move beyond the military agreements with France to a full alliance policy. The French, he asserted, were minimising the significance of the defensive accords of December 1935 so as not to excite Italy; in reality, 'both powers are interested in raising a screen behind which they can patiently and slowly rebuild their alliance'.[59] As far as the immediate crisis over Abyssinia was concerned, he had no doubt that England had secured assurances of a military contribution from Turkey, Greece and Yugoslavia in the event that Italy used force to resist a further development of the sanctions imposed by the League of Nations. In the longer term she would aggressively seek to transform the Locarno policy into a guarantee against Germany and 'invisibly transform the Locarno undertakings into an Anglo–French alliance'.[60] Attolico chimed in with the view, derived from German sources, that London aimed to reduce Italy to the rank of an enlarged Greece or Spain.[61]

Britain's determined attempt to persuade the League to impose oil sanctions on Italy during the first months of 1936 earned the new foreign secretary, Anthony Eden, the lasting loathing of Mussolini. Any fears of an Anglo–French alliance were set more or less at rest when the two powers fell apart over the twin issues of France's unwillingness to apply oil sanctions against Italy and Britain's unwillingness to apply economic and financial sanctions against Germany in the aftermath of the reoccupation of the Rhineland.[62] With a large slice of the British political establishment – including Winston Churchill – against sanctions, Mussolini was able to use the German threat and hollow declarations of interest in revivifying the Stresa Front and Locarno to encourage Britain to abandon her support for sanctions. His ultimate objective at this stage was legal recognition of Italy's new Abyssinian empire. There was, as Sir Robert Vansittart rightly remarked, 'a touch of blackmail' in all this.[63] Eden's announcement to the House of Commons on 18 June 1936 that the British government intended to abandon sanctions, and the League's decision a month later to do so also, suggested that it had partially worked. However, recognition was still withheld.

The outbreak of the Spanish Civil War on 17 July 1936 – the day on which the London embassy reported the naval attaché's confirmation that the Royal Navy units temporarily in the Mediterranean were returning to their home stations – immediately created another point of contention in the shape of British fears that Italy had designs on Ceuta and the Balearics. Grandi's outright denial of any intention to seek their cession was designed to quieten these anxieties, but in his speech announcing the formation of the Rome–Berlin Axis on 1 November Mussolini revived them by returning to one of the basic themes of his foreign policy – the need for Italian security in and control over the Mediterranean. For Great Britain it was no more than 'a short-cut' to its 'peripheral territories', whereas for Italy 'it is life'.[64] His demand that Italy's 'vital interests' be respected, and his direct but imprecise invitation to the British government in November to conclude a bilateral accord struck a responsive chord. On 2 January 1937 the two governments signed the so-called 'Gentlemen's Agreement', in which both undertook not to seek to modify the status quo in the Mediterranean and the Italian government undertook not to engage in any negotiations with Franco with this in mind. Since at that juncture Mussolini's policy was not to lever territorial concessions out of Nationalist Spain but to help ensure that Franco defeat the Bolshevik spectre there, he lost nothing by engaging in what was a diplomatic charade. The following day he revealed where and what his immediate interests were by sending three thousand Italian 'volunteers' to Cadiz. Even before the agreement was signed, Ciano reassured von Neurath that it represented no more than a *modus vivendi* and that Fascist Italy was united with Nazi Germany 'in a common struggle for the triumph of a common ideal'.[65]

Vansittart's opinion that in concluding the agreement the Italians had behaved 'accommodatingly' and that as a consequence 'we shall automatically loosen the Italo–German tie' was a complete misapprehension of Mussolini's position in regard to both England and Germany.[66] In April 1937, the Duce provided the heads of the armed services with a rare statement of political guidance in the form of a summary of the current state of European politics which was to inform and shape Italian military planning. Recent accords with Yugoslavia, reached in March and designed both to weaken the Little Entente and to block German penetration, had 'notably reinforced' the Rome–Berlin Axis. Notwithstanding the authoritative voices and sympathetic gestures which suggested closer Anglo–Italian relations, 'Great Britain is and will remain for many years to come decidedly hostile to Italy'. However, it was unlikely that she would provoke a single-handed war against Italy, or that France, despite her ties with England, would act against Italy unless her national interests were directly threatened. After commenting briefly on Turkey's attempt to construct a four-power pact including Greece, a country on which he put no weight whatever, Mussolini instructed marshal Badoglio to ensure that the armed forces perfected the arrangements for the security of the Mediterranean they had begun in 1935.[67] Clearly, if war transpired in the next few years the Duce expected Italy and England to be ranged against one another.

It was evident by the early summer of 1937 that her policy of supporting international non-intervention in the war in Spain and the increasingly menacing attitude of Germany together made England potentially receptive to Italian approaches over recognition of Abyssinia – provided that the obstacle presented by Anthony Eden could be circumvented. The advent of a new prime minister, Neville Chamberlain, offered an opening. At the beginning of July an evidently friendly Chamberlain gave Grandi a broad hint that London was reading his ciphered telegrams.[68] At the end of the month skilful orchestration, which included a press campaign to pump up Italian anger and a successful mixture of subterfuge and flattery by Grandi, lured a willing Chamberlain into offering to take part in talks with Mussolini. It also led Chamberlain to reveal his hand: as well as admitting that Britain had already accorded Italy de facto sovereignty over Abyssinia, which was equivalent to de jure recognition, he identified his concerns – anti-British radio broadcasts and press controversy, and the military reinforcements that were appearing in Libya.[69]

An unwelcome development in the Spanish Civil War in the shape of attacks by Italian submarines unleashed by Mussolini on 5 August 1937 in response to a request by Franco helped delay the planned talks with Rome and momentarily tipped the balance in British diplomacy in Eden's favour. The Nyon Conference (10–11 September) which resulted was in the end something of a success for Italy, as will be seen. The repositioning of British policy towards Italy which it represented was brief and within a fortnight of its conclusion Chamberlain was again in pursuit of *détente* with her.[70] In the circumstances, Mussolini had every reason to believe that the diplomatic balance in Anglo–Italian relations was tilting in his favour.

The military balance was another matter. In October 1936 Ciano was assured by the British ambassador, Sir Eric Drummond, that rearmament was proceeding rapidly; 'no difficulties' were being met in providing either materials or manpower for the Navy and Air Force, though Drummond did acknowledge difficulties in recruiting the army.[71] The Yugoslav minister, Stoyadinovich, flatteringly discounted Britain as compared to Italy, telling Ciano in December 1937 that in his view England 'will never be in a position to possess an army, in view of her strong objection to compulsory service'.[72] However, British rearmament began to pose an increasing threat. In January 1937 Mussolini learned from Goering that if he wanted Germany's support in a war with England then he would need to wait for three or four years before the navy was ready. Even then it would only be built to the 35 per cent quota agreed with England in 1935.[73] The reichsmarschall emphasised England's considerable economic power, which was allowing her to make a 'gigantic effort', and remarked on the fact that while her weakness in manpower affected her land capability it was not an important factor in respect of her naval or air rearmament. To face the threat, Italy needed at least another pair of battleships and an air force with the reach to cover the whole of the Mediterranean up to and including Gibraltar.[74]

As the year went on Britain's capacity to produce armaments began demonstrably to expand, nowhere more so than in the air. In February Grandi told Mussolini that in the 'lazy British mentality' naval and air armament played the role of a 'miraculous specific against the outbreak of a terrible malady, war'. In October, subtly changing his tune, he told Ciano that England saw Italy as 'potential enemy number one', that war was regarded as inevitable and that while Eden had full control of foreign policy he intended to use it to seek a military confrontation.[75] At the same time reports reached Rome that Milch had been very favourably impressed by the impressive strides being made by the British aircraft industry after his visit and believed it would be ready in two years.[76]

Although they were naturally her greatest concern, Italy's Mediterranean position and ambitions were not threatened only by the actions being taken, or apparently so, by the major powers. Relations with Yugoslavia were improving all the time, and Italy kept to the secret accord of 25 March 1937 by putting the lid on Croat dissidents. Turkey was altogether more problematical. A ciphered message to the Turkish military high command at the end of December 1935 which came into the Italian military attaché's possession indicated that the government had decided to collaborate 'in all points' with England, had passed information to her about the Soviet–Turkish defensive military alliance as a gauge against future arms supplies, and had been asked to prepare a revolt in Tripolitania.[77] The accreditation of a British naval attaché to Istanbul in February 1936 and the arrival of a British air mission was believed to have resulted in an agreement for British aircraft to use bases at Smyrna and along the Aegean coast in the event of 'Italian aggression', and the British were also believed to be putting pressure on the French through acquisition of rights to use air bases along the Syrian border in order to force France at least to facilitate if not to aid British action against Italy.[78]

Mussolini was violently angry at Turkey's behaviour during the Mediterranean crisis, not least because she appeared to be one of the obstacles blocking the lifting of sanctions. In mid-April he told the Italian naval attaché in London, count Capponi, that it had taken forty years to settle accounts with Ethiopia but ten would be enough to settle accounts with Istanbul.[79] Turkey's interest in remilitarising the Straits added to Italian anxiety and anger. She was believed to be acting in accord with Britain's wish to close off Italy's third avenue of supply and encircle her, and the Montreux convention of June 1936 was interpreted as reflecting Britain's fear of an Italo–Soviet accord and her using Turkey to block Russian entry into Mediterranean.[80] It was characteristic of Fascist diplomacy that it chose not to see the positive advantage of the convention, namely that it prevented the Russians from joining hands with their French ally in the Mediterranean.

Suspicion that Turkey was willing to become England's catspaw continued. In mid-July, Ciano believed that Britain planned to hold naval talks with Turkey to strengthen its Mediterranean naval position. When Greece and Yugoslavia dropped the Mediterranean accords, Great Britain was believed to be trying to keep Turkey in them.[81] In an attempt to make use of Turkish hostility to France, Ciano tried to trick her into seizing Alexandretta by letting her believe France was about to cede it to Italy. The scheme failed, and Italy had to face an expansion of British economic influence in Turkey against which she did not have the means to compete.[82] Turkish links with Greece also tightened as Bulgaria began to rearm. In the eastern Mediterranean, diplomatic circumstances exacerbated the difficulties faced by the navy and the air force in contemplating either defensive or offensive military action against England. Turkish control of one of the three entrances to the Mediterranean was of heightened strategic significance when set alongside the difficulties besetting Italy's war economy.

Conquest, conflict and the defence agenda

The defence environment which confronted the Commissione suprema di difesa as it prepared for its annual round of meetings in 1936 was significantly different from that in which it had convened a twelvemonth earlier. The acquisition of Ethiopia presented both problems and unknowns. The 'immense riches' to which many experts attested, and which according to them would in time produce liquid fuels, iron, copper and the like, were at present something of an unknown. The only available statistics on Ethiopian external trade, deriving from the Djibuti railway which carried some 75 per cent of the entire traffic, revealed that annual exports averaged approximately 26,000 tons, over 90 per cent of which was made up of coffee and hides. By contrast, 1,293,552 tons of fuel, foodstuffs and other materials would be needed to keep the colony going during the first year of a war, permanently occupying thirty-one ships. While some of the necessities – oats, barley, coffee and fresh meat in particular – could sooner or later be produced locally, much of the shopping list would have to be imported.[83]

The war had made considerable inroads into Italy's military capacity to defend herself in Europe, and therefore into the substrata of her foreign policy. Between February 1935 and January 1936 six army divisions and five blackshirt divisions had been sent to Eritrea, and one infantry division and one Blackshirt division to Somalia, amounting in all to

301,772 officers and men, along with 65,000 horses and 11,000 motor vehicles. The intense activities of mobilisation, which had thinned out the permanent cadres, and of replacing the troops sent overseas with seven new metropolitan divisions had their effects on the army's capacity to face a major war in Europe. In February 1936 it could field twenty-five infantry divisions in a general mobilisation and not forty as had been the case twelve months earlier, along with three celeri and four alpini divisions. Shortages of ammunition, clothing, boots and automobiles were now evident, but the Army Council was airily reassured that there was no need to worry about them 'given the firm will of the DUCE to replace the stocks with timely and concrete measures'.[84]

In twenty-four hours, the army could put into the field five alpini divisions (one of which was in East Africa), three celeri divisions and two motorised divisions) (one of which was in Cyrenaica). As soon as circumstances allowed, the military intended to create two new motorised divisions and two *autotrasportate* (lorry-borne) divisions so as to be able to put a force of twelve to fourteen divisions into the field immediately. The four reserve classes of 1912–14 could already produce a force of 1,250,000 'perfectly trained' soldiers, to which the class of 1915 would shortly be added. The programme for rearming the infantry presented to the Army Council in January 1935 was now 'a reality': among the new weapons in use were 47-mm anti-tank guns, 45mm and 81 mm mortars and light assault tanks.[85]

As far as new developments were concerned, the Po division was in the course of motorisation, and planning was under way for the creation of a motor-mechanised brigade designed to meet 'special operational needs in particular terrain which require small units that are highly mobile and have heavy firepower'.[86] The new *Regulations for Divisional Combat* completed the roster of operational regulations 'perfectly appropriate for the moral and war-like (*guerriero*) climate of the Regime'.[87] On them, as will be seen, was engraved the personality of the army's current commander.

Both the air force and the navy were manifesting considerable interest in Albania. The navy was preoccupied with the hostile attitude of Great Britain and France and their evident intention to increase the extent of their encirclement of Italy, possibly by constructing a naval base at Alexandria, air bases in Egypt and air and naval bases in the Aegean and Ionian seas. If they achieved these objectives they would 'deprive our advanced positions east of Tobruk and Leros of any value and thereby inexorably restrict our options in the areas close to the coasts of the mainland'.[88] Given the difficulties of keeping open the sea lines of communication, the necessity of keeping open the land and sea communications with the markets of the Balkans put a premium on control of the Adriatic.

To exercise this, the navy needed to command both sides of the Otranto channel. Hence the dual importance of Albania as a bridgehead to the eastern markets of the Mediterranean and the Red Sea and of Valona and Brindisi to keep enemy fleets out of the Adriatic. Given the range of modern bombers, the Regia Aeronautica saw no need to concern itself with Albania or indeed the entire Balkan and Danubian–Carpathian region as far as offence was concerned. However, Albanian air bases would be useful for defensive purposes in the event of an Italo–Yugoslavian war. After a convention signed on 20 March 1935 the Albanian domestic air service was under Italian control for a period of ten years, safeguarding Italy from the possibility of any foreign air service establishing itself in the country.[89]

In its preparation for the annual gathering of political and military luminaries, the navy reviewed the arrangements for construction of ships in time of war. In 1934, the Consiglio superiore di difesa had agreed on the production of 170,540 tons of shipping in addition to those under construction according to peacetime programmes, the first elements to be ready by the ninth month of war and the whole programme to be completed by the twentieth month. New calculations showed that the shipyards could produce no more than 50,000 tons of shipping a year, and that no wartime construction could be ready for at least six months. Construction time and the amounts of raw materials and labour required dictated that new shipping be limited to a maximum displacement of 5,000 tons. As regarded the types of ships, the navy wanted heavier destroyer leaders which could operate both inside the Mediterranean against Britain and France and outside it, where they could watch German naval traffic, and also submarines which could operate throughout the Mediterranean basin and outside the Straits.[90]

The unique perspectives on war planning for which the Fascist machinery had a marked predilection were apparent in the calculations of the amounts of raw materials that would be needed in wartime. The ministry of communications estimated that 20,864,000 tons of coal, fuel, minerals, chemicals, wood and foodstuffs would be needed in the first year of a war. The fact that this was two million tons less than the actual importation in 1934 and almost four million tons less than the expected import total for 1935 was brushed aside with the argument that these figures had been artificially swollen due to the requirements of the Abyssinian War and the need to confront the consequent world situation and were therefore abnormally large.[91] For at least one branch of the Italian government, the practical experience of war was being deliberately discarded in favour of a comforting best-case scenario.

Detailed calculations about the carrying capabilities of the various land routes by which imports could be brought in produced the conclusion that the railways could import 11,000,000 tons from either France or Germany, and the roads could in theory carry 15,400,000 tons but because of the foreseeable shortage of lorries could in practice bring in between 960,000 and 1,760,000 tons according to whether and how the army was operating. To carry the entire amount required by land would need an additional 15,650 railway wagons. If one or both frontiers were closed, the amount of goods which could be imported shrank to a minimum of 4,888,000 tons – 'never enough for our complete resupply' – in which event the shortfall would have to be made up by sea and by utilising neutrals' railway wagons.[92]

Given the likelihood that in a major war a part of Italy's merchant fleet would not be able to get home before hostilities began, some 1,260,000 tons of shipping would probably be available with a total annual carrying capacity of 7,566,000 tons. Since this amounted to only one third of the estimated requirements, the country would have to rely for the remainder on land routes and on neutral shipping. The obvious probability that in wartime enemy action, particularly a co-ordinated naval blockade, would make serious inroads into the amounts of materials Italy could import produced the conclusion that the only ways to escape from this reality were to decrease dependence on foreign production by improving national output of key products, to build up stocks, to develop relations with potential wartime suppliers, and to keep ready the organisation necessary to ensure that Italian merchant ships were warned of the approach of war so that they could get to national or neutral ports. Any improvement, the ministry acknowledged, was going to take some time.[93] These conclusions did not sit entirely comfortably alongside the navy's recommendation that the state should look to maximise the possibilities offered by land transportation 'in order to limit sea transportation to a minimum and thereby limit the demands made by the defence of maritime traffic, which always absorb a notable part of the means of war'.[94]

When the Commissione suprema di difesa convened on 4 February 1936 for the first of five meetings over the coming ten days it had an agenda of twenty-one items to digest. Some issues – for example the measures to be taken for protection against incendiaries or the air defences of the Marghera industrial zone – were matters which a more efficiently co-ordinated bureaucracy could and should have handled at a less exalted level. Others – such as the situation with regard to petrol, lubricants and alcohol – produced a mass of detailed figures on supply, demand and reserves, and identified products such as castor oil whose output could be expanded. In a monologue of which Hitler would not have been ashamed, Mussolini reviewed in detail the situation with regard to raw materials and asserted that utilisable coal did exist in Italy and imports could be halved, that sufficient iron existed in Italy for there to be no need to import any more, that manganese had been discovered in Pisa, that nickel mines which had been reactivated after falling into disuse in 1793 could produce four or five thousand tons a year, and that where problems existed the technicians must solve them. 'More than being guided by the "fact" of war, the entire national economy must be absolutely dominated and obsessed by it', the Duce declared.[95] Evidently, success in war was to be achieved not as the consequence of rational calculation but would instead result from the triumph of the will.

Ducking every one of the major problems identified in the memoranda submitted by the ministry of communications and the navy, the commission agreed that studies of supply in wartime would be annually updated and reported to it. The navy's wartime building proposals were accepted even more swiftly. Baistrocchi reported major deficiencies in motor vehicles which were partly due to the demands of the East African campaign, and after a short discussion on the relationship between the kind of trucks needed to meet civilian requirements and those appropriate to the military the task of advising on the qualitative and quantitative requirements to be imposed on the automotive industry was handed to the ministry of communications and the war ministry to sort out.[96] The problem presented by the railway situation was passed to the ministries of finance, war, communications and public works with the injunction that they were to come up with a gradual programme which was in harmony with the financial possibilities.

When Albania came up, the military and naval members of the commission came into their own. Reviewing its importance, Pariani pointed out that previously it had been of purely politico-military interest because of its function in blocking the Adriatic and its potential role as the jumping-off point for military operations either to support Montenegrin movements or, in collaboration with the Bulgarians, to cut Yugoslavia off from her access to the sea at Salonika. Now there was a logistical dimension to consider – petroleum – and since this was the priority diplomatic and military initiatives must be taken to secure, protect and transport it from Albania to Italy. Mussolini pointed out that Italy could not yet take on the anti-aircraft protection of the petroleum fields directly without causing a national uprising. Cavagnari rehearsed the by now familiar naval arguments about the need to possess Valona in order to control the Adriatic; without it, the arrangements for blocking the Otranto channel 'would collapse'. While accepting that the occupation of Valona would be a necessary act in war which must be studied in peacetime, Mussolini pointed out that although king Zog was *italofilo* the country was under pressure from England, which controlled the gendarmerie, and the population was hostile. The meeting concluded that Italy's political and economic supremacy in Albania must be guaranteed and reinforced, and planning should continue for military, naval and air action 'to confront any of the various situations which could arise'.[97] The discussion did serve to focus attention on a problem whose full dimensions had not previously been grasped; by the summer, the army general staff was working on plans to provide an efficient anti-aircraft defence for the petroleum field of Devoli, Valona and Durazzo, to improve the Albanian road network to make it suitable for use by Italian motorised units, and to strengthen the Albanian army so that it could resist an enemy for at least ten to twelve days and thereby allow Italy to send in sufficient reinforcements.[98]

One of the last acts of the commission was to approve the devising of measures to create a nucleus of officials capable of serving in the office of the Capo di stato maggiore generale. Balbo argued that such officers would inevitably get entangled in conflicts with the general staffs of the three armed forces and suggested that the real necessity was to give the staff defined functions. Ignoring the first point but taking up the second, Mussolini also invited Badoglio to submit proposals defining his functions in wartime. The army's view, as expressed by Pariani, was that the Duce was the central functional link between the king, who fixed 'the great final objectives', and the chief of the general staff of the armed forces, who transmitted to the various services technical instructions on the general lines to be followed to achieve the objectives and the ways in which these lines were to be developed. The chiefs of staff then acted on their own authority in respect of their individual services.[99]

In December, Badoglio's proposals were finally forthcoming. He predictably proposed that the conduct of operations in wartime should be given to him, or to any subsequent holder of his post, since he was the authority responsible for co-ordinating the military preparations of all three services and acting as technical consultant to the head of government. Given that it was proposed to employ both the air force and the navy as autonomous bodies in war, it was evident that a single mind was necessary to co-ordinate them. Shrewdly picking his arguments, he pointed out that now that the prime minister also had constitutional responsibility for all three service ministries he would in wartime be responsible not only for the conduct of the war but also for the conduct of operations. There would inevitably be conflicts with and between the three heads of the services to be adjudicated. A further complication to which he had the answer was the fact that the three under-secretaries of state were simultaneously chiefs of the general staffs of their respective arms. Debate between the two posts had therefore disappeared, and a change in one office would be a change in both. Badoglio was bidding for the role and title of *Commandante Superiore delle forze armate*, a deputy and an office with twelve divisions including his own intelligence and cipher sections.[100] When the issue came before the Commissione suprema di difesa on 10 February 1937 as an agenda item, Mussolini ruled that it lacked the competence to consider it.

When the Commissione suprema di difesa met again in February 1937, it included for the first time among its member the marshals of the army and the air force, the grand admirals of the navy, the chiefs of staff of the three services and the secretary of the Fascist party – evidence that organisation for war was likely to give way more directly to war preparation.[101] Noting Hitler's success in expanding German automobile manufacture, Mussolini opened a discussion on motorisation. Alberto Pariani, who had succeeded Baistrocchi as both under-secretary of state for war and chief of the army general staff on 7 October 1936, emphasised the central role motor vehicles would play in the army's 'war of rapid decision'. The minister of communications assured the meeting that the problem of provision could be resolved with appropriate tax reliefs. After a brief argument between him and the finance minister about exactly how much motoring tax was not being paid, and a discussion about how many kinds of motor fuel should be used in the course of which the finance minister declared sal-ammoniac 'the most national' of all fuels, general Dallolio pointed out that Italian industry could only produce what it was equipped to produce and urged that the present twenty-three types of trucks be reduced to two if the country was to have any hope of meeting the demand for spare parts in wartime. Badoglio pointed out that it was useless to talk about a war of movement, which he supported in preference to one of attrition, if the army was not given the means necessary to wage it. Evidently impressed by Hitler's Four Year Plan – 'we must aim at this [kind of] autarchy' – Mussolini decided on the 'two lorry' solution but simultaneously backed development of a variety of fuels including Albania's ten to fifteen million tons of petroleum, Italian lignite ('a secure source which we can rely on for 150 years'), alcohol, methane and sal-ammoniac.[102]

An upbeat report from an inter-ministerial committee on forty-two types of raw materials that were in short supply reached an encouraging conclusion:

[W]ith the growing development of hydro-electricity and electro-chemicals, the geographical privilege of those powers controlling iron, coal and steel is ceasing; copper, brass and bronze are being dethroned; Italy's servitude in metals and in part in coal is losing ever more significance.[103]

A survey of special metals concluded that Italy could at least meet her normal needs in almost all of them with the exception of copper. General Dallolio was less happy. It was 'blind faith' to think that at a given moment all the factories in the war industries sector could take part in a leap in production when in current conditions they had run through supplies and stocks of raw materials. He wanted much greater control exercised in stock rotation and more cover for vital industries in respect of supplies, stocks and reserves. Mussolini reassured everyone that the problem of supply was 'at the head of his thoughts', but had to tell the commission that until 31 July wheat and oil seed had priority as far as financing imports was concerned.[104]

With the recent experience of sanctions to profit from, general Dallolio believed that as far as industrial mobilisation was concerned the co-operation between his own office for war manufacture and the ministry of exchange and currency was proving able to meet every new request and overcome every fresh difficulty. Key minerals – coal, copper, iron and nickel – were bought from abroad under monopoly purchasing arrangements by the state railway authorities and distributed through his office. This system was exercising an accurate check on whether imports were really essential. While the system for distributing nationally produced minerals was working effectively, Dallolio produced figures which showed that it simply could not meet demand. With total national output of aluminium amounting to 16,017 tons, he had been confronted with short-term requests for 5,642 tons from the military and 4,530 tons from civil industry. Comparisons between the 1935 and 1936 figures showed that the metallurgical industries were now in difficulties. While production of cast iron and the amount of scrap-iron collected in Italy had both risen, production of raw and finished steel had fallen as had the amount of imported scrap-iron.[105]

On matters of military policy the commission made little progress. After listening to informed arguments by Cavagnari against a proposal to develop large transport submarines and to Badoglio's reasoned objections to developing the large-scale air transport of troops, the Duce over-ruled them both and ordered further exploration of the possibilities in both spheres. A discussion on the unification of the support services for the armed forces which aimed at greater harmonisation of weapons, equipment and supplies, in which Pariani supported the idea of a special office attached to the Stato maggiore generale to try to harmonise things, led Cavagnari to say that the navy and the air force had done as much as they could but that both were 'eminently technically specialised forces'. Valle backed him up, leaving Badoglio to remark somewhat forlornly that the proposals before the committee were modest ones. Mussolini concluded a very brief discussion with one of his customary flourishes. The results of unification hitherto achieved were satisfactory and as much more should be done as possible which did not 'disturb the particular functions and needs of the individual armed services'.[106] Whether in recognition of their recent achievements or in anticipation of future calls on them, the three armed services were essentially to be left undisturbed.

Naval necessities

The navy performed well during the Ethiopian war – a fact which may have encouraged Mussolini to make unjustified assumptions about what it might do if called on to fight a larger war demanding great exertions. Between February 1935 and July 1936 it shipped 595,304 men, 40,859 animals, 634,900 tons of supplies and 10,084 vehicles to Eritrea and Somalia.[107] Four transatlantic liners were used in order to keep up a rate of 60,000 men a month from the end of September, and the capacity of the port of Massaua was expanded so that the unloading rate of four ships a day in 1934 reached fifty a day when military operations began. All this was achieved under extremely testing tropical conditions: as well as 90 per cent humidity, the crews had to withstand temperatures in the Red Sea which reached 60 degrees in the engine rooms of *Pantera*-class ships.[108] In international terms, the outcome of the war could easily be interpreted as due to the intimidatory effect of the Italian navy in the Mediterranean acting in support of the policy of the state. To admiral Bernotti, commanding a light cruiser squadron at La Spezia, the victory in East Africa 'allowed the illusion to develop that Italy was capable of obtaining quick victories in a European conflict, just as she had carried out the Ethiopian war'.[109]

Supporting colonial campaigns was not what the navy thought it existed to do. Its official view, enunciated in the *Enciclopedia Militare* published in 1933, defined the object of maritime strategy as the control of communications, to be obtained only by defeating the bulk of the enemy's forces. Three years later, in the no less official *Enciclopedia Italiana*, admiral Bernotti ennumerated the navy's tasks as protecting the nation's seaborne supplies and attacking those of the adversary, protecting its own troop transports while preventing the enemy from moving his troops between territories, defending the coasts of the *madrepatria* and attacking those of the enemy, all of which was summed up in the concept of preserving the free use of the sea while denying it to the enemy. In the face of this cautious formulation, admiral Oscar di Giamberardino issued a clarion call for action in *L'arte della guerra in mare* ('The Art of War at Sea'), published in 1937. Eager to escape from what he saw as the extension of the immobilisation of the First World War from the land to the sea, Giamberardino dismissed both the defensive and the defensive–offensive and called for the strategic offensive pure and simple: 'The objective of every offensive at sea can only be the enemy fleet . . . [and] the goal is always and only its destruction'.[110] Where a combatant did not have superior mass, a true defensive did not consist of sitting in port as a 'fleet in being' but acting offensively in other regions and seeking to break the enemy into fractions spread over the seas so that its separate detachments could then be defeated by a locally stronger fleet. While Giamberardino's theories won a considerable following in the navy, a cautious Cavagnari preferred to opt for Fioravanzo's defensive–offensive.

The immediate preoccupation of the navy, however, was not so much with the higher reaches of strategy as with the practicalities of international disarmament negotiations. After a series of bilateral conversations begun in 1934, and after the Japanese announcement on 29 December 1934 that it did not intend to adhere to the naval arms limitation treaties after they terminated in 1936, London indicated to Rome and Paris early in August 1935 that it proposed to hold a new conference to seek qualitative arms limitation. At the moment when the Anglo–Italian naval crisis began to reach its height, the Italian navy ministry signalled its eagerness to reach new agreements on maximum displacements and gun calibres which should be 'the lowest possible' in order to avoid a new competition in areas in which Italy, with its limited financial resources, would find it difficult to participate.[111] Despite the tension between the powers, both recognised that international co-operation in the naval sphere was in their best interests. Accordingly when, on 24 October 1935, London invited the five signatory powers of the Washington and London Conferences to a further conference, Rome accepted after a brief delay.

The chief task of the Italian delegation was to avoid any regulatory system such as the communication to other powers of naval construction programmes for a period of six years which might raise the question of naval parity between Italy and France. Alongside this technical consideration other important political considerations had to be borne in mind. Being present at the conference would provide Italy with useful information on the construction programmes planned by other powers. Every concession offered by Great Britain would be of great value in the present political situation. And considerable care must be taken if the Italian delegation found itself having to consider a policy line which would be unwelcome to France, with whom naval co-operation since the January 1935 accords had been good.[112] Like Italy, who already had two 35,000-ton/381-mm gun battleships on the slipways, France was ready to see a maximum limit of 30,000 tons displacement and 330-mm guns for new battleship build.[113]

The London Conference opened on 9 December 1935. En route the deputy chief of naval staff, admiral Wladimiro Pini, learned from ambassador Cerruti in Paris that as far as the current conflict was concerned Laval could not detach France from Great Britain.[114] At first the Italian delegation took no major part in the discussions because it was in sympathy with the Japanese proposal that there should be a common upper limit of tonnage for all powers. However, when the Japanese delegate proposed to restrict this to Japan, Great Britain and the United States, Italy joined France in objecting to what was in effect a return to a system of ratios. The unspoken corollary was that such an agreement would finally put the Royal Navy beyond the legal reach of Italy, thereby condemning Italy permanently and publicly to a place among the least of the naval great powers. Italy then joined France and Japan in opposing the British proposal that naval building plans be communicated in advance to other powers and then be binding on the grounds that every power would be bound to set a high level in order to confront any eventualities and would then tend to build up to it. Instead, the Italians relaunched their preferred option of annual declarations. At this point the Japanese insistence on reaching prior agreement on the common upper limit threatened to torpedo the conference.[115] Japan's subsequent withdrawal from the London Conference had positive implications for Italy for it suggested that Great Britain was going to face a growing Japanese navy and further Japanese aggression in the Far East in the coming years. This, Grandi thought, would make England more aware of the fact that reaching an agreement with Italy in the Mediterranean was in her best interests.[116]

The decision to continue without the Japanese produced relatively straightforward agreement on an annual publication schedule of construction based on the Italian proposal. Both Italy and France objected to the Anglo–American proposal to limit battleship size at 35,000 tons and 356-mm (14-inch) guns, and both the size limits and the British proposal for a 'construction gap' which would outlaw battleships displacing 10,000 to 20,000 tons proved serious sticking points for Rome and Paris. A further bone of contention was the question of whether Germany and the USSR should be invited to adhere to a treaty after the four remaining powers had signed it. There were soon clear indications that the French were willing to abandon their opposition to the American proposals regarding battleships.[117] With the ground shifting underneath it, the Italian delegation was called back to Rome to consult with Mussolini.

The Duce was preoccupied with the decision on a possible petrol embargo which the League of Nations committee of experts was scheduled to consider on 8 March and wanted to trade. The British should be told that, despite her initial reservations, Italy had offered 'a very effective technical collaboration' in the hope that the political situation would improve during discussions, thus allowing her to adhere to an agreement 'which [was] not just technical, but also political'. There were precedents for a British *revirement* in the shape of the conclusion of the Anglo–German naval pact two months after Germany had been censured for rearming, and the withdrawal of the Hoare–Laval plan. The Italian naval delegation were given the task of securing an undertaking from the British that petroleum sanctions would not be applied on 8 March and that the application of new sanctions would be halted.[118] Characteristically, Mussolini gave Grandi different instructions: that Italy should not subordinate the signing of an agreement to a specific undertaking to stop the process of extending sanctions, but should maintain her attitude of reserve on the details of the proposed treaty.[119]

The Italian delegation duly did as it was instructed, holding discussions with the British on 24 and 27 February 1936. The immediate British reaction – that if they had known that Italy was going to link the signing of the treaty to the current political situation they might have taken a different decision over the convening of the conference – did not augur well for Rome.[120] The desired quid pro quo was not forthcoming, and after resisting manoeuvres by London to try to get them to agree in principle to the terms of the treaty even if not yet actually signing it, Raineri-Biscia and his team announced that Italy was not in a position to sign because of 'difficulties of a technical character'.[121] At the final plenary session, Grandi offered a vigorous defence of Italy's position as a power under economic attack and facing a potential naval threat in the Mediterranean.

Summarising the final treaty for Mussolini, Cavagnari suggested that the outcome, if not quite a triumph for Italy, was something from which she could draw considerable cheer. The proportional ratios established at Washington were dead. The 35,000-ton limit for battleships was 'not prohibitive with regard to the logistical possibilities of our ports'. The 'building holiday' on 10,000-ton cruisers gave the four *Zara*-class ships an advantage because of their additional armour, and the 'holiday' for 8,000-ton cruisers prevented the construction of ships superior to the types Italy had and ones she did not need. Also, while the displacement of aircraft carriers had been reduced (a consideration Cavagnari passed over in near-silence), there was no limit to the numbers of aircraft that could be flown off other types of warship.[122] However, for Italy the real significance of the London Treaty was not naval but political. France had accepted the 35,000-ton limit on battleships and had signed it, thus pulling away from Italy and beginning the process of aligning herself with Great Britain.

Although economic sanctions were restricting Italy's economic room for manoeuvre, the outcome of the London Conference confirmed that a naval building competition was now under way: over the years 1935–9 the French government expanded its naval programme to comprise four new capital ships, two aircraft carriers, three cruisers and fifty-one smaller ships. In response, the Italian naval budget for 1935–6 rose by 305,010,000 lire to 1,609,891,000 lire to accommodate new naval construction. International competition whetted naval appetites. In January 1936, as the culmination of planning studies begun the previous May, the naval staff drew up an ambitious plan for a *flotta d'evasione* comprising nine or ten capital ships, four aircraft carriers, thirty-six cruisers and up to seventy-five new submarines, designed to break out of the Mediterranean and operate in the open oceans alongside Germany or other friendly powers. However, unless Italian dockyards were considerably expanded the programme would take twenty-four years to complete. Therefore the alternative was a *programma minima* under which two new *Littorio*-class battleships, three heavy cruisers, eight destroyer leaders, twenty-two destroyers and torpedo craft and four submarines would be constructed between 1936 and 1942. While the *programma massimo*, which was so evidently beyond reach as probably to represent simultaneously a strategic dream and a budgetary ploy, signalled an unmistakeably anti-British stance, the naval staff preferred the reduced plan as unlikely to cause undue international alarm.[123] The two new battleships, *Impero* and *Roma*, were not in fact begun until May and September 1938 respectively and the former was never completed.

For a year Italo–French naval relations improved. In March 1936 the Rhineland crisis forced the French navy to acknowledge that it could not act alone against both Germany and Italy, and three months later the French naval general staff recognised that a 'two power standard' was now beyond reach and that henceforth France must try to ensure a decisive superiority over either Germany or Italy. However, an analysis of publicly announced naval construction programmes and estimated rates of completion which every naval staff could compute, although with varying degrees of inaccuracy as regarded the latter, suggested that a dangerous window of opportunity for Italy would open up between 1938, when the *Vittorio Veneto* and the *Littorio* were due for completion, and 1941 when the *Richelieu* and *Jean-Bart* would be ready. (In fact the Italian battleships were not completed until April and May 1940 respectively.) Faced with the awful prospect of a simultaneous war in two oceans the French chief of naval staff, admiral Durand-Viel, became a proponent of the policy of recognising Italy's imperial conquests in East Africa and signing a Mediterranean agreement with her, a line of policy which continued until the italophobic admiral Darlan succeeded Durand-Viel in January 1937.[124]

While there was clear evidence that Laval was making serious efforts to prevent the application of an international embargo of all raw materials on Italy, and while the evidence emerging from the French war and air ministries suggested that Anglo–French conversations were limited to technical matters related to the application of article 16 of the League Covenant, initially it appeared highly probable that staff conversations were in fact underway. They were thought to deal not merely with Anglo–French naval co-operation in the Mediterranean but also with possible British support on the French Alpine frontier and on the Rhine. Judging Durand-Viel's stance correctly, the Italian naval attaché in Paris believed that in the face of German naval rearmament France could have no interest in anything other than a three-power equilibrium in the Mediterranean. He also relayed to Rome Durand-Viel's flat denial that there had been any conversations between the British and French naval staffs, a statement he was very much inclined privately to believe.[125] While his opposite number in London, count Capponi, thought the British press was correct in declaring that there had been a complete resurrection of the entente cordiale, Ferreri did not agree: although France was gradually moving closer to England 'she has hesitations, doubts, does not really know how far she will be able to rely on her friend across the channel in future'.[126]

The German reoccupation of the Rhineland on 7 March 1936 produced what could only be regarded from Italy's point of view as favourable reactions. The 'first glacial impressions' given by the British press suggested that not much was going to come to Paris by way of cross-channel assistance, and both naval and military circles looked to Italy for a degree of support after a rapid liquidation of the Ethiopian question.[127] Durand-Vial passed on to Rome the information that Anglo–Franco–Belgian staff talks in April had stuck to broadly generic issues relating to the protection of a British expeditionary force going to France and had made no reference whatever to Italy or to the Mediterranean. He hoped for a rapid solution to the Ethiopian conflict 'so that Italy can reassume her position alongside France'.[128] The Italian victory there in early May produced further expressions of friendly sentiment among military and naval circles. The announcement that Léon Blum's Popular Front cabinet approved the lifting of sanctions on Italy on 19 June – partly due, the naval attaché believed, to the effect of the advent of Ciano as minister for foreign affairs – and the mounting domestic difficulties it faced after the ending of the strike waves that month both augured well for Italy. With the lifting of sanctions the French determined that the Mediterranean accords with Turkey, Greece and Yugoslavia had ceased to exist. At the 14 July celebrations, the Italian naval and military attachés were the recipients of a sympathetic public demonstration.[129]

Although the political signs were positive, the Italian naval staff believed that the French were planning for a conflict in which they would face the combined naval resources of Germany and Italy, whilst the British would be almost entirely preoccupied with the Far East whither they would be impelled by a likely Russo–Japanese conflict. They were thought to be intending to place long-range guns on Corsica to bombard the Tuscan, Ligurian and Sardinian coasts, to make offensive use of the Russian fleet in a war and to launch a land campaign in the Balkans.[130] Although Capponi was reporting from London that in all likelihood recent Anglo – French naval conversations had centred on the possibilities of French assistance in a war against Italy, the only specified co-operation between the two powers in this plan was in the channel and the North Sea.

As far as Great Britain was concerned, the naval intelligence coming from London was by no means entirely unreassuring. While there was evidence of Anglo–French naval collaboration – much trumpeted in the British press – which pointed to the joint imposition of sanctions on Italy, Capponi reported at the beginning of 1936 that although the country in general and the Royal Navy in particular was continuing gradually to put itself on a war footing, this had nothing directly to do with the Abyssinian crisis. Rather it was to be explained as part of 'the general plan of rearmament policy resulting from the instability of Europe'. Senior figures at the Admiralty were evidently losing interest in the Italo–Abyssinian question. However it would be unwise, he warned Rome, to assume that the British government had given up the policy of exerting pressure on Italy in the Mediterranean or that the British naval presence there would not be permanently reinforced.[131]

During the spring Capponi learnt from a string of British admirals that the Royal Navy did not share the Foreign Office's view of the Mediterranean situation and that they wanted it settled on amicable terms as soon as possible. Called back to Rome in mid-April, Capponi reported his impressions to the Duce. 'So then', Mussolini remarked towards the end of the interview, 'the English won't act'.[132] Within a month the Abyssinian War was over, and as British policy shifted to what would become an increasingly positive stance towards Italy Capponi learned that the Home Fleet and units from the China, Australia, New Zealand and East Indies stations were being returned to their bases and that the

Mediterranean fleet would then be held at the strength it had been before the Mediterranean crisis.[133]

With the war in Africa won, Mussolini turned to the question of a new naval programme which he had left in abeyance at the start of 1936. The situation was scarcely favourable: raw materials shortages had already slowed down the building of the two *Littorio*-class battleships, and the immense gaps in the service inventories caused by the Abyssinian campaign had to be made good. In late June, abandoning his temporary support for the construction of small motor boats and human torpedoes, Cavagnari renewed his bid for a large surface fleet. By the following month Mussolini had allocated an extra one billion lire for naval building, but was not prepared to fund or find the large warships Cavagnari preferred. The new 'surge' programme, to be carried out in the space of twelve months, comprised twelve destroyers, sixteen torpedo boats, twenty submarines (twelve of which were ocean-going) and twenty-five MAS boats. In Italy's present economic circumstances this was a realistic move, but it left the naval planners complaining that 'the relativity between our fleet and that of the British will not be improved to our advantage'.[134] In early August Cavagnari put an end to the vexed question of whether Italy should build aircraft carriers by flatly ruling out any discussion of the need for them – thereby widening the future gap between the two fleets.[135]

As the Abyssinian War moved towards its conclusion, naval planners developed designs from which to fight a Mediterranean war. In February, the navy passed to the air force the list of targets in which it was interested in the event of a war with Great Britain; as well as warships which might be spread across the Mediterranean from the Balearics to the Aegean, it included specific targets at Malta, Alexandria, Haifa, Aden, Berbera, Perim and Port Sudan.[136] The navy's own plans provided for the offensive mining of the Sicilian channel, along with night patrols of the Gulf of Lyons and the zone south of Sardinia. War planning put much weight on night-time sweeps by light Italian surface craft on the presumption that the English would in all probability use aircraft carriers standing some 200 miles off the coasts to attack targets on the mainland and that they would do so at night to avoid Italian air and sea defences.[137] As well as aerial bombardment of coastal targets by carrier-borne aircraft, the enemy's aims were presumed to be to bring on a daylight action and to attack sea-borne traffic. The task of the Italian flotillas was to bring on daylight cruiser actions under favourable conditions wherever possible, 'profiting from extreme readiness and determination', and when faced by superior enemy numbers to draw them onto lines of submarines.[138] By now, however, tension was definitely easing and the likelihood of having to carry out such operations in the immediate future was diminishing.

The possibility of conflict with the British stimulated the Italian navy's interest in the Indian Ocean. In the event of war with Britain, the need to reinforce Kenya and Somalia and maintain a blockade on the Red Sea would give added importance to British bases at Simonstown, Trincomalee and Aden. Rerouting shipping because of the closure of the Suez canal was calculated to produce a daily traffic of 44,000 tons of shipping around the Cape of Good Hope. In a war with France there was less to be gained from attacking the enemy: she would have to protect Djibuti and a merchant traffic amounting to 2,000,000 tons a year. Submarines were the ideal and obvious instrument. To use them against Great Britain would require clandestine bases which would be best situated in the region of the Mozambique channel. In the case of war with France, existing Italian bases in the Red Sea and Somalia would suffice. Orders were duly issued at the start of July for a clandestine exploration of the coasts of Tanganyika, Mozambique, Madagascar, the Comoro islands and the coast south of Kisimaio.[139] The navy also contemplated seizing the Seychelles in the event of war, perhaps assisted by the prior insertion of a clandestine colony on Silhouette island.[140]

Over the summer the redistribution of the British fleet eased the strategic position in the Mediterranean to a degree. By September 1936 Malta was empty save for a few light cruisers, British battle cruisers were at Gibraltar, and Alexandria was being turned into the main English base. However, evident problems remained. War materials had been shipped from France to North Africa, suggesting that the French intended to occupy Libya as a first move in any war. The presence of the French fleet at Toulon also suggested that it might intend to try 'a prestige action in grand style' off the Ligurian coast, notwithstanding the risks posed by submarines, torpedo boats and mines.[141]

With the onset of the Spanish Civil War and Italy's participation in it the naval planners realised that they were trying to maintain too many hypothetical conflicts. It appeared evident that the conflict between the forces of conservative nationalism and those of communism and anarchy in Europe had now begun. Even when it was over the probability was that the conflict would shift to other parts of Europe. It was therefore logical now to divide Europe into two groups of powers, Italy and Germany on the one side and France and Russia on the other. England and Japan were playing a waiting game, and while the orientation of Turkey, Greece and Yugoslavia was uncertain it was likely that Turkey's ambitions in the Aegean and in the zone around Antioch would cause her to line up with France. The other two powers would probably follow England. Whichever side won the civil war in Spain was likely to emerge exhausted, but the war provided the opportunity for Italy and Germany to make use of the Balearics, the Canaries, and possibly a port near Gibraltar such as Cadiz. The scenario of a future war in which Italy, Germany and Albania faced France, Russia and Turkey – Beta 3 – took its place in the menu of hypothetical conflicts for which plans were now being worked up: Alfa 0-4 (Italy versus England with various combinations of powers attached to both sides), Beta 1-5 (Italy and Germany against France, Yugoslavia, the USSR and others), and Gamma 1-3 (Italy, Albania and possibly France against Germany and Yugoslavia with Greece and Turkey as possible allies).[142]

By the end of 1936 the international arms competition was becoming increasingly intense. British defence spending, embodied in the defence white paper of March 1936, was given a push by the ending of the Abyssinian War. In May 1936 Capponi estimated that within a year the re-equipment of the Royal Air Force and the army would have reached 'a satisfactory stage' and within two to two-and-a-half years the same would be true of the Royal Navy.[143] He dissented from the French naval attaché's judgement that the preference being given to light surface craft in the early stages of the new tranche of naval building and the delay in starting the two battleships envisaged in the programme indicated that the British were no longer seriously considering the possibility of a conflict in the North Sea but were instead preparing a 'defensive wall' around their East African empire and making ready to confront Italian aeroplanes and submarines in the Mediterranean. He simply interpreted the timing as due to the provisions for replacing capital ships embodied in the previous naval treaties.[144]

In the face of mounting naval competition, the navy produced a rationale for focusing on battleships. It had enough heavy and light cruisers and there was no point in building more when their use in the restricted Mediterranean basin 'appears problematic', and when their lack of range meant that they were unusable in the open oceans because Italy had no bases to support them. What the navy now needed was the modernisation of either the *Doria* or the *Duilio* – preferably both – and a third *Littorio*. Remodernising the two old battleships would cost the same amount as building two *Garibaldi* class light cruisers, would take no longer (two-and-a-half-years), and would result in warships whose use was self-evidently more convenient for Italy. Along with them, the navy wanted four *Oriani* class destroyers and eighteen 600-ton torpedo boats to escort convoys and launch night attacks against an enemy fleet. The programme, which concentrated on 'a strong offensive battle fleet well equipped to defend itself', supported by one or two 'anti-aircraft ships', reflected the turn away from the *flotta d'evasione* and embodied at least some of the navy's traditional priorities.[145]

Projecting current construction programmes forward to their completion in July 1940, the navy calculated that it would then have 6 battleships and 19 cruisers as compared with Great Britain's 17 battleships and 50 cruisers, France's 10 battleships and 20 cruisers, and Germany's 6 battleships and 11 cruisers. What now worried it was not this balance but that between light surface craft and submarines. Italy would have 56 destroyer leaders and destroyers to match England's 107, France's 68 and Germany's 34. This force was 'absolutely inadequate' given the needs of the naval commands and the number of new battleships coming into service. Italy's 98 submarines would be the absolute minimum necessary in comparison to England's 72, France's 100 and Germany's 36 in the light of the additional light craft which it was expected that 'the lesser Mediterranean nations' would provide for Great Britain in the event of an Italo–British war. What the navy needed were 16 additional destroyers and destroyer leaders, 8 specialised submarine chasers (a type of ship of which it had none) and 4 minesweepers in the 1938–9 building programme.[146]

While the planners focused on revising the appreciations for Alpha Uno and Beta Zero, and on compiling the relevant war instructions, training exercises concentrated on defending Italian convoys and attacking the enemy's.[147] By the end of the summer, however, the events in Spain led to the consideration of a possible war in which Italy, Germany and Nationalist Spain faced England, France, the USSR and minor powers. War under hypotheses A–B, pitting Italy and Germany against France, Russia and Turkey, would close the Dardanelles and the Straits of Gibraltar save for neutral traffic and leave the Suez canal as the only route through which supplies could reach Italy. Using the calculation that Italy would need 21,200,000 tons of imported fuel, raw materials and foodstuffs in the first year of a war, the navy estimated that 4,253,700 tons could be imported via the Suez canal (including half the oil and petroleum requirements), a further 9,550,000 tons (including half the coal requirement) could be brought in from Europe via overland routes, and the remaining 7,396,000 tons would have to be borne by neutral shipping carrying cargo either openly for their own countries or covertly for Italy.

While it was presumed that the enemy would respect neutrals' rights and that the neutrals' interest in freedom of commerce would coincide with Italy's, the navy confessed that it was impossible to calculate how much material could reach Italy by such means via Gibraltar and the Dardanelles. Nevertheless, using the most favourable hypothesis, it was estimated that the Dardanelles route could carry 1,000,000 tons of oil from Romania, while the Gibraltar route would provide coal from Great Britain, petrol and phosphates from the United States, wood from

Finland, salt cod from Norway, and phosphates and meat from Central and South America. The planners dutifully calculated the number of voyages merchant ships would have to make to Italy (140 a month), but ignored completely the most self-evident conclusion to be drawn from the figures: that Italy could not hope to sustain a war of any length against both Great Britain and France.[148]

The prospect of a Mediterranean war against France, Russia and Turkey, first raised in the previous December, had advanced by February 1937 to the point at which studies of the possibilities of attacking enemy communications in the western Mediterranean and employing submarines had been completed. The Montreux Convention, to which Ciano was now prepared to adhere, and the probable closing of the Straits to Russian ships in time of war removed the USSR from the possible combinations of enemies the navy calculated it might have to face. England was now at or near the top of that list, 'too interested in retarding the development of our Nation and undoubtedly hoping to have revenge for the check it suffered over the Ethiopian question'. The course of the Spanish Civil War had shown that a fairly concrete understanding existed between England and France, the 'Gentlemen's Agreement' notwithstanding.[149]

Relaying Mussolini's politico–strategic directive, Badoglio confirmed that England was and would remain for many years hostile to Italy, but that neither she nor France was likely to provoke a war unless her interests were directly threatened. The Yugoslavian accords improved the situation, and the Mediterranean pact which Turkey was seeking to concoct with Italy, Yugoslavia, and Greece would at least result in her neutrality. As far as the navy was concerned, the present shape of Mediterranean politics and the importance now acquired by Libya, which the Duce intended to reinforce with a second army corps during 1938, meant that it could reduce the priority it gave to the Adriatic and concentrate on completing its preparations in the Mediterranean and the Red Sea.[150]

By the late summer of 1937, Italian planning for a war with England had taken on a long term perspective and had settled on the '50 per cent formula': that the total tonnage of the combined Italian and German fleets must be at least half that of the combined French and British fleets. The force strength derived for Italy from this formula indicated that she required a fleet equivalent to 80 per cent of the French fleet, 110 per cent of the German fleet, and 40 per cent of the English fleet. The planners presumed that in wartime England would not be able to put more than 20 per cent of her modern units into the Mediterranean to join 90 per cent of the French fleet, and calculated that the relativities would be such that the Italian fleet would be 60 per cent the size of the combined fleets opposing it.

Some complicated arithmetic, based partially on guess-work as to the
rates at which over-age ships would be put out of commission and partly
on presumed construction capacities, produced the calculation that at
the end of the period 1936–44 the British fleet would comprise 21
battleships, 11 aircraft carriers, 15 heavy and 51 light cruisers, 176 flotilla
craft and 83 submarines. By July 1944 the French, with the capacity to
construct half the annual tonnage that the British could manage, would
possess 10 battleships, 4 aircraft carriers, 7 heavy and 18 light cruisers,
91 flotilla craft and 104 submarines. The Germans, constrained by the
35 per cent ratio of the Anglo–German Naval Agreement but with no
over-age ships to put out of commission, would by then possess 10 battleships, 4 aircraft carriers, 5 heavy and 17 light cruisers, 66 flotilla craft
and 101 submarines. Since the respective building rates of these three
powers were assumed to be 116,000 tons, 55,600 tons and 68,000 tons
annually, the mathematics showed that Italy would have to build 44,500
tons of shipping a year in order to reach the '50-per cent' formula by July
1944. This, it was acknowledged, would require a 'notable contribution'
from the country but it was not thought to be beyond Italy's capacity:
average annual construction between 1932 and 1935 had totalled 27,000
tons, but during 1933–4 the yards had reached the maximum annual rate
of 71,250 tons.[151]

The air of unreality enveloping the navy's numerical calculations was
equally evident in the political calculations it was making at the same
time about the possibilities of coming to an understanding with England.
There were supposedly two possible bases for an accord. The first was the
fact that both were on the side of 'order'; here British incomprehension of
'the value, effectiveness and continuity of our Regime' had led to a failure
properly to appreciate the great contribution it could make to 'the general
progress of peoples'. The second was the Duce's manifest awareness of
the fact that the white races must combine to protect 'their thousand year
civilisation ... [against] the invading wave emerging especially in the Far
East'. If England recognised the need to embrace these two realities then
a friendly understanding could be reached with her.

Italy's power to offer or deny the prospect of safe transit across the
central Mediterranean was taken to be a tradeable asset. Another possible opening could be a joint agreement to prevent naval expansion by
Yugoslavia, an occurrence which would certainly dent the basis of the
'Gentleman's Agreement'. As far as access to the eastern Mediterranean
was concerned, the principles of the 1888 Convention must be confirmed
to keep open the Suez canal and counter 'acrobatic interpretations' of
Article 16 of the League of Nations Pact. British control of access to the
western Mediterranean through possession of Gibraltar might perhaps

be countered by friendly accords with Nationalist Spain allowing for the use of Ceuta in wartime without violating the principle of maintaining the status quo in the Mediterranean. On the other hand developments in which the British might be interested such as the military expansion of Cyprus and Haifa, the arming of Aqaba and the creation of a Zionist state in Palestine certainly went against the spirit if not against the letter of the 'Gentlemen's Agreement' and were therefore potential matters for discussion. In all this the naval staff perceived an opportunity to develop an atmosphere of 'solid friendship based on mutual trust'. There was everything to be gained from such a union, not least the fact that the immense problem of securing the sea-borne supply of Italy would be solved.[152]

For its consummation to occur Great Britain would have to come to its senses as they were perceived in Rome – a transformation which Neville Chamberlain's policies now apparently seemed to suggest was at least possible. However, the navy recognised the counter-balancing factors influencing British policies which stood in the way of any such understanding. They included a sense of political superiority which Italy could not accept; a hostility towards Fascism and an unwillingness to accept its 'eminently democratic political ideals'; a policy not merely of conserving the British empire but of extending its influence in Iraq, Transjordan, Arabia, the Persian Gulf, Tibet and elsewhere; and the threat Italy posed to Britain's use of 'our sea'.[153]

A similar analysis of the pros and cons of an understanding with Germany produced six favourable factors – affinity of political ideals, identical demographic problems, the need for territorial expansion, the raw materials question, the need to form a political block to counterbalance others in and beyond Europe, and the need to combat the spread of bolshevism – and three unfavourable ones, namely anschluss, German designs on the Adriatic and Mediterranean, and Germany's expansionist policy in the Balkans which caused the Little Entente countries to link themselves up to France.[154] As for France, the bases for possible understanding comprised a 'psychological affinity' which went back to their common Roman origins, the possibility of forming a joint bloc of eighty millions to counter-balance Germany and to assure absolute joint predominance over the Mediterranean, and the strengthening of the links between the Little Entente and a Franco–Italian grouping which the navy supposed would result 'for obvious reasons'. Among nine 'divergent' factors pushing the two powers apart were the differences in political ideology and the line of foreign policy these inspired in France; France's 'incapacity to utilise its vast empire for the demographic expansion of the race' which Italy could do differently; the questions of Nice, Savoy and Corsica; and the political competition for influence in Spain. As this analysis made clear, the forces of repulsion pushing Italy and the western democracies apart were at least as strong as the forces of attraction drawing her towards Germany.

The conclusions the navy reached were that in case of conflict 'England will be against us', as would France, and that France provided such an important bulwark against Germany that England could not permit her to be sunk. Although both parties evidently wanted an understanding with Germany, and though Germany's acceptance of the 35 per cent naval ratio made it evident that she would prefer not to find England arrayed alongside her enemies in future, 'the problem of German colonial demands seems not to be resolvable without recourse to arms'.[155] These reflections led to a further conclusion:

A precipitation of events in the immediate future would lead to us facing a Franco–British partnership; the question of having Germany with us must be given careful attention since, without her participation [in a war], the task which our forces would presently face would be difficult to resolve successfully.[156]

Two current international crisis could improve Italy's position. If Franco's Nationalists won the Spanish Civil War this would put her in a position to act against England's Atlantic shipping routes via the Cape of Good Hope, and if the Japanese were quickly successful in China and threatened British possessions in the Pacific, London would be forced to send a very large part of its forces to Singapore. The navy regarded these 'diversions' as more practicable than a land campaign against Egypt or Tunisia – overseas operations being 'very delicate if one does not possess command of the sea' – or an advance from Ethiopia which would require the creation of 'a solid, loyal black army capable of acting autonomously in long-range undertakings'.[157]

In the new strategic world which the planners were facing, the idea of action in the Red Sea and the Indian Ocean began to appear less attractive. While Italy could control the central and northern parts of the Red Sea, Aden barred her routes to the south. Calculating on a local superiority for five days before British and French reinforcements arrived, the best the Italians could do would be to put the port out of action for light cruisers for a period of several months. As far as interrupting traffic in the Indian Ocean went, the main traffic nodes south of Madagascar and around the Cape of Good Hope were in range of Italian submarines, but the lack of surface units with the necessary 10,000-mile range and the primitive state of the ports of Mogadishu and Kisimaio made surface action against enemy shipping routes there presently impossible.[158]

While the planners were generating these conclusions, international politics projected the actualities of Italian naval policy to the foreground. On 18 November 1936 Italy recognised the Franco government and at the same time Mussolini ordered the navy to begin using submarines to attack 'Red' naval and merchant shipping heading for Republican ports. The first Italian submarine campaign, which ended in mid-February 1937, produced only four hits on fourteen ships. The second offensive, which began in early August, brought Italy close to war with Britain and France when Italian submarines covertly at work in the Mediterranean narrowly missed the British destroyer *Havock* on 1 September and shortly afterwards sank the British tanker *Woodford*.[159] On 3 September Franco requested that Mussolini intercept Soviet ships that were reportedly ferrying large quantities of arms to Republican Spain, and three days later Mussolini agreed to impose a blockade on all west-bound shipping south of Sicily and to sink both enemy ships and suspicious neutral merchantmen. With the British cabinet at odds over whether or not to recognise Italy's conquest of Abyssinia, and the Royal Navy at odds over the complex question of asserting and defending neutral and belligerent rights at sea, the British and French proposed an international conference at Nyon to resolve the issue of the sinkings. The Italians and the Germans both refused invitations to attend.

The conclusions of the conference, which carefully avoided any general condemnation of Italian actions at sea and even invited her participation in anti-submarine patrols in the Tyrrhenian sea, were far from being a diplomatic triumph for the democracies, as Eden subsequently claimed, and can only have appeared to the Italians as further evidence of the extent to which Great Britain under Chamberlain's leadership was prepared to appease Italy.[160] The terms of the agreement were regarded by the Italian as unacceptable because they implicitly classified Italy as a second-rank Mediterranean power and effectively revived the anti-Italian Mediterranean accord created during the imposition of sanctions. The navy wanted recognition of full equality of rights and appropriate arrangements for policing the various zones into which the Mediterranean was divided – either by giving responsibility to the powers whose coasts bordered them or by common action carried out by all three powers. However, this could give rise to problems in distinguishing Italian submarines ceded to Nationalist Spain from those still genuinely part of the Italian navy.[161]

The position was clarified by admiral Godfroy, deputy chief of the French naval staff, when an Italian delegation visited Paris at the end of September. The patrols were intended to suppress piracy but not to prevent either the Nationalists or the Republicans from stopping, visiting, capturing or even sinking a French, Italian or Greek ship provided that the rules agreed at the London naval conference of 1930 were adhered to. However, the proposed zones excluded Italy completely from the western Mediterranean, interrupted her communications with Libya, put the Greek coast and access to the Adriatic under English control and put the Dardanelles–Gibraltar route under joint Anglo–French control. Agreement was reached on the two issues which were central to Italian concerns, control over the Sicilian channel and over one of the three access points to the Mediterranean. The agreement, signed on 30 September, gave Italy everything she wanted: a continuous zone which extended from Leros to Port Said and Tobruk, control over the Dardanelles and the coasts of Greece and Turkey, access to Port Said and therefore to the East African empire, and an arrangement of individual zones which avoided the possibility of France and England operating together in some parts of the Mediterranean and Italy operating alone in others.[162] On 30 October admiral Bernotti, admiral Esteva and admiral Pound met on board the *Barham* off Biserta and swiftly agreed the details of executing the naval patrols, a jovial Pound remarking at one point that there was now less patrolling activity than previously 'because the submarines appear to have gone'.[163]

Having attended on Mussolini during the latter's meeting with Hitler in September and been briefed on German naval manoeuvres – during which submarines had proved notably effective in breaking up convoys, attacks on surface traffic had succeeded, and (in an action calculated to reassure the Italian navy about its own tactical doctrine) destroyers had kept a battleship away from the main action for an entire day – Cavagnari now had first-hand knowledge of the German navy.[164] With this in mind, and taking account of the planners' calculations, international circumstances and what he could fathom of Mussolini's Axis policy, in mid-November 1937 he presented Badoglio with the navy's current politico-strategic conspectus.

Things had changed since April, when Mussolini had identified Great Britain as Italy's likely main rival and had suggested that the issue of whether or not France supported her depended on Italy's attitude towards her Latin sister. The Anglo–French relationship was closer, as the Nyon Accords demonstrated, while Italy's relations with France had worsened; the Italo–Yugoslav accord had not led to a four-power Mediterranean agreement and in fact Turkey had on occasion acted in ways decidedly not favourable to Italy; and the Soviet Union should probably be numbered among Italy's potential adversaries in the event of a Mediterranean war. While 'Our actual situation appears, when examined objectively, to be more complex than it was last spring', the moves towards closer links with Germany were a counter-balancing factor. Italian naval war planning was accordingly taking it into account, and although German naval power in the Mediterranean was virtually non-existent it could cause both England and France to retain substantial forces in northern waters to defend their metropolitan territories. A nationalist victory in Spain and the pressure Japan was exerting on Britain's Far Eastern empire were further positive factors, though for the moment the Mediterranean 'constitutes the central problem for Great Britain'. If there was a threat to the dominions, Cavagnari believed this could have a 'notable impact' on a European war, making it possible with Japanese support for Italy to dominate the Red Sea and the Indian Ocean. This in turn would make possible major operations in Africa whose favourable outcome could contribute to final victory economically by securing transit of the Suez canal and politically by influencing the Islamic and Indian populations that were being subjugated by England.[165]

Evidently well aware of the risks of a war with Great Britain, Cavagnari did not rule one out. Indeed, as a loyal servant of the Duce he could not do so. But he was making it clear that to the navy success depended on a constellation of factors over many of which Italy had little or no control, and also that the success of a land campaign in Africa was contingent on the prior satisfaction of naval requirements. By the end of 1937 war planning was therefore in need of adjusting to take into account the possible strategic consequences of three important developments in international politics: the likely neutrality of Yugoslavia, the possibility of a Nationalist Spain being an ally in a war against England and France or of a Republican Spain being an enemy, and the effect which the newly made alliance with Japan might have on the various scenarios envisaged in the Alpha, Beta and Gamma plans.[166] While Hitler prepared for his second 'year of surprises', the Italian navy entered 1938 with doctrinal and construction policies shaped largely by operational considerations, an acute awareness of the many difficulties which a war in Mussolini's *mare nostrum* would pose, and no strategy at all with which to confront the power now identified as its chief potential enemy in wartime.

A new model army for new Fascist wars

In 1936, partly under force of circumstances, partly as a result of the lessons drawn from the Abyssinian War, but chiefly as a consequence of the designs of Baistrocchi and of the deputy chief of staff, Alberto Pariani, the army moved gradually towards the two-regiment *divisione binaria* which would be the basis of the structure with which it entered the Second World War. In September 1935, three divisions were sent to

Libya to increase its protection; partly through force of circumstance at a time when heavy demands were being made on the manpower pool, and partly because 'lighter' divisions would be easier to move and supply in desert conditions, all three were *binaria*. When, in November, two of them were sent to Eritrea and the third returned home, they were replaced by the newly created Trento motorised division and a new infantry division, both of which were composed of two regiments.[167]

The forces in Libya were intended both to counter any attempt by the French to take advantage of Italy's preoccupation elsewhere and attack from Tunisia, and to act as a coercive threat to the British in Egypt. The idea that major operations might actually be mounted in North Africa against the British gathered pace as a series of proposals were developed or commissioned which suggested that such a course of action might be both viable and effective. In November 1935, Mussolini instructed Italo Balbo, the governor of Libya, to draw up a design for operations to be launched from Libya against Egypt and the Sudan. When it arrived in Rome, Balbo's plan embodied a force of five Italian divisions, 300 guns, 3,500 motor vehicles and 256 tanks but had no obvious operational objectives beyond driving along the coast. Assuming that Cairo and Alexandria were its objectives, Pariani pointed out that it was too weak, particularly in artillery, to overcome the British defences if it took the coastal route, and too heavy if it chose to go via Jarabub and the Siwa oasis, for which more motorised units and fewer infantry divisions were needed. Despite his own calculation that the British had a thousand tanks in Egypt, Balbo remained blithely optimistic that he could undertake an offensive if he were given a motorised division, 100 anti-aircraft guns and the maximum possible number of tanks, trucks and aircraft. The figures available to Rome, which were gross over-estimations, suggested that while the 75,000 British in Egypt barely outnumbered the 71,000 Italians in Libya in manpower, they were greatly superior in guns, tanks, armoured cars and aircraft, and that only in respect of Sudan, Kenya and Somalia did the Italians enjoy a local superiority.[168]

In the dying weeks of the Abyssinian War, proposals for possible Italian action in North Africa multiplied. Pariani argued that if hostilities were to break out with the British, Italy should act along the axis of the Siwa oasis and against Port Sudan and Atbara from Eritrea. General Ugo Cavallero, ordered by Mussolini to produce his own proposal, argued that the Sudan was a secondary theatre which should only be activated if Italian forces were successful in annihilating the enemy in Egypt, an outcome he suggested could be achieved if a motorised and two infantry divisions, equipped with as many tanks as were available, drove along the coast to Mersa Matruh while native troops carried out an encircling movement through the desert. Thereafter the retreating enemy would have to be sought out and beaten again before he could withdraw to Alexandria. Otherwise the result would be a war of position which the Italians, far from their own logistical bases, could not win. The colonial section of the general staff in Rome produced a study that followed Cavallero's conception, employing 75,000 men, 186 tanks, 300 guns and 8,450 trucks to get from Bardia to Alexandria and from Jarabub via Siwa to Cairo.[169] While suggesting a vision of strategy compounded of impracticalities and indecision, the array of plans can also be seen as way stations en route to the formulation of a North African land strategy by 1938. In the meantime the plan for a Libyan offensive was still-born, its only immediate legacy being a decision to build up Tobruk as a base for a future Mediterranean struggle which Baistrocchi thought might not be far off.

After a six-month gap in their meetings, Badoglio called the chiefs of staff together on 5 November 1936 and instructed them that in the light of the recently formed Axis and the Duce's observation that for Italy the Mediterranean was a life and death matter they must examine how they could guarantee it, as well as providing security for the frontiers and the national territory.[170] To prepare for the debates to come, Pariani, who had replaced Baistrocchi as under-secretary of state for war and chief of the army general staff the previous month, ordered that the plans for war in North Africa which he had drawn up the previous spring be dusted off and brought up to date. The characteristics of the campaign that he foresaw – combining motorised units and aviation to produce 'extreme lightness and mobility with great potential [for] rapid fire' – married exactly with those of the new *binaria* units with which he proposed to refit the army.[171] The urgency of the issue was underlined when Mussolini had the question of 'the organisation of Italian territories overseas' put on the agenda of the forthcoming annual meeting of the supreme defence commission.

In a preliminary discussion with the chiefs of staff to explore the ground, Badoglio gave it as his opinion that in the case of 'any complications' East Africa would not be able to intervene and Libya would need help from the *madrepatria* against either the French or the British. After securing Badoglio's support for the proposition that in future the war ministry and not the colonial ministry should have charge of any war involving the empire, Pariani suggested that in a war with England Italy could launch an offensive into Egypt from Cyrenaica via Wadi Halfa, agreed that Ethiopia was not yet in a position to launch a converging attack through the Sudan, and proposed that the western frontier of Libya should be fortified against the French. On the basis of his experience as governor of Libya, Badoglio did not think the western frontier could be effectively defended: 'if we fortify a particular point, the enemy can easily cross it a few kilometres away'.[172] Shortly afterwards Graziani confirmed that Abyssinia was not likely to be able to play a significant role in a war against England and France. It could pose active threats in three directions, towards Djibuti and Somaliland, Kenya, and the Sudan where in cooperation with another unspecified colony (Libya) it could take decisive action, and it could also attract enemy forces on all three fronts, thus weakening their capacity to act elsewhere. Although cut off from the *madrepatria*, it could look for supplies to the Indian Ocean via Somalia. In what was a brief but nonetheless comprehensive survey of the situation, Graziani was acknowledging that the colony was going to be of no economic and only questionable military benefit to Italy in wartime.[173]

In considering how to shape the Italian army for the as yet imprecisely defined tasks which might face it, Baistrocchi was influenced by the difference between the Piedmontese caution shown by Badoglio in the second phase of the Abyssinian war and the Fascist-style flair with which Graziani was operating on the Somalian front. Contrasting the two, he told Mussolini in January 1936 that 'One has the impression that on this [Eritrean] front a static mentality may already have taken root according to which solutions are based more on time than on action.'[174] The force that had been committed to Abyssinia had been a motorised army equipped with light CV 35 tanks; apart from the unfortunate episode at the battle of Dembeguina in December 1935, when six of them were separated from the troops and destroyed (and their crews decapitated), losses had been very light. The army had emerged from that war with an inventory in which one thousand of its total of 1,223 tanks were light tanks, but it was evident that as special purpose vehicles with fixed forward fire built for mountain warfare they had serious deficiencies; thus during 1936 Ansaldo began work on a new tank while the army introduced its first anti-tank gun.[175]

As the army began to demobilise from the Abyssinian War, Baistrocchi emphasised the need to keep the celeri units – 'the force for immediate action' – in a state of high readiness, improve the logistics organisation and carefully maintain the stock of motor vehicles.[176] The static war of 1915–18 was long gone, though he clearly felt that this fact had not been completely absorbed by the gunners. In keeping with a doctrine now oriented towards a war of movement and in conformity with 'our will to act quickly, to arrive before the enemy [does], to overcome his defences and [any] difficulties of terrain', divisional artillery was to act as regimental batteries closely linked to the fighting infantry and not as more distant support artillery. The infantry divisions themselves, now composed of ten and not twelve battalions, 'must be small blocs, agile, [and] capable of manoeuvre and penetration'.[177]

Pariani fully shared his chief's views, putting a premium on celeri and motorised units and the alpini who could act swiftly – *poco ma pronto* ('few but ready') was his motto.[178] The infantry was to be supplied with new 81-mm mortars and 47-mm anti-tank guns which were designed to be light and easy to manage in order to meet the requirements of practicality, rapidity of deployment and mobility. Partly influenced by the Russian example, Pariani also proposed to create a parachute battalion to add more tactical and operational mobility to the army.[179] The new tanks should be of two types: fast tanks armed with anti-tank guns or solely machine-guns, and assault tanks, two thirds of which should carry machine-guns and one third a mix of flame-throwers and machine-guns.[180]

After a senior staff ride in March involving army, corps and divisional commanders to test arrangements for a war against France and Yugoslavia in which Italy launched a counter-offensive on the eastern front while operating an active defence in the west, Baistrocchi explained to the generals the roots, purposes and aims of his reforms. Stressing the revolutionary characteristics of the new army that had been created in line with those of the Fascist regime in whose wake it had followed, particularly since 1933, and which had helped it stand up to 'English pretensions', he underlined the fact that the Abyssinian War had signalled the 'triumph' of motorisation – 'a necessity, especially for we Italians in whom the dynamic spirit predominates'.[181] Italy's possible enemies included France, Yugoslavia, and England. He was unable to say where and against whom Italy might have to march or when, Baistrocchi told his audience, but it was this very indeterminacy which 'imposes on us the duty to give the army an elastic organisation which allows us to employ our forces immediately according to the rule of the offensive'.[182] Thus, frontier defence against Yugoslavia was to rely as little as possible on fixed strong points but instead to favour semi-permanent works coupled with mobile nuclei on the principle that to defend meant to attack. Pursuing the new doctrinal goal of a war of movement, Baistrocchi issued a series of directives which were simultaneously firm and vague. The artillery, for example, was instructed to abandon 'doctrinaire tactics' and focus on the contribution it could make to the tactical situation, though it should not function simply as close support fire since that was a task for the mortars.[183]

On 15 September 1936, Baistrocchi put to Mussolini a programme for twelve motorised divisions and three motorised assault brigades to be created by 1937. The dual army which would thus be created – which

Mussolini called a 'diarchy' – would require expenditure of 30,000,000 lire out of a total budget of 78,700,000 lire in the budgetary years 1935–6 and 1936–7.[184] When Mussolini, contemplating intervention in the Spanish Civil War and beyond that a general war between the two camps into which Europe had already divided, called for the withdrawal of all 'superfluous' weapons and materiel from Abyssinia, Baistrocchi felt compelled to tell him that in the event of a major war the colonies were a point of weakness and not a source of strength and also tacitly to admit that his operational formula for war would not work in the face of a coalition of powers which would comprise Great Britain, France and in all likelihood the United States as well.

The war that you foresee will be long, very long – the lightning war to which the hack strategists, who are utopians, allude is a pleasing aspiration for [us] all, [but] realisable only when there is an enormous discrepancy in strength between the belligerents – look at Italy with more than 400,000 men, 1,200 guns and 400 aeroplanes against Abyssinia without guns or aircraft.[185]

Baistrocchi's observation that in a general war the side would win which had foreseen the need to prepare and supply itself, and been able to do so, was evidently not what Mussolini wanted to hear. On 7 November 1936 he was sacked as chief of the army general staff and under-secretary of state for war and replaced by general Alberto Pariani.

As well as being ready to accommodate Mussolini's desire to send aid and troops to Spain, which Baistrocchi had opposed, Pariani pressed on with the reorganisation of the army. A week after taking up office, instructing his staff to study the transformation of the twenty-five infantry divisions into *divisioni binarie*, he acknowledged that tasking and equipping the army corps for logistic and general support was in part a way of economising on resources, as otherwise every division would have to be given its own support arms.[186] Senior commanders were asked whether the motorised divisions were light enough and reminded that units should be equipped with the minimum weaponry necessary to carry out their tasks on the assumption that higher formations could provide extra units or artillery to support them where necessary.[187] Pariani noted that a report on the war in East Africa suggested that the light tank needed to be faster. Although the two motorised divisions that currently existed and nineteen of the twenty-nine infantry divisions were not fully equipped for immediate mobilisation, he reassured Mussolini shortly after entering office that a production rhythm had been achieved which would complete the necessary stocks 'shortly' unless the demands from Abyssinia grew unexpectedly.[188]

Pariani's formula for the new-style fast war whose instruments he was constructing – *guerra brigantesca* ['brigandish' war'] – quickly won Mussolini's approval.[189] The under-secretary's enthusiasm for the new light-weight army, unlike Baistrocchi's, rested not only on operational theory but on a strategic conception of the next war which conformed to the characteristics of the emerging force. Believing, unlike many of his conservative predecessors, that the western Alps formed 'an insurmountable obstacle' for both parties, he calculated that a war with France would be most likely to take place on Tunisian soil. It was 'even more obvious' that a war with England would be likely to occur in Egypt and the Sudan, regions which 'when our organisation is developed we shall be able to "pincer" however and whenever we wish'. This 'fortunate premise' allowed Italy to accentuate her theory of fast war even more because it put a premium on developing 'that part of the army which, because of its lightness, elasticity and dash, is the most suited to be launched into theatres of operations outside the mainland'. Accordingly, the army would concentrate its energies on developing the new mobile units, behind which the mass of the infantry divisions would act as covering forces, manoeuvre reserves and the 'consolidators' of the successes won by the fast units.[190]

In February 1937, Pariani ordered the transformation of all the three-regiment divisions into *divisioni binarie* by spring of the following year, and an examination of possibility of creating an army corps of two motorised *binarie* divisions especially for Libya. He put his scenario of a war on the Libyan frontiers to the Commissione suprema di difesa that same month. Although hedged with qualifications – the overseas colonies would absorb resources for at least another two years and the defences on both frontiers were not yet adequate to resist attack – land offensives against Tunisia and Algeria or against lower Egypt or the middle Nile between Aswan and Wadi Halfa promised favourable outcomes in a struggle 'which would perhaps be wearyingly prolonged and without possibilities [if fought] on the French Alps, or which would not find a [favourable] solution if fought only at sea or in the air'.[191] Under Badoglio's lead, the chiefs of staff were already paying considerable attention to improving the defences of Tobruk. Accordingly, feeling confident of the eastern border, Pariani ordered immediate work on the defensive arrangements for the Tunisian frontier, the organisation of bases for possible operations beyond the frontier, and the possibilities of landing troops from Italy either in Cyrenaica or Tripolitania.[192]

In April 1937, Mussolini's view of the politics of the European situation caused him to give Libya particular prominence in the question of Mediterranean security. Badoglio conveyed to the service chiefs the Duce's intention to transfer a second army corps there in 1938. The army must look to ensure the inviolability of the western land frontier of the *madrepatria* and the security of the coasts and islands and make ready a project for the reinforcement of Libya. The navy was to consider the requirement to strengthen the port of Tripoli, and the construction of a new port on Pantelleria, and the air force should relocate its units away from the Yugoslav border towards France and the islands.[193] Strategy and policy alike appeared to be moving in Pariani's direction.

Backed by a scenario to which he could provide the solution, Pariani pressed ahead with the reorganisation of the army. As well as having to overcome military conservatism, he had to resolve a debate over the relative merits of motorisation and mechanisation. The exact worth of tanks was a debatable quantity after the battle of Guadalajara (8–23 March 1937), during which their weaknesses had been exposed in conditions in which mud, rain and difficult terrain deprived them of the mobility and of the speed which was their one means of escape when confronted by Republican tanks armed with cannon.[194] Summer manoeuvres in the Veneto tested the three theories of war then current: attritional war in which primary resources were plentiful, manoeuvre was freely possible and time was an ally; counter-offensive war after initial positional warfare when time was not on one's side; and 'war of rapid decision' in which time was an enemy. These manoeuvres and others held in the north-east tested the relative fighting powers of a motorized and an armoured division and compared motorised and celeri divisions. They produced the conclusions that tanks needed better cross-country ability if they were to be able to defend the land borders in the west and north, that the use of motorised units in combat with mechanised units be reconsidered, that a new tank armed with a cannon was needed, and that tanks be used in greater numbers and in independent roles even though 'for now it is not possible to adopt a mechanised vehicle the equal of the horse, either as a fast means of transportation or as a weapon'.[195]

Pariani planned to transform the army over a period of ten years, producing a force which included three motorised divisions, three armoured divisions, twenty-four 'auto-transportable' *binarie* divisions, twenty-four 'normal' divisions and twelve mountain divisions. Taking advantage of motor vehicles meant that much of the regimental transport could be passed back to *binarie* divisions and then in turn back to corps headquarters, thereby applying 'the theory of pressing forward with weight applied by weapons while shifting the logistical encumbrances to the rear'.[196]

At the end of November 1937 sixty-five generals were assembled to discuss the results of the Veneto manoeuvres, the formation of armoured divisions and the introduction of the *binaria* division. Pariani explained that decisive actions in future wars were unlikely to be fought in the

Alps, but would in all probability take place in colonial wars which would require small, easily transportable units. If the army was not facing imperial wars, it could have to fight political or religious wars – 'fascism against bolshevism, etc'. – when it would again be likely to be fighting not in mountains but in lowlands.[197] Some serious doubts were expressed about whether the new division had the fire-power and the strength in reserve necessary for effective combat, whether corps could manoeuvre multiple divisions well enough to compensate for their lack of weight, and whether the new smaller divisions would not add a new and potentially complicating link to the chain of command, but the overwhelming majority were in favour of the new model army. Obviously in no mood for a real debate, Pariani swatted objections without much ceremony: when general Trezzani remarked that Italy could never have 'an army which works as well for the Sahara desert as for Lake Ladoga', he replied loftily that neither Napoleon nor Graziani had fought two battles with the same formation – effectively admitting the bankruptcy of his own argument – and then threw in the homily that 'the smaller the bricks that are used to construct a building, the easier it is to build it quickly'.[198]

When the assembly turned to the discussion of tanks and armoured divisions a wide range of views were expressed. While some favoured light tanks armed with machine-guns as at present, several participants suggested that their armament was presently too weak. This caused Pariani to observe that the fast tank (*carro veloce*), which was then and would remain the backbone of the force, 'acts more with its mass than with its machine gun, like a horse' and that therefore the fast tank was all right 'as small as it is'.[199] Visconti Prasca was in favour of armoured divisions with their own complement of artillery, a sensible suggestion given the tanks' exiguous armament, but then added that it had to be borne in mind that 'in the theatres of central Europe there is fog for a good part of the year and that tanks cannot function when they lack visibility'.[200] Many participants stressed the importance of mobility in tank design and construction, several echoing Pariani's observation about cavalry, which doubtless gratified him; some wanted to strengthen armour protection while others did not. A substantial number of participants emphasised the need for armoured divisions to have their own 75-mm self-propelled artillery, though Trezzani thought it pointless since tanks would not be able to advance beyond ground swept by corps and divisional artillery.

References to Italian experience in Abyssinia and Spain and to the lessons to be learned from other powers prompted Pariani to observe that a leading French military journal pronounced the tank 'the arm of the future' on the basis of Spanish Republican experience. However, he did not think that Italy could afford to wait to profit from the experience of other powers because 'we would always be behind'. His answer to this dilemma was that 'since we always want to be [on the] offensive, we can see what other states do so as to put ourselves in a position to attack them with certain superiority'.[201] General Maravigna discounted the setback suffered by the tanks at Dembeguina as unrepresentative, and Visconti Prasca reported that the French were in the process of shifting from a counter-offensive doctrine to an offensive one based on a large number of tanks which their financial resources allowed them to build.

General Ettore Bastico, who had served as commander of the Italian forces in Spain from April to October 1937 offered the most informed judgement. The *carro veloce*, which stalled on very wet ground, was vulnerable and lacked fighting power, had had its day. Without close co-operation between tanks and infantry, the former would achieve nothing. In deserts it might be possible to use large masses of tanks, but in Europe divisions of 150 were the limit because of the difficulties of controlling larger numbers.[202] Summing up a meeting which had 'demonstrated its faith in the utility of the tank', Pariani adopted Bastico's observations about the size of an armoured division but not his remarks about the light tank. It would retain its machine-guns, while a new 'break-through tank' would have a 20-mm gun mounted on the hull.

At the close of the year, Pariani was facing serious budgetary problems which necessitated his reducing the size of the army to a cadre for most of the year in order to fill formations with conscripts and reservists for manoeuvres and training exercises in the summer months. His financial needs were considerable: as well as 1,939,000,000 lire to make good the shortfall in the monies set aside for the war in Abyssinia, he wanted a further 650,000,000 lire in extraordinary funds over the coming two financial years to meet mobilisation needs and improve frontier organisation.[203] Preparations were under way, for which funding had already been allocated, to send the second army corps to Libya. His immediate wish was to show off one of his new divisions on a war footing to Mussolini as early as possible in the new year.

In keeping with the increasingly pro-German orientation of Mussolini's foreign policy, military collaboration began to develop between Rome and Berlin from the start of 1936. After Hitler had agreed to military contacts proposed by Canaris during a visit to Milan, colonel Efisio Marras was sent by Mussolini to Berlin in February 1936 to take soundings about how they might develop. Italy's objective, as he explained to von Ribbentrop, was to develop efficient military links out of collaboration on the basis of a 'moral solidarity' which future events could transform into a 'material solidarity'. Pressed as to what these future events might be, Marras replied cautiously that, apart from preventive enemy action against her, Germany might one day collide so forcibly with the interests of other states as to lead to an armed conflict or a political conflict 'in which the armed forces will represent the determining element'. At this, von Ribbentrop looked at him silently for a moment and then smiled.[204]

Canaris warned Marras that despite Hitler's instructions there was among many of the senior officers 'a certain reluctance' to follow up his directive, partly because Italy was regarded as closely linked to France and fundamentally inclined towards England. Von Ribbentrop's personal secretary told him that the Abyssinian War had made clear the divisions in Europe and that Germany and Italy formed a 'true front' because they were the only two powers which could defend Europe against bolshevism. Von Ribbentrop himself, after opining that Italy's common interests were not with Britain and France, which were defenders of the status quo, but with Germany whose 'needs and aspirations' conflicted with their programme, expanded on Russia's aims of world revolution and assured Marras that Germany 'would fight tooth and nail against Russia, to the last man, and he thought would finish by stopping the Soviets'.[205] After some direct remarks about the commonalities of race, culture and kinship that existed between Germany and Austria, and some vague observations about there being at the moment 'more important cats to skin', he left Marras with the impression that he regarded England as friendly until proved otherwise.

General von Stülpnagel, alone among Marras's contacts, remarked that Germany had no faith in England and that she looked for territorial expansion in the colonies and mandates, but not in Europe, as an outlet for her industries. Germany's armed forces would be ready in two years, he added. Von Blomberg declared Germany ready to participate in the joint development of weapons and munitions, joint training, and the preparation of common operational plans. Regarding the latter, he warned that the Franco–Soviet Pact excluded the possibility of a conflict limited to the eastern front alone and added that Hitler wanted a further step in the secret tightening of military relations between the two powers before concrete operational plans were drawn up. Canaris agreed to the exchange of intelligence information on England and Yugoslavia, and von Blomberg left it to Italy to produce concrete proposals for the further development of military contacts.[206] Keitel, alone among the officials with whom Marras had dealings, indicated that before closer links were developed Italy would have to disengage from her military links with France. Marras, giving what was undoubtedly an officially authorised response, replied that the Rome Accord, the Stresa Front and the Badoglio–Gamelin accords were separate issues, that the latter were narrowly technical and could only come into operation on the basis of precise political premises which had not been realised, and that in any case 'it was our intention to free ourselves from it, at the opportune moment, in order to be scrupulously correct'.[207]

The Italian military authorities were ready to develop a programme of officer exchanges with Germany and to share preliminary studies, but not to discuss operational plans.[208] An Italian mission comprising representatives of all three services, which arrived in mid-May to find the principal heads of section away on a staff ride, agreed the bases of the technical and training exchanges but nothing more.[209] When finalised during the summer, the exchanges were limited: the Germans proposed sending only one officer to the war college, one each to the Italian infantry and artillery schools and the geographical institute but none to divisional commands and would take two Italians into the Kriegsakademie. The Italians were invited to send a mission to attend the manoeuvres in Saxony at which armoured units would be tested – the only other invitees being the Hungarians – and asked to receive a German mission at annual manoeuvres in Irpinia in return. German unwillingness to host Italian officers at divisional level was attributed to 'their wish to avoid having our observers in positions where they can follow the feverish work of army expansion'.[210]

The military collaboration with Germany yielded something, but not very much. The Italian military attaché attended the 1936 summer manoeuvres, and although he was not able to see much of some aspects of the exercises such as reconnaissance, he did note the success with which tank and infantry attacks were co-ordinated rather than tanks being used as infantry supports.[211] The German mission attending the 1937 manoeuvres in the Veneto, although impressed by Trezzani's attention to reconnaissance and 'manoeuvre spirit', were unimpressed by the 'lack of intrinsic offensive capacity' of his motorised columns, by the slowness and passivity of the force opposing him, which got itself into a position in which it faced annihilation, and by the qualitative and quantitative deficiencies of the non-commissioned officers.[212]

In June 1937, a group of SIM officers went to Berlin to exchange information on French mobilisation, motorisation and armaments, and on England and Russia. The mission came away with the impression that they had 'a more realistic knowledge of the French possibilities on the two frontiers', and were surprised at their hosts' lack of detailed knowledge of Britain's military organisation and her industrial capacity to sustain her rearmament programme which was, by inference, as limited as their own.[213] At the follow-up meeting in Rome in September the Germans, although full of information on the location, organisation and armament of the French army, gave the impression of possessing only 'vague and imprecise ideas' about its mobilisation, likely deployment zones and intentions. Italian military intelligence concluded that 'Our German friends want to know a lot and to give us little or nothing positive [in exchange].'[214]

War planning continued to concentrate in 1936 on the two most probable conflict scenarios in the European theatre: war with Austria, Germany and Yugoslavia in which France was a benevolent neutral (PR 9), and war with France and Yugoslavia in which Germany and Austria were benevolent neutrals (PR 10). The major objectives of the plans were in the first case to prevent German and Yugoslav pincers closing on the northeastern frontier of Italy, and in the second to eliminate or neutralise the weaker of the two opponents before she had time to make her strength count.[215] In line with the tension over Austria which was publicly evident, Plan Z (a variant of PR 9) to move from Verona into the Tyrol and Carinthia along the river valleys in the event of disorder in Austria was updated in April 1936, and the commander was allocated three celeri divisions and the Po motorised division. The action would occur in support of the Austrian authorities. Whatever the immediate contingencies which might trigger it, the aim was to act with 'maximum resolution and speed'. Although the circumstances in which the plan would be put into operation were contingent and the initial situation was uncertain, there were 'ambient' factors which could be foreseen: initial police operations would probably turn into war operations, the zone of operations was vast, and a large part of the population would be hostile. Troops must therefore be deployed in blocks equally capable of decentralised operations in the principal centres of population and communications and of concentrating quickly. The troops were to act calmly, firmly and decisively; the civilian population was to be treated 'correctly but without weakness' while 'maximum repressive energy' was to be used against insurgents and if faced by hostile acts.[216] The plan, which was updated in the spring and early summer of 1937 and was unchanged in essentials, envisaged the employment of a force comprising eight infantry divisions, four alpini divisions, two celeri divisions and the Trento motorised division, and foresaw the possibility that intervention in Austria could lead to armed conflict with Germany.[217] By this time it was purely an office exercise as there was no likelihood of Mussolini's ordering its implementation.

In an attempt to widen Italy's strategic options, Pariani ordered in March 1936 that a variant of PR 10 be drawn up in which Austria and Hungary collaborated in a war against Yugoslavia. Over the following three months the scenario occupied an increasingly prominent place in the day-to-day work of the general staff as the possibility developed that the Duce might call for it to be put into action. In an interview on 19 May with the Hungarian military attaché, colonel Laszlo Szabo, Mussolini confided that if the League of Nations did not lift sanctions on Italy he would leave it, and if it tightened sanctions he would attack Yugoslavia with the aim of carving an independent Croatia out of it. In a second interview nine days later he intimated that if he quitted the League he would attack Yugoslavia.[218] The Hungarian general staff had interests of its own to pursue – it believed that in the event of war Yugoslavia would attack Hungary and not Italy and wanted the Italians to deal with her and leave their troops free to fight Czechoslovakia. When Szabo accordingly suggested staff conversations Mussolini did not discourage them.

Pariani gave Szabo an outline of the war plans against Yugoslavia and the proposed direction of attack towards Laibach and Zagreb, which did not accord with Mussolini's intention to launch Italian forces down the Dalmatian coast to Zara if it came to war. However, he was not overly keen on starting talks. From a strictly operational point of view he was prepared to allow that Hungary might be the most suitable area in which to deploy Italian troops, but there were two reasons why he was reluctant to develop the idea. First, the basis of any Italian attack was the concept of surprise which would be destroyed if troops had to be moved by rail into Hungary, thereby disclosing Italian plans and giving the enemy time to take military and political counter-measures. Secondly, as long as Germany's attitude was unclear Italy could not risk giving her a pretext to intervene in Austria by transporting troops across the country.[219] He was, however, willing to consider the idea; given Mussolini's involvement he could scarcely do otherwise. Accordingly an officer was sent to Hungary to study the situation on the frontier and the use that could be made of Hungarian railways for deployment.[220] The idea foundered when the Austrians showed no interest in participating in it, leaving the Italians to contemplate acting along the axis of the Drava.[221]

In April 1936, in keeping with the new accent on tempo in military operations which Baistrocchi was seeking to impart, and also perhaps with Mussolini's penchant for the idea of launching surprise attacks, Pariani ordered the designated army commanders who would have command in the event of war against France and Yugoslavia (PR 10) to draw up directives which stressed the time factor. The commander-designate of 2nd Army at Bologna complied, proposing to use his forces (which included the Po motorised division) in a concentric attack along three routes converging on Lubljana.[222] Austria was already shifting out of the planning spotlight: instructing his subordinates to initiate immediate study of concentration plans for the eastern and western frontiers, which should not involve the four army corps located south of Rome, Pariani decreed that only 'simple watchfulness (*vigilanza*)' needed to be maintained in the north.[223]

In June 1936, with the Hungarian option already a dying if not a dead letter, the general staff completed a variant of PR 10 which provided for a surprise attack against Yugoslavia alone. This plan, which was also in keeping with the accent being put on speedy operations, aimed to nullify the Yugoslavian defensive deployment process, disrupt mobilisation and strike at Zagreb via the Lubljana basin and Karlovać. The forces were to act 'with maximum aggression' and give the enemy no pause, chasing him in order to prevent him creating a defence on rear positions.[224] The southernmost of the two armies – Army 'J' based on Trieste – which would have only two infantry brigades, two battalions of bersaglieri and one battalion of support tanks was tasked with providing support for the northern army aiming at Zagreb by creating a threat in the south.[225] Because of their emphasis on surprise and of the depth of penetration into enemy territory they envisaged, the new plans put a premium on speed and therefore on the employment of the new motorised and lorry-borne divisions, as well as of celeri and alpini troops. The army commanders were evidently not yet fully aware of how best to match the new units and the new plan while conforming to the new concept of operations: Rome criticised the Bologna army commander for packing all his celeri and motorised divisions into the first wave instead of keeping some back as reinforcements to push action forward when and where needed.[226]

Summarising the work of the planners in the *biennio* 1935–6, Pariani was able to point to substantial developments. The two main war scenarios were now covered, and a series of variants covered the Austrian option, the defence of the islands of Sardinia and Sicily, and the sending of an Italian force to Albania. The creation of a territorial organisation with its own troops to provide cover along the frontiers had freed the field army for the offensives specified in the new plans. However, Pariani's plans did not develop war scenarios very far; 'They do not constitute schemes to be followed', he told Badoglio on 2 November 1936, 'but [are] simple orientation directives, inasmuch as the real action will be based exclusively on the situation at the time'.[227] This implied a deficiency in the process of which he was unaware, because the study of objectives but not of the modalities of achieving them made the accurate calculation of means in relation to ends difficult if not impossible. It also reflected an acknowledgement that the forces Italy had to hand were limited for funding reasons and that planning had to make the most of them by inculcating a spirit of aggression. 'The fewer we are, the more we must make ourselves felt', Pariani remarked in February 1936 with specific reference to PR 10.[228]

If Pariani did not see anything wrong with his planning concept, there was a more obvious lacuna to which he was most certainly sensitive. The army had drawn up its plans more or less by itself, although they depended on co-operation from the other two services which had done likewise. There were thus no unified plans for the concentration of force on defined objectives, and it was not even certain that the army's plans could be carried out without unduly interfering with those of the navy and the air force. In asking for further meetings of the chiefs of staff 'to establish the direction of operations of war in the most likely contingencies', to examine their implications for war preparation and to co-ordinate action, Pariani was both illuminating Badoglio's shortcomings and challenging him to exert his potential authority as chief of the armed forces general staff.[229]

Three days after Pariani communicated his concerns about planning, Badoglio summoned the chiefs of staff to consider the situation in the light of Mussolini's declaration of the Rome–Berlin Axis. Mussolini had informed him that he intended to adopt a benevolent stance towards France but that the military accords reached in 1936 were no longer operative. The Duce's statement that the Mediterranean was for Italy 'a question of life' led him to the conclusion that, while waiting for the international political situation to develop, the problem had to be examined from three perspectives: the absolute guarantee of Italy's position in the Mediterranean, the safety of the frontiers, and the security of national territory. Reminding them that Mussolini had given them the figures for the extraordinary budgets in August and had told them not to ask for changes for two years, Badoglio added that according to the minister of finance a shortfall of 5,000 million lire was forecast on the coming year's budget. A chorus of protests greeted this remark. Cavagnari declared that he had already committed the budget assigned to him and that no savings could be made on the navy budget. Pariani laid out the parlous position of the war ministry: its budget was 1,800 million lire in debt, Abyssinian expenses were continuing, the orders to replace the mobilisation equipment used there had already absorbed the allocations for the next three budgetary years (1936–7 to 1938–9), and a new programme would require another 2,200 million-lire. Badoglio concluded the brief but lively meeting by remarking that since the new situation made demands on monies which were already insufficient he would seek a meeting with Mussolini to end the uncertainties about problems which had to be resolved if the armed forces were to ensure Italy's position in the Mediterranean. 'Military preparation[s] must be in correlation with the political line', he remarked, somewhat optimistically.[230]

With the question of the military function of the overseas colonies in a future war on the agenda for the coming meeting of the Commissione suprema di difesa, Badoglio raised the issue at the next meeting of the chiefs of staff on 17 December 1936. Coming to any definite conclusions about how the colonies might intervene in the case of 'European events' he regarded as 'a little premature'. For the immediate future both Abyssinia and Libya, far from being able to make active contributions, would need help from the *madrepatria*. Pariani believed that Italy should make use of the colonies as part of her military organisation; presently, the army was excluded from doing more than producing studies for the organisation of the empire. Sketching his scenario of a war with Great Britain, he suggested that Abyssinia could in due course act against the light Anglo–Egyptian forces which would be holding the Sudan. Motorised units and aircraft occupying the line of oases which followed the old course of the Nile could split Egypt from the Sudan. Libya should be fortified along its western border against the French, while Tobruk should be prepared as a base for operations to the east or the south. Badoglio shared Pariani's view that for the time being Ethiopia could do nothing, but was unconvinced by his Libyan scenario: Italy still had 200,000 troops in Abyssinia, Libya had 10,000 troops there, and the western border was as good as indefensible against the French, who would simply find a way round any fortifications. As was its wont, the meeting went off on a tangent to discuss the vexed but absorbing question of the powers of command of the governors of the overseas territories, which were in theory limited to matters of defence only, and how the central military authorities could ensure that they took charge of matters which they thought were within their realms of interest.[231]

With Badoglio evidently unenthusiastic about the prospects of a war in North Africa, the co-ordinated planning process continued its necessary but somewhat plodding progress during 1937. Four meetings surveyed the problems of defending the Aegean islands, the coasts of Messina and Reggio Calabria and Pantelleria between January and June, after which the chiefs of staff were not summoned to another meeting until December. The general staff updated the war plans and made minor alterations to them, but by the middle of the year the transport office was still compiling the schedules for assembling the troops to be used for the eastern element of PR 10 and the Yugoslav variant (Plan J), and had not yet begun to compile the necessary documents for PR 9.[232] However, the improvement of relations with Yugoslavia considerably eased the situation as far as Pariani was concerned. The garrisons on the eastern frontier could be reduced and some units could be sent to Libya as part of the second army corps being transferred there, while preparations were made to 'hermetically seal' the French frontier which, far from being a potential field of combat, he had long regarded as 'an insurmountable dividing obstacle' for both sides.[233]

Badoglio summoned the final meeting of the chiefs of staff on 2 December 1937, prompted by a proposal from Cavagnari that in the light of the good relations now existing between Italy and Yugoslavia the naval plans for operations in the upper and lower Adriatic could be abandoned. There was general agreement that the latter operation must be kept on the books, and that the Albanian plans needed reorienting away from Yugoslavia and towards Greece, from whose territory the British could easily launch bombers against the petroleum depots at Devoli. Looking at the broader picture in which England and France were now Italy's likely enemies, Pariani reiterated his view that France was very unlikely to launch a major attack across the Alps and thought that the decisive actions would take place on the Egyptian or Tunisian frontiers. Badoglio confirmed that Mussolini wanted two metropolitan army corps in Libya, in addition to the two native divisions already there, to be able to parry a French attack. What was now needed was detailed examination by the army and navy of the possibilities of shipping a specified number of divisions from Italy to Libya, and whether this had to be carried out before war began, as Cavagnari believed. With the discussion sliding into issues such as the fuel supplies and other resources that the air force would need to ship to North Africa, and Cavagnari settling into a potentially obstructive stance, Badoglio closed this part of the meeting by calling for Pariani to produce some proposals and for close co-operation between the army and the navy and then between the navy and the air force in examining the details.[234]

Decisive but undecided: the Regia Aeronautica

The Abyssinian experience and the Spanish war that followed it gave Rome the sense that it was in possession of a strong and effective air force. The air force's intervention in the Abyssinian war, in which it dropped 1,853,000 kilos of bombs and 1,074,000 kilos of supplies, did not cause it much material loss; official figures recorded eight aircraft lost and forty-eight personnel killed. What damaged it more – or so its leaders appear to have felt – was the fact that it was under the orders of a soldier, Badoglio, who consulted little with the airmen and reduced their high command to little more than postmen passing on orders while expecting the aeroplanes to be ready at all times to cover any emergency in the field. The result was, or was presented as being, a wearing down of the force together with a tangible restriction on its operational and strategic independence.[235]

At the end of the Ethiopian war, the air force drew up Programme R. Scheduled for completion between July and December 1940, the so-called 'three-thousand plane' plan provided for an air force of 3,161 aircraft, of which 2,064 were undeveloped prototypes. Of the total, 1,191 were to be land-based bombers, 971 fighters and 75 assault planes of the type favoured by Mecozzi. The programme, which was characterised by technological backwardness and rested on refining types which had won prizes and competitions in the past, embodied serious technical deficiencies: the prototypes were soon surpassed by aircraft under development in other countries and the aero engines could produce a maximum of only 1,000 horse power. Its twenty-two types of aeroplane indicated an intention to try to fulfil every kind of operational demand and also reflected its doctrinal confusion. The programme was not completed by the time Italy entered the Second World War, partly because of her involvement in the Spanish Civil War and partly because of the government's decision to sell aircraft overseas to earn much-needed foreign currency. Between 1937 and 1939 more than 2,000,000,000 lire-worth of aircraft was sold to thirty-nine countries in a process Valle was powerless to stop.[236]

Valle also faced internal problems due to 'infiltration' and interference from outsiders. He modified the system whereby Balbo had been able to nominate anyone to a reserve lieutenancy, but between 1934 and 1940 1,093 new officers entered the service in this way. Party members got in and brought their feuds with them. Valle was unable – or unwilling – to prevent the increased politicisation of the air force which resulted from this policy but which was also partly the consequence of the participation of a number of senior Fascist figures (*gerarchi*) such as Roberto Farinacci and Galeazzo Ciano in the Abyssinian War. The latter particularly took it upon himself to interfere in air force policy thereafter. Having got to know him in Abyssinia, Ciano tried to get Aimone Cat made under-secretary of state by splitting that office from the post of chief of staff. Valle blocked this move and instead of going to Libya Cat was given command of the *Scuola di Guerra Aerea*.[237]

Although the Italian air force had provided facilities for the covert training of German pilots during Balbo's time as air minister, this programme had been ended in 1934 and official contacts between the Italian air force and its German opposite number had been limited thereafter.[238] Valle's visit to Germany in June 1936 – the first time he had been there since 1922 – was therefore of considerable importance both for the political intelligence he was able to bring back to Mussolini and also because it shaped the picture of the technical and professional development of the Luftwaffe in the mind of the head of the Italian air force. Everywhere he found evidence of great social discipline – 'exaggeratedly formalistic in accordance with the German character' – and feverish industrial activity.[239] The German air force already numbered 1,500 planes, half of which were bombers, and it was expected to rise to 3,000 in the spring of 1937 and 6,000 a year later, thanks to an output of 400 planes a month. 200 new airfields under construction and when they were completed Germany would be able to employ at least 10,000 aircraft in war. Valle was impressed, as was undoubtedly intended, not least by the secrecy which enveloped every aspect of German air rearmament and which contrasted starkly with the openness of military and naval developments. His conclusions were that 'by the beginning of 1938 Germany will possess the strongest air force in Europe', that German air power already constituted 'a factor of formidable weight', and that it was better to have her as a friend than an enemy.[240]

The ongoing continuing doctrinal conflict between Douhetism and Mecozzism was complicated still further by the vexed question of how to interpret the experiences in Ethiopia and Spain and what to learn from them. The gauntlet was thrown down in 1936 when the culturally prestigious and politically authoritative *Enciclopedia Italiana* declared that 'Aerial strategy, which governs the battles between aeronautical rivals, has no precedents in this field and cannot for the moment be confined within any [particular] formula.'[241] Harmonising with this anti-Douhetian fanfare, Mecozzi refined his arguments for assault aviation, drawing a distinction between air actions that were co-ordinated with land action, which he favoured, and direct air support of ground operations, which was only justified in respect of reconnaissance and air transportation, and arguing for planes operating at short range with light bomb loads which would have greater penetrative capacity than heavy bombers because they would be equipped with the means to fight off enemy aircraft. The assault planes should aim at the most sensitive targets, which were not simply the largest ones. The aim was not mass concentrated bombing action as propounded by Douhet but simultaneous separate actions; the targets were to be found in the zone between fifty and four hundred kilometres behind the front lines where the enemy's armed forces were to be found. Mecozzi did not, however, close the door entirely to action directed against enemy populations, industry and communications. Not only might assault aviation take part in initial actions designed to produce the rapid industrial, economic and moral collapse of the enemy nation, but it could be used with particular effect to strike at political and administrative buildings in great cities and at the major thoroughfares.[242]

Mecozzi's ideas were, as he himself pointed out, particularly applicable to colonial wars, where major cities were few and targets small and vulnerable, to wars against small European countries lacking major population centres, where terrorising the population by mass bombing would not work, and against countries where industry was dispersed. They also fitted with the theory of rapid and decisive land war developed by Baistrocchi and Pariani, though from an airman's rather than a soldier's point of view: occupying the Rhône valley or lower Bavaria would be a decisive action from the point of view of the air war because it would put Italy's most precious cities beyond the reach of hostile air power while simultaneously increasing the possibility of attacking those of the enemy.[243] However, the air force contained many officers who either still kept faith with undiluted Douhetian principles or who regarded them as the foundations of an evolving doctrine and, like Valle's successor Francesco Pricolo, saw limited tactical collaboration with the army as exceptional and not as negating Douhetian doctrine.

The course of the Ethiopian War gave ammunition to both sides in the debate over the relationship of air power to land power. When military commentators argued that the close collaboration between fast military units and the reconnaissance planes and bombers that had contributed greatly to the success of Badoglio's and Graziani's columns pointed the right way forward, Mecozzi entered the lists once more to reiterate his theories, arguing that the aeroplane was 'a cannon that fires at a distance and not an impervious flying gun-carriage'.[244] Douhetians stuck to their guns. Purists argued that the absence of an enemy air force to be defeated and the lack of major cities to be bombed had allowed the air force to move immediately to the third stage of Douhetian war, direct attack on the land forces, and had thus demonstrated the crushing power of the aeroplane when it enjoyed mastery of the skies. Lieutenant-colonel Vincenzo Lioy gave this argument a twist: circumstantial command of the air had enabled the bombers to hinder the enemy's mobilisation, weaken his resistance on the ground, and deliver the *colpo di grazia* after battles such as Amba Aradam and Tembien.[245]

Air force authorities, not unnaturally, argued that the experience of the Abyssinian War had shown that the aeroplane's capacity to attack where ground offensives had stalled made it potentially the decisive arm in deciding the outcome of future wars. The same line of thinking validated Douhet's proposition about resisting on the ground while massing in the air; in his account to the senate on 28 March 1936 of air operations in Ethiopia, Valle declared that the experiences in Eritrea and Somalia had confirmed their validity, though in fact a good deal of what he had to say was about the tactical rather than the strategic use of air power. The doctrinal confusion which Valle perpetuated was clearly apparent in the conflict between the bomber regulations (AD 2 *Criteri generali di impiego dell'aviazione da bombardamento*) published in 1936, which specifically excluded the bombing of cities, Valle's repeated declaration that the air force did not have a doctrine, and his equally fervent adherence to the concept of the air force as 'the terror arm'. Valle's ambiguous attitude to Mecozzi, whom he encouraged to continue publishing polemics in favour of assault aircraft when Mecozzi was inclined to give up, was evident when he allowed general Mario Cebrelli to criticise him for continuing to engage in them. In 1937, at the suggestion of his deputy chief of staff general Pietro Pinna – a Douhetian – Mecozzi was moved to Somalia and his place in command of the assault brigade taken by Cebrelli, who was a telecommunications expert.[246]

The somewhat confused state of air power doctrine was no secret. Indeed, by highlighting its pragmatism it could be made to accord with Fascist worship of action over thought. Mussolini, obviously aware at least in general terms of the state it was in, did exactly this when he summarised the situation of the armed forces for the senate on 30 March 1938, three weeks after he had ordered the bombing of Barcelona. 'Our doctrine of air war was applied before it was taught with academic authority (*dalla cattedra*),' he announced proudly. Air war would be conducted in such a way as to break up the enemy's dispositions, dominate the skies and exhaust the morale of his population. When stripped of its 'impassioned polemicism' – not an easy task – Douhet's vision was the 'precursor' to current thinking.[247] The bombing of Barcelona on 16–18 March, which Mussolini calculated would depress Republican morale and increase Italy's standing in the eyes of the Germans 'who love integral pitiless war', did indeed have Douhetian overtones.[248]

As the war in Abyssinia came to an end, air force planning naturally focused on the requirements of a war in the Mediterranean against Great Britain. In April 1936, a month before Badoglio declared victory, the tasks which the nine air districts which covered mainland Italy, the major islands, the Aegean and Libya would have to undertake were updated. As well as coastal defence on the eastern and western sides of the mainland, they had to be ready to undertake possible offensive action against Yugoslavia, attack British ships if they were located in Greek ports and harbours, and launch 'reprisal operations' from the Upper Tyrrhenian zone against London – an action which, given the current range of Italian aircraft, would have been a one-way trip at best. Attacks would be launched from Sicily and Sardinia on Malta and on enemy shipping in the western and central Mediterranean, and from Libya on the British aircraft carriers, battle-cruisers and battleships (in that order of priority), on Malta, and then on the ships, airfields and fuel dumps in Egypt and Palestine.[249]

Some three weeks after Badoglio's declaration, with the likelihood of a war still looming if sanctions continued to be enforced against Italy, deputy chief of staff Pietro Pinna sought guidance from Valle on the likely adversaries Italy would face, the zones in which action might take place, and the targets against which the air force should direct its initial activities. The answer was that Italy's likely adversaries were '[e]veryone except Austria, Hungary and Germany', and that the air force had to be ready to act simultaneously against Malta, Haifa, Alexandria, Gibraltar, London, Belgrade and Athens. To Pinna's question as to what actions by the other armed services the air force would be required to support, Valle simply noted 'Ask the other chiefs of staff.'[250] In June 1936, undoubtedly acting either under Mussolini's instructions or with his consent, Valle wrote to the French air minister, Pierre Cot, to inform him that if sanctions continued the air accord reached the previous year would be abrogated.[251] Two months later, with sanctions gone, the status of Plan B was lowered from that of likely immediate activation to one of being a 'normal foreseeable requirement'.[252]

The announcement of the Axis in November 1936 changed the foundations on which air force planning had to be based. The political assumptions used during 1936 and 1937 to guide the thinking of the advanced course of the Air War School, which the air force used like its naval equivalent as a 'think tank' to explore planning options and test solutions to practical strategic and operational problems, embodied the likely new international configurations of future war. They were grounded on the 'open [and] incurable' conflict between National–Fascist and Communist systems which characterised the current European political situation. Germany's increasingly combative attitude to Russia made an early conflict between the two powers a strong possibility. If it occurred, France's alliance with Russia would bring her in against Germany. Italy, 'linked to Germany by the recent protocols and determined to fight all-out (*a fondo*) against actual Communism in Russia and that which is fast developing in France', must align herself with Germany.[253] Japan would join the latter group, as would Austria and Hungary. England's traditional policy of opposing hegemonies would lead her to line up against Germany, Italy and Japan; however, 'given that the social agitation consequent on a Russian victory is substantially against all her interests', she might maintain her neutrality during the first stages of a conflict.[254] Poland and Yugoslavia would probably stay neutral though aligned to the German–Italian–Japanese bloc, Czechoslovakia and Romania likewise but aligned to the Franco–Russian bloc.

In January 1937, Valle sought guidance from Badoglio on the war plans his service should now be developing. The scenarios on which it had hitherto been concentrating were for war against Germany and Yugoslavia (PR 9), against France and Yugoslavia (PR 10), and against England (PR B). However, given the recent change in the political situation, the air force now needed to know whether all three should still be kept in an active state and if so in what order of precedence, whether there were additional war scenarios it should prepare for, and what the politico-military situation and the general directives from the government were likely to be in the event of war.[255] The reply, which did not come for a month, was no help. The current political situation did not allow the forecasting of any specific concrete case or even of establishing an order of precedence for the updating of war plans. Everything should kept up to date and completed, where necessary, in conformity with the army's plans. About Plan B Badoglio was prepared to say nothing at this time.[256]

The extant plans were now deficient in several respects. In particular they either completely or partially failed to incorporate new units created since 1935, and the transportation elements were going to be invalidated when the state railways introduced a new general timetable for 1937.[257] In order to produce plans which would not need constant updating, the planners also needed to know what the structure of the air force would be on 1 July 1938, how units would be grouped, what new ones would be in existence and where, and where and how the supporting services would be organised.[258] They got some assistance when, in late April 1937, Valle passed on Mussolini's directive identifying England and France as Italy's likely opponents in war and identifying the Mediterranean as her pre-eminent security problem. For the air force, this meant examining ways to thin out air cover on the eastern frontier, increase protection on the western frontier and the islands of Sardinia and Sicily, and transform the air force in East Africa so as to make it capable of carrying out long-range actions against distant objectives.

We must anticipate stationing bombers and fighters – with the necessary supplies – so as to be able to carry out offensive and defensive tasks that are somewhat more vast than those hitherto contemplated in the organisation of the East African Air Force, while limited to search and defence actions on the borders of the Empire in case of a war in Europe.[259]

The task Valle now set his planners was neither clear nor easy, though this was perhaps not entirely his fault. For some reason, though, he entirely neglected to mention Libya.

Pinna's response was reasonably encouraging. Presently there were very few English aircraft in Sudan, Kenya and Aden. However, it had to be borne in mind that in April 1936 there had been 46 bombers, 67 fighters and 147 other aircraft in the region and that such a situation could recur, particularly since the stores and magazines set up along the Suez canal in the aftermath of the Anglo–Egyptian Treaty would enable England to build up her position in the area rapidly. Italy had 320 aircraft in the area, 140 of which were bombers and 90 reconnaissance planes. They were more than a match for the enemy quantitatively, but not qualitatively 'if, as is to be expected, they are faced with more modern aircraft'. Italy needed to be able to strike at the aero–naval bases at Aden and on the Upper Nile to aid naval operations in the Red Sea and Indian Ocean, and to hit targets in the Sudan and Kenya. In his opinion, an additional thirty-six fighters and twenty-four bombers would provide the wherewithal to carry out all these tasks successfully.[260]

Contradictions now began to emerge in Italian war planning as a result of Mussolini's requirement that the colonies should be self-sufficient in matters of supply from 1 July 1938. In East Africa, Marshal Graziani interpreted this to mean that the colony would be isolated in the event of war and would have to sustain itself for at least a year. The men on the spot had insufficient intelligence about the strength of the air forces in neighbouring countries to be able to work out for themselves how many planes they would need to carry out offensive operations. The matter was accordingly referred to the air ministry in Rome with the warning that special attention would need to be given to the network of permanent and temporary airfields which would be needed to give 'full elasticity of manoeuvre' to the forces operating there.[261]

The inter-relationship between planning, doctrine and action in war came most clearly to the fore when the vexed question of co-operation with the other two services resurfaced in the summer of 1937. When the army produced a list of targets it wanted the air force to strike to assist it in carrying out its own plans, aimed particularly at disrupting enemy mobilisation and deployment, it provoked a Douhetian response from Pinna. At the start of a war, the deputy chief of staff informed the army general staff, the air force 'has the greatest interest in seeking to reduce the enemy's air power [by] hitting the air bases in enemy territory, the forces located there and the air resources which are for immediate use'. To get the maximum return, such action must be immediate and intense; only thus would Italy obtain the greatest possible security for its national territory against enemy air offensives and thereby make it possible subsequently to strike at other enemy targets with the bulk of its air forces. From this it followed that for the first two or three days of war nothing could be allowed to distract the air force from this task. In any case, striking at enemy communications would have a greater disruptive effect when mobilisation had been under way for several days and the transportation systems were fully employed. Although this represented the general criteria for employing the air force, Pinna allowed that a particular set of political and military circumstances could change them so that second phase objectives could have priority. However, it would take special orders from Badoglio for this to happen. Nevertheless, Pinna assured the soldiers, the air force would study their list of targets so as to be ready to act against them at any time.[262]

Badoglio's April directive identifying England and France as Italy's prime potential enemies also prompted Cavagnari to suggest to Valle that their respective general staffs carry out a combined study of the objectives they would need to identify, the means employed to attain them and the tactical employment of the navy and the air force in the process. Coordination was especially urgent in respect of the Upper Tyrrhenian, Red Sea and Adriatic zones, where only limited numbers of submarines and light surface craft were available for defence; since they could only act at night, it was hoped that the air force could provide defence by day. Cavagnari also wanted air detachments created to defend naval operations and logistical bases. Finally, the participation of offensive and defensive air power in naval operations was necessary 'if we do not wish consciously to worsen our unfortunate [naval] inferiority'.[263]

Cavagnari got more or less the same response that Pariani had received. The air force had studied all the objectives that it might be called on to attack but because of the vast size of the prospective theatre of operations it could not hit them all simultaneously. Priorities would be determined by the circumstances of the moment and according to the judgement of the High Command. In any case, for the air force 'the fundamental and absolutely pressing objective' in any conflict was the complex of enemy air power. To reduce its potential at the outset would be to aid all three armed services, giving them a greater freedom of movement and allowing operations on land and at sea to unfold in greater security. The air force was deployed in such a way as to allow it to operate almost anywhere in the Mediterranean, while the long-range aircraft with which it was currently equipped enabled it to strike Gibraltar and London. As far as indirect support for naval operations went, the air force was studying ways to reduce the effectiveness of enemy air forces and the efficiency of their naval bases; direct support, involving attacking enemy surface units and taking part in naval battles, would be given as agreed with the navy.[264]

The Regia Aeronautica had its own views about the major naval strategic problems Cavagnari had identified. All that was necessary in the Upper Tyrrhenian sea was for the navy to use its own naval and air resources to avoid surprise so that the bombers stationed in Tuscany, Liguria, Piedmont and Lombardy could intervene in time. No enemy attack was currently foreseeable in the Adriatic, and in any case the air force was deployed so as to be able to confront any threat in that area. In the Red Sea, Italian air superiority was such that it could neutralise any enemy air offensive. The question of defending naval bases was already incorporated into the organisation of fighter defence for mainland Italy. Having served up this revealing combination of operational optimism and strategic certitude, Valle concluded by inviting his naval opposite number to send across the information being used in the compilation of naval objectives in the Mediterranean so that his staff could work out the details of the air offensive there in advance.[265]

While shaping its plans for an air war the Regia Aeronautica had ongoing experience in Spain to absorb and accommodate. Its involvement began when on 29–30 July 1936 twelve SM 81 aircraft were sent secretly to Melilla in Morocco to neutralise Republican naval forces patrolling the Straits and escort a convoy of five ships carrying troops and munitions for Franco from Ceuta to Algeciras. By the end of August twenty-two Fiat CR 32 fighters had been despatched and in October another twenty-one Ro 37 aircraft were sent. On 18 December, two days after his arrival to take command of Italian land and air forces in Spain, Roatta wrote to Franco and to the Spanish and German air commanders dividing up the air tasks. The *Aviazione Legionaria* in mainland Spain would mainly use fighters while the Condor Legion deployed bombers, and the units on the Balearics would use fighters, bombers and reconnaissance aircraft on the islands, over the seas around them and 'on the Red areas [on the mainland] within their range of action'.[266]

Following this division of responsibilities, the Italian air force on the mainland was mainly employed in direct support of ground combat operations and in tactical interdiction, bombing enemy troop concentrations and communications targets, as well as reconnaissance operations. Thus only the units stationed in the Balearics carried out the systematic bombardment of ports, industrial targets, communication routes and airports which corresponded to the strategic concept of *guerra integrale* ('integrated war') during the later stages of the war. Experiences in the air were misleading. The Italian SM 79 three-engined bombers and BR 20 twin-engined bombers enjoyed a temporary and deceptive superiority in 1937–8 because they were faster than all but the most recent models of Polikarpov fighters, which were frequently employed on other tasks and had in any case to confront the faster Messerschmidt 109 B from the spring of 1937. The arrival of the German aeroplane also contributed to the deceptively successful record of the CR 32 biplane, which was slower than the early Russian fighters but more manoeuvrable and equipped with a pair of heavier machine-guns with longer range.[267]

The Spanish experience did not help to resolve the fundamental doctrinal conflicts which bedevilled the air force – indeed it exacerbated them. Mecozzi argued in 1937 that Spain showed that the fastest and best-armed bombers then available could not escape from fighters, and could only obtain good results by low-level or dive bombing. Bombers had unloaded massive amounts of explosives on the starving Spanish population without causing it to give up. He neatly evaded the charge that special considerations applied in Spain because it was a civil war by arguing first that it was already an international war and secondly that 'much evidence allows us to forecast that the next European war will have the character of a civil war ... it will perhaps not be a war between countries but a war of ideals (which everyone claims to be his position) against ideologies, which everyone claims to be the other side's'.[268]

Others for whom Mecozzi's views on the proper role for assault aviation did not seem to square with recent experience or with doctrinal rectitude offered differing versions of the relationship between tactical and strategic air power. Pinna allowed that the tactical use of bombers had been very effective against enemy troops and behind their lines. Military commentators such as Emilio Canevari and general Ambrogio Bollati went further, arguing that experience demonstrated that low-level and dive bombing were the most effective forms of air action and that assault aviation was the pre-eminent new element in war.

Douhetians of all degrees were able to find in what did and did not happen in Spain evidence to support their views. The air force had had 'a decisive function, though acting against targets (trenches, troops, artillery concentrations) which are among the least appropriate to the particular offensive capacity it possesses'.[269] Assault aviation had its place in the air war acting in a tactical role, while fighters secured freedom of action and bombers acted against strategic objectives. To Aimone Cat, who had commanded the air force in Ethiopia, that war and the Spanish Civil War together had shown that although it had not been intended to follow the Douhetian maxim of resisting on the ground to mass in the air, it had often been necessary to mass air power in order to resist on the ground. To overcome the inevitable phases of stabilisation that would occur in future conflicts, it would therefore be necessary to look to air power. Francesco Pricolo held that putting too much weight on the existence or absence of targets was a fundamental error: 'today the effective weapon of the air force is terror, that of the navy is hunger, and that of the army is the effective occupation of ground'.[270] Objecting forcefully to the way in which the air force had been subordinated to the army in Ethiopia and in Spain, he held that there were targets in the latter war which could have been attacked, such as naval traffic, and could have led to the rapid surrender of the enemy.

Valle himself remained a Douhetian, holding that the 'imposing development' of tactical bombing in Spain had been the result of the particular and unrepeatable characteristics of that war. While he acknowledged the value of ground attack techniques, especially in the opening phases of the campaign, he saw evidence that the high level bombing of the coasts and ports of Republican Spain had 'notably reduced the moral and material resistance of the enemy'.[271] More could have been achieved had not political and international considerations restricted the bombers' freedom of action.

The lessons of the Spanish Civil War, embodied in reports on bombing tactics, bomb-sights, bomb types and related technical issues, went unlearned. The reasons were complex and included lack of money (the sums earned in aircraft sales did not go into the air force budget or for the purchase of much-needed raw materials), Mussolini's decision to prioritise production of aircraft suitable for tactical co-operation with the ground forces, an inability to make good the losses suffered in Ethiopia and Spain, and the poor choices made by the air force's leadership such as Pinna's insistence on the efficacy of using light 15–50-kilo bombs against 10,000 ton warships. The air industry contributed to the sorry state of affairs by producing a string of aircraft which were soon discarded as technically inadequate.[272] A further factor, though, was the inability of the air force collectively to decide on the lessons to be learned from the Ethiopian campaign and the Spanish Civil War. Balbo believed that there were none because neither had had the totalitarian characteristics of a European war. Like the navy, but unlike the army, the air force entered a year in which the likelihood of an Axis war against the western democracies became more pronounced with no clear strategic plans that could offer a prospect of victory.

Fig. 8 Hitler and Mussolini reviewing troops prior to the Munich
Conference, 1938

Hitler professed much respect and admiration for Mussolini both
before and after January 1933, but Munich was only the fourth
occasion on which they met. Their first encounter, at Venice in May
1934, did not go well, but Mussolini returned from a visit to Berlin in
September 1937 convinced of Germany's burgeoning military power.
Shortly afterwards he announced the creation of the Rome–Berlin
'Axis'. When Hitler left Florence after his second visit in May 1938,
Mussolini told him 'No force can separate us any more.' At Munich,
Mussolini read from a script written by Hitler and won himself an
ill-deserved reputation as a peace-maker.

Mussolini's policy during the Munich crisis, when military and diplomatic factors necessarily became intimately inter-mixed, has been the subject of sharply conflicting interpretations. They range from the view that he had 'no policy' and was content to sit on the sidelines and watch events through his having had 'a profound desire for confrontation with the Western democracies' but choosing not to go to war to the depiction of a warmonger who chose war and mobilised his military machine early in September for a 'violent ... undeclared' strike but was forced to abandon his design as a result of contrary and pessimistic military and naval advice.[1] Exactly which factors acted in which ways to shape his decisions it is impossible at present to say. However, the diplomatic and military dimensions of Italian policy provide a series of inter-locking explanations which suggest that the best answer lies somewhere in the middle ground and not on either historiographical extreme.

Going to war in September 1938 would have presented Italy with well-nigh insuperable difficulties, but in any case Mussolini did not feel that he had to do so. His diplomatic and intelligence sources gave him sufficient reason to think that a general war would probably not break out, but if it did Italy had no need to hurry to get into it. Ambassadors, service attachés and consuls provided him with evidence which confirmed his enmity for England, and had she chosen to fight over Czechoslovakia he would almost certainly have done so too. Otherwise his ambitions pointed rather to localised theatre wars and the calculations, plans and representations of his service chiefs added up to a counsel of delay – at least for the time being.

Foreign policy before and after Munich

At the end of 1937, Ciano believed that 'on an historical plane' conflict between Italy and Great Britain might be inevitable, and at the start of February 1938 Mussolini was sure of it. The military dimension was something on which, as will be seen, Ciano and Mussolini received increasingly enthusiastic noises as a confident Pariani prepared for a war in North Africa. Meanwhile there were goals which could benefit Rome, especially British recognition of the East African empire, and London soon made it apparent that she was ready to take this step.[2]

An obvious campaign to woo the Italians assured Rome that she possessed the leverage she required. In Paris, the British naval attaché told his Italian opposite number early in January that both countries had much to gain from a sincere and friendly collaboration, and was told in return that Italy suspected that friendly words were being used to gain the time necessary for British rearmament to put her in a position to dictate terms to Italy. As a poor nation with little to lose, captain Hamill was informed, Italy would prefer to fight if she found her back to the wall rather than surrender to threats.[3] In what was obviously a concerted campaign, the British military attaché in Paris reiterated the message, acknowledging that the situation in the Far East was such as to magnify the significance of the Italian threat in the Mediterranean.[4]

Ciano's policy was straightforward: Grandi was instructed to look for an agreement with Chamberlain before German pressure for anschluss with Austria weakened Italy's negotiating position by suggesting that she was being forced to turn to London, but at the same time to give no indication that Italy was pursuing England to get a general agreement.[5] Even without resorting to duplicity, Ciano was able to manipulate Great Britain into an agreement which met all of Italy's immediate objectives in the Mediterranean. In return for agreeing to put the question of recognition of Italy's Abyssinian empire in front of the League of Nations on 9 May, London secured a statement from Rome that Italy did not have any territorial or political aims in Spain and did not seek a privileged economic position there – which was more or less Italian policy anyway – and an offer to adhere to the 1936 London Naval Treaty. As a sweetener, Mussolini announced that he had decided to withdraw troops from Libya at the rate of 1,000 a week, a move which was demonstrably inconsistent with the direction in which Italian military strategy was moving and one which he reversed less than four months later when, on 14 July, he ordered that the Libyan garrison be reinforced.

As well as securing discussions on Italy's interests in Palestine and Syria, Ciano was able to fend off British attempts to secure the withdrawal of Italian 'volunteers' from Spain. His refusal to agree to France's joining the agreement, on the grounds that such a tripartite arrangement would look as if it were directed against Germany, furthered the twin aims of splitting England and France apart wherever and whenever possible while maintaining good relations with Hitler's Germany.[6] Speeches by Halifax in Bristol and Chamberlain in Birmingham, reported by Grandi in early April, which made it plain that the British Government was no longer inclined to look to the League of Nations to uphold international order, sought an 'honourable peace' and wanted to improve relations with Italy, made Ciano's task even simpler.[7] The 'Easter Agreement' signed on 16 April 1938 made British recognition of Italian East Africa dependent on a settlement in Spain. The accord did not signal a change of direction in Italian foreign policy: Ciano told the Japanese ambassador a month after it was signed that it was 'no more than a matter of routine'.[8] It was however a little more than that, for as well as securing Italy's immediate Mediterranean goals it was deliberately aimed at weakening France.[9] It was also intended to influence the internal balance within the Axis, for it was seen as a counter-balance to Germany which would force her to act more cautiously in her relations with Italy.[10] Mussolini and his son-in-law no doubt also calculated – correctly – that with this document in their pocket time was for the moment on their side.

During the negotiations in March which preceded the signing of the Easter Agreement, London supplied Rome with the information that its troops movements in the Mediterranean amounted to shipping 1,070 men to Egypt and 1,300 to Palestine. The picture developing in Rome during the spring and early summer preceding the Munich crisis looked rather different. A string of telegrams from the Italian consul in Port Said and the legations in Cairo and Alexandria between December 1937 and June 1938 reported the arrival of large stocks of ammunition, explosives, machine-guns, artillery, anti-aircraft guns, armoured cars, tanks and parts. Fortifications were also apparently being constructed near Alexandria, at Aboukir and along the Suez canal. In mid-March the consul-general at Gibraltar reported the news 'from a confidential source' of the arrival there over recent months of 120 light tanks, 30 armoured cars, 100 heavy mortars, 100 75-mm guns and a large quantity of machine-pistols.[11] In May, the British were believed to be about to sow underwater mines to protect the approaches to Alexandria, and in June 2,000 British troops were reported to have disembarked there. The fortifications at Gibraltar were also being improved. In mid-September, at the height of the crisis, quantities of munitions were reported to be arriving at Aden.

A further reason to be suspicious of British policy was supplied in March when Italian military intelligence reported that the British were putting pressure on the sultan of Yemen to agree to fortification of the eastern side of the Strait of Bab el Mandab, which he was resisting. SIM interpreted this move as one element of a design to extend the British protectorate of Aden into the Yemen.[12] In August 1938, Ciano decided to send arms and advisers to the Yemen, violating the agreement to preserve the regional status quo contained in the Easter Accords.

To a leadership prone to paranoid suspicions as it pursued its ambitions in the Mediterranean, signs of potential hostility and resistance multiplied during the early months of 1938. The military attaché in Ankara, lieutenant-colonel Gabriele Boglione, reported on closer co-operation between Greece and Turkey in the advanced defence of Thrace and Macedonia ostensibly against the possibility of Bulgarian attack, though the joint defence of Thrace seemed to the ambassador conceivable only in the context of a general war or of a Mediterranean conflict between England and Italy.[13] A visit by Metaxas to Ankara in January, and a simultaneous visit by the Greek deputy chief of general staff to Istanbul, gave rise to suspicions that Greece and Turkey were about to sign a mutual defence pact. Given that neither intended to attack the other and that neither had the strength to give the other much support in the event of a wider Mediterranean conflict, the conclusion drawn by the Foreign Ministry was that the pact must be anti-Italian in design and British by inspiration.[14] The Italian ambassador surmised that since Britain could never raise a large army it might be intended that Turkish troops go to defend the Suez canal on her behalf.[15] For a brief period after Italy adhered to the Montreux Convention on 2 May Italian diplomats optimistically forecast that Ankara, impressed by Italy's power, was moving out of the British orbit. The Franco–Turkish accords signed on 3–4 July appeared to give the lie to that view and presented a tangible threat. In a counter-move Rome sought to undercut the Little Entente by persuading Hungary and Rumania to spearhead the four-power Bled Agreement of 23 August in which France's eastern allies agreed to allow Hungary parity of arms and to renounce force.[16]

The British ambassador in Rome thought that the British decision to rearm had come as an unpleasant surprise to Rome 'owing to the fact that they had come to look upon Great Britain as decadent, fat, lazy and unfit for effort'.[17] In fact, it did not significantly affect the perceptions of British military power which circulated in Rome as the international climate grew more unsettled. After a courtesy visit from the British secretary of state for war, Leslie Hore-Belisha, in late April Mussolini was inclined to lower his rating of British military capacity yet further. He did not think that the British army could become 'a serious army' as long as it had 'that "little chick" ' as its leader.[18] If British armaments did not give cause for great concern – something which would be confirmed by the military attaché in London before the Munich crisis blew up – the configurations of Middle Eastern politics and their military corollaries did. Although the Anglo–Italian accords had lessened the fear of war in the Middle East, the Egyptians were arming and Iraq and Palestine would probably follow suit. Were they doing so to defend their own interests or those of Great Britain?[19]

In many respects, French policy too played into Rome's hands in the first half of 1938. Rather than accept reports that Rome's Mediterranean ambitions made her willing to turn a blind eye to the German absorption of Austria, which was in fact the case, Paris first chose to believe that Mussolini was ready to 'escape from under the thumb of Berlin' if he could obtain western recognition of the Italian empire and efface the stain of Guadalajara, and then to try to secure a joint statement in which France and Britain declared themselves wholly opposed to anschluss.[20]

The foundation on which this policy rested was evident to Rome. Large sections of French public opinion were permeated by the opinion that close collaboration with England was indispensable to ensure the integrity of France and her empire and the navy, unlike the army, was 'anglophile to the core'. The explanation was to be found in reasoning not sentiment, the Italian naval attaché reported: English naval power was such that a Franco–Italian alliance could not counter-balance it, and the day that France detached herself from England, her erstwhile partner would ally with Germany.[21]

A policy which was barely afloat was holed below the waterline when Chamberlain's naive diplomacy allowed Grandi to offer the bait of a possible opposition to anschluss in return for recognition of the empire and the settlement of Mediterranean questions, thereby reinforcing the prime minister's illusion that he could secure the best results by dealing directly with Mussolini and leaving France to one side. Despite urgent pleas from the political Right, the French government refused to emulate the British prime minister. The anschluss went ahead, and was subsequently interpreted as the fruit of a wrong-headed policy which had resulted in a lost opportunity. When the Popular Front collapsed on 10 April, French diplomacy duly changed tack.

French attempts to open up a better relationship with Italy and to knit together the Anglo–Italian accords and the protection of her own interests in Syria, the Middle East, the Red Sea and elsewhere started on the day that the accords were signed but soon foundered – as was probably their destiny. The chief sticking point was Spain, over which Italy refused to declare its disinterest, construct reciprocal agreements for non-intervention or agree to withdraw volunteers and war materiel. The Italian position, as Ciano explained to the Japanese ambassador, was straightforward: by helping the republican government in Valencia, France was delaying the conclusion of the Spanish Civil War.[22] Additionally Mussolini did not want to extend to France the agreements on the Red Sea already reached with Great Britain. French demands may well have been too big for Mussolini to accept, but they could never have shrunk to a size he was likely to be able to swallow. Nor did he wish to do so, despite the evidence that Europe was splitting into two factions. Asked by the British secretary of state for war on 23 April whether, having come to an understanding with Germany, he would not do so with France, his reply was indirect but clear: war would come, he told Leslie Hore-Belisha, although not in the near future.

There was little comfort for France in the speech Mussolini gave at Genoa on 14 May. Stresa was 'dead and buried' and as far as Italy was concerned it would not be resuscitated. Explaining why Italy had not done in March 1938 what she had done in August 1934, Mussolini told the citizens of Mazzini's birthplace that Italy would not play the part of Habsburg Vienna and mobilise every four years to prevent 'the inevitable outcome of a national revolution'. In a speech shot with Axis colours, Mussolini declared that he was going to be circumspect about the conversations with France that were currently going on:

I do not know if they will reach a conclusion because in respect of a very current issue, that is to say the war in Spain, we are on opposite sides of the barricade. They want Barcelona [i.e. the Republicans] to win; we, on the other hand, want and wish for Franco's victory.[23]

When, at the end of July 1938, the French looked to reopen conversations with Italy they got no response. Mussolini would not contemplate resuming them until the Gentleman's Agreement with Britain was actually in force.

Events in Berlin at the start of the year suggested that Nazi Germany had not lost its predilection for sudden dramas and dramatic shifts in policy. The crisis which led to the resignation of the Reichswehr minister, general Werner von Blomberg, in February and the Führer's assumption of supreme executive authority over the military suggested that greater nazification of the armed forces was now on the cards.[24] When coupled with the replacement of von Neurath by von Ribbentrop at the foreign ministry, and the former's translation to the headship of a new committee of government, the puzzling features of the crisis took on a satisfactory hue for Rome. Since von Blomberg was a well-known anglophile and von Ribbentrop a notorious anglophobe, ambassador Attolico interpreted the change of guard as one that was unfavourable to England and therefore favourable to Italy.[25]

Hitler's Reichstag speech on 20 February 1938 confirmed initial impressions about a new course in German policy and led Attolico to conclude that there was more to the current events than just a change of personnel and the insertion of a new rung in the bureaucratic ladder. German foreign policy had now abandoned its collaborative attitude, taking up a clearly anti-British position in which colonies figured large – thus making German policy appear consonant with Italy's aims in respect of French overseas territories – and emphasising a concentration on increasing its military power and on its need for new armaments. The general tone of Hitler's policy, Attolico concluded, had 'profoundly changed'.[26] The crisis, and its likely consequences, had a more immediate aspect, however: Hungarian intelligence, conveyed to Mussolini by Pariani, suggested that the change of guard made anschluss much more likely.[27]

Safeguarding kinship relations within his preferred primary group against any misunderstanding about the course he was temporarily pursuing, Ciano reassured Berlin in early February that the negotiations with London did not betoken any weakening of the Axis. Mussolini had fully accepted by the beginning of 1938 that the nazification of Austria was inevitable and indeed favoured it. The best that Italy could hope for was to delay it for as long as possible.[28] When anschluss came on 12 March, without any specific forewarning as far as Rome was concerned, Ciano confirmed the now well-established line of Italian policy by rejecting French pleas to concert common action and reassuring Berlin that 'we observe, and take part in nothing which is directed against Germany'.[29]

Mussolini portrayed the anschluss as the 'test' of the Axis. 'Now the Germans know,' he told the Chamber of Deputies on 16 March, 'that the Axis is not [just] a diplomatic construction efficient only in normal circumstances, but has shown itself to be solid especially in this exceptional hour in the history of the German world and of Europe'.[30] Unenthusiastic about German absorption of Austria but a political realist, Mussolini looked immediately for reassurance that Germany's guarantees regarding the Brenner frontier still stood. Confirmation that, far from contemplating action against Germany, he saw the two powers to be ideologically aligned came when he explained to the new German ambassador, von Mackensen, in mid-April that he was rejecting French approaches which involved withdrawing Italian 'volunteers' from Spain because Italy would not jeopardise the achievements of her troops there who 'were not fighting directly for their homeland but in a "political" war'.[31] Speaking at Genoa on 14 May, Mussolini portrayed his policy as one based on foresight which had frustrated Italy's anti-Fascist enemies who had wanted a collision between the two totalitarian states and maybe a war 'even if this had opened the gates to the triumph of bolshevism in Europe'.[32]

On 20 April von Mackensen reported, on the basis of information from a confidential informant with access to the thinking of the Foreign Ministry, that Italy expected the Czech problem to come to a head swiftly and that she 'will cause no difficulties whatsoever with respect to the solution which Germany deems most suitable'.[33] Mussolini's determination to 'hermetically seal' the borders with Germany, noted by Ciano the following day, was a defensive measure which is best interpreted as insurance against some unpredictable future 'turn' by a Germany that had demonstrated twice in two years that she could move with great rapidity when Hitler made up his mind to overturn the established order. Of more lasting concern were the economic consequences of anschluss. In 1937, 19.4 per cent of Italy's exports went to Germany and 3.68 per cent to Austria while Italy took only 5.3 per cent of German exports. In 1938 the proportion of Italian exports going to an expanded Germany was forecast to rise to 24.2 per cent. The imbalance made Italy acutely vulnerable to German price manipulation, and the balance across the exchanges could be worsened by moves such as a cut in German tourism.[34] In fact, economic forces were moving Italy inexorably under Germany's wing: coal imports from the Reich rose from 7,930,000 tons in 1937 to 9,000,000 tons in 1938, while at the same time exports of bauxite from Italy to Germany increased from 111,217 tons to 150,000 tons.[35]

Hitler's visit to Italy between 3 and 9 May 1938 was designed in part to showcase Italian power. Planning for 'Demonstration H', which took place on 5 May, began on 23 January. In the naval exercise, the battleship *Cavour* with the two heads of government on board was attacked by submarines and torpedo boats covered by smoke. After they were driven off, Hitler was then treated to a firing exercise.[36] The air force's share of the show, scheduled to last fifty minutes, involved a simulated attack on a naval-industrial centre which was contested by air defences, an exhibition of acrobatics by four squadrons of Cr. 32 aircraft, and a fly-past of fighter aircraft.[37] In the event assembling the aircraft over the target proved difficult as some of the formation leaders showed an 'inexplicable and stubborn incomprehension' of the need to synchronise watches.[38] Nevertheless, Hitler's visit 'further fed the illusion of power' of the Regia Aeronautica.[39]

The naval and air manoeuvres were reported to have had a profound effect on the visitors and on German newsreel audiences alike.[40] Mussolini was told that Hans Frank had regarded the naval review as 'stupefying', the Italian air force as having reached a level of perfection beyond that attained in Germany, and the army as impressive for its abilities and audaciousness – though he did add that it had carried out 'dangerous manoeuvre[s] which are not done in Germany'.[41] As was often the case, the desire to please and the wish to flatter combined to adulterate Italians' reporting about themselves.

In the course of the official visit von Ribbentrop made it plain that Germany might settle the Czech problem by force of arms, in which case she would move quickly before anyone else had time to react. When this might happen remained a matter of guesswork. Colonel Tripiccione, head of SIM, had left Berlin after an earlier visit with the strong impression that Germany would 'very soon' solve the Czech problem by force. After talking with admiral Canaris on the eve of Hitler's arrival in Rome, he was convinced that the Germans had changed their minds.[42] After Hitler had left Pariani asked Mussolini about the chances of military action and the scope of an Italian involvement in it. Mussolini's reply suggested that he was at least ready to back Hungarian territorial ambitions:

If nothing is asked of him, he would not force anything on the Hungarians. On the other hand, if the Hungarians demand anything we will do anything for them as we always have done.[43]

During Hitler's visit to Rome, von Ribbentrop offered Italy a military assistance pact which Ciano refused. In late June he broached the idea of a military alliance, reassuring Attolico that Germany would take on the 'liquidation' of Czechoslovakia herself – a task he thought could be done in a week – and would not expect Italian aid if a war broke out.[44] Shortly afterwards Pariani presented Mussolini with a proposal for a convention for technical military collaboration between Italy and Germany in which Hungary, which already had a similar convention with Italy, might also join. Although Mussolini and Ciano were favourable to the idea of an alliance, they were not yet ready to go ahead because the ground had not been prepared and because they had not yet squeezed everything out of the British. Pariani's proposal was accepted as a timely one.[45] It was also another step on Italy's road from Axis partner to ally.

Mussolini's readiness to step further down the path towards a full-blown military alliance was tempered by caution. Not only were Germany's designs on Czechoslovakia now evident but so were her interests elsewhere. At the end of June the Duce received a report from SIM that the Germans were undertaking what was evidently a co-ordinated programme of industrial and commercial penetration into countries of great interest to Italy. In Spain, they were trying to secure a monopoly on post-war civil, military and industrial reorganisation; in Hungary they were monopolizing the arms trade; in Yugoslavia they were looking for industrial control; and in Albania it was not clear what they were doing, but it was not in conformity with Italian interests.[46] Sent to Berlin on 10–11 July to prepare the ground for closer military collaboration, Pariani was told by Hitler that if England by diplomatic manoeuvrings towards either party were to split Germany and Italy apart then both would fall one after the other. Italy and Germany did not have 'conflicting' interests as Italy's 'line of march' was south to the Mediterranean while Germany's was north and east, but if there were any then they should be cleared up 'in order to establish clear lines of action in such a way as not to be open to any interpretative doubts'.[47] Germany was preparing for actively for war, but was still short of officers, men and raw materials. By 1940–1, Pariani estimated, she would have reached 'substantial efficiency'.[48]

After Munich the first thing on Mussolini's mind was the Anglo–Italian accords, which the British cabinet decided to bring into force on 26 October. Immediately thereafter, in what Ciano saw as a new order of things, he began to pursue his next objectives: the reduction of France's power in North and East Africa and the consolidation of Italian security in the Mediterranean. His initial goals were a condominium in Tunisia, joint control of the port of Djibouti and Italian control of its railway, and a revision of the tariffs on the Suez canal.[49] He also wanted direct control of Corsica. The Easter Accords, formally implemented by England on 16 November, would have no effect on his policy. In Europe the Axis remained 'fundamental', in the Mediterranean Italy would collaborate with the English for 'as long as it is possible', but France stayed 'out' and Italy's claims towards her were now specific.[50]

Mussolini's programme was publicly applauded when on 30 November 1938, after a speech by Ciano on foreign affairs, the Italian Chamber of Deputies rose in an orchestrated chant 'Tunisia, Corsica, Nice, Savoy!' Next day, in answer to a question from the French ambassador as to whether the 1935 Tunisian accord still stood, Ciano linked it to 'presuppositions' which had not occurred, first among them France's unfriendly attitude during the Ethiopian campaign.[51] From Paris, Guariglia reported that the French did not seem to understand that in going along with sanctions they had broken their agreement to give Italy a 'free hand' as embodied in the January accords. In his mind, the most pressing arguments for Italy's claims to Tunisia were not irredentist or nationalist but strategic and naval – the ease with which the narrow Sicilian channel could be blocked and the 'radical change which aviation has brought to the organisation of military defence in the Mediterranean'. The same argument held true for Corsica. France should be made aware of the menace that the two French possessions posed to Italian security, the possibility that England might one day consider a change in the Mediterranean status quo in Italy's favour, and the fact that Germany was prepared to press her support of Italy to the limit to obtain such a change.[52] On 17 December Ciano told ambassador François-Poncet that the January accords could no longer be considered in force.

If Mussolini's appetite for expansion was growing, Hitler's was evidently far from assuaged. It was clear, Ciano's brother-in-law reported from Berlin, that the Führer did not intend 'to go peacefully along the path of international co-operation'.[53] Even before the Munich crisis was over colonel Marras thought that Hitler's next targets were already clear: the Polish Corridor, Schleswig, Danzig and Memel.[54] Hungarian military intelligence and the Berlin embassy both considered Danzig and the Polish Corridor to be next on his list, and Hitler himself evidently did not regard the Czech question as liquidated. Another – and possibly larger – potential conflict also now loomed: 'the next big problem that will face us is the attack on Russia', Milch told Marras in mid-November.[55]

Somewhere and at some time in the future a war was evidently in the offing. As the two Axis powers' appetites grew keener, their military partnership began to solidify. The prospect of external support in the shape both of a tripartite pact and a set of secret bilateral military and naval accords covering specific war hypotheses was raised by the Japanese on the day of the Munich meeting. Mussolini felt that the Axis had no need of a defensive military pact with Tokyo. Until the aims to be achieved had been clearly defined by the three powers and a genuine friendship had come to exist between their peoples, an offensive alliance would be premature. When these preconditions had been met, and it was clear that a clash was inevitable, such an alliance would come naturally into being.[56] Pariani was more enthusiastic. A military agreement with Japan had great potential strategic importance as she would be able to exert pressure against Russia, England, and France on land and along the sea lanes to the Persian Gulf and the Red Sea.[57]

At the same time the German army high command revived the proposal for technical military collaboration between the two partners, limited for the time being to weapons and munitions, military vehicles, war production and anti-aircraft defence. Mussolini passed it on to Pariani with his imprimatur, and by the third week in December it had been agreed that the exchange of officers and information would be the basis for collaboration and an Italian military mission headed by the inspector of artillery was in Berlin to start an exchange of views. The fact that the German military seemed at last to have abandoned their reservations about their Italian opposite numbers, which 'favourably surprised' its head, suggested that joint military power was becoming an ever more important ingredient in the Italo–German political partnership.[58]

Reviewing the sinews of war

When the Commissione suprema began its annual *tour d'horizon* on 3 February 1938, Mussolini pointed out that little progress had been made in anti-aircraft defence. Spain provided some object lessons. The most recent bombardment of Barcelona had lasted eighty-nine seconds, during which time six- or seven-storey houses had been opened up 'like the pages of a book' by 200-kilogramme bombs while the sixty anti-aircraft batteries had not had time to fire a shot.[59] A rambling discussion which included the issue of whether or not to put up the price of cinema tickets to fund an expansion of the civilian national union for anti-aircraft protection produced some interesting statistics: Italy had only 168 batteries of modern anti-aircraft guns and could produce 250,000 gas masks a year but the public had only acquired 8,000 – at which point Mussolini asked if they had enough for the troops and had anyone thought of providing gas masks for horses. The answer to both questions was no. Eventually it was agreed that the war ministry, now in charge of anti-aircraft defence, must have enough money, that the air and naval ministries must chip in to cover the costs of defending their bases, and that Badoglio would 'formulate the provisions to define all the questions . . . relating to the defence of the objectives of pre-eminent interest to the Army, Navy and Air Force'.[60]

The discussion of economic autarchy was one of the lengthier sessions, lasting the whole of one meeting (which ran from 4 p.m. to 6.45 p.m.) and part of the next. Targets had been set by the National Council for Scientific Research, and the commission measured them against actual and forecast production – for once a useful procedure. Lantini, the minister for corporations, announced that the plans – most of which were for autarchy in peacetime – were expected to reach fruition in 1940–1. Grain supplies were sufficient, but imports were having to make up shortfalls in meat and fish – the latter providing the opportunity for a characteristically shapeless discussion which included a demand by Balbo that fishing with dynamite be heavily punished and another by Rossoni that the privileges of the Borromeo princes allowing them to prevent fishing on much of Lake Maggiore be withdrawn. Italy was also having to import leather and animal fats. She could produce only 35 per cent of the target in glycerine but five sixths of the cloth she would need in wartime. At the end of the day's session, during which Guarneri, the minister for financial exchange, had reported that during the current year Italy would have to pay 100,000,000 lire for fish imports and 90,000,000 lire for frozen meat and had paid out 300,000,000 lire in 1937 for meat on the hoof, Ciano thought that Italy was bankrupt. Mussolini disagreed: 'The situation in reality is very sound.'[61]

The next day the commission examined the situation as regarded minerals and fuel oils. Italy was almost wholly deficient in chrome, vanadium, molybdenum, tungsten, titanium and manganese. Aluminium, zinc and lead were all being produced at close to target amounts. Wartime consumption of rubber was put at 40,000 tons a year, but Italy's production of synthetic rubber (like Germany's) was a mere trickle: an experimental plant could produce a maximum of 50 kilos a day, and an industrial plant would not be ready for two and a half years. Showing great personal interest in this question, Mussolini wanted production speeded up and the necessary new factories located in central-southern Italy and the islands. His reasoning betrayed the influence that the First World War exercised in his mind: if this were not done then in the event of war 'once again the rural peasants of the islands and the south will go to the front to fight while the workers of the Po valley go into the factories'.[62]

The discussion ended with congratulations all round and the assertion that in wartime Italy must aim at all-round self-sufficiency as far as was humanly possible, 'given that she will be facing a complete blockade by land and sea'.[63] A complex discussion over the production of petroleum and ethyl alcohol, which grew bad-tempered when two members of the commission suggested that the authors of some of the background papers were either liars or fools, ended with Mussolini declaring that the Albanian wells would produce 80,000 tons of petrol in the current year and 200,000 tons in the following one and expressing pleasure that improvements in refining would make it possible to produce aviation fuel from it – something Valle had hitherto believed impossible.[64]

Leading a discussion on arms production on the penultimate day of the gathering, Cavagnari questioned whether Breda, the sole Italian manufacturer of automatic weapons, would be able to keep up with demand in case of war and pointed out that while the Fiume torpedo plant had produced a total of 300 torpedoes the navy needed 2,400 of them in order to have 3 for every tube. Indirectly raising a query over the policy being pursed by the *Commissariato generale per le fabbricazioni di guerra* under the direction of the aging general Alfredo Dallolio, he also stated that the navy needed special plant to manufacture such items as heavy guns and reinforced armour that was not suitable for meeting the army's needs. Dallolio was absent that day, but his deputy general Palcani responded by repeating his master's credo that it was not appropriate to split up interdependent parts of the 'industrial mobilisation complex', and reading out a chunk of a memorandum written by Dallolio in 1915 to justify his philosophy. The only way to overcome the shortage of war industries in peacetime, Dallolio believed, was to increase arms exportation. Mussolini wound up the discussion by backing two horses at once – as so often. Cavagnari was to establish a plan to bring the construction capacity in guns, armour and munitions into line with the navy's wartime needs and co-ordinate with Dallolio in realising it. Meanwhile the commission reaffirmed the principle of 'the unity of industrial mobilisation' so that all three armed services 'can rely completely on the totalitarian industrial sector and any element of that sector can be put at the service of any of the armed forces'.[65]

The likelihood of war with England in North Africa was reflected in the consideration the commission gave to the military organisation and offensive/defensive capabilities of Libya and Italian East Africa. A paper produced on Mussolini's behalf as minister for Italian Africa by his under-secretary, Teruzzi, acknowledged that it had not been possible to reduce the numbers of troops in Ethiopia from 300,000 to 68,000 by the end of December 1937, as had been planned, because of 'rebellions' and 'symptoms of revolt' in Gojjam and Showa. The numbers of colonial and metropolitan Italian troops in action had in fact never descended below 210,000. However, with entirely unwarranted optimism, Teruzzi announced that crisis had 'reached its culminating point and was now moving, albeit slowly and with hard work, towards a solution'.[66] The obvious military value of the colony was such that England was conducting a campaign on the borders of the Sudan, at times open and at times concealed, to foment rebellion. In a war against England and France, its military functions would be to threaten Djibuti and Somaliland, French Somalia and Kenya, and take decisive action against the Sudan. If isolated from Italy, either by the closure of the Suez canal or because the *madrepatria* chose not to reinforce and resupply East Africa, it must be able to stand on its own.

The outlook was far from gloomy though – or so Teruzzi professed to believe – because the colony could be supplied by unspecified allies (presumably Japan) or neutrals via the Indian Ocean. The Duce had ordered that a 'black army' of at least 300,000 be raised, of which number 116,000 men were already under arms fighting the rebels. As well as for home defence, they might be used either in unspecified 'extra-European countries' where combat conditions were more suited to them or, more likely, in operations against neighbouring colonies.[67] To them would be added 100,000 white colonists (four fifths of whom were already in place), 400 aircraft and sufficient ships to protect the ports and their approaches. On the issue of stocks, the minister painted an equally rosy picture. The colony possessed 300,000 rifles with 1,000 rounds of ammunition each, 800 artillery pieces with 2,712,000 rounds, three and a half months' supply of petrol, seven months' worth of diesel and lubricants, and modern automobile repair plants at Asmara, Addis Ababa and Mogadishu.[68]

The air force saw the central and eastern Mediterranean and the Red Sea as a single theatre of operations which could not be divided into separate operational sectors 'without producing a dangerous fragmentation of force'.[69] A lack of sufficient bases and logistical difficulties in keeping those available supplied meant that only limited forces could be maintained on the Aegean islands; they would be employed to attack the coasts of Syria and Palestine, the Suez canal and possibly the south-east coasts of Greece. Libya, which had a good network of airports, was regarded as the hub of strategic operations in the region and would have need of little or no aid from the metropole. Although vague about the details of the situation in Italian East Africa, the air ministry was confident that it was already in a condition to be able to develop 'operations of large proportions and at long distances' and therefore to 'contribute directly or indirectly to our operations based on Libya and the Aegean'.[70] While it was prepared to allow the units in east Africa a large degree of autonomy, those located in Libya and the Aegean should not as at present come under the authority of the governors of those colonies but should be fully at the disposal of the chief of air staff in Rome.

The navy reported that Benghasi, the least exposed port in wartime, could handle only five to seven ships at a time, could not undertake disembarkations from the roadstead in wartime due to the danger from submarines, was subjected to strong winds, and lacked port defences against air and naval attack. Urgent works were necessary, but as far as the latter requirement was concerned the navy could only indicate the problem 'not being able to contribute in any way to its solution because of innumerable other obligations'.[71] Tobruk lacked quays and needed a protective breakwater and water tanks before it could be used to disembark major units. Only Tripoli was in a state to undertake immediate landing operations, though its wharves lacked cranes and it was close to French bases in Tunisia. As far as operations in the Red Sea and Indian Oceans were concerned, they could only be prepared by the local force commanders under the direction of the viceroy.

Pariani took much the most positive line. The army saw mastery of the eastern Mediterranean and the Red Sea as being 'probably the decisive factor' in a war against Britain, France and Russia since this would hold open a vitally important supply artery when the enemy was trying 'to close central Europe in a ring of steel'.[72] Moreover such mastery would be a severe setback for English prestige. North Africa was presently self-sufficient only in salt, but could have oil, meat, fish, wool, leather, alcohol, wine, beer, tobacco and paper in abundance. Everything else would have to be imported. Italian East Africa was better off, being already self-sufficient in such products as meat, coffee, salt, bananas and wood, but would certainly need to import fuel and lubricants. Given the difficulties of developing major operations in the Alps, North Africa would become the pre-eminent theatre of war because of its role in dominating the central Mediterranean and as the starting point for an offensive directed on the Suez canal. Defensive works were under way in Libya, but logistic support in the shape of port facilities, magazines and depots, supplies and communications were all lacking. In East Africa, where development was being slowed down (by the increasing resistance to Italian rule, although Pariani did not say so), supplies and communications were the priorities. He urged that the necessary works be undertaken immediately.

Teruzzi began the discussion, briefly describing the poor condition of the ports in the former Abyssinia and loyally confirming that in accordance with the Duce's orders and intentions the empire was 'marching with a markedly accelerated step' despite the outbreaks of rebellion which were on the decline.[73] In this respect at least his servile optimism was entirely misplaced. Mussolini then took over. The country was six times the size of Italy, he told his assembled notables, so that it would take longer than five years to put it on a sound economic footing. The costs of the necessary road building, for one thing, were high but unavoidable. While the peripheries – Somalia, Harrar and Eritrea – were calm, the situation in the Amhara centre of the country was 'not serious but simply bothersome'. Referring to his recall of Rodolfo Graziani the previous November and his replacement by the Duca d'Aosta, he explained that he had ordered a change of scene because policy had been wrong and the Italians had not been racially prepared.

When you promise an Abyssinian something, you must give it; when you take a carpet, you must pay him. And above all you must not lower the prestige of our race. When an Italian soldier robs and kills an Abyssinian, it will be said that Italy cannot bring civilisation to the country.[74]

Given Mussolini's exhortations to slaughter Abyssinians eighteen months earlier, and his support of Graziani's brutal policy of reprisals after the attempt on his life in February 1937, this was a remarkable volte-face. The explanation lay in his next remark. The Showans and the Amhara were the warrior races of Ethiopia and it was they whom he proposed to make the core of the million-man army he expected to quarry from the conquered population.

Balbo, who had previously submitted two papers on Libya, briefly summarised what he described as the gradual economic advance in cereal production and animal husbandry he was overseeing before passing to the question of the military organisation of the colony In the most likely war scenario, Libya would have to withstand an attack on her western frontier by 100,000 French troops with 30–35,000 forces of her own. When taken together with the construction of fortifications between Medenine and Gabes, these numbers dictated a strategic defensive on that front. To that end, a *progetto di copertura* was now under way to block the main invasion routes and organise the appropriate garrisons and mobile troops, the latter based on the fortified camp at Tripoli. Balbo was taking a number of steps to improve the quality of the troops in Libya, including the 'cautious' employment of motorisation and the introduction of obligatory military service for a term of three months backed by regional centres of recruitment and mobilisation. If all went well, he expected to complete his arrangements before the year was out.[75] All was approved, with the rider that all the Italian territories overseas and East Africa in particular should be put in conditions of 'absolute self-sufficiency for a long period' as soon as possible and as much as possible.[76]

Opening the final session of the commission, Mussolini responded to criticisms of Italy's tardiness in imposing economic discipline by pointing out that no one should think other countries were in a 'particularly brilliant situation'. England faced problems that were 'almost insoluble' and were acknowledged in an official report which concluded that in the event of war the country could consider itself 'a maritime fortress under siege'. To feed her population she had to import 70,000,000 quintals of grain a year – almost four times the amount Italy imported. Added to this were 20,000,000 tons of food imports, 17,000,000 tons of mineral imports and 12,000,000 tons of petrol. In the event of war this 'colossal provisioning' would be possible only if there were adequate port facilities and a sufficient merchant fleet, but 'well-informed circles' believed that the British fleet was short of 1,000 merchant ships. Thus England too would face serious difficulties, especially if a fleet of submarines could operate along the trade routes for fifty or sixty days.[77] Since neither of the Axis powers possessed a fleet of ocean-going submarines and Germany was planning a cruiser campaign against English shipping, it was far from obvious how advantage could yet be taken of the weakness that the Duce had identified to his own evident satisfaction.

The difficulties Italy would face in the event of war were underlined when Galeazzo Ciano provided the commission with a written commentary on the new American Neutrality Act which had been ratified by president Roosevelt on 1 May 1937. It posed greater difficulties for Italy than the legislation it replaced. Not only had Roosevelt extended the new laws to include civil wars, and substituted a general ban on American citizens travelling on belligerents' ships for the discretionary power he had previously enjoyed, but most important of all he had extended the ban on direct or indirect trading with belligerents to include goods other than arms, munitions and war materials. 'Cash and Carry' meant that belligerents would now have to collect and transport goods on non-American ships and pay for them in advance. If applied to Italy, it would mean 'the almost complete closure of the American market as a source of supply [for us]'.[78] Substitute supplies of coal and cotton would be particularly hard hit, but so would mineral oils, copper, scrap iron, machine-tools and parts. The new legislation would also mean that a power having effective control of the ocean could deny its adversary access to American goods even on the new terms. In effect, the United States was siding with the western democracies against Germany and Italy.

Notwithstanding all this, the foreign minister was able to look on the bright side. The law had a term of only two years. If it were to be applied during that time, there would inevitably be an interlude between the embargo on munitions of war and that on other goods during which

American public opinion might move in such a way as to make the president think again. Moreover, it had failed its first test of fire when Roosevelt had chosen not to apply it in the Sino–Japanese war because it would have favoured the Japanese. Nevertheless, 'the maximum account' had to be taken of it when sizing up the international situation and determining Italy's line of conduct.[79]

There was no discussion whatsoever of the implications of the new legislation for Italy's programme of autarchy. After listening to a brief report to the effect that 5,000 new railway carriages would be in service by the end of the biennial 1937–8, and being told that if the railways had to provide more transport than they had done in the world war then the country would face grave difficulties, Mussolini approved Ciano's conclusion that 'Cash and Carry' had to be taken into account in the dispositions made for provisioning the nation in war without giving any clue as to exactly how this was going to be done.[80]

Although Mussolini expressed only positive reactions to the progress apparently being made in the progress towards autarchy and war, the battery of negative statistics clearly made some impression on him. Three weeks after he closed its final session, he travelled with Ciano by car to attend D'Annunzio's funeral. 'Throughout the entire journey', his companion recorded, 'he did nothing but observe the large quantities of unnecessary iron that is found lying about in the countryside'.[81]

Naval strategies and suppositions

It was apparent at the beginning of the year that the British naval building programme for 1938–9 was expected to include five new battleships, some of which could displace more than 35,000 tons, seven cruisers and various light craft. Whether the battleships would exceed the 35,000-ton and 14-inch gun limits seemed initially unlikely.[82] The British building programme was a response to the evident Japanese intentions to build cruisers and battleships which exceeded the limits laid down in the Washington Treaty. There was thus also the possibility that the British would equip the new *King George V* class battleships with 16-inch guns not the 14-inch ones initially planned. The *Queen Elizabeth* and the *Warspite*, which were still under construction, were being given more powerful engines, thicker deck armour and improved secondary armament.[83] The Defence white paper published in March 1938 indicated that Britain expected to bring some sixty new warships totalling 130,000 tons into service between April 1938 and March 1939 and by the start of June London indicated that it was prepared to build 40,000-ton battleships.[84]

While the British naval programme added to the negative side of the international balance as far as the Italian navy was concerned, the Japanese programme worked to the advantage of the Axis. Japan's intention to make what the Italian naval attaché in Tokyo described as 'a weighty increment' to their navy was a new factor in international naval calculations. Despite the web of secrecy surrounding her intentions, it appeared that since she was unable for financial reasons to compete in quantitative terms with the United States and Great Britain, she intended to do so qualitatively. Her programme was the expression of political intentions to expand not merely in China but also southwards, so that Japanese naval circles were now studying offensive war 'in theatres of operations at some distance from their homeland'. Translated into tangible factors, this meant greater concern with the speed and range of warships, increasing numbers of long-range submarines, five new 9,000-ton cruisers, a 14,000-ton aircraft carrier, and four high speed and long-range 46,000-ton battleships with 406-mm guns (three were already under construction) – the latter built on the assumption that it would be difficult for Britain to concentrate a squadron of equal strength at Singapore.[85]

All this was good news for Rome. So was the information that the Japanese navy regarded the new naval building being undertaken by the United States as a sign that she was trespassing beyond her legitimate interests in the Eastern Pacific and challenging Japan's defensive interests in the Western Pacific, for it represented a potential distraction for a democratic power whose intentions might not be threatening but whose potential most certainly was – as Ciano had demonstrated to the Commissione suprema di difesa.[86]

As far as the French navy was concerned, Darlan made it plain at the start of the year that, while recognising the need for the combined action of surface craft, submarines and aircraft, he was at heart a 'battleship admiral'. They were, he claimed, cheaper in unit costs per ton than any other type of ship or aeroplanes, had a much longer working life, and in the case of battleships over 25,000 tons were virtually impervious to sinking by submarines.[87] In the discussions carried on during the spring and early summer, in which the French appeared to be seeking to persuade the British to preserve the 35,000-ton limit by persuading Germany, Italy and Russia to do the same, the Germans made it clear that they were not disposed to bind themselves in any way that might trigger automatic limitations on their rights as laid down in the Anglo–German naval treaty. France was evidently anxious to limit the naval building competition that had just begun, but Rome noted her failure to persuade London and Washington to commit to building only two battleships that exceeded treaty limits.[88]

In Rome Capponi, speaking with the authority of one who had closely observed British policy and with acquaintances in the highest naval circles, believed that British public opinion about Italy had changed markedly over 1935–6: 'first surprise, then growing irritation and finally a deeper aversion and a growing respect for us'. English anti-Italianism had steadily intensified and was now 'an established fact'. One of the decisive features of the moment was the centrifugal tendencies of the British empire, evident since the Statute of Westminster in 1931, which was encouraging the Foreign Office to move towards a return to the entente cordiale with France and to attempt to revive the League of Nations as a coercive force so that the empire could be mobilised on its behalf. The other was the possibility that 'the two great pillars of the Empire', sterling and the Royal Navy, might suffer blows, as the former had done in China and the latter in the Mediterranean. In the event of war he had no doubt that the English would attempt at all costs to hold on to the Mediterranean; the evidence lay in the work going on at Malta, Alexandria, Haifa and Cyprus and in the determined wooing of Turkey presently evident. Since she could not hope to maintain her position in the Central Mediterranean without coming to an understanding with Italy, she would defend her route to India and her Cairo-Cape axis by concentrating on the Eastern Mediterranean.[89]

The supplementary Italian naval programme officially announced on 7 January 1938 comprised two battleships, twelve destroyer leaders, four ocean-going and twelve other submarines. It was planned to take four years and reach completion in June 1942. Its justification lay, in the navy's eyes, in a multitude of factors: the requirement to get men and materials from the new empire, the failure of the London Naval Conference, the 'politics of incomprehension' which seemed to be established in several governments, and the naval arms race which had demonstrably restarted. Italy needed a navy which was 'no longer Mediterranean but oceanic'. Like that of other countries, the 'dorsal spine' of her programme was the battleship.[90] By no means everyone shared Cavagnari's fixation with battleships, and elements within the naval staff were not entirely happy with the programme. It contained no aircraft carriers, although they had been recommended in the 1937 force study. They were seen as 'indispensable' in future programmes and two should be constructed between 1940–2 and 1942–4. Nor did the plan contain any cruisers, though naval planning for operations in the Indian Ocean depended on them, and the naval staff recommended that eight should be built between 1939 and 1943. The submarine programme was the only element which offered the prospect of qualified superiority: by July 1944 Italy would have 119 submarines to France's 104, Germany's 101 and England's 83. The navy staff wanted an expanded programme with a total cost of 3,500,000,000 lire.[91] The plan – typical of the 'blue seas' thinking of which the navy was demonstrably capable – would doubtless have foundered on budgetary considerations had Cavagnari not publicly pronounced roundly against aircraft carriers in March.

The programme hit trouble immediately when Dallolio said it could go ahead only if the ministry for currency and foreign exchange could provide the necessary money to buy in raw materials. The minister said he could not and that Dallolio must make use of what he already had. Dallolio thereupon at once ordered that no material be supplied for the new programme. Cavagnari appealed to Mussolini to prevent it being strangled at birth: the yards needed to produce 2,000 tons of worked material if the *Impero* was to be started as planned. In all, 35–40,000 tons of metal 'with a very limited value in foreign currency' was needed; he asked for it to be committed in advance of funding 'while waiting for a final resolution of the general problem which will presumably take some weeks'. A partial answer was initially found by juggling the year's 84,000-ton steel allocation to the navy to 'advance' 1,500 tons from the December amount.[92] In the event, Dallolio, who believed that new programmes should be covered by new allocations from newly available raw materials, was forced to cede ground: from June onwards he had to increase the naval allocation from 7,000 tons of metals a month to 10,000 tons and assign an extra 31,000 tons of iron to the navy with only limited increases in the stocks he controlled.[93]

While the construction programmes for 1934–5 (including the *Littorio* and *Vittorio Veneto*), 1936–7 and 1937–8 were all on time, the 1938–9 programme depended on material allocations that had not been made. However, they were by no means the only problem the navy faced. Even supposing that everything that was requested was forthcoming, delays of between four and ten months were forecast in completing eight out of twelve destroyer leaders, four ocean-going submarines and twelve smaller submarines because the factories could not keep up with the work. Torpedo reserves ordered in 1936–7 and 1937–8 would not be ready until 1940, and those ordered in 1938–9 were due to be completed by June 1942 – unless there were problems providing the necessary raw materials.[94] Nor could the navy afford to lengthen the naval basin at Naples to 300 metres so that it could take the new battleships.

The funding to pay for the programme, which amounted to a total of 4,220,000,000 lire, was spread by the Finance ministry through the annual naval budgets from 1940–1 to 1943–4. The navy found itself being asked to pay for the reequipment of shipyard plant, now particularly in need of additional specialised machine tools from Germany to cut armour plate and gears, as well as a variety of lathes, shears, fast iron-cutting saws and the like.[95] One of the two steel plants, SIAC, declared that it would need fifty-four months to produce the steel needed for a 19,000-ton ship and then only if the other, Terni, took over the manufacture of the 381-mm guns and ceded an equivalent proportion of the smaller guns to SIAC. After a lengthy argument over the price the navy would have to pay per kilo of steel, for which it offered 5.50 lire a kilo and the steel companies asked 15.20 lire per kilo, both sides settled at Cavagnari's suggestion on 8.75 lire.[96]

Paying for the programme was not merely administratively complex but generally difficult: the Italian trade deficit in 1938 amounted to 776,000,000 lire, and as the minister for exchange and currency pointed out to Cavagnari, Italian exports were in continuous decline in both quantity and in value.[97] By July 1938 the navy was anticipating that it would have to delay staged payments to the shipyards and pay interest on the late payments.

News of the Italian naval building programme, picked up by French naval intelligence the previous November, and the realisation that for the next four years and more the French navy could be beaten if it acted alone in any theatre triggered a response which saw six billion francs invested in a five-year programme to build 743,558 tons of shipping by 1943.[98] Italian naval intelligence reported that the French intended before the end of the year to start building two aircraft carriers, a cruiser, three destroyers, five submarines and a number of torpedo boats. In April 1938 the British and American governments announced their intention to derogate from the 35,000-ton limit on battleship size imposed under the Washington Treaty. Although they did not announce the calibre of the guns on their new battleships, in early June the French confirmed their intention not to build beyond the treaty limit in size unless other continental naval powers did so. In July came the news that an additional one billion francs had been added to the French naval budget in order to fund the construction of two new battleships, a 24,000-ton cruiser and various light craft. The 26,300-ton battleship *Strasbourg*, sister to the *Dunkerque*, was now finished and ready to undergo trials.[99]

German reaction to the prospect that the Washington Treaty limits on battleships were about to go up in smoke was founded on the possibility that Britain might initially undertake a three-ship 40,000-ton programme but then up-rate the third to 45,000 tons, leaving Germany (with a single 40,000-ton ship) at a greater disadvantage, and on the probability that since Japan was building 45,000-ton warships Russia would do the same. Berlin therefore hoped that she could act in concert with Italy in reacting to the proposed new limits.[100] The Italian naval staff was not persuaded either by the German arithmetic or by the likelihood that Britain would disrupt an 'organic' programme by altering a third warship. They did, however, register a strong interest in holding London to the 40,000-ton limit 'because given the rhythm of our naval construction it is not very likely that we shall lay down any new battleships before 1940–41, at which time British construction characteristics can [then] be clear'.[101] Behind this lay the recognition that Italy could only afford 'an exiguous number' of the *supercolossi* that Japan and America were proposing to build, which would weaken her strategic position, that they brought in their wake additional expense in reconstructing ports and basins and dredging deeper channels to accommodate them, and that up until December 1942 there would be no financial margin in the sums already voted from which to fund any expansion in size.[102]

As well as announcing its construction programme, the Italian naval staff updated its plans for war against a combination of powers including England, France, Greece, Turkey and Egypt, making provision in them for the possibility of German participation alongside Italy (Alpha 1), and also its studies for a single-handed war with Albania against France, Yugoslavia, the Soviet Union and possibly Turkey and Spain, again possibly with German help (Beta 3). Plans for war against Germany were not updated, 'not being urgent'. The various naval directives which defined the operational tasks for the main war plans changed to reflect some of the shifts in Italian foreign policy. Thus the plans for war in the Lower Adriatic now replaced Yugoslavia with Greece as a potential aggressor against Albania. A new set of directives was in preparation for the defence of naval traffic, based on the period of Anglo–Italian tension in 1935–6. While directives for operations in East Africa and the Eastern Mediterranean were ready, those in respect of the central and western Mediterranean were still waiting for clarification on two major matters – how the defence of the Sicilian channel was going to be organised and what the expeditionary force would be that would have to be transported to North Africa. As far as directives for naval operations in the Atlantic and Indian Oceans were concerned, 'very little has been done'.[103]

A number of major questions remained unresolved. Plan AA to send a one-division expeditionary force to Albania to defend the petroleum basin against a possible Greek coup-de-main was under study. As far as operations in North Africa were concerned, Pariani had ruled out an offensive on the Sudan and Egypt from East Africa, leaving on the table a defensive on the Tunisian frontier and an offensive on the Egyptian frontier. The former operation would require six divisions, the latter ten. The navy had begun provisional study of the transportation and maintenance of the army forces in Libya but was still awaiting official confirmation of their exact make-up.[104] It did not know under what circumstances it would be called on to carry out Plan AZ for operations in the Upper Adriatic; in its opinion this should not be done in the event of a general conflict in which England was involved, but only in a war against France and Yugoslavia. It wished to transfer resources from the region to the North African coast in particular. Despite having enquired in December, it had no idea in January of the composition of an expeditionary force it might have to convey to North Africa and protect and was still waiting for information two months later.[105]

As part of the development of plans for Italo–German co-operation, the naval staff produced a study in January 1938 of how Italy might obtain supplies in a war in which Italy, Germany and Japan fought England, France and Russia. Little could be expected to come from the Scandinavian states since, provided that their foreign policies allowed it, their export surpluses would be largely taken up by Germany. Consequently, the sources on which Italy could draw comprised the central and eastern European states, Central and South America and the United States. The likely effect of the American Neutrality Acts – confirmed by Ciano a few days later – and the fact that the Suez canal and the Straits would certainly be barred to Italy by England and Turkey led the navy to conclude that maximum use had to be made of continental European sources of supply. The 'alliance' with the Nationalists meant in theory that some goods could transit Spain, and that the consequent 'devaluation' of the British naval base at Gibraltar and the free use of the Balearics would make it worth risking running traffic into the western Mediterranean. However, the navy dismissed the possibility of running five or even three ships a day through the Straits to make up the shortfalls in supplies as 'inadmissible' in the conflict under consideration, and concluded that the solution had to be found in the formation of stockpiles of supplies, the realisation of the plan for autarchy and a reduction in wartime consumption.[106] In this respect, naval policy and strategy was in tune with the conclusions of the supreme defence commission and at odds with economic reality.

A rehearsal of what were by now well-known statistics about Italy's import requirements produced the conclusion that the European railway system could carry over 90 per cent of the 12,170,000 tons of imports which came from the continent, an amount that represented 58 per cent of her total requirement of 20,800,000 tons. The most prominent problem was fuel oils. Romania exported some 7,000,000 tons a year, and it was intended to import 1,000,000 tons of that amount by rail via Yugoslavia. The problem of autarchy might be solved as far as fuel oils went if the number of railway tankers was increased, greater use was made of the Danube, and a 900-kilometre oil pipeline was built between Romania and Fiume which could carry 2,000,000 tons of oil a year.[107] As the navy effectively admitted, the only way to make supply balance demand was to make optimistic assumptions: that substitutes would be found for minerals and foodstuffs, that the population would cut its consumption, that stocks would be built up, and that one day the policy of autarchy would free the country – to 'a presently incalculable extent' – from its subjection to external suppliers of wood, meat, oils and fertilisers.[108]

As far as Italian East Africa was concerned, the navy looked unpalatable truths straight in the face. The empire was cut off from all sources of supply save North and South America, and supplying it with fuel alone would require twenty-three of the eighty-five tankers Italy possessed and some hired vessels as well. Costs, climatic problems such as monsoons, and vulnerability to enemy attack meant that imports in wartime would be minimal and therefore that for military operations the empire 'would have to rely almost entirely on its own stocks and its local resources'.[109] No help could be expected from Japan as regarded supplies. Combined operations by the two navies in the Indian Ocean and the Gulf of Aden might improve matters, but they in turn depended on getting the naval base at Kisimaio ready to support them.

As well as using its own staff, the naval planning process called on the services of a 'think tank' in the shape of the Sezione Alti Studi, a group of middle-ranking officers temporarily attached to the Istituto Superiore di Guerra. In January 1938 it was tasked to examine five war scenarios involving England, France and Spain as enemies in various combinations and Germany and Japan as allies waiting to intervene and was specifically requested to look at the possibilities for Italian naval operations in the Atlantic near Gibraltar. A second area of analysis, daytime and night-time escort and protection of naval forces and convoys, reflected the navy's obsession with what it had seen for more than a decade and still saw as its most important task.[110]

Detailed planning for Alpha 1 (Italy and Germany versus England, France, Turkey, Greece, Egypt and the USSR) and Beta 1 (Italy versus France, Greece, the USSR and Turkey) was complete by 1 July 1938, though the material was only in draft form and needed the agreement of the top staff officials before it could be published and distributed to the fleet.[111] In the first case, the enemy was expected to conduct a war of exhaustion. In order to keep open communications with the eastern Mediterranean they were expected to have to fight an active war in the central Mediterranean, perhaps attempting the occupation of Sicily or of the coast of Tripolitania. If the war was short and decided on the land frontiers, the Italian navy would adopt an aggressive stance and risk heavy losses. If it were long, action in the western Mediterranean would be dangerous and bring no concrete results. In these circumstances the navy would undertake a counter-offensive in the central Mediterranean and take the offensive in the eastern Mediterranean, covering Tobruk and the Aegean, perhaps provoking the defection of minor states, and combining with land operations to open the Suez canal. In the former case, Pantelleria and Taranto would be of major importance as operational bases for surface craft, cruisers and submarines. In the latter case, Tobruk and Augusta would be Italy's main bases and underwater weapons such as human torpedoes would have first to be used to weaken the enemy fleet before it would be possible to launch surface actions co-ordinated with the army to open the Suez canal. Surface action in the Atlantic was excluded, but submarines would be used against commercial traffic. In any such war, the Italo–German forces would be notably inferior to those of their enemies. However, the planners believed that if Italy took the initiative and started the conflict by surprise '[we] will be able to secure initial successes that will improve the strategic situation in a way indispensable for the prosecution of the war in conditions that are not entirely unfavourable'.[112]

In a single-handed war against France and her allies, the planners expected the French to seek to isolate Italy, safeguard their communications with North Africa and link up with their eastern allies. To obtain these ends the French fleet would seek to bring the Italian navy to battle in order to weaken or destroy it by luring it into attacking French transports. In the eastern Mediterranean, the navies of France's smaller allies would attack the route from Suez to Italy, the islands and Italian traffic in the Aegean, the Adriatic coasts and traffic there. To meet this threat the Italian fleet would be held together to take advantage of its position on interior lines, acting on the defensive in the eastern Mediterranean, the counter-offensive in the west, and the offensive in the centre. Exactly how the French were to be forced or encouraged into battle was not clearly specified, though it was thought that the careful selection of coastal objectives might fire the traditionally combative French morale which would be unwilling to stomach Italian initiative.[113]

The naval planners picked up some information about how their plans might fare against potential opponents from their naval exercises. A British exercise carried out at Malta between 1–3 June in which an attempted landing was driven off showed the effectiveness of the air defences in spotting attacking forces and trailing them through the night, but also showed how MAS boats could be used for night-time attacks.[114] French naval exercises simulating a war with Italy and Germany, carried out 21–3 June 1938 as part of its accelerated planning for a Mediterranean war in the aftermath of the anschluss, gave the Italians important cryptographical information about the codes the French would use on mobilisation and equally useful information about the initial French moves in the event of such a war, particularly the staging of troop convoys from North Africa.[115]

Pariani's preparations and plans

During the spring of 1938 Pariani carried forward the transformation of the army he proposed to use either in North Africa or in Europe, though not without some internal criticism – particularly for disregarding the lessons of the Spanish Civil War. Three-regiment divisions were to be transformed into two-regiment divisions (*binaria*) at a rate to be determined by the needs of the defences on the French Alpine frontier.[116] Motorised units must aim, in order of importance, for autonomy (the capacity to operate for twelve hours at fifteen kilometres an hour over varied terrain), speed, armament (not to be to the detriment of the former two), and armour protection. The army was to be freed of the idea that tanks were 'for breakthroughs in the sense of beating down obstacles' and to develop the concept that they were 'the essential element in manoeuvres *en masse*'.[117] As part of his revolutionary new schema for war, Pariani also wanted to mobilise ten million men and to have an equal proportion of combatants and non-combatants.[118]

A last-ditch stand by general Ottavio Zoppi in the senate on 29 March 1938 failed to halt the reforms, in part because he was largely unsupported but also because his arguments were so complex as to be, at least on the surface, self-contradictory. Zoppi claimed that because they had the same amount of artillery as the old three-regiment divisions, the *binaria* divisions were not in fact lighter but heavier, and then rebutted the argument that to match other European armies they needed more guns by claiming on the basis of his experience in the First World War that artillery could be 'manoeuvred' and concentrated where it was most needed. For the same reason, Zoppi acknowledged that the new divisions had a greater penetrating power – but only as far as the artillery could reach. Beyond that point, extra divisions would have to be brought forward.[119] In fact, the new formations brought with them a number of other problems which included an increased burden on the mobilisation machinery, a shortage of suitably qualified senior officers and a need for more and particularly better weaponry.

When Mussolini had allocated extraordinary funds of 5.5 milliard lire for the years 1936/7 and 1937/8, Baistrocchi had signed an undertaking not to ask for any more money until 30 June 1938. Bound by his predecessor's undertaking, Pariani was seriously short of the money needed to arm and equip his army. The consequences were particularly apparent as regarded artillery. In response to an enquiry from his office, Badoglio learned in early February that the army possessed only 307 guns, mostly of 20-mm to 75-mm calibres; a further 2,286 were on order of which only 88 were medium and heavy calibre; and 2,714 guns were 'programmed', almost all of them light calibre and with no specified delivery dates.[120] Alarmed by this news, and by further information that of the 18,586,870 rounds of ammunition needed Pariani's plans would produce only 5,386,142 by the end of 1938, Badoglio warned Mussolini and asked for more money, which he wanted spent solely on the artillery.

Aware of the need for greater firepower to strengthen the *binaria* divisions, as well as the competing demands of frontier defence, anti-aircraft defence and motorisation, Pariani sought a five- or ten-year arms and munitions programme and also wanted the levels of production in war to be determined 'so as to be able to give an indication to industry of what will meet [our] needs'.[121] In May 1938, he put forward a ten-year rearmament programme for 24,500,000,000 lire which would have improved matters. On 27 July Mussolini gave him 5,000,000,000 lire to spend in five years; in the event he received two fifths of his original requested sum between August 1938 and April 1939. The 1938 arms programme which these monies funded provided for 1,098 light howitzers and guns for the new *binaria* divisions and 1,108 anti-aircraft guns. This pattern of reequipment, which accorded with Pariani's designs but did not meet Badoglio's preference for an army stocked with lots of artillery of all calibres, was to an extent unavoidable. A lack of productive capacity which was the consequence of the army's failure to place substantial orders up to now and of a stock of aged machine-tools which proved difficult to replace meant that Italian industry could only manufacture sixty-five guns a month. On 1 September, as the Munich crisis began to accelerate, the central armaments manufacturing commission presented a programme to raise output to 250 guns a month.[122]

The transformation of the experimental armoured brigades into armoured divisions went ahead to the accompaniment of a debate as to whether they should have more than two battalions of motorised infantry and some artillery (presently they had none), whether they first needed more tanks (210 instead of the current strength of 120), and whether they were best used to break through the enemy or to exploit success, in which case the infantry, artillery, engineers and support services would need armoured vehicles. The answer to these questions came in the shape of a *Stralcio e promemoria sulla Divisione Corazzata* issued in May 1938. The development of anti-tank weapons made tanks less useful as weapons of breakthrough and more useful as instruments of exploitation. The new armoured divisions would comprise four tank battalions, a company of armoured cars, two battalions of bersaglieri on motorcycles, a regiment of artillery and two batteries of 20-mm anti-aircraft guns. *La Dottrina tattica nelle realizzazioni dell'anno XVI*, a circular published on 28 October 1938, put mechanisation firmly at the heart of the *guerra di rapido corso*. The armoured divisions would use tanks *en masse*, preferably against the flanks of the enemy positions, and the infantry likewise to break the enemy line, after which the motorised forces would exploit their success.[123]

The concept of combining armoured and motorised divisions into a new kind of mass assault unit which was already tested in war and which would be always ready to act on Italy's land frontiers grew partly out of the likelihood that elements of the CTV would soon be repatriated from Spain (a notion which was quickly abandoned) and partly out of Pariani's desire to have an army in the Paduan region which would be available for immediate employment, as dictated by the war plans.[124] The new formation, named the *Armata del Po* and constituted in November 1938 under the command of general Ettore Bastico, was made up of one army corps of three celeri divisions and a second comprising two of the new armoured divisions (Ariete and Centauro) and two motorised divisions. For the time being – and at least on paper – Pariani had put Italy 'in the vanguard in the matter of mechanisation'.[125]

The planners' conceptions of how the *Armata del Po* might be used in wartime were not clearly spelled out until the end of December 1938, and then only after Bastico had complained that although he had been given various zones of concentration to study he did not know on what operational designs they had been prefigured. As far as the western frontier was concerned, the defensive posture proposed in PR 12 ruled out its use in initial offensive operations; its role would therefore be to act as a manoeuvre force to re-establish a situation 'compromised by a sudden enemy irruption' or to undertake a counter-offensive manoeuvre. On the northern front it could expect to have to undertake immediate operations to occupy the Carynthian pocket around Tarvisio; the possibility that it would be based on Mila and employed against the Swiss frontier was much less likely. On the eastern front, where operations of a 'distinctively offensive character' were envisaged, it would be deployed east of a line from Udine to Trieste with Lubljana as its objective. Although no specific plans to use it elsewhere currently existed, the planners kept their options open by noting that the scenarios they had laid out applied provided that the *Armata del Po* was not employed overseas or beyond the Alps.[126]

Plan PR 12 for war against England and France with Germany as a benevolent neutral was drawn up in January 1938 and turned into directives by the regional army commanders at the end of March. It covered three theatres: the Western Alps, the Mediterranean and Africa. As far as the Alpine theatre was concerned, the distance of important objectives, the nature of the terrain and the French defences meant that there was no expectation that the covering forces in that zone would gain 'rapid results of real importance'. The task of the fourteen divisions holding the western front was to bear the shock of enemy attacks and block any offensive operations.[127] The army commander in charge of the Alpine sector, general Angelo Tua, translated the general directive into a posture of active defence involving cover particularly against incursions by motorised units and initial local offensives across the border.[128] Two army corps were allotted the task of guarding the northern frontier in case of rapid enemy action across Swiss territory and three corps protected the eastern frontier in case of aggressive action as a result of a change in Yugoslavia's attitude.[129]

In the Mediterranean theatre, the general staff expected the enemy to try landings on the western and southern coasts of the peninsular, to attempt to seize one or more of the islands of Elba, Sardinia, Sicily and Pantelleria, and to occupy the Italian islands in the Aegean. Enemy landings on the Ligurian and Tuscan coasts – a familiar nightmare which had figured prominently in military planning before the First World War – would be particularly damaging. Loss of control of any of the islands and the naval bases they harboured – an equally familiar scenario – would be no less damaging as it would expose the Sicilian channel and the mainland naval bases and add greatly to the navy's strategic burdens.[130] The army updated and revised its plans for the coastal defence of Italy, either in the event of a two-front war or in the scenario of a war involving only the defence of the Tyrrhenian and Ionian seas, to address the new scenario.[131]

In the North African theatre, the chief strategic tasks were to guarantee the integrity of Libya and to secure the possession of the main bases of Tripoli and Tobruk as the necessary preliminaries to a possible counter-offensive. Of the three sectors into which this theatre of operations was divided, the Tunisian front offered limited possibilities for offensive action and lacked any natural lines of defence, exposing the Italians to attacks along the coast or through the Djebel. To meet such an offensive, the Italians would have to slow down and weaken the French attack before looking to give battle. In fact, as Italian intelligence revealed, the French felt strong enough only to resist an attack but intended to launch a counter-offensive if the need and the opportunity arose, and were re-equipping three armoured battalions with modern tanks.[132] In the east, a British attack from Egypt along the coast using motorised forces was to be expected. The Italian position turned on the successful defence of Tobruk and Bardia – although the planners gave no indication of how they thought this was to be achieved. The French were likely to attempt attacks from the south through the Sahara; here air action would be of major importance in counter-attacking the enemy columns. SIM was accordingly tasked with watching French troop movements in southern Algeria and Chad.[133] Italian East Africa was likely to face attacks from north-east Sudan and British Somalia, which would be met by blocking the access routes and organising counter-attacks.[134]

Pariani's conception of the force levels that would be required to carry out the main operations in North Africa envisaged moving from an 'initial stage' in which four metropolitan divisions and two Libyan divisions would be supplemented by the gradual arrival of four additional divisions, through an 'intermediate stage' to a 'final stage' when eight metropolitan divisions, two Libyan divisions and an armoured division would be in place, reinforced by fourteen infantry divisions and two motorised divisions shipped across from Italy.[135] Balbo's tasks were to maintain sufficient troops to cover the colony and start initial operations, to construct barracks for at least four more metropolitan divisions, and to build up enough stocks of arms, munitions, fuel and supplies to support operations for six months. Pariani proposed initially to mask the troop build up by adding a third division to each of the two army corps presently in Libya and then doubling the number of corps when the other two divisions arrived.[136]

Convinced of the inevitability of a war with the western powers, and excessively confident about the effect which his organisational changes would have on Italy's military capabilities, Pariani believed that 'an instant and surprise war' in the spring of 1939 would most favour Italy. Victory would be won 'at Suez and in Paris' by means of attacks on Egypt, southern France (possibly by way of Switzerland, Ciano suggested) and the fleets of the western powers. The idea persuaded Ciano of the need for a secret Italo–German war committee, though nothing concrete was to be forthcoming for another year.[137] Something of his army chief of staff's enthusiasm for a war in the Western Desert evidently percolated through to Mussolini. After reassuring the German ambassador in early July about the state of Anglo–Italian and Franco–Italian relations, the Duce suddenly changed tack:

He added abruptly that the British were undoubtedly splendid sailors, but it was something else again to fight in the desert at 50 [degrees] centigrade. His Italians were accustomed to it, and the state of health of the Italian troops in Libya and also in Abyssinia was excellent.[138]

As formulated and conveyed to Cavagnari in May, the army's tasks in a war against Britain and France in the Mediterranean were to bar the Alpine frontier, assure the best conditions for the aero–naval contests in the Mediterranean basin by guaranteeing the safety of the coasts and the bases, and develop offensive action in Africa.[139]

That same month Balbo carried out annual manoeuvres in Libya designed to test the capacity of local and metropolitan troops to operate together to defend the western frontier against French incursions, a move which the French general staff had begun to consider the previous December. The manoeuvres, during the course of which a motorised division was moved along the coast from Benghasi to Tripoli at speeds of up to thirty kilometres an hour and was attacked by air and sea at the western end of the coast, was decided when a 'French' aero-transportable division landed behind 'Italian' lines after a parachute regiment had secured the landing ground. Balbo's report emphasised the 'brilliant success' of the air-transportable division, whose 'vertical turning movement' opened new doctrinal horizons for 'the war of quick decision, typically Italian and Fascist'. He also trumpeted the achievements of the auto-transportable division, which showed that large units could carry out 'noteworthy changes of location at appropriate speeds' even when operating in enemy territory or under the pressure of events and therefore without prior arrangements. When analysed in more detail, however, the auto-transportable divisions experienced problems with off-road supply and because of the time they took to switch from march formation to combat formation. The motorised columns were also vulnerable to attack by air assault planes and bombers, and the fighters had not been able to do much to counter either threat.[140]

The air force was quietly pleased with the success of the 'air transportable division' which had been watched with evident pleasure by Vittorio Emanuele III and had most enthused 'the old [army] generals'. Preceded by 200 parachutists, flights of 3 aircraft landing at two-minute intervals had deposited 1,500 men, 3 batteries of trench artillery, 20 motorcycles and several machine-gun companies which had assembled and begun their advance in under two hours. The problem the airmen recognised – but Balbo did not – was whether what was technically possible in peacetime could be carried out successfully in wartime. A few hundred parachutists could never hold a bridgehead large enough to protect landing aircraft against artillery or heavy machine-guns. What was possible in the empty spaces of the Libyan desert would be impossible in more populated zones in Europe or elsewhere unless landing grounds were chosen which were so far from the front lines as to render the action of the force ineffective. Modern communications also made such a landing highly vulnerable to interdiction by enemy fighters and bombers. There could, Pinna admitted, be tactical–strategical situations which suggested such an 'audacious strike'; however it was necessary to avoid being carried away by enthusiasm and believing in the possibility of 'acts of war which for their success require the favourable concurrence of innumerable moral and material factors'.[141]

Pariani wanted to be in a position to undertake either defensive or offensive action on both the eastern and the western frontiers of Libya. As far as defending the western frontier was concerned, the French objective would obviously be Tripoli.[142] Balbo's experiment opened up new possibilities and accordingly in June the general staff in Rome examined the use of air transportable forces for a 'vertical turning movement' to defend western Libya. In the most favourable circumstances, which entailed a rising by anti-French Italians and Arabs, they could occupy Tunisian territory. In less favourable circumstances, they could hold off the threat of a rapid French invasion and win the time needed to disembark reinforcements to defend Tripolitania and attack Egypt. Given the slowness with which Libyan divisions could mobilise and the time taken to send reservists from mainland Italy, the defence of Tripoli could not be guaranteed until such time as her fixed defences were fully efficient. Nor could a mobile defence be expected to succeed when the enemy had a three-to-one advantage in troops.

Faced with these facts and the likelihood that the enemy would choose to launch a lightning attack, if only to wreck any prospect of attacking Egypt, the only hope for Italy was to take the offensive using initiative and surprise as force multipliers and thus gain space and time. Timely troop reinforcements from Italy could not be guaranteed. The one advantage Italy would enjoy was in the air. Using bases in Sardinia, Sicily, Pantelleria and Tripolitania, surprise should give her temporary command of the air initially and 'a certain prevalence' thereafter since the enemy could not detach many aircraft from the skies of Paris and London. An air offensive in Tunisia would not just aid the navy; as well as representing 'an aeronautical glory' it would achieve a strategic objective of great value to the air force, enabling it to guard the Sicilian channel more economically and giving it offensive possibilities to the west and north.[143]

Having decided that the only way presently to defend Tripoli was by an offensive supported by sufficient air power to dominate the enemy, and having dealt with the likely objections of the Regia Aeronautica by deciding that this would not prevent the air force putting up serious opposition in the face of possible enemy air attacks on Italy and would 'only delay by a few days the actions of city bombing to which the air force seems to attribute decisive value', the army general staff turned to the question of how and where to use the airborne forces.[144] The target would be Gabes. A force of 18–20,000 men would take the French fortification line from the rear and crush the local forces before reinforcements could come from the north, while all available forces in Tripolitania would launch a motorised drive on the enemy's front and flank. The planners admitted that their imaginative scheme was merely an initial statement of the task. Given the strategic improbability that Italy would fight France alone and the operational and tactical issues which had to be solved or resolved before 'vertical turning' could hope to succeed, the scheme was no more than a flight of fantasy. Ever inventive, Pariani was much taken by the possibilities inherent in Balbo's experiment for a special air-transportable *binaria* division with a battalion of parachutists attached. However, neither air-transportable troops nor the 'vertical turning manoeuvre' figured in his decision that the defence of the western frontier of Libya would comprise mobile covering forces, a system of strong points in the field and a belt of defences covering Tripoli itself.[145]

Although Pariani's preferred strategy was for a land war against Britain and France in North Africa, he was sufficiently aware of the directions in which Italian foreign policy was travelling – and sufficiently attuned to Mussolini's way of exercising control – to recognise that other scenarios might either open up or be forced upon him. The structure and allocation of his forces were intended to provide a central reserve of at least twenty divisions over and above the forces needed for the defence of the frontier with France and 'the realisation of our strategic goals in Libya'. 'These forces,' he told colonel Szabo two weeks before the anschluss, 'will be used either against Czechoslovakia or, for example, against Serbia'. At that moment, nobody knew where they would be needed. If Britain entered the war they would be deployed against her, as it would be pointless to employ them against Czechoslovakia while losing the war against Britain and France. If not, they could be employed elsewhere. Evidently contemplating the possible dismemberment of Czechoslovakia by force, and Budapest's territorial ambition to regain sub-Carpathian Ruthenia, Pariani asked what the Hungarians needed 'to reach their goals in the critical area'.[146]

Although his own strategic sights were firmly set on North Africa, Pariani had to consider a new strategic scenario in the aftermath of the anschluss. Obeying an instruction from Mussolini, Pariani ordered the preparation of plans in case of an Italo–German conflict. Although the western frontier defences were nearing completion and arrangements for watching the Swiss frontier were progressing, the new German–Yugoslav frontier and in particular the Tarvisio basin represented 'our Achilles' heel' in the event of a German–Yugoslav alliance.[147] Although the

Germans had seventy divisions to Italy's fifty, the staff expected the numbers to be more or less equal after troops had been drawn off to watch the French, Czech, Yugoslav and Polish frontiers. Given her doctrine, her organisation (three quarters of her wartime effectives were always under arms) and her equipment, Germany could be expected to undertake a 'decisively offensive' campaign.

Of the three lines of attack open to her, a move on the Alto Adige would be the least likely because of the mountain barrier protecting the Po valley. Taking Tarvisio would be easier, but would not expose any vital objectives. To prevent this, the planners proposed actions to occupy the mountains north of the Drava river and the valley trench from Lienz to Villach. A rapid drive through western Switzerland – easy prey to the Germans – would put the attackers within one hundred kilometres of Milan. Pre-emptive occupation of the high passes would counter this, and the Italians might consider cutting off the Ticino salient using the Spluga and St Gotthard passes.[148] While the Duce might one day have need of such a contingency plan, nothing in his policy or diplomacy at this time suggested that he intended to put it into effect.

Valle's tribulations

At the Air Ministry, Valle suffered what he afterwards portrayed as a series of insurmountable trials and tribulations during these years. He was apparently unable to prevent the intrusion and interference of outside political and industrial agencies – indeed it grew steadily worse despite his reputation for Sardinian sternness. Mussolini apparently interrogated him regularly and forcefully on the basis of information from outside sources, a practice which he saw as evidence that his ministry was a victim of intrigue and gossip but which can equally be seen as a manifestation of the Duce's need to check on his somewhat fitful progress. Ciano, who had gathered a circle of airmen around him while in Abyssinia, interfered from time to time, trying unsuccessfully to get Aimone Cat appointed as under-secretary of state for air and passing on to Mussolini details of the poor night-flying performance of the S 79 – an aircraft for which Valle was said to have a mania.[149]

Mussolini's policy of aircraft sales worried Valle, according to his own later account. The Consorzio Esportazioni Aeronautiche, which he set up at this time to manage the business and which was then put under the Ministry of Exchange and Currency rather than staying under the wing of the Air Ministry, sold over two billion lire's worth of aircraft and materials in two years. Valle's complaint that the monies it earned were neither given to Air Ministry nor used to buy valuable raw materials was

intended to support his basic plaint that the air force was being starved
of funds. It was also untrue: between 1937 and 1943 half the value of
the exports of aircraft, engines and parts came back in the form of raw
materials through clearing arrangements.[150] The charge was self-serving,
as Mussolini in all probability very well recognised.

The budget allocated to the Air Ministry rose in 1937–8 to
4,086,000,000 lire or 31 per cent of overall military spend, an increase of
358,000,000 lire and a rise of 9 per cent in the air force's share compared
with the previous year, and in 1938–9 it rose again to 4,490,000,000
lire, representing 30 per cent of overall spend.[151] Later, Valle claimed
that money was being denied to the air force in order to give it to the
navy. This was also untrue. The navy received 23 per cent of the budget
allocation during these years, almost exactly its average since 1935.

Procurement remained a nightmare for which Valle and the Regia Aeronautica bore more responsibility than they or their apologists afterwards
cared to admit. The system of competition for new aircraft types and
the awarding of contracts to the winners produced eight *concorsi* for aircraft during 1937–9 in which 50 per cent of aircraft were rejected, and
three for aero engines which resulted in the approval of a single project.
Valle's grouping of the fifty-odd aircraft manufacturing groups into a Cor-
porate Technical Committee – set up partly to decentralise the aircraft
industry and shift it away from northern Italy – had little impact on the
problem. To the airmen – and their historiographers – the situation was
elementally simple: industry built prototypes and imposed them on the
air force.[152] In reality, poor technical selection played at least as large a
role in retarding the development of the air force. In 1938 seventy-three
Caproni Ca 135 and Ca 135*bis* twin-engined bombers were acquired
and then retired after only ten months' service, thirty-two twin-engined
Piaggio 32 and 32*bis* bombers were junked after two months, and thirty-
six S 85 dive-bombers were taken out of active service a year after they
had been delivered.[153]

During an inquest by the chamber of deputies on the state of the air
force on 11 December 1939, twelve days after he had been sacked by
Mussolini, Valle maintained that his policy of aircraft procurement had
been driven by a shortage of funds and the need for a quality force, and
that he had not wanted to bog the air force down in series production of
a small number of aircraft types because rapid technical progress would
have made them obsolete in comparison to foreign planes. In fact, the
air force's decision in the summer of 1938 to maintain a rate of aircraft
production of 140 planes per month, which was designed to parcel out
orders between the different aircraft companies in order to keep them in
business, meant that it lost all the technical and economic advantages of

long production runs, to which it was apparently oblivious, with seriously deleterious consequences when war came.[154]

Of the three services the air force enjoyed the best relations with Germany, largely because Goering was an airman. When the new air attaché, general Liotta, arrived in Berlin in April, the reichsmarschall greeted him warmly, taking care to reaffirm both the solidarity and the importance of the Axis from Germany's point of view. Italy and Germany, Liotta was reassured, shared both a 'style' and a political doctrine, had the same enemies, and operated in complementary spheres of interest.[155] Germany's overtures, which amounted to little more than the maintenance of an additional channel of political and diplomatic communication, gave the air force no real assistance either in dealing with its internal problems or in confronting its putative external enemies. Meanwhile, on 2 June the French air minister, Guy La Chambre, announced a programme to spend nine milliard francs building 2,600 new aircraft during 1938 and 1939.

The air force made no more progress in resolving its doctrinal debates and dissensions than it did in solving its procurement and personnel problems. In terms both of theory and practice, and when put alongside the Abyssinian campaign, the Spanish Civil War posed a central question about the meaning of current experience: was it either a special form of war or a half-way house between colonial war and general war? Mecozzi took it to be more universal and saw in it confirmation of his view that fighters were likely to dominate over bombers and that the latter required escorts of they were to survive in the air and could not hit targets at altitude as effectively as low-level or dive-bombing. To his mind bombing the civil population was a second-order use of air power which served to force the enemy to divert resources to protection and defence and could function as reprisal for raids launched by the enemy on Italian population centres. While not sharing Mecozzi's privileging of assault bombing, Pietro Pinna put the weight of the deputy chief of air staff behind the idea that tactical bombing of troops and of areas immediately behind the front lines had been shown to be effective during the war.[156] Aimoni Cat, who had commanded the air force in Ethiopia, pointed out that the air force had acted as the only operational reserve in halting or slowing enemy advances until fresh divisions came up and had struck the enemy after they had enveloped the Italian right wing at Adua-Axum.[157]

Douhetian purists were able to accommodate the specific circumstances in Ethiopa and Spain and still find validation of their general theories. Since Ethiopia lacked both a sizeable air force to defeat and large centres of population to bomb, the air war had moved straight to Douhet's third phase, attacking the enemy's ground forces. The special circumstances operating in Spain – which included the use of slow S 81 and Ju 52 bombers vulnerable to fighters – would not be repeated in a European war where, for one thing, the moral effect of air attacks on well-prepared troops would be much less. For Francesco Pricolo, who would succeed Valle at the end of 1939, the true potential of air power had been frustrated during the Ethiopian and Spanish wars not so much by the particular circumstances of those conflicts as by the fact that in both it had been under to the command of military men who did not understand it and had used it as an appendix to the ground forces. Targets had existed – Pricolo singled out sea traffic to Barcelona – which, if attacked continuously could have had decisive strategic effects. While allowing some room for other ways of using air power, Pricolo remained wedded to Douhetian fundamentals. 'Still today', he believed, 'the effective weapon of the air arm is terror, that of the navy hunger, and that of the army the occupation of territory'.[158]

The serving head of the air force was also fundamentally Douhetian in his doctrinal outlook. Since entire populations would be ranged against one another in modern war, Valle believed that it was necessary to attack an enemy's territory in order to weaken his moral power to resist and dry up his main sources of life and production. Moral forces had precedence as targets, Valle believed, because 'they give the conduct of war its tone, they determine the character of combat, and they rule the struggle and all the tests'.[159] Tactical bombing such as had been seen in Spain Valle regarded as the exception to the norm; fundamentally it was an uneconomic use of air power that ran risks out of proportion to the returns to be gained by it and the value of the means used to carry it out. The chief of the air staff stamped on Mecozzi: :

In the tactical field of land war, it is artillery which must have the exclusive role. Modern armies possess sufficient fire-power to make the intervention of aviation in the zone beaten by the guns absolutely superfluous. This does not signify a disinterest in what happens on the battlefront, but a wish to contribute in the most effective way to victory by working in a more rewarding field.[160]

Valle's doctrine for the air force was thus substantially unaffected by any of the experiences in Spain which suggested that there might be new things to learn about air war. Apart from establishing the Blind Flying School, he did little else which derived from the many reports and studies of that war. While the air force benefited from the practical experience it had gained, it suffered from the losses in aircraft that participation entailed (some 1,530 were committed in Ethiopia and Spain), from disruptions to and exhaustion of personnel, and from 'the illusion they created that war was easy'.[161]

The armed forces and the Munich crisis

Relations with Germany grew closer in the spring of 1938. As part of the ongoing programme of intelligence collaboration a delegation from SIM went to Berlin at the end of March to exchange information with their German opposite numbers on French military organisation and the defence of her north-eastern and south-eastern frontiers and to discuss future collaboration. The Germans gave their guests information on Britain's rearmament programme and, as part of the agreed programme, SIM gave the Germans material on Czech military organisation and on Czech fortifications along the former Austrian frontier. The Italian intelligence officers noted 'a particular interest in everything to do with Czechoslovakia which was not evident last year and the purpose of which is obvious'.[162] Both parties agreed that Russia was not ready for war, particularly because of the low state of morale among her military personnel. A further sign of German friendliness, no doubt welcome to the Italian treasury, came early in May when the German authorities agreed to assume the burden of repaying the debt of 4,544,000 lire which the former Austrian government owed for the purchase of Italian arms and munitions. The programme had been suspended since June 1936 because of the needs of the Spanish Civil War.[163]

When the May crisis occurred, Mussolini already had an insight into German thinking. At the beginning of April the Italian military attaché in Berlin, colonel Marras, reported a conversation with a senior officer in the Wehrmacht high command in which it was made clear that conceding autonomy to the German minority in Czechoslovakia would not resolve the matter and that the Germans believed that if they took action France could only intervene with difficulty and then only in the air. Admiral Canaris also told Marras that Hitler wanted to avoid any new step until after his visit to Italy at the start of May.[164] Information from Hungarian sources shown to Mussolini at the time of Hitler's visit suggested that Czechoslovakia would be broken up in September and that joint German and Hungarian action would last two weeks.[165]

In the course of the May crisis, during which Mussolini received a stream of daily reports from the Italian military attachés in Germany, Czechoslovakia and Hungary, Marras reported German measures that were designed to threaten Prague but no direct response to Czech mobilisation. He attributed Germany's inaction to the loss of surprise as a result of Czech mobilisation and a wish to avoid Hungarian and Polish participation. The game, Marras thought, had merely been postponed. It was also clear that Britain's firm attitude had played a significant part in what looked increasingly like a military climbdown.[166]

Italian intelligence detected a distinct change of attitude in French military circles as a consequence of the May crisis. Whereas they had been largely favourable to the Italian action in Ethiopia, sympathetic to the nationalists in Spain and strongly opposed to the idea of sending troops there, the highest military authorities were in favour of armed intervention against Germany if she used force to invade Czech territory. However, in the course of somewhat confused discussions about France's absolute and relative obligations to Czechoslovakia a number of matters had come to light, including the autonomist tendencies of various racial groups in the country besides the Germans and the 'unjust domination' of the Czechs over other races, which were leading elements of the French General Staff towards the notion of 'a peaceful settlement of the Czech question by means of successive degrees of administrative autonomy in the German zone, even if these provisions were to be the prelude to a future German annexation, excluding the use of violence'. The general hope was for a peaceful agreement which would lead to a partial dismemberment of the country 'without touching French prestige'. Among the questions in play in Paris were the issues of whether the British would join in a defence of Czechoslovakia and how any direct assistance could be given to Prague given the state of the French air force and the distances involved. The official answer to the latter point was that the conflict would become a general war, but the democracies were as yet unprepared for that. The Czechs themselves were thought to be capable of putting up resistance for between three weeks and three months.[167]

Early in June, general Valle paid an official visit to Romania. While Mussolini may very well have been hoping to gain some additional insight into Bucharest's fidelity to Paris, Valle's main task was to further arms sales to the Romanians in general and their air force in particular. Rome knew in the early spring that the Romanian air force was in a sorry state and was looking to buy twenty to thirty Italian bombers.[168] It soon became evident that the shopping list was lengthening as enquiries came via the Italian military attaché, lieutenant-colonel Della Porta, about the possibilities of ordering chemical weapons plants, torpedo boats, MAS boats, submarines and later one hundred Alfa Romeo aero-engines.

Valle noted a clear Romanian volte-face away from France and towards Italy accompanied by an evident anxiety not to forfeit French or Czech protection – especially the latter. There was, he reported, a chance for Italy both to undertake an industrial penetration of Romania and to gain access to her raw materials and primary products but this would have to be done with the maximum care and tact so as not to excite French and especially Czech alarm.[169] In the event the negotiations dragged on for six months as the Romanians looked to the United States as a possible source for aero-engines, haggled over prices and repayment terms and entertained what Della Porta described as a 'veritable avalanche' of representatives of the German aircraft industry before finally reaching a commercial agreement on arms acquisition in December. Italy put up to two milliard lire into the clearing accounts for repayment over four to five years. The aircraft contract was worth 26,000,000 lire and in exchange for her arms Italy would receive 35,000 wagon-loads of grain and 160,000,000 lire worth of petroleum products.[170] Given the revelations about the resource needs of the Impero Romano, these economic gains were every bit as important as the political ones of displacing France and competing with Germany in a region of increasing interest.

After Valle's visit the head of Romanian military intelligence, Mihail Moruzow, sent him a fulsome letter disowning on behalf of all thinking elements of the country Titulescu's earlier policy of distancing Romania from Fascist Italy, casting Italy as 'the hope and the guarantee for Romania's existence' and expressing gratitude for Italian recognition of Romania's claim to Bessarabia. While such a communication was, as Della Porta pointed out, highly unusual and while it was cast entirely in political terms, Romanian military intelligence doubtless hoped to get something more out of its new partners than it had managed to do before Valle's visit. Then the Romanians had sought to take advantage of their impending order to get information about the western military districts of the USSR, but SIM had refused to give it unless specifically directed by higher political authority – which apparently never transpired.[171]

A month after Valle's visit to Bucharest, Pariani went to Berlin to explore further technical collaboration with Germany. What he saw led him to conclude that military preparations were not yet complete and that the German army lacked materiel. Arms plants were being expanded and would be completed in 1939, and a big effort to produce weapons would be made in 1940. The army was short of reserve and junior officers, but it impressed by its concentration on character and energy. The former was a major concern in the officer training schools, where there was little general culture and much practical training. The latter was generally evident in calm will power and a lack of impulsiveness. Goering told him that because of the concentration on the air force, which was already larger than those of England and France combined, relatively little had been done for the army so far, but now it was being equipped in its turn. Germany and Italy together represented a formidable force, the reichsmarshall told him; united with Japan 'they can hold everyone in check'.[172] Perhaps partly as a consequence of receiving Pariani's report on German military preparations, Mussolini authorised his five milliard lire extraordinary military budget at the end of July. The immediate and pressing needs were for arms and munitions, anti-aircraft defence and transport, but he proposed not to neglect the completion of defences and Libya.[173]

Surveying Italy's strategic situation in the third week of June, the army planners noted that Italy's land frontiers with France and Switzerland required guarding while those with Austria and Yugoslavia offered good opportunities for offensive action. This much conformed to the conclusions they had reached in January. When they went on to claim that Libya offered the opportunity for 'rewarding land offensives' either against Tunisia or Egypt, they were stepping somewhat beyond their earlier conclusions. The rosy glow being cast over Italy's strategic options was also evident in the claim that East Africa offered 'a new base of Italian power in the Indian Ocean' (which it did not until Kisimaio was made into a proper base) and the statement that Suez was 'directly threatened by the convergence of our strategic lines coming from Libya and Ethiopia'.[174]

The land defences along the Alps were believed generally to be in good shape, although the barriers blocking the four main routes from Switzerland were inadequate. To complement them, an army of three corps which was organised for immediate employment should be created and based in the Paduan plain. The elements for two of them – a celeri corps and an auto-transportable corps of three infantry divisions – already existed. A motorised division was available for the third, a motor-mechanised corps, but a new armoured division was required to complete it. Thirty-nine divisions, thirty of which were *binaria* infantry divisions, could be mobilised at once, with thirty more infantry divisions following along in two batches.

When the operations staff looked at the likely war scenario in which these forces would be employed, things were less straightforward. A war against France and England would be simultaneously continental, Mediterranean and oceanic. Italy's strategic position gave her 'a role of the very first order' in such a conflict, but 'to decide which [theatre] is pre-eminent is difficult'.[175] However, the soldiers had no real difficulty in coming to a logical conclusion on the matter. With no possibility of securing rapid and decisive results on the continent, the decision had to be sought either by intervening in another continental theatre alongside an ally or in the Mediterranean and oceanic theatres (the latter meaning Italian East Africa). For Italy as a Mediterranean power, Libya was politically and strategically the most important card to play:

Libya is able now to hurt the whole of the French forces in North Africa; to draw strong British forces to Egypt; as the strategic centre of the Mediterranean to dominate the adversary by developing operations which, as a result of the favourable geographic–strategic situation, can have a decisive character.[176]

Translated into geographical objectives, this meant defending western Libya while launching an all-out (*decisa*) offensive to conquer the Egyptian Delta and the Nile. Other operations that would be necessary or desirable in a war against England and France included the occupation of Corsica, Corfu and Malta and intervention in Albania to secure petroleum resources and control the Straits of Otranto.

Although Libya might be the strategic trump card, there was still a great deal to be done before it could be played. The four divisions of Libyan native troops needed better organisation and training before they could be combined with metropolitan units in European-style operations. More Italian troops – at least four divisions – were needed to defend the western borders and more again to undertake an offensive in the east. The land defences in western Libya had still to be completed, as did the sea and anti-aircraft defences throughout the colony. The arrangements for water supplies were only sufficient for normal use and could not support offensive operations, and there were currently no fuel stocks. Arrangements were still being made so that Libya could last for six months and Italian East Africa for twelve on their own resources. The strategic conspectus was artfully drawn up so that optimists could see a glass that was more than half full; presented with such a picture, it would take a strong-minded pessimist to point out that it was half empty. Unlike their naval counterparts, the army's planners were presently not so minded.

While the planners considered the broad scenario, Pariani's attentions were temporarily focused elsewhere – as would Mussolini's be during much of the coming August. On 24 June he ordered his staff to ready Plan V, for intervention in Spain, for rapid action. The plan had originally been devised as part of an attack on Valencia and then revised in January in order to be able to hit the republicans in the rear if the nationalists launched an attack in the direction of Teruel. As again revised, it now envisaged landing a motorised division and an alpini division, supported by a regiment of bersaglieri and a battalion of assault tanks, on the coast between Vinaroz and Castellon de la Plana with the objective of driving south on Valencia and cutting Madrid off from the sea. Pariani rated the probability that such action might prompt French intervention quite high. When and if put into action, the plan would also require mobilising the frontier defences with France, the alpini and the army corps based on Alessandria and Turin, and calling up at least one class of reservists for all the other army corps.[177]

Pariani had also to consider the possibility that the mounting pressure on Czechslovakia might result in a war to which the Italian army would be expected to contribute. In May he had expected to be able to help the Hungarians in the event of war if his reserve was available to be disposed freely, but had warned them that in the event of a simultaneous attack by Yugoslavia, France and Great Britain Italy would have to concentrate her forces on her main adversary and not on Yugoslavia.[178] On 25–26 July he met the Hungarian war minister and the army chief of staff to discuss a *guerra di rapido corso* against Great Britain, France and Russia with the aim of preventing them from encircling the Axis powers or breaking them up. The foremost question in his mind was whether in such circumstances to attack the strongest state – France – by surprise or to attack the weaker states – Czechoslovakia and Romania – which had the raw materials Italy wanted and contemporaneously take the Suez canal. The Hungarians, who professed themselves ready to launch immediate operations against Prague, were allocated the task of concentrating their military effort against Czechoslovakia and Romania and reassured that they had no need to worry about a hostile Yugoslavia. While such assistance was no doubt welcome, Pariani was in no hurry to tie the Hungarians down to specifics: the next meeting was scheduled for November.[179]

At the end of June, Pariani summoned all the Italian military attachés from their posts overseas for the first of what he intended to be a regular series of annual gatherings. He was thus in possession of the most up-to-date information and advice on the armies of all the states which might be directly or indirectly involved when the Munich crisis blew up two months later. Among the lesser powers, Hungary with a small but well-trained army of 80,000 men would look to avoid losing any territory and gaining its objectives in Czechoslovakia quickly; Yugoslavia, whose armaments situation would not permit her to take the offensive at the start of a war, would not move if Hungary acted in Czechoslovakia; Poland, anti-Bolshevik, anti-German but enjoying good relations with Hungary and with an appetite for additional territory, could field an army of 700,000 but was somewhat backward in doctrine, equipment and weaponry. Russia, which was in the midst of industrialisation and undergoing mass purges, shared an interest in Czechoslovakia with Britain and France but would probably not intervene there directly, limiting herself to using air power. Czechoslovakia, 'weak and surrounded by enemies,' could be attacked from any direction. She could not hope for help from the Little Entente, and the encouragement she received from Russia, France and England amounted to little more than political posturing.[180]

As the May crisis had made abundantly clear, Britain's stance was likely to be crucial in any replay of events in central Europe and that in turn would depend to a very considerable extent on her military capabilities. Lieutenant-colonel Cesare Laderchi reported that although Chamberlain's position as prime minister was strong, it would be shaken if an Anglo–Italian pact were not reached. As for national policy: 'England wants peace at all costs, and looks only to safeguard the conquests [she has] made in the world'.[181] A military alliance certainly existed between England and France, but the support that could be given to Paris would be limited to air power alone. The British army, having taken the decision to mechanise, was in the middle of a two year process of re-equipment and retraining and would not be ready for war until 1940. Pariani took the fact that England could field a total of only 170,000 men as the explanation for England's wish for peace at any price.

France, according to Visconti Prasca, was a country undergoing a period of moral and political crisis, thanks largely to the cross-currents and conflicts of 'so many parties, all strong and looking to dominate, which create real chaos'.[182] Everyone was united by fear of Germany. This, together with her preoccupations over Spain, Belgium and Switzerland, forced France into partnership with England despite a long-standing aversion towards her. French doctrine was based on a concept of defence followed by a counter-offensive, and the French general staff believed that as the German army was not yet at maximum efficiency it could still hold it off with the aid of the frontier fortifications. Further evidence about the Anglo–French security relationship arrived at the start of July, when the naval attaché in Paris reported the belief that a general agreement existed between the British and French navies for collaboration of their aero–naval forces in case of war, and that special attention had been given to using the French base at Corsica.[183]

Reporting on Germany, Marras depicted an army with a standing force of 850,000 and a total of some 4,000,000 trained men, well equipped, well trained and imbued with a doctrine of manoeuvre warfare. Morale among the rank and file was high, but the officer corps suffered from numerical and qualitative deficiencies, particularly in the higher ranks where 'a good number of generals are of somewhat limited capacity'.[184] England and France were regarded as enemies, though there was a healthy respect for the French army; although Russia was held at a distance, there was some sympathy for her. Germany's expansionist aims were directed towards the east and south-east. In action her army, which was highly efficient but not yet able to sustain a lengthy war, would take the offensive in the east while using fortifications and the natural lie of the land to fight delaying actions in the west.

Although the shape that any Italian military action might assume was not as yet clear, Mussolini's policy preferences were. Attolico told von Ribbentrop on 27 July that in the event of a localised war Italy would remain neutral, but if either France or Great Britain (or both together as many indicators already suggested in August would be likely) entered it then Italy would join in. By late August he also had from the military attaché's office in Berlin a clear and remarkably prescient forecast both of the likely development of the crisis by Hitler and of the broad contextual circumstances in which it would play out. Hitler would stir the Sudeten Germans to action, thereby providing himself with a pretext for action if president Beneš reacted, at a moment when France was not ready for war and Britain would do everything possible to avoid one.[185]

By mid-August both the civilian and military authorities in Rome knew, thanks to Marras and his deputy, that the military in Germany were divided over the use of force to resolve the Czech situation. Canaris, von Brauchitsch and Beck feared that it would trigger a general war in which Germany would have to fight Britain and France while Keitel and others favoured what they believed would be a localised war in which Britain would not take part. Marras's deputy reported at the end of August that Hitler appeared not have made up his mind what to do, that the military generally thought a limited conflict between Germany and Czechoslovakia inevitable and that 'the critical moment' would come between the end of September and the first half of October. For his part, Badini thought it unlikely that Germany would unleash a conflict until its armaments were more complete and its fortifications along the western frontier finished, which would take at least another two months.[186] Throughout the month Attolico was unable to get a clear answer from von Ribbentrop as to what Hitler proposed to do, though when Goering proposed on 9 September that the two dictators should meet during the next fortnight Mussolini showed no immediate interest in learning any more about his Axis partner's intentions.[187]

Additional materials were now added to the flood of diplomatic cables which informed Mussolini's decision-making. On 25 August, Pariani ordered the head of SIM, colonel Tripiccione, to prepare a weekly synthesis of the politico-military situation in Germany, France, England, Hungary, Yugoslavia, Turkey and Russia in addition to the daily communications he provided. By 10 September, tension had heightened to the point at which Tripiccione was ordered to provide a daily summary for Mussolini of the situation in France and French North Africa with special focus on the Alps and Libya, and of developments in Czechoslovakia, England, Russia and Germany.[188] This material provided valuable evidence of the military relativities which now came to feature so prominently in diplomatic calculations.

At the beginning of September, the Italian naval attaché in Paris found it difficult to say with certainty what the French attitude would be in the event of a violent solution to the Czechoslovakian problem. Officially, Bonnet put faith in the likelihood of British and American support in the event of armed German intervention in Czechoslovakia; but French diplomacy was patently willing to settle for administrative autonomy for the Sudetenland which would ultimately lead to Germany's preferred solution. However, the military attitude was not one ready to face the worst. At the end of August the naval base at Brest had been on a peace footing; the air force was in no state to face a war in the immediate future; and while the army was ready to mobilise at short notice there was no sign of any unusual troop movements.[189]

On 5 September, the attaché learned that sailors on leave from the Mediterranean squadron at Toulon were being recalled and the ships were being loaded with supplies and munitions. However, a strike at the port of Marseilles and the threat of further trade union action by the communists and the CGT complicated the situation for the French navy. Five days later the naval base at Toulon was reported to be on a full war footing. As the French government proposed a cantonal solution to the Czech crisis, Margottini reported that the attitude of the population in Paris was unhappy and worried at the idea of war but that this 'transitory state of mind' would disappear in the event of war when French steadfastness would be reinvigorated. The general attitude to Italy, demonstrated on film and in the press, was that she was of no account and played second fiddle to Germany. Margottini was of the view that Italy could never reach any agreement with France 'until we have fought her so as to show her ... who we are and what we are worth'.[190]

During August, admiral Cavagnari was occupied with the question of the amphibious resources to be provided for operations on the Albanian coast and against Malta. Towards the end of the month, he had to give the Duce the unwelcome news that a number of the newest warships were failing their initial trials and would have to go back into dry dock.[191] On 2 September, presumably stimulated by the tensions now developing on the international scene, the naval staff produced a plan for a surprise war in the Mediterranean against England and France. Italian submarines and surface craft would attack enemy warships at sea, including those currently in Spanish waters, but the main actions proposed were the blockading of Malta and Biserta by means of blockships. For the Malta operation, which was acknowledged to be 'daring' but which had a good chance of success if the enemy did not learn about the preparations for it (which would take twenty days), the navy proposed to use the liner *Roma* loaded with 6,000 tons of cement. In a conscious imitation of Rizzo's successful action against the Austrian navy in Pola harbour in December 1917, MAS boats would attack French warships anchored in Toulon harbour. Once these operations had provided temporary security in the Mediterranean, Suez and Tunisia would be the most profitable targets for action. For maximum reward, the three operations required follow-on air attacks by the Regia Aeronautica. Here the naval staff envisaged a problem: given the general circumstances in which this plan would enfold, the air force would undoubtedly choose to attack the main enemy population centres.[192]

By 8 September, when detailed orders were issued to the submarine command, the navy's perspective had changed slightly. Cavagnari now envisaged either a war that started with a surprise attack by the Italian navy or one in which open hostilities began after 'a very brief period of diplomatic tension'. While the British ships in Spanish waters were expected to fall back on Gibraltar and the French on Toulon, all or most of the heavier units in Malta would be transferred to Alexandria – as indeed happened on 22 September. The Italian submarines were therefore tasked to hit the enemy during the first phase of the conflict when their ships would be moving within or to the Mediterranean, to prevent enemy bombardments of the Italian coast and bombing raids on Rome, Naples and Taranto by aircraft carriers and warships, and to attack French transports travelling between North Africa and metropolitan France and any carrying troops and equipment to Corsica. Forty-seven submarines were allotted to the nine routes to be patrolled.[193]

On 10 September, Cavagnari warned admiral Lais of the 6th Division that it could be decided to launch 'surprise hostilities' against Britain and France, in which case he should be ready to put the most important enemy units in Spanish waters out of action.[194] Admiral Iachino and admiral Goiran were likewise ordered to prepare MAS attacks on Malta and Toulon. Two days later Cavagnari informed all naval commands that while the developing crisis over Czechoslovakia could easily lead to war, in accordance with orders received he did not intend to order a major mobilisation of the fleet.[195] The source of these instructions can only have been Mussolini, whose intention was evidently to avoid a move which might propel Britain and France into countering what would appear an act of war.

The German military attaché in Paris, general Kuhlenthal, told Visconti Prasca at the start of September that in the event of a European war the French would immediately exert their maximum force in an offensive war against Italy, a choice reflecting Britain's interest in having Italy annihilated so as to ease the naval problem and turn the geo-strategical situation to their joint advantage.[196] This scenario, as Tripiccione's intelligence reports would soon confirm, was a German fiction. The French military authorities, evidently sensitive to the effects of any such miscalculation, took swift steps to set the record straight. Visconti Prasca was called to the French war ministry on the morning of 5 September to be told by the chief of the general staff, general Colson, that German troops, artillery and tanks were massing on the Rhine frontier on what was nearly a war footing, and that the French were taking no special measures on the Italian frontier, contrary to rumour. However, the French naval attaché who was en route to Marseilles to observe the situation there reported seeing a number of trains carrying reservists south to Provence.[197]

As events unfolded, the French high command was demonstrably concerned to keep Italy fully abreast of its actions in order to avoid any misunderstanding. Visconti Prasca was called in by the deputy chief of the general staff, general Dentz, on 14 September and shown official documents, including telegrams exchanged with the French military attaché in Rome, to prove that reports of Moroccan troops being sent to the French frontier were fabrications and that, apart from the pre-arranged recall of reservists which was scheduled to take place between March and November but which had been compressed because of the international situation, military activity in the Alps and Tunisia was simply the continuation of normal maintenance and construction work on roads and forts respectively. The movement of supplies in the fortified zone of the Alps was tied in with the precautionary measures being taken on the eastern frontier. The French, Dentz assured Visconti Prasca, were anxious to initiate no measures there which might provoke corresponding moves by Rome.[198]

At this point the one thing Mussolini ruled out was a localised war. If Germany took military action against Czechoslovakia on her own he was sure that she could not succeed. France, Great Britain and Russia would intervene; Germany, Italy, Hungary and Poland would line up against them; and 'the war will be hard and long'. In such circumstances, he told Szabo, 'colonial and submarine war have to be expected'. He intended to stir up Arabs and Muslims. However, if Hitler accepted a compromise 'Czechoslovakia will fall into his hands like a ripe fruit, as happened with Austria'. If by 12 September Germany's intentions were still unclear, Mussolini intended to mobilise some classes because 'he cannot remain passive'.[199]

The intelligence picture that Mussolini possessed by the time that Neville Chamberlain went to Berchtesgaden on 15 September to offer agreement in principle to the incorporation of Sudeten areas into the German Reich did not provide any reason for him to change his posture. Both Germany and Czechoslovakia had recalled their reservists and were mobilising: on 13 September the Germans were estimated to have 1,300,000 men under arms; next day, Czech strength was estimated at 1,100,000; and on the day of the Berchtesgaden meeting itself the Germans were reported to have recalled two thousand pilots and mobilised their air force. Apart from supplying Czechoslovakia with aircraft, the

Russians appeared to be doing nothing. Nor, apparently, were the British. The first news of any consequence about their activities came on 17 September when it was announced that seven infantry battalions were reinforcing Palestine, partly in case of 'Mediterranean complications'. France appeared to be making no unusual military moves; in particular, military activity along the Alpine front was normal and not much activity was to be observed in North Africa other than regular work on defences.[200] Ciano's knowledge of the military attaché's reports from Paris enabled him to engage in some safe posturing. 'Italy was so strong on her Alpine borders,' he told the German ambassador on the day of Chamberlain's first encounter with Hitler, 'that she could only hope that the French would attempt a thrust there'.[201]

During the third week in September, the navy stayed below the diplomatic radar as instructed. Precautionary measures were now in place which involved keeping alert for possible enemy moves; men and ships were allocated to surprise operations; and submarines were ready for initial deployment. Personnel, munitions and artillery were shipped to Leros, Tobruk and Benghasi to complete their readiness for war. Care was taken to carry out these moves without recalling reserve personnel.[202]

The picture provided by his intelligence sources may well have encouraged Mussolini to take a public step to exert what he most likely conceived as a pressure strategy on the western democracies. In a speech at Trieste on 18 September he called for plebiscites for all the national minorities in Czechoslovakia and declared his hand: as a solid member of the Axis, Italy hoped for a peaceful solution to the crisis or, if that was not to be, for a 'limited and circumscribed' conflict. However, if everyone took sides for or against Prague, 'everyone knows that Italy's position is already chosen'.[203] His very public association of Poland, Hungary and Romania with the German, Ruthenian and Slovakian minorities under Czech domination, reiterated at Treviso on 21 September, was calculated to recruit diplomatic and possibly military allies, while his review of Yugoslav troops at Caccia on the border the day after the Trieste speech publicly underlined the friendly relations now existing between the two powers. It also subtly communicated an important message to Belgrade which weakened France's ability to call on one of her eastern allies, namely that in any upcoming conflict neither party had any reason to fear the other. That Yugoslavia was refraining from playing any active role in the crisis was confirmed by Tripiccione. Other than moving three infantry divisions and one cavalry division to the Hungarian border region for autumn manoeuvres on 17 September, Belgrade took no unusual steps until 28/9 September, when garrison troops were moved to the Hungarian border, the release of recruits called up for retraining in August was suspended and troops on leave were recalled, and a partial call-up of specialist troops and air elements was begun.[204]

Assessing the process of military calculation that had been going on in the French general staff, Visconti Prasca concluded on 20 September that it had discounted arguments about Czechoslovakia's military and political value, considering the military support Czechoslovakia could give France as 'risky and in some circumstances more dangerous than useful'. Given the unpopularity of war in the public mind, the general staff had settled for a 'face-saving' solution. However, like the majority of the public, it believed that German demands would soon be renewed and that situations analogous to that of Sudetenland were increasingly likely as German power grew.[205] Margottini could report little more about French naval preparations than that there was intense activity at Rue Royale in which the British naval attaché had taken part before his departure for London on 12 September. Attitudes were hardening against a partial dismemberment of Czechoslovakia, especially on the political Right, on the grounds that such an outcome would not guarantee peace but simply postpone war. Never the less, Margottini believed that France would accept the detachment of the Sudetenland as long as it was proposed by England and presented in such a manner as not to appear to be a submission to Hitlerian threats.[206]

Between 18 and 22 September, information came in from the Italian consulates that naval mobilisation in Corsica and on the coast of Provence had been completed, and in the latter case anti-torpedo and anti-submarine defences were being emplaced. Of thirty-five submarines based at Toulon only sixteen were in port, suggesting that the remainder were at sea and watching the Italian fleet. More generally, there was a notable difference between the policy of reassurance adopted by the French army and the measures being taken in the Mediterranean by the French navy – the most hostile to Italy of the three services – which went beyond what was needed to carry out the government's policy of demonstrating strength. The state of mind of the French population at large, facing diplomatic defeat as a result of British policy and Italy's forceful stance over Czechoslovakia, appeared to Margottini to be that of a people who had already ignominiously lost a war and were looking to a future which would soon make new demands and require fresh sacrifices.[207]

By the time that Chamberlain journeyed to Bad Godesberg on 22 September to receive Hitler's expanded demands, the military configuration of the crisis suggested that the tensions had heightened but the parameters had not yet changed. England had done nothing more than intensify anti-aircraft precautions and distribute gas masks. France had recalled 350,000 reservists for the north-east frontier and had 800,000 men under arms by 20 September, since when no further moves had taken place. The first signs of preparations were visible in Russia: reservists were not being released after their terms of service were completed and the road and rail transport organisation from Moscow was being hurried up. Germany was the only power – other than Czechoslovakia – in a state of advanced preparation for war. Large amounts of heavy and medium calibre artillery, tanks and war materiel had arrived on the Rhine frontier on 18 September, and three days later Germany was estimated to have sixty-four divisions under arms, twenty-two to twenty-four of them on the Czech frontier and between fourteen and sixteen on the western frontier. On the day that Hitler and Chamberlain met at Bad Godesberg, Tripiccione reported that the army units and 'an imposing mass of aviation' were believed to be ready to intervene immediately.[208]

Not until the third week of September did Pariani begin to bring the Italian army up to a war footing. On 12 September, faced with mounting tension, and still preoccupied with Spain, he ordered that the final decisions on what was necessary for the Po Army be made as quickly as possible and that first priority in the creation of the new type divisions be given to those in the army corps which would be part of it. Next day generals Marinetti and Grossi, the commanders of 1st and 4th Armies which defended the western Alps, were ordered to their wartime command headquarters and general Ettore Bastico was ordered to Verona to assume command of the nascent Po Army, which consisted of two celeri divisions, two motorised divisions, one armoured division and three auto-transportable divisions. Work on the frontier defences there was to be pushed to the maximum.[209] The intendants of the two armies were ordered to their posts, though Pariani was concerned that they should act with maximum calm while checking that all the necessary dispositions for deploying the armies were in place. At the same time preparations were made for a call-up of the Frontier Guard, which now provided initial front-line defence, and for reinforcing the alpini guarding the western frontier.[210] Between 15 and 19 September, Pariani went on a rapid inspection tour of the frontier defences of the Alps.

On 23 September, Ciano told the German ambassador in Rome, von Mackensen, that Italian military preparations had been completed. This was a gross exaggeration, as he probably very well knew. That same day, thinking that the situation had 'grown darker', Pariani began to make the preparatory arrangements needed to bring the army up to full strength by recalling reservists from the classes of 1903 to 1915, deciding to exclude the classes of 1911 and 1913 because they had already served in Abyssinia. The political developments of the next two days, and the military intelligence that accompanied them, finally led Mussolini to accept that Italy now needed speedily to be readied for possible war. On 24 September, Ciano learned from Keitel via ambassador Attolico that unless further concessions were made Hitler had set a deadline of 1 October for military action, information which the prince of Hesse confirmed the following day. Military intelligence reports indicated that four German armies, including nine armoured, motorised and light divisions, and an estimated 3,500 aircraft were poised for action along the Czech frontier. The Czechs had begun general mobilisation on 23 September and instituted blackouts that same night. On the north-eastern frontier of France 200,000 reservists, recalled for training only two or three days after they had been sent on leave, were coming to their war stations regularly and quickly.

At this moment the navy had two concerns. One was whether in the event of war Franco would bring Spain in on Italy's side, as the Spanish naval attaché had said, or whether, as Cavagnari believed, British pressure would incline him to neutrality. Admirals Campioni and Cattaneo were united in believing that whatever the circumstances the navy should not waste any of its ships defending the Balearics. The other was what England's designs were. Campioni thought they might assert control over the exits of the Mediterranean and carry on a form of passive warfare. The French, on the other hand, could launch joint air–sea actions against Genoa and the Ligurian industrial region at the outset of a war. The admirals found it hard to reach an agreed position: Cavagnari thought naval bombardments unlikely, but Campioni warned that they could not be ruled out because of their moral effect and the lack of risk if they were carried out quickly.[211]

No less significantly, the military parameters of a crisis which Ciano had thought on 22 September could be regarded as 'fundamentally settled' were now beginning to widen. Poland was massing more troops on the Czech border and there was tantalisingly incomplete evidence to suggest that the Soviets had moved three army corps into the Kiev military region.[212] The contrast which the attachés were reporting in the attitudes of the French army and navy grew as the climacteric approached. On 24 September, Margottini reported that while the majority of the army general staff were against armed intervention in Czechoslovakia and the further call-up of reservists was to be explained in part as a political move by the government to counter accusations of weakness, the majority of the navy was inclined to immediate war on the grounds that a peace would be precarious and war sooner or later inevitable.[213]

Mussolini informed Ciano on 26 September that mobilisation would start on the morrow. Pariani ordered the frontier guard put on a war footing, purely as a precautionary measure, and the personnel required to man the anti-aircraft defences of peninsular Italy and eight major naval bases were mobilised. Next day, Mussolini told the heads of all three armed services to 'start a mobilisation sufficient to ensure initially an armed neutrality'.[214] The measures Pariani put in place corresponded exactly with that instruction. Reservists of three alpini divisions were called up; the Turin and Alessandria army corps and the *Armata del Po* were brought up to three-quarters of wartime strength, as were the army corps stationed in Sicily and Sardinia; the reservists for the XX and XXI army corps in Libya were recalled; the garrisons on Pantelleria, the Aegean islands and Elba were reinforced; and the anti-aircraft defences along the Tyrrhenian coast were mobilised.[215] Great care was taken to avoid any misinterpretation of these measures. The German and Hungarian military attachés were to be informed about the moves that same day. The following day the Yugoslav military attaché was to be told that precautionary measures were being undertaken but no steps taken along the eastern frontier, and the British and French attachés were to be informed that the measures were not being taken directly against France.

On 27 September, Pariani offered Mussolini his advice on the politico–military situation. If France went to war she would initially adopt a defensive stance on the German border and the Alpine frontier, but would take the offensive against Spanish Morocco and the Balearic islands and perhaps also from the Pyrenees. The troop concentrations on the Moroccan and Tunisian borders, the concentration of the fleet at Toulon and the closure of the port of Biserta were evidence for this. If England entered the war, she would initially act against the Aegean islands and Leros in particular to remove a thorn from her eastern Mediterranean flank and as compensation for the forced abandonment of Malta. On the basis of this somewhat imaginative assessment, Pariani recommended defending the Balearics, Pantelleria and the Dodecanese, as well as the Alpine frontier, and taking the offensive against Egypt.

Actually, Pariani admitted, Italy was in no position to undertake such an action immediately. Mobilisation stores for two army corps had been pre-positioned there, but manpower and fuel were both lacking. Even when complete, the XX and XXI army corps would not be enough and six more divisions would have to be sent from the mainland. They might come from the *Armata del Po*, which was in the course of formation, or elsewhere, but all their equipment, supplies and weaponry would have to be shipped across to Libya. Pariani therefore recommended that the transportation of materiel and fuel from Italy be started so as to reduce shipping needs to a minimum if it became necessary to pass from preparation to action.[216]

Much of this appreciation cannot have come as a great surprise to Mussolini: he was, for instance, very well informed about the resource situation in North and East Africa and aware that both colonies were incapable of sustaining a war without considerable additional support from the *madrepatria*. One of Pariani's main arguments, though, can only have rung hollow. SIM told Mussolini the same day – as it had done since the outset – that nothing new or untoward was being done by the French either in Tunisia or in Algeria.

The following day the commanders of 1st and 4th Armies were put generally in the picture as to the war scenario. Now worried about leaks and concerned that there was too much chattering in the war ministry, Pariani issued orders that no one was to be allowed to pause in the corridors. On 29 September, when he was in Munich, Mussolini was informed that the mobilisation orders would involve 244,000 men in all, that the troop movements would take place that day and the next, and that reinforcements would be shipped to Libya starting on 1 October.[217]

By that time, any question of mobilisation leave alone of war had dissolved. Chamberlain's appeal through the British ambassador, Lord Perth, for a last-ditch Italian intervention met with energetic acceptance in Rome and reluctant acquiescence in Munich. The news that Mussolini was going to intervene in the crisis, which began to spread through Paris at about 4 p.m. on 28 September, produced evident signs of relief.[218] Mussolini duly produced Germany's demands next day and then wandered restlessly around the conference room while his fellow statesmen hammered out the final details. Afterwards Italy experienced a small military humiliation. Evidently expecting that Italian forces would be involved in some way in the dismemberment of Czechoslovakia, the Duce instructed Pariani to be prepared to transport Sardinian *granatieri* and bersaglieri to Czechoslovakia.[219] They were never required.

The Aftermath of Munich

No sooner was the Czechoslovakian crisis over than reports began to flow into Rome about how the great powers had handled it and how they now felt about the new situation in Europe. General Gamelin called in the Italian military attaché, colonel Visconti Prasca, at the beginning of October to express his satisfaction that the crisis had been solved and that the situation of having to fight Italy – 'deprecated by the whole of the French army' – had been avoided. At the same time, he took care to pass on the statistic that thirty French divisions had been ready for action on 28 September and that at the end of partial mobilisation the French army had numbered over 1,200,000 regulars and reservists.[220] Margottini thought – somewhat at variance with his reports during the previous month – that during the Munich crisis the mass of the French people had shown 'a high sense of patriotism and notable balance'. The reservists recalled to the colours, although unenthusiastic, had shown discipline and a sense of duty. Parisians had shown much less nervousness and anxiety than Londoners, according to those who had visited England. Morale was fundamentally sound and had only been superficially touched by propaganda and communist intrigue. The line of French policy was evident though mistaken: emphasis on the closeness of Anglo–French relations, on Britain's new undertakings in respect of central Europe, and on American sympathy.[221]

To the naval attaché in London the most striking thing about British action during the crisis had been the preparations to receive air attacks which had included the evacuation of some 700,000 people. London had been protected with barrage balloons to a height of 2,000 metres; Brivonesi believed this would be effective in keeping attackers from descending below cloud level. The mobilisation of the Royal Navy on 28 September had not been very evident, partly because recall notices had been issued some weeks previously and partly because the annual Home fleet manoeuvres at the end of the summer masked the preparations. The Admiralty had carried out the mobilisation of the fleet without any significant intensification of its habitual rhythm of work, a fact ascribed to the fruits of past experience, attentive study and digestion of its lessons, and an increase in personnel. Mobilisation of the territorial army for anti-aircraft defence had been effective. Troops had been sent to Palestine and Transjordan; Gibraltar had been reinforced with local volunteers; a mobile division had been created in Egypt; and Anglo–Indian units had reinforced Singapore. In addition, the government had readied an expeditionary force consisting of two infantry divisions and a mobile division.[222]

General Kuhlentahl, the German military attaché in Paris, gave a clear indication of the German view of the future two days after the meeting at Bad Godesberg on 22 September. It was time for Europe to form a united and compact federation of states in order to face both the eventual drive of the Japanese towards the west and the attempt at economic subjection which would come from America. Germany and England could co-operate because there existed no real conflict between them since Germany's colonial demands had been no more than bargaining chips. The colonies Germany wanted lay close to her frontiers on the continent.[223] When it came to matters of detail, however, Germany was less enthusiastic. Pressure from Pariani to open Italo–German staff talks, the absence of which during the September crisis the Italian chief of staff described as '[a] palpable omission and a voluntary curtailment of the prospects of success', met with a dilatory German response. Admiral Canaris instructed the German military attaché in Rome, colonel von Rintelen, to reply favourably but to reserve the decision on place and time.[224]

At the height of the crisis, Pariani had remarked that the experience of putting precautionary measures into action would be of undoubted value in revealing 'inconveniences' which would be avoided in the future. In future, full mobilisation in one go would be exceptional and troops would be recalled in batches even in the case of urgent need 'because it is better to have few [troops] but good [ones]'.[225] Some of these inconveniences were soon apparent. Reservists had frequently to travel from their homes in the north to their regimental depots in the south to be clothed and equipped before returning north again to their war stations. Many were recalled to tank regiments when they had never seen a tank, or to motorised divisions in which they had never previously served when few of them could drive. Among the measures Pariani now believed necessary were inspectors to report on shortcomings of future test mobilisations and a period of forty-eight hours' continuous working for telegraph offices and telephone exchanges involved in calling-up reservists. Because he believed that one of the causes of bureaucratic slowness and complication was excessive centralisation he looked forward to the day when regiments provided for their own mobilisation.[226]

Reports of the irregular and chaotic character of the partial mobilisation of the army, which had apparently even left some of the military shaken, soon reached Mussolini's desk. Reservists complained that they had worn out their own shoes as they had not been issued with boots, that in the field rations had arrived late, cold and covered in dust because the canisters had no covers, and that meanwhile their families had gone without support.[227] Pariani's response to the specific complaints was that boots had been issued to everyone but that the reservists had had to turn them back in and wear their own shoes when going home; that in cases where units had not had their own field kitchens they had been supplied with food from elsewhere but always in covered containers; and that the local authorities and not the war ministry were responsible for meeting the needs of reservists' families after they had made appropriate application.[228] His reply to the broader charge of chaos was that '[o]verall partial mobilisation went pretty regularly'. He had made changes, particularly ordering that the most recent classes of reservists should go straight to their respective corps instead of going first to their military district headquarters, which some people had interpreted as a criticism of the system previously in use. There had been no significant inconveniences even though 250,000 reservists had been on the move in a very brief time span. Mobilisation was bound to be a disruptive affair, he told the Duce, and there would always be some whining; 'The important thing is that the people presents [itself,] and I can assure [you] that the mass presented itself well.'[229]

Pariani's solutions to the mobilisation problems, which threatened to produce as much chaos as the system he had applied during the Munich crisis, were complicated by an age-old problem: the inability to keep the army permanently on full strength because of lack of funds. His solution – harking back to the debates of the early 1920s – was a period of four months during which the army would be at *forza massima* (maximum strength) between mid-May and mid-September, and eight months at *forza minima* when most of it would be at a quarter or a third of full war strength save for the six divisions of the *Armata del Po*, the frontier guards and possibly the troops in the Aegean and Libya.[230] A structure which harked back to the army of the 1890s reflected his failure to escape from the army's traditional preoccupation with numbers to the detriment of quality, despite his modernising tendencies.

Just as the international environment in which Italy operated changed in the aftermath of the Munich crisis, so did the strategic and operational environment. In the latter case it was not yet easy to discern exactly what these changes might amount to. There were signs of weakness in the colonial positions of both Britain and France. Britain had been caught not merely by a generic crisis due to the incomplete state of her rearmament programme for the army in particular, but also by a contingent crisis in the shape of the Palestine situation.[231] The Egyptian army was being strengthened in accord with the Anglo–Egyptian treaty; among the new weaponry being supplied were guns, howitzers, anti-aircraft guns, machine-guns and anti-tank guns.[232] SIM interpreted French moves in North Africa during the Munich crisis as indicating that she had looked in the event of war to attack Spanish Morocco first while parrying any Italian threat from Tripolitania before launching a counter-offensive action of her own there. As far as likely action in the immediate future was concerned, France was in no state to undertake offensive operations against Libya until she had assembled more troops and of higher morale than those presently in Tunisia. Until she did so, she might launch a motorised attack on Zuara but would attempt to slow down an Italian attack and wear down the enemy's motorised columns by using a combination of defensive positions and two or three infantry divisions behind them. Due to the distances involved, any Italian attack could not hope to take the French by surprise.[233]

Munich confirmed Pariani's particular blend of operational and strategic thinking. As a power occupying a central position from which she was able to manoeuvre but short of raw materials and money, confronting enemies who had both and for whom time was a friend and not an enemy,

Italy faced encirclement and dying in a trap. Her choice was therefore simple: avoid encirclement or break out of it using 'violent manoeuvre war of rapid decision'. To achieve such a break-out required a powerful mass of men and means. The only way to amass such forces, in every dimension from grand strategy to local tactics, was to divide the front into defensive and offensive sectors and to stabilize the former by 'hermetically sealing' them while using massed forces to break through the enemy in the latter. Cover – *copertura* – would be thinner in offensive sectors and thicker in defensive ones. Where once the defence of northern Italy had rested solely on fortifications, Pariani now saw it as a combination of three elements: frontier guards, the *Armata del Po* always ready for immediate action, and rapid surprise attacks in depth by fast-moving units able to manoeuvre behind a combination of distant barriers and road blocks. Offensive 'breakthrough' war – *guerra rottura* – would rely on the new *binaria* divisions.[234]

In the view of the army general staff, in the event of a European conflict between the 'authoritarian' powers and the democracies it was of 'pre-eminent importance' for Italy to 'act against its own objectives and reach the Suez canal' while at the same time for moral and political reasons 'it must not suffer setbacks on the western frontier of Libya 'and worse, lose Tripoli'.[235] The studies being carried out suggested that in the event of war an expeditionary force of ten divisions must be sent to Libya along with the reservists of the XX and XXI divisions currently stationed there. However the problems of sea transport, which faced heavy demands and very great risks in the event of war, meant that the numbers must be kept to a minimum and compensated for by quality, armaments and motorisation, and by recourse to permanent fortifications. In addition, the most would have to be made of local troops by arranging as quickly as possible to mobilise three or four Libyan divisions.

The total bill for putting the necessary logistical infrastructure in place amounted to over 1,500,000,000 lire. Recognising the impossibility of getting its hands on that much money, the general staff laid out a 'minimal' programme for provision of water supplies, fuel and fuel depots, barracks, magazines, roads and telegraph and radiotelegraph facilities which would cost 377,000,000 lire. Equipping the ports to handle the large ships on which the expeditionary force and its supplies would travel required another 100,000,000 lire. The army suggested that the responsibility for seeing to this and for paying the bills be handed to the Africa Ministry. Unquantified in the programme were the costs of civil construction necessary to handle the troops, increasing agricultural output and adding to the numbers of locally available automobiles. Nor was any figure put on the cost of bringing the coastal and anti-aircraft defences of Tripoli,

Zuara and Benghasi up to a satisfactory level. Finally, the supplies and administrative back-up to mobilise three or four Libyan divisions would cost another 100,000,000 lire.

As far as Italian East Africa was concerned, the ministry had to acknowledge at the end of the year that there were still parts of Amhara, Showa and Gojjam in which the population remained hostile to Italian rule. Evidence of the strength and character of the resistance in the first two regions came in the shape of the statistic that garrisoning them required 140,000 of the 227,000 men stationed in the empire.[236] Despite a determinedly optimistic tone, the facts that the ministry had to report with regard to economic self-sufficiency were by no means reassuring. Grain production had gone down in 1937–8 for a variety of reasons, including the abolition of slavery and the destruction of stores by rebels or by Italian columns, and as a result the colony did not produce enough to feed the Italian immigrant population. Production of primary products such as cotton, castor oil seeds, sugar, milk and butter was being expanded. Deposits of copper, tin, manganese, tungsten, lignite and gold were to be found, though no estimates were made of possible quantities.

Supplies varied – there were enough munitions for 60 days' fighting – but perhaps the most serious problems lay in transportation. Assuming that 28,000 motor vehicles were in operation in wartime, there was fuel for only five to ten days, largely because of the three companies operating there only AGIP kept stocks of any size and then only enough for one month's peacetime consumption.[237] As to manpower, the colony could produce the 50,000 white soldiers Mussolini had demanded for the Armata coloniale by 1940, but would need 3,000 officers and 3,000 non-commissioned officers from the *madrepatria*. Of the 300,000 native troops which made up the bulk of the Armata coloniale, 170,000 still had to be recruited and trained, for which purpose censuses were being conducted. The true strategic uselessness of Italian East Africa came in the concluding acknowledgement that if the Suez canal were closed to Italian shipping the only way to get to the colony would be by air, over-flying Anglo–Egyptian Sudan from bases in the Libyan Sahara, or by sea using long-range submarines to travel round the Cape of Good Hope to Kisimaio and Massaua.[238]

In the immediate aftermath of the Munich crisis, the naval planners analysed the factors which favoured an alliance with England and those which indicated a divergence from her. The range of considerations favouring an alliance was considerable, including financial, commercial and economic advantages, securing free access to the Mediterranean, putting a brake on the arms race with consequent benefits to the budget, opening the way to friendly relations with the United States, Turkey,

Greece and Yugoslavia, and being able to speed up the economic development of the Italian empire. Some of the same factors were 'divergent': Great Britain's direct and indirect control of the three exits from the Mediterranean and the leverage which Malta, her alliance with Egypt and garrisoning of the Suez canal, Cyprus, the Palestine mandate and her control of the Sudan and Kenya gave her. Others were of a different order, namely the English mentality which produced 'an attitude of political superiority which Italy cannot acknowledge' and an unwillingness to recognise 'the eminently democratic political ideals' of Fascism. Finally, English policy looked 'not only to conserve her already immense empire but to extend her influence into Iraq, Arabia, the Persian Gulf, Tibet, etc'.[239] There was nothing in this analysis to encourage Cavagnari to question the current line of Italian policy, something which he was not in any case temperamentally inclined to consider.

Following this, the naval planners analysed the options in a joint Italo–German naval war. The results were scarcely encouraging. Little or nothing could be done against the enemy's bases at Gibraltar, in Egypt, Syria or Cyprus. Once again, the planners concluded that Italy would have to concentrate on defending the central Mediterranean, attacking the enemy's communications and preventing the linking up of his fleets. In a war, Malta and Albania should both be occupied, and the Dalmatian archipelago, Aden, Djibuti and the Seychelles seized. Apart from the neutralisation of Malta – a task which the navy accepted as necessary in December 1938 but for which no plans were developed until spring 1940 – this amounted to not much more than what the Americans would later call 'periphery pecking'.[240]

The navy was not the only service facing difficulties. There were huge obstacles to the North African strategy that Pariani propounded. Mounting a large-scale military operation there was hindered, as the Commissione suprema di difesa had noted in February 1938, by the lack of enough merchant shipping to transport it quickly and by the inadequacy of the ports, especially Benghasi. By 1941 the planned build would produce a total stock of forty-two ships capable of fifteen knots, of which the authorities expected to be able to make use of twelve or thirteen, but this number was not enough.[241] The inadequacies of inter-service communication presented another set of barriers to designing a strategy: the navy waited ten months before it received in the autumn the information it needed from the army and the air force about the size of an expeditionary force, its equipment and the monthly requirements for resupply.[242]

By October 1938 the shape of a major land campaign in North Africa was clear enough for the navy to work out detailed plans to carry it out. After shipping 39,478 officers and men to bring the units already there up to war effectiveness, it would have to transport 42,160 troops to the Tunisian front and 89,669 to the Egyptian front, along with 12,717 assorted motor vehicles and tanks, 4,849 horses and 48,365 tons of supplies. The air force's contribution to the expeditionary force would amount to 3,170 officers and men, 66 fighter aircraft and 2,227 tons of materials. On top of this, the navy would have to provide for the monthly shipping of reinforcements, calculated at 6,000 soldiers, 276 airmen, 18,727 tons of arms and munitions, 20 aircraft, 155 vehicles, 1,171 tons of aircraft fuel and lubricants and 44,760 tons of materials. Finally, the local population would need 45,000 tons of supplies a month from mainland Italy to keep it going.[243]

Tripoli could handle ten ships at a time (although only six could moor at quay-side), Benghasi and Tobruk five each. Creative calculations, which included sending the troop-carrying ocean liners ahead of the main convoys and turning them round in twenty-four hours, increased the total capacity of the Libyan ports to thirty-four ships at a time.[244] Further arithmetical exercises involving time at sea and turn-around times produced the conclusion that Italy might expect to have fifteen troop transports available (ten fewer than were calculated to be necessary), twenty-five ships capable of carrying vehicles and roughly fifty for men and horses (well over the forty-eight ships thought necessary for the two tasks together). However, this could only be the case if one precondition was met:

[I]n the period of diplomatic tension adequate provision should be made to keep in the Mediterranean a number of our ships which otherwise on the opening of hostilities would find themselves outside the Straits [of Gibraltar], and if we are able to make use of a certain number of German ships which will take refuge in our ports and perhaps also enemy ships which we have detained.[245]

Besides these considerations, there were other strategic issues which rendered the operation problematical. Alexandria would probably be the main British naval base in the Mediterranean. In the worst case imaginable, the British might station their entire fleet of seven battleships and battle-cruisers, fifteen cruisers and forty-five destroyers there – a force far larger than the entire Italian fleet. During the Munich crisis, the British and French had stationed only light units at Malta and Biserta; if, as seemed probable, they would return in strength to those bases this could render the entire transportation operation impossible. The only ways to avoid this situation were to take Malta or to keep it bottled up by air and naval forces while maintaining interception forces in the Sicilian channel.[246]

As well as grappling with what looked like almost insoluble operational and strategic problems, the navy also faced a serious issue with regard to future naval build which had important ramifications as far as the as yet fairly tenuous naval relations of the Axis were concerned. The question was whether a 40,000-ton limit on battleship size should be accepted by continental European powers, and whether Germany and Italy should come to a joint position on it. The Germans did not wish to be bound by such a limit if other powers were allowed to build beyond it. Cavagnari's advice to Mussolini revealed that he was as much concerned about the Italo–German naval balance as about any wider issues. It was worthwhile trying to persuade the Germans to change their mind, he suggested, because while Italy had already laid down two 35,000-ton battleships, the *Roma* and the *Impero*, in addition to the *Littorio* and the *Vittorio Veneto*, which would keep her shipyards occupied until 1941–2, Germany had only two 35,000 ton ships under construction. The proposed new limit would allow her more room for manoeuvre and provide greater possibilities for her to expand her build during that time.[247]

Mussolini approved the idea, but the German navy put off discussion until November and then December. They were inclined to agree as long as there would be some counter-balancing compensation, the Italian naval attaché believed, but thought that Anglo–German relations were not in the best state to initiate such a discussion.[248] On 16 December, admiral Raeder told captain Pecori Giraldi that Germany intended immediately to begin the construction required to bring her submarine fleet up to parity with Britain's and to arm the last two of five 10,000-ton cruisers in construction or preparation with 203- and not 150-mm guns. Both moves were within the parameters of the Anglo–German naval treaty. He also told the attaché that Germany was prepared in principle to accept the 40,000-ton limit, that Germany had secure information that British battleships would not exceed this, and that the next two German battleships would probably be 40,000-ton 406-mm gun ships since Hitler had decided that German ships must be equal in power to the largest English ships.[249]

The matter took on a new diplomatic complexion with the impending visit of Chamberlain to Rome, when the question of whether Italy would adopt a 40,000-ton limit as England had said she intended to do would likely be raised by the visitors. The British also proposed that all powers having naval agreements with London should exchange intelligence on naval building. Since Italy had adhered to the London treaty on 2 December 1938, she now had a formal mechanism through which to exchange information on naval construction with Britain, the United States and France. No such formal arrangement existed with Germany, and the Foreign Ministry suggested making one so as not to have to go via London to get details of Germany's programme. Rome already knew that

Hitler did not intend to join any naval agreement which obliged him to exchange information with the Soviet Union, and was equally aware that it ought not to get out of step on this issue, though Cavagnari generally favoured such an idea. Nor did the navy want to respond to France's proposal to operate a 35,000-ton limit as long as the other continental powers did likewise – which it was not disposed to accept – until it knew more about German thinking.[250] Vittetti was convinced of the political advantages of a direct Italo–German naval pact which would further solidify the Axis and combine the two powers in a common front in future discussions, and ordered that discussions take place on 7 January 1939 so that he would have something in his hands by the time that the British arrived four days later.

Admiral Raineri Biscia returned to Rome just in time to arm the Foreign Office with German views. The Reichsmarine accepted the 40,000-ton limit 'for now' and had included such a ship in its 1939 programme but reserved the right to respond to bigger ships in the future by building ones of equal size. It would not accept the proposal for a limit applying only to the continental European powers, and neither would it enter into any system for the exchange of naval information which included the Soviet Union. Not only were the two powers now aligned on a central issue of international policy, but admiral Schniewind also undertook to begin a bilateral exchange of naval information at once.[251] Although the Italian navy had had to chase the Reichsmarine throughout, in at least one respect it could feel that it had more to give than to receive: during the course of the conversations Schniewind had asked if the Italians could provide him with the locations of the British warships during the Sudetenland crisis. As Mussolini's policy moved the Italian armed forces towards a closer relationship with their German opposite numbers there was one piece of good news for the navy: the *Richelieu* was eight months behind schedule and the *Jean Bart* eleven months.[252]

Immediately after the Munich crisis was over, Valle instructed his deputy, Pietro Pinna, that the air force's war plans must be ready by March 1939. His perception of the present parameters in which planning must operate showed that he was unable – either because of excessive bureaucratic caution or an inability to fathom what his leader was up to – to impart any clear direction to his staff. To his mind, the political situation required that plans be drawn up under four general hypotheses: war against France with Germany an ally of Italy or neutral, war against France and England with Germany allied, war against Germany with France and England allied, and war against Germany with France and England neutral.[253] Valle was covering all the options. He was also unaware that he had no need to do so. A month later, he was informed by Pinna that the first two scenarios were covered by PR 12 and the latter two by PR 9, both of which were already in existence.[254]

In late November, Pinna was sent to Germany. He was well received by the German chief of air staff, Stumpff, who discussed matters openly with him 'without assuming a lecturing manner like other German generals', and more coolly by Erhard Milch, who had 'a tendency to exaggerate the figures with the evident aim of making an impression and falsifying reality'.[255] A visit to the Air Academy revealed a confusing doctrinal division between the 'retrograde' ideas its commandant was disseminating of close co-operation with the army and navy, which were shared by many Luftwaffe officers, and those of his host Stumpff. He was told by Stumpff, Milch and the director of the Heinkel aircraft factory that Germany was two years ahead of its nearest rival, Great Britain, in air power and during his visit Hitler ordered that that distance must be maintained at all costs. The German airmen hated France and treated Russia with a mixture of contempt and envy for the economic riches she controlled which left Pinna with 'the clear impression that their designs, or rather their dreams, go very much further than the Ukraine'.[256] The general atmosphere enveloping Germany was that of imminent war.

Pinna was not very impressed by the bomber and fighter exercises he watched at Schwerin and Doberitz:

The bombing formations were a little confused, the combats between fighters and the demonstrations they put on not very sparkling and in every way [they were] very far distant from the marvellous performances of our fighters and bombers.[257]

He was, however, struck to the point of stupefaction by the care and precision of the organisation that was going on, by the numbers of workers in the factories, and by the amounts of materials and spare parts he saw. So great were the resources available to the Luftwaffe that he wondered whether the tens of milliards of lire that had obviously been given to it were being well spent, and speculated whether such a complex machine could function when it lacked some small but vital component. Would the units fight as well when they did not have such rich supplies of manpower and materiel at their disposal, he wondered. Although he was sure that the efficiency that the Italian air force had displayed in Spain was at least the equal of that of the Condor legion, there was one fact that he had to acknowledge: the spirit of sacrifice and initiative of the Italian soldier was not the equal of his German counterpart. In that respect and in others Fascism still had a long way to go before Italy was ready to fight the wars which Mussolini and Hitler were now contemplating.

8 'Speak of peace and prepare for war', 1939–1940

Fig. 9 Neville Chamberlain and Mussolini, 1938

Prime minister between 1937 and 1940, Neville Chamberlain believed that the path to Berlin and a peaceful negotiated settlement with Nazi Germany ran through Rome. His perception of Mussolini as potentially an 'honest broker' was seriously awry. The agreements he reached with Mussolini in April 1938 (the 'Easter Accords') opened the door to the recognition of Italy's new East African Empire without gaining much in return. Chamberlain's visit to Rome in January 1939 was a well-orchestrated charade: a week before he arrived, Mussolini had decided to sign a pact with Germany and Japan. Nothing of consequence came of the meeting, but Chamberlain returned to London convinced that Mussolini was 'a charming host and a man of peace'.

At the start of 1939, Fascist Italy aggressively tied its future to that of its ideological partner, Nazi Germany. The partnership was intended to aid Mussolini in reaching his goals, but the realities of economics and the currents of international politics forced him at least temporarily to abandon longer term objectives and look to security closer to home. Temporarily displaced, the Balkans reappeared in the centre of his sights as, aided enthusiastically by his son-in-law, he sought to profit from Germany's evident intention to crush Poland. A local war, it seemed, could well be conducted either on its own or under the shelter of a general one. When the moment came, in August 1939, the Duce was forced by the reality of military unpreparedness to retreat to neutrality and then to non-belligerence.

During the 'phoney war' which followed the collapse of Poland, the regime tried by a change of personnel to effect a belated recovery from what turned out to be a parlous situation as far as the progress of rearmament and war preparation went. Nothing could change the situation as far as the economics of autarchy were concerned – and nothing is what Mussolini did. Strategically Italy faced considerable difficulties, but there were also slender possibilities to take better advantage of the situation. Mussolini's wilful and autocratic decision-making during the spring of 1940 ensured that the best could not be made of a bad job. Thus, on 10 June 1940, bearing on their shoulders the weight of decisions made by their predecessors and by themselves, and now carrying the burden of conducting a war on behalf of a state whose reach greatly exceeded its grasp, Fascist Italy's military leaders took the first step towards ultimate defeat.

International politics and Fascist goals

On 4 February 1939, in his notorious 'March to the Sea' address, Mussolini expanded on the goals he had announced at the end of the previous November. To be truly independent Italy needed access to the oceans. Instead, she was locked in an inland sea, its bars Corsica, Tunisia, Malta and Cyprus and its gatekeepers Gibraltar and Suez. Italy's only objective on the European continent was Albania. In the Mediterranean Corsica and Tunisia were 'pistols' pointing at the heart of Italy and at Sicily, while Malta and Cyprus threatened 'all our positions in the eastern and western Mediterranean'. Greece, Turkey and Egypt were ready to join with England in completing Italy's politico–military encirclement and had therefore to be regarded as 'vital enemies of Italy and its expansion'. Once the bars were broken, Italy would march either towards the Indian Ocean via Sudan or the Atlantic Ocean via French North Africa.

In either case she would face Anglo–French opposition. The Axis – 'an historical necessity of the most basic kind' – provided the necessary protection for her back in Europe.[1]

The Duce did not initially propose the use of force to solve the most pressing of these problems. Corsica would be annexed after first encouraging its autonomist tendencies and then its independence; the French protectorate over Tunisia would be replaced by an Italian one once the Arab world's backing had been won; and negotiations would secure territorial and economic concessions at Djibuti. There were, Mussolini suggested, three ways of dealing with Italy's requirements: to wait on better times, to negotiate smaller details, or to present France with the programma massimo at an opportune moment, when she might agree to discuss it and so remain in the diplomatic process or reject it, in which case the only solution would be a recourse to arms.

There was no question that a test of force must come one day, 'not least because France only respects those people who have defeated her'.[2] However, Mussolini's survey of the shape a future Italo–French war might take shows that he had abandoned Pariani's idea of a North African war at least for the time being. Of the three potential theatres for a land war only Somalia offered some hope of success, though that was less promising than it had been; both on the Alpine front and in Libya the defences of both sides were too powerful to overcome. Therefore a war with France would become an 'aero–naval war'. Such a war could last a long time unless other factors intervened to accelerate it or it became a European and world war. Italy would be in a much better position to confront a war in 1941–2, when among other things she would have completed her artillery renewal programme, she would have eight battleships at sea, and the East African empire would be completely pacified, For the time being, therefore, Italian diplomacy would work to secure the best solution while the armed forces speeded up their preparations so as to be ready to face any eventuality.

The German occupation of the rump of Czechoslovakia on 15 March convinced Mussolini that the weight of power in the Axis had turned in Germany's favour. She had twice the number of divisions that Italy had and an air force five times the size, as well as a larger population. The only area in which Rome was superior was the navy, which was twice as big as Germany's. Yet Italy still had a crucial political card in her hand, he told the Fascist Grand Council on 23 March: whether Germany was encircled or not depended on Italy.[3] Five days later, in a speech to the Fascist squadristi, Mussolini told his audience that France could refuse to discuss Tunisia, Djibuti and the Suez canal if she wished, but the Mediterranean was for Italy a *spazio vitale*. The order of the day was

'More guns, more ships, more planes, at whatever the cost and whatever the means, even if I have to sweep away everything that is called civil life.'[4]

The turns of international politics in the early months of 1939 forced Mussolini to recognise that his *spazio vitale* was as much European as Mediterranean and that rather than being encircled he was in some danger of being shut out. In early January Attolico detected pressures to abandon the policy of autarchy inside Germany for one of economic autonomy in an area which included south-east Europe. These pressures might, he thought, be 'the essential determinants' of Germany's external policies in the coming year.[5] On 30 March, in a speech to the central committee of the Reichsbank which Mussolini read with some attention, Walter Funk declared that Greater Germany would in the future be a single economic block which must extend from the Baltic to the Black Sea, and it became increasingly clear that Germany considered south-east Europe to be more or less exclusively part of her *spazio vitale*.[6] Six weeks later the news that Moscow was negotiating with the Turks for a possible Treaty of mutual assistance and had made what she regarded as satisfactory contacts with Romania, Bulgaria and Poland raised the spectre of a Soviet bloc extending from the Baltic to the Black Sea.[7] The Russians were already believed to have been encouraging French resistance to Italy's demands since the start of the year and to be looking to form a 'democratic bloc' centred on Great Britain and France which they would then join or with which they would sign an accord.[8]

Economic, diplomatic and military considerations all seemed to indicate that some form of alliance with Germany would benefit Italy. Believing that a conflict with the western powers was inevitable, Mussolini told Ciano on 1 January 1939 that he was ready to transform the Anti-Comintern Pact of 1937 into a three-way alliance. When Japan proved obdurately determined not to extend its focus beyond the Soviet Union, he was happy to enter a bilateral agreement with Berlin. Both dictators were contemplating aggressive action in due course and therefore future war formed the backdrop to the discussions. The timing of the future general war was clarified to a degree, though ambiguities remained. In late March Hitler appeared to believe that a delay of between eighteen months and two years was necessary before it could be contemplated. In discussions with Mussolini on 15 and 16 April, citing the pace of the German naval programme and the introduction of the new Ju 88 aeroplane, Goering first thought that a delay of nine months to a year would produce a more favourable military situation for the Axis and then, pressed by Mussolini, favoured 1942/3 when the armaments ratio between Germany and Great Britain 'would be appreciably more favourable, especially in the naval sphere' and France would be hampered by a shortage of manpower. The pair then agreed on the policy to be pursued during the coming two or three years while the Axis prepared for a general conflict: 'Talk of peace and prepare for war, i.e. victory.'[9]

With the exception of Albania, which he seized on 7 April 1939, Mussolini's declared objectives were all in France's hands. Having shelved the idea of attacking Egypt and taking Suez, he now needed German support and assistance for a colonial war against France. Although he told Goering on 16 April that he did not intend taking action against her for two or three years, the enthusiasm with which he supported the closer military partnership which was embodied in a secret protocol to the Pact of Steel signed on 22 May 1939 suggested that he might want German help sooner than that. It was also possible that he might have to give help. The alliance, which contained no reference to the period that should elapse before war and became operative only if one party was simultaneously at war with both Great Britain and France, covered neither localised nor single-handed wars. However, even before it was signed there were indications that Germany intended to impose demands on Poland which could result in conflict.[10] The British guarantee to Poland on 30 March, and Hitler's violently anti-English diatribe at the launching of the *Tirpitz* two days later, suggested to Attolico that light had been shed 'on what will be the origins of the war of tomorrow'.[11] Ten days before Hitler denounced both the Polish–German agreement and the Anglo–German naval accord on 28 April, Attolico reported that German action against Poland was 'imminent' and suggested that although Hitler did not want a European war 'He could decide to attempt a coup against Poland in the supposition that neither England nor France would intervene.'[12]

The shape of the Pact of Steel was hammered out by Ciano and von Ribbentrop in Milan on 6 and 7 May. Four days before the two foreign ministers met, Mussolini was under no illusions as to the possible course and outcome of Germany's present policy. 'Germany cannot be under the delusion of being able to do to Poland what it did to the others without shedding blood,' he told the papal representative father Tacchi Venturi; 'Poland will resist; will be overcome by the greater German power; and this will start a new international war.'[13] On 12 May, sticking to the spirit of the imminent Pact, Ciano informed Warsaw that if a crisis was provoked Italy would stand beside Germany. A fortnight after it was signed, father Tacchi Venturi asked Mussolini if he now thought war inevitable. 'Most certainly, was his reply.'[14]

France's declaratory stance in the face of Italian demands appeared to be one of intransigence. 'France will not cede an acre of her territories to Italy, even if maintaining such a policy results in armed conflict,' Daladier told the chamber of deputies on 13 December 1938.[15] To drive home the point, he made a well-publicised visit to Corsica, Tunisia and Algeria between 2 and 6 January 1939. Behind the scenes, however, the French government put out a series of feelers to Rome. In January, using the banker Paul Baudoin as a back-channel, Daladier suggested that he was prepared to go a little bit beyond what French public opinion would permit to get a settlement. In mid-March, using Baudoin again, Bonnet and Daladier signalled that they were ready to negotiate if they got a public indication that Mussolini was open to talks. At the same time a second back-channel, Roberto Suster of the Agenzia Stefani in Paris, reported that Laval and the Right were keen to open negotiations. Suster was ordered to let the matter fall.[16] A letter from Daladier on 21 March offering too little, and a speech by Mussolini the same day condemning France for intransigence in resisting the peaceful revision of the Versailles settlement and jealousy of Italian colonial conquests, showed how little ground there was on which to try to construct an amicable settlement.[17]

Germany's occupation of the rump of Czechoslovakia in March produced no significant reaction in metropolitan France, but a notable flurry of activity in Tunisia. Reservists of two annual classes were recalled and intelligence reached Rome suggesting that substantial numbers of motorised forces had been brought over from France and additional artillery moved in from the metropole and from Algeria. SIM also reported precautionary steps by France's allies. Yugoslavia moved elements of six infantry battalions to the Julian frontier under the guise of improving fortifications and suspended leave for frontier garrisons, her populace clearly alarmed that Italy intended to occupy Slovenia. Poland also intensified its guard along the German frontier.[18]

Although Daladier publicly reiterated his determination to cede neither an acre of France's territories nor a single one of her rights, French attempts to open up channels were not yet over. Indirect approaches by Bonnet at the beginning of April and in mid-May were immediately closed off – the latter by direct order of Mussolini – and another by the pro-Italian minister of public works, De Monzie, was left to wither on the vine.[19] The news that Italy and Germany had agreed a pact generated an increased sense of uncertainty and alarm in Paris. However, Daladier's government showed no signs of buckling in the face of the new empowerment of Rome – if anything quite the reverse. Guariglia reported that the premier's stance was backed by 'an undeniable strengthening of France's military, social, political and financial situation' and that his optimism over France's capacity to resist stood on 'pretty secure foundations'.[20] In more desperate circumstances, the French tried one more time. On 7 September 1939, using the Polish and Hungarian military attachés as intermediaries, they indicated that while they were not prepared to discuss Corsica, Nice and Savoy they were ready to examine all non-metropolitan questions. 'Don't take this any further,' Mussolini scrawled at the foot of the memorandum.[21] As these episodes all demonstrate, he had as little interest in reaching a peaceful agreement with France before the European war broke out as he did afterwards.

Mussolini's bargaining position at the start of 1939 was growing stronger, as some in the British Foreign Office acknowledged. Thus the fact that Neville Chamberlain came to Rome on 11–12 January to talk with Mussolini 'without gifts in his hand' was one reason why their conversations were destined to be unproductive.[22] The other was that Italy now had no interest in embarking on the line of policy to which the British hoped to attract her. Chamberlain's objective in coming to Rome was to give Mussolini 'a greater freedom of movement than he possessed at present and help him, if he so desired, to escape from German toils'.[23] It made him irrelevant because the Duce had no wish and sensed no need to do so. Asked by the Japanese ambassador, Shiratori, whether Italy had any particular object in view in regard to the English prime minister's forthcoming visit, Ciano replied that Italy had no concrete proposals to make and expected no concrete results from it.[24]

Britain was a nation whose weight was now being thrown on to the international scales of power to counter that of Italy and whose diplomatic initiatives put obstructions in the way of Italy's attainment of her goals. Some sanguine intelligence analysis of a 'best case' variety enabled Rome to discount her military capability. SIM put a reassuring spin on the British defence budget, published in March. The emphasis on the air force, which was to have 2,000 front-line planes, showed what England feared most in the event of war, and the rearmament programme, though 'colossal', presented 'the grave structural defect of being fundamentally based on the mechanical factor rather than on that of men'. The 'spiritual and material deficiencies' which this demonstrated were regarded as self-evident.[25]

Britain's diplomatic weight, though, was another matter. Besides her guarantees to Poland, Greece and Romania, she was perceived to be manipulating Turkey into an anti-Axis policy (with Ankara's active encouragement) and pulling France into positions that were not ones she would otherwise naturally adopt.[26] The news that Britain was building a naval and air base at Cesme overlooking the Gulf of Smyrna and anchoring the northern end of a 370-kilometre line of Turkish fortifications extending down the coast of Anatolia as far as Antalya, trumpeted by the press as 'the future Singapore of the eastern Mediterranean', heightened both concern and hostility in Rome.[27]

When, on 4 July, the recently arrived British ambassador told Ciano that if Germany put unacceptable pressures on Danzig and if Italy backed her with promises of military support there would be war, Ciano was ordered to reply that if England was ready to back Poland's position with force 'Italy will do the same for Germany's demands.'[28] Given the circumstances, it is hardly surprising that Mussolini completely ignored Dino Grandi's suggestion that the Pact of Steel opened up the opportunity to manipulate Great Britain by encouraging her obvious desire to conciliate Italy in order to separate her from Germany. In an action at once symbolic and practical, Grandi was removed on 12 July and was not replaced for two months.[29]

Italo–German military collaboration

Mussolini's moves to tighten the military links between Italy and Germany moved in parallel and in partnership with his strides towards an alliance with Germany. On 23 February 1939 Attolico was instructed to tell von Ribbentrop that it seemed advisable to the Duce 'in the current state of affairs' to set up agreements between the general staffs of the two powers which might initially be drawn in broad terms and could be set out in detail later.[30] On 9 March Rome was told that Keitel intended to develop communications with the Italian military in two phases: first the drawing up of an inventory of equipment, a process expected to last several months, and then a discussion of military problems after the tripartite accord with Japan which von Ribbentrop was vainly trying to engineer had been signed. Three days later Hitler gave the talks his blessing.

Pariani responded with alacrity to Keitel's invitation to talks, conveyed to him by the German military attaché on 22 March 1939, expressing admiration for the rapidity with which the Germans had occupied Bohemia and Moravia. In terms of a future war, it was his view that Britain, France and the United States would have rearmed and be fully prepared for war from 1942 onwards. The war, when it came, would be one of 'rapid decision' and it was therefore essential that the two armies get to know one another well before it occurred. As von Rintelen reported, Pariani wanted what was presently a 'betrothal' gradually to become a 'marriage'.[31]

The immediate stimulus to military conversations came from the prospect of a war against France. Mussolini made Berlin aware of his thinking in this regard as soon as Hitler had agreed that they might begin. As far as German military assistance to Italy was concerned, in the case of a conflict with France it was his intention that Italy would fight alone.

We do not have need of foreign military intervention and we shall not ask for reinforcements of manpower from anyone. We shall be satisfied if Germany is able to furnish us with arms, means [i.e. equipment] and raw materials.[32]

Pariani and Keitel met at Innsbruck on 5–6 April and exchanged ideas on the military situation and on the general operational postures which it suggested. After Keitel had relayed Hitler's assurance that in any war Germany would be by Italy's side, confirming the assurance given to the Duce by letter on 23 March, Pariani unveiled a scheme for a localised 'colonial' war against France for which Italy would need material aid but not manpower. Keitel thought that in such a case a European war would be inevitable and suggested that if things were going badly England would join in.

It must be plainly stated: this we would not have. We should be losing all opportunities for surprise and be letting our ability to take the initiative ourselves slip from our hands, as the others would then be fully prepared.[33]

Faced with outright dissent, Pariani at once abandoned his design and acknowledged that in the circumstances it would be much better for Italy and Germany to attack together.

Both men agreed that a war with the western powers was inevitable. Pariani suggested 1941–2 as the most favourable time for Italy. According to the German account of the meeting Keitel did not specify any dates, but suggested that war might come in a few years time when their rearmament was complete but England's was not. The Italians presumed he meant that war would occur within three or four years. Then, and over a vital issue, the two men apparently parted company. Keitel believed that they had both concurred that a war must be decided quickly since Italy was even less well placed to endure a long war than Germany. Pariani came away from the first meeting believing they had agreed that they had to take into account the possibility of a long war as well as a short war, and that their countries must give one another reciprocal economic as well as military support.[34] Next day both men described the organisation of their respective frontier defences. Pariani indicated that the Italians expected to be able to prevent a French breakthrough along the Alpine frontier. Both agreed on the importance of a single plan, but left the related issue of unified command untouched.[35] Keitel made no mention of the order to prepare for military operations against Poland that he had signed on 3 April, and Pariani likewise made no reference to the attack on Albania which began on 7 April.

In raising the prospect of a localised war against France, Pariani was following instructions given him by Mussolini. Personally he agreed with Keitel that such a war would be bound to spread, or so he told the

German military attaché von Rintelen during their journey back from Berlin. Such a war, he reassured his travelling companion, 'need hardly be reckoned with; at all events Italy has no intention of attacking France single-handed'.[36] Setting out his thoughts for Mussolini on the next stage in developing the military relationship with Germany, Pariani made no reference to the issue of war scenarios or to questions of strategy. To his mind the essential elements were the efficiency of the two armies and of fortifications and the potentiality of communications. What was being considered at this stage was chiefly an exchange of information about how the respective armies organised their command structures and their corps and divisions, about their arms and weapons production potential, and about how to improve rail communications between the two countries.[37]

The agreements reached with general von Brauchitsch during his visit to Libya and Rome between 29 April and 10 May followed the outline that Pariani had given to Mussolini. Technical collaboration would continue through the mechanism of five sub-commissions. No operational co-operation would take place 'for the time being' since no collective plan of operations was to hand and joint operations were 'not envisaged at the moment'. This was an outcome which was agreeable to both parties.[38] In von Brauchitsch's case this may have been because his visit confirmed the reservations about military Italy which many in the Wehrmacht shared. Visiting Venice, he left admiral Vittorio Tur with the impression that while he admired the Italian troops, he did not think that their armament was up to the requirements of modern war. This in turn was due not to any deficiencies among the employees in the arms industries but to poor organisation of the work and a lack of modern machine tools.[39]

When he learned of the signing of the Pact of Steel, Pariani greeted it with an enthusiasm which was in equal parts ideological and professional. It was not encumbered with 'the mass of casuistry' with which treaties were so often 'engorged', but instead spoke of 'a compact mass' which, 'sharing ideals, training and technical conceptions', was ready to throw itself on whatever point was selected. Militarily, what pleased him about the alliance with Germany was that it put weight on trained manpower reserves which other countries did not have.[40] To have come to such a conclusion, which more or less totally disregarded the technological and economic dimensions of the future war which both men had discussed the previous month, suggests that Pariani was quite unable to envisage the kind of war he and his ally would now face.

A week after the Pact of Steel had been signed, von Ribbentrop suggested that it be put into effect through the creation of military and economic commissions. The former would play a co-ordinating role and develop contacts between each of the three services, as well as dealing with general questions and those needing decisions by government.[41] Mussolini selected general Ugo Cavallero, rather than Pariani or Badoglio, to act as his co-ordinator and sent him to Berlin with a memorandum re-emphasising the fact that Italy needed the next three and a half years to organise Libya, pacify Abyssinia, complete the six battleships currently in the yards and renew all her medium and heavy artillery. Only from 1943 onwards could a common military effort have the best prospect of victory. As to the shape such a war would take, Mussolini assumed that it would be one of attrition and 'reciprocal defensives' on the Rhine, the Alps and in Libya. Offensives would be possible from Ethiopia against the neighbouring British and French colonies. More importantly, 'from the very first hours of war we must make ourselves masters of the entire Danube basin and the Balkans'. A 'lightning' operation which used Hungary and Bulgaria as launching pads and was 'conducted with extreme resolution' would knock out Greece, Romania and Turkey and would 'secure our backs'.[42]

During Cavallero's encounters with the Germans in early June he raised three dimensions of the military alliance, preparation, military co-ordination and the war economies, but made little progress with any of them. Von Ribbentrop was ready to set up a military–political commission to establish the general lines for the conduct of a joint war – 'according to superior directions' – but evidently saw the task as one for the future and refused to specify what might be entailed. Keitel thought that effort should be directed at pushing on with preparations, but led Cavallero to believe that 'a premature outbreak of war may be excluded'.[43] At one moment the nascent military collaboration seemed about to move in the direction Mussolini evidently wanted. German officials suggested convening the military–political commission at the end of the month to determine Italo–German needs in case of war, taking account of the availability of Yugoslavia, Hungary, Romania and Bulgaria 'which will be neutral or occupied', and to improve transportation by arranging for the double tracking of the railway lines through the Brenner Pass and Tarvisio. Von Ribbentrop quickly intervened to postpone it.[44]

Cavallero came away from Berlin with the organisational outlines of a military–political and an economic commission, but disagreements about exactly how they should be composed led Ciano to seek to engineer an invitation to Badoglio which would allow him to 'complete the exchange of useful ideas' between the alliance partners. In late July Keitel was minded to invite his Italian opposite number in the middle of the following month. Almost inexplicably – though resentment at Hitler's unilateral high-handedness may have had something to do with it – Mussolini was ready to postpone a meeting between Badoglio and Keitel until the *Parteitag* in November.[45] With information starting to pour in from Italian diplomatic and military sources in Berlin indicating that Germany was very close to moving against Poland come what may, Mussolini received an invitation from Hitler on 28 July to meet on the Brenner on 4 August. Three days later the Germans postponed it. The meeting never took place. Instead Ciano was sent to Salzburg on 11–13 August where he found an 'implacable' Hitler determined to crush Poland. The measure of Italy's unreadiness for either of the wars Keitel and Pariani had discussed in April lay in the enormous list of raw materials and goods which the Italians presented to Germany on the eve of the outbreak of war as a justification for their coming neutrality – a list, as Ciano memorably remarked, which was 'enough to kill a bull – if a bull could read it'.[46]

Economic accounts and security surveys

In preparation for the annual meeting of the Commissione suprema di difesa between 6 and 11 February 1939, the ministries assembled the customary mass of statistical data and created overviews of the economic and security situations. As far as East Africa was concerned, the colonial ministry had to acknowledge that while 'the great majority' of the population were peaceful and loyal, the situation in the provinces of Showa, Gojjam and Amhara was 'not completely tranquil'. The figures told their own story: Showa and Amhara, where the most warlike inhabitants were to be found, were tying up 140,000 of the total force of 227,000 troops presently in Italian East Africa. Much remained to be done before it would be possible to enrol in wartime the great colonial army Mussolini wanted. From a mass of varying figures a picture emerged of a colony with approximately six months' supplies of food and clothing, ten days' supply of petrol in wartime (the planners presumed that the peacetime total of 8,000 motor vehicles would expand to 28,000 in wartime, though they offered no ideas as to where they were to come from or how they were going to get there), and enough aviation fuel for five months' wartime consumption. If the sea routes were cut off in wartime, the only ways to reach the colony would be by over-flying the Sudan from south-east Libya or by sending long-range submarines (a type of vessel Italy did not possess) via Gibraltar and the Cape of Good Hope to Kisimaio or Massowa.[47]

Italo Balbo's report on Libya was prefaced with the assurance that although material preparations were not yet complete, spiritually 'everyone, soldier and civilian, Italian and Muslim, is more than ready to face any eventuality'. What he actually had to say can only have confirmed

Mussolini's shift away from the idea of a North African war. In the west, improved French fortifications along the frontier now made it impossible to turn the fortifications guarding the Straits of Gabes, while improvements to Tunisian communications meant that four times as many enemy motor vehicles could use some roads. In the east, British forces in Egypt had been doubled to two divisions, one of which was wholly motorised, and a 'vast programme' to increase Egypt's military capabilities was under way. In the event of war, Balbo still intended to launch a 'lightning offensive' against Tunisia. To carry it out he would now need not four but eight divisions from the *madrepatria* to add to the four metropolitan and two Libyan divisions he already possessed. Balbo's own figures showed how far his feet were from the ground. Eight additional infantry divisions would require 6,000 trucks, 2,000 motorcycles, 400 tanks and 500 guns. No supplies or mobilisation stores were available for any of them. Libya had about three months' supplies of petrol, and for the troops already in place there was rifle ammunition for ten days and artillery ammunition for six.[48]

When the three service chiefs surveyed the situation Cavagnari reported that work being carried out on Tripoli would, when finished, render the port suitable for the disembarkation of major troop units but that Benghasi and Tobruk were a long way from such a situation. Nothing at all had been done to build a naval base at Kisimaio, as the navy had recommended in November 1937, and the naval chief of staff requested 45,000,000 lire to transform it from an anchorage to 'a naval base able to give support and shelter to the naval forces conducting the war in the Indian Ocean'. The navy hoped that by the end of 1940 'the greater part' of the fuel supplies necessary to sustain twelve months' fighting would be in place.[49] The army acknowledged that the logistical underpinning which was needed to give Libya the capacity for autonomous military operations was 'still much below the minimum limit [necessary]'. A complete solution to the logistical problems would require over one billion lire. Most urgently needed were water stations, pipelines and storage tanks, completion of the barracks for the four divisions already in Libya and the construction of magazines for the war stores of those to be brought in, road works along the eastern frontier, and telephone and radio-telephone communications. Mussolini had already allocated 80,000,000 lire for this work, but another 238,000,000 lire would be required to complete it. There was as yet no properly co-ordinated scheme at all for the coastal and anti-aircraft defence of the colony.[50]

Valle was more up-beat. Libya had stocks sufficient for seventy-five days' fighting and these would 'gradually' be brought up to the required six months' worth as the development of the programme allowed. Twelve airports and over a hundred temporary airfields gave the air force more than enough freedom of movement. The planes to use them would be detached from metropolitan Italy and added to the two squadrons based at Tripoli and Benghasi as circumstances dictated.[51]

The Commissione suprema gathered on 6 February to begin six days of discussions on the customarily varied agenda. A lengthy debate on anti-aircraft defences produced clear directions from Mussolini that 4,000 anti-aircraft guns were required, and that 10 million gas masks should be distributed to the population within five years. An attempt by Valle to systematise anti-aircraft defence along German lines, with the army and the navy using guns to defend 'the very limited number of vital objectives requested by the air force' while it defended the designated locations of the other two services with interceptor fighters was resisted by Cavagnari. Mussolini effectively scotched the idea by ruling that it be left to the three services to decide the question together 'relative to the funds which the air force will make available to the army and navy'.[52] In one of the shortest discussions on record the proposal by the commission's secretary, general Fricchione, to create a special organ to prepare for and conduct economic war was summarily dismissed by Mussolini after Badoglio declared it unnecessary since competent bodies already existed and since there already was 'the indispensable linkage between the Supreme Command and the Government'.[53]

Mussolini was in a position to know with some exactitude how pressing the problems were as far as rearmament and industry were concerned, for just over a week before he convened the meeting he had received a report indicating that while industry was capable of meeting the targets for 1941 raw material stocks were scarcely sufficient to keep normal day-to-day working going. In an emergency, which would increase demand and reduce imports, the raw materials crisis which would immediately occur would practically halt production. Stocks of all sorts had to be built up: as one example, the army would need 5,500,000 quintals of grain in the first six months of war but had none in store. A solution to the war materials question, he was warned, could not be delayed any longer.[54]

Statistics were liberally scattered about. Italy was now producing domestically 10 per cent of the 3,000,000 tons of liquid fuels she consumed each year – an amount which would probably double in wartime. This was, Mussolini admitted, 'the weak, and you could say dramatic, point of our preparation ... If the motors do not work for lack of fuel the Nation is beaten, even if composed of lions and heroes.' In some respects, the drive to autarchy appeared to be going well, though the absolute quantities were small. Domestic production of refined tin had risen from 77 tons in 1937 to 275 tons in 1938 and looked to be on course for 350 or 400 tons in 1939. Experiments were still going on to get the best results out of the 320 tons of rich copper ore mined in 1938; here Mussolini hoped for 3,000 to 4,000 tons a year from Albanian mines. Coal was a problem – supplies for gas works had reached their lowest level in January as a result of the effects of the mobilisation in September, and stocks which should by law suffice for a year existed only for ten to fifteen days. Obtaining coal through clearing arrangements with Germany offered a way out, though Guarneri pointed out that delivery was difficult. Mussolini cut this Gordian knot by simply resetting the target at three months' supply.[55]

The discussion on the role of Italy's overseas colonies in war was entirely empty of any serious meaning. Mussolini introduced it by observing that since the authorities had moved the entrance to the port of Bari so that it now faced north instead of east the ships were blown into the streets. As Benghasi could not be used for 270 days each year there was no point in spending money on it. Marshal Graziani bemoaned the fact that neither of the roads from Addis Ababa to Mogadishu and Kisimaio had yet been built, and Balbo praised the possibilities of the air route as a direct link between Benghasi and Addis Ababa. When Valle objected that the British would not give permission for flights via Sudan Mussolini said that 'given the state of things' it was foreseeable that England would concede over-flying rights. With that vague observation, and after recording a blanket approval for all the measures the various ministries said they were going to undertake, Mussolini moved the discussion on to the next item.[56] Although Pariani provided a characteristically up-beat report in mid-June, Badoglio's office concluded a month later that Italian East Africa and Libya were still in much the same boat, with war stocks running down or being built up only slowly.[57]

The armaments that Mussolini wanted needed steel, and here again the picture was less than comforting. Steel output at 2,399,000 tons was at the highest level ever reached between 1914 and 1938, but correspondingly stocks were down by almost two thirds. Mussolini thought an annual output of 4,000,000 tons was needed to meet the minimum needs of war and blamed the entire industry for relying too heavily on foreign-sourced scrap-iron. Although France was going to cease supplying it, Italy had 150,000,000 tons of iron ore deposits from which to make up the deficiency. The fundamental issue, Dallolio pointed out, was not one of stocks but of the means to purchase them. This was particularly the case because hitherto Italian steel producers had depended mainly on imported scrap iron to which they made small additions of domestic wrought iron. Once again, the figures were striking: between 1934 and 1938 Italy had imported 3,098,387 tons of scrap at a total cost of 831,592,000 lire. In this respect at least, as Dallolio pointed out, industry had hitherto worked at odds with the policy of autarchy.[58] At the end of the day, the issues all remained the same: finding the financial resources to fund the necessary imports, managing industry in such a way as simultaneously to cut those imports down and produce the high-quality metals that were needed for the armaments industry in particular, and co-ordinating the massive and conflicting demands of the armed services. They also remained unresolved.

Military preparations

On 7 January 1939, in order as he put it 'to avoid the chaplain at Gobes becoming the first French bishop of Tripoli', Mussolini announced that he intended to recall 50,000 reservists the following month, some of whom would be sent to flesh out the 'overly skeletal' units comprising the two army corps presently in Libya. In doing this, he intended to avoid tying up the entire Italian navy for three months protecting convoys heading there.[59] Pariani's immediate priorities were strengthening the cover on the western Alpine frontier and the defences in Libya. Balbo was advised that the Tunisian frontier fortifications and the wall protecting Tripoli must be ready by May, and the army staff were ordered to explore the use of old tanks to stiffen fortifications especially in Libya.[60] SIM reported no signs of any unusual activity on the French frontier and a modest increase in the size of the garrison at Djibuti – which Pariani deliberately exaggerated in his report to Mussolini, increasing it from an initial estimate of 3,500 to 8,000.[61]

Mussolini's perspective on international politics was relayed to the armed forces chiefs of staff by Badoglio on 26 January 1939. In making his demands on France, the Duce did not intend to raise the issues of Corsica, Nice or Savoy; they were initiatives taken by individuals and did not enter into his plans. Nor did he intend to make territorial demands of France because he was sure she could not grant them, thus putting Italy into a situation in which she had either to withdraw such demands or go to war – 'and that is not in his intentions'.[62] There existed no firm undertaking by Germany to come to Italy's aid such as Mussolini had given Hitler the previous September. In terms of specifics not much was forthcoming. Libya should stay wholly on the defensive; relations with Yugoslavia were very good though her internal situation was delicate because of Croat secessionism; and in the event of a conflagration in the west the military did not need to worry over the situation on the eastern frontier.

From this limited guidance Badoglio developed a military conspectus. An Italian offensive into Egypt was no more. Reinforcing the colony was much easier for France than for Italy, whose navy would be very vulnerable to hostile submarine actions, and air transport offered no practical alternative: Pariani had asked for 1,000 planes, Mussolini had reduced that number to 100, and Valle announced that ten S 82 transports would be ready by July, each capable of carrying fifty men. Supplies, including 200-days' ammunition, would have to be built up over the coming months for the extra four divisions it was planned to put into Libya, so that only the men would have to be shipped over. Neither the airmen nor the soldiers were happy with the quiescence imposed on them. Valle pointed out that half of Italy's fleet of 200 civil aircraft could be used to fly 1,000 men at a time across the Mediterranean, and put in a bid to neutralise the French air force on Corsica as the most pressing defensive action that had to be taken. Pariani chafed at the restrictions being imposed on planning and argued that defensives resolved nothing. Anything more than strictly defensive planning evidently waited, however, on Hitler's speech and on how Mussolini interpreted it.

Briefing the army commanders on 4 February, the day on which Mussolini spoke to the Fascist Grand Council, Pariani saw nothing in the international situation at the start of the year to cause the military any alarm, though the need for preparations was evident. Relations with England were more relaxed, partly because of the Mediterranean accords and partly because England was neither ready for war nor inclined towards it. France had taken measures to improve her defences in Tunisia, to counter which Italy was recalling 60,000 men from the older classes with the least possible disturbance to civil life. As far as Germany was concerned, Hitler's speech on 30 January had made it clear that 'we are passing from friendship to military co-operation'.[63] Pariani was still unrepentantly in favour of a Libyan offensive and tried to use the air force's preference for a pre-emptive move against Corsica as a lever to revive it. If Corsica were bombed as the opening act of hostilities, he advised Badoglio, it would provoke war and would thus be 'inconclusive and dangerous'. If Italy proposed to strike, then it should inflict a mortal wound: 'If we must go in for brigandage – let us do it well!'[64]

Badoglio's directives set the army's immediate priorities. Everything had now to be concentrated on securing the defences on the Alpine and Tunisian fronts and bringing the war plan (PR 12) up-to-date.[65] At the beginning of February general Dallolio reported that the Libyan defences would be ready by May.[66] At the end of the month Badoglio went there and on returning told Mussolini that it would take at least another six or seven months to complete the programme and prepare western Libya for war. Not until spring 1940 would Libya be in a condition to be able to undertake possible offensive operations.[67] Three months later he revised that estimate: if it was not possible to speed up the supply of materials necessary to do the work, Libya would not be in an adequate state of defensibility until the end of 1940.[68]

Pariani contributed to the strategic shift now taking place by reorienting his new mobile army. Laudatory reports about the performance of the Littorio division – one of Pariani's new *binaria* divisions – in the closing stages of the campaign in Spain, passed to Mussolini, noted that it had done notably well in the Catalonian campaign where, operating in hilly and broken ground with no proper road network, it had proved particularly effective at manoeuvre and penetration.[69] Annual manoeuvres of the *Armata del Po* were set up so as to test the swiftness with which the combined mechanised, motorised and celeri units could protect Milan against an attack by the French across the central part of the Western Alps by blocking their advance in the foothills. General Grossi's 4th Army was ordered to carry out a practice counter-offensive manoeuvre on the frontier of the western Alps against a French attack along the frontier from the Alpes Maritimes to the open line of the Italian Cornice by mid-March.[70]

In February and March the army carried out precautionary measures which amounted to a limited mobilisation. They were designed to have sufficient trained forces in position on the mainland, in Libya and in the Aegean by the spring to be able to meet 'the immediate demands of the international situation' and to carry out general mobilisation quickly and smoothly if and when required. All or parts of nine annual classes of reservists were recalled, as a result of which the Libyan army corps were brought up to full war footing (62,000 men), 244,000 men were assembled on the western, northern and eastern frontiers of Italy (bringing them up to roughly half of war strength), the Aegean garrisons were brought up to 80 per cent of war footing (13,000 men) and the remaining units on the mainland were reinforced to a total of 290,000 men.[71]

The invasion of Albania on 7 April, an extemporised operation triggered by Hitler's occupation of the rump of Czechoslovakia, revealed some of the deficiencies in Pariani's army. Hurried arrangements were made in mid-March to call up the 1912 class of reservists in order to have a force of between seven and nine divisions on a war footing and ready to move in six hours. Details of the troops to be deployed and their locations were available within a fortnight. The attack itself was ill co-ordinated, clumsy and laborious.[72] It also used up munitions worth 176,000,000 lire. Pariani asked for a total of 876,000,000 lire to replace them and to provide infantry and artillery ammunition for six months of war in addition to the 5 billion lire already deployed.[73]

The calling-up of reservists made it apparent that the problems in the system revealed the previous September had not been resolved.

Recalling reservists by means of postcards, the method that had been used in 1914–15, showed serious defects; there were shortages of accommodation, clothing and supplies; and the system of checking and inspection was not working properly.[74] The postcard system was still in place in September 1939, when Pariani asked that the idea of using radio instead be explored. The chief of staff's despairing order in late September that a prize be offered to anyone who could find a way of getting rid of useless bureaucratic work suggests that he was unable to control the machinery under his charge.[75] Among the deficiencies that were thrown into relief as Pariani worked on mobilisation during May and June was the shortage of non-commissioned officers – an age-old problem.

If Albania was a less than dazzling feat of Italian arms, it opened up the prospect of action elsewhere than in North Africa. Pariani saw a range of strategic possibilities arising as a consequence of the Italian occupation, and on 10 April ordered his staff to study the occupation of Corfu, Cephalonia and Xante as well as possible operations against Salonika, Montenegro and Serbian Macedonia.[76] Clandestine over-flights of British and French naval bases began that day and provisional naval directives for a Greek operation were issued three days later, to be combined into a unified directive at the end of July.[77] On 1 May Mussolini told colonel Laszlo Szabo that if the West attacked Germany and a general war broke out, Italy would move against Greece. A little over a month after Ciano had flown over the landings that were to secure him his personal fiefdom, he and Pariani were exploring the options its possession opened up: attacking Romania to get control of its oil, and moving into the eastern Mediterranean via Greece to weaken the position of the British fleet there.[78] On 26 May, inspired by the possibilities which might open up as a result of Germany's evident ambitions in Poland, Mussolini and Ciano added a third Balkan target, Serbia. As well as the long-standing plans for war with Yugoslavia, Pariani's staff had drawn up a scheme in March (*Progetto 'C'*) under which twelve Italian divisions would move into Croatia on the back of regional disturbances, in tandem with ten German and three or four Hungarian divisions.[79]

While Pariani explored the new Italian options, Italian military intelligence sought to discern what the western democracies might do in the event of war. Assuming the Anglo–French military agreement to be in practical activation, SIM expected the British to send five or six divisions to France immediately and another thirteen or fourteen within the course of a year. France would take the defensive everywhere in Europe, though what she would do regarding Spain was not yet clear. In North Africa, she would in all probability undertake an immediate offensive to gain possession of Spanish Morocco and would adopt an offensive posture in Tunisia towards Libya, as would Anglo–Egyptian forces. Because the French were expected to take Ceuta, SIM believed that the British might vacate Gibraltar as being no longer of such strategic importance. They might also leave Malta as they would have access to the French base at Bizerta. Forces in Egypt would take the offensive against Libya to tie down Italian troops, and aero–naval action in the Red Sea would aim at cutting off Italian East Africa. Putting together all the signs – concentration of forces, movement of weapons and munitions, translocation of air units, naval exercises, the recall of specialist personnel and the like – SIM concluded that England and France intended to be ready by the end of March to confront any possible crisis.[80]

In mid-April news reached SIM that Gamelin was recalling a total of a million men and strengthening the occupation of the Maginot Line, while the fleet was being put on a war footing and concentrating in the Mediterranean. Units were being moved up to the Italian and Swiss Alpine frontiers. The French calculated on being able to mobilise 800,000 men in North Africa by degrees. SIM concluded that as the 'feverish rhythm' of activity was not justified by any threat of imminent external danger it could be a demonstration of some kind. However, the possibility existed that France was readying herself for a sensational move.[81] The French were believed to have allocated one army to the Italian Alpine front which would take the offensive in war. This news confirmed the need to put the Italian frontier defences in good order. In Yugoslavia a partial call-up was under way which would bring the army up to 400,000 men. This was thought to be a reaction to the possibility of internal disorder after negotiations with Croat leaders had been broken off.[82]

By late April activity in metropolitan France seemed to be quietening down and indications suggested that troops were being returned from Tunisia to Morocco. Focus shifted to England, where the cabinet was about to discuss the introduction of conscription. SIM noted an increase in the number of aircraft and anti-aircraft guns on Malta and believed that a British official was on the way to Cairo to discuss the future deployment of Indian troops in Egypt. Britain's decision to introduce peacetime conscription was seen as a sign that she was willing to face a possible future conflict; however, it could not be expected to have 'appreciable effects' for at least a year.[83]

Although the international military situation was temporarily static, there was intense diplomatic activity as the great powers sought to ensure that smaller powers adhered to their policies. SIM noted in particular Soviet activity in Turkey and the Balkans which was presumed to be aimed at securing concrete links with Britain and France in pursuit of an 'anti-totalitarian' policy. Everyone now waited for Hitler's next public pronouncement, which would decide whether the conclusive phase of the crisis would be one of peace or war.[84] His birthday speech on 28 April, though full of bombast, did not signal any open aggression and immediate tensions began to die down. For Italy, perhaps the most significant thing about the exercise in French defensive mobilisation that she had just witnessed was the fact that France had been able to put 200,000 men under arms in North Africa, 40,000 of them ready to act on the southern Tunisian front with Libya.[85]

In order that the army was fully aware of its responsibilities under the scenario he was developing, Mussolini summoned the army council to a special meeting at Palazzo Venezia on 8 May – a highly unusual occurrence. The papers that accompanied the gathering told Mussolini that at that moment the army comprised fifty-one infantry divisions, fifteen of which were 'auto-transportable', two armoured and two motorised divisions which together formed an armoured corps, three celeri divisions which formed another corps and the other half of the *Armata del Po*, and five alpini divisions. Following Balbo's experiment in Libya the previous year, a two-division 'air-transportable' corps was also being planned.[86] The main lesson drawn from the partial mobilisation of September 1938 was that it would be more effective to recall the youngest classes of reservists aged 23 and under rather than those aged between 26 and 35 as had occurred at the time of Munich.[87]

The Duce began by telling the two marshals (Badoglio and Graziani) and eleven generals assembled before him that the artillery question was keeping him awake at night. The fact that he had been told three months earlier that the first guns of the new artillery programme would not emerge from the Pozzuoli works until 1940 doubtless heightened his concern. Output had to be raised from the current figure of 65 guns a month to at least 200 and if possible 300 a month, together with the required ammunition. Even this figure would only be half France's output. On current schedules, the first medium and heavy guns would be available in 1941–2.

The army was then given as clear a picture of Mussolini's intentions and priorities as they could reasonably expect from him, liberally seasoned with statistics about the monies being allocated for the various activities. 'What was urgent', he told the soldiers, 'was barring the doors of the house'. All of them must be 'hermetically sealed', including Libya.[88] Hence the fortifications programmes in Libya, the Aegean and Italian Somaliland: 'with these works [completed], we shall be safe'. After that the next priority was in the Balkans, where Italy's control of Albania put her in the dominant position. Italy's move into the country had an important strategic rationale: it put her 'at the back of Yugoslavia and Greece'.[89]

Maintaining 60,000 men and twelve airfields in Albania would allow Italy to dominate the peninsula. The navy would make appropriate arrangements and would neutralise Corfu, which was 'now undervalued'.

Pariani responded by presenting Mussolini with an almost uniformly rosy picture of the present and future state of the army. Despite having to provide for the wars in Abyssinia and Spain, stocks of machine-guns, light field guns and mortars, ammunition of all kinds, motor vehicles and tanks – of which he claimed the army now had 1,377 – had all risen.[90] The army already had 13,000 guns and a further 1,600 were in production. The 149-mm gun would be available by the end of the year and the 210-mm gun during the coming year; distribution of 81-mm mortars (a key component for the new *binaria* divisions) and 47-mm guns had been delayed because they were being sold abroad. Petrol stocks, which had been doubled in Italy and in Libya, were sufficient for two or three months of war. By 1941 there would be munitions enough for four and perhaps six months of war. In fact although according to the planned provision metropolitan Italy was supposed to have 145,000 tons and Libya 42,000 tons of fuel, which were calculated to be enough to last three months and six months respectively, by 21 August 1939 there were only 110,000 tons of fuel in Italy and 15,000 tons in Libya.[91]

On the eve of the announcement of the Pact of Steel, Pariani outlined for Mussolini his perspective on war in general and Italy's strategic options in particular. The democratic powers were seeking to encircle the Axis and cut off the supplies of raw materials that were essential for making war. They would look to wage a war of attrition founded on positional warfare while attempting sharp blows at the weakest points. By contrast, the Axis looked for quick decisions in war by means of breakthrough and manoeuvre. In present circumstances, there were three possible strategic solutions to the problem: they could act against France, secure 'vital space' in the Ukraine and the Baltic, or take control of North Africa to free the Mediterranean and the Red Sea. France offered 'the most decisive solution but the most difficult'. She could not be attacked through the Alps, and although Switzerland could be taken rapidly attack across the terrain would make it difficult to secure a quick success. This left the Rhine and the Maginot Line. Breaking open the French defences there would not be easy, but Pariani believed that it was far from impossible. His recipe for success embodied his conviction of the value of the twin components of the ideal Fascist war machine: concentrated fire-power and chemical weapons, and action with 'violence which by virtue of mass and impulsion is overwhelming'. After that it would be a question of being fully prepared to break the enemy's counter-offensive and then bring about his swift collapse.[92]

The themes of his reorganisation of the army were summed up and reconfirmed in his speech to the chamber of deputies on 10 May 1939. The *guerra di rapido corso* was based on adequate moral, material and technical preparation. The new division had been tested in the last phase of the Spanish Civil War. Provided no crisis intervened, the transformation of all units would be completed during the year 1939–40.[93] This was a wildly optimistic assertion. A little over a week before Pariani made it general Giacomo Carboni, soon to be head of SIM, alerted Ciano to the 'disastrous' state of Italy's armaments.[94] Recent discussions had demonstrated that the army was drastically short of almost everything from boots to motor cars, and as future events would soon show the bulk of it consisted of unreformed infantry divisions most of which were not fit to take the field.

Naval preparations for war

In January 1939, the naval planners drew up an outline of Italy's naval requirements to match a scenario in which Italy and Germany were ranged against Britain and France. The aim was that the Axis powers should have at least 50 per cent of the tonnage of the democracies, but at present the figure stood at 41 per cent. Basing their calculations on the assumption that Germany would adhere to the Anglo–German naval agreement ratio of 35 per cent for 'a certain number of years', that Italy could build 60,000 tons of naval shipping a year, and that it was in her interests to slow down the rate at which ships were declared obsolescent, the planners calculated that Italy could reach the amount required by the formula in seven years. The 260,000-tons of new shipping required to do so would comprise two 35,000-ton battleships, two 15,000-ton aircraft carriers, six 8,000-ton cruisers (four of them ocean-going), twenty destroyers, sixteen 1,100-ton submarines and assorted torpedo and MAS boats, mine-sweepers and minelayers. By 1945, the Italian navy would thus be 80 per cent of the size of the French navy, 10 per cent larger than the German navy, and 40 per cent the size of the Royal Navy – though given the difficulties of deploying more than three fifths of the latter in the Mediterranean, the proportion climbed to 70 per cent.[95]

Such a programme was, as the planners acknowledged, beyond Italy's industrial and financial capability. They therefore narrowed down their sights to what could be built in three years and what could be done with it. The strategy attached to this revised programme acknowledged that there was little that Italy could do on her own in the Atlantic other than deploy a few long-range submarines. However, if sufficient naval forces were diverted to the Red Sea to block it, this would force Great Britain to divert traffic around the Cape of Good Hope. With Italy controlling the central Mediterranean, she would then have to rely on a route passing through the eastern Indian Ocean and the Persian Gulf before transshipping materiel for transport along the land route via Iraq and Palestine in order to resupply the canal zone. The resulting shipping flows would require the enemy to increase the shipping travelling the new routes by at least half, giving Italian submarines good targets between Karachi and the Gulf of Oman. If threatened from Kisimaio they would be forced to organise convoys, which would further lower shipping efficiency and to provide both close and distant escorts.

To carry out the strategy would require Italy to build another dozen ocean-going submarines and three long-range cruisers supported by two tankers to operate from the Red Sea in the Indian Ocean and China Sea, a dozen destroyers, a dozen submarines and six minelayers to shield the eight battleships in the Mediterranean and control the central section, and get the money to build up Kisimaio. In all, the planners estimated that this plan would require 89,400 tons of new shipping and would cost 2,644,000 lire. It could all be done, they believed, by the end of 1942.[96]

Having tailored his coat, Cavagnari ordered the cloth. On 8 April he presented his building programme for 1939 and got Mussolini's approval for it. By early 1940 he planned to lay down two *Garibaldi*-class ocean-going cruisers, eight destroyers, half-a-dozen torpedo boats, six colonial and six ocean-going submarines. The full programme included a third cruiser, four more *Soldati*-class destroyers, six coastal and six ocean-going submarines and two fast tankers.[97] The list was ambitious and greatly exceeded Italy's current capabilities: in January 1939 the navy had still not laid down twelve *Capi Romani* destroyers and nine submarines from the 1938 programme.[98]

Even as Cavagnari presented his desiderata, the calculations on which it was based were being overturned. At the beginning of February the naval attaché in London, rear-admiral Bruno Brivonesi, offered the reassuring view that England had no wish to go to war because in doing so she would have everything to lose and nothing to gain.[99] Then, in quick succession, came the news that in the coming year the Royal Navy would lay down two new battleships, an aircraft carrier and four cruisers, doubling the previous year's commitments, as well as seventeen destroyers and four submarines and then the announcement of the British naval budget for 1939–40. Britain planned to lay down sixty new naval vessels, including six battleships, and her annual rate of construction was being raised from 125,000 tons to an average of 220,000 tons.[100] Italy once again faced a yawning naval gap which was growing rapidly wider.

Cavagnari's budget presentations to the chamber of deputies and the senate differed markedly, a reflection of the fact that the former was composed of ideological enthusiasts while the latter contained a number of retired admirals. The deputies were told that the quality of ships was more important than their numbers but that Italy was close to getting the fleet she required. She would soon have four modernised 26,000-ton battleships, four new 36,000-ton battleships, thirty-one cruisers, some sixty destroyers and over a hundred submarines and MAS boats. The new programme comprised nine large cruisers and several squadrons of destroyers.[101] This was something of an exaggeration, especially where the second pair of new battleships was concerned, and Cavagnari chose at least some of his words more carefully when addressing the senate nine days later. The programme that Mussolini had agreed was reported accurately. The situation of the navy was 'satisfactory'. Its most salient characteristics were the submarine arm and fast ships; although battleships remained its 'backbone', what was now needed was ships that could stand greater wear and tear and be put into service faster. Arriving at his climax, Cavagnari gave the senate a sizeable hostage to fortune. Sufficient reserves had been gathered, he declared, 'even for a conflict of long duration'.[102]

While it dreamed up its own war scenarios, the navy continued to work on the requirement to ship troops to Libya to fight Pariani's – and Balbo's – preferred war there. In mid-January it calculated that it could ship the 41,808 men of the XX and XXI corps, together with the 11,874 tons of materials they and the air force would need and all 2,596 motor vehicles they would require to Benghasi, Tripoli and Tobruk within 23 days of the order initiating the operation, using 83 ships and sending them in three batches.[103] At the start of February the tables had to be readjusted when the army operations bureau reduced the number of divisions from ten to eight and indicated that all would be of the 'auto-transportable' variety rather than being armoured, motorised or horse-drawn divisions. Matters quickly became more complicated, for although the army envisaged that the measures presently under way would bring the two army corps up to a war footing of 36,500 men, it now envisioned two different war scenarios. If it was only defending the western frontier of Libya, 58,110 men, 985 motor vehicles, 164 motor bikes and 13,242 tons of materials would have to be shipped to Tripolitania and 25,000 men to Cyrenaica in a second batch. If it was defending the western frontier and attacking across the eastern frontier, 56,130 men, 3771 motor vehicles, 84 tanks, 1096 motorcycles and 27,091 tons of supplies would have to be shipped to Cyrenaica along with the forces required in Tripolitania under the first scenario. If operating according to the first scenario, the navy calculated that it could get the troops to North Africa in twenty-three days and the supplies in twenty-nine days; if operating according to the second scenario, the troops and supplies would take seventy-one days to get to Cyrenaica if they were disembarked at Benghasi and Tobruk, and fifty-one days if Tripoli too was used.[104]

These calculations were based only on the supposed availability of shipping and the logistical capacity of the ports. When the navy thought about the need to take longer routes than normal in order to try to reduce the likelihood of attack by enemy surface craft and the numbers of flotilla craft that could be allocated to protect the convoys, the times required increased. When the time taken to ship two months' supplies, the need to escort the full convoys out and the empty ones home, and the requirement to replenish the escorts and rest their crews were all added in, the final calculation revealed that it would take between 77 and 101 days from the start of transport operations to get the army ready to launch an offensive into Egypt.[105] From the naval perspective alone, the Libyan war looked an increasingly impractical venture.

Although personally somewhat austere and uncommunicative, Cavagnari had to move with the currents of Mussolini's policy which meant deepening links with Berlin. When, in late November 1938, Hitler laid down the principles that were to govern negotiations between the heads of the armed services of the two Axis powers, they were founded on the prospect of a joint war against France and Britain and envisaged independent action by the two powers in separate theatres. Italy's chief naval tasks would be to interrupt French communications with North Africa and eliminate Gibraltar.[106] In January 1939, Admiral Raeder indicated that he would soon make a proposal to the Italian naval staff for the exchange of operational information between the two fleets, a significant advance on the construction information that was being passed between them.[107] However, little of substance transpired until Hitler gave his formal permission for the three services to enter into negotiations with the Italians on 11 April.

Cavagnari learned indirectly about Germany's plans for naval action in a war against the western powers when his official representative at Hitler's fiftieth birthday celebrations, admiral Salza, talked to general Pariani on the train to Berlin on 19 April. The Reichsmarine planned to defend the central Baltic in order to secure iron ore supplies from Sweden and to use its surface forces in the North Sea to sweep the coasts of Norway. At Berlin neither admiral Raeder nor his staff showed any inclination to raise the question of Italo–German naval co-operation until Hitler remarked that he hoped that the moves towards initial collaboration begun in the Keitel–Pariani talks could be extended to all other fields, after which he expressed a readiness to confer with Cavagnari.

Ambassador Attolico then lifted a ban on following up earlier and less explicit offers from Raeder imposed on the Italian naval attaché after Germany had announced the protectorate of Bohemia and Moravia without prior warning to Rome. Salza came away from Berlin feeling that the Germans had wished to give the impression of a navy ready for a decisive offensive and that if Italy adopted a similar attitude – 'albeit without excessive boasting' – this would encourage Raeder to take them further into his confidence.[108]

A 'decisive offensive' did not figure in the Italian navy's strategic lexicon. Nevertheless, Cavagnari followed up the invitation on 3 May, expressing a readiness to enter conversations and asking what the Germans proposed to put on the agenda. The answer, which arrived five days after the signing of the Pact of Steel, was that the German navy wished to discuss the objectives and principles of further collaboration between the two navies, to determine the separate theatres in which they would act, and to reach general agreement on how to proceed in future meetings.[109] The two admirals agreed in early June to meet at Friedrichshaven on the 20th and 21st of the month. In the interim, Cavagnari gave rear-admiral Zieger of the German navy permission to look over one of the newest Italian destroyers, a submarine, and the battleship *Littorio* presently being completed at the Ansaldo yard in Genoa. Zieger's visit to Italy's newest battleship posed no difficulties for the Italians: an engineer officer, he only asked to see a boiler room and inspect the turbines, showed no interest in the ship's protection and was 'very discreet in his requests for information'.[110]

Before Cavagnari went to Friedrichshaven, the naval staff computed the naval balance between the Axis partners and the Anglo–French fleets. Their conclusions suggested that the Axis would shortly be at least a match for their potential opponents and that Italy was bringing a substantial contribution to the table. The French navy had a larger tonnage of ships afloat than Italy (546,332 tons to 464,407 tons), but five of France's seven battleships were unmodernised whereas Italy possessed four modernised battleships. In the Mediterranean, therefore, the staff concluded that the two powers were on level terms. Italy had more submarines than France (105 to 77), and they were expected to be more effective than in the past notwithstanding the British Admiralty's claim that anti-submarine measures had dramatically improved. The German pocket battleships and battle-cruisers, though fewer in number than those of Britain and France, were of the most modern type. As far as the newest 35,000-ton battleships were concerned, in 1941 the two sides would be evenly matched with three each. The arithmetic was creative, and tended to minimise the overwhelming preponderance of the Royal Navy;

for example, whereas Italy and Germany could count nine 10,000-ton cruisers built and four building, Britain and France presently possessed twenty-two. So were the strategic observations which accompanied it. The geographical position of the Axis would force their opponents to split their forces, a problem which would be increased when they had to defend territories spread out across the globe. The enemy powers would face serious problems defending sea traffic for 'The Axis would certainly make its presence felt both in the North Sea and in the Mediterranean'.[111]

The Italian navy had never seen much opportunity for decisive actions of any kind, but when Cavagnari went to meet his German opposite number the limited options he perceived had narrowed even further. French naval manoeuvres in the Atlantic in March, conducted for the first time at a strategic rather than a tactical level, appeared to be designed to practise the protection of traffic in the eastern Atlantic against German submarines and cruisers. The French clearly feared that German surface craft could escape from the North Sea in time of war, and were also taking into consideration the political orientation of a nationalist Spain. More significantly for a Mediterranean war, France now had enough troops available in the metropole for her no longer to need to transport them from North Africa. Nor had she need of their contribution to an offensive, since the strength of German fortifications along the frontier greatly reduced the likelihood that France would undertake such a strategy. Thus, at the start of a war the targets on which the Italian navy had counted for so long would not be there. Even if, as seemed probable, the French used their numerical superiority in Tunisia to attack Libya they already had enough forces on the spot and would need only modest supplies from France to augment their war stocks.[112]

On 20–21 June, Cavagnari and Raeder met at Friedrichshaven. At the first meeting Raeder spoke of a war against Great Britain and France which would be 'a matter of life and death' for both powers. For Germany it was a question of gaining 'living space' but that was to be achieved by politics if possible: war was 'not in the Führer's sights' and would be a last resort. When Cavagnari suggested that in such circumstances Greece, Turkey and the Soviet Union would have to be added to the list of enemies Raeder did not demur, and added in the United States. Japan he expected to show benevolent neutrality towards the Axis unless Britain made an agreement with Russia, in which case it would join Germany and Italy.[113]

A divide opened up when Raeder turned the discussion to naval strategy. Having erred during the previous war in not attacking the enemy's Atlantic traffic from the outset, the Reichsmarine proposed to do so in the next one, using its submarines and surface forces first against the North Atlantic and then gradually extending the action to the southern

Atlantic and the Indian Ocean. What he looked for from the Italian navy was collaboration in the form of operations by Italian submarines in the Atlantic south of Lisbon and possibly in the Indian Ocean. Cavagnari saw things from a completely different perspective. The weight of the enemy's naval strength would be felt in the Mediterranean, the French in the western and the British in the eastern basins. When Raeder suggested that a French move against the Balearics would give Italy a good opportunity to concentrate its forces in the western Mediterranean and win command of that sector, Cavagnari replied evasively: any such operation was demanding and not likely to be brief, but would provide Italy with 'a good opportunity to act'. The Germans took away the impression that for the Italian navy defence was 'the only possibility' as far as both the Balearics and the Dodecanese were concerned, and that offensive operations were 'excluded by the given balance of forces'.[114]

Raeder continued to press the advantages of energetic action in the western Mediterranean on his fellow mariner as one way to encourage Spain to join in on the Axis side, or at least adopt an attitude of benevolent neutrality. When he suggested that such action there would also force the French to shift their lines of communication with North Africa out into the Atlantic, making them more vulnerable to German action, Cavagnari revealed that the Italians did not think that the French intended to ship troops from Algeria and Morocco to France. Cavagnari's positive contribution to a future wartime partnership was twelve ocean-going submarines to operate in the Atlantic; however, whether Italy would be able to undertake such action at all depended on the availability of Spanish bases. What Cavagnari wanted, it became clear, was for Germany to keep the British fast battleships out of the Mediterranean while the Italian navy 'fixed' the British units in the eastern Mediterranean. The only possible area of direct collaboration was in the Indian Ocean. Presently the possibilities there were 'very limited' but they would increase over time. When Cavagnari talked about the development of Kisimaio as a base for submarine warfare, Raeder saw possibilities for German cruisers to operate there too.[115]

At their second meeting Cavagnari raised an issue close to the Italian navy's heart – how to secure supplies in wartime. Raeder, who expected sea-borne trade across the world's oceans to drop dramatically as soon as war broke out, suggested that as well as northern Europe some supplies might come from across the Atlantic via Spain. Cavagnari expressed open scepticism that Spanish road and railways could cope, but was reassured that Italy could get its supplies from Europe and particularly Sweden. Cavagnari then asked how much reliance Germany was going to place on supplies from Yugoslavia and Romania. After Raeder told him that

Germany hoped to get wheat and petroleum from Romania and was considering building an oil pipeline the Italian backed hastily away from what could turn out to be a very delicate diplomatic matter, asserting that he had only been considering the problem from a naval point of view and that the question of provisioning Italy was not within his competence. In discussing various technical and organisational issues, Cavagnari asked for 2,000 tons of cast steel, 20,000 tons of steel plate and a number of anti-aircraft batteries, requests which he made 'openly and frankly with the aim of speeding up the Italian navy's preparation' but which cannot have left Raeder with a favourable impression of his potential ally.[116] The discussions closed with both admirals agreeing that any influence either could exert on Spain should be directed towards discouraging her from building battleships and encouraging her to build cruisers. Italy would shortly do exactly the opposite.

After the conclusion of the formal discussions between the principals, their deputies met to go over Italian strategy in more detail. The Italians intended to remain on the defensive along the Libyan–Tunisian frontier, admiral Sansonetti explained; then, departing somewhat from the facts as the naval staff understood them, he reassured the Germans that, after taking into account the fortifications built and building there, 'Italy believed that ... she could put the necessary forces into Libya in good time'. The Italians aimed at taking offensive action against Egypt and the Suez canal, but might not be able to do so in the light of the British agreement with Turkey. The 'most important and urgent task' for the Italian navy was to keep open the sea route to Libya; this 'would not permit of conducting a simultaneous offensive in the western Mediterranean'. Unconvinced by the land strategy and unimpressed by the naval strategy, the Germans privately concluded that in a combined war they had to ensure that

Italy does not go running after all sorts of prestige targets (protection of Libya or taking possession of Tunisia or Egypt) but that, in the interests of our common goal, she displays the most vigorous activity in the Western Mediterranean and, at the same time, persists in the strategic defensive in the Eastern Mediterranean'.[117]

The ending of the Spanish Civil War altered the strategic situation for the navy with consequences which were both positive and negative. On the one hand, fears abroad in March of a Republican attack by air and naval forces on the Italian coast were dissolved with the end of the Spanish fleet in April. On the other, the failure of the Nationalist landing at Cartagena on 7 March increased the navy's reluctance to contemplate developing plans for the seizure of Malta. More broadly, the prospect of being able to use bases in the Balearics and on the Spanish mainland was not thought likely to do much to help the interruption of enemy traffic, which could simply be switched to the Atlantic. However, if British and French forces attempted to occupy the Balearics this might present the opportunity for a major naval engagement on relatively favourable terms for Italy.[118]

Elsewhere in the Mediterranean the picture looked equally mixed. The occupation of Albania and the opportunity to make use of Valona put the navy in a good position to be able to neutralise Corfu and to support military action against Yugoslavia or Greece. The news that the army now had materiel and supplies in Libya for seven of the eight divisions to be employed there in war meant that the navy's task in a defensive war was eased since it only had to transport the manpower for the four additional divisions. Supporting an offensive war in that theatre would be very difficult if the transports had to sail after war had been declared, and practically impossible if the enemy had a base on Crete. The presence of 300 aircraft on Malta, reported by Italian air intelligence, meant that naval bases on Sicily were now more exposed and ships would have to be moved away. The Anglo–Turkish accord raised another spectre – the possibility that Anglo–French forces would be able to make use of air and naval bases in Anatolia and the Aegean in war. This speculative anxiety had support: intelligence already suggested that the British were exploring the possibility of joint Anglo–Turkish action against the Italian Aegean islands and trying to secure the use of Marmaris as a naval base in war, and in late August the British were reported to be studying a plan to build a naval and air base near Smyrna.[119]

In July, the naval staff lifted its eyes from the present to the coming year. By autumn 1940 it would have six battleships. Until the extension to Taranto harbour was completed at the start of 1942 they could not all be sheltered in the only anchorage available in the area, and accordingly urgent work was undertaken to extend the basin at Naples.[120] The positive reaction of the Germans to the idea of using Kisimaio as a base for surface and submarine warfare in the Indian Ocean provided a lever with which to press for funding to undertake the necessary work there and to speed up construction of the ships that comprised Cavagnari's April programme.[121] Cavagnari also put to Mussolini a typical piece of naval arithmetic to support an acceleration in the battleship programme. By September 1940 both the two reconstructed Italian battleships and the two new 35,000-ton vessels would be in service, at which time the navy calculated that they would face sixteen Anglo–French battleships out of a total of twenty-three. Since the western powers were already experiencing difficulties basing four warships at Mers-el-Kebir and six at Alexandria, speeding up that part of the programme would exacerbate their problems. The second pair of 35,000-ton Italian battleships were due to enter service in December 1941 and August 1942 respectively. Between the autumn of 1941, when the British and French would have another four brand new battleships, and the autumn of 1942, when the Germans were scheduled to launch a pair of 40,000-ton warships, the Axis powers would have no new build and would be in a relatively more disadvantageous position 'compared to the more favourable relationship in the period between autumn 1940 and summer 1941'. This justified an acceleration in the building programme for the second pair of new Italian battleships. Cavagnari also wanted to speed up work on the twelve *Regolo*-class cruisers so that they would all be ready by the autumn of 1941, and on the four *Saint Bon*-class ocean-going submarines so that they were complete by the end of 1940 rather than between March and June 1941. To achieve all this, Cavagnari wanted priority in the allocation of raw materials, absolute possession of any metals coming from Germany as a result of agreements between the two navies, and an increase in the working week.[122] Mussolini immediately agreed to all Cavagnari's suggestions save the last one. He perhaps remembered Cavagnari's incautious remarks about the battleship balance in the second half of 1940 when he made the decision ten months later to propel Italy into the European war.

Readying the Regia Aeronautica

Like the other two services, though in some respects less obviously, the air force under Valle was gradually but inexorably falling behind its rivals. A combination of factors which included a 'small orders' policy intended to keep aircraft factories in business by ordering a few examples of a large number of different models, many of which were obsolescent before they appeared, and an industry which could only produce on average 146 aeroplanes and 350 aero-engines a month during 1939, meant that the 3,161 aircraft Programma 'R' was already running behind schedule. In September 1939 it had to be revised and rescheduled for completion by 1 July 1940.[123] The true extent of the Regia Aeronautica's problems would only become apparent, however, in September and October.

Valle's contribution to the strategic problems which the navy saw itself as facing in the late spring of 1939 as it attempted to safeguard the central Mediterranean was airily optimistic. The twelve and a half *stormi* stationed on Sicily, Sardinia and Libya, which could be reinforced if and as necessary with units from Puglia and Tuscany, would be able to assist in the defence of the central Mediterranean against attacks from either east or west. Malta and Biserta were particular targets, and Valle was confident that his planes be able to render them unusable by significant enemy naval forces.[124] In July the air force took part in an exercise to test troop convoying to North Africa against attacks by British and French air and naval forces coming from the western and eastern Mediterranean respectively. As the design made clear, the task of the Italian air force in this scenario was to prevent the junction of the two enemy fleets and thus allow the Italian navy to defeat them separately, while at the same time defending the convoy both directly (especially near its ports of departure and landing) and indirectly.[125] How effectively they could do so if simultaneously engaged elsewhere remained an open question.

The main air staff exercise for 1939 took as its theme a war in which Italy was ranged against England and France, Greece was allied with England, and Germany was ready to intervene on Italy's behalf after a very short time. The offensive tasks which the air force was required to experiment included the defence and attack of protected convoys, attacking enemy ports and naval bases, and attacks by bombers and fighters on enemy naval formations escorted by aircraft carriers. A lengthy list of defensive tasks which pointed to the main concerns in such a war included the defence of Palermo, Trapani, Messina, Catania, Augusta and Siracusa, as well as assessing the role of Malta as an advanced fighter base.[126] From it the air force learned that the enemy's naval and air assets made the best targets in the opening phase of a war while the army was still mobilising and deploying and that all the targets in Algeria and Tunisia were in reach save Algeri. It also showed up a number of operational deficiencies, although they did not appear to worry the directing staff unduly: orders were sometimes inexact or incomplete, targets were not clearly identified, and insufficient account was taken when attacking ships of their possibilities for manoeuvre.[127]

Air components also took part in the summer exercises of the *Armata del Po*. The 'Red' (French) elements were tasked to slow the movements of the mechanised force westward by hitting vital road communications and zones where they had to pause and lay up, while bombing road and rail nodes where the land forces had to cross or receive fresh supplies by night and day. All this was to be done under a protective fighter screen. 'Blue' (Italian) air units had to slow the enemy's advance, protecting the assembly, advance and deployment for battle of the Po Army. The manoeuvres, which turned out to be chaotic for the army, were rendered less realistic by the decision not to test the fighter screens to the full due to a shortage of available aircraft and a wish 'not to create aerial conflicts which would be entirely extraneous to the aims of what is essentially a land manoeuvre'.[128]

Like his fellow chiefs of staff, Valle had to pursue closer links with the Germans during the early part of 1939. Hitler's approval for conversations between the German and Italian air forces in March 1939 was given only within very narrow parameters: the topics for discussion were limited to the exchange of target data, co-operation in air defence, matters to do with the meteorological service and the mutual use of ground organisations. Milch came to Rome immediately after the signing of the Pact of Steel, and between 24 and 26 May he and Valle discussed developing co-operation between the two air forces. The agreement they reached accorded closely with Hitler's wishes. Both sides agreed to exchange information on their own, their allies' and their potential enemies' air forces and on potential targets for air warfare, to consider exchange posting of units and individuals, and to establish mixed commissions to examine the exchange of information on new projects and developments and on communications and meteorology.[129] The Germans did not intend to take collaboration any further. The Italian air force was to be given access only to aeroplanes and weapons currently in use and was not to be given any insight into weapons under development, and nothing was to be done to institute a liaison staff during the current year.[130]

A month later Valle paid a return visit to Berlin. Once again the agreements reached did not amount to very much. Strategically the two sides agreed that since their probable enemies were located around the peripheries of their joint territories they must act on internal lines, bringing their common strength to bear against a single weaker enemy. To safeguard national sensibilities – thereby complicating the issue of strategic collaboration – it was agreed that the Italians would command all air units south of the Alps and the Germans all units north of them. Other than agreeing to set up two teleprinter links between Venice and Klagenfurt and Bolzano and Innsbruck, and to establish four short-wave radio-telegraphy stations for the exclusive use of the two air forces, the two parties did not get very much further. In the course of his visits to Milch and Goering, Valle was told that the Luftwaffe already numbered 4,000 front-line aircraft (a figure not reached a year later) as well as having 2,000 planes in reserve. He in turn exaggerated the position of his own service, telling Ciano that the Luftwaffe's torpedoes and bombs were inferior to Italy's, which was untrue. The Italian airman learned something of Goering's air strategy, which was to starve England by using dive-bombing against her merchantmen and her navy, and of his view of Italian strategy, which the reichsmarschall held should concentrate on occupying Corsica, Minorca and Malta and relegate Libya to secondary importance. In an aside, Goering remarked that he was not excessively bothered either by France or by Russia.[131]

From ally to non-belligerent, August–September 1939

On 18 August general Mario Roatta reported from Berlin that it was now obvious that Germany was preparing to undertake major military operations aimed at incorporating into the Reich the eastern territories which had been taken from her at Versailles 'if not more'. Aggressive attacks by a combination of armoured and mechanised units supported by continuous air bombardments 'and where necessary extensive use of chemical weapons' were expected to knock Poland out in two to three weeks before she could receive any aid from Britain or France. Although he was uncertain of the exact size of the standing army, Roatta estimated that Germany had between 1,500,000 and 1,800,000 men under arms (600,000 of whom were reservists), and expected Germany ultimately to field roughly forty divisions. He did not think the fifteen German divisions guarding the western frontier would be sufficient and expected a massive recall of reservists and further extensive mobilisation before the Germans risked a war. Having served as military attaché in Poland in the 1920s, he believed that the German High Command was 'singularly undervaluing' the Polish army's powers of resistance and was 'extraordinarily optimistic' in its estimates of the time it would take to crush it. He reported the logic underlying the Germans' disregarding of the likelihood of war in the west – that if they could not break through the Maginot Line by surprise then neither could the French break through the Westwall, leaving both sides with the prospect of a war of attrition – but clearly did not entirely concur in it.[132]

Two days earlier, Mussolini summoned Badoglio and told him that the Germans proposed to solve the question of Danzig and the Polish Corridor by force around the 21st of that month. They believed that the conflict would remain a localised one between themselves and Poland and would therefore not require any assistance from Italy. Mussolini profoundly disagreed, believing that a clash between Germany and Poland would draw in the other powers. If France and England joined in the hostilities which he expected would break out very shortly, Italy would maintain a strictly defensive posture 'undertaking no action that could indicate our adhesion to the German initiative'. If, notwithstanding such a posture, she was attacked, Italy would first make every effort to secure the inviolability of her frontiers both at home and in the colonies; then, after a brief pause, she would attack Greece with the aim of seizing Salonika. Should circumstances permit, and only after internal anti-Serbian riots had broken out, Italy would also take control of Croatia in order to make use of her material resources. Badoglio pointed out that a conflict would catch Italy in the midst of renewing her equipment and that Libya was particularly vulnerable to likely enemy action. Mussolini accepted the latter point, though he did not indicate what he proposed to do about it. What he did intend was to take advantage of the preoccupation of the northern European powers to strengthen his position in the Balkans and the Mediterranean. The staffs of the three armed forces were ordered to prepare plans for attacks on Greece and Yugoslavia.[133]

Pariani already knew of – or had anticipated – parts of Mussolini's directive. At the beginning of August he told the Hungarian chief of staff, colonel-general Henrik Werth, that 'England and France will be our enemies, that is for sure'. Italy was encircled, and defeating France would be the best but also the most difficult option. The alternative was to over-run the British and French allies in the Balkans and the east – in which event Yugoslavia could not remain neutral.[134] On 9 August the planners were told that in the event of a German action on Danzig leading to a general war with the democracies Italy would stand on the defensive along the French and Swiss frontiers and launch a high speed offensive against Yugoslavia aimed at 'submerging' her and linking up with Bulgaria unless Belgrade clearly sided with Rome.[135] A week later Mussolini ordered plans for attacks on both Yugoslavia and Greece.

As far as a jumping off point for an attack on Yugoslavia was concerned, the planners had already scrutinised the frontier with Montenegro, Kosovo and Macedonia. Their conclusions were not particularly encouraging. Although the sympathies of most of the inhabitants lay with Albania and not with Belgrade and the Yugoslav defences consisted only of old lines of fortifications dating from the First World War, roadways in the mountainous region were few and poor, there was no railway in Albania, and the Yugoslav army was acknowledged to be durable and of 'high military quality'.[136] Albania was therefore disregarded as planning altered the established shape of PR 12 according to which, in exercises planned for August, the *Armata del Po* was scheduled to defend the Swiss border against possible incursions by the French coming via the Sempione or Great St Bernard passes.[137] The plan for the Yugoslavian operation envisaged a force spearheaded by the *Armata del Po*, with the 2nd Isonzo Army under Ambrosio in tow, aiming at Zagreb and the Danube before linking up with a Hungarian force coming via the Sava.[138] The best routes for an Italian attack would be via Lubljana and Fiume–Karlovac, and the planners saw attractive possibilities for linking up with a German advance from Klagenfurt or Graz and combining with a Hungarian drive on Zagreb or Belgrade. Although Yugoslavia could be expected to deploy eighteen divisions against Italy in a single-handed war, the need to guard four other frontiers would probably reduce that figure to seven or eight divisions. The Po and Isonzo armies would be able to field fourteen or sixteen divisions. Great faith was put in surprise and speed, which would make the operation not so much one of conquest as of 'rapid occupation'.[139] The planned Italian campaign hinged on the prior outbreak of anti-Serbian riots; if they did not occur, then the Yugoslavs would put twenty or twenty-two divisions into the area between the Drava and Sava rivers and unless the assault on Greece was abandoned the attack could only hope to succeed with the assistance of six German and four Hungarian divisions.

The attack on Greece would be a three-pronged assault. Eight divisions, headed by a celere detachment and an armoured division, would drive the 250 kilometres from Albania to Salonika, while a force of five divisions struck through the Epirus aiming at Kalamos, supported by subsidiary landings on the islands of Cephalonia, Zante [Zakinthos] and St Maura which would deny the Greeks the possibility of support along the west coast from 'an enemy fleet' – presumably the Royal Navy – and aid the main thrust with turning actions towards Missolonghi and Corinth. Guzzoni, who would command the main drive on Salonika, could expect the Greeks to try to halt his action by blocking the road and would accordingly go south of it via Florina.[140] The improvement in Italo–Greek relations over the next two months was to lead to the temporary shelving of this operation, leaving the Yugoslavian campaign as the lone option.

Pariani saw the two operations as complementary, since with Salonika in Italian hands Yugoslavia would be almost completely encircled. He also saw Greece as the jumping off point for yet wider operations in which Italy would act in concert with Hungary against Romania or with Bulgaria against Turkey. A feature of his ideas which doubtless would have pleased Mussolini was that they did not demand full mobilisation. Two divisions would be freed from guarding the western frontier and one from guarding the eastern frontier by using 'valley battalions' of alpini. Thus, while the Po Army was to be put on 90 per cent of its war footing, the army corps on the western and eastern frontiers needed only to go to 50 per cent war footing.[141]

Probably as a consequence of these likely demands, Pariani told Mussolini on 23 August that he proposed to recall a third class of reservists – that of 1913 – which would increase the total size of the standing army from 520,000 to 860,000 men. Two days later he decided to recall the 1903 class, which had just been stood down, as well.[142] In all, Pariani expected to have 680,000 men under arms on 1 September 1939, of whom 64,500 would be in Albania, 46,000 in Libya and 13,000 in the Aegean.[143] At this point, the command headquarters of army group west had been set up, the major formations slated to operate on the western front were being readied and brought forward, the Pavia division was about to embark for Libya next day followed by the Brescia division, fourteen divisions of blackshirts had been mobilised to cover the western frontier and another twenty-four divisions were being readied to go to Libya.[144]

The navy's strategic analysis, produced on 20 August, presented a very unpromising picture. The British and French fleets, each with three battleships and assorted other ships already, would have control of the eastern and western basins of the Mediterranean. They would also have the assistance of the Greek, Turkish and Yugoslav navies, which included light modern surface ships, fifteen submarines and a battleship, and of the Russians, who might send into the Mediterranean one or more modernised battleships, accompanying surface craft and 'a very significant (notevolissimo) number of submarines'. The enemy could simply block the exits to the Mediterranean, but would in all likelihood challenge Italy's control of the central Mediterranean. The inferiority of the Italian fleet and the absence of 'decisive objectives' at either end of the Mediterranean prevented the fleet from contemplating 'actions in grand style' there. Escorting convoys to Libya was 'extremely risky' since it would expose almost the entirety of the surface fleet to superior enemy forces in a zone that was within reach of enemy air bases in Tunisia, Egypt and Greece. Nor could the Aegean count on intervention by Italy's principal warships. In sum, the navy was going to hang back and rely on local engagements with equal or superior forces to erode the enemy's strength while waiting to seize its only opportunity for a major fleet action – if the enemy got into difficulties with local defences while trying to seize the Balearics.[145] The hollowness of Cavagnari's position was now finally and completely revealed: he had no workable strategy for a war against England and France. In answer to a question from Mussolini in a ministerial council meeting he apparently admitted as much, saying that in a war the navy would 'do its duty and fight, but no more'.[146]

Faced with Pariani's acknowledgement that Italy could not launch a Balkan offensive on her own, the king's opposition to war, and Badoglio's warnings as to Italy's vulnerability to French attack, the dangers of relying on German aid and the weakness of Hungary and Bulgaria as possible allies, Mussolini was forced to abandon his plans. The French stance gave him some security: on 23 August Gamelin assured the Italian military attaché in Paris that France would take no measures along the Italian frontier as long as Italy did not increase her troops on the border.[147]

The notion of an offensive against Egypt was now firmly shelved. Badoglio directed Balbo to ensure Libya's territorial integrity in the likely event that in war the colony would be isolated from the madrepatria.

Transporting large numbers of troops to North Africa would then be difficult or impossible, though air transport might be able to provide some relief. Having overseen the vicious suppression of the Senussi in Cyrenaica only a decade earlier, and therefore well aware of the likelihood that local hostility to Italian rule might spill over into conflict once a European war broke out, Badoglio warned that the first and particular objective in Libya was to take the necessary steps to safeguard the colony against armed uprisings. Beyond that, it must prepare the co-ordinated defensive plans and logistic arrangements to be able to function effectively for at least twelve months.[148] The only offensive operations the colonies were to consider undertaking were attacks from Italian East Africa on Djibuti and British Somaliland, and operations on the north-eastern frontier of Abyssinia designed to aid the defence of Libya by tying down Anglo-Egyptian forces.[149]

Following Badoglio's directions, Pariani began reinforcing Libya. In the last days of August, along with the twenty-four battalions of blackshirts and two regular divisions, he ordered that 1,300 new trucks be sent to Balbo. The army's reckless requisitioning of tractors in particular caused Mussolini to intervene. The Duce's reasoning encapsulated the ill-considered and unexplored conflict between Pariani's conception of a Fascist war and the likely reality of a conflict with economically stronger enemies:

The theories of rapid war are to be followed technically, but we must not lose from view [the fact] that the life of the nation (and therefore of the army) must be assured in case the war might last longer.[150]

On the very last day of the month Badoglio noted that there was 'not even the beginnings of a practical solution' to the problem of anti-aircraft defence for all the airports and other air-related targets save for those few under the protection of the navy or the army.[151]

On 1 September, as Germany went to war and Italy declared her non-belligerence, Badoglio ordered the three chiefs of staff, while keeping their war plans updated, to ensure as their first priority that the frontiers of Italy and her colonies were inviolable.[152] The navy was now coming to acknowledge what it had been unwilling to admit throughout the peacetime years: that its operations depended to a significant extent on contributions by the air force. Cavagnari sent Valle a list of targets at the end of the first week of September. In the Mediterranean they were enemy ships at sea, likely be found around the Balearics, off the Ligurian coast, in the area of the Italian islands in the Aegean and around Tobruk. Malta was the second priority and Cavagnari listed ten separate targets starting with the floating dock and including fuel dumps, magazines and radio stations. A list of eight targets in the Red Sea included gun batteries and water supplies, along with ships under way. Targets at Berbera and a non-specific request to help with the possible occupation of Perim concluded the navy's wish list.[153]

The navy made only halting progress in improving its collaboration with the air force. A list of a dozen officers nominated to service as air observers was produced early in September.[154] It then had to fight off an attempt by the air force to reduce the numbers of aircraft allotted to it for naval reconnaissance on the grounds that substituting multi-engined planes for single-engined ones would allow coverage of larger areas.[155] The battle over naval aviation rumbled on throughout that winter. The navy pointed out that their allocation of reconnaissance planes essentially dated back to 1930, and that their tasks were now 'much larger and more complex'. Adding up the numbers needed to carry out tasks that included anti-submarine observation and the escort of warships and merchantmen at sea produced a requirement of 991 aircraft plus all the associated hangers, repair shops and fuel dumps.[156]

Pricolo, newly installed as chief of air staff following Valle's dismissal, rose to the challenge. The navy wanted 33 per cent of the total available force of 3,000 planes in order to meet all its theoretical needs, leaving only 67 per cent to meet some of the other services' actual requirements. Doing calculations this way – that is, the way the armed forces had been accustomed to doing them in peacetime – would produce requirements which, Pricolo pointed out, would put the industrial and economic resources of any nation in serious difficulty. While the navy had genuine needs, which Pricolo was prepared to acknowledge, the air force held that they should be worked out by inter-relating the needs of all services while taking account of the war economy, and not separately and individually.[157] With barely concealed irritation, the navy responded that it had not dealt with 'a theoretical problem in abstract terms' but with real and novel needs, listing ten different kinds of tasks for which it needed daily aerial cover. It presently had 204 planes, but was prepared to limit its immediate expansion with current models in order to get new ones that were better capable of meeting its requirements, and calculated that it now needed 491 aircraft to meet its needs.[158]

At the beginning of January 1940, having read this correspondence and discovered 'with great pleasure' that it was characterised by 'a praiseworthy spirit of understanding between the two general staffs', Badoglio asked them to make the contacts necessary to come to a common agreement about what was 'an important and urgent problem' while taking account of 'the real possibilities of the nation, the augmentation of which may be gradual'.[159] The air force then told the navy that the burden of air defence was so great that it could not protect every potential naval target, and that therefore the defence of naval bases was considered as part of general territorial defence. The arrangements made to protect the ten major naval bases on the mainland and in Libya were nevertheless in its view reasonable: only La Maddalena, Messina and Augusta could not be protected from nearby airfields.[160]

At the end of the first week in September 1939, a month he regarded as 'the most critical', with the Po Army complete Pariani ordered the gradual mobilisation of the troops guarding the western frontier and Sardinia, the three auto transportable divisions and the 2nd, 7th and 8th armies.[161] Although in the light of current politico-military developments the timeliness of an attack on Greece appeared to be shrinking, he still thought a Yugoslav campaign might be on the cards and shifted some troop deployments accordingly, increasing the force available for the Yugoslav operation from fifteen to twenty-one divisions. As *binaria* divisions they were the minimum force possible, the planners warned him; to be sure of success Italy would need the assistance of five or six German or Hungarian divisions 'given that Yugoslavia is now united, ready to resist and vigilant'. Pariani was also warned that the previous plan had been based on a surprise action undertaken while Yugoslavia was in a situation of domestic crisis and told – somewhat to his surprise – that the plans needed to be reworked as a breakthrough operation against an enemy who was already mobilised and deployed along the frontier with well-organised defences.[162]

With the likelihood of French operations against Italy fast diminishing, Pariani was able to stand down half the troops on the western frontier in the middle of September. By joint agreement Italy and Greece both withdrew their troops from the Greek–Albanian frontier, to the accompaniment of protestations by Athens of appreciation and of her determination to preserve her neutrality at all costs.[163] Pariani kept the Yugoslav plan alive however, ordering that a breakthrough operation in the central sector be devised on the basis of 'no great political preparation', but did not give up his optimistic operational ideal readily. If there were to be effective political work, then the resulting reversal would allow a rapid advance with the lightest of breakthroughs required to overcome weak resistance.[164] Only days before he was sacked, he sketched out his ideas for the benefit of Ambrosio, who would command 2nd Army tasked with the initial breakthrough, and Graziani, who with the Po Army and 8th Army would follow Ambrosio up and develop operations. In the event of a 'very favourable situation' in Yugoslavia, the forces would move swiftly on Zagreb taking the better route from Gorizia via Lubljana. If, as seemed more probable, the enemy's defences had first to be broken open this would be done by means of a 'crushing' artillery action along the

Gorizia–Lubljana axis and also that of Fiume–Karlovac, after which operations would be developed along whichever of the two lines promised to be the more rewarding.[165] A revised plan was duly drawn up in outline, though the possibility of German assistance seemed now to have disappeared.[166] A SIM report in mid-November of mutinies and desertions among some Yugoslavian military units and signs that communist propaganda was affecting reservists suggested that she remained potentially vulnerable to an Italian blow.[167]

A crucial issue which would now help shape Mussolini's thinking was the question of how determined the French were to continue the war. Perhaps to test Italian reaction, the German High Command passed a message via Roatta asking if Italy could confirm their impression that 60 per cent of the French population was little in favour of war and 40 per cent decidedly against it. This did not concur with the estimates in Rome. According to their information, the highest levels of military and civilian officialdom supported fighting the war to a finish, morale in the army was good, and the majority of the population was in favour of the war but without great enthusiasm. If a solution could be found which did not directly damage French interests, the view in the Italian general staff was that both officialdom and the general population would end up by accepting it.[168]

The heads of the Italian military and naval intelligence services, general Tripiccione and admiral Lais, met admiral Canaris in Munich on 17 September to exchange information about the Polish campaign and estimates of French strength in North Africa but chiefly, Tripiccione believed, so that the Germans could communicate their views about the political situation. Italy's neutrality suited them because it tied down enemy forces but not German ones and ensured 'stagnation' in the Mediterranean. It also ensured that Turkey, which might otherwise ally herself with Britain and France, remained neutral. Yugoslavia was overtly neutral but inclined towards the democracies, Bulgaria clearly on the Axis side, Romania determinedly neutral, and Hungary aligned with Germany on account of her geographical position and her interests. The Germans expected Italy to seek compensation from the enemy for her neutrality 'in everyday small change'.[169]

The Russo–German Pact and the joint elimination of Poland made the political situation in late September confused and future developments not easy to discern. Might Russia create confusion in the eastern Mediterranean by launching a drive through eastern Turkey and Syria towards the Suez canal, as the Hungarian military attaché suggested, or might she and Germany together put intolerable pressure on Romania in order to secure the supplies of grain and petrol that both powers wanted, as the Yugoslav military attaché hazarded and the Romanian attaché evidently feared?[170]

Information from SIM that the Soviet Union had moved from a partial mobilisation of the western military districts to a situation in which she had about 114 mobilised divisions, of which 35 were strung along the Romanian frontier and another 25 along the frontier with Turkey and Iran, made either move look possible.[171] All the Balkan states were now evidently much more eager to put themselves under Italian protection. However, the configurations of Soviet military strength and the threats they might represent began to alter as it became apparent towards the end of October that the Soviet Union was responding to growing tensions with Finland by shifting troops from the Baltic states and Poland to the Leningrad military region.[172]

There were also indications of German unease about the new geopolitical shape of eastern Europe. Tripiccione learned from the head of Hungarian military intelligence that the presence of Soviet forces on the Ruthenian border had led to an agreement between Germany and Hungary to exchange intelligence about Russian attempts at infiltration and propaganda. Colonel Ujszaszy also relayed admiral Canaris's views that the Russo–German agreement did not presage close future military collaboration between the two powers and that nationalist tendencies, rather than Bolshevik internationalism, were evident in Molotov, Voroshilov and other Soviet leaders.[173] SIM's liaison officer with German military intelligence confirmed that senior officers there were less than happy at the Russo–German pact and that almost all the officers in the Oberkommando der Wehrmacht showed signs of ill-concealed concern and suspicion.[174]

With war at some time in the more or less immediate future now likely, leading generals began to criticise Pariani's regime and its supposed achievements. General Giacomo Carboni, shortly to become head of SIM, painted a 'very dark picture' of military unpreparedness and disorganisation; general De Bono described the state of the army as 'materially and morally disastrous'; and general Guzzoni pointed out that only ten divisions were complete while thirty-five others were 'patched up, incompletely manned, and with poor equipment'.[175] The critics were right. From 25 August until the end of September, Pariani recalled half a million reservists and by 1 October a force of 1,310,000 men stood under arms. However, partial and incomplete mobilisation of units – some of which were at only half their wartime size – and a muddled arrangement for exemptions produced chaos and a real crisis in the system.[176] From North Africa Balbo complained about the officers he was getting, who lacked liveliness (*vivacità*), and troops who exuded a sense of resignation and lacked 'spiritual soundness'.[177]

Although the armaments programme and the discussions in the Commissione suprema di difesa had all pointed to readiness in 1941–2, Pariani produced reports on the state of supplies and a series of seductive graphics suggesting that ammunition output would be at the requisite levels by November or December of the current year, leading Mussolini to conclude in late September that Italy would be in the best (*ottima*) situation by June 1940.[178] Mussolini also quizzed Bastico closely on the state of the *Armata del Po* and got satisfactory answers. In fact, Pariani's optimism would shortly be exposed for what it was. Output figures can only have been encouraging to a self-deluding optimist: Italy would produce a total of 234 Breda 38-mm machine-guns during the whole of 1939, a figure which would rise to 100 a month in 1940, and the M 11 tanks for which they were destined were coming off the production lines at a rate of only 20 a month.[179] On 27 September Mussolini told the king of the excessive 'inconveniences' of Pariani's mobilisation and the 'uneasiness' it had created in the army and the country and three weeks later the Duce decided to sack him.[180]

Having successfully concentrated in the early summer on persuading Mussolini to build ships designed for a campaign in the Indian Ocean, the naval staff now woke up to the 'not to be ignored necessity' of at least twelve and ideally sixteen new *Camicia Nera*-type destroyers to provide protection for the four new battleships joining the fleet, and two new minelayers which were needed to ensure that the mines which were to block the Sicilian straits were properly laid and regularly replaced. The mine-layers would take a year to build, and the programme would cost 1,015,000,000 lire if carried out in full and 775,000,000 if four destroyers were left off it. As it was, the navy did not possess the means to lay more than one of four lines of mines in an offensive mode, and then only if the weather was good.[181]

Despite its inability to promise decisive action in war, Mussolini was evidently less displeased with the navy's leadership and Cavagnari stayed in post as Valle and Pariani went. However, all was not well in the highest reaches of the navy. An intercept by SIM revealed that admiral Somigli had told the British naval attaché that the Italian people were tired by the recent campaigns and did not want war, that the British guarantee to Poland had been right, and that there would be no peace in Europe until an end was put to German aggression.[182]

New men, new programmes

According to the establishment laid down in 1938, the Italian army at full strength was to consist of fifty-one infantry divisions, two armoured divisions, two motorised divisions, three cavalry divisions and five alpini divisions. In January 1939 Pariani had stated that all sixty-three divisions could be mobilised at full strength by spring of the following year. Despite the addition four 'blackshirt' divisions to the total, it became clear in the discussions that occurred after the proclamation of *non-belligeranza* that a larger force would be needed. At the end of October Pariani proposed increasing the total immediately to seventy-three divisions and ultimately to ninety divisions, equalling the total size of the army mobilised during the First World War.[183] He claimed that the army already comprised seventy-one divisions, of which thirty-eight were at full strength, together with another seventeen divisions on paper, and told Badoglio that in May 1940 it would consist of eighty-eight divisions of which sixty-four would be at full strength.[184]

On 1 November, Badoglio gave Mussolini a stock-taking survey of all three armed forces with a projection of how they would look on 1 May 1940. His commentary on Pariani's claims was damning. At the moment, he told the Duce, there were only ten complete divisions; twenty-nine of the remainder were suffering from minor shortages of equipment, thirty-two were incomplete and twenty-two had yet to be constituted. The *binaria* divisions had lighter artillery than modern divisions in other armies, and there were shortages everywhere – in artillery, munitions, motor vehicles (up to 50 per cent in some divisions and corps), tanks and uniforms. Italy was defended by 225 antiquated anti-aircraft batteries with little ammunition and the requisite new equipment would not be complete until the summer of 1942.[185] Even in the areas where Pariani had claimed to be concentrating effort, the shortcomings were considerable: the army was short of a third of its 45-mm mortars and a half of 81-mm mortars, and though it had almost all the Breda 37-mm machine-guns it was supposed to possess, the majority of them lacked magazines.[186] Two days later Pariani was fired. Mussolini split the two functions he had fulfilled, appointing general Ubaldo Soddu as under-secretary of state for war and marshal Rodolfo Graziani as army chief of staff.

Badoglio's staff assembled data on the other two services for his report to Mussolini which was scarcely less discouraging. The navy's fleet strength consisted of 2 battleships, 22 cruisers, 61 destroyers, 71 torpedo boats, 107 submarines and 71 MAS boats. Not too much account should be taken of the 4 additional battleships coming into service in 1940, Badoglio warned: it would take some time for them to become fully efficient. There was currently enough fuel for five months' fighting in Italy and Libya, for two and a half months in the Aegean and for one and a half months in Italian East Africa.[187] The Regia Aeronautica currently possessed 1,769 aircraft fit for war. It was short of 319 pilots, a figure which would rise to 1,124 by 1 May 1940. However, Badoglio was not unduly worried by this since the shortages could be made up with personnel currently in service and reservists. Fuel supply was a more complicated matter. The air force calculated that it would have 3,000 planes in action by 1 May 1940, a figure which Badoglio was disinclined to believe, and according to the volume of activity believed it could fight on its fuel stocks for between three and six months.[188] Badoglio did his own calculations, and told Mussolini that by the following spring there would be enough aircraft fuel for little more than two months' fighting. He did not pass on to the Duce the observation by his own air staff officer that since it was impossible to store enough fuel to last 3,000 aircraft through a year of war (700,000 tons), it was of 'vital importance' that the air force receive continuing supplies from external sources for otherwise it could only fight for eight to ten months at best.

The men now in charge of Italy's military fortunes were operating in the dark and did not know what Mussolini intended to do. On the basis of the available figures they were able to make reasonably educated guesses as to when they would be able to do anything of any consequence. Soddu thought at the start of November 1939 that the army might be ready for action eleven months hence. Badoglio thought that with hard work Italy might be ready to intervene in two years' time, but only if the other combatants were by then worn out. The Capo di stato maggiore generale made little secret of the fact that he would rather fight against the Germans than with them.[189] Although for the moment Badoglio privileged the defensive, all the various military options were still on the table. By the beginning of November the improvements in Libya's defensive and logistic organisation, and the increases in the forces stationed there, led the military planners once again to consider the possibility of offensive action from Cyrenaica into Egypt if the circumstances were favourable.[190]

By mid November, the chiefs of staff of the three armed services were unable to say what turn events might take, whether there would be military actions and how such actions might develop. The one signpost they had was the Polish campaign, from which they must learn the appropriate lessons quickly. Italy, they were agreed, must not repeat the mistake she had made in 1915, when she had entered the world war having ignored what had happened during the previous ten months on the western front. The armed forces also had to resolve the problem of co-operation between one another and with Badoglio's office. In a belated attempt to solve a problem that had bedevilled the armed forces for twenty years and more, it was proposed that each service nominate a liaison officer to communicate with the other two and with the armed forces general staff. Those problems which could not be dealt with by agreement would be the subject of discussion at meetings chaired by Badoglio.[191]

The Capo di stato maggiore generale called the heads of the armed forces together on 18 November for what was only their second collective meeting that year. In the interim heads had rolled and only Cavagnari survived as chief of his service. Badoglio ceremoniously welcomed the new army chief of staff, marshal Graziani, though the two men loathed one another. After echoing Mussolini's declaration that things should no longer be said to have been done when they had not, and exhorting everyone to eschew politics and simply get on with preparing the armed forces for war – a remark which may have been aimed at Graziani, who from his time in Libya in the 1920s had been a loudly and fervently self-proclaimed Fascist – Badoglio made his priorities clear. 'It has always been my concern in [making] preparations,' he told the assembled top brass, 'to close the doors of the house [first] and then think about [taking] the offensive'.[192]

As the various chiefs of staff ran over the supply situation it became evident that the colonies were far from ready for war. The army had stocks sufficient to last six months in the Aegean, three months in East Africa and three months in North Africa, though the latter was being brought up to six months. It was particularly short of fuel without which, Graziani pointed out, Italy's strength, which lay in rapidity of movement, would disappear. The navy had fuel stocks for five to six months in North Africa, two and a half months in the Aegean, and one and a half months in East Africa; all three theatres had munitions enough to last five months, and North Africa had eight or nine months' anti-aircraft munitions. In North Africa the air force had fuel for two months and munitions for five, in East Africa fuel for one month and munitions for five, and in the Aegean fuel for one month and munitions for four. The new men were not inclined to smooth things over, as Badoglio had often succeeded in doing in the past. Graziani said that to bring North African supplies up to a level that would last a year would take another two billion lire, and complained that because East Africa came under the authority of the *Ministero per l'Africa Orientale* he could not get planning information from the local military authorities quickly or easily. Pricolo pointed out that the figures they were throwing about were more or less meaningless since each service used a different method of calculation. Badoglio's observation that even the army's method of calculating ammunition stocks when used in relation to the western front did not mean much testified to one of the weaknesses of the process over which he was presiding.

Shortly after this meeting, Carboni gave Cavallero a digest of the most important features of the Polish campaign according to the Germans.

First in importance, and contrary to the assertions made by many after the First World War about the strength of the defence thanks to fire-power, was the fact that in modern war large turning movements were possible at long range, making possible the complete destruction of enemy forces. The speed of German action had paralysed the Poles, protecting the Germans from surprises, as well as surrounding Poles in pockets and making counter-action impossible. Another new feature of warfare, unlike that of the world war, was the possibility of commanders of major units directly and personally intervening on the battlefield thanks to the petrol engine. The German conquest of the air was of the greatest importance and showed the 'sinister consequences' for any army of losing control of the skies from the opening days of operations.[193]

For the 1940 rearmament programme the new regime at the War Office abandoned its predecessors' practice of creating new corps, armies and command organisations which would simply worsen the 'anaemic' state of the army. Instead it proposed to concentrate on building up the officer corps, adding the units and support arms that should be in the extant army but were not, and completing the mobilisation stores. 1,500 sub-alterns and 6,500 non-commissioned officers were being recruited and one fifth of the officers embedded in the headquarters of higher military units were being returned to service in the active corps. Over the winter, 18,000 reserve officers were to be given intensive training to improve their quality. The exiguous amounts of raw materials available would be used to provide the weapons and munitions for sixty divisions, to continue an artillery programme 'characterized by slowness and long gestation', to continue with motorisation (though lack of raw materials had reduced output to fifty vehicles a month), and to produce the first tranche of the 400 M 13 tanks that had been ordered. Money was committed to increase the output capacity of the explosives and munitions industries, to build up fuel supplies to levels sufficient for three months' consumption in Italy and twelve months' in Libya and the Aegean, and to order 3,126 light and medium anti-aircraft guns which would be available by 1942–3. Funds were also going on frontier defences, barracks, magazines and stores in Italy, the colonies and Libya.[194]

Graziani and Soddu concentrated their efforts on a 71-division army. The situation was worse even than Badoglio had reported: at the end of November only ten divisions were fully complete (including two motorised divisions), twenty were 'war efficient' (including three mecha-nised divisions), thiety-eight were incomplete, and three were 'inefficient'. There were deficiencies of all sorts at corps and divisional level and in the reserve territorial and auxiliary forces, which lacked on average 50 per cent of the weapons and 70 per cent of the equipment they were supposed to have. The army was short of half its establishment of 34,000 trucks and possessed only fifty of the 660 M 11 and M 13 tanks with which it should have been equipped.[195] Faced with these extensive shortcomings, Mussolini instructed Graziani on 13 December to have 1,000,000 trained men in sixty divisions ready by August 1940 with the supplies necessary for a year of war. Infantry weapons were to have priority in the armaments programme and the artillery, 'whose realisation according to the recent construction programme is very far off', was to take second place.[196]

As the head of COGEFAG, the body tasked with supplying the raw materials for the armaments programmes and co-ordinating demand, general Favagrossa asked the service ministries to convert the requirements for Mussolini's 60-division army into specific quantities of raw materials. The war ministry responded in two days. To create and equip 60 divisions would require 792,950 tons of iron, 60,718 tons of copper, 20,943 tons of zinc, 12,477 tons of lead, 15,844 tons of aluminium and large amounts of wool, cotton, timber, cement and coal. To keep the force going during the first year of a war would require in metals alone a further 1,727,272 tons of iron, 211,464 tons of copper, 70,988 tons of zinc, 59,968 tons of lead and 26,156 tons of aluminium.[197]

The figures went way beyond the bounds of possibility. As Graziani pointed out to Ciano early in January 1940, simply to keep the current programme running required twice as much iron per month as had been available in 1939, more than three times as much copper, fifteen times as much nickel and six times as much tin. To meet Mussolini's demands he was obliged to suspend the medium artillery programme, so that the 149-mm and 210-mm guns would not now be available in 1941–2 as scheduled, in order to concentrate manufacture on infantry weapons, light artillery and anti-aircraft guns. In all probability aware that Ansaldo wanted to sell its 11-ton medium tank to Belgium, Graziani also warned Ciano, who was responsible for the trade, that Italy could not afford to sell arms to other countries and could only use her spare manufacturing capacity to export munitions and motor vehicles if the raw materials needed to make them were forthcoming first.[198] Ciano came away from this meeting with the conviction that Graziani, who had 'more ambition than brains', was influencing Mussolini in the dangerous direction of intervention, which was a misperception.[199] In fact, the broad lines of Graziani's programme had Mussolini's full approval and the chief of army staff was only working according to his master's wishes.[200]

At the beginning of February, Soddu reported that ten divisions were fully complete, twelve were efficient and lacked only some motor vehicles, twelve had varying deficiencies which did not rule them out of combat, thirty four were incomplete and three were inefficient. Now, unlike in

Pariani's day, Mussolini was being given precise details of deficiencies in tanks, guns and the like.[201] Fitting the roll-out of completed divisions to the production schedules was a massive problem. Favagrossa warned that sixty divisions could only be ready by the start of 1941 'if industry works two shifts of ten hours a day, and provided that we have triple the amount of raw materials that we have today', and even then they would be without reserve stores. Otherwise at the current pace of output it would take three times as long. Nineteen divisions were complete and at Mussolini's direction the war office agreed to programme the roll-out of additional completed divisions in batches of ten up to an interim total of fifty, accelerating the process on the back of supplementary allocations of raw materials which the Duce intended to make available.[202]

Along with men and weapons, fortifications – a traditional preoccupation of the Italian army – were still very much on the agenda. Aware that Germany was building fortifications either side of the main routes through the Brenner and along the Drava and Tarvisiano valleys, Graziani ordered improvements to fortifications along the northern frontier to be completed by May 1940.[203] The army's programme for 1940 envisaged constructing 345 large defensive works, 1,115 medium-sized works and 460 small works requiring in all 1,600,000 tons of cement. When general Favagrossa promised them at least half that amount, the generals decided to go ahead with the full programme at the best pace they could. Their rationale combined the traditional Italian preoccupation with fortifications with the contemporary reality that a number of states, including Holland, were fortifying their borders. In support, Graziani quoted Mussolini's dictum that in the middle ages cities had been enclosed whereas in the present day the tendency was to enclose states.[204]

The two elements of the military programme now under way – the fortification of the frontiers and the readying of fifty or more divisions – fitted together to form a single strategic conception on which Soddu, Graziani and his deputy chief of staff, general Mario Roatta, all agreed. The army was, for the moment at least, in no condition to be able either to fight outside Italy's borders or to give battle in open field inside them. It must therefore fight on lines of fortifications which themselves had to be located on the actual frontiers and not in positions which might be more secure or more economical. Italy's overseas possessions must be left as they were and not given any more resources. As Roatta put it, 'We must concentrate everything on the mainland.'[205] On 22 March 1940, the war office was able to report that it now fulfilled Mussolini's directive, having 1,010,000 men under arms.[206]

While the military used available funds to patch up the army, the sailors found new holes in the navy as the fruits of earlier investment came on line. Bringing two new divisions of battleships into service during 1940 weakened Italy's naval position. In January the staff calculated that an extra squadron of four destroyers had to be found to protect each of them, which could only be done by withdrawing one squadron from Brindisi and the other from the Aegean. The *Navigatori*-class destroyers now being pulled back from the Aegean had originally been sent there to ensure that the Italian navy would be able to defeat Turkish light surface forces in those waters. Given the state of relations between the two powers, the naval planners now assumed that Turkish naval forces would have support from British fleet units. Together, the new circumstances determined that the Italian navy could only adopt a defensive strategy in the area and seek to maintain communications between the islands. To do this, the navy would have to rely on submarines and MAS boats; the only possible reinforcements for the Aegean were the *Crispi*-class destroyers based at La Spezia, but if they were removed then the operational possibilities in the Gulf of Liguria would be even more limited than they were now.[207] Juggling the thirty-six modern and twenty-five more or less antiquated destroyers they possessed around the Mediterranean, the naval staff calculated that they needed at least four more in order to provide the requisite levels of protection for the battle squadrons and another eight properly to equip the naval regions and to have something in reserve.[208]

By February, the figures looked worse: now the navy needed another eight destroyers to protect the two divisions of battleships and heavy cruisers, and ten more for the defence of the Aegean and metropolitan waters.[209] In support of the new build, the planners pointed out that Salonika would be 'an important land objective within the general picture of the war'. The additional destroyers would both help to achieve it and control enemy surface traffic with the Dardanelles and Macedonia by putting the Italian navy in a better position relative to the Greek, Turkish, Egyptian and British units which would likely be in and around the Aegean. Cooler heads pointed out that local superiority was unobtainable, that the Aegean islands were 'geographically abandoned' and that the best that could be done was to put them in a state to be able to defend themselves for a year.[210]

While the staff did its strategical calculations, the navy used the Sezione Alti Studi, its 'think tank' at the Istituto Superiore di Guerra, to work through some of the operational problems it now had to resolve. Air reconnaissance to locate and keep track of the movement of enemy forces during the hours of daylight was going to be a central feature of a sea war in the Mediterranean; likewise, submarines would carry out the task during the hours of darkness. Studies concluded that forty naval aircraft and twenty-four from the Regia Aeronautica would be needed to watch the nine enemy bases that would need daily surveillance and another twelve which would only need occasional surveillance after the opening days of a war, as well as flying along a series of lines stretching round the mainland and into the eastern Mediterranean. Seventy submarines would complement their activity by watching six ports and guarding similar lines at sea. Aerial anti-submarine work was thought 'in general of limited effectiveness', but fifty naval aircraft were allotted to the task in specified zones. With an allocation of 186 aircraft, the navy for once had enough means to carry out its share of the task. However, it need a faster, better-armed and longer range aircraft to watch enemy bases than the Cant Z 501 currently in use. Also no naval air units were actually ready to hunt down submarines.[211]

Pricolo, more co-operative than his predecessor, recognised both the necessity to overfly enemy bases periodically and the difficulties this task posed for the naval reconnaissance aircraft, and offered to provide the service within the limits of availability of aircraft. He could not, however, guarantee that every enemy naval base would be observed once a day – or even sometimes twice – as the relevant naval directive required.[212]

While the new team worked on the army, the war ministry wanted Germany kept at arm's length. The navy felt much the same way: admiral Somigli, Cavagnari's deputy chief of staff, was more than content not to be too closely involved with the Germans as that preserved Italy's freedom of manoeuvre. The initial and skeletal framework of collaboration had fallen into disuse after the Polish campaign, but in mid-January 1940 the Germans indicated that they wanted to revive and develop the machinery of sub-commissions, showing a particular interest in defensive and offensive chemical warfare. The war ministry presumed that one of the main purposes behind the proposal was to find out more exactly what the true state of things was with their ally, and since it saw no 'purely technical–military reasons' for tightening the relationship it proposed adopting 'a dilatory attitude' and waiting until things were clearer.[213]

At the beginning of April, the Germans accepted an Italian suggestion that the deputy chief of the Italian general staff, general Mario Roatta, visit Berlin during the month. They also offered to send colonel Ritter von Thoma to Rome to share his experience of using tanks in Spain and Poland. Finally, Goering promised to speed up the delivery to Italy of three batteries of 88-mm anti-aircraft guns.[214] Strongly encouraged by Badoglio to believe that Italy's intervention in war, when it came, must not be chained to Germany but must be exclusively with Italian troops and at a moment and in a direction which he selected as opportune, Mussolini vetoed the visit.[215] The Germans then suggested that a mission go to Berlin to establish the bases for common military action. The Italian army staff immediately rejected out of hand the three German suggestions: a Libyan offensive was impossible because of the lack of tanks, armoured cars and artillery, an attack across the Alps would be difficult and would require German tanks and guns, and contributing twenty or thirty divisions to the German left wing 'would have a less Italian appearance' and could not be organised until Italian intervention was 'at least looming'.[216] A week before the German attack on France Soddu did acknowledge that it would be useful to find out what the Germans wanted to know and what Italy could hope to acquire. However, he did not think the matter 'particularly urgent'.[217]

For the Italians, without closer contacts with the Germans, forecasting their ally's next move was not much more than semi-educated guesswork. During the autumn Cavallero hazarded that since German action appeared to be directed chiefly against England she would likely try to get control of the North Sea coast, turning the Maginot Line with an offensive through Holland and Belgium.[218] Information from the Belgians suggested that Germany might repeat her 1914 strategy or attack the Luxembourg portion of the Maginot Line or launch a frontal attack on it from the Saar.[219] In a conversation with Marras in December, general Halder had hinted at the possible nature of German action with the remark that if France lost a few battles it could quickly give up, and had suggested that since France was very vulnerable in North Africa, a big Italian offensive from Libya could achieve great results.[220] At the end of March 1940, the German naval high command sketched out to the Italian naval attaché Germany's intention to strike England in its vital points, and if necessary land troops along its coasts. The central point of the conversation – and probably its chief purpose from the German side – was to invite Mussolini to join in such a campaign at the crucial point, thereby avoiding a long war which Italy could not sustain. The navy doubted the Luftwaffe's ability to do more than intimidate England and thought that land and sea action would be essential. At the moment, Pecori Giraldi reported, Germany was calmly awaiting the great offensive which would cost France 'more men than she is able to replace' and would force England to recognise the power of German arms.[221]

Last orders

No one who had attended previous sessions of the Supreme Defence Commission can have been in any doubt as the final peacetime assembly gathered about the yawning gap between the services' demands for raw materials to feed their armaments programmes and the volume of supplies available to satisfy them. The outbreak of war in Europe and the consequent acceleration in activity demanded of the armed forces made the problem worse in two respects. First, as Cavagnari pointed out, not merely had it been impossible for the navy to grow stocks to the levels required under previous programmes but demand had run them down to the point where they could practically be considered non-existent. It had calculated the amounts of raw materials it needed to survive five months of war – a list headed by 20,000 tons of iron – and had sought the necessary licences from Favagrossa. He had said that the materials would be forthcoming as soon as the ministry of finance gave him the necessary money – 130,000,000 lire – but up to the present no funds had been forthcoming. The programme was therefore currently suspended.[222]

The army reported a similar run-down of stocks, though not apparently as severe as the navy's, and added another dimension to the problem. Monies had been allocated for the raw materials needed by the military's own factories, but the supplies available for the civil arms industry were far below what it needed to meet defence orders. In the event of war demand would go up and even if arms exports were contracted yet further 'there would at once be a crisis of raw materials which would practically halt production'. The war ministry wanted 'an untouchable stockpile' to be built up, with reserves sufficient to last for six months' wartime consumption. It also pointed out that if new and secure sources of supply were not located then 'replacing the heavy consumption [of raw materials] in wartime presently appears highly chancy'.[223]

The commission began with a discussion on anti-aircraft defence and the announcement by Mussolini that Italy probably possessed the best gun in the world in the shape of the 90-mm gun. The problem was that the first one would not be available before the end of the year. In his view Italy would have an adequate defence when she had two thousand guns, half of them modern. Evacuating the cities would be no defence – Italy was small, and it would simply produce crowding elsewhere. The best protection was the threat of reprisals, but passive defence could be provided if most people used their cellars or protected their ground floor rooms with sand-bags. The problem of how families of six or seven could afford gas masks at thirty-five lire each was raised but not directly resolved. All agreed that preparations should be speeded up and that the ministries involved in the business should be given the extra funds and raw materials allocations they required.[224]

An examination of the situation with respect to fuel and lubricants revealed a mixed but generally unhopeful picture. Soddu warned that the production of lubricants was inadequate for peace and for war. Only the navy was in a good position as far as diesel oil was concerned: for the first time it had more stocks than it could hold in its tanks. Although Russia had stopped supplying diesel oil in September 1939, adequate supplies were reaching Italy from Mexico and the United States. Mussolini wanted the navy to have two million tons of fuel by 1942, which would be enough for up to twelve months of war. To enter a war, the air force needed at least 400,000 tons of fuel and the army 500,000 tons. By June 1941, domestic refineries would be able to produce 100,000 tons of aviation fuel, 140,000 tons of motor fuel and 60,000 tons of lubricants a year.[225]

The committee's discussion of raw materials shortages was sharpened by the fact that Europe was now at war and a greater premium than ever was therefore being placed on trying to maximise domestic production. This meant that a much greater degree of broad industrial co-ordination was needed if there was to be a realistic chance of hitting targets. General Favagrossa pointed out that it took 300 million kilowatt hours of electricity to manufacture 10,000 tons of aluminium; therefore it was not enough simply to build factories to produce aluminium without simultaneously expanding power plant capacity at the same time. Mussolini declared that Italy needed an annual output of 4 million tons of steel to face the needs of peace and war. She must reach 2.5 million tons during 1940 and the rest would become available 'when the process of integral steel making is fully functioning'. Adding up the amounts of iron ore to be found up and down Italy, he concluded that there was no obstacle to Italy's having a great steel-making capacity. The Dolomites contained 'incalculable amounts' of magnesium. High quality deposits of common clay, which the Germans worked to get aluminium, could be found in Istria and on the Gargano. Domestic production of aluminium would reach 52,000 tons in 1941, about 10 per cent of world output; because the shortages of copper and tin had made it ever more important Favagrossa agreed with Mussolini that output must reach 70,000 tons a year if he was to meet demand.[226]

Textiles and foodstuffs seemed to present a fairly good picture as Mussolini glissaded over more mounds of statistics, remarking off-handedly that the meat situation did not concern him 'as twenty million Italians have the wise habit of not eating it and they do very well'.[227] It was left to the secretary, general Fricchione, to point out that there existed no proper plan for agricultural mobilisation in wartime. The minister of agriculture, Tassinari, was instructed to draw one up as quickly as possible. The parlous state that Italy was in with regard to raw materials began to become obvious when the discussion turned to coal, iron and copper. Many of Mussolini's solutions to the problems did not promise much relief. Coal consumption could be reduced by cutting the number of trains using it and by adjusting the timetables so that they stood still in stations for as short a time as possible. When the need arose, the country could produce

500,000 tons of scrap iron. And there were, he believed, at least a million copper utensils in homes and on farms up and down the country, most of which could be requisitioned.[228]

When the commission reached item eleven on the agenda, an apparently innocuous one dealing with the transport of supplies from abroad in wartime, the minister for currency and foreign exchange, Raffaello Riccardi, made the bravest and most critical intervention ever seen at any of its gatherings. The minister for communications, producing the paper for discussion, had calculated that Italy would need to import 22,000,000 tons of goods in 1940. This would cost 22,000,000,000 lire. The commission might as well stop calculating there, Riccardi told it, because it no longer had its feet on the ground. In an earlier session he had raised the question of how Italy, with exiguous gold supplies and a rapidly shrinking export trade, was going to pay for its imports; now he complained that every time one of his staff raised this question Mussolini replied that whether or not the requisite goods could be paid for was no concern of theirs.

Warming to an impossible task, Riccardi went further. The studies were being done by people who still lived mentally in the world of 1914 '[t]hat is to say, with the freedom of the seas, abundant means to pay and secure [sources of] provisioning'.[229] The services were playing their part in the unrealistic exercise by grossly inflating their demands: the army had asked for five million pairs of shoes in April 1940. Why was there not greater interchangeability between the services? Why, for example, did the army, the navy and the air force each use a different type of bed sheet? The internal market was prey to casual and thoughtless treatment and the military authorities were consuming more than they actually needed. And how did the services propose to import seven million tons of liquid fuels in wartime when all three entrances to the Mediterranean were going to be closed to traffic?

Riccardi was asking pertinent but highly awkward questions of a kind that no one else had dared to raise before. He also sought to educate the commission to the facts of financial life as he saw them. The most that could be imported in peacetime was half the amount that had been suggested by the minister of communications. 55 per cent of the bill could be paid for by clearing, but he still had to find a total of 7,045,000,000 lire. Income from tourism had disappeared and the receipts sent home by Italians abroad were a drop in the bucket. Even with the best effort he would still be short of 2,245,000,000 lire, a sum much too large to be covered by Italy's meagre gold reserves. Since Italian industry had oriented itself to meeting military orders and not to exporting, the only way out of the situation was to cut back on everything which was not strictly essential for the military and reduce domestic demand. 'Hannibal is not at the gates,' Riccardi told the assembled company, 'but he has crossed the threshold'.[230]

Badoglio once again displayed the bureaucratic subtlety which enabled him to appear simultaneously to be both a critic and a supporter of the regime. After thanking Riccardi for his 'detailed and convincing exposition', he completely rejected it as far as the army was concerned. It was being entirely honest in its demands and telling Mussolini the truth 'complete and entire'. Using a turn of phrase which situated the armed forces as a disinterested but untouchable servant of the regime, he told the commission: 'We must say to the DUCE: if this is what is wanted, this is what we need.'[231] Mussolini, who was infuriated by the speech, replied with a series of disconnected remarks which avoided addressing any of Riccardi's substantive points. The minister was not being asked for anything he could not give. If and when he himself thought it necessary, he would spend all the gold reserves. He would sell trucks to a belligerent if asked, but not artillery. The air force had earned Italy more than one milliard lire which gave it the right to ask for things. When he heard about the episode Ciano, who was not present at the meeting, thought that Riccardi had 'acted courageously in sounding the alarm'.[232]

The commission wandered on through the thickets of Fascist bureaucracy, learning on the way that no real progress had been made in relocating industry to the south, that three quarters of the machine-tools being used in the aircraft industry had to be imported, and that the artillery programme was being held up through lack of raw materials. At one point, acknowledging representations from Badoglio and Graziani about not going too far in respect of weapons sales abroad, Mussolini explicitly admitted that his policy on arms was politically determined: he was willing to sell weapons to smaller states such as Finland, Greece, Bulgaria and Turkey, he declared, because their needs could be 'legitimate' but not to large ones.[233]

When the commission got to discussing the overseas territories it learned that the navy had begun to construct a base at Kisimaio, though it presently had less than one third of the money needed to improve the port facilities. With the 160,000,000 lire to be allocated for the purpose it expected to be able to make it into a good military and commercial port.[234] Opening a window on to the Indian Ocean was a well-calculated way to win Mussolini's sympathy. The air force expected soon to have 100 airfields around the Mediterranean, enabling it to concentrate rapidly where and when needed. Balbo's account of the work carried out over the past two years to prepare Libya for action against regular armies rather than rebel bands depicted a colony where much had been done but much remained to be done. In September 1939, 80,000 Italian and native troops had faced between 290,000 and 360,000 enemy troops on the western and eastern borders supported by 'hundreds of aeroplanes'. There were now 105,000 active troops in Libya, a number which would rise to 120,000 in mid-February, but they were short of officers and non-commissioned officers and in want of machine-guns, anti-tank guns and mortars. Some progress had been made with respect to fortifications, particularly those at Tripoli and Ain Zuara, but much had yet to be done to reach the levels recently set by Graziani for Bardia and Tobruk. The most chronic deficiencies were in anti-aircraft defences: Tobruk was defended by the navy and Tripoli had only five batteries of 76-mm guns. Nevertheless, Balbo was optimistic. If it came to war, he expected the colony to be able 'without any doubt to put up an effective resistance, to break down the probable enemy offensives and to think of the possibility of offensive action'.[235]

When Balbo, glossing his report to the commission, emphasised the impressive amount of work done in Tripolitania over recent years starting effectively from nothing, Badoglio intervened. His inspection visit had revealed that the forts had indeed been built but could not be used because they lacked both furnishings and armaments. If all Balbo's requests were to be met 'we should have completely to empty out the *madrepatria*'.[236] Mussolini gave his customary brand of advice, cluttered with detail but entirely lacking any clear overall sense of priorities and direction. There were twelve divisions in Libya (eight had been sent in September 1939), which was enough for the time being, but the four divisional magazines were empty and needed refilling. The colony was also short of seventy-four steel turrets. The services should look at sending divisions across to North Africa by air in wartime. In the meantime, since Italy possessed the best anti-tanks guns in Europe they should be sent across to Libya as soon as possible. Still, things were not too bad: 'today, with the means that we have, we are in a position to look to the future I would not say with tranquillity but with firmness'.[237]

At the close of what was to be the last peacetime session of the defence commission, Mussolini allowed Graziani to go off the agenda and introduce the subject of frontier defences. After spiritedly defending the army general staff from the implicit and explicit criticisms in Riccardi's earlier remarks without directly addressing any of the minister's specific charges, Graziani reminded the Duce that he himself had said that they would be stained with infamy by posterity if they ever allowed a foreign army to cross the frontier and 'violate' the Paduan plain. Calling in aid the same passion that had motivated Riccardi's call to defend the currency, the army chief of staff demanded that the frontiers be safeguarded at all costs whatever the sacrifices that had to be made and the privations that had to be imposed on the Italian people. Riccardi seized the chance to apologise for what had perhaps been the excessive fervour of his earlier polemic, but did not cede any ground on his fundamental criticism. 'The secret of victory,' he concluded, 'lies in the exact proportion[ality] between programmes and the means to realise them'.[238]

Mussolini had no time for the kind of money worries that underlay Riccardi's interventions: at a meeting of the council of ministers in January he had over-ridden his minister of finance, Thaon di Revel, declaring that states did not collapse from debt but only from defeat or internal dissolution.[239] He now brushed aside Riccardi's concerns. After sanctions had been imposed on Italy in 1935, the minister's predecessor had told him at least twenty times that they were not going forward and would end by going down. They had now reached 1940 and no doubt at the end of the year Riccardi would say that the ship was still afloat. The army's programmes, he affirmed, were not 'idiotic' but matched the means available and the domestic possibilities – a reassurance he could scarcely avoid giving since they had his explicit approval. The armed forces' requests for materials must therefore be met because they were the necessary minima below which Italy could not go. He closed with a ringing endorsement of Graziani's programme to fortify all Italy's northern land frontiers.[240]

Giuseppe Bottai, who as minister of education attended the meetings of the commission, noted at the end of its session that he had never seen so much paper and so many programmes, plans and forecasts in any other body – without any firm check on whether they had been put into effect. The way in which it reached decisions almost defied analysis:

Now a mythical date blooms amid uncertainties: between the end of '41 and the spring of '42. Everyone says that they will be ready by then, if they are given the money.[241]

Over the brink of war

While the generals were making what progress they could with armaments, Mussolini oscillated backwards and forwards about when to move. At the beginning of January 1940 he spoke of intervention alongside Germany in the second half of 1941. By the end of the month he thought Italy could make a move in the second half of the current year but would do better in the first half of 1941. At the end of March he set out his assessment of the situation for the king. Building on the certainty that there would be no compromise peace, the Duce ruled out both an Anglo–French attack on the Westwall and a German attack on the Maginot Line or on Holland and Belgium. His grounds for reaching the latter conclusion were that Germany had already achieved its war objectives and could await the enemy's attack and that the likelihood of an adverse popular reaction if the attack failed made it too risky – a spectacular misreading of Hitler's personality. Germany would therefore resist a blockade and launch a land offensive only when she was mathematically certain of crushing her enemy or as a desperate last card. If the war continued Italy could neither remain neutral nor wage a long war. She must break the bars imprisoning her in the Mediterranean and to do this she would fight a *guerra parallela*. When spelled out, Mussolini's 'parallel war' did not amount to much: other than neutralising French air bases on Corsica, Italy would adopt the defensive everywhere but in East Africa, where attacks would be launched on Kassala and Djibuti. The Duce appeared to put most faith in the navy: while the air force would act offensively or defensively according to what happened on each front and whether the enemy took the initiative, the Regia Marina would take the offensive in the Mediterranean and beyond.[242]

Despite what he said to the king, which probably did not represent his complete list of the strategic options, Mussolini appears at this moment to have flirted with yet another possible action – direct intervention alongside the Germans in the land campaign against France which was now evidently imminent. At the start of April the war office prepared for him an outline of the arrangements initiated in 1888 and renewed on the eve of the First World War to send Italian troops to the Rhine to fight alongside the Germans.[243] With the Austrian railways in German hands this was certainly not an impossible option, but by the same token it was not one which could be improvised. Even on the eve of Italy's intervention, Mussolini was apparently thinking of putting into action a version of Italy's pre-1914 undertaking and sending Italian units to fight alongside the German army in France. Rather than send half a dozen battalions of bersaglieri – the idea originally in mind – the war office suggested sending the Trento and Trieste motorised divisions. Well equipped and well trained, they would be particularly suited to the lie of the land in northern France with its dense road network.[244] No Italian soldier ever actually turned up on the Franco–German front in June 1940, but Mussolini had the pre-1914 documents with him in his briefcase when he was captured by partisans four years later.

When the chiefs of staff met on 9 April Badoglio's main concern, besides reiterating that Italy had to stand on the defensive everywhere, was to ensure that contacts with the Germans were no more than 'purely informative'. No undertakings could be made in order, as he put it, not to 'limit in any way the Duce's decisions'. When Graziani asked if he was authorised to consider 'operational hypotheses' for joint action he received a flat refusal. 'Then we will be able to do nothing, even if France collapses, while moreover we [shall] have an uncertain Yugoslavia at our back,' the chief of staff observed.[245] Cavagnari pointed out that the naval situation was worse than in 1939: now, because there were no German ships in the Atlantic, the Royal Navy could concentrate forces in the Mediterranean. When Badoglio suggested that the navy's strategy should not be to go head down for the enemy but to use its submarines to attack his convoys, Soddu pointed out that this would be a commerce war without targets. Pricolo questioned whether people were not nourishing 'too many illusions about aero–naval offensives, the possibilities of which are few'. He would have 2,300 aircraft by 1 August, but what really concerned him was 'having to make an operational deployment without having any precise direction[s]'. Sinuously evading what was a crucial issue, Badoglio dismissed the chiefs with the injunction 'Study and then report back on your possibilities.'[246]

Mussolini received a summary of the meeting two days later. Both Cavagnari and Pricolo were 'uncertain' about the efficacy of future offensive action given the 'numerous and demanding' defensive tasks their forces had to fulfil and the lack of means available to carry them out. All three services agreed that the demands of defending Italy's frontiers were such that, even if preparations were complete, they could not undertake offensive operations in any sector.[247] The following day Soddu told the chiefs of staff of the army corps that Italy would never fight alongside France and England, nor would she remain neutral, but that at the opportune moment she would fight a 'parallel' war 'not "for" or "with" Germany, but one for ourselves'. They hoped to determine the opportune moment for themselves, but the troops must be ready to do go at any time. The real benefits of the rearmament programme would start to come on stream from 1941; if war should break out during the current year, Soddu told the staff officers, 'we shall do our best'.[248]

The re-equipping of the army was in fact even farther off than Soddu optimistically forecast. Mussolini decided at this time to start off a new programme of artillery rearmament designed to produce 2,330 medium and heavy guns (90-mm, 149-mm and 210-mm) – exactly the ones Pariani had neglected in his mania for speed. On 20 April he was informed that the first production outputs would be available between May and September 1943 and that the runs would be complete in October 1943, May 1945 and October 1945 respectively.[249] Soddu visited the western and northern defences in the last week of April and produced upbeat reports for his master. The state of army morale on the western frontier was excellent: the army was 'profoundly healthy, working intensively, preparing itself seriously and permeated in every fibre with that vibrant spirit which You have infused in it'. On the northern frontier the defensive works could be considered complete by August. Mussolini could be reassured that everyone was carefully looking after the cement.[250]

As far as the naval staff was concerned, the German occupation of Norway and Denmark on 9 April did not greatly change the complexion of the war. Germany now had access to the northern exits to the Atlantic and could deploy aircraft against naval bases in Scotland and northern industrial zones from bases in Norway. The new situation did give Germany advantages but was not thought likely significantly to change the positions of the British and French fleets; at most, they might have to pull back some forces from other theatres for traffic protection.[251] Where the naval staff saw a glass half empty, admiral Bernotti saw a glass at least half full. Calculating the likely distribution of heavy British and French warships in the new circumstances, and taking into account factors arising from the new shape of the war in the North Sea such as the additional strain posed on the Royal Navy by the longer hours of daylight and greater German submarine and air action against sea traffic, Bernotti reckoned that between September and December 1940 the British and French would be least able to deploy warships in both theatres capable of meeting the Axis heavy ships and that the six Italian battleships then available would have a good chance of success in an encounter with either the Anglo–French forces in the western Mediterranean basin or the British forces in the eastern Mediterranean basin.[252]

Probably aware that the news of Germany's successes might encourage Mussolini to move farther and faster down the road to the war he so palpably wanted, Cavagnari now presented the Duce with a deeply but not quite unredeemedly pessimistic survey of the strategic situation. After dwelling briefly on Italy's naval and geographical inferiorities, and remarking as an aside that if the air force could provide the means then the best thing from the navy's point of view would be the conquest of Greece, Cavagnari succinctly summed up the strategic position in the Mediterranean. Britain and France had already deployed their troops and did not need to transit from the eastern to the western basins, so that Italian control of the Sicilian channel was valueless. If the Allies simply sat in their ports at either end of the Mediterranean it would be difficult to do anything. As merchant traffic there was non-existent, submarine warfare could have little effect; nor could it do much in the Atlantic due to the lack of bases and the enemy's convoys. Mussolini had issued him with a directive to take the offensive 'all along the line'. No strategic objective had been defined. Without it, and without the possibility of defeating the enemy's forces, 'entering the war on our own initiative does not seem justified'. However the war in the Mediterranean turned out, Cavagnari warned, Italian naval losses would be heavy and she could arrive at the peace table 'without either a navy or an air force'.[253]

Mussolini, who assured Hitler on the day that he received Cavagnari's memorandum that the Italian fleet would be fully on a war footing by noon on the morrow, was furious. What, he asked Ciano rhetorically, was the use of building 600,000 tons of warships if they were not used to take advantage of the current opportunity and pitted against the British and French?[254] At that moment, though, the naval balance was at its worst from Italy's point of view. The two new *Littorio*-class battleships arrived at Taranto in the second half of May but problems with their main armament were not sorted out until October, while the reconditioned *Duilio* and *Doria* reached the base in mid-July and late October respectively but both needed two months' work before they were fully ready to put to sea.

On the eve of the German attack on France Mussolini's attention was temporarily elsewhere. Ordered to examine reinforcing Libya, the chiefs of staff met on 6 May and agreed to add another 90,000 men to the 120,000 already there, whom they believed entirely erroneously to be facing 100,000 British and Egyptians, 314,000 French troops in North Africa and another 200,000 in Syria.[255] The moment was closer at hand than anyone expected. On 9 May Badoglio thought it would take six months and a million men to break the Maginot Line, and when the campaign in the west began next day Soddu dismissed the struggles on the Dutch and Belgian borders as amounting to nothing, believing that the French defences would be 'absolutely unbreakable'.[256] The German move completely disrupted Mussolini's plans. At a meeting with the three under-secretaries of state for the armed services that same day he ordered that action against Yugoslavia, which had been planned to start that day, be temporarily suspended.[257] At that moment nineteen army divisions were fully ready, forty were almost ready, half or fewer of the air force's 2,000 aircraft were in line and there were supplies for only four months. 'Our situation,' concluded general Quirino Armellini, newly arrived at the Comando supremo, 'is not brilliant'.[258]

Three days after the German attack on France had begun, Mussolini told Ciano that he had decided to declare war on England and France within a month. Although supposedly opposed to the war, Ciano hoped to make gains from it both diplomatically by agreeing conditions for Italy's entry with Hitler and militarily by independent Italian action. His goals were extensive: protectorates over Croatia and Greece, the absorption of Dalmatia and the expansion of Albania to its ethnic borders, Italian occupation of Crete, protectorates over Egypt, Tunisia, Algeria and Morocco, and the absorption of Corsica.[259] Italy had military plans for offensive action against Yugoslavia and naval plans for an action against Corfu. Ciano believed that the moment was ripe to move against both countries, and while visiting Tirana on 25 May he told general Carlo Geloso that his forces must be ready to attack Greece. Geloso refused to do so on the grounds that he had only half the number of troops that had been available the previous year when the idea had last been on the table and was sacked twenty-four hours after Ciano got back to Rome in favour of one of Mussolini's favourite soldiers, Visconti Prasca.[260] The Greek option had however for the moment to be shelved, as on 12 June was the Yugoslav operation.

With intervention coming ever nearer, the question loomed as to how the Fascist regime was to organise the running of the war. Soddu proposed an amalgam of the German system with the present Italian system. The Duce would head the Comando supremo, directing the overall conduct of the war, fixing its scope, determining the military objectives and assigning them to the various armed forces. With Badoglio functioning as his assistant to co-ordinate the activities of the services this would put him, he was shown, in a position very much akin to Hitler's. Beneath this superstructure Soddu proposed a system very much like that operating in France, in which the war ministry was responsible for organising the military effort and the respective chiefs of staff carried out military operations as directed. There was no place in this design for the kind of political and military consultative machinery which, as Mussolini was also shown, operated in the United Kingdom.[261] For it to work Mussolini had to wrestle de facto control of the war out of the hands of the king, who was persuaded to derogate his constitutional powers to the Duce. The Comando supremo as designed by Soddu was inaugurated at the Palazzo Venezia on 29 May 1940. 'Rarely have I seen Mussolini so happy,' Ciano recorded.[262]

On 10 May, as the Germans unleashed their attack on France and the Low Countries, Mussolini promised Balbo that within the month 80,000 men would be sent to Libya together with the guns, munitions and supplies required to sustain them for six months. Balbo needed not just men but the means to fight, and responded with four separate lists of 'urgent requirements' which included 390 47-mm anti-tank guns, 1,357,200 rounds of artillery ammunition, 90 radio sets, 12 field hospitals, 4,000 tons of frozen meat, 3 million quintals of cement and a great deal else besides.[263] It was enough, in Ciano's words the previous August, to kill a horse – and since Balbo was no friend of the Germans it may indeed have been designed in part to cause Mussolini indigestion. A partial solution, provided by Soddu, was to juggle with the very limited resources available. The arms industry could produce a total of 120 47-mm guns during

May and June. If the last tranche of 50 guns from an order of 200 for Romania were withheld, then the entire output could be sent to Balbo.[264]

Balbo's demands exposed a fundamental weakness in Mussolini's direction of the war departments: the disconnectedness of strategy. Soddu warned him of the danger:

[These] individual improvised pressures to act in favour of various theatres (Italian East Africa, the Aegean, Libya) as if they were each self-contained theatres of war in themselves for all of which the process of preparing for war did not have to provide a single [i.e. unified] military organisation – given also the eminent personalities who are in charge of them – could end by dangerously interfering with the general efficiency of the country for war.[265]

Soddu was prepared to do what he could to satisfy a bare minimum of Balbo's demands but they went far beyond what was available either now or in the immediate future. As one example, Balbo had asked for 23 batteries of 77-mm guns and 437,000 rounds of ammunition: the guns might be provided within six to eight months but there was no ammunition available at all. Soddu urged Mussolini to consider the requests in the light of the overall picture and to consult Badoglio and Graziani before reaching any decisions.

Mussolini's options were, as his subordinates pointed out to him, severely circumscribed by the situation in which the army still found itself. He was warned three days after the German onslaught in the west began that the maximum force the army could mobilise amounted to 1,500,000 men and that they could be kept operational for only two months. The need to economise on resources and to maximise production meant that full mobilisation of this force must be delayed until the last possible moment, which in turn meant giving the war office three weeks' warning of full mobilisation.[266] One obvious way to relieve the pressure on the arms situation was to get them from Germany, which not only produced enough weapons to be able to sell them abroad for hard currency but also now had captured Norwegian, Danish and Dutch stocks. Since Germany had gone to war well ahead of the moment when Italy's rearmament was due for completion, it was logical that if Italy was going to intervene alongside her then she should provide in plenty of time the weapons Italy had not been able to produce. Soddu suggested that the time had come to put co-operation with Germany on what he termed 'concrete bases'.[267] This was not something Mussolini was prepared to do.

Graziani, who since the beginning of May had been opposed to any war action, now joined Soddu in pointing out the consequences of the slow pace of rearmament, the failure to secure concrete support from the Germans, and the stripping of materiel from the metropolitan army to shore up Italian forces overseas. Twenty four of Italy's seventy-three divisions were overseas, fourteen of them in Libya. Of those in metropolitan Italy the two armoured divisions were equipped only with light tanks apart from seventy M 11 medium tanks; the infantry divisions had only three fifths of the artillery possessed by French divisions, and no medium guns like those possessed by its potential enemy. There were only fifteen batteries of modern 75-mm anti-aircraft guns in the entire country. Lest Mussolini mistake the meaning of this analysis, Graziani warned him directly: his was not an army that 'possesses those armoured instruments (*mezzi*) and general modern equipment that permitted the recent rapid German penetration'.[268]

The litany of shortcomings went on. The army was severely short of regular officers and non-commissioned officers. It needed to requisition 20,500 trucks to mobilise completely, but if it took every one not exempted that amounted to only 12,600. Thus 'while the army is in a condition to be able to live and to fight a static war, <u>it is in no condition to operate on the move</u>'. There was only enough clothing and equipment to fit out 400,000 incoming reservists and the situation would not get any better before the winter. Only the few batteries of anti-aircraft guns had their full ration of ammunition; the rest of the artillery was short by between half and five sixths of requirements.

As to military operations, Graziani had in mind only two possible scenarios besides defensive war on the frontiers: an action against Yugoslavia with the 2nd, 8th and Po Armies which would reduce the reserves available to zero, or a fairly peaceful occupation of Croatia and Slovenia, which would leave the six divisions of 8th Army as the only possible reserve. His conclusions were uncompromising. As long as full mobilisation of Italy's manpower remained impossible because of the shortage of equipment and weapons, and as long as there was any chance that the French might launch an offensive across the Alps, the army should stand on the defensive. When the general military situation allowed, it might act in the east or the west, or send forces to the German front.[269] Two days later, Graziani forecast that by the first fortnight in June the Po Army would be ready, all the covering forces would be up to war strength in men but not in vehicles or horses, and the eastern and western army groups would have 60 per cent of their war strength in manpower and 50 per cent in motor vehicles and horses.[270]

On 29 May Mussolini summoned Badoglio, Cavagnari, Pricolo and Graziani to tell them that having initially fixed the date for Italian intervention in the war for spring 1941, and having then advanced it to September 1940 after the German successes in Denmark and Norway, he had decided in the light of the present situation to advance it yet again to any time from 5 June. To his mind, the risks of staying out were greater than those of coming in because the Allies' days were numbered. Germany still had by his count 165 divisions to throw in against the 70 or 80 French divisions – the British no longer counted for anything – and a crushing superiority in the air. The French had nothing to hope for either from their own industry, which the Germans would bomb, or from the United States. As to what action the services were to take, the programme outlined in May 1939 remained operative. Apparently heeding Graziani's advice, Mussolini decreed that the land theatre would be defensive, though something might in due course transpire regarding Yugoslavia. The navy would attack the enemy's forces in port and at sea. The important thing was to get involved now and not in two or three weeks' time when it would look as though Italy was coming in after the deed was done and when there was no risk. After the Duce had outlined how the Comando supremo would function there was a brief and somewhat desultory discussion about whether Cavagnari and Pricolo should continue to fulfil the twin roles of under-secretaries of state and chiefs of staff for their respective services. No one thought it appropriate – or worthwhile – at that moment to discuss the strategy of the hour, and certainly not that of the coming weeks and months.[271]

Badoglio summoned the chiefs of staff and warned them to ready the defences. Enemy attacks were likely across the French Alps and from either side of Libya – 'the zone of most concern to us'. Cavagnari, who well knew by now that the navy could do little more than defend the Sicilian channel, pointed out that 475 Italian merchant ships were still at sea and explained that the ones that could not avoid capture had been ordered to scuttle themselves. When Pricolo complained that he did not know which of a variety of operations he might be called on to carry out, Badoglio explained that they had not yet gone into that matter. He would call the chiefs together again 'and we shall see what we can do'.[272] His personal view, which he did not share with the chiefs of staff, was that things were not going as well for the Germans and that Italy should intervene when they broke through on the Somme, some time between mid-June and early July.[273]

After pondering on the meeting for a couple of days, Badoglio suggested to Mussolini that there were good grounds to delay entry into the war. Italy was already detaining over a million enemy troops in North Africa, Corsica and on the mainland. The Germans were about to unleash another offensive and expected to crush France in six or seven weeks; however, it could take longer than they expected and after that there was the war against England to face. 'We have therefore [more] time available in which to intervene without looking like crows'. Balbo needed the whole of June to gather the materiel necessary to put up 'an honourable resistance', and the raw materials on their way during that month would be of great assistance. Premature entry into the war could produce some successes for Italian submarines but also offered the English and French the chance of gaining successes in Libya which would be counter-productive for Italy. His advice was therefore that Italy ought 'at all costs' to stay out of the war in June, during which she could benefit from the guidance she could get by observing 'the quick or not so quick successes the Germans will obtain in France'.[274]

Cavagnari, too, wanted at least a few days more before sending his fleet to war. The first service head to learn that Mussolini had decided to enter the war alongside Germany – he had been told on 25 May – he had managed to amass enough diesel fuel to run the navy for sixteen months and not the three that Mussolini forecast by inflating his needs from 75,000 tons a month to 200,000 tons a month and then asking for enough to last six months. On 28 May 95 per cent of the reservists had been recalled, the fleet was at or near its wartime stations and the coastal defences were ready save for the emplacement of last-minute minefields and barriers.[275] On 3 June, he got Mussolini to agree to put back the start date for war by two days in order to get Italy's transatlantic liners back home – not least the *Roma*, which was returning from the United States and was destined in theory to be converted into an aircraft carrier. Perhaps because he sensed it was fruitless to do so, he appears to have made no mention of the need to safeguard the Italian merchant fleet, an eventuality for which plans had been drawn up some years earlier.

Ciano hoped at the last for a spontaneous wave of French resistance which might hold out for three months, thereby increasing the value of Italy's assistance. 'Why, the French are magnificent soldiers,' he told the Russian counsellor Leon Helphand on 1 June. 'They have an incomparable record!'[276] More realistically, Mussolini calculated their resistance in terms of weeks. He also abandoned, at least temporarily, the idea of capitalising on the war to launch attacks in theatres of his own choosing. On 5 June he directed Badoglio to order a defensive strategy on all fronts so that the army and navy would be saved 'for future events'. The navy was ordered not to bombard the French coast or lay mines. Refining these general instructions two days later, he ordered the navy to attack if it encountered mixed British and French forces but not to be the first to attack French forces alone unless this put it at a disadvantage, and encouraged Italian submarines to attack French warships 'if they can get off a good anonymous shot'. He also ordered the air force not to bomb

Alexandria, and instructed that operations against Malta and Gibraltar were only to proceed when he had given explicit confirmation.[277]

On 10 June, their hands tied by Mussolini's decisions, the military had no choice but to step into the maelstrom. 'When the guns start to go off,' Graziani declared at the penultimate chiefs of staff meeting before the war began, 'everything will automatically fall into place'.[278] As an expression of Piedmontese military loyalty, Fascist ardour and professional positivism, his words embodied the values that had shaped the Italian military as they served Mussolini after 1922 in peace and in war.

Conclusion

The politics of military policy in Fascist Italy were far from straightforward. While the party sheltered 'leftists' such as Roberto Farinacci, who wanted military power to follow organisational power and reside within it, and Giuseppe Bottai, whose service in Ethiopia led him to despise generals who enjoyed rank and privilege while being fixated with minutiae and whose Fascist aesthetic rebelled at the 'vulgarity' of Marshal Pietro Badoglio's physique, it also included figures such as Galeazzo Ciano who were powerful enough to interfere in the selection of the high-ranking officials according to their own amateurish predilections.[1] Such people created currents which Mussolini had to ride – but that is exactly where one of his talents lay. More importantly perhaps, while Mussolini was able to use his position as head of government to direct the armed forces he was never in full control of them. With the Duce lodged in Palazzo Venezia and king Vittorio Emanuele III ensconced in the Quirinale palace as rival poles of attraction, loyalty and obedience were always at least potentially in doubt. However, unless and until the opening of the Royal Archives proves otherwise too much should not be made of this. There is no substantive evidence to suggest that the pull of the monarchy ever significantly affected the strategic postures or military policies of any of the services, and in moments of tension for Italy their members seem to have managed to link the security of the state with the well-being of the realm.

As military master of Italy, Mussolini brought to his work the limited perspectives of his frontline experience and a confident assertiveness founded on ignorance. The result was judgement by prejudice which then had to be tempered when reality obtruded. Privileging manpower as a military factor led him in 1936 to congratulate the French on beginning to realise that the problem they confronted was not one of armaments alone but of demographics and that it was no good relying only on 'a belt of iron stretched along the frontier' before realising himself three years later that this was just what Italy needed.[2] His understanding of the economic sinews of war seemed initially to be more penetrating.

Writing in 1924, when his cabinet ministers were grappling with legislation designed to organise the nation for war, he recognised that the fortunate circumstances of 1915–18 were not likely to recur:

> The conditions in which this war was fought, with mastery of the sea and the financial possibilities of being resupplied from abroad which one cannot be sure of having every time, will also certainly be more difficult in a future war; industrial effort will have to be much greater and accompanied by a productive effort in agriculture and mining, as well as a considerable reduction in consumption.[3]

In practice, he proved quite unable to deal with – or even squarely confront – the problems he faced when preparing Italy for another war. As the tortured proceedings of the Commissione suprema di difesa demonstrate, this was in part the consequence of his penchant for simplistic solutions to his problems, such as collecting all the 'unnecessary iron' that he saw lying around in the country. In part also it was the product of his belief that he could solve the pressing problems of scarce resources simply by imposing an order of priorities on the system of raw materials allocation and thereby resolving ministerial conflicts.[4] Fascism was a command economy in which only commands were plentiful.

The advent of the Fascist regime perhaps complicated the problem to the point of insolubility, for on more than one occasion attempts to impose a solution to a problem of supply ran into massive practical obstacles resulting from the fact that the party had simply laid a new system of bureaucracy on top of an old one. However, the root of Italy's problems lay in the fact that neither Mussolini nor his chief military advisers ever grasped the fact that the next war would be a capital-intensive war – with the possible exception of the navy, which pitched its demands for funds on the basis of calculations of relative strength but did not directly spell out the consequences of its inescapable inferiority until the eleventh hour. What passed between Mussolini and Cavagnari during their regular meetings is unknown, but either the admiral did not explain the situation objectively or Mussolini did not take in the explanation. When he did understand the naval position, his solution was to throw caution to the winds in a characteristic miscalculation of the outcome. 'The Italian fleet will not lay passively in the fjords of Istria as happened in the last war,' he told the Hungarian military attaché in April 1940. 'I won't be careful with them, a part of the ships will be sunk but there will not be English–French traffic on the Mediterranean.'[5]

To say, as James Burgwyn has done, that '[n]one of Mussolini's war talk in the 1920s was followed up by fine-tuned operational plans and military mobilisation' is to draw something of a false distinction between the decades, as well as setting the services a high but ill-defined hurdle to jump.[6] As early as June 1924 the army and the navy were drawing up plans to land a 70,000 man expeditionary force around Hammamet in Tunisia – an operation for which an aircraft carrier was deemed to be one of the essential preconditions of success.[7] Other plans may well have preceded it and there is enough evidence to suggest that operational – and perhaps mobilisation – plans for an operation against Turkey shortly afterwards may once have existed. What is undeniable is that from an early stage the armed forces drew up operational designs for a variety of scenarios. Each service did so in its own ways, following its own traditions, from its own perspectives and according to its own characteristics. Military planning tended to be defensive when the Piedmontese traditionalists were in charge and aggressive when 'young Turks' of a modernising frame of mind were in command. Its defining characteristic was not so much the balance between these two poles as the very narrow and entirely depoliticised view of what a plan was which went not much further than identifying geographical objectives, computing the balance of forces and determining the deployment of Italian troops.[8] Naval planning dealt with large ocean areas and their inter-relationships, was task specific and was much influenced by threat analysis. Air force planning, so far as one can tell from the limited traces of it that have survived the archival turmoil of the war and its aftermath, dealt with tasks in broad rather than specific terms, was much influenced by operational factors of range and flying time, and always had as a backdrop an awareness that air power was a highly mobile weapon which could therefore be shifted about with no prior warning and more or less at whim by soldiers who did not understand it.

While the plans have intrinsic importance and say much about what the armed services thought they might have to do and what they thought they were capable of doing, they were no more than contingency plans. Some were generated by directives from Mussolini or Badoglio, but others were the product of a functional elite doing what its professional sense told it to do. This makes it unwise to build too large a political edifice on planning alone and to suggest that mapping its geographical preoccupations and charting the ebb and flow of its aggressivity provides conclusive evidence of Mussolini's designs or intentions.[9]

Mussolini thought of wars and his soldiers, sailors and airmen planned them, but lack of clear direction meant that his wishes did not mesh with their designs and his choices ultimately did not square with their capabilities. With no way of reaching the trans-oceanic sea routes, and little chance of winning a fleet encounter unless the imbalance in odds had somewhat improbably been lessened, Cavagnari's navy could not win a short war and faced a long one on the back foot. The army under

Baistrocchi and Pariani could not face a long war but was designed and intended to win a short one through a combination of speed, firepower and movement. In theory this made it an appropriate instrument for Mussolini to seize Greek ports, Yugoslav metals or Romanian oil. In practice, as even the aggressive and ideologically committed Marshal Graziani more or less acknowledged once the European war had begun, its lack of weight and punch made it a poor prospect for either a short or a long war. The air force was stranded between a short war which it had neither the ideas nor the means necessary to win and a long one in which industrial inferiority condemned it to defeat.

In June 1940 a disconsolate subordinate of Badoglio's noted in his diary, 'after many years' talk of fast offensive war ... we are starting by standing fast on our frontiers, without a plan of operations, taking great care that we are not attacked'.[10] Mussolini was certainly chiefly responsible for this state of affairs but so to a degree were most if not quite all of his generals and admirals. What had brought them to this pass was not bluff, nor even straightforward incompetence although there was certainly a deal of that, but a combination of individual inadequacies and multiple institutional failures on a massive scale.

Notes

INTRODUCTION

1 For a concise summary of the many fundamental differences between the two schools by the doyen of English historians of Italy, see Denis Mack Smith, 'Mussolini: Reservations about Renzo De Felice's Biography', *Modern Italy* vol. 5 no. 2, 2000, pp. 193–210.

2 Denis Mack Smith, *Mussolini as Military Leader*, University of Reading Stenton Lecture 1973, p. 15; Mack Smith, *Mussolini* (London: Weidenfeld & Nicolson, 1981), p. 237.

3 Giorgio Rochat, *L'esercito italiano da Vittorio Veneto a Mussolini* (Bari: Laterza, 1967), p. 586.

4 Brian R. Sullivan, 'The Italian Armed Forces, 1918–1940', in Allan R. Millett and Williamson Murray, eds., *Military Effectiveness* vol. II: *The Interwar Period* (Boston: Allen & Unwin, 1988), pp. 169–217; MacGregor Knox, 'The Italian Armed Forces, 1940–3', in Allan R. Millett & Williamson Murray, eds., *Military Effectiveness* vol. III: *The Second World War* (Boston: Allen & Unwin, 1988), pp. 136–79.

5 MacGregor Knox, 'The Sources of Italy's Defeat in 1940: Bluff or Institutionalized Incompetence?', in Carol Fink, Isobel V. Hull and MacGregor Knox, eds., *German Nationalism and the European Response, 1890–1945* (Norman, OK: University of Oklahoma Press, 1985), pp. 247–66; Knox, *Mussolini Unleashed, 1939–1941: Politics and Strategy in Fascist Italy's Last War* (Cambridge: Cambridge University Press, 1982), chap. 1.

I THE BEGINNING OF THE FASCIST ERA, 1922–1925

1 Pierre Milza, *Mussolini* (Rome: Carocci, 2000), p. 97.

2 *Ibid.*, pp. 222–3.

3 His hospitalisation and extended convalescence were apparently the consequence not of his wounds but of his having contracted neuro-syphilis: Paul O'Brien, *Mussolini in the First World War: The Journalist, the Soldier, the Fascist* (Oxford: Berg, 2004), p. 121.

4 Antonio Sema, '1914–1934: guerra e politica militare secondo Mussolini', in Virgilio Ilari and Antonio Sema, *Marte in Orbace: Guerra, esercito e milizia nella concezione fascista della Nazione* (Ancona: Nuove Ricerche, 1988), pp. 15–49, 54 (quos. pp. 41, 43, 44, 54).

5 *Ibid.*, pp. 95–6, 100–1.

6 Mario Roatta, *Otto milioni di baionetti. L'esercito italiano in Guerra dal 1940 al 1944* (Milan: Mondadori, 1946), p. 86.

7 Ubaldo Soddu, 'Memorie e riflessioni di un Generale (1933–1941)', (unpubl. mss. 1948), pp. 1–8.

8 Raffaele Guariglia, *Ricordi 1922–1946* (Naples: Edizioni Scientifiche Italiane, 1950), pp. 17–21. Mussolini's insistence on being met at Territet, near Montreux, by Curzon and Poincaré before the Lausanne conference opened on 20 May 1922 was not solely motivated by considerations of prestige, as Guariglia explains: *contra* Briton Cooper Busch, *Mudros to Lausanne: Britain's Frontier in West Asia, 1918–1923* (Albany NY: State University of New York Press, 1976), pp. 363–4. On the other hand, his arrival at Locarno on 15 October 1925 by racing car and then speed-boat was undoubtedly designed for effect.

9 H. Stuart Hughes, 'The Early Diplomacy of Italian Fascism', in Gordon A. Craig and Felix Gilbert, eds., *The Diplomats 1919–1939* vol. I: *The Twenties* (New York: Athenaeum, 1967), p. 225.

10 MacGregor Knox, 'Conquest, Foreign and Domestic, in Fascist Italy and Nazi Germany', *Journal of Modern History* vol. 56 no. 1, March 1984, pp. 7–11, 17–20; Giorgio Rumi, *Alle origini della politica estera fascista (1918–1923)* (Bari: Laterza, 1968), p. 24 (quo.).

11 O'Brien, *Mussolini and the First World War*, pp. 17, 42, 43, 160; Rumi, *Alle origini della politica estera fascista*, p. 159; Glenda Sluga, 'Italian national identity and Fascism: aliens, allogenes and assimilation on Italy's north-eastern border' in Gino Bedanti and Bruce Haddock, eds., *The Politics of Italian National Identity: A Multidisciplinary Perspective* (Cardiff: University of Wales Press, 2000), pp. 163–174.

12 ASMAE. T.2910/554, Frassati to Mussolini, 11 November 1922. Affari Politici: Germania, b.1135. The sentence is underlined by Mussolini.

13 Rumi, *Alle origini della politica estera fascista*, pp. 244–5, 246; Milza, *Mussolini*, p. 445.

14 The nature of Italian foreign policy in this period, and its relationship to domestic policy, is much contended; for one, by Renzo De Felice, who posits the primacy of domestic policy in Mussolini's thinking throughout the 1920s. For an introduction to these debates, see Alan Cassels, 'Was there a Fascist Foreign Policy? Tradition and Novelty', *International History Review* vol. 2 no. 2, May 1983, pp. 255–68; Stephen Corrado Azzi, 'The Historiography of Fascist Foreign Policy', *Historical Journal* vol. 36 no. 1, March 1993, pp. 187–203; Borden W. Painter, jr., 'Renzo De Felice and the Historiography of Italian Fascism', *American Historical Review* vol. 95 no. 2, April 1990, pp. 391–403; Denis Mack Smith, 'Mussolini: Reservations about Renzo De Felice's Biography', *Modern Italy* vol. 5 no. 2, 2000, pp. 193–210.

15 Mussolini to Thaon di Revel and Diaz, 24 February 1923; Mussolini to Diaz, 12 April 1923; Mussolini to Diaz, 24 April 1923. *DDI* 7th series vol. I nos. 548, 705, 742; pp. 393, 503, 528.

16 Alan Cassels, *Mussolini's Early Diplomacy* (Princeton NJ: Princeton University Press, 1970), p. 99.

17 UKNA, Mussolini to London Embassy, 10 January 1923, HW 12/42/012275. Mussolini to Della Toretta, 25 May 1923, *DDI* 7th series vol. II no. 55, pp. 37–8.

18 ASMAE. T.573, De Bosdari to Esteri, 14 September 1923. Gabinetto del Ministro GM 156 b.5/f. 2.

19 Cassels, *Mussolini's Early Diplomacy*, pp. 226–9; Dilek Barlas, 'Friends or Foes? Diplomatic Relations between Italy and Turkey, 1923–36', in *International Journal of Middle Eastern Studies* vol. 36, 2004, pp. 234, 236.

20 UKNA. N.1240, Della Torretta to Mussolini, 19 December 1922. HW 12/41/012182.

21 Rumi, *Alle origini della politica estera fascista*, pp. 40–1, 66. UKNA: T.132, Mussolini to Italian Embassy London, 13 January 1923; HW 12/42/012328-30.

22 AUSSME. N. 209, Martin-Franklin to Carletti, 23 February 1923; n. 810, Martin-Franklin to War Ministry, 29 June 1923. Rep. G-29 racc. 45/1, 45/2.

23 H. James Burgwyn, *Il revisionismo fascista: la sfida di Mussolini alle grandi potenze nei Balcani e sul Danubio 1925–1933* (Milan: Feltrinelli, 1979), p. 48.

24 William I. Shorrock, 'France, Italy, and the Eastern Mediterranean in the 1920s', *International History Review* vol. 8 no. 1, February 1986, pp. 70–8; Burgwyn, *Il revisionismo fascista*, p. 38; Avezzana to Mussolini, 7 December 1923, *DDI* 7th series vol. II no. 499, pp. 335–7.

25 Avezzana to Mussolini, 17 May 1923. *DDI* 7th series vol. II, no. 44, pp. 30–1.

26 ASMAE. T.310, Romano to Foreign Ministry, 11 March 1924. N.R. 1412, French Embassy, 22 March 1924. Gabinetto del Ministro b.GM 156.

27 ASMAE. T.3968, Romano to Foreign Ministry, 24 June 1924. Affari Politici: Francia, b.1102 f. 1. On the issue of Italian national rights in Tunisia, guaranteed under a convention of 1896 which France threatened unilaterally to abrogate, see William I. Shorrock, *From Ally to Enemy: The Enigma of Fascist Italy in French Diplomacy, 1920–1940* (Kent OH: Kent State University Press, 1988), pp. 49–53.

28 ASMAE. T.2910/554, Frassati to Mussolini, 11 November 1922. Affari Politici: Germania, b.1135.

29 ASMAE. T.2007/446, De Bosdari to Mussolini, 13 October 1923; T.2092/461, De Bosdari to Mussolini, 27 October 1923. Affari Politici: Germania, b.1139.

30 Mussolini to De Bosdari, 14 September 1923; De Bosdari to Mussolini, 17 September 1923; De Bosdari to Mussolini, 19 September 1923. *DDI* 7th series vol. II, no. 360 p. 238; no. 373 p. 247; no. 389, pp. 254–5.

31 ASMAE. Denti di Piraino to De Bosdari, 27 November 1923. Gabinetto del Ministero GM 156 b.5/f. 2.

32 *DDI* 7th series vol. II, pp. 329–30 fn. 2.

33 ASMAE. N.1594, 'Notizie pubblicate circa la costituzione dell'esercito tedesco', 28 December 1923. Affari Politici: Germania, b.1142.

34 'Relazione del Gen. L. Capello a Mussolini sulla sua missione in Germania (marzo 1924)': Renzo De Felice, *Mussolini e Hitler: I rapporti segreti 1922–1933*, (Florence: Le Monnier, 1977), pp. 90, 115.

35 ASMAE. N. 4869, De Bosdari to Mussolini, 18 March 1924; N.4870, De Bosdari to Mussolini, 18 March 1924. Gabinetto del Ministro, b. GM 156. Capello would be involved in a plot by socialists, ex-combatants, freemasons and dissident Fascists to assassinate Mussolini on 4 November 1925.

36 AUSMM. N.600, Cattanei to Marina, 5 October 1922. Cartelle Numerate b.1700/f. 11.

37 ASMAE. T.443.2, Raineri-Biscia to Ufficio Informazioni Marina, 19 February 1924. Gabinetto del Ministero GM 156 b.5/f. 2.

38 Della Torretta to Mussolini, 5 January 1924, *DDI* 7th series vol. II no. 534, p. 371.

39 John Gooch, *Army, State and Society in Italy, 1870–1915* (London: Macmillan, 1989), *passim*; Giorgio Rochat and Giulio Massobrio, *Breve storia dell'esercito italiano dal 1861 al 1943* (Turin: Einaudi,1978), part I, part II ch. 1.

40 Mario Isnenghi, *I Vinti di Caporetto nella letteratura di guerra* (Vicenza: Marsilio, 1967), *passim*; Nicola Labanca, *Caporetto: storia di un disfatta* (Florence: Giunti, 1997), *passim*; Luigi Cadorna, *Lettere famigliari (1915–1918)*(Milan: Mondadori, 1967), pp. 230, 234.

41 Lucio Ceva, *Le forze armate* (Turin: UTET, 1981), pp. 183–4.

42 Brian R. Sullivan, 'The Primacy of Politics: Civil–Military Relations and Italian Junior Officers, 1918–1940' in Elliott V. Converse III, ed., *Forging the Sword: Selecting, Educating, and Training Cadets and Junior Officers in the Modern World* (Chicago: Imprint, 1998), pp. 67–8; Carlo De Biase, *Aquila d'Oro: Storia dello Stato Maggiore Italiano (1861–1945)* (Milan: Edizione Borghese, 1969), p. 356.

43 Brian R. Sullivan, A Thirst for Glory: Mussolini, the Italian Military and the Fascist Regime, 1922–1936, PhD Columbia University 1984, pp. 91–8.

44 Milza, *Mussolini*, p. 311.

45 Ferrucio Botti and Virgilio Ilari, *Il pensiero militare italiano dal primo al secondo dopoguerra* (Rome: Ufficio Storico dello Stato Maggiore dell'Esercito, 1985), p. 47.

46 Rochat, *L'esercito italiano da Vittorio Veneto a Mussolini*, pp. 224–3.

47 As originally constituted, the army council comprised the war minister as non-voting president, Diaz as vice-president, the *generali d'esercito* who had commanded armies during World War I, and the designated army commanders in a future war.

48 AUSSME. 2a Relazione riassuntiva delle deliberazioni prese dal Consiglio dell'Esercito fra il 30 novembre 1921 ed il 24 giugno 1922, sec. XI. Rep. F-9, racc. 3 f. 2.

49 *Ibid.*, sec. I.

50 *Ibid.*, sec. XI.

51 *Ibid.*, sec. XI.

52 *Ibid.*, sec. XIII.

53 De Biase, *Aquila d'Oro*, p. 363.

54 AUSSME. 3a Volume dei verbali delle sedute tenute dal Consiglio dell'Esercito, verbale della 62a seduta, 23 October 1922, pp. 44–6, 48. Rep. F-9, racc. 3 f. 3.

55 *Ibid.*, p. 51.

56 3a Volume dei verbali delle sedute tenute dal Consiglio dell'Esercito, verbale della 63a seduta, 24 October 1922, pp. 59–60. *Loc. cit.*

57 Renzo De Felice, *Mussolini il fascista* vol. I: *La conquista del potere 1921–1925* (Turin: Einaudi, 1966), pp. 322, 325; Emilio Canevari, *La guerra italiana: Retroscena della disfatta* (Rome: Tosi, 1948), vol. I p. 79 fn. 1.

58 Pier Paolo Cervone, *Enrico Caviglia l'anti Badoglio* (Milan: Mursia, 1997), pp. 144–5.

59 Luigi Emilio Longo, *Francesco Saverio Grazioli* (Rome: Ufficio Storico dello Stato Maggiore dell'Esercito, 1989), pp. 347–8; De Felice, *La conquista del potere* pp. 361–2. De Felice discounts the contacts with Grazioli and Baistrocchi as important in deciding the king's action: De Felice, *Mussolini il Fascista* I, pp. 361–2.

60 Antonino Repaci, *La Marcia su Roma* (Rome: Canesi, 1963), vol. 2, p. 386. However, Seton Watson claims that Diaz was in Florence that night and that communications were cut: Christopher Seton Watson, *Italy from Liberalism to Fascism, 1870–1925* (London: Methuen, 1967), p. 627.

61 Gian Franco Venè *Cronaca e storia della Marcia su Roma* (Venice: Marsilio, 1990), p. 260.

62 Rochat and Massobrio, *Breve storia dell'esercito italiano*, pp. 206–7.

63 Longo, *Grazioli*, pp. 308–9, 337, 342–3.

64 *Ibid.*, p. 351.

65 Ceva, *Le forze armate*, pp. 196–7.

66 AUSSME. 4a volume dei verbali delle sedute tenute dal Consiglio dell'Esercito, verbale della 70a seduta, 1 February 1923, p. 9. Rep. F-9, racc. 4/ f. 1.

67 AUSSME. 4a volume dei verbali delle sedute del Consiglio dell'Esercito, verbale della 73a seduta, 4 February 1923, pp. 29–35. Rep. F-9, racc. 4/ f. 1.

68 AUSSME. Commissione suprema mista di difesa: Appunti per la seduta del 29 giugno 1923, pp. 9, 10. Rep. F-9, racc. 12/ f. 1.

69 *Ibid.* p. 26. In this copy, the amounts of time necessary to mobilise at 'minimum' levels and to move to 'maximum' strength are both blanks.

70 ACS. N.5396, Di Giorgio to Ministro delle Finanze, 31 October 1924. Presidenza del Consiglio dei Ministri 1924, fasc. 1/2-2/2956.

71 AUSSME. Relazione riassuntiva dell'esame fatto dal Consiglio dell'esercito dell'Ordinamento Di Giorgio nelle sedute dal 10 al 12 novembre 1924 (1925), pp. 6–7. Rep. F-9, racc. 4/ f. 4.

72 ASMAE. N.126, 'Relazione supplementare dell.on Fabry sul progetto di legge concernente la organizzazione generale dell'esercito', 25 January 1924; N.245, 'Progetto di legge sull'organizzazione generale della nazione per il tempo di guerra', 14 Feburary 1924 [quo.] Affari Politici: Francia, b.1102 f. 39-1.

73 ASMAE. N.325, 'Relazione supplementare sul "Progetto di legge di quadri ed effettivi" ', 26 February 1924; N. 452, 'Relazione parziale del progetto di legge sui quadri ed effettivi concernante la fanteria', 21 March 1924 [quo.]; N.1837, 'Progetto di bilancio della guerra per il 1925', 22 November 1924 [quo.]; N. 1898, 'Relazione sul bilancio della guerra per l'esercizio 1925',

8 December 1924., Affari Politici: Francia b.1102 f. 39-1 [nn. 325, 452], b. 1102 f. 1 [nn. 1837, 1898].

74 N.1478, 30 November 1923. *Cit.* Luigi Emilio Longo, *L'attività degli addetti militari italiani all'estero fra le due guerre mondiali (1919–1939)* (Rome: Ufficio Storico dello Stato Maggiore dell'Esercito, 1999), pp. 165–8 [quo. p. 168].

75 AUSSME. 5a volume dei verbali delle sedute tenute dal consiglio dell'Esercito, verbale della 90a seduta, 10 November 1924, pp. 2–4. Rep. F-9, racc. 6 bis.

76 *Ibid.*, pp. 5–8; Massimo Mazzetti, *La politica militare italiana fra le due guerre mondiali, (1918–1940)* (Salerno: Edizioni Beta, 1974), pp. 13–15.

77 *Ibid.*, verbali della 92a seduta, 11 November 1924, pp. 21, 23–4.

78 *Ibid.*, p. 26.

79 *Ibid.*, verbali della 93a seduta, 11 November 1924, p. 33.

80 *Ibid.*, verbali della 94a seduta, 12 November 1924, p. 43.

81 Sullivan, 'A Thirst for Glory', pp. 142–52; Milza, pp. 367–85.

82 Giorgio Rochat, *L'Esercito italiano da Vittorio Veneto a Mussolini*, pp. 495–501, 540, 546; De Felice, *Mussolini il fascista* vol. II, *L'organizzazione dello Stato fascista* 1925–1929 (Turin: Einaudi,1968), p. 54.

83 'Per la riforma dell'esercito', 2 April 1925: *OO* XXI, pp. 270–9 (quo. p. 278).

84 Paul G. Halpern, *The Mediterranean Naval Situation 1908–1914* (Cambridge MA: Harvard University Press, 1971), pp. 187–219; Lawrence Sondhaus, *The Naval Policy of Austria–Hungary 1867–1918* (West Lafayette, IA: Purdue University Press, 1994), pp. 173–4, 183–4, 191–204, 232–44; Mariano Gabriele and Giuliano Friz, *La politica navale italiana dal 1885 al 1915* (Rome: Ufficio Storico della Marina, 1982), pp. 146, 161–7, 213–4.

85 Giuseppe Costa, *La nostra flotta militare* (Torino: Lattes, 1912), pp. 5–12; Giuseppe Fioravanzo, *A History of Naval Tactical Thought* (Annapolis MD: Naval Institute Press, 1979), p. 145.

86 Romeo Bernotti, *Fondamenti di tattica navale* (Livorno: Raffaele Giusti, 1910), pp. 19, 30, 32, 62–3, 233.

87 Paul G. Halpern, *The Naval War in the Mediterranean 1914–1918* (London: Allen & Unwin, 1987), p. 516.

88 Guido Po, *La guerra marittima dell'Italia* (Milano: Corbaccio, 1934), pp. 30, 32, 45–6, 48, 62; Halpern, *Naval War in the Mediterranean*, pp. 85–6, 133.

89 Po, *La guerra marittima*, pp. 291–9.

90 Giuseppe Fioravanzo, editorial introduction to Domenico Bonamico, *Mahan e Caldwell* (Rome: Edizioni Roma, 1938), p. 11.

91 Ezio Ferrante, *Il Grande Ammiraglio Paolo Thaon di Revel* (Rome: Rivista Marittima, 1989), pp. 71–3.

92 Halpern, *Naval War in the Mediterranean*, p. 470.

93 Oscar di Giamberardino, *L'Ammiraglio Millo dall'impresa dei Dardanelli alla passione dalmatica* (Livorno: Società editrice tirrena, 1950), pp. 113–26, 146–8, 157–8, 183.

94 'Discorso pronunciato in Senato dall'Amm. Revel in occasione della ratifica del Trattato di Rapallo', 15 December 1920: Ferrante, *Paolo Thaon di Revel*, pp. 201–2.

95 AUSMM. Schema di uno studio sulla potenzialita' marittima dell'Italia (1921). Direttive Generali DG 1/D1.

96 Ferrante, *Paolo Thaon di Revel*, p. 78.

97 Walter Polastro, 'La marina militare italiana nel primo dopoguerra (1918–1925)', *Il Risorgimento* 1977, no. 3, pp. 134–7.

98 Romeo Bernotti, *Cinquant'anni nella marina militare* (Milan: Mursia, 1971), pp. 110–13.

99 *Ibid.*, p. 138 (8 July 1920).

100 'Discorso', 15 December 1920; Ferrante, *Paolo Thaon di Revel*, p. 202.

101 Giorgio Pini, *Vita di Umberto Cagni* (Milan: Mondadori, 1937), pp. 415, 417–8.

102 Polastro, 'La marina militare italiana', pp. 146–7.

103 Thomas H. Buckley, *The United States and the Washington Conference 1921–1922* (Knoxville TN: University of Tennessee Press, 1970), p. 32.

104 Brian R. Sullivan, 'Italian Naval Power and the Washington Disarmament Conference of 1921–22', *Diplomacy & Statecraft* vol. 4 no. 3, November 1993, pp. 227–8.

105 Carte Capponi. De Lorenzi to Ministro [Bergamasco], 6 October 1921 [draft]. 'Ruspoli'.

106 Carte Capponi. Promemoria 'Conferenza di Washington', 5 October 1921, p. 1 [attached to De Lorenzi to De Vito, 6 October 1921]. 'Ruspoli'.

107 *Ibid.*, p.3.

108 Giovanni Bernardi, *Il disarmo navale fra le due guerre mondiali (1919–1939)* (Rome: Ufficio Storico della Marina Militare, 1975), pp. 42, 43.

109 *Ibid.*, pp. 46–8.

110 Carte Capponi. Acton to Ministro della Marina & Capo di Stato Maggiore della Marina, 17 November 1921. 'Ruspoli'.

111 Bernardi, *Il disarmo navale*, pp. 73–7.

112 Bernardi, *Il disarmo navale*, pp. 52–8, 65–94; Sullivan, 'Italian Naval Power', pp. 229–37.

113 AUSMM. Relazione del Ministro degli Affari Esteri alla Camera dei Deputati della seduta del 16 marzo 1922, p. 15. Cartelle Numerate b.3183, f. 6.

114 Polastro, 'La marina militare italiana', pp. 149–51; Bernardi, *Il disarmo navale*, p. 144; Sullivan, 'Italian Naval Power', pp. 238–9, 243.

115 Joel Blatt, 'The Parity that meant Superiority: French Naval Policy towards Italy at the Washington Conference, 1921–22, and Interwar French Foreign Policy', *French Historical Studies* vol. 12 no. 2, Fall 1981, pp. 228–9, 233; Joel Blatt, 'France and the Washington Conference', *Diplomacy & Statecraft* vol. 4 no. 3, November 1993, p. 204.

116 Bernardi, *Il disarmo navale*, p. 144.

117 AUSMM. N.10816, Capo di Stato Maggiore della Marina to Ministro della Marina, 20 July 1922. Cartelle Numerate b. 1651.

118 AUSMM. Pro-memoria per il Sottocapo di S.M.: Dislocazione delle forze navali per la protezione del traffico marittimo nel bacino orientale del Mediterraneo, 16 January 1922. Cartelle Numerate b. 1662/ f. 3.

119 AUSMM. Lorenzi to Ministro della Marina, 29 April 1922. Cartelle Numerate b.1640.

120 AUSMM. 'Le prove di siluramento aereo navale', n.d., p. 5. Cartelle Numerate b.1700/f. 2.

121 AUSMM. Verbali delle adunanze tenute dal Comitato degli Ammiragli per esaminare il problema generale delle necessità dell'aeronautica e dell'aviazione nei riguardi degli scopi militari marittimi, 2 May 1922, pp. 18–19. Cartelle Numerate b. 1700/ f. 2.

122 *Ibid.*, 6 May 1922, p. 28.

123 AUSMM. Relazione: Ordinamento del servizio aeronautico della Ra Marina, 16 May 1922, p. 2. Cartelle Numerate b.1700/ f. 2.

124 *Ibid.*, pp. 3–5, 12, 14, 18.

125 AUSMM. Comitato Ammiragli, adunanza del 10 ottobre 1922, p. 2. Cartelle Numerate b.1684.

126 *Ibid.*, p. 9.

127 AUSMM. 'Dislocazione del naviglio in caso di mobilitazione', 20 March 1922. Cartelle Numerate b.1700/ f. 5.

128 AUSMM Comitato Ammiragli, 10 Ottobre 1922, pp. 3, 4, 7. Cartelle Numerate b. 1684.

129 *Ibid.*, pp. 2–3.

130 Rumi. *Alle origini della politica estera fascista*, pp. 37, 40, 158.

131 Di Revel to general Cittadini [n.d.], Ferrante, *Paolo Thaon Di Revel*, p. 83; Milza, *Mussolini*, p. 331. Cagni was if anything more in sympathy with the Fascists, passively disobeying an order to move his ships so that they were not available for public order duties when the March on Rome took place : Pini, *Umberto Cagni*, pp. 423–4.

132 AUSMM. N.40, Gabetti to Capo di Stato Maggiore della Marina, 18 December 1922; N. 41, Gabetti to Capo di Stato Maggiore della Marina, 22 December 1922. Cartelle Numerate b. 1651/ f. 3.

133 Philippe Masson, 'La "Belle Marine" de 1939', in Guy Pedroncini, ed., *Histoire militaire de la France* vol. III *De 1871 à 1940* (Paris: Presses Universitaires de France, 1992), p. 446.

134 ASMAE. N. 178, Ducci to Di Revel, 9 October 1924. Gabinetto del Ministro, b.156.

135 AUSMM. N.600, Cattanei to Capo di Stato Maggiore della Marina, 5 October 1922. Cartelle Numerate b.1700 f. 11.

136 AUSMM. Bianchi to Ambassador De Martino, 1 November 1922. Cartelle Numerate b.1640.

137 Carte Capponi. 'Trattato di Washington per la limitazione degli armamenti navali', December 1922. 'Ruspoli'.

138 AUSMM. N.2808, Ministero della Marina Direzione Generale delle Costruzioni Navali to Comando in Capo del Dipartimento Militare Marittimo: Lavori alle navi maggiori, 26 August 1922. Cartelle Numerate b.1662/ f. 3.

139 AUSMM. N.2241, Solari to Ministero della Marina, 15 December 1922. Cartelle Numerate b. 1662/ f. 3.

140 AUSSME. Commissione suprema mista di difesa: Appunti per la seduta del 29 giugno 1923. Rep. F-9, racc. 12 /f. 1.
141 AUSMM. Il Dodecaneso: Copia di Studio inviato all'I.G.M. in Aprile 1923, pp. 4, 2. Cartelle Numerate b. 1666.
142 Vittorio Tur, *Plancia Ammiraglio* (Rome: Canesi, 1963), vol. III p. 36; Ferrante, *Paolo Thaon di Revel*, p. 102.
143 AUSMM. Relazione della missione eseguita dal giorno 3 all'8 agosto 1923, 13 August 1923. Cartelle Numerate b. 1669.
144 AUSMM. Relazione di fine comando, December 1923, p. 15. AUSMM Cartelle Numerate b. 1689.
145 AUSMM. N.442, Vice-admiral Solari to Ministero della Marina, 1 September 1923. Cartelle Numerate b.1668.
146 Bernotti, *Cinquant'anni*, pp. 132–3; Ferrante, *Paolo Thaon di Revel*, p. 106.
147 Di Revel to Mussolini, 13 September 1923. *DDI* 7th series vol. II, no. 347, pp. 229–30, no. 348, pp. 230–1.
148 AUSMM. 'Difesa del Dodecaneso', Ducci to Mussolini, 13 September 1923. Cartelle Numerate b.1668.
149 AUSMM. N.399, Vice-admiral Simonetti to Ministero della Marina, 18 December 1923. Cartelle Numerate b.1668.
150 AUSMM. N.137, Captain Luigi Bianchi to Naval General Staff, 4 October 1923. Cartelle Numerate b.1672/ f. 4.
151 Brian R. Sullivan, 'The Italian Armed Forces', pp.171–2; Massimo Mazzetti, *La politica militare italiana fra le due guerre mondiali*, pp. 73, 92–3; Lucio Ceva, *Le forze armate (1918–1940)* p. 202.
152 AUSMM. 'Premesse al preventivo del bilancio 1924–925', 22 November 1923. Cartelle Numerate b. 1682/ f. 2.
153 ASMAE. N.299, 'Predisposizioni emanate dal Governo francese all proprie forze navali', 23 February 1924, Affari Politici: Francia, b. 1102/ f. 48-2.
154 AUSMM. 'Esercizio finanziario 1924–1925', 12 December 1923. Cartelle Numerate b. 1682/ f. 2.
155 AUSMM. 'Previsioni per il bilancio 1924–1925', 18 January 1924. Cartelle Numerate b.1682/ f. 2.
156 AUSMM. Di Revel to Mussolini, 6 March 1924. Cartelle Numerate b.1682/ f. 2.
157 AUSMM. 'Nuove costruzioni', 29 December 1924. Cartelle Numerate b. 1682, f. 2. The navy costed construction as follows: 'Trento' type cruiser L.140,000,000; 38-knot destroyer L.24,000,000; long-range submarine L.25,000,000; medium range submarine L.19,000,000.
158 ASMAE. N.762, 'Il progetto di Legge allo "Statut Naval"', 29 December 1924. Affari Politici: Francia b.1103 f. 1. The calculations of ship numbers were the attaché's own, as the Statut simply fixed global tonnage allocations for battleships (177,800), aircraft-carriers (60,960), light surface craft (390,000) and submarines (96,000).
159 Masson, 'La "belle marine" de 1939', pp. 447–8.
160 Ferrante, *Paolo Thaon di Revel*, p. 89.

161 Polastro, 'La marina militare italiana', pp. 157–8.
162 AUSMM. 'Esercitazione navale estate 1923', 23 April 1923. Cartelle Numerate, b.1662.
163 AUSMM. 'Relazione sull'attività dell'Armata navale durante l'anno 1924', 31 March 1925, pp. 3–4. Cartelle Numerate b.1689.
164 AUSMM. 'Relazione riassuntiva del comandante del partito avversario', n.d., pp. 7–8, 12; 'Il giudice capo del partito avversario', 29 August 1924. Cartelle Numerate b.1689.
165 Tur, *Plancia ammiraglio* vol. III p. 48.
166 AUSMM. Comitato degli ammiragli, adunanza 8 March 1924. Cartelle Numerate b.1684.
167 Antonio Pelliccia, 'L'aviazione navale in Italia', Italo Balbo Aviatore: Convegno internazionale del centenario (1896–1996), Roma 7–8 novembre 1996, unpubl. mss.; Ferrante, *Paolo Thaon di Revel*, p. 98. Secchi's two volume *Elementi di arte militare marittima* (1903–6) argued for both absolute and temporary control of the sea and presented the concept of the fleet-in-being at sea rather than in port. He was influential in persuading the pre-war Italian government to build fast dreadnoughts.
168 Ezio Ferrante, *Il pensiero strategico navale in Italia* (Rome: Rivista Marittima, 1988), pp. 37–8, 40–3; Bernotti, *Cinquant'anni*, p. 112.
169 Vice-admiral Luigi Donolo and James J. Tritten, *The History of Italian Naval Doctrine*, United States Naval Doctrine Command 3-00-009, 1995, pp. 22–3; Polastro, 'La marina militare italiana', pp. 129–31.
170 Ferrante, *Il pensiero strategico navale*, p. 40.
171 Bernotti, *Cinquant'anni*, p.134.
172 Achille Rastelli, 'I bombardamenti sulle città' in Paolo Ferrari, ed., *La grande guerra aerea 1915–1918: Battaglie–industrie–bombardamenti–assi–aeroporti* (Valdagano: Gino Rossato, 1994), pp. 183–249.
173 Alessandro Massignani, 'La guerra sul fronte italiano' in *ibid.*, pp. 17–55.
174 Vittorio Giovine, 'L'Arma aerea italiana nella sua crisi e nella sua rinascita', in Tomaso Sillani, ed., *Le forze armate dell'Italia fascista* (Rome, La Rassegna Italiana, 1939), p. 244; Andrea Curami and Giorgio Apostolo, 'The Italian Air Force from 1919 to 1923', in *Adaptation de l'arme aérienne aux conflits contemporains et processus d'indépendence des armées de l'Air des origines à la fin de la Seconde Guerre mondiale* (Paris: Fondation pour les études de defense nationale, 1985), pp. 258–9.
175 This is the conventional chronology; however, D'Avanzo claims that Mussolini began flying in 1918, temporarily gave up his course in 1921 and was only granted his licence in 1933 when the normal requirement to take off solo was waived: Giuseppe D'Avanzo, *Ali e poltrone* (Rome: Ciarrapico, 1976), pp. 49–50.
176 Gianni Rocca, *I disperati. La tragedia dell'Aeronautica italiana nella seconda guerra mondiale* (Milano: Mondadori, 1993), p. 10.
177 Giuseppe Valle, *Uomini nei cieli* (Rome: Centro Editoriale Nazionale, 1958), p. 91.
178 Andrea Curami and Giorgio Apostolo, 'The Italian Aviation from 1923 to 1933', pp. 269–70.

179 D'Avanzo, *Ali e poltrone*, p. 79.

180 The highest scoring wartime ace, lt. col. Francesco Barracca, had 34 'kills' at the time of his death on 18 June 1918; the second highest was lt. Silvio Scaroni, with 26 'kills'.

181 D'Avanzo, *Ali e poltrone*, pp. 60, 65–7; Curami and Apostolo, 'Italian Aviation from 1923 to 1933', p. 272.

182 Curami and Apostolo , 'Italian Aviation from 1923 to 1933', p. 275. The engines in question were Hispano Suiza 300 h.p., which Finzi had selected in 1923.

183 ASAM. L'aviazione alle manovre del Garda 1923, n.d., pp. 3–4, 10–12, 15, 17–20. Fondo Esercitazioni b.1.

184 ASAM. Relazione sulle manovre navali svoltesi nel Mare Ionio dal 20 al 24 agosto 1924, n.d., pp. 12–13, 16, 18, 22. Fondo Esercitazioni b.1.

185 ACS. B.3083, Thaon di Revel to Mussolini, 19 September 1924. Presidenza del Consiglio dei Ministri 1924, fasc. 1/2-2/2374.

186 ACS. N.31, Bonzani to Mussolini, 24 November 1924. Presidenza del Consiglio Ministri 1924, fasc.1/ 2-2/2374.

187 'Politica aeronautica', *Il Popolo d'Italia*, 19 October 1922.

188 Giorgio Rochat, 'Douhet and the Italian Military Thought 1919–1930', in *Adaptation de l'arme aérienne aux conflits contemporains*, pp. 22–6. See also Frank J. Capelluti, The Life and Thought of Giulio Douhet, PhD Rutgers University 1967, pp. 159–60.

189 Ferrucio Botti and Mario Cermelli, *La teoria della guerra aerea in Italia dalle origini alla seconda guerra modiale (1884–1939)* (Rome: Ufficio Storico dell' Aeronautica Militare, 1989), p. 333.

190 *Ibid.*, pp. 361–2.

191 *Ibid.*, pp. 422–8.

2 DOMESTIC CHECKS AND INTERNATIONAL BALANCES, 1925–1929

1 The burden of Italy's repayments was significantly greater than France's: in August 1926 Italy owed Great Britain $570,000,000 and had paid $76,000,000 whereas France owed $600,000,000 and had paid $227,000,000. T.869, Della Torretta to Foreign Ministry, 5 August 1926. ASMAE Ambasciata di Londra b.617 f. 3. Under the terms of the agreements of 14 November 1925 and 27 January 1926, Italy was released from 80 per cent of her legal debt to the United States and 50 per cent of her debt to Great Britain, and paid interest rates of 0.4 per cent and 0 per cent respectively on the remainder over sixty-two years: Alan Cassels, *Mussolini's Early Diplomacy*, pp. 262–71.

2 The claim made in Raffaele Guariglia, *Ricordi 1922–1946*, pp. 39–40. Nor, to go to the other extreme, did he regard Locarno as the 'basis of European policy': *contra* Richard Lamb, *Mussolini and the British* (London: John Murray,1997), p. 84.

3 Mussolini to De Bosdari, 30 May 1925; De Bosdari to Mussolini, 9 June 1925; Scialoja to Mussolini, [arr. 4] June 1925; Della Torretta to Mussolini, 24 June 1925; Della Torretta to Mussolini, 26 August 1925; Avezzana to

Mussolini, 18 September 1925. *DDI* 7th series vol. IV, nos. 13, 26, 32, 44, 110, 126, pp. 9–11, 22, 26, 34–5, 83–5, 95–6.

4 Avezzana to Mussolini, 20 May 1925; Appunto (Mussolini), 2 March 1927 [quo.]; Mussolini to Primo De Rivera, 21 March 1927. *DDI* 7th series vol. IV, no. 3, pp. 2–4; vol. V, nos. 39, 87, pp. 39–40, 94–5.

5 ASMAE. T.1482/1177, Romano Avezzana to Esteri, 27 October 1926. Affari Politici: Francia, b.1104 f.1. Unlike the copy published in *DDI* 7th series vol. IV, no. 417, pp. 363–5, this one bears Mussolini's underlinings (which appear under the phrase about the vagueness of French responses), and his annotation '*Interessante e nullo*'. See also William I. Shorrock, *From Ally to Enemy*, pp. 56–7, 110–11, 246–7.

6 AUSSME. Memoria sulle possibilità operative nel teatro di operazioni albano-jugoslavo (1926). Rep. L–10 racc. 85/1.

7 Paulucci de' Calboli Barone to Mussolini, 12 December 1927. *DDI* 7th series vol. V no. 674 p. 613.

8 Bodrero to Mussolini, 7 July 1925; Bodrero to Mussolini, 7 November 1927; Petrucci to Mussolini, 12 November 1927; Mussolini to Chiaramonte Bordonaro, 14 November 1927 [quo.]. *DDI* 7th series vol. IV no. 59, p. 46; vol. V nos. 506, 535, 542, pp. 489, 511–12, 519.

9 Grandi to Mussolini, 17 September 1925; Bodrero to Mussolini, 5 October 1925. *DDI* 7th series vol. IV, nos. 123, 139, pp. 93, 105.

10 Dino Grandi Diary, 15 October 1929.

11 Carte Badoglio. Promemoria sull'attività svolta dall'Ufficio Situazione nel periodo Maggio 1925–Febbraio 1927, 4 March 1927, pp. 1–2, 26. ACS 48/6 Scat. 2.

12 On Turkey, see Orsini Barone (Constantinople) to Mussolini, 17 April 1926; *DDI* 7th series vol. IV no. 298, p. 215; T.6271/499, Berlin Embassy to Esteri, 12 October 1926; ASMAE Affari Politici: Germania, b. 1166. On Romania, see Mussolini to Durazzo, 23 July 1926; Appunto (Mussolini), 31 August 1926; Mussolini to Vittorio Emanuele III, 16 September 1926; Promemoria, Guariglia to Mussolini, n.d. (between 23 February and 7 March 1927) [quo.]. *DDI* 7th series vol. IV nos. 379, 401, 428 , pp. 286–8, 309–10, 332; vol. V no. 54, p. 62.

13 ACS. Principali questioni trattate dall'Ufficio Operazioni durante la permanenza di S.E. il Maresciallo d'Italia Badoglio allo S.M. dal R. Esercito, 15 February 1927. Carte Badoglio 48/6 scat. 2.

14 Cassels, *Mussolini's Early Diplomacy*, p. 309.

15 Promemoria, Guariglia to Mussolini, n.d. (between 23 February and 7 March 1927). *DDI* 7th series vol. V no. 54, pp. 62–3.

16 ASMAE. T. 2108/730, Aldovrandi to Esteri, 23 December 1926; Affari Politici: Germania b.1166. Orsini Barone to Mussolini, 7 May 1927; *DDI* 7th series vol. V no. 190, pp. 196–7.

17 ASMAE. T.334, Mussolini to Ambassadors and Consuls, 28 April 1925. Affari Politici: Germania b.1157.

18 ASMAE. Colloquio Scialoja–Stresemann, 17 March 1926; T.2108/730, Aldovrandi to Esteri, 23 December 1926; Affari Politici: Germania b. 1166. Della Toretta to Mussolini, 26 August 1925; Mussolini to Scialoja, 12 March 1926; *DDI* 7th series vol. IV nos. 110, 276, pp. 83–5, 215.

19 Mussolini to Scialoja, 9 December 1926; *DDI* 7th series vol. IV no. 528, pp. 409–10. The Yugoslavs played their part in this process, exaggerating the extent to which Mussolini wanted to collude with them against French interests in the Balkans while telling Rome that they were being pressed to join the French alliance system in order to cut Italy off from eastern Europe. For their part, Italian diplomats 'bent' reports from Yugoslavia. H. James Burgwyn, *Il revisionismo fascista*, pp. 95–6, 145–6.

20 Avezzana to Mussolini, 24 December 1924; *DDI* 7th series vol. IV no. 558, pp. 436–8.

21 Avezzana to Mussolini, 25 November 1926; *DDI* 7th series vol. IV no. 500, pp. 389–90; Cassels, *Mussolini's Early Diplomacy*, pp. 369–72.

22 Della Toretta to Mussolini, 23 June 1926; Chiaramonte Bordonaro to Mussolini, 13 September 1927; Chiaramonte Bordonaro to Mussolini, 16 September 1927; Chiaramonte Bordonaro to Mussolini, 28 November 1927; Manzoni to Mussolini, 10 September 1928; *DDI* 7th series vol. IV no. 344, pp. 250–2; vol. V nos. 415, 423, 630, pp. 397–8, 408–9, 585–6; vol. VI no. 640, pp. 559–61. ASMAE. T. 2208/848, Bordonaro to Mussolini, 16 September 1927; Affari Politici: Francia b.1107 f. 1-1.

23 ASMAE. N.735, Notiziario No. 57, 12 December 1927, p. 2. Ambasciata di Londra b.644 f. 2.

24 ASMAE. T.1765, Mussolini to London and Paris Embassies, 22 May 1926; T.1867, Mussolini to London Embassy, 30 May 1926; T.431/635, Della Torretta to Foreign Ministry, 6 June 1926; T.2110, Bordonaro to Paris and London Embassies, 13 June 1926; To.232476, Mussolini to London Embassy, 5 August 1926; To.234054, Guariglia to Colonial Ministry, London and Paris Embassies, 17 August 1926; T.3047, Grandi to Addis Ababa Legation, London and Paris Embassies, 28 August 1926. Ambasciata di Londra b.620 f.4. Strictly speaking, only the Abyssinian state was authorised to import arms under the agreement; Ras Tafari did not represent it. In his 30 May telegram, Mussolini explained that the purpose of the link with Great Britain was partly 'to guarantee us in the event of any more or less distant radical change in the Abyssinian situation'. See also Cassels, *Mussolini's Early Diplomacy*, pp. 289–302.

25 Lamb, *Mussolini and the British*, p. 85.

26 Guariglia, *Ricordi*, pp. 47–50, 63; Mario Donosti, *Mussolini e l'Europa: la politica estera fascista* (Rome: Edizione Leonardo, 1945), pp. 13–14.

27 'I compiti della diplomazia italiana: discorso alla Camera dei Deputati il 19 maggio 1926': Dino Grandi, *La politica estera dell'Italia dal 1929 al 1932* (Rome: Bonacci, 1985), vol. I, pp. 95–112.

28 Paulo Nello, *Dino Grandi: La formazione di un leader* (Bologna: Il Mulino, 1987), pp. 262–3, 273–4. Guariglia's depiction of Grandi as maintaining the 'traditional' line of Italian foreign policy, that of friendship with Great Britain and France, is not the whole truth: Guariglia, *Ricordi*, pp. 63–4.

29 Appunti, 14 December 1927; *DDI* 7th series vol. VI no. 653, p. 601. The list of demands was put to the French ambassador in Rome on 30 January 1928.

30 Grandi Diary, 29 January 1929. *Cit.* Nello, *Grandi: La formazione*, p. 268 fn.

31 ASMAE. 'Questione dei confini meridionali della Libia', 30 March 1928, p. 1. Affari Politici: Francia b.1110 f. 1-7.

32 *Ibid.* (capitals in original).

33 ASMAE. T.1751/273, Mussolini to Manzoni (Paris), 13 April 1928. Affari Politici: Francia b. 1110 f. 1-7.

34 ASMAE. T. 2459/403, Manzoni to Mussolini, 23 April 1928. Affari Politici: Francia b. 1110 f.1-7.

35 Durazzo to Mussolini, 16 January 1928; *DDI* 7th series vol. VI no. 25, pp. 17–27.

36 Grandi to Preziosi, 2 May 1928; *DDI* 7th series vol. VI no. 295, p. 254 & fn. 4. A month after becoming foreign minister, Grandi recorded with approval Guicciardini's observation that 'It is necessary to deceive your own ambassadors first if you wish to deceive foreign princes': Dino Grandi Diary, 13 December 1929.

37 Mussolini to Durini di Monza, 6 January 1928; Mussolini to Paulucci, 16 January 1928; Durini di Monza to Mussolini, 30 January 1928; *DDI* 7th series vol. VI nos. 6, 23, 73, pp. 4, 17, 72–3.

38 Oxilia to War Ministry and Durini di Monza, 18 February 1929; Promemoria per il Sottosegretario degli Esteri, Grandi, [c.2–5 May 1929]; *DDI* 7th series vol. VII nos. 267 all., 408 all., pp. 291–4, 411.

39 Cerruti to Mussolini, 12 December 1928; *DDI* 7th series vol. VII no. 108, pp. 129–31.

40 Colloquio Mussolini to Titulescu, **25** January 1928.; *DDI* 7th series vol. VI no. 46, p. 53.

41 Mussolini to Aldovrandi *et al.*, 17 September 1928; Mussolini to Nochira, 28 December 1928; *DDI* 7th series vol. VI no. 658, pp. 573–4; vol. VII no. 132, p. 157.

42 Appunto . . . colloquio Mavroudis, 6 February 1928; Appunti colloquio Suad Bey, 8 February 1928; Mussolini to Arlotta, 21 February 1928; Mussolini to Chiaramonte, 30 March 1928; Orsini Barone to Mussolini, 11 November 1928; *DDI* 7th series vol. VI no. 86, 88, 120, 202, pp. 82, 85, 109–10 , 173–4; vol. VII no. 65, pp. 74–5.

43 Mussolini to Arlotta, 26 June 1928; *DDI* 7th series vol. VI no. 438, p. 381.

44 Barlas, 'Friends or Foes?' p. 235.

45 Galli to Mussolini, 19 March 1929; Galli to Mussolini, 9 April 1929; *DDI* 7th series vol. VII nos. 326, 364, pp. 341–2, 373–5.

46 'L'Italia alla conferenza di Locarno', 16 October 1925. *OO* XXI, pp. 411–2.

47 'Celebrazione della vittoria', 4 November 1925. *OO* XXI, p. 444.

48 Sullivan, A Thirst for Glory, pp. 166–8.

49 'Del Capo di Stato Maggiore' in Ferrante, *Paolo Thaon di Revel*, pp. 209–11; Lucio Ceva, 'Costituzione e funzionamento del Comando dell'esercito dal 1918 al 1943' mss., pp. 30–2.

50 Ferrante, *Paolo Thaon di Revel*, pp. 107–10.

51 'Per la riforma dell'esercito', 18 May 1925. *OO* XXI, pp. 311–14 [quo., pp. 312–3].

52 *Il Popolo d'Italia*, 25 May 1925; quo. Giorgio Rochat, *L'esercito italiano da Vittorio Veneto a Mussolini*, p. 563.

53 Carlo Cavallero, *Il dramma di Maresciallo Cavallero* (Milan: Mondadori, 1952), pp. 44–52.

54 Enrico Caviglia, *Diario (aprile 1925–marzo 1945)* (Rome: Casini, 1952), p. 4 (26 May 1925).

55 Badoglio to Mussolini, 1 May 1925; *cit..*, Longo, *Francesco Saverio Grazioli* p. 361. Grazioli only found out what Badoglio thought of him when, after the war, he read Mussolini's *Storia di un anno* in which Badoglio's letter was reproduced.

56 AUSSME. N.256, Mussolini to Badoglio, 7 January 1926. Rep. H-5 racc. 10/f. 11.

57 Antonio Sema, '1914–1934: Guerra e politica militare secondo Mussolini' in Ilari and Sema, *Marte in Orbace*, pp. 77–9.

58 The move seems to have worked, at least temporarily : on 7 July 1929 Balbo wrote to an acquaintance, 'Politics doesn't interest me any more. Let them do what they want. I'm fully occupied (*preoccupato*) with the air force'. De Felice, *Mussolini il fascista* II, p. 69. fn. 1.

59 Claudio Segrè, *Italo Balbo: A Fascist Life* (Berkeley CA: University of California Press, 1987), p. 276.

60 Luigi Federzoni, *1927: Diario di un ministro del fascismo* (Florence: Passigli, 1993), pp. 27–8 (entry for 6 January 1927).

61 Federzoni, *1927*, pp. 39, 75 (entries for 11 January & 4 February 1927).

62 Canevari, *Retroscena della disfatta* vol. I, pp. 158–9, 161; Lucio Ceva, *Le forze armate* (Turin: UTET, 1980), p. 208; Ceva, 'Costituzione e funzionamento dell'Comando dell'Esercito', pp. 32–6.

63 Mussolini to Badoglio, 2 October 1926; *DDI* 7th series vol. IV no. 446, pp. 346–7.

64 AUSSME. Badoglio to Mussolini, 4 October 1926. Rep. L-10 racc. 1/1.

65 Sedute del 18 giugno, 3 luglio [discussion of Austrian war plan], 10 luglio, 23 luglio, 27 luglio, 1 agosto, 5 agosto, 20 agosto 1925: Antonello Biagini and Alessandro Gionfrida, *Lo stato maggiore generale tra le due guerre (Verbali delle riunioni presiedute da Badoglio dal 1925 al 1937)* (Rome: Ufficio Storico Stato Maggiore dell'Esercito,1997), pp. 59–91.

66 Seduta del 18 luglio 1927, allegato: 'Promemoria del Maresciallo Badoglio relativo ai piani di guerra'; *ibid.*, p. 108.

67 Federzoni, *1927*, pp. 90, 136 (entries for 13 February & 19 March 1927).

68 Mussolini to Cavallero, 30 November 1928: *OO* XXIII, pp. 311–12.

69 Botti and Ilari, *Il pensiero militare italiano dal primo al secondo dopoguerra*, pp. 80–1.

70 AUSSME. Verbali della quarta serie di sedute della Commissione suprema di difesa, 30 June 1925, p. 1. Rep. F-9 racc. 13/f. 7.

71 *Ibid.*, pp. 5–6. The outcome was an allocation of 29 million lire over ten years to increase and improve the stock.

72 AUSSME. Principali questioni trattate dalla Commissione suprema di difesa (1923–1927), January 1928, p. 11. Rep. F-9 racc. 12/ f. 5.

73 AUSSME. Verbali della terza serie di sedute della Commissione suprema di difesa, 9 October 1924, p. Rep. F-9 racc. 13/f. 2.

74 AUSSME. Principali questioni trattate dalla Commissione suprema di difesa (1923–1927), January 1928, pp. 2–4, 5–7, 16. Rep. F-9 racc. 12/f. 5.

75 AUSSME. N.1245, Promemoria: Funzione delle Colonie nella mobilitazione civile, 28 November 1927. Rep. F-9 racc. 15/f. 5.

76 AUSSME. Commissione suprema di difesa: Verbali della quarta serie di sedute, 30 June 1925, pp. 2–5, 8–9. Rep. F-9 racc. 13/f. 7.

77 AUSSME. Relazione sommaria sul lavoro compiuto ed in corso dalla Commissione suprema di difesa, 15 February 1928, pp. 2–4. Rep. F-9 racc. 12/f. 5.

78 *Ibid.*, p. 5. *Loc. cit.*

79 AUSSME. Produzione delle Artiglerie, December 1928, p. 4. Rep. F-9 racc. 15/ f. 3.

80 AUSSME. Relazione sommaria sul lavoro compiuto ed in corso dalla Commissione suprema di difesa, 15 February 1928, p. 8. Rep. F-9 racc. 12/f.5.

81 AUSSME. Principali questioni trattate dalla Commissione suprema di difesa (1923–1927), January 1928, pp. 4–5. Rep. F-9 racc. 12/f. 5.

82 D'Avanzo, *Ali e poltrone* p. 858. See also the figures in Rochat, *Balbo* p. 119, which differ.

83 Segrè, *Balbo*, p. 157. The British air budget grew between 1927 and 1928 by 71 per cent, and in 1929 was 79 per cent higher than in 1927; the French air budget increased by 14 per cent in 1928 and in 1929 was 144 per cent of the 1927 figure.

84 ACS. Memoria sull'organizzazione dell'esercito italiano in tempo di pace e sulla sua trasformazione in esercito di campagna, October 1925. Carte Badoglio 48/6 scat. 2. Badoglio specifically distanced himself from the *lancia e scudo* model, according to which the army was at first small and could only ward off enemy attacks 'if it could even do that' while gaining time for general mobilisation.

85 AUSSME. Consiglio dell'esercito: verbale della 95a seduta, 16 November 1925, p. 2. Rep. F-9 racc. 6 bis.

86 AUSSME. Consiglio dell'esercito: verbale della 96a seduta, 17 November 1925, pp. 1–8 and addendum. Rep. F-9 racc. 6 bis.

87 AUSSME. Consiglio dell'esercito: verbale della 97a seduta, 18 November 1925, pp. 2–3. Rep. F-9 racc. 6 bis.

88 Rochat, *L'Esercito italiano*, pp. 575–86; Canevari, *Retroscena della disfatta* vol. I p. 153. Figures on the size of the officer corps differ; the following are Rochat's figures, with Ceva's in parentheses: generals 164 – 189 (194); senior officers 2500–3320 (4114); captains 4350-4800 (6129); lieutenants 7150–3730 (5283): Ceva, *Le forze armate*, p. 214.

89 Sedute del 10 luglio, 27 luglio, 5 agosto, 20 agosto 1925: Biagini and Gionfrida, *Lo stato maggiore generale*, pp. 63–6, 71–4, 82–8, 89–91.

90 Sullivan, A Thirst for Glory, p. 173. ACS. Mussolini to Ferrari, 15 January 1928. Segretaria particolare del Duce b.5.

91 Ferrari to Capo del Governo e Ministro della Guerra [Mussolini], 28 January 1928: Canevari, *Retroscena della disfatta* vol. I, pp. 236–44 [quo. p. 243].

92 *I capi di S. M. dell'esercito: Alberto Bonzani* (Rome: Comando del Corpo di Stato Maggiore dell' Esercito, n.d. [1938]), pp. 8–10, 12–13, 16–17. Although born in Rimini, Bonzani had Piedmontese parents and was educated at the *Accademia militare* in Turin.

93 Federzoni, *1927*, p. 134 (19 March 1927).

94 Botti and Ilari, *Il pensiero militare italiano*, pp. 274–80, 316–9. Significantly, Botti and Ilari find no strategic theorist of note, and only two writers on *pedagogia militare* of significance (Alfredo Baistrocchi and Carlo De Risky), in the years up to 1929.

95 Antonio Sema, 'La cultura dell'esercito', in AA. VV., *Cultura e società negli anni del fascismo* (Milan: Cordani, 1987), p. 92.

96 Rochat, *L'esercito italiano*, p. 469. Declarations such as these, Rochat points out, 'opened the way to the policy of "eight million bayonets" without tanks or guns': *ibid.*, fn. 15.

97 Botti and Ilari, *Il pensiero militare italiano*, pp. 131–71.

98 MRR. N.232, Esercitazioni sperimentali nei pressi del Lago Trasimeno, 19 June 1926. Archivio Pecori Giraldi b.9.P.82.

99 Sema, 'La cultura dell'esercito', p. 100.

100 *L'esercito italiano tra la 1a e la 2a guerra mondiale novembre 1918-giugno 1940* (Rome: Ufficio Storico Stato Maggiore dell'Esercito, 1954), pp. 87–91, 96–7; Botti and Ilari, *Il pensiero militare italiano*, pp. 137–9.

101 ASMAE. N.198. Notiziario No. 60, 22 March 1928. Ambasciata di Londra b.670 f. 2.

102 ASMAE. N.552, Notiziario No. 65, 17 September 1928, pp. 31–5; N. 660, Notiziario No. 66, 17 November 1928, pp. 38–41, 46. *Ibid.*

103 Luigi Emilio Longo, *L'attività degli addetti militari italiani all'estero fra le due guerre mondiali (1919–1939)*, pp. 380–4 [quo. p. 384].

104 Sema, 'La cultura dell'esercito', pp. 106, 116 fns. 64, 65.

105 Mussolini to Acton, 7 June 1925; *cit.* Lucio Ceva, 'Appunti per una storia dello Stato Maggiore generale fino alla vigilia della "non belligeranza" (giugno 1925–luglio 1939)', *Storia Contemporanea* vol. 10 no. 2, April 1979, pp. 211–2.

106 AUSMM. Il Bilancio della Marina per l'esercizio finanziario 1927–8, 1928–9; Cartelle Numerate b.3172/f. 3.

107 Romeo Bernotti, *Cinquant'anni nella Marina Militare*, p. 193.

108 AUSMM. Comitato Ammiragli, adunanza del 25 febbraio 1925. Cartelle Numerate b.1684.

109 AUSMM. 'Nuovi incrociatori', 27 January 1925. Cartelle Numerate b. 1684.

110 AUSMM. 'Promemoria sulle grandi manovrc navali da svolgere nell'estate del 1925: Attacco e difesa della Sicilia', 24 October 1924. Cartelle Numerate b.1683/f. 1.

111 AUSSME. Appunti circa le condizioni strategiche dell'Italia in Mediterraneo in caso di conflitto con la Francia, specialmente dal punto di vista della protezione del traffico maritime con l'Oriente, 8 May 1926, pp. 9–10. Rep. L-10 racc. 61/c. 2.

112 AUSMM. Comitato Ammiragli, adunanza del 12 agosto 1925. Cartelle Numerate b.1684.

113 Carlo Di Risio, *Tempesta sul ponte di volo* (Rome: Adnkronos, 1987), p. 26.
114 The navy was prepared to gamble to get the ships it wanted. In 1926, as part of a new build of twelve destroyers to be begun that year, it agreed to order four 38-knot destroyers from the Cantiere Navale del Quarnero at a price of L.20,750,000 per ship without specifying a time limit for their delivery and before trials of the Belluzzo turbine with which they were to be equipped were complete. AUSMM. N. 729, Consiglio Superiore di Marina, adunanza 28 luglio 1926; Consiglio Superiore di Marina b.25.
115 AUSMM. N.103 RRP, Promemoria a S.E. il ministro circa la situazione al 16 dicembre 1926. Cartelle Numerate b.1683.
116 AUSMM. N.107RRP, Situazione navale Italo–Francese, 19 December 1926. Cartelle Numerate b.1683.
117 AUSMM. Costruzione di naviglio sottile, subacquee e sussidiario in tempo di guerra, 17 December 1934, p. 1. Cartelle Numerate b.1727.
118 Ferruccio Botti, 'La strategia marittima negli anni venti', *Bollettino d'Archivio dell'Ufficio Storico della Marina Militare* anno II no. 3, September 1988, p. 255.
119 Ezio Ferrante, *Il pensiero strategico navale*, p. 48.
120 Ferrante, *Il pensiero strategic navale*, pp. 40, 42–4. The army, too, took a more aggressive line, believing that in a war with France the navy's tasks were to attack ocean traffic, to block the Sicilian channel, and to counter-attack the enemy in the eastern Mediterranean basin: Appunti circa le condizioni strategiche dell'Italia in Mediterraneo, *op. cit.*, pp. 7, 8, 12. *Loc. cit.*
121 Botti, 'La strategia marittima negli anni venti', pp. 252, 256.
122 Bernotti, *Cinquant'anni*, pp. 185–7.
123 Giorgio Rochat, *Italo Balbo aviatore e ministro dell'Aeronautica 1926–1933* (Ferrara: Bovolenta, 1979), pp. 96–8.
124 Ferrante, *Il pensiero strategico navale*, pp. 39–40.
125 Bernotti, *Cinquant'anni*, p. 155.
126 *Ibid.*, p. 169.
127 Mussolini to Sirianni, 23 October 1927; *ibid.*, p. 172.
128 Botti and Cermelli, *La teoria della guerra aerea in Italia*, p. 398.
129 *Ibid.*, pp. 399–419.
130 Naval General Staff to Foreign Ministry, 28 April 1926: Giovanni Bernardi, *Il disarmo navale*, p. 188 fn. 10.
131 *Ibid.*, pp. 190–3.
132 Carte Capponi. [Ruspoli] to Acton, 17 October 1926. 'Trattati e disarmo'.
133 Bernardi, *Il disarmo navale*, pp. 212–3.
134 Acton to Ministry of Foreign Affairs, 14 February 1927; Bernardi, *Il disarmo navale*, pp. 224–5.
135 Carte Capponi. Conferenza internazionale del dopoguerra, January 1928. 'Trattati e disarmo'.
136 Carte Capponi. Appunti, January 1928. 'Trattati e disarmo'.
137 AUSMM. N.208101–42, Memorandum del 21 febbraio 1927-V diretto dal Regio Ministero degli Affari Esteri all'Ambasciata degli Stati Uniti d'America in Roma, in risposta al memorandum americano del 10 febbraio circa una nuova conferenza per la limitazione degli armamenti navali fra le

potenze firmatorie del Trattato di Washington del 1922. Cartelle Numerate b.3183/f. 6.

138 Carte Capponi. La marina e la politica del disarmo, 1 October 1927. 'Trattati e disarmo'.

139 AUSMM. In 1928, Italy ordered two 32-knot 10,160-ton cruisers, *Fiume* and *Zara*, at unit costs of L.107,000,000 and L. 112,000,000: N. 8426, Consiglio Superiore di Marina, adunanza 14 luglio 1928. Consiglio Superiore di Marina, b.25.

140 Carte Capponi. Conferenze tripartite e tendenze di politica navale, 27 January 1928. 'Trattati e disarmo'.

141 ACS. Mussolini to Sirianni, 15 August 1927. Segretaria Particolare del Duce b.4.

142 'L'Italia nel mondo', 5 June 1928. *OO* XXIII p. 184.

143 Memorandum del Sottosegretario degli Esteri, Grandi, per l'Ambasciatore di Francia a Roma, Beaumarchais, 6 October 1928; *DDI* 7th series vol. VII no. 22, pp. 20–1.

144 Promemoria dell'Ufficio Trattati dello Stato Maggiore della Marina, 10 November 1928; *DDI* 7th series vol. VII no. 61, p. 69.

145 ACS. Verbali delle riunioni del Consiglio dei Ministri, 25 January 1929.

146 UKNA. Bonzani to Mussolini, 7 December 1925. GFM 36/438/fr.087621–6.

147 UKNA. Dubbi sulla efficienza della aeronautica, 6 December 1925; n.136, Bonzani to Mussolini, 6 July 1926. GFM 36/438/fr.087627, 087637–44.

148 Rochat, *Italo Balbo aviatore*, p. 54.

149 Pelliccia belives that he was 'technically and professionally prepared': Antonio Pelliccia, *Il Maresciallo dell'aria Italo Balbo* (Rome: Ufficio Storico Aeronautica Militare, 1998), p. 146.

150 ASMAE. N.532/M, Sulla limitazione degli armamenti, 19 February 1926, p. 7; N.3920 N.S., Notiziario dell'Aeronautica, 30 November 1927. Ambasciata di Londra b.620/f. 3; b.644/f. 1.

151 Segrè, *Italo Balbo*, pp. 150–1. Handing over to Valle in 1933, Balbo gave slightly different figures: 399 aircraft had taken off and approximately 200 had completed the test, 'almost all unarmed'. Canevari, *Retroscena della disfatta* vol. I, p. 180.

152 Pelliccia, *Il maresciallo dell'aria*, p. 134. The apparently insuperable practical difficulties to be overcome in any attempt to produce an agreed set of figures are expertly summed up in Rochat, *Italo Balbo aviatore*, pp. 115–6.

153 Seduta del 28 febbraio 1927: Biagini and Gionfrida *Lo stato maggiore generale*, p. 98. Badoglio announced that he had informed Mussolini that Italy must have at least 600 aircraft to be able to counter the Yugoslavs, apparently unaware that as far as Balbo was concerned she already possessed that number.

154 However, the differences between the 'organic' figure embodied in the legal establishment, the annual budgeted figure and the actual size could vary considerably: in 1928 the air force calculated it needed 1,650 officers the following year, but the 1928/9 budget allowed for 1,750: Rochat, *Italo Balbo aviatore*, p. 135.

155 Segrè, *Italo Balbo*, pp. 177, 270–1; Rochat, *Italo Balbo aviatore*, pp. 71 fn. 2, 73–4.

156 Giuseppe Santoro, *L'Aeronautica italiana nella seconda guerra mondiale* (Milan: ESSE, 1957), p. 15.

157 Another unusual feature of the furnishings was that the desks had open shelves instead of drawers. The building, which is an historical document in its own right and exceptionally interesting, is not open to the public, but a good idea of its striking quality can be had from Franco Borsi, Gabriele Morolli, Daniela Fonti and Giuseppe Pesce, *Il Palazzo dell'Aeronautica* (Rome: Editalia, 1989). A photograph of the 'standing lunch' can be found on p. 175. I am grateful to Dr Paulo Balbo for giving me a personal tour of his father's offices. See also Segrè, *Italo Balbo*, pp. 186–7.

158 ACS. Promemoria circa l'ordinamento tecnico fianziario delle forze armate, 8 June 1928; Sirianni to Mussolini, 11 July 1928; n.1022, Aeronautica to Presidenza, 7 August 1928. Presidenza del Consiglio dei Ministri 1928 fasc. I/2–2/3096.

159 D'Avanzo, *Ali e poltrone*, p. 98.

160 Pelliccia, *Il maresciallo dell'aria*, p. 149.

161 *Ibid.*, pp. 136–7.

162 *Ibid.*, pp. 148–9, 201, 203–4.

163 ASAM. Relazione sul funzionamento ed impiego dell'aviazione da ricognizione (1o gruppo aeroplani) assegnato alla divisione di manovra (parte azzurra), September 1926, pp. 7, 59, 60–1, 64, 70 [quo.]. The report, by general Porro, claimed that the airmen got a little too absorbed with 'preoccupations of a technical–experimental character'. Fondo Esercitazioni b.1.

164 ASAM. Esercitazioni navali giugno 1927: Apprezzamento della situazione, 14 June 1927. Fondo Esercitazioni b.1.

165 ASAM. Manovre Armata Aerea: Ordine di massima-Esercitazioni aeree, September 1927; Manovre aeronautiche, September 1927. Fondo Esercitazioni b.2.

166 ACS. T.4848, Balbo to Mussolini, 15 September 1927; T.48759(5), Balbo to Mussolini, 16 September 1927; T.48817(4), Balbo to Mussolini, 17 September 1927; T.49169/4/Pi, Balbo to Mussolini, 19 September 1927 [quo.]. Presidenza del Consiglio dei Ministri 1927, fasc. 1/2–2/3748.

167 ASAM. Relazione sulle esercitazioni aeree settembre 1927, pp. 115–6. Fondo Esercitazioni b.1.

168 *Ibid.*, pp. 117, 119, 122, 124, 125.

169 ASAM. Direzione esercitazioni aeree 1927: Conferenza finale tenuta a Padova da S.E. il C.S.M., direttore alle esercitazioni, il giorno 21 settembre 1927, p. 14. Fondo Esercitazioni, b.2. This was the only passage of his concluding remarks not included in the printed version.

170 ASAM. Esercitazioni aeree 1928, pp. 8–11, 30–1, 116–21. Fondo Esercitazioni b.3.

171 ASMAE. N.3978/N.S., Notiziario dell'Aeronautica (1–10 dicembre 1927), 12 December 1927, p. 1; N.552, Notiziario No. 65, 17 September 1928, pp. 70–96. Ambasciata di Londra b.644/f. 1; b.670/ f. 2.

172 Pelliccia, *Il Maresciallo dell'aria*, pp. 292–5 [quos. p. 295].

173 ASAM. Memoria sulla preparazione alla guerra della R. Aeronautica e sui provvedimenti relativi per la sua intensificazione (1928), p. 8. Relazioni per il Capo di Stato Maggiore Generale c.9. [From internal evidence the memorandum was produced between January and June 1928.]

174 Pelliccia reproduces the original memorandum, which is not dated, together with Balbo's blistering response to the generals: Pelliccia, *Il Maresciallo dell'aria*, pp. 109–200, 202.

175 Rochat, *Italo Balbo aviatore*, pp. 98–9.

176 Claudio Segrè, *Italo Balbo*, p. 156. There is no agreement between scholars as to the extent to which Balbo was a 'Douhetian': Pelliccia suggests that he shared Douhet's fundamental principles but did not accept their extreme consequences, while Rochat argues that he 'instrumentalised' Douhet's theories as cultural cover for a fascist aeronautical policy in which publicity was the dominant consideration: Pelliccia, *Il maresciallo dell'aria*, p. 275; Rochat, *Italo Balbo aviatore*, pp. 88, 144. Segre stands somewhere in the middle.

177 Claudio Segrè, 'Douhet in Italy: Prophet Without Honor?', *Aerospace Historian* June 1979, pp. 75–6; Giorgio Rochat, 'Douhet and the Italian Military Thought 1919–1930', *Adaptation de l'arme aérienne aux conflits contemporains et processus d'indépendence des armées de l'Air des origines à la fin de la Seconde Guerre mondiale* (Paris: Fondation pour les études de défense nationale, 1985), pp. 27–8.

178 Botti and Cermelli, *La teoria della guerra aerea* , pp. 364–73, 375–7, 380–4.

179 *Ibid.*, pp. 447–57 (quo. p. 457). For a digest of these debates in English, see Frank J. Cappelluti, The Life and Thought of Giulio Douhet, pp. 200–18.

180 Segrè, *Italo Balbo*, pp. 161–5.

181 AUSSME. Commissione suprema di difesa VIa serie di sedute, verbale del 13 febbraio 1929, p. 24. [Balbo's intervention p. 23]. Rep. F-9 racc. 15 f. 2.

182 *Ibid.*, verbale del 13 febbraio 1929, p. 25.

183 Pelliccia, *Il Maresciallo dell'aria*, pp. 206–10.

184 Federzoni, *1927*, p. 76 [diary entry 4 February]; D'Avenzo, *Ali e poltrone*, p. 108. In the course of the discussion on Piccio, Federzoni noted, Mussolini referred to 'the worrying [*preoccupante*] deficiency of the entire Italian air force, planes, pilots, [and] organisation'.

185 Among other incidents causing bad blood, De Pinedo's supporters had made supposedly threatening remarks about replacing Balbo at a restaurant and De Pinedo had been accused of losing 300,000 lire at poker; despite the strained relations between them, Balbo denied that De Pinedo had ever been a gambler: D'Avanzo, *Ali e poltrone*, pp. 116–7, Rochat, *Italo Balbo aviatore*, p. 77 fn. 27.

186 Promemoria, n.d., att. to De Pinedo to Mussolini, 22 August 1929: Rochat, *Italo Balbo aviatore*, pp. 189–93 [quos., pp. 192, 193].

187 'Considerazione sulla situazione del materiale aeronautica', 18 August 1929: *ibid.*, pp. 193–207 [quo. p. 206].

188 AUSMM. Italia contro Francia: Apprezzamento della situazione, n.d. [18 November 1924], p. 4. Direttive Generali DG 1/D1.

189 *Ibid.*, p. 6.

190 AUSMM. Italia contro Francia: Piano generale di operazioni [1924], p. 2. Direttive Generali DG 1/D1.

191 *Ibid.*, p. 6.

192 For the conceptual relationship, see Fortunato Minniti, 'Piano e ordinamento nella preparazione italiana alla guerra degli anni trenta', *Dimensioni e problemi della ricerca storica* n. 1, 1990, pp. 121–2.

193 AUSMM. Italia contro Francia: necessità politiche internazionali [1924], p. 1. Direttive Generali DG 1/D1.

194 Gabetti to Acton, 10 January 1928; *DDI* 7th series vol. VI no. 15 (att.), pp. 9–10.

195 AUSMM. Italia contro Francia: necessità politiche internazionali [1924], p. 4. *Loc. cit.*

196 AUSSME. Memoria preliminare per il piano di operazione alla frontiera austriaca: Nota al piano 1A, 1927 [1926], p. 2. Rep. H-6 racc. 2.

197 *Ibid.*, p. 16. The Germans, it was calculated, would have to use civil aircraft for bombing and reconnaissance, and would at least initially be unable to deploy fighters; bombing should concentrate on the railway net – not an activity which was currently in the Regia Aeronautica's lexicon; *ibid.*, pp. 25–8.

198 ACS. Carte Badoglio. Principali questioni trattate dall'Ufficio Operazioni durante la permanenza di S.E. il Maresciallo d'Italia Badoglio allo S.M. del R. Esercito, 15 February 1927. ACS 48/6 scat. 2. See also Fortunato Minniti, 'L'ipotesi più sfavorevole. Una pianificazione operativa italiana tra strategia militare e politica estera (1927–1933)', *Nuova Rivista Storica* anno LXXIX fasc. III, 1995, p. 614.

199 Seduta del 28 ottobre 1928; Biagini and Gionfrida, *Lo stato maggiore generale*, p. 171.

200 Minniti, 'L'ipotesi più sfavorevole', p. 622.

201 Seduta del 18 luglio 1927, allegato: promemoria del Marsceiallo Badoglio relative ai piani di Guerra; Biagini and Gionfrida, *Lo stato maggiore generale*, p. 106.

202 Seduta di 21 gennaio 1928: *ibid.*, p. 157.

203 Sedute di 13 gennaio, 14 gennaio, 16 gennaio 1928; *ibid.*, pp. 124, 128, 133, 135–6, 140–3, 150.

204 Premessa letta dal Capo di Stato Maggiore dell'Aeronautica generale Armani [21 January 1928]; *ibid.*, p. 159.

205 Seduta di 22 gennaio 1928; *ibid.*, p. 167.

206 AUSMM. N.5176, Ferrari to Burzagli , 27 December 1927. Direttive Generali DG 3/B1.

207 AUSSME. N. 22RRF, Necessità della R. Marina, 10 March 1928. Rep. H-6, racc. 2.

208 AUSMM. Italia contro Yugoslavia: premessa-esame della situazione-condotta delle operazioni, n.d. [1927/8], pp. 2 (original italics), 4. Direttive Generali DG 1/D5.

209 AUSSME. N.106R, Relazione sulla prima fase della manovra sulla carta (Ipotesi Est), 30 March 1928, pp. 4, 10. Rep. H-6, racc. 2.

210 *Ibid.*, p. 11.

211 AUSSME. Schema dei piani d'operazione No. 1 P I e No. 4 P I, 20 October 1928. Rep. H-6 racc. 2.
212 AUSSME. Traccia per la compilazione delle memorie preliminari sui piani di operazioni, 26 October 1928. Rep. H-6 racc. 2.
213 AUSSME. Opinioni dello stato maggiore e degli ambienti militari jugoslavi su alcune questioni militari e politiche, January 1928; n.8622, Visconti Prasca to War Ministry 15, May 1928 and all.: Considerazioni politico militare dell'alto comando e dell'ambiente militare S.H.S. per il caso di conflitto tra l'Italia e la Jugoslavia. Rep. M-3 racc. 37/f. 1. The latter document is reproduced in Longo, *L'attività degli addetti militari*, pp. 665–76.
214 Seduta del 13 ottobre 1928; Biagini and Gonfrida, *Lo stato maggiore generale*, p. 172.
215 Seduta del 20 settembre 1928; *ibid.*, pp. 178–9.
216 Sola to Mussolini, 17 September 1928. *DDI* 7th series vol. VI no. 661, pp. 576–7.
217 Promemoria del capo dell'Ufficio Albania, Lojacono, 16 January 1929; *DDI* 7th series vol. VII no. 173, p. 201. Lojacono pointed out that three or four Albanian divisions could occupy five of Yugoslavia's sixteen divisions; if Yugoslavia deployed the eight divisions necessary to conquer the country, Italy would be able to reach all her objectives on the other front.
218 Seduta del 16 gennaio 1929; Biagini and Gionfrida, *Lo stato maggiore generale*, pp. 182 5.
219 Promemoria dello Stato Maggiore Regia Marina relativo ai provvedimenti attuabili in fase di sicurezza, 14 January 1929; *ibid.*, pp. 188–94.
220 Seduta del 16 gennaio; *ibid.*, p. 185.
221 Seduta del 17 gennaio; *ibid.*, pp. 194–8.
222 Commissione suprema di difesa VI a serie di sedute, verbale del 18 febbraio 1929, p. 35. AUSSME Repertorio F-9 racc. 15/ f. 2.
223 Verbale del 22 febbraio 1929, pp. 36–9 [quo. p. 39]; *ibid.*
224 Dino Grandi Diary, 1 February 1929.
225 Galli to Mussolini, 17 January 1929; *DDI* 7th series vol. VII no. 185, pp. 212–3. Dino Grandi Diary, 27 February 1929.

3 MILITARY CONSTRAINTS AND DIPLOMATIC RESTRAINT, 1929–1932

1 Grandi Diary, 12 September 1930.
2 Mario Donosti [Mario Luciolli], *Mussolini e l'Europa*, p. 32.
3 AUSSME. Rapporto da S E Mussolini, 7 August 1929. Rep. L-13 racc. 202/f. 1.
4 AUSSME. Udienza Gazzera–Mussolini, 30 June 1930. Rep. L-13 racc. 202/f. 1.
5 AUSSME. Udienza Gazzera–Mussolini, 23 December 1930. Rep. L-13 racc. 202/f. 1.
6 AUSSME. Udienza Gazzera–Mussolini, 29 January 1931. Rep. L-13 racc. 202/f. 1.
7 Grandi Diary, 24 December 1929; 8 October 1929.

8 Grandi Diary, 2 December 1929.
9 Grandi to Mussolini, 31 August 1930; *DDI* 7th series vol. IX no. 234, p. 322.
10 'Discorso al Gran Consiglio del Fascismo', 8 October 1930 [misdated 2 October 1930]; Grandi, *La politica estera dell'Italia*, vol. I, pp. 277–327.
11 'Discorso alla Camera dei Deputati', 14 March 1931; *ibid.*, pp. 451–71 [quo. p. 471].
12 'Discorso di Livorno', 11 May 1930; 'Discorso di Firenze', 17 May 1930. *OO* XXIV, pp. 227–8, 235. Paolo Nello, *Un fedele disubbediente: Dino Grandi da Palazzo Chigi al 25 luglio* (Bologna: Il Mulino, 1993), pp. 106 fn. 37, 122–4. The speeches awakened fears of a possible armed conflict in the world of French finance: Manzoni to Grandi, 31 May 1935; *DDI* 7th series vol. IX no. 68, pp. 95–6.
13 'Messaggio per l'anno nono', 27 October 1930; *OO* XXIV, pp. 278–85.
14 ASMAE. N.3444/1969, Manzoni to Mussolini, 15 June 1929. Affari Politici: Francia b.1113/f. 1.
15 Manzoni to Mussolini, 10 July 1929; Boscarelli [chargé d' affaires Paris] to Grandi, 22 September 1929. *DDI* 7th series vol. VII no. 531, p. 517; vol. VIII no. 13, pp. 25–6.
16 Grandi Diary, 22 October 1929, 1 January 1930.
17 Colloquio Mussolini–Chamberlain, 2 April 1930; Relazione Guariglia–Grandi, 24 May 1930; Auriti to Grandi, 24 May 19330. *DDI* 7th series vol. VII no. 348, p. 357; vol IX no. 55, pp. 75–6, no. 58, pp. 82–4.
18 Grandi to Mussolini, 31 August 1930; *DDI* 7th series vol. IX no. 234, pp. 320–3.
19 Guariglia to Grandi, 25 June 1930: Guarglia, *Riccordi 1922–1946*, pp. 111–27; also, pp. 71–2, 110.
20 Manzoni to Grandi, 4 April 1931; Manzoni to Grand, 30 April 1931; Colloquio Grandi–Poncet, 23 May 1931; Colloquio Grandi–Beaumarchais, 25 June 1931; Grandi–Mussolini, 14 July 1931; Grandi to Mussolini, 25 July 1931. *DDI* 7th series vol. X no. 189, 234, 286, 357, 397, 413, pp. 284, 358–9, 447, 562–3, 631–5, 652–9 [quo. p. 654].
21 AUSSME. Udienza Gazzera–Mussolini, 5 May 1931. Rep. L-13 racc. 202/f. 1.
22 Relazione De Bono–Mussolini, 22 March 1932; *DDI* 7th series vol. XII, p. 51 fn. 2.
23 Grandi to Manzoni, 23 May 1932; *DDI* 7th series vol. XII no. 55, pp. 72–3.
24 Mussolini to Durini di Monza, 31 May 1929; Grandi to Balbo, [–] October 1929. *DDI* 7th series vol. VII no. 459, p. 454; vol. VIII no. 130, p.147.
25 Grandi to Mussolini [?17] May 1930; Colloquio Grandi–Neurath, 4 June 1930; Grandi to Orsini Barone, 3 July 1930. *DDI* 7th series vol. IX no. 43, 76, 129, pp. 61–2,104, 173–4.
26 ASMAE. T.2422/1251, Orsini Barone to Mussolini, 28 July 1930. Affari Politici: Germania b.1183. The passage relating to France was underlined by Mussolini.
27 ASMAE. To.1888/983, Orsini Barone to Gandi, 12 June 1930; N.3735/298, Capasso to Grandi, 16 September 1930. Affari Politici: Germania b.1183, 1184.

28 Colloquio Grandi–Litvinov, 26 November 1930; Grandi–Mussolini, 2 February 1931; Grandi to Orsini Barone, 24 March 1931. *DDI* 7th series vol. IX no. 411, pp. 589–95; vol. X no. 52, 161, pp. 76–90 [quo., p. 85], 250–1.

29 Colloquio Grandi–Curtius, 15 May 1931; Grandi to Mussolini, 17 May 1931; Colloquio Grandi–Curtius, 22 May 1931. *DDI* 7th series vol. X no. 269, 272, 284, pp. 406–9, 418, 442.

30 Grandi to Mussolini, 14 July 1931; *DDI* 7th series vol. X no. 397, pp. 631–5 [quo., p. 634].

31 AUSSME. Udienza Gazzera–Mussolini, 15 March 1931, 5 May 1931, 11 January 1932 [quo.]. Rep. L-13 racc. 202/f. 1.

32 ASMAE. T., Pittalis [Munich] to Mussolini, 30 September 1932. Affari Politici: Germania b.6/f. 1. Pittalis's phrase was underlined by Mussolini.

33 Cattaneo to Burzagli, 14 December 1929; *DDI* 7th series vol. VIII no. 258 all., p. 273.

34 Colloquio Grandi–Marinkovitch, 22 January 1931; Colloquio Grandi–Rakitch, 23 April 1931; Appunto Guariglia-Grandi, 29 April 1931. *DDI* 7th series vol. X no. 30, 216, 230, pp. 44, 335–6, 353–5.

35 Colloquio Grandi–Jeftič, 8 January 1930; *DDI* 7th series vol. VIII no. 302, p. 334. Emphasis in original.

36 Grandi Diary, 18 October 1929.

37 Guariglia to Grandi, 25 June 1930: Guariglia, *Ricordi*, pp. 111–27; Nello, *Un fedele disubbediente*, pp. 87–8.

38 Colloquio Grandi–Marinkovitch, 12 May 1930; Galli to Guariglia, 12 May 1930; Galli to Grandi, 27 May 1930; Colloquio Grandi–Mussolini, 14 July 1930; Galli to Grandi, 1 August 1930; Colloquio Grandi–Marinkovitch, 9 September 1930; Galli to Grandi, 6 November 1930; Grandi to Mussolini, 12 November1930; Galli to Grandi, 29 November 1930. *DDI* 7th series vol. IX no. 29, 33, 62, 148, 189, 241, 352, 370, 425, pp. 46–7, 52–5, 88–9, 201–2, 265–9, 330–3, 502–5, 525–8, 610–14.

39 Burgwyn, *Il revisionismo fascista*, pp. 145–6, 271 fn. 25.

40 Sola to Mussolini, 5 August 1929; Soragna to Grandi, 1 July 1931; Grandi to Gazzera, n.d. [20 July 1932]. *DDI* 7th series vol. VII no. 581, pp. 568–72; vol. X no. 375, pp.598–9; vol. XII no. 163, pp. 241–4.

41 AUSSME. Udienze Gazzera–Mussolini, 23 September 1930, 27 December 1930, 5 May 1931, 8 August 1931 [quo.]. Rep. L-13 racc. 202/f. 1.

42 Orsini-Barone to Mussolini, 11 June 1929; Orsini Barone to Mussolini, 3 July 1929; Koch to Grandi, 3 February 1930; Colloquio Grandi–Tewfik Ruscdi Bey, 14 April 1932. *DDI* 7th series vol. VII no. 482, 523, pp. 473–4, 589; VIII no. 344, pp. 386–7; XII no. 13, pp. 10–11.

43 Cesare Falessi, *Balbo Aviatore* (Milan: Mondadori, 1983), p. 74.

44 Arlotta to Mussolini, 17 May 1929; Grandi to Aloisi, 29 December 1930; Grandi to Aloisi, 15 January 1931. *DDI* 7th series vol. VI no. 429, p. 430; IX no. 480, pp. 712–4; X no. 14, p. 21.

45 Grandi to Mussolini, 23–4 May 1931: *DDI* 7th series vol. X no. 287, pp. 448–53.

46 Burgwyn, *Il revisionismo fascista*, p. 214.

47 Badoglio to Grandi, 31 March 1931; *DDI* 7th series vol. X no. 174, p. 276.

48 Relazione Grandi, November 1929: *cit.* Nello, *Un fedele disubbediente*, pp. 19–22.
49 Chiaramonte Bordonaro to Mussolini, 2 June 1929; *DDI* 7th series vol. VII no. 466, pp. 458–9. ASMAE. Notiziario politico–militare Nos.6 & 8, 1 July 1929 & 6 September 1929: Ambasciata Londra b.691/f. 1.
50 Grandi to Mussolini, 23 March 1930; Colloquio Grandi-Henderson, 1 April 1930; Chiaramonte Bordonaro to Grandi, 8 December 1930. *DDI* 7th series vol. VIII no. 445, 459, pp. 538–9, 567–9; vol. IX no. 445, pp. 655–6.
51 Nello, *Un fedele disubbediente*, pp. 110-12.
52 Ghigi to Grandi, 23 August 1931: *DDI* 7th series vol. X no. 441, p. 701.
53 Guariglia to Mussolini, 27 August 1932: *Ricordi*, pp. 763–73.
54 AUSSME. 'Relazione sulla costruzione del naviglio sottile in caso di guerra', December 1929. Rep. F-9 racc. 16/f. 3. Sirianni also claimed that the ship-yards could produce four destroyers, four *torpedinieri*, four submarines, four submarine chasers and eight MAS boats every month.
55 AUSSME. Commissione suprema di difesa VIa serie di sedute (31 gennaio-4–13–18 e 22 febbraio 1929–VII), seduta del 31 gennaio, pp. 4–11. Rep. F-9 racc. 15/f. 2.
56 *Ibid.*, seduta del 4 febbraio 1929, pp. 15–16, 19.
57 AUSSME. 'Relazione sulle principali questioni trattate dalla CSD nel periodo 1928–30', 15 November 1930, pp. 14, 15, 18, 19. Rep. F-9 racc. 12/f. 6.
58 *Ibid.*, p. 6.
59 AUSSME. Riunione del 30 dicembre 1929 al Ministero delle Colonie sotto la Presidenza di S. E. il Ministro De Bono per l'argomento "MOBILITAZIONE CIVILE DELLE COLONIE', p. 2. Rep. F-9 racc. 25/f. 5.
60 AUSSME. Promemoria alle superiori autorità, 29 January 1930. Rep. F-9 racc. 25/f. 5.
61 AUSSME. Mobilitazione civile delle colonie, 8 February 1930. Rep. F-9 racc. 25/f. 5.
62 AUSSME. N.1858, Organizzazione civile delle Colonie, 24 June 1930. Rep. F-9 racc. 25/ f. 5.
63 AUSSME. N.2525, Punto di vista circa la funzione militare delle varie Colonie e le necessità cui dovrà far fronte la corrispondente organizzazione civile, 28 July 1930. Rep. F-9 racc. 25/f. 5.
64 AUSMM. N.2924, Sistemazione difensiva di alcune località costiere delle Colonie, 29 January 1930. Cartelle Numerate b.2535/f. 1.
65 AUSMM. Funzione militare–Marittima delle Colonie, 29 July 1930. Cartelle Numerate b.2535/f. 1.
66 AUSSME. N. 319, Badoglio to Mussolini, 22 August 1930. Rep. F-9 racc. 21/f. 4.
67 De Bono had presented a request for an extraordinary allocation of 100,000,000 lire to the Commissione suprema di difesa in February to remedy the munitions deficiencies.
68 The weapons undergoing test comprised a 75-mm anti-aircraft gun, 149-mm and 210-mm howitzers, a 75-mm pack howitzer, a 149-mm heavy gun, a 20-mm antiaircraft/anti-tank gun and a mechanised self-propelled anti-tank gun.

AUSSME. Relazione sulla fabbricazione delle artiglierie, 25 January 1931. Rep. F-9 racc. 16/f. 3.

69 AUSSME. Verbale della VIIIa sessione della C.S.D. (Febbraio 1931-IXo), seduta del 2 febbraio 1931, pp. 11–12. Rep. F-9 racc. 18/f. 2.

70 AUSSME. Costruzione del naviglio sottile–Relazione, [February 1931]. Rep F-9 racc. 22/f. 1.

71 VIIIa sessione della C.S.D., seduta del 6 febbraio 1931, pp. 18, 20. *Loc. cit.*

72 *Ibid.*, pp. 20–2.

73 *Ibid.*, p. 24.

74 *Ibid.*, pp. 23–7.

75 *Ibid.*, pp. 27–31.

76 AUSSME. IX sessione della CSD (a) Difesa c.a. territoriale (Relatore S.E. il Ministro dell'Aeronautica), [n.d.]. Rep. F-9 racc. 22/f. 1.

77 AUSSME. IX sessione della C.S.D. (a) Difesa territoriale (Relatore S. E. il Ministro della Guerra), [n.d.], pp. 1–5. Rep. F-9 racc. 22/f. 1.

78 *Ibid.*, p. 8.

79 AUSSME. Commissione suprema di difesa: verbali della IX sessione (febbraio–marzo 1932-X), seduta del 26 febbraio 1932, p. 31. Rep. F-9 racc. 21/f. 1.

80 *Ibid.*, pp. 31–4.

81 AUSSME. Difesa aerea territoriale: Riferimento alla relazione di S.E. il Ministro dell'Aeronautica, 27 February 1932, p. 3. Rep. F-9 racc. 22/f. 1.

82 Commissione suprema di difesa, seduta del 27 febbraio 1932, pp. 35–6. *Loc. cit.*

83 *Ibid.*, p. 37.

84 *Ibid.*, p. 38.

85 *Ibid.*, p. 40.

86 Carte Capponi. Conferenza tripartita, [?August] 1927. 'Trattati e Disarmo'

87 Carte Capponi. La marina italiana e la politica del disarmo, 1 October 1927, pp. 2–3. 'Trattati e Disarmo'

88 Grandi Diary, 23 November 1929. Carte Capponi. Appunti, January 1928. 'Trattati e Disarmo'.

89 Carte Capponi. Conferenze internazionali del dopoguerra, January 1928, p. 4. 'Trattati e Disarmo'.

90 Carte Capponi. Conferenza tripartita e tendenze di politica navale, 27 January 1929, pp. 15–17 [quo., p. 17]. 'Trattati e Disarmo'.

91 AUSMM. Dichiarazione di S.E. il Capo del Governo sulla politica militare italiana nella seduta del Senato di martedì 5 giugno 1928. Cartelle Numerate b.3183/f. 6. Mussolini added a third condition – *interdipendenza* of all kinds of armaments – designed to tie any naval agreements to the outcome of the forthcoming Geneva Disarmament Conference on land and air armaments. Nominally at least, he still adhered to it in entering the London Conference.

92 AUSMM. La Nostra politica marittima, February 1929, p. 24. Cartelle Numerate b.2536.

93 The programme comprised 2 light cruisers (one 'Zara' type and one 'Trento' type), 6 destroyer leaders, 14 fourteen hundred-ton destroyers, 14 700-ton

destroyers, 40 300-ton submarine chasers (a new type), 20 MAS boats and 28 submarines: *ibid.*, pp. 46–7.

94 This represented an increase of 190,000,000 lire a year on the combined ordinary and extraordinary allocation for 1929–30. The programme costed out at 2,381,000,000 lire over the five year period, leaving a surplus more than large enough to absorb the over-run of 250,000,000 in 1929–30: *ibid.*, 3–4, 46–7.

95 'La giusta pace fra le nazioni: Discorso alla Camera dei Deputati il 9 maggio 1930': Grandi, *La politica estera dell'Italia* vol. I, pp. 219, 229–30 [quo., p. 229, italics in original].

96 AUSMM. Conferenza navale Londra 1930: Il problema della limitazione degli armamenti navali nei suoi aspetti tecnico-politici, 1929, pp. 65–9 [quos., p. 69]. Cartelle Numerate b.3172.

97 Grandi Diary, 29 October 1929.

98 Grandi Diary, 28 October 1929 [marked 'domenica' and therefore misdated since 28 October 1929 was a Monday].

99 Grandi Diary, 30 October 1929; Promemoria per S. E. il Capo del Governo, 31 October 1929 [incorporated into diary for 6 November 1929].

100 Radicati 12 November 1929 att. to Manzoni to Grandi, 19 November 1929; *DDI* 7th series vol. VIII, p. 189 fn. 1.

101 Grandi to Ambassadors Paris, Tokyo, Washington, Gazzera, Sirianni, Balbo, 14 October 1929; Grandi to Ambassadors London, Tokyo, Washington, 17 October 1929; Briand to Grandi, 18 October 1929; *DDI* 7th series vol. VIII nos. 72, 81, 86, pp. 93–4, 105, 108. Grandi Diary, 18 October 1929.

102 Grandi to Manzoni, 12 November 1929; *DDI* 7th series vol. VIII no. 152, pp.171–2; Dino Grandi Diary, 25 October 1929. Grandi was partly wrong-footed himself when Briand indicated that he would be generally in favour of a Mediterranean understanding, though at the same time confirming that France was in favour of submarines and against the question going to the naval conference: Manzoni to Grandi, 19 November 1929, *DDI* 7th series vol. VIII no. 171, pp. 188–9.

103 Sola (Tirana) to Grandi, 5 December 1929, Galli to Guariglia, 9 December 1929, Galli to Grandi, 12 December 1929, Galli to Grandi, 6 January 1930; *DDI* 7th series vol. VIII nos. 218, 233, 244, 298, pp. 228–9, 240–1, 248–54, 320–3.

104 Grandi Diary, 28 November 1929 [italics in original].

105 In the light of this piece of evidence alone – and there is more – Nello's assertion that in the winter of 1929–30 Mussolini was 'hesitant' (*titubante*) and uncertain whether to conciliate France or Yugoslavia is unconvincing: Nello, *Un fedele disubbediente*, p. 27.

106 Carte Capponi. Immunità delle navi trasportanti viveri, 21 December 1929. 'Trattati e Disarmo'.

107 Grandi Diary, 13 October, 12, 13, 14, 19 November 1929.

108 Grandi Diary, 27 November 1929; quo. Nello, *Un fedele disubbediente*, p. 41 fn. 46.

109 AUSMM. T.4923, Rogeri to Esteri Roma, 10 December 1929. Cartelle Numerate b.3181/f. 1.

110 AUSMM. T.5023, Rogeri to Esteri Roma, 18 December 1929. Cartelle Numerate b.3181/f. 1.

111 AUSMM. T.5029, Rogeri to Esteri Roma, 21 December 1929. Cartelle Numerate b.3181/f. 1.

112 Carte Capponi. Conferenza navale di Londra, 30 December 1929, pp. 1–6. 'Trattati e Disarmo'. The main parts of this memorandum are reproduced in Bernardi, *Il disarmo navale*, pp. 267–72. Since reducing the maximum displacement would reduce British and American tonnage from 525,000 tons to 375,000 tons, the Italian proposal to retain 175,000 tons would increase her relative strength from the original Washington figure of 1.67:5 to 2.33:5. This would raise the combined force of either European power plus Japan from 4.75:5 to 5.33:5, something Britain could never accept.

113 Conferenza navale di Londra, *op. cit.*, p. 6.

114 *Ibid.*, p. 12.

115 *Contra* Bernardi, *Il disarmo navale*, p. 270 and fn. 48.

116 Conferenza di Londra, *op. cit.,*, p. 10.

117 AUSMM. Il Convegno di Londra, February 1930. Cartelle Numerate b.1718/ f. 2.

118 Grandi to Manzoni, 12 November 1929, Grandi to Graham, 14 December 1929; *DDI* 7th series vol. VIII nos. 152, 250, pp. 171–2, 258–9.

119 Bernardi, *Il disarmo navale*, pp. 256, 274.

120 Mussolini to Grandi, 10 January 1930; *DDI* 7th series vol. VIII no. 304, p. 335.

121 AUSMM. Sirianni to Mussolini, 8 February 1930; Sirianni to Russo, 13 February 1930. Cartelle Numerate b.2542.

122 AUSMM. Situazione dei lavori della Conferenza di Londra, 10 February 1930. Cartelle Numerate b.2542.

123 AUSMM. Lavori Conferenza di Londra, 18 February 1930. Cartelle Numerate b.2542.

124 AUSMM. Sirianni to Mussolini, 4 March 1930. Cartelle Numerate b.2542. The final result of some complicated arithmetic is that, in comparable terms, France had a total of 470,000 tons of warships in service in 1930 and would have 684,000 tons in 1936, of which 292,000 would be new build, plus another 100–120,000 tons under construction: Bernardi, *Il disarmo navale*, pp. 292–4.

125 Grandi to Mussolini, 13 February 1930; Promemoria sul colloquio Grandi–MacDonald, 27 February 1930; *DDI* 7th series vol. VIII nos. 362, 392, pp. 410, 458. AUSMM. Situazione dei Lavori della conferenza [Burzagli], 18 March 1930. Cartelle Numerate b.2542.

126 Mussolini to Grandi, 3 February 1930, Grandi to Mussolini, 13 February 1930; *DDI* 7th series vol. VIII nos. 343, 362, pp. 386, 410–13.

127 Grandi to Mussolini, 15 March 1930; *DDI* 7th series vol. VIII no. 430, pp. 508–13.

128 AUSMM. Sirianni to Russo, 3 and 9 April 1930. Cartelle Numerate b.2542. The latter is reproduced in *DDI* 7th series vol. VIII no. 483, pp. 591–2.

129 UKNA. Mussolini to Grandi, 20 and 21 March 1930. HW 12/126/N.C.275. The originals are reproduced in *DDI* 7th series vol. VIII nos. 439 and 441,

p. 533. Eight of Grandi's cables from London were deciphered by the British during the conference.

130 AUSMM. Colloquio Sirianni con Dumesnil alla presenza di Stimson, 10 April 1930; 'Situazione dei lavori della Conferenza' (Burzagli), 12 April 1930. Cartelle Numerate b.2542.

131 UKNA. Grandi to Ministry of Foreign Affairs, 24 and 28 January, 12 April 1930 [quo.]. HW 12/126/N.C.93, 94, 388.

132 Grandi to Mussolini, 13 April 1930; *DDI* 7th series vol. VIII no. 489, pp. 600–5 [quos., pp. 601, 602].

133 Bernardi, *Il disarmo navale*, pp. 320–32.

134 Promemoria per il Capo di Stato Maggiore della Marina, 14 April 1930; *DDI* 7th series vol. VIII no. 493, pp. 609–10.

135 AUSMM. Estratto del discorso del Ministro degli Affari Esteri (Grandi) al Senato del regno (seduta del 3 giugno 1930-VIII). Cartelle Numerate b.3183/f. 6.

136 Bernardi, *Il disarmo navale*, pp. 380–425. Under the terms of the 1 March 1930 agreement Italy would build 26,407 tons a year and France 27,550 tons; when the agreement concluded on 31 December 1936 the Italian fleet would total 441,256 tons and the French fleet 670,716 tons.

137 AUSMM. N. 7388, Concorso della R. Marina in fase di copertura nella Ipotesi Est, 14 March 1929, p. 3. Direttive Generali DG 3/B1.

138 AUSMM. Presumabile utilizzazione delle basi e porti del Mediterraneo da parte della Marina francese, 3 May 1929. Direttive Generali DG 1/D2. A detailed schedule of likely troops numbers, sailings and routes was compiled in 1932: Promemoria n. 58, Trasporto in continente delle truppe francesi del Nord Africa, 10 May 1932. Direttive Generali DG 10/A3.

139 AUSMM. Documento di consultazione – B – (Biserta) [May 1929]. Direttive Generali DG 10/B11.

140 AUSMM. Promemoria per gli studi operativi nell'ipotesi di guerra su due fronti, 18 September 1929. Direttive Generali DG 0/1.

141 AUSMM. Libro di guerra Parte II (Piani operativi): Piano III (Ipotesi Italia contro Francia e Jugoslavia), 2 October 1929. Direttive Generali DG 0/1.

142 AUSMM. Questioni la cui definizione implica la collaborazione della Regia Aeronautica [n.d. but prepared for sessions of Commissione Superiore di Guerra on 3 and 4 October 1929]. Direttive Generali DG 0/1.

143 Seduta del 4 ottobre 1929: Biagini and Gionfrida, *Lo stato maggiore generale*, pp. 212–3.

144 AUSMM. Istituto di Guerra Marittima IX sessione 1929–30 Studio T: Il problema della Tripolitania nella Ia ipotesi di conflitto, pp. 10, 43–4, 46, 51–2. Direttive Generali DG 1/D [unnumbered].

145 AUSMM. Esercitazioni a parti contrapposti – Conferenza, [April 1930], pp. 5–6. Cartelle Numerate b.2551.

146 AUSMM. Difesa del traffico nel Mediterraneo orientale, May–June 1930. Direttive Generali DG 5/C5.

147 AUSMM. Funzione Militare–Marittima delle Colonie, 28 July 1930, p. 4 Cartelle Numerate b.2535/f. 1.

148 *Ibid.*, p. 5.

149 AUSMM. B.5607, La 'Corsa' nella Ia ipotesi di Guerra, 11 November1930. Cartelle Numerate b.2536/c. 5.

150 Seduta del 23 ottobre 1930: Biagini and Gionfrida, *Lo stato maggiore generale*, pp. 229–31.

151 AUSMM, Località di sbarco per la spedizione 5.E (Durazzo), 3 April & 4 May 1931. Cartelle Numerate b.1713/f. 1.

152 AUSMM. Promemoria circa eventuali azioni in Mar Rosso, 11 September 1931. Direttive Generali DG 8/A.0.

153 Seduta dell'8 novembre 1931; Biagini and Gionfrida, *Lo stato maggiore generale* p. 262.

154 *Ibid.*, p. 266.

155 Seduta del 9 novembre 1931; *ibid.*, pp. 275, 279, 280.

156 AUSMM. Verbale della riunione tenuta presso il Capo reparto operazioni il 7 gennaio 1932 – X – alle ore 16, 30; Isole italiane dell'Egeo, 16 January 1932. Direttive Generali DG 9/A1.

157 AUSMM. Promemoria n. 41: Considerazioni sull'isole italiane dell'Egeo, 10 February 1932. Direttivi Generali DG 9/A1.

158 AUSMM. Promemoria n. 26: Osservazioni al documento di consultazione B del maggio 1929, 9 January 1932 [italics in original]. Direttive Generali DG 10/B11.

159 AUSMM. Mar Rosso ed Oceano Indiano, 17 November 1931. Direttive Generali DG 8/A0.

160 AUSMM. Ducci to Sirianni, 12 January 1932. Direttive Generali DG 12/A0.

161 AUSMM. N.297, Ducci to Sirianni, 30 November 1932. Direttive Generali DG 12/A0.

162 Emilio Canevari, *Graziani mi ha detto* (Rome: Magi-Spinetti, 1947), p. 266.

163 Claudio Segrè, *Italo Balbo*, p. 159.

164 Emilio Canevari, *Retroscena della disfatta* vol. I, p. 189.

165 *Ibid.*, pp. 191, 192.

166 Antonio Pelliccia, *Il Maresciallo dell'aria Italo Balbo*, pp. 267–72.

167 Canevari, *Retroscena della disfatta*, vol. I, p. 198 (3 May 1933).

168 Pascal Venesson, 'Institution and Air Power: The Making of the French Air Force', *Journal of Strategic Studies* vol. 18 no. 1, March 1995, pp. 54–5, 66, 67; Robert J. Young, 'The Strategic Dream: French Air Doctrine in the Inter-War Period, 1919–39', *Journal of Contemporary History* vol. 9 no. 4, October 1974, pp. 57–76.

169 Segrè, *Italo Balbo*, p. 165.

170 Giorgio Rochat, *Italo Balbo aviatore*, pp. 122–4.

171 'Bilancio dei Previsioni, 1932–3'; *cit.* Segrè, *Italo Balbo*, pp. 167–8. In 1941, the peak wartime production year, the Italian aircraft industry produced 300 aircraft a month.

172 Canevari, *Graziani mi ha detto*, pp. 265–6.

173 ASAM. Ipotesi di guerra sulla fronte ovest. Ipotesi di guerra sulla fronte est. Ipotesi di guerra sulle due fronti. Considerazioni generali, May 1929, pp. 1–3. Fondo Esercitazioni c. 9.

174 *Ibid.*, pp. 12–13. De Pinedo did not define what 'the sources of enemy air power' were, but his usage suggests a Douhetian turn of mind.

175 *Ibid.*, pp. 13–16.
176 *Ibid.*, pp. 19–20.
177 Seduta del 3 ottobre 1929: Biagini and Gionfrida, *Lo stato maggiore generale*, pp. 205–7.
178 AUSSME. Relazione sulle principali questioni trattate dalla C. S. D. nel periodo 1928–30, 15 November 1930, pp. 7–8. Rep. F-9 racc. 12/f. 6.
179 UKNA. Appunti stenografici sulle dichiarazioni di S. E. il Capo di S. M. nella sedute del 21 febbraio 1930 (n.d.), att. to Gazzera to Mussolini, 25 March 1930. GFM36/194/ fr. 035644-6.
180 Seduta dell' 8 aprile 1930: Biagini and Gionfrida, *Lo stato maggiore generale*, pp. 215–6.
181 *Ibid.*, pp. 217–8.
182 UKNA. Balbo to Mussolini, 16 June VII [1930]. GFM 36/194/ fr. 035649-53.
183 Rochat, *Italo Balbo aviatore* , pp. 104–5.
184 Seduta del 23 ottobre 1930; Biagini and Gionfrida, *Lo stato maggiore generale*, p. 233.
185 Seduta del 23 ottobre 1930, *op.cit.*, pp. 234–6.
186 ASAM. Memoria sulla copertura delle unità della RG. Aeronautica nell'ipotesi est–ovest, August 1930. Relazione per il C. S. M. G. c.9.
187 ASAM. Relazione interessante l'impiego delle forze aeree nello svolgimento delle manovre coi quadri Febb.–Marzo 1930, pp. 2–13, 36, 48 [quo.]. Fondo Esercitazioni b.4.
188 ASAM. N.255, Direttive per l'addestramento in sede dei reparti M.A., 11 March 1930, p. 3, 5. Fondo Esercitazioni b.4.
189 *Ibid.*, Allegato – A, pp. 1–13.
190 Rochat, *Italo Balbo aviatore*, p. 110 (29 April 1931).
191 ASAM. Grandi manovre 1931 – Relazione conclusive, p. 3. Fondo Esercitazioni b.5.
192 Pelliccia, *Il Maresciallo dell'aria*, p. 308.
193 Canevari, *Retroscena della disfatta* vol. I, pp. 195–6.
194 Pelliccia, *Il Maresciallo dell'aria*, pp. 313–5.
195 *Ibid.*, pp. 315–20.
196 'Per l'arte della guerra aerea' (May 1928) : Giulio Douhet, *La guerra integrale* (Rome: Campitelli, 1936), pp. 176–9, 183, 185.
197 'Caccia, combattimento, battaglia' (September 1928): *ibid.*, pp. 260–96 (esp., pp. 263–5).
198 Botti and Cermelli, *La teoria della guerra*, p. 457; for a detailed summary of the debates, *ibid.*, pp. 446–57.
199 *Ibid.*, p. 470. Mecozzi favoured bombing at very low altitudes in level flight over bombing at an angle and vertical dive-bombing, his least favoured method.
200 Pelliccia, *Il Maresciallo dell'aria*, p. 283.
201 Seduta del 9 novembre 1931; Biagini and Gionfrida, *Lo stato maggiore tra le due guerre mondiali*, p. 270.
202 *Ibid.*, pp. 271, 273.
203 *Ibid.*, p. 277.

204 *Ibid.*, pp. 280–2.
205 Renzo De Felice, *Mussolini il Duce* vol. I: *Gli anni del consenso 1929–1936* (Turin: Einaudi, 1974), p. 133 fn. 1.
206 UKNA. Note, 5 May 1931. GFM 36/194/ fr. 035658.
207 Grandi Diary 3 February 1932 (referring to the previous day): *cit.* Nello, *Un fedele disubbediente*, pp. 207–8. This entry is missing from the archived versions of the diary.
208 Canevari, *Graziani mi ha detto*, pp. 265–6; De Felice, *Mussolini il Duce* vol. I, pp. 283–4; Rochat, *Italo Balbo aviatore*, pp. 147–8. Rochat inclines to disbelieve the 'plan' though accepting that Balbo wanted Badoglio's job: Giorgio Rochat, *Italo Balbo* (Turin: UTET, 1986), p. 216. There was a Douhetian tinge to the programme: in May 1928, Douhet had used a speech of general von Seeckt to reinforce the idea that a small army could play a decisive role in war if supported by a powerful air force: Douhet, *La guerra integrale*, pp. 173–4.
209 UKNA. Mussolini to Balbo, 12 November 1933. GFM 36/194/ fr. 035631. Even this number may not be correct: the printed version of the 'Verbale di consegna' gives a total of 3,095, the photo reproduction a total of 3,125 (numbers in two categories differ), and the hand-written corrections on the photo reproduction a total of 3,184 (again numbers in two categories differ from the printed version, and a third category has been counted twice): Canevari, *Retroscena della disfatta* vol. I, pp. 180–1. No one seems to have been very good at arithmetic.
210 UKNA. Balbo to Mussolini, 16 November XII [1933]. GFM 36/94/ fr.035633-5/1. The remainder of the total of 3,125 aircraft comprised 344 planes in flight schools and 957 for touring and training. In the face of an enemy deprived of his air fleet at the outset, Balbo added, touring planes could serve in an aerial reconnaissance role.
211 UKNA. Promemoria per S. E. il Capo del Governo, n.d. [att. to Balbo to Mussolini, 16 November 1933]. GFM 36/194/fr.035636-9.
212 AUSSME. Note sulla efficienza complessiva dell'Esercito alla fine del 1928 e sui provvedimenti necessari per continuare la preparazione, 8 January 1929. Rep. L-13 racc. 202/f. 2. Gazzera prepared only four copies of his annual surveys; one went to the king, one to Mussolini, one to Bonzani and the fourth he kept himself.
213 AUSSME. Bonzani to Mussolini, 11 March & 14 March 1929. Rep. L-13 racc. 202/f. 2.
214 AUSSME. Mussolini to Bonzani, 17 March 1929. Rep. L-13 racc. 202/f. 2.
215 AUSSME. Udienza Gazzera–Mussolini, 16 February 1929; Rapporto a S. E. Mussolini, 16 March 1929; Udienza Gazzera–Mussolini, 28 March 1929. Rep. L-13 racc. 202/f. 1.
216 AUSSME. Gazzera to Mussolini, 11 June 1929. Rep. L-13 racc. 202/f. 2.
217 AUSSME. Rapporto a S. E. Mussolini, 11 June 1929. Rep. L-13 racc. 202/f. 1.
218 AUSSME. Gazzera to Mussolini, 11 August 1929; all. La preparazione bellica jugoslava, 10 August 1929; marginal annotation, 22 August 1929; Rep.

L-13 racc. 202/f. 2. Rapporto da S. E. Mussolini, 7 August 1929; Rep. L-13 racc. 202/f. 1.

219 Lucio Ceva, *Le forze armate*, p. 216.

220 AUSMM. Relazione sulla Fabricazione delle Artiglierie, 23 January 1930. Cartelle Numerate b.2531/f. 1. In 1930, with the collaboration of Ansaldo and Terni, the war ministry were testing models of a 75-mm anti-aircraft gun and a 149-mm howitzer, had a design for a 149-mm heavy gun, and were studying a 75-mm pack gun, a 20-mm anti-tank gun and a self-propelled anti-tank gun. At that time, the rate that the arms industry could replace guns in wartime was estimated at less than 4 per cent a month.

221 AUSSME. Colloquio Gazzera–Mussolini, 11 October 1929; Rep. L-13 racc. 202/f. 1. Gazzera to Mussolini, 11 October & 12 December 1929. Rep. L-13 racc. 202/f. 2.

222 AUSSME. N.5500RR, Piano 5L: Direttive per la copertura, 16 December 1929. Rep H-6 racc. 3. See also Minniti, 'L'ipotesi piu sfavorevole', pp. 632–3.

223 AUSSME. Piano 5M: Direttive per la copertura 20 December 1929. Rep. H-6 racc. 3.

224 AUSSME. Memoria circa un eventuale intervento italiano nel Burgenland, October 1929; Rep. H-6 racc. 3. Studi e provvedimenti per una eventuale azione attraverso l'Austria, 20 November 1929; Rep. L-10 racc. 1/f. 1.

225 Sedute del 3 & 4 ottobre 1929: Biagini and Gionfrida, *Lo stato maggiore generale*, pp. 202–5, 213–4.

226 AUSSME. Efficienza complessiva dell'Esercito al 1o gennaio 1930 (VIII) e sue essenziali necessità, p. 2. Rep. L-13 racc. 202/f. 2.

227 *Ibid.*, p. 15.

228 *Ibid.*, pp. 14–15, 18, 19, 24–8, 29.

229 AUSSME. Gazzera to Mussolini, 18 June 1930. Rep. L-13 racc. 202/f. 2.

230 AUSSME. Mussolini to Gazzera, 5 June 1930. L-13 racc. 202/f. 2.

231 Seduta del 22 ottobre 1930; Biagini and Gionfrida, *Lo stato maggiore generale*, p. 224.

232 *Ibid.*, p. 225.

233 Seduta del 23 ottobre; *ibid.*, pp. 236–7.

234 AUSSME. Udienza Gazzera–Mussolini, 6 November. Rep. L-13 racc. 202/f. 1.

235 Giuriati to Mussolini, 22 February 1931: Renzo De Felice, *Gli anni del consenso*, pp. 283–4.

236 AUSSME. Gazzera to Mussolini, 25 February 1931. Rep. L-13 racc. 202/f. 2.

237 Brian R. Sullivan, 'The Primacy of Politics', p. 75.

238 Longo, *Francesco Saverio Grazioli*, pp. 376–80. See also Antonio Sema, 'Pensiero militare e fascistizzazione delle forze armate' in Virgilio Ilari and Antonio Sema, *Marte in Orbace*, pp. 150 *et seq.*

239 UKNA. Mussolini to Grazioli, 12 November 1930. GFM 36/217/fr. 039826.

240 UKNA. Draft speech attached to Grazioli to Mussolini, 26 May 1931. GFM 36/217/fr. 039795–039814 [quos. fr. 039797, 039799].

241 UKNA. Note esplicative. GFM 36/217/fr. 039815–039825. The celeri units Grazioli favoured were not the ones created in 1928 from bersaglieri cyclists and cavalry and formed into two divisions in 1930, but hybrid units which also included motorcycles, motor vehicles and light tanks.

242 Francesco Grazioli, 'Della guerra e della pace (Meditazioni di un combattente)', *Nuova Antologia* 1 July 1931, pp. 15–16. An incomplete copy can be found in GFM 36/217/fr. 039758–039767/2 [quos. fr. 039767/1, 039767/2].

243 UKNA. Bonzani to Grazioli, [–] July 1931. GFM 36/217/fr. 039771.

244 AUSSME. Gazzera to Mussolini, 5 July 1931. Rep. L-13 racc. 202/f. 2.

245 AUSSME. Mussolini to Gazzera, 7 July 1931. Rep.L-13 racc. 202/f. 2. Longo, presumably without the original to hand, gives *incriminato* for *incriminabile*: Longo, *Grazioli*, p. 392.

246 One of these was Roberto Farinacci, sometime ally of Balbo, strident critic of most soldiers and, Mussolini was told by the *Pubblica Sicurezza*, associated with Grazioli: Undated note on 'X' [Grazioli], UKNA. GFM 36/217/fr. 639828–9.

247 UKNA. Efficienza complessiva dell'esercito al 1o gennaio 1931 (Anno X) e sue essenziali necessità, pp. 4–5, 9, 10–11. Rep. L-13 racc. 202/f. 2. Gazzera pointed out that Italy had 6,700,000 men between the ages of 21 and 55, enough to form ninety divisions, but that lack of training, weapons, equipment and support services meant they could not all be used.

248 *Ibid.*, pp. 21–2, 25. The ten classes of reservists that had served between 1920 and 1929 and would be recalled first in wartime also presented problems as they had had maximum periods of training varying between twelve and seventeen months; *ibid.*, p. 27.

249 AUSSME. Udienza Gazzera–Mussolini, 29 January 1931. Rep. L-13 racc. 202/f. 1.

250 AUSSME. Condizioni di efficienza dell'esercito in relazione alla situazione politico–internazionale, 12 August 1931. Rep. L-13 racc. 202/f. 2.

251 Seduta del 5 novembre 1931: Biagini and Gionfrida, *Lo stato maggiore generale*, p. 241.

252 Lucio Ceva, 'Appunti per una storia dello stato maggiore', pp. 219–20.

253 Seduta del 5 novembre 1931: Biagini and Gionfrida, *Lo stato maggiore generale*, pp. 241–2.

254 *Ibid.*, pp. 244–6.

255 Seduta del 7 novembre 1931; *ibid.*, pp. 251–7.

256 AUSSME. Note sulla efficienza complessiva dell'esercito al 1o gennaio 1932 – Xo – e sulle sue essenziali necessità, 22 January 1932, pp. 1–2. Rep. L-13 racc. 202/f. 2.

257 *Ibid.*, pp. 4–6, 9–10, 14.

258 *Ibid.*, p. 16.

259 Gazzera to Grandi, 13 June 1932; *DDI* 7th series vol. XII no. 92, p. 121.

4 MOVING TOWARDS AGGRESSION, 1932–1934

1 *Contra* Richard Lamb, *Mussolini and the British*, p. 94.

2 Grandi Diary, 20 March 1932.

3 ASMAE. To.223314, Esteri to London Embassy etc., 29 July 1932. Ambasciata di Londra b.775/f. 1. On the Beneš resolution, which among other things proposed absolutely to prohibit aerial attacks on civil populations and chemical, bacteriological and incendiary war, and to limit the size of tanks and the calibre of heavy artillery, see Giovanni Bernardi, *Il disarmo navale*, pp. 481–5.

4 Pittalis to Mussolini, 30 October 1932; Cerruti to Mussolini, 19 November 1932. *DDI* 7th series vol. XII nos. 375, 443, pp. 471–4, 560–1.

5 AUSSME. Udienza Gazzera–Mussolini, 15 July 1932; Udienza Gazzera–Mussolini, 3 September 1932 [quo.]. Rep. L-13 racc. 202/f. 1. There is no evidence to support the claim that in adopting this line Mussolini was in part acknowledging 'the importance of preventing the Nazis coming to power', *contra* Lamb, *Mussolini and the British*, p. 96.

6 ASMAE. T.1192, Esteri to Paris Embassy etc., 23 November 1932; T.1299, Esteri to Paris Embassy etc., 12 December 1932. Ambasciata di Londra, b.786/ f. 1.

7 ASMAE. N. 537, Mancinelli to Ministero della Guerra, 11 July 1932; T.4356/1882, Cerruti to Esteri, 19 December 1932. Affari Politici: Germania b.8/f. 4; b.7/f. 1.

8 ASMAE. 'Situazione politica della Germania – dicembre 1932' (Cerruti). Affari Politici: Germania b.7/f. 1.

9 ASMAE. T.3536/1580, Chargé d'affaires Berlin to Esteri, 20 October 1932. Affari Politici: Germania b.7/f. 1.

10 Renzo De Felice, *Mussolini e Hitler*, pp. 211–58.

11 ASMAE. T., Pittalis to Esteri, 10 June 1932. Affari Politici: Germania b.5/f. 2. The passage was underlined by Mussolini.

12 Grandi Diary, 20 March 1932. See MacGregor Knox, 'The Fascist Regime, its Foreign Policy and its Wars: An "Anti-Anti-Fascist" Orthodoxy?', *Contemporary European History* vol. 4 pt. 3, November 1995, p. 358.

13 Renzetti to Chiavolini, 31 January 1933; Cerruti to Mussolini, 9 February 1933; Cerruti to Mussolini, 8 March 1933. *DDI* 7th series vol. XIII nos. 61, 76, 182, pp. 63, 81, 192 [quo.].

14 Aloisi to Mussolini, 13 March 1933; Cerruti to Mussolini, 15 May 1933. *DDI* 7th series vol. XIII nos. 198, 596, pp. 211, 655–7.

15 Cerruti to Mussolini, 14 March 1933; Cerruti to Mussolini, 16 March 1933; Cerruti to Mussolini, 2 May 1933; Prezioisi to Mussolini, 10 August 1933; Cerruti to Mussolini, 13 August 1933; Cerruti to Mussolini, 10 March 1934. *DDI* 7th series vol. XIII nos. 202, 212, 515, pp. 214, 229–30, 515; vol. XIV nos. 79, 89, 791, pp. 90, 97–8, 879–80.

16 Manzoni to Mussolini, 15 August 1932; Manzoni to Mussolini, 17 September 1932; Colloquio Aloisi–Berenger, 15 October 1932; Cerruti to Mussolini, 14 March 1933. *DDI* 7th series vol. XII nos. 204, 267, 343, pp. 286–7, 366, 442–3; vol. XIII no. 203, pp. 215–7.

17 Pignatti to Mussolini, 15 February 1933; Colloquio Suvich–Jouvenel, 22 February 1933. *DDI* 7th series vol. XIII nos. 94, 127, pp. 96–7, 128–9.

18 Colloquio Mussolini–Jouvenel, 2 March 1933; Preziosi to Mussolini, 29 January 1933; Mussolini to Cerruti, 13 February 1933. *DDI* 7th series vol. XIII nos. 157, 56, 83, pp. 96–7, 57–9, 83.
19 ASMAE. N.214/0.1, Pralormo to War Ministry, 1 March 1933. Affari Politici: Francia b.8/f. 1–6 (Pralormo admitted that most of his informants were Italian). Pignatti to Mussolini, 28 February 1933; Pirazzoli to Mussolini, 27 February 1933: *DDI* 7th series vol. XIII no. 148 and all., pp.151–2.
20 ASMAE. N.602/D.1, Pralormo to War Ministry, 10 May 1933; N.1211/C.1, Pralormo to War Ministry, 15 November 1933. Affari Politici: Francia b.8/f. 1–6, f. 1.
21 ASMAE. N.867, Pralormo to War Ministry, 19 July 1933. Affari Politici: Francia b.8/f. 1–6.
22 AUSSME. Consiglio dei ministri, 27 May 1933. Rep. L-13 racc. 202/f. 1.
23 Lowe and Marzari come closest to this interpretation of the Four Power Pact: C. J. Lowe and F. Marzari, *Italian Foreign Policy 1870–1940* (London: Routledge & Kegan Paul, 1975), p. 222. For other interpretations of its meaning see H. James Burgwyn, *Italian Foreign Policy in the Interwar period, 1918–1940* (Westport CT: Praeger, 1997), p. 80; Denis Mack Smith, *Mussolini's Roman Empire* (Harmondsworth: Penguin, 1979), p. 49.
24 Mussolini to Cerruti, 29 May 1933. *DDI* 7th series vol. XIII no. 729, pp. 780–2.
25 Cerruti to Mussolini, 29 May 1933; Cerruti to Mussolini 6 July 1933 [quo.]. *DDI* 7th series vol. XIII nos. 735, 942, pp. 785–8, 980–4.
26 ASMAE. N.572, Mancinelli to War Ministry, 27 July 1933. Affari Politici: Germania b.13/f. 1.
27 ASMAE. T.1628, Esteri to London Embassy etc., 7 September 1933. Affari Politici: Francia b.8/f. 1.
28 Colloquio Suvich–Chambrun, 12 September 1933. *DDI* 7th series vol. XIV no. 169, pp. 179–81.
29 ASMAE. N.1857, Suvich to Berlin Embassy etc., 22 October 1933. Affari Politici: Germania b.11/f. 2. Palazzo Chigi still had ambitious plans for the pact and wanted to bring Poland, Belgium, Turkey and the USSR into it: Appunto per S. E. il Sottosegretario di Stato, 25 October 1933, with marginal note by Aloisi. Affari Politici: Germania b.16/f. 1.
30 Colloquio Aloisi–Paul-Boncour, 18 January 1934. *DDI* 7th series vol. XIV no. 579, pp. 659–61.
31 ASMAE. Colloquio Suvuch–Chambrun, 28 May 1934. Affari Politici: Francia b.11/f. 1.
32 Cerruti to Mussolini, 16 May 1933. *DDI* 7th series vol. XIII no. 606, pp. 665–6.
33 ASMAE. N.867, Pralormo to War Ministry, 19 July 1933. Affari Politici: Francia b.8/f. 1–6. N.736, Mancinelli to War Ministry, 20 September 1933. Affari Politici: Germania b.13/f. 1. On 2 May 1933 Mancinelli passed on to Rome the opinion of the departing Yugoslav military attaché that it would take Germany more than a year to be able to put an army of three million men in

the field: Luigi Emilio Longo, *L'attività degli addetti militari italiani*, p. 254 fn. 60.

34 ASMAE. N.1332, de Courten to Maristat, 4 September 1933; T.1477, Esteri to London Embassy etc., 24 July 1933. Affari Politici: Germania b.11/f. 2; b.13/f. 1.

35 ASMAE. N.18, Cavagnari to Esteri, 26 December 1933 [Raeder memorandum]; N.1823, De Courten to Maristat, 8 December 1933. Affari Politici: Germania b.10/f. 2; b.19/f. 7. Raeder told De Courten that he had given the memorandum to Mussolini.

36 ASMAE. T.1017, Esteri to Paris Embassy etc., 4 October 1932. Ambasciata di Londra b.775/f. 1.

37 ASMAE. T.1248, Esteri to London Embassy etc., 3 December 1932. Ambasciata di Londra b.775/f. 1.

38 Shorrock, *From Ally to Enemy*, pp. 67–8, takes the French perception as accurate. Among other things, Mussolini had shown his contempt for the League of Nations when, on 8 April 1932, the Fascist Grand Council had passed a resolution pronouncing in favour of revision of the peace treaties and against the over-frequent convocation of international conferences, and reserving the right to examine Italy's position in the League of Nations in October: Nello, *un fedele disubbediente*, pp. 194–5.

39 Colloquio Suvich–Hitler, 13 December 1933. *DDI* 7th series vol. XIV no. 476, p. 533.

40 ASMAE. T.2212, Suvich to London Embassy etc., 22 December 1933; Affari Politici: Germania b.10/f. 2. Colloquio Mussolini–Chambrun, 8 January 1934; *DDI* 7th series vol. XIV no. 535, pp. 608–9.

41 ASMAE. N.2166/877, Cerruti to Mussolini, 6 June 1934. Affari Politici: Germania b.22/f. 2.

42 ASMAE. T.230818 all., Relazione sul viaggio di esercitazione della 2a divisione (manovra d'intendenza), 24 September 1934. Ambasciata di Londra b.832/1.

43 ASMAE. N.026, Teucci [air attaché] to Cerruti, 24 November 1934; N.1367, Promemoria per S. E. l'Ambasciatore [De Courten], 28 November 1934; N.1369, De Courten to Cerruti, 29 November 1934; Riassuntivo dell'attività della Reichswehr nel 1934 [Mancinelli], 30 November 1934. Affari Politici: Germania b.21/ f. 5 [Teucci & Mancinelli]; b.25/f. 3 [De Courten]. De Courten expected the two new ships to be 10,000-ton *Deutschland*-class ships; as *Scharnhorst* and *Gneisenau* they were designed at 26,000-tons displacement and when launched displaced 31,000 tons.

44 ASMAE. T.3183, Pignatti to Mussolini, 17 August 1933. Affari Politici: Germania b.11/f. 2.

45 ASMAE. N.96/S, Kellner to War Ministry, 13 June 1934; Promemoria per S. E. l'Ambasciatore [Parona], 14 June 1934. Affari Politici: Francia b.11/f. 1.

46 ASMAE. T.3168/1253, Pignatti to Esteri, 15 June 1934. Affari Politici: Francia b.11/f. 1.

47 AUSMM. N.987, Gli avvenimenti interni in Germania, 9 July 1934 [de Courten]. Cartelle Numerate b.3277/f. 4.

48 ASMAE. N.508, Mancinelli to War Ministry, 11 July 1934. Affari Politici: Germania b.27/f. 4. The passage was underlined by Mussolini.

49 ASMAE. T.45/24, Ponzone to Esteri, 19 July 1934; T.50/29, Ponzone to Esteri, 24 July 1934. Ambasciata di Londra b.832/ f. 1.

50 ASMAE. T.2481/1094, Cerruti to Mussolini, 2 July 1934. Affari Politici: Germania b.22/f. 4. T.1069, Esteri to London Embassy etc., 8 August 1933; To.230940, Esteri to London Embassy etc., 25 September 1933; T.1308, Esteri to London Embassy etc., 27 September 1934. Ambasciata di Londra b.832/f. 1. Cerruti, who had previously been at the Moscow embassy, saw parallels between the SS and the OGPU troops.

51 ASMAE. N.1514, Quaroni to Paris Embassy etc., 2 August 1933. Affari Politici: Germania b.13/f. 1.

52 ASMAE. N.2056, Colonna to Esteri, 28 May 1934. Affari Politici: Germania b.22/f. 2.

53 ASMAE. T [unnumbered], Esteri to Italian Legation Budapest, 21 June 1934. Affari Politici: Germania b.24/f. 1.

54 AUSSME. N.2992, Situazione austriaca, 5 June 1934. Rep. H-6 racc. 6 bis/f. 5.

55 ASMAE. T.1308, Esteri to London Embassy etc., 27 September 1934 [repeating Cerruti to Esteri, 16 September 1934]. Affari Politici: Germania b.22/f. 3.

56 ASMAE. T.6791, Pittalis to Esteri, 31 July 1934. Ambasciata di Londra b.832/f. 1.

57 ASMAE. T.1058, Esteri to London Embassy etc., 6 August 1934. Ambasciata di Londra b.832/f. 1.

58 ASMAE. Vittetti to Suvich, 7 August 1934. Ambasciata di Londra b.840/f. 1. T.1106, Esteri to London Embassy etc., 13 August 1934. Affari Diplomatici: Francia b.11/f. 1.

59 Burgwyn, *Italian Foreign Policy*, pp. 73–5; Burgwyn, *Il revisionismo fascista*, pp. 223–8.

60 AUSSME. Udienza con S M il Re, 9 January 1933; Udienza Gazzera–Mussolini, 8 January 1933. Rep. L-13 racc. 202/f. 1.

61 AUSSME. Udienza Gazzera–Mussolini, 13 January 1933, 18 January 1933, 14 February 1933; Rep. L-13 racc. 202/f. 1.

62 Galli to Mussolini, 9 January 1933, Galli to Mussolini, 13 January 1933, Sola to Mussolini, 17 January 1933, Suvich to Cerruti *et al.*, 19 February 1933. *DDI* 7th series vol. XIII nos. 21, 28, 46, 114, pp. 20–7, 32, 50, 118–9.

63 AUSSME. Udienza 4 March 1933. Rep. L-13 racc. 202/f. 1.

64 Colloquio Cosmelli–Avakumovic, 26 September 1933; colloquio Cosmelli–Avakumovic 29 September 1933; Avakumovic to Cosmelli, 10 November 1933, Galli to Mussolini, 4 December 1933; colloquio Cosmelli–Avakumovic, 5–6 December 1933; Aloisi to Mussolini, 18 January 1934; Aloisi to Mussolini 22 February 1934. *DDI* 7th series vol. XIV nos. 218, 235, 357, 441, 452, 575, 654, pp. 235–41, 265–7, 393–4, 482–4, 497–505, 652–5, 733–6.

65 Colloquio Mussolini–Galli, 2 September 1934. *DDI* 7th series vol. XV no. 757, pp. 807–11.

66 Galli to Mussolini, 14 August 1934; Umilta to Mussolini, 22 August 1934; Aloisi to Mussolini, 12 September 1934; Suvich to Galli, 13 September 1934; Suvich to Galli, 15 September 1934; Galli to Mussolini, 21 September 1934; Aloisi to Mussolini, 25 September 1934; Mussolini to Galli, 26 September 1934; Galli to Mussolini, 27 September 1934. *DDI* 7th series vol. XV nos. 702, 724, 801, 808, 815, 842, 871, 877, 893, pp. 744–5, 771, 866–7, 872–3, 879, 920, 948, 951–2, 970.

67 Buti to Suvich, 30 March 1933; Lojacono to Mussolini, 6 April 1933; Lojacono to Mussolini, 9 May 1934. *DDI* 7th series vol. XIII nos. 329, 382, pp. 352–3, 404; vol. XV no. 201, pp. 215–6.

68 Attolico to Mussolini, 4 April 1933; Lojacono to Mussolini, 28 April 1933; Lojacono to Mussolini, 5 May 1933; Aloisi to Mussolini, 6 May 1933; Aloisi to Mussolini, 13 September 1933; Mussolini to Lojacono, 21 November 1933; Suvich to Grandi, 21 January 1934. *DDI* 7th series vol. XIII nos. 371, 492, 537, 545, pp. 394–5, 544–7, 593–5, 606–7; vol. XIV nos. 173, 397, 594, pp. 185, 428–31, 682–3.

69 ASMAE. Notiziario politico–militare N.30, 30 April 1932; Notiziario dell'Addetto Navale a Londra N. 257, July 1932; Notiziario dell'Adetto Navale a Londra N.301, August 1932. Ambasciata di Londra b.781/f. 2.

70 ASMAE. Notiziario dell'Addetto Navale a Londra N. 259, July 1932: Ambasciata di Londra b.781/f. 2. Notiziario dell'Addetto Navale, January 1933; Notiziario N. 192, 10 March 1933, Notiziario N. 703, 24 November 1933. Ambasciata di Londra b.811/f. 2.

71 ASMAE. T.239, Berardis to Berlin Embassy etc., 14 February 1933; Affari Politici: Germania b.12/ f. 1. Cerrruti to Esteri, 15 February 1933; *DDI* 7th series vol. XIII no. 95, pp. 98–100.

72 Lamb, *Mussolini and the British*, pp. 99, 107.

73 ASMAE. T.764, Grandi to Mussolini, 4 December 1934; T.0162, Grandi to Mussolini, 20 December 1934. Ambasciata di Londra b.832/f. 1. Simon and Drummond were pleased at retaining Grandi as their interlocutor with Mussolini in October 1934 instead of losing him to the ministry of corporations: Nello, *un fedele disubbediente*, pp. 239–42.

74 ASMAE. Mancinelli to Cerruti, 24 November 1934; Mancinelli to War Ministry, 3 December 1934. Affari Politici: Germania b.21/f. 5.

75 ASMAE. T.232494, Quaroni to London Embassy etc., 10 October 1934. Affari Politici: Germania b.23/f. 1.

76 AUSSME. Udienza Gazzera–Mussolini, 1 May 1933. Rep. L-13 racc. 202/f. 1.

77 AUSSME. N.85, Stato delle scorte dei metalli e di quelli correttivi degli acciai, 6 February 1933; N. 62, Stato delle scorte dei combustibili liquidi e provvedimenti per aumentarle, 3 February 1933. Rep. F-9, racc. 26/f. 1.

78 AUSSME. Il problema del petrolio, February 1933, pp. 2–4. Rep. F-9 racc. 26/f. 1.

79 *Ibid.*, pp. 11–12.

80 *Ibid.*, pp. 20–1.

81 AUSSME. Stato delle scorte di combustibili liquidi e provvedimenti per aumentarle, February 1933. Rep. F-9 racc. 26/ f. 1.

82 *Ibid.*

83 AUSSME. Trasporto dei rifornimenti della nazione in guerra, February 1933, p. 4. Rep. F-9 racc. 26/ f. 1.
84 AUSSME. Trasporto dei rifornimenti della nazione in guerra, February 1933, p. 4. Rep. F-9 racc. 26/f. 1.
85 AUSSME. Commissione suprema di difesa verbale della X Sessione (Febbraio 1933–XI); Seduta del 2 febbraio 1933, pp. 2–3, 6. Rep. F-9 racc. 24/ f. 2.
86 *Ibid.*, seduta del 3 febbraio 1933, p. 14.
87 *Ibid,* seduta del 4 febbraio 1933, p. 44.
88 AUSSME. Minsitero delle Corporazioni: SITUAZIONE dei depositi di combustibili liquidi in Italia – trasporti, 1934, p. 4. Rep. F-9 racc. 7/f. 4.
89 AUSSME. Combustibili liquidi, 5 February 1934. Rep. F-9 racc. 30/f. 2.
90 AUSSME. Ministero della Marina Argomento IX-b: Stato delle scorte di combustibili liquidi e provvedimenti per aumentarle, February 1934. Rep. F-9 racc. 30/f. 2.
91 AUSSME. Commissione suprema di difesa verbale della XI sessione (Febbraio 1934–XII); seduta del 13 febbraio 1934, pp. 28, 29. Rep. F-9 racc. 29/f. 2.
92 *Ibid.*, pp. 34–7.
93 *Ibid.*, pp. 55–6.
94 *Ibid.*, pp. 74–6.
95 AUSSME. Riassunto dei lavori compiuti dalla C.S.D. fino alla XI sessione compresa (1934), November 1934, pp. 26–8.
96 *Ibid.*, pp. 35–7.
97 *Ibid.*, pp. 45–50.
98 Emilio Canevari, *La guerra italiana*, vol. I, p. 203.
99 The Italian estimate was the French conscript system added 4 per cent to overall costs. Italian and French lieutenants and captains were paid more or less exactly the same (12,000 lire and 22,000–23,600 lire respectively), but French colonels and major-generals earned considerably more than their opposite numbers (the former 49,400 lire and 82,500 lire and the latter 33,880 lire and 56,320 lire). AUSMM. Confronto fra le spese militari della Francia e dell'Italia negli ultimi anni, 3 March 1933, pp. 31, 35. Cartelle Numerate b.3293/f. 16.
100 *Ibid.*, pp. 19–20. On the statistical pitfalls inherent in the figures, see below fn. 143.
101 Italy spent 1,487,199,532 lire on all combined; France spent 3,255,000,000 lire on weapons and materiel, and a further 2, 475, 000, 000 lire on fortifications. *Ibid.*, p. 37.
102 AUSSME. Io = Piano 6, February 1932. Rep. H-6 racc. 5.
103 AUSSME. Udienza Gazzera–Mussolini, 8 January 1933. Rep. L-13 racc. 202/f. 1.
104 AUSSME. Note sulla efficienza complessiva dell'esercito al 1o gennaio 1933 –XIo – e sulle sue essenziali necessità, 28 January 1933, p. 9. Rep. L-13 racc. 202/f. 2.
105 *Ibid.*, p. 20. In 1932 the overall odds had been 1:2.8, now they were 1:2.6 or 1:2 locally.
106 *Ibid.*, p. 28.

107 *Ibid.*, p. 30.
108 *Ibid.*, p. 35.
109 *Ibid.*, pp. 52, 53, 57.
110 *Ibid.*, p. 71.
111 AUSSME. Cenno riassuntivo sull'organizzazione difensiva, September 1933, section I. Rep. H-6 racc. 5.
112 'Le guerre segrete di Mussolini', *La Stampa* 9 January 1982.
113 AUSSME. Piano 34–Direttive, 30 November 1933. Rep. H-6 racc. 5.
114 AUSSME. N. 430, Bonzani to Baistrocchi, 4 February 1934. Rep. H-6 racc. 6/ f. 1.
115 Appunti 29 April 1934; quo. Ceva, 'Appunti per una storia dello Stato Maggiore', p. 226 fn. 7.
116 AUSSME. La preparazione militare nei principali state esteri durante il 1933–Svizzera, [n.d.]. rep. H-3 racc. 31/ f. 12.
117 AUSSME. Dal notiziario quindicinale riguardante gli state esteri nos. 5 and 6, 1 March 1934 and 1 April 1934. Rep. H-3 racc. 31/ f. 12.
118 AUSSME. N. 13783 all., Proposta di urgenti lavori di fortificazione sulle frontiere nord e nord-ovest, 19 July 1934. Rep. H-3 racc. 31/f. 12.
119 AUSSME. Operazioni offensive con obbiettivo Monaco e Vienna, February 1934, sec. I. Rep. H-6 racc. 6.
120 *Ibid.*, secs. VII (a), IX (a), IX (b).
121 AUSSME. N.2/1094, Austria–Notiziario n.1, 1 March 1934. Rep. H-6 racc. 6 bis/f. 5.
122 AUSSME. N. 2/1125, Austria–Notiziario n.2, 2 March 1934. Rep. H-6 racc. 6 bis/f. 5.
123 AUSSME. Appunti sulla riunione tenuta a Verona il 2 marzo 1934-XII-ore 8.45, da S.E. il Capo di S.M. dell'Esercito. Bonzani issued detailed instructions to the army commander at Florence and the corps commanders at Verona, Bologna, Udine and Milan on matters such as powers of command, legal controls, equipment, munitions and transport six days later: N. 1460, Piano 34, 8 March 1934. Rep. H-6 racc. 6/ f. 1. The final version of Plan K, incorporating and expanding on Bonzani's remarks at Verona, was issued on 20 April 1934.
124 AUSSME. N. 173, Situazione austriaca–Notiziario giornaliero n. 22, 22 March 1934. Rep. H-6 racc. 6 bis/ f. 5.
125 AUSSME. Stralcio del bollettino giornaliero no. 30 del 9/4/1934-XII. Rep. H-6 racc. 6/f. 2.
126 AUSSME. N.2245, Bonzani to Baistrocchi, 13 April 1934. Rep. H-6 racc. 6/f. 2.
127 AUSSME. Riassunto delle principali notizie sulla situazione austriaca alla data del 4 maggio [1934]. Rep. H-6 racc. 6 bis/f. 5.
128 AUSSME. Austria: Notiziario No. 2, 27 July 1934; Austria=Notiziario n. 4, 20 July 1934; Austria: Notiziario no. 6, 1 August 1934. Rep H-6 racc. 6 bis/f. 5.
129 AUSSME. N.4607, Piano K, 28 July 1934. Rep H-6 racc. 6 bis/f. 5.
130 AUSSME. Austria: Notiziario no. 9, 13 August 1934. Rep. H-6 racc. 6 bis/ f. 5.

131 AUSSME. Piano Z Direttive, 4 November 1934. Rep. H-6 racc. 6.
132 AUSSME. Piano 5 L Direttive per la copertura, 1 February 1934. Rep. H-6 racc. 6.
133 ASMAE. N.200/0.1, Pralormo to War Ministry, 25 February 1933. Affari Politici: Francia b.8/f. 1–6.
134 AUSSME. Piano 5 B Direttive per la copertura, 1 February 1934. Rep. H-6 racc. 6.
135 AUSMM. Mussolini to Undersecretaries of War, Navy and Air, 10 August 1934. Direttive Generali DG 8/G1.
136 Seduta del 3 settembre 1934: Antonello Biagini and Alessandro Gionfrida, *Lo stato maggiore generale*, p. 312.
137 Direttive date da S.E. il Capo di S.M. generale nella riunione del 17 novembre 1934; *ibid.*, pp. 325–6.
138 AUSSME. Baistrocchi to Mussolini, 26 November 1934. Rep. H-9 racc. 1/f. 1.
139 AUSMM. Dichiarazioni alla Camera del Ministro della Marina Ammiraglio Sirianni, 23 April 1932, p. 3. Cartelle Numerate b.3267/f. 1.
140 *Ibid.*, pp. 8–9.
141 AUSMM. Dichiarazioni al Senato del Ministro della Marina Ammiraglio Sirianni, 31 May 1933. Cartelle Numerate b.3267/f. 1.
142 AUSMM. Confronto fra le spese militari della Francia e dell'Italia negli ultimi anni, 8 March 1933, p. 34. Cartelle Numerate b.3293/f. 16.
143 *Ibid.*, pp. 19, 20 [recalculated in lire]. The innumerable statistical pitfalls inherent in any such comparisons are laid out in full in the first eighteen pages of this memorandum. The lire remained more or less static during this period, averaging 0.75 to the franc: *ibid.*, p. 5. Economists will raise issues of comparative costs and purchasing power. Italian calculations suggested that raw materials cost less in France but labour cost more, so that overall *materiale bellico* was about as expensive in both countries, while higher costs of living added 5 per cent to French costs: *ibid.*, pp. 28–31, 36.
144 AUSMM. Programma di costruzioni navale, 29 November 1933, para. 7. Direttive Generali DG 0/C0.
145 *Ibid.*, para. 12.
146 *Ibid.*, para. 39.
147 AUSMM. N.404/M/5, Radicati di Marmorito to Capo di stato della R. Marina, 23 July 1930; Notiziario Addetto Navale in Francia no. 326, 29 November 1933. Cartelle Numerate b.3272/ f. 1.
148 AUSMM. Memorandum, 2 March 1934; 'Visita fatta dal commandante de Larosière al Ministero della Marina per precisare le comunicazioni fatte durante l'udienza ottenuta il 2 Marzo 1934.XII', 3 March 1934. Cartelle Numerate b.3272/ f. 1. De Larosière told Cavagnari France was sticking to the Washington 'platform' of 175,000 tons, and justified the 330-mm guns of the *Dunkerque* on the grounds of the superior ballistic quality of German guns of lesser calibre as demonstrated in the last war. The *Deutschlands* had 280-mm guns.

149 AUSMM. Questione delle grandi navi e situazione italo-francese nel caso che il trattato di Washington non venisse denunciato, 5 March 1934. Direttive Generali DG 0/C1.

150 AUSMM. L'impostazione di una moderna nave di linea considerata alla luce dell situazione politica, March 1934; unheaded memorandum, 19 March 1934. Cartelle Numerate b.3268/ f. 3.

151 AUSMM. Questione delle navi di linea, n.d. Cartelle Numerate b.3268/f. 3. The Washington limit for Italy was 175,000 tons.

152 AUSMM. Mussolini to Cavagnari, 10 February XII [1934]. Direttive Generali DG 8/G1.

153 AUSMM. N.185, unheaded memorandum, 27 March 1934. Cartelle Numerate b.3268/f. 3.

154 AUSMM. N. 376, Jachino to Maristat, 15 June 1934; N.151, Parona to Maristat, 29 June 1934; N.407, Nota per S.E., 5 July 1934. Cartelle Numerate b.3268/f. 3. ASMAE. Colloquio Suvich–Chambrun, 3 July 1934. Affari Politici: Francia b.11/f. 1. Suvich thought the resentment came more from de Chambrun than from French naval circles.

155 AUSMM. Promemoria per S.E. il Capo del Governo, 6 July 1934. Cartelle Numerate b.3268/f. 3.

156 AUSMM. Promemoria per S.E. il Capo del Governo, 27 August 1934. Cartelle Numerate b.3268/f. 3.

157 Enrico Cernuschi, *Domenico Cavagnari: Storia di un Ammiraglio* (Rome: Rivista Marittima, 2001), pp, 54–5 [which gives 29 October as the day the ships were laid down]. Fitting a main armament of nine 381-mm guns, a secondary armament of twelve 152-mm guns, the necessary armour protection and the engines and fuel capacity to run at 30 knots meant that both ships exceeded the published limit, ending up with a standard displacement of 40,516 tons: William H. Garzke Jr. and Robert O. Dulin Jr., *Battleships: Axis and Neutral Battleships in World War II* (Annapolis MD: Naval Institute Press, 1985), pp. 379–81.

158 AUSMM. Direttive impartite dal Capo di S. M. della Marina sulla compilazione del 'Libro di guerra', January 1932. Dirrettive Generali DG 1/A1.

159 AUSMM. Promemoria per S. E. il Capo di Stato Maggiore, 8 December 1931. Direttive Generali DG 1/A1.

160 AUSMM. Promemoria n. 58: Trasporto in continente delle truppe francesi del Nord Africa, 10 May 1932. Direttive Generali DG 10/A3.

161 AUSMM. Promemoria n. 26: Osservazioni al documento di consultazione B del maggio 1929, 9 January 1932. Direttive Generali DG 10/B11.

162 AUSMM. Promemoria: Condotta e Difesa del Traffico, April 1933, pp. 6–8, 19–24. Direttive Generali DG 5/C8.

163 AUSMM. Bacino di operazioni nel Mar Rosso, 14 February 1933. Direttive Generali DG 8/A0.

164 AUSMM. Promemoria: Difesa ed organizzazione marittima delle colonie in Mar Rosso ed Oceano Indiano, 18 December 1934. Direttive Generali DG 8/A0.

165 AUSMM. N. 6237, Bonzani to CSMM, 20 December 1933. A hand-written note at the foot of the letter [by Ducci?], begins: 'Asked many times by me about the most likely issues, Bonzani has always, I say always, answered that

he does not think the help of the fleet necessary'. Direttive Generali DG 11/B4.

166 AUSMM. Operazioni in piccolo stile contro il littorale nemico nella ipotesi '1', 17 January 1934. Direttive generali DG 11/B5.

167 AUSMM. N.54, Ducci to Bonzani, 18 January 1934, paras. 22, 27. Direttive Generali DG 11/B4.

168 AUSMM. Direttive di massima nella ipotesi di guerra su due fronti = valevoli per l'anno 1934, n.d., pp. 3–10. Direttive Generali DG 1/D3. [The memorandum must predate 1 June 1934 when admiral Ducci, who signed it, ceased to be chief of naval staff.]

169 AUSMM. Cavagnari to Vanutelli, 14 May 1934. Direttive Generali DG 1/D7.

170 Seduta del 3 settembre 1934: Biagiani and Gionfrida, *Lo stato maggiore generale*, pp. 312, 314.

171 AUSMM. Studio di preparazione navale: Ipotesi di conflitto nord con eventualità di complicazioni ad est, 16 September 1934, p. 7. Direttive Generali DG 1/D6.

172 AUSMM. N.919, Badoglio to sotto segretario guerra, marina, aeronautica, 19 September 1934. Direttive Generali DG 1/D7.

173 Seduta del 17 novembre 1934: Biagini and Gionfrida, *Lo stato maggiore generale*, p. 322.

174 AUSMM. Ipotesi Nord-Est: Note per la riunione presso il Capo di stato maggiore indetta per il Dicembre 1934, 6 December 1934. Direttive Generali DG 1/D7. Either the meeting for which this memorandum was prepared never took place or the record has been lost.

175 Giuseppe Santoro, *L'aeronautica italiana nella seconda guerra mondiale*, vol. I, pp. 16–17.

176 AUSMM. Confronto fra le spese militari della Francia e dell'Italia negli ultimi anni, 8 March 1933, p. 33.

177 *Ibid.*, pp. 19–20.

178 Gregory Alegi, 'Sette anni di politica aeronautica', in Carlo Maria Santoro, ed., *Italo Balbo: Aviazione e potere aereo* (Rome: Aeronautica Militare, 1998), pp. 137–67.

179 Giuseppe D'Avanzo, *Ali e poltrone*, pp. 211–5. Pelliccia claims that Valle took measures to limit this influx by requiring educational and flying qualifications, but broadly accepts both the figures and their consequences: Antonio Pelliccia, *Giuseppe Valle: Una difficile eredità* (Rome: Ufficio Storico dell'Aeronautica Militare, 1999), p. 115.

180 ASAM. Manovre coi quadri a partiti contrapposti Anno XI: Parte IVa, Osservazioni sugli studi dei partiti e sullo svolgimento delle operazioni, February–April1933, p. 2. Fondi Esercitazioni b.7.

181 *Ibid.*, Parte Va, Direzione della manovra–Deduzioni–Conclusioni, pp. 11–16, 19–20, 24–9. *Loc. cit.*

182 ASAM. Esercitazioni Aero–Navali EN1, February 1934; Esercitazioni Aero–Navali EN 4 [23 May 1934]. Fondo Esercitazioni b.8 *bis*.

183 ASAM. Partecipazione della Regia Aeronautica alle grandi esercitazioni terrestri–Agosto1934/XIIIo: Considerazioni e deduzioni sulla manovra, n.d., pp. 28–35 [quo., pp. 34–5]. Fondo Esercitazioni b.8.

184 Pelliccia, *Giuseppe Valle*, p. 93.
185 *Ibid.*, pp. 96–7, 197–200.
186 UKNA. Valle to Mussolini, 5 April 1941. GFM 36/162/ ff. 030013/A-030015/A.
187 UKNA. Pricolo to Sebastiani, 10 April 1941; memorandum by Pricolo, 16 April 1941. GFM 36/162/ff 030016/A, 030017/A-030027/A.
188 Air Staff report 8 March 1933, *cit.* MacGregor Knox, 'Fascist Italy assesses its enemies', in Ernest R. May, ed., *Knowing One's Enemies: Intelligence Assessment before the Two World Wars* (Princeton NJ: Princeton University Press, 1984), p. 357.
189 AUSSME. Udienza Gazzera–Mussolini, 31 July 1930, 22 July 1932. Rep. L-13 racc. 202/f. 1.
190 ASAM. Studio circa le possibilità di azione di neutralizzazione della Corsica mediante l'Armata Aerea, 11April 1932. OP 1.4.
191 AUSSME. Seconda seduta, 13 February 1934, pp. 23–4. Rep. F-9 racc. 29/f. 2. Elmas is not in the list of twenty new airfields opened in October and December 1937 given by Pelliccia: *Giuseppe Valle*, pp. 65, 67.
192 Seduta del 3 settembre 1934: Biagini and Gionfrida, *Lo stato maggiore generale*, pp. 312–3, 315.
193 ASAM. Memoria sullo schieramento della Regia Aeronautica nell'ipotesi Nord-est, December 1934, pp. 1–8. OP1.4.
194 *Ibid.*, pp. 15–16.
195 AUSMM. N. 117, Ducci to Valli, 25 March 1932. Cartelle Numerate b.1725/ f. 3.
196 AUSMM. N.800, Ducci to Badoglio, 22 September 1933. Cartelle Numerate b.1725/ f. 3.
197 Ferrante, *Il pensiero strategico navale in Italia*, pp. 46–7 [quo., p. 47].
198 *Ibid.*, pp. 50–1.
199 Alberto Baldini, *Elementi di cultura militare per il cittadino italiano* (Rome: Nazione militare, anno XIII [1934–5]), pp. 79, 84, 90–2.
200 Giuseppe Sirianni, 'Appunti sulla costituzione degli organi di comando in guerra', *Nuova Antologia*, December 1933, p. 527.
201 *Ibid.*, p. 530. According to admiral Tur, no attempt was made by Mussolini to 'fascistise' the navy during Sirianni's period of office, and he defended admirals unjustly accused of being 'anti-fascist': Tur, *Plancio Ammiraglio*, vol. III, p. 140.
202 Botti and Ilari, *Il pensiero militare italiano dal primo al secondo dopoguerra*, p. 173.
203 *Ibid.*, pp. 174–6; J. J. T. Sweet, *Iron Arm: The Mechanization of Mussolini's Army 1920–1940* (Westport CT: Greenwood Press, 1980), pp. 32, 80–4.
204 Sebastiano Visconti Prasca, *La guerra decisiva* (Milan: Grossi, 1934), pp. 45–6, 53, 57, 65–6, 72, 74, 79–80, 90–1.
205 *Ibid.*, p. 114; Botti and Ilari, *Il pensiero militare italiano*, p. 186.
206 Visconti Prasca, *La guerra decisiva*, pp. 11, 13.
207 Antonio Sema, '1914–1934: Guerra e politica secondo Mussolini'; Sema, 'Pensiero militare e fascistizzazione delle forze armate': Virgilio Ilari and Antonio Sema, *Marte in Orbace*, pp. 102–4; 176–7.

208 Botti and Ilari, *Il pensiero militare italiano*, p. 198.

209 The German PZKW Mark I B, manufactured between August 1935 and June 1937, weighed 5.8 tons and carried two 7.92-mm machine guns; the PZKW II, produced between May 1936 and February 1937, weighed 7.6 tons and carried one 20-mm gun and one 7.92-mm machine gun.

210 Longo, *Francesco Saverio Grazioli*, p. 404.

211 ASMAE. Appunto per Sua Eccellenza il Capo di Governo (Suvich), 27 August 1934. Affari Politici: Francia b.11/f. 1.

212 'Memoria riassuntiva della missione militare italiana in Russia', n.d. [1934]: Canevari, *La guerra italiana*, vol. I, pp. 246–9.

213 Ferriccio Botti and Mario Cermelli, *La teoria della guerra aerea*, p. 470.

214 *Ibid.*, pp. 471–2.

215 *Ibid.*, p. 482.

216 *Ibid.*, p. 481.

217 *Ibid.*, pp. 486–90.

218 *Ibid.*, pp. 494–8, 539, 556–7.

219 Grandi to Benni, 4 April 1932; Grandi to Manzoni, 23 May 1932. *DDI* 7th series vol. XII nos. 2, 55, pp. 2, 72–3.

220 Guariglia to Mussolini, 26 August 1932; Guariglia, 27 August 1932. *DDI* 7th series vol. XII nos. 222, 223, pp. 311–14, 315–23 [quos., pp. 313, 321].

221 Sullivan, A Thirst for Glory, pp. 258, 266–8.

222 De Bono to Mussolini, 22 March 1932. *DDI* 7th series vol. XII, p. 51 fn. 2.

223 Luigi Emilio Longo, *La campagna Italo-Etiopica (1935–1936)* (Rome: Ufficio Storico dello Stato Maggiore dell'Esercito, 2005), vol. I, p. 47 fn. 44.

224 Riunione al Ministero delle Colonie, 5 November 1932. *DDI* 7th series vol. XII no. 393, pp. 502–7 [quo., p.506].

225 De Bono to Gazzera, 29 November 1932; De Bono to Balbo, 29 November 1932: Giorgio Rochat, *Militari e politici nella preparazione della campagna d'Etiopia: Studi e documenti 1932–1936* (Milan: Franco Angeli, 1971), pp. 276–91, 291–3.

226 Mussolini to Vinci, 4 January 1933. *DDI* 7th series vol. XIII no. 7, pp. 7–8.

227 Baistrocchi to De Bono, 15 September 1933; Rochat, *Militari e politici*, pp. 294–8.

228 Badoglio to De Bono, 23 October 1933; *Ibid.*, pp. 298–300.

229 Piero Pieri and Giorgio Rochat, *Badoglio* (Turin: UTET, 1974), p. 649; Rochat, *Militari e politici*, pp. 37–9, 43–5.

230 Massimo Mazzetti, *La politica militare italiana*, pp. 150–5.

231 De Bono to Mussolini, 8 January 1934. *DDI* 7th series vol. XIV no. 536, pp. 609–11.

232 Badoglio to Mussolini, 20 January 1934; Rochat, *Militari e politici*, pp. 301–4.

233 De Bono Diary, 8 February 1934; *cit.*, Rochat, *Militari e politici*, p. 39.

234 De Bono to Mussolini,14 February 1934. *DDI* 7th series vol. XIV no. 696, pp. 782–4. The meeting referred to in this document (p. 782), of which the editors were unable to find any trace, is the one identified in footnote 227 above.

235 Mussolini to De Bono, 23 February 1934. *DDI* 7th series vol. XIV no. 739, pp. 818–9.
236 Mussolini to Badoglio, 1 March 1934; Badoglio to Mussolini, 3 March 1934. *DDI* 7th series vol. XIV nos. 766, 771, pp. 850, 855–7.
237 De Bono to Mussolini, 12 March 1934. *DDI* 7th series vol. XIV no. 797, pp. 884–5.
238 Appunto Bonzani, 27 March 1934. *DDI* 7th series vol. XV no. 40, pp. 51–2.
239 Badoglio to Mussolini, 26 April 1934; Rochat, *Militari e politici*, pp. 323–4.
240 Seduta del 7 maggio 1934: Biagini and Gionfrida, *Lo stato maggiore generale*, p. 293; Pelliccia, *Giuseppe Valle*, pp. 105–6.
241 Badoglio to De Bono, 12 May 1934: Rochat, *Militari e politici*, pp. 324–7. Copies were sent to Valle and on 16 May, at De Bono's request, to Mussolini.
242 *Ibid.*, p. 61; the full report *ibid.*, pp. 327–49.
243 Colloquio Mussolini–Suvich–De Bono–Badoglio, 31 May 1934. *DDI* 7th series vol. XV no. 325, p. 344.
244 Rochat, *Militari e politici*, pp. 64–9. Badoglio did not rule out the possibility of an improvised Ethiopian attack: n. 860, Badoglio to Bonzani, 21 July 1934. ACS 48/6 b.3/n. 79.
245 ACS. De Bono to Valle, 18 July 1934. Carte Badoglio 48/6, b.3/n.76. The same day, De Bono recorded in his diary that he did not think an enemy attack in September probable! *Cit.* Rochat, *Militari e politici*, pp. 69–70.
246 ACS. N.80805, De Bono to Bonzani, 19 July 1934. Four days later, De Bono was excluding the likelihood of 'an Abyssinian *colpo di testa*': N.80837, De Bono to Badoglio, 23 July 1934. Carte Badoglio 48/6 b.3/n. 77, 81.
247 ACS. N.80984, De Bono to Bonzani, 4 August 1934; n.80987, De Bono to Bonzani, 4 August 1934. Carte Badoglio 48/6 b.3/n. 88, 90. General plans for the defence of Somalia, about the lack of which De Bono complained in September, were only initiated in November: Rochat, *Militari e politici*, pp. 83–7.
248 Promemoria Visconti Prasca to Badoglio, 25 July 1934: Rochat, *Militari e politici*, pp. 354–5.
249 ACS. Promemoria: Forze aeree per l'Eritrea, 25 July 1934. Carte Badoglio 48/6 b.3/n. 83.
250 ACS. Promemoria: Spedizione O.M.E. in Eritrea, 26 July 1934. Carte Badoglio 48/6 b.3/n. 84.
251 Seduta del 27 luglio 1934; Biagini and Gionfrida, *Lo stato maggiore generale*, pp. 299–302.
252 *Ibid.*, pp. 303–8 [quo., p. 307].
253 *Ibid.*, pp. 308–9.
254 Promemoria Cavagnari, 18 July 1934. *DDI* 7th series vol. XV no. 541, pp. 579–83.
255 ACS. N.241, Ducci to Bonzani, 9 May 1934. Carte Badoglio 48/6 b.3/n. 80 all.
256 ACS. N. 731, Cavagnari to Badoglio and De Bono, 30 July 1934. Carte Badoglio 48/6 b.3/n. 86 all.
257 AUSMM. Mussolini to De Bono, Baistrocchi, Cavagnari, Valle and Badoglio, 10 August 1934. Direttive Generali DG 8/G1.

258 Costo operazioni militari in Africa Orientale, 9 September 1934; Longo, *La campagna Italo Etiopica* vol. II, p. 129.

259 Promemoria del generale di brigata Dall'Ora, 7 November 1934: Rochat, *Militari e politici*, pp. 367–9 [quo., p. 368].

260 Badoglio had held aloof from a tussle for command of the war between De Vecchi, Balbo, Graziani, Baistrocchi and Lessona, playing on his seniority as a *Maresciallo d'Italia*, though it had not secured him command: Longo. *La campagna Italo–Etiopica* vol. I, p. 57.

261 AUSMM. Direttive e piano d'azione per risolvere la questione italo–abissina, 30 December 1934, pp. 1–3, 4. Direttive Generali DG-8/G1. The sentence quoted is a hand-written addition at the foot of the latter page. Copies also went to De Bono, Lessona and Badoglio; the latter is reproduced in Rochat, *Militari e politici*, pp. 376–9.

262 Pignatti to Mussolini, 20 November 1935; Colloquio Pignatti–Leger, 21 November 1934; Colloquio Suvich–Chambrun, 24 November 1934; Colloquio Suvich–Chambrun, 1 December 1934; Appunto, 5 December 1934. *DDI* 7th series vol. XVI nos. 166, 171, 188, 225, 245 all. VI, pp. 175, 179, 191, 231, 259.

263 Appunto di Mussolini, 10 December 1934. *DDI* 7th series vol. XVI no. 276, p. 290.

264 *Ibid.*, p. 6. Underlined in original.

265 *Ibid.*, p. 4. Underlined in original.

266 Carte Badoglio. Badoglio to De Bono, 18 December 1934. ACS 48/6 b.3/n. 119.

267 *Contra* Rochat, *Militari e politici*, pp. 105–7.

268 Vitetti to Mussolini, 28 December 1934. *DDI* 7th series vol. XVI no. 348, p. 323.

5 THE TRIAL OF FORCE: ABYSSINIA, 1935

1 *Contra* Esmonde M. Robertson, *Mussolini as Empire Builder: Europe and Africa 1932–36* (London: Macmillan, 1977), p. 74.

2 Renato Mori, *Mussolini e la conquista dell'Etiopia* (Florence: Le Monnier, 1978), p. 27. See also Memorandum by Foreign Minister, 2 May 1935, Grandi to Mussolini 3 May 1935, Colloquio Suvich–Chambrun, 27 May 1935. *DGFP* series C vol. IV n. 63, p. 114; *DDI* 8th series vol. I nos. 134, 289, pp. 127, 308.

3 Mussolini to Grandi, 25 January 1935. *DDI* 7th series vol. XVI no. 492, pp. 518–20.

4 Grandi to Mussolini, 27 February 1935. *DDI* 7th series vol. XVI no. 670, p. 711.

5 Colloquio Suvich–Chambrun, 27 May 1935; Hassell to Foreign Ministry, 31 May 1935; Colloquio Suvich–Drummond, 18 June 1935; Colloquio Mussolini–Eden, 24 June 1935. *DDI* 8th series vol. I no. 289, p. 308; *DGFP* series C vol. IV no. 121, p. 234; *DDI* 8th series vol. I nos. 403, 431, pp. 421, 457–8. Mussolini to Chambrun, 15 July 1935, *cit.* Mori, *Conquista dell'Etiopia*, p. 50 [quo.].

6 'Il "Dato" Irrefutabile', 31 July 1935; *OO* XXVII, pp. 110–11. See also Drummond to Hoare, 1 August 1935: Drummond–Suvich, 17 August 1935; *DBFP* series 2 vol. XIV nos. 412, 463, pp. 407, 502.

7 Cerruti to Mussolini, 16 February 1935; Colloquio Suvich–Drummond, 20 February 1935; Grandi to Mussolini, 20 February 1935; Colloquio Suvich–Drummond, 18 March 1935; Cerruti to Mussolini, 21 March 1935. *DDI* 7th series vol. XVI nos. 602, 624, 626, 756, 779, pp. 637–8, 661–2, 663–4, 803–4, 835–6.

8 Teucci to Valle, 29 December 1934; Cerruti to Mussolini, 24 January 1935. *DDI* 7th series vol. XVI nos. 362 att., 486, pp. 371–2, 512–4. Robertson, *Mussolini as Empire Builder*, p. 59.

9 ASMAE. Unheaded memoranda, Innsbruck 24 and 30 April 1935. Affari Politici: Germania b.27/ f. 1.

10 ASMAE. T.938, Quaroni to Paris Embassy etc., 27 May 1935. Affari Politici: Germania b.26/f. 1.

11 ASMAE. Pinna to Valle, 31 March 1935. Affari Politici: Germania b.28/ f. 1.

12 ASMAE. N.383, Mancinelli to War Ministry, 18 April 1935. Affari Politici: Germania b.27/f. 1.

13 Robertson, *Mussolini as Empire-Builder*, pp. 111–2.

14 Viola to Mussolini, 11 April 1935. *DDI* 7th series vol. XVI no. 905, p. 962.

15 ASMAE. To. 216309/178, Quaroni to Berlin Embassy, 18 May 1935. Affari Politici: Germania b.26/f. 1

16 ASMAE. N.1141, Mancinelli to War Ministry, 13 September 1935. Affari Politici: Germania b.27/f. 1.

17 ASMAE. N.1224, Mancinelli to War Ministry, 25 September 1935. Affari Politici: Germania b.27/f. 1.

18 ASMAE. N.293, De Courten to Maristat, 27 February 1935. Affari Politici: Germania b.30/f. 3.

19 ASMAE. Promemoria per S. E. l'Ambasciatore, 18 March 1935. [Marked 'V/M', i.e. read by Mussolini]. Affari Politici: Germania b.30/f/3.

20 ASMAE. Armamenti marittimi della Germania, 30 March 1935, p. 4. Affari Politici: Germania b.28/f. 1. Shorrock's assertion that Britain was preparing to negotiate a naval accord with Germany on the eve of the Stresa conference [11–14 April] 'unbeknownst to her French and Italian partners' is demonstrably incorrect as far as Rome is concerned, and the implication that Rome did not know what was in the wind until formally informed of the impending accord in mid-June is misleading: Shorrock, *From Ally to Enemy*, pp. 129, 134.

21 ASMAE. N. 510, De Courten to Maristat, 2 May 1935; Affari Politici: Germania b.28/f. 1. Robertson, *Mussolini as Empire Builder*, p. 132. De Courten knew, as his British and French opposite numbers did not, that although the Germans had announced that they planned to build twelve 250-ton submarines – information which they accused the British naval attaché of leaking and only gave the French naval attaché casually and after telling the British – they planned to follow them up with 450–500 ton submarines. N. 508, De Courten to Maristat, 1 May 1935. Affari Politici: Germania b.28/f. 1.

22 Vitetti to Grandi, 7 June 1935; Cerruti to Mussolini, 22 June 1935; Cavagnari to Mussolini, 12 August 1935. *DDI* 8th series vol. I nos. 353, 422, 719, pp. 359–60, 443–5, 731.

23 ASMAE. T.3137/0178, Cerruti to Mussolini, 6 June 1935. Affari Politici: Germania b.26/f. 1.

24 ASMAE. To.2605/1085, Cerruti to Mussolini, 18 July 1935; Affari Politici: Germania b.26/f. 2. Cerruti to Mussolini, 18 July 1935; *DDI* 8th series vol. I no. 565, pp. 588–90. Robertson, *Mussolini as Empire Builder*, p. 143.

25 Attolico to Mussolini, 17 September 1935. *DDI* 8th series vol. II no. 131, p. 120.

26 ASMAE. To.3892, Pittalis to Esteri, 5 June 1935; Affari Politici: Germania b.28/f. 2. Von Hassell to Foreign Ministry, 26 May 1935; *DGFP* series C vol. IV, 26 May 1935, p. 209.

27 Colloquio Mussolini–von Hassell, 15 July 1935; Cerruti to Mussolini, 6 August 1935. *DDI* 8th series vol. I nos. 540, 675, pp. 564–5[quo.], 691–3.

28 ASMAE. T.1263, Quaroni to London Embassy etc., 13 July 1935. Affari Politici: Germania b.26/f. 2.

29 H. James Burgwyn, *Italian Foreign Policy in the Interwar Period*, pp. 103–7, 115; Robertson, *Mussolini as Empire Builder*, pp. 66, 73, 82.

30 Riunione del 5 febbraio 1935; Biagini and Gionfrida, *Lo stato maggiore generale tra le due guerre*, p. 341.

31 Von Hassell to Foreign Ministry, 14 May 1935; *DGFP* series C vol. IV no. 87, p. 154 [author's italics].

32 For example, Hungary wanted Czechoslovakia dismembered but Austria did not as this would increase German power. *See* Viola to Suvich, 26 February 1935; *DDI* 7th series vol. XVI no. 660, pp. 695–7. Suvich to Mussolini, 9 May 1935; colloquio Mussolini–Schuschnigg, 11 May 1935; Aloisi to Mussolini, 19 June 1935; Suvich to Mussolini, 3 July 1935; colloquio Suvich–Chambrun, 6 July 1935; Preziosi to Mussolini, 25 July 1935; *DDI* 8th series vol. I nos. 172, 180, 405, 480, 504, 610, pp. 186–7, 197–201, 423–6, 500–1, 529–30, 628–9.

33 ASMAE. T.3602/1456, Attolico to Mussolini, 2 October 1935. Affari Politici: Germania b.26/f. 2.

34 Von Hassell to Foreign Office, 3 October 1935. *DGFP* series C vol. IV no. 322, p. 685.

35 ASMAE. T.3654/1485, Attolico to Mussolini, 7 October 1935. Affari Politici: Germania b.28/f. 2.

36 ASMAE. T.3967/1605, Attolico to Mussolini, 29 October 1935. Affari Politici: Germania b.26/f. 1. Mussolini underlined the passage in question.

37 Grandi to Mussolini, 25 July 1931. *DDI* 7th series vol. XVI n. 413, pp. 652–9 [quos., pp. 654, 655]. Grandi used the term *gallo* ('Gaul'), which also means 'cockerel' or 'strutting cock'.

38 Piccio to Mussolini, 5 August 1931. *DDI* 7th series vol. X n. 423, p. 673.

39 Pignatti to Mussolini, 25 October 1934. *DDI* 7th series vol. XVI n. 91, pp. 87–9.

40 Pignatti to Mussolini, 31 October 1934; Pignatti to Mussolini, 20 November 1934; Colloquio Pignatti–Léger, 21 November 1934. *DDI* 7th series vol. XVI n. [unnumbered], 166, 171, pp. 88 fn. 1, 175, 179.

41 Colloquio Suvich–De Chambrun, 24 November 1934; Pignatti to Mussolini, 21 November 1934; colloquio Suvich–De Chambrun, 1 December 1934. *DDI* 7th series vol. XVI n. 188, 189, 225, pp. 191, 191–2, 231.

42 ASMAE. N.7984, Chambrun–Laval, 26 December 1934; N.8069, Chambrun–Laval, 30 December 1934. GAB 332 b.131. Romania was afraid of being at the mercy of Hungarian revisionism if she was not a party to the agreement.

43 ASMAE. N.8005, Chambrun–Laval, 27 December 1934; N.8069, Chambrun-Laval, 30 December 1934 [quo. fl.84 – author's italics]. GAB 332 b.131.

44 Colloquio Mussolini–Laval, 5 January 1935. *DDI* 7th series vol. XVI n. 391, pp. 404–7. An English translation is given in G. Bruce Strang, 'Imperial Dreams: The Mussolini–Laval Accords of January 1935', *Historical Journal* vol. 44 no. 3, September 2001, pp. 802–5 [quos., p. 805].

45 Colloquio Mussolini–Laval, 6 January 1935. *DDI* 7th series vol. VXI n. 399, pp. 416–7; also Strang, *op. cit.*, pp. 806–7. See also Renzo De Felice, *Gli anni del consenso*, pp. 524–32.

46 Mussolini to Laval, 7 January 1935. *DDI* 7th series vol. XVI all. no. VII, p. 426.

47 Colloquio Suvich–Chambrun, 27 May 1935; Drummond to Hoare, 24 June 1935. *DDI* 8th series vol. I n. 289, p. 308; *DBFP* 2nd series vol. XIV n. 320, p. 332. Shorrock concludes that Laval did not 'endorse' an Italian conquest of Ethiopia: William I. Shorrock, *From Ally to Enemy*, pp. 108–116. Burgwyn concurs but perceives enough ambiguity in Laval's posture to allow Mussolini to presume French acquiescence in the use of force: Burgwyn, *Italian Foreign Policy*, pp. 110–11.

48 AUSSME. Nota, 29 January 1935. Rep. H-5, racc. 54.

49 SHAT. M. Catoire, *Journal de ma mission à Rome 1934–1937*, 12, 30 & 31 January 1935.

50 N.50/A-S, Parisot to War Minister, 28 March 1935: Pascal Krop, *Les Secrets de l'espionnage francais de 1870 à nos jours* (Paris: J. Clattes, 1994), pp. 670–81.

51 ASMAE. N.313/S, Kellner to Captain Gustavo Strazzeri, 13 February 1935. Affari Politici: Germania b.28/f. 1.

52 ASMAE. N.355/S, Kellner to Paris Embassy, 14 March 1935. Affari Politici: Francia b.16/f. 1–2. AUSSME. N.357/S, Kellner to War Ministry, 14 March 1935; n. 358/S, Kellner to War Ministry, 14 March; SIM to Under-Secretary of State for War/Deputy Chief of General Staff, 20 March 1935. Rep. H-3 racc. 2/f. A/10.

53 Mario Montanari, 'Il "Progetto A. O." e i suoi sviluppi', *Studi storico-militari* 1987, p. 708 fn. 3.

54 ASMAE. N.422/S, Kellner to SIM, 10 April 1935. Affari Politici: Francia b.14/f. 1.

55 ASMAE. N.645, Kellner to Chief of the Armed Forces General Staff, 1 August 1935. Affari Politici: Francia b.16/f. 1–2.

56 ASMAE. T.5135/0112, Cerruti to Esteri, 28 August 1935. Affari Politici: Francia b.14/f. 1.

57 ASMAE. To.206182, Suvich to Paris Embassy etc., 26 February 1935. Affari Politici: Francia b.14/f. 1.

58 Accordo di collaborazione aerea tra Italia e Francia [12–13 May 1935]; *DDI* 8th series vol. I no. 196, pp. 214–7.

59 Von Hassell to Foreign Ministry, 41 May 1935; *DGFP* series C vol. IV no. 87, p. 153.

60 Riunione dei rappresentati degli stati maggiori dell'Aeronautica francese e italiano, 12 September 1935; *DDI* 8th series vol. II no. 99, pp. 82–7.

61 Suvich to Mussolini, 3 July 1935 all: Riassunto dell'accordo Gamelin-Badoglio; *DDI* 8th series vol. I no. 480, p. 501. The Germans were told of the military accords by Roatta on 4 July 1935: Memorandum by an Official of Department II, 22 October 1935; *DGFP* series C vol. IV no. 373, pp. 766–7.

62 SHAT. Catoire, *Journal* 3 July 1935.

63 ASMAE. T.1337, Pignatti to Esteri, 14 March 1935; Colloquio Suvich–Laval, 23 March 1935. Affari Politici: Francia b.16/f. 1–2.

64 ASMAE. T.1885/587, Pignatti to Esteri, 27 March 1935. Affari Politici: Francia b.18/f. 48. His estimate was in fact two years out.

65 Pignatti to Mussolini, 17 June 1935; Colloquio Suvich–Chambrun, 24 July 1935; Bova-Scoppi to Mussolini, 30 August 1935; *DDI* 8th series vol. I nos. 387, 602, 864, pp. 402, 620, 894–6. Shorrock, *From Ally to Enemy*, pp. 138, 143–4, 147–8.

66 Mussolini to Cerruti, 25 August 1935; *DDI* 8th series vol. I no. 815, p. 845. Suvich repeated the argument, adding the Balkans to the list of probable German acquisitions, in mid-September: Colloquio Suvich–Chambrun, 16 September 1935; *DDI* 8th series vol. II no. 124, pp. 109–11.

67 Shorrock, *From Ally to Enemy*, pp. 146–7.

68 Vitetti to Buti, 23 April 1935, Grandi to Mussolini, 3 May 1935, Grandi to Mussolini, 21 May 1935, Aloisi to Mussolini, 14 June 1935; Grandi to Mussolini, 2 July 1935, Grandi to Mussolini, 15 August 1935; *DDI* 8th series vol. I nos. 71, 134, 250, 377, 475, 740, pp. 63–7, 123–38, 268–9, 389–91, 495–8, 750–2. Mussolini to Grandi, 5 August 1935: Mori, *Mussolini e la conquista dell'Etiopia*, pp. 56–7. On the same day that Grandi told Mussolini that London was likely to fold in the face of the possibility of Italy leaving the League, the British ambassador told him that if forced to a choice Britain would likely choose the League: Drummond to Foreign Office, 21 May 1935: *DBFP* 2nd series vol. XIV no. 244, p. 239.

69 Robert Mallett, *Mussolini and the Origins of the Second World War, 1933–1940* (Basingstoke: Palgrave Macmillan, 2003), p. 45.

70 Grandi to Mussolini, 27 August 1935; Grandi to Mussolini, 19 September 1935. *DDI* 8th series vol. I no. 835, pp. 865–72; vol. II no. 146, p. 135.

71 ASMAE. To. 221257, 221722, 223656, Esteri to Colonial Ministry etc., 27 June 1935, 2 July 1935, 16 July 1935. Ambasciata di Londra b.873/f. 1.

72 ASMAE. T. Solazzo [Calcutta] to Esteri, 29 July 1935; T., Ghigi [Cairo] to Esteri, 3 August 1935. Ambasciata di Londra b.873/f. 1. Further reports that Great Britain was strengthening the defences of the Suez canal and Aden

arrived in Rome during September: Mallett, *Mussolini and the Origins of the Second World War*, p. 51.

73 Carte Capponi. N.464, Capponi to Marina, Questione Italo–Etiopica, 28 May 1935; no. 478. 'Questione Italo–Etiopica', 31 May 1935.' Rapporti Londra'.

74 Carte Capponi. N.12, Attività informativa nei riguardi dell'atteggiamento inglese (questione A-O), 19 July 1935. 'Rapporti Londra'.

75 Carte Capponi. N.23/S, Atteg/to inglesi A.O.-Movimenti di navi, 30 August 1935. Rapporti Londra. The Admiralty's precautionary measures included transferring the Home Fleet to Gibraltar, reinforcing the Mediterranean fleet and sending the latter from Malta to the eastern Mediterranean at the end of the month: Marder, 'The Royal Navy and the Ethiopian Crisis of 1935–6', pp. 67–8. On British public opinion at this time, see Daniel, P. Waley, *British Public Opinion and the Abyssinian War 1935–6* (London: Temple Smith, 1975), pp. 29–32; Mori, *Mussolini e la conquista dell'Etiopia*, pp. 68–70; Richard Lamb, *Mussolini and the British*, pp. 125–6.

76 Carte Capponi. N.25/S, Atteggiamento inglese nella questione A.O.-Movimenti di navi, 6 September 1935. 'Rapporti Londra'.

77 Christopher Andrew and Vasili Mitrokhin, *The Sword and the Shield: The Mitrokhin Archive and the Secret History of the KGB* (New York: Basic Books, 1999), pp. 35–6, 49–52, 54, 78.

78 Francesco Costantini and Lino Rizzo, 'Gli occhi del SIM nell'Ambasciata inglese Pt. IV: Chiudo la partita con il colpo più grosso: il rapporto Maffey', *Candido* 1 December 1957, p. 16; Annamaria Borgonovo, 'Parlano gli uomini che furono gli protagonisti del spionaggio italiano Pt. 2', *L'Europeo* 17 August 1967, p. 78; Mario Toscano, *Pagine di storia diplomatica contemporanea* II: *Origini e vicende della seconda Guerra mondiale* (Milan: Giuffré, 1963) . For British and Soviet perspectives on the Costantini affair, see David Dilks, 'Appeasement and "Intelligence"' in Dilks, ed., *Retreat from Power: Studies in Britain's Foreign Policy of the Twentieth Century* (London: Macmillan, 1981), pp.150–5; Dilks, 'Flashes of Intelligence: The Foreign Office, The SIS and Security before the Second World War' in Christopher Andrew and David Dilks, eds., *The Missing Dimension: Governments and Intelligence Communities in the Twentieth Century* (London: Macmillan, 1984), pp. 105–18; Nigel West and Oleg Tsarev, *The Crown Jewels: The British Secrets at the heart of the KGB archives* (New Haven CT: Yale University Press, 1999), pp. 96–102.

79 Mori, *Mussolini e la conquista dell'Etiopia*, p. 71 [original italics].

80 Carte Capponi. N.1153, Promemoria per la R. Ambasciata d'Italia a Londra: Situazione aeronautica inglese in relazione alla questione abissina, 16 August 1935. Ambasciata di Londra.

81 ASMAE. T., Conti [Port Said] to Esteri, 4 September 1935; T.5041/556, Conti to Esteri, 13 September 1935; T.5088/560, Conti to Esteri, 16 September 1935. Ambasciata di Londra b.873/f. 1

82 ASMAE. To.231633, Esteri to Colonial Ministry etc., 11 September 1935. Ambasciata di Londra b.873/f. 1.

83 ASMAE. To.7249/1174, Fontana [Alexandria] to Esteri, 7 September 1935 [quo.]; T.233487, Esteri to Colonial Ministry etc., n.d. [23 September 1935]

[quo.]. Ambasciata di Londra b.873/f. 1. In the latter telegram, the minister at Cairo estimated that there were 300 British aircraft in Egypt.

84 ASMAE. T.233887, Esteri to Colonial Ministry etc., 25 September 1935. Ambasciata di Londra b.873/f. 1.

85 Paolo Nello, *Un fedele disubbidiente*, pp. 254–6, 258–9.

86 Carte Capponi. N.509, Mondadori to War Ministry, 23 September 1935. 'Ambasciata di Londra'.

87 Carte Capponi. Atteggiamento inglese in relazione alla questione A.O., 27 September 1935. 'Rapporti Londra'.

88 Colloquio Mussolini–Kanya, 20 October 1934. *DDI* 7th series vol. XVI n. 75, pp. 71–2.

89 Colloquio Mussolini–Gömbös, 6 November 1934. *DDI* 7th series vol. XVI no. 112, pp. 121–2.

90 Galli to Mussolini, 5 December 1934. *DDI* 7th series vol. XVI, p. 237 fn. 2.

91 Viola [Belgrade] to Suvich, 26 February 1935. *DDI* 8th series vol. I no. 660, pp. 695–7.

92 Viola to Mussolini, 27 July 1935; Viola to Mussolini, 20 September 1935; Mussolini to Viola, 21 November 1935; *DDI* 8th series vol. I no. 631, p. 644; vol. II nos. 152, 679, pp. 140, 650.

93 Mussolini to Sapuppo [Sofia], 26 March 1935; colloquio Jacomoni–Villari, 10 April 1935. *DDI* 7th series vol. XVI nos. 807, 899, pp. 857, 957.

94 Mussolini to Sapuppo, 11 May 1935. *DDI* 8th series vol. I no. 183, p. 203.

95 AUSSME. Promemoria per S.E. il Sottosegretario di stato: Materiali per l'Austria, 15 January 1935; Promemoria per il capo del servizio informazioni militari: materiali per l'Austria, [?January], 1935; Promemoria per S.E. il Sottosegretario di stato: Materiale per l'Austria, 22 February 1935. Rep. H-3 racc. 2/f. A/2.

96 AUSSME. N.L/30, Baistrocchi to Minister of Finance, 4 March 1935. Rep. H-3 racc. 2/f. A/2.

97 AUSSME. Promemoria per S.E. il Capo del Governo: Cessione materiali bellici ad altri Stati, 1 April 1935. Mussolini scrawled 'Sta bene' ['OK'] on the memorandum.

98 AUSSME. Promemoria per S.E. il Sottosegretario di stato: Carri veloci per l'Austria e l'Ungheria, 10 April 1935. Rep. H-3 racc. 2/ f. A/2.

99 AUSSME. Colloquio con addetto militare austriaco, 1 August 1935; L/98, Forniture carri veloci all'estero, 3 August 1935; L/111, Roatta to Pugnani, 20 September 1935; Pugnani to Ufficio Autonomo Approvvigionamenti Automob., 24 September 1935. Rep. H-3 racc. 2/f. A/2.

100 Colloquio Mussolini–Schuschnigg, 11 May 1935, *DDI* 8th series vol. I no. 180, pp. 197–201 [quo., p. 197].

101 AUSSME. N.5083, Suvich to Baistrocchi, 25 June 1935. Rep. H-3 racc. 2/f. A/2.

102 AUSSME. N.1038, Promemoria per S.E. il Sottosegretario di stato alla Guerra: Relazione sulla missione compiuta in Austria ed Ungheria, 7 July 1935. Rep. H-3 racc. 2/f. A/6.

103 AUSSME. N.769, Di San Martino to War Ministry, 7 August 1935; SIM to Pariani, 25 August 1935. Rep. H-3 racc. 2/f. A/6.

104 AUSSME. N.7/1308, Roatta to War Ministry, 19 July 1935. Rep. H-3 racc. 2/f. A/6.
105 AUSSME. N.914, Mattioli to War Ministry/SIM, 28 September 1935. Rep. H-3 racc. 39/f. 1.
106 AUSSME. N.390/XXVI/35, Liebitsky to Roatta, 9 October 1935; SIM to Baistrocchi, 10 October 1935; L/135, Fornitura da e per l'Austria, 18 October 1935. Rep. H-3 racc. 2/f. A/2.
107 AUSSME. Roatta to Mussolini, 14 October 1935; SIM to Inspector of Engineers, 24 October 1935; SIM to Inspector of Engineers, 29 October 1935. Rep. H-3 racc. 8.
108 AUSSME. T.15227, De Bono to Colonial Ministry, 3 November 1935. Rep. H-3 racc. 8.
109 AUSSME. Badoglio to Baistrocchi, 1 December 1933. Rep. L-13 racc. 69/b.25.
110 Massimo Mazzetti, *La politica militare italiana*, pp. 124–8; Sullivan, 'A Thirst for Glory', pp. 354–6; Sullivan, 'The Primacy of Politics, pp. 72–3.
111 Giorgio Rochat, ''L'esercito di Mussolini visto dalla Francia', *Storia e memoria* no. 2, December 2003, pp. 33–4; SHAT, Catoire, *Journal*, 24–31 August 1935.
112 AUSSME. Badoglio to Baistrocchi, 19 July 1934. Rep. L-13 racc. 69/b.28.
113 AMR. Pariani to Baistrocchi, 5 March 1935; Pariani to Berti, 4 May 1935; Pariani to Bancale, 29 June 1935. Quaderni Pariani V, VI, VII. Pariani wanted to call the new motorised divisions *folgore* ('lightning'), *rapida* ('swift') or *veloce* ('fast').
114 Dorello Ferrari, 'Dalla divisione ternaria alla binaria: una pagina di storia dell'esercito italiano', *Memorie Storiche Militari* 1982, pp. 51–3, 55.
115 AMR. Pariani to Berti, 10 August 1935. Quaderni Pariani IX.
116 AUSSME. Relazione al Consiglio dell'esercito nella seduta del 12 gennaio 1935, p. 2. Rep. F-9 racc. 5/f. 1.
117 *Ibid.*, p. 7.
118 *Ibid.*, p. 10.
119 AUSSME. Verbale della prima seduta del Consiglio dell'esercito tenuta il giorno 12 gennaio 1935. Rep. F-9 racc. 5/f. 4.
120 AUSSME. Verbali della seconda seduta del Consiglio dell'Esercito tenuta il giorno 15 gennaio 1935, p. 10. Rep. F-9 racc. 5/f. 5.
121 *Ibid.*, pp. 13–14.
122 AUSSME. Verbale della terza seduta del Consiglio dell'Esercito tenuto il giorno 17 gennaio 1935, p. 5. Rep. F-9 racc. 5/f. 7.
123 AUSSME. Verbale della quarta seduta del Consiglio dell'esercito tenuta il giorno 21 gennaio 1935, p. 3 (tank). Rep. F-9 racc. 5/f. 7.
124 Sweet, *Iron Arm*, pp. 87–8; Botti and Ilari, *Il pensiero militare italiano*, pp. 173, 181
125 Botti and Ilari, *Il pensiero militare italiano*, p. 199.
126 Mario Montanari, *L'esercito italiano alla vigilia della 2a guerra mondiale* (Rome: Ufficio Storico dello Stato Maggiore dell'Esercito, 1982), pp. 252–74.
127 AUSSME. Badoglio to Baistrocchi, 13 June 1935. Rep. L-13 racc. 69/b.29.
128 AMR. Pariani to Berti, 29 November 1934. Quaderni Pariani II.

129 AMR. Pariani to Berti, 13 December 1934. Quaderni Pariani II.

130 AMR. Pariani to Berti, 29 March 1935. Quaderni Pariani VII.

131 AUSSME. Baistrocchi to Mussolini, 24 May 1935. Rep. H-9 racc. 1/f. 2.

132 AUSSME. Piano Z, 21 May 1935, p. 5. Rep. H-6 racc. 7.

133 AUSSME., P.R.10-Frontiera Est, 19 December 1935. Rep. H-6 racc. 7.

134 De Felice, *Gli anni del consenso*, pp. 638–40.

135 Capponi to Maristat, 3 March 1935; cit. Robert Mallett, Italian Naval Policy and Planning for War agaist Great Britain, 1935–1940, Ph D University of Leeds 1996, pp. 22–3.

136 Cavagnari to Mussolini, 4 March 1935; *DDI* 7th series vol. XVI, no. 694, pp. 732–6.

137 AUSMM. Ipotesi Nord-Est: Intervento della Francia nel conflitto a lato dell'Italia, 29 March 1935, pp. 4–5, 7, 9, 18. Direttive Generali DG 1/D6.

138 Enrico Cernuschi, *Domenico Cavagnari*, pp. 75–6.

139 AUSMM. B.2739, Cavagnari to Vanutelli, 14 April 1935. Direttive Generali DG 1/D7.

140 AUSMM. Promemoria (Riferimento al foglio B.2739 in data 14 aprile 1935 di 'Marina' sull'argomento =Piani di guerra=), 16 April 1935, pp. 6–7 [underlining in original]. Direttive Generali DG 1/D7.

141 *Ibid.*, pp. 9–10. This may not have been the first time that the staff examined the scenario of a war against Great Britain, as Cavagnari apparently asked them to prepare plans in May 1934: Cavagnari to Vanutelli, 14 May 1934, Direttive Generali DG 1/D7.

142 AUSMM. B.2954, Cavagnari to the Office of the Chief of Naval Staff, 24 April 1935. Direttive Generali DG 1/D7.

143 AUSMM. Studio sulle operazioni successive alla mobilitazione contemplata nel documento L.G. no. 9, 2 May 1935. Direttive Generali DG 1/D6.

144 AUSMM. Ipotesi di contrasto italo-britannico, 15 May 1935, p.13. Direttive Generali DG 1/D9.

145 *Ibid.*, p. 15.

146 *Ibid.*, p. 20.

147 Mallett, Italian Naval Policy, pp. 38, 283 fns. 65, 66.

148 Cernuschi, *Domenico Cavagnari*, pp. 80–1, 83, 84. In August, Valle began to study a one-way bombing mission against London as a solution to the problem of restricted range.

149 AUSMM. Promemoria a S. E. il Capo di Stato Maggiore [Vanutelli], 6 June 1935. Direttive Generali DG 2/A7.

150 AUSMM. N.90356, Lessona to De Bono & Balbo, 10 June 1933. Direttive Generali DG 0/N3.

151 AUSMM. Promemoria a S.E. il Capo di Stato Maggiore [Vanutelli], 15 June 1935. Direttive Generali DG 2/A7.

152 AUSMM. N.150, Cavagnari to Valle, 19 June 1935; N. 11373S, Valle to Cavagnari, 27 June 1935. Direttive Generali DG 2/A7.

153 AUSMM. Cavagnari to Mussolini, 19 June 1935. Direttive Generali DG 8/G1.

154 Cavagnari's calculations were designed to ensure that Italy stayed within the limit of 52,700 tons of submarines agreed by the United States, Great Britain

and Japan at the 1930 London Naval Conference, even though Italy had not signed the agreement and France possessed an estimated 82,511 tons of submarines.

155 AUSMM. Mussolini to Cavagnari, 26 June 1935. Direttive Generali DG 8/G1.

156 Carte Capponi. N.400, Capponi to Maristat, 10 May 1935: N. 389, Capponi to Maristat, 18 June 1935: Patto navale anglo–germanico maggio 1935. Visita captain Wassner, 10 July 1935; nota, 27 July 1935: 'Interviste e colloqui'. See also Vittetti to Grandi, 7 June 1935: *DDI* 8th series vol. I no. 353, pp. 359–60.

157 Marginal addendum to Rotti to Cavagnari, 23 May 1935; *cit.* Reynolds M. Salerno, The Mediterranean Triangle: Britain, France, Italy and the Origins of the Second World War, 1935–40, PhD Yale University 1997, p. 69.

158 AUSMM. N. 342/U.T., Cavagnari to Foreign Ministry, 15 June 1935. Cartelle Numerate b.3188/f. 3. This document makes no mention of the possibility that the Anglo–German naval agreement might trigger an increase in French naval building, unlike the letter from Cavagnari to the Foreign Ministry also of 15 June 1935 cited in Mallett, Italian Naval Policy, p. 48.

159 Mussolini to Cerruti, Grandi etc., 14 June 1935. *DDI* 8th series vol. I, no. 376, p. 388.

160 AUSMM. Promemoria per S.E. Il Capo del Governo: Considerazioni sull'accordo navale anglo-tedesco, 23 June 1935. Cartelle Numerate b.3188/f. 3. For Cavagnari, not losing touch with France translated into a technical issue which he believed to be of considerable importance, namely adhering to the French proposal that respective countries' naval programmes should be publicly announced each year, thereby allowing Italy to escape from earlier sterile discussions about parity and giving all sides a considerable degree of latitude, and not adopting the British proposal the programmes should be declared for a six-year period, which could 'crystallise a period of inferiority' for far too long.

161 Carte Capponi. N.592, Capponi to Maristat, 25 June 1935. 'Rapporti Londra'.

162 AUSMM. Promemoria sugli eventuali accordi navali pel 'Piano C'. [Vanutelli], 3 July 1935. Direttive Generali DG 1/D6.

163 AUSMM. 'Piano C'. (Situazioni speciali), 1 July 1935. Direttive Generali DG 1/D6.

164 AUSMM. N.167, Cavagnari to Colonial Ministry, 3 July 1935. Direttive Generali DG 0/N3.

165 Mussolini to Cerruti, 10 July 1935; *DDI* 8th series vol. I, no. 521, p. 547.

166 AUSMM. Mussolini to Cavagnari, 2 August 1935. Direttive Generali DG 8/G1.

167 AUSMM. Nota da tenere in evidenza in caso di applicazione del documento 'L.G. no.1' per il piano 'B', 5 August 1935. Direttive Generali DG 0/E2.

168 AUSMM. Processo verbale della riunione del 13 agosto 1935, p. 6. Direttive Generali DG 8/G1. The record of this meeting is not included in Biagini and Gionfrida, *Lo Stato Maggiore Generale*.

169 *Ibid.*, p. 11.
170 *Ibid.*, pp.12, 14. In the light of what was to happen in June 1940, it is interesting to note that the Navy recorded that instructions had been given to merchant navy captains as to what to do in the event of war breaking out. These instructions, which had existed for some time, were to head for Italy if time allowed or to go into neutral ports.
171 Carte Capponi. N.18, Capponi to Marina, 13 August 1935. 'Addetto Navale a Londra: Rapporti'.
172 Carte Capponi. N.1153, Situazione aeronautica inglese in relazione alla questione abissina, 16 August 1935. 'Londra – Embassy File'.
173 AUSMM. Piano B: Dislocazione iniziale ed impiego del naviglio di superficie, 20 August 1935. Direttive Generali DG 0/E2.
174 AUSMM. Dislocazione iniziale delle forze di superficie: Confronto fra una dislocazione preponderante ad Augusta ed una preponderante a Taranto, 27 August 1935. Direttive Generali DG 0/E2.
175 AUSMM. N. 244, Castagna (Ufficio Piani) to Ufficio di Stato Maggiore della Regia Aeronautica, 22 August 1935. Direttive Generali DG 2/A7.
176 AUSMM. Riunione del 26 agosto 1935. Direttive Generali DG 2/A7.
177 AUSMM. Conversazione fra l'amm. Pini ed il gen. Pinna, 28 August 1935. Direttive Generali DG 2/A7.
178 AUSMM. Conferenza degli ammiragli, 3 September 1935. Direttive Generali DG8/G1.
179 AUSMM. N. 284, Piano B.= Obbiettivi, 6 September 1935. Direttive Generali DG 0/M10.
180 AUSMM. N.297, Ordine generale di operazione No. 1 Op. N. A., 12 September 1935. Direttive Generali DG-1/XVI/(1)b.See also Fortunato Minniti, '"Il nemico vero". Gli obbiettivi dei piani di operazione contro la Gran Bretagna nel contesto etiopico (maggio 1935–maggio 1936)', *Storia Contemporanea* anno XXVI n. 4, August 1995, pp. 581–2.
181 Mallett, Italian Naval Policy, pp. 61–2.
182 AUSMM. Esame della situazione, 20 September 1935. Direttive Generali DG 8/G1.
183 Giuseppe Bottai, *Diario 1935–1944* (Milan: Rizzoli, 2001), p. 60 (19 November 1935).
184 Suvich to Mussolini, 15 September 1935; Suvich to Mussolini, 16 September 1935; Aloisi to Mussolini, 19 September 1935; Colloquio Mussolini–Drummond, 23 September 1935; Grandi to Mussolini, 30 September 1935. *DDI* 8th series vol. II nos. 120, 125, 140, 166, 209, pp. 103–6, 111–2, 130, 149, 192–5. Mori, *Mussolini e la conquista dell'Etiopia*, pp. 97–101.
185 AUSMM. Cavagnari to all naval departments, 9 October 1935. Direttive Generali DG 1.
186 AUSMM. Promemoria sulle possibilità d'azione britannica nel Mediterraneo, 12 October 1935. Direttive Generali DG 1/D7.
187 AUSMM. N.3, Direttive provvisorie di massima per l'impianto dei mezzi aerei, in queste prime operazioni della campagna, 20 September 1935. Direttive Generali DG 8/C4.

188 AUSMM. Questioni trattate allo S.M. della Regia Aeronautica, 11 October 1935. Direttive Generali DG 0/M1.

189 AUSMM. N.16475, Cavagnari to Valle, 12 October 1935. Direttive Generali DG 0/D1.

190 AUSMM. N.41429, Valle to Pini, 23 October 1935. Direttive Generali DG 0/D1.

191 AUSMM. N.13290, Valle to Pini, 26 October 1935. Direttive Generali DG 0/D1.

192 AUSMM. Mussolini to Baistrocchi, Cavagnari, Valle and Dallolio, 19 October 1935. Cartelle Numerate b.2684. *Contra* Salerno, there is no direct evidence that Cavagnari's programme was the result of his having 'panicked' at the prospect of war with Great Britain: Salerno, The Mediterranean Triangle, p. 28.

193 AUSMM. N.1266, Direzione generale delle costruzione navali e meccaniche to Marina, 24 October 1935; N. 38001, Direzioni generali armi ed armamenti navali, 26 October 1935. Cartelle Numerate b.2684.

194 AUSMM. N.669 U.T., Promemoria per S.E. il Capo del Governo: Considerazioni circa la necessità di aumentare la flotta [Cavagnari], 24 October 1935, p. 2. Cartelle Numerate b.2684.

195 *Ibid.*, p. 4.

196 AUSMM. Cavagnari to Presidente del comitato progetti navali, 12 May 1935. Cartelle Numerate b.2675/f. 5.

197 Cernuschi, *Domenico Cavagnaro*, pp. 97–101; Mallett, Italian Naval Policy and Planning, pp. 74–5; Fortunato Minniti, 'Il problema degli armamenti nella preparazione militare italiana dal 1935 al 1943', *Storia Contemporanea* anno X no. 1, February 1987, pp. 42–4.

198 Bernotti, *Cinquant'anni*, p. 234.

199 Valle to Badoglio, 12 January 1935: Rochat, *Militari e politici*, pp. 379–81 (italics in original).

200 Seduta del 14 gennaio 1935; Biagini and Gionfrida, *Lo stato maggiore generale*, pp. 326–36.

201 Badoglio to Mussolini, 19 January 1935; Rochat, *Militari e politici*, pp. 381–9 (quos., pp. 387, 389).

202 Valle to Badoglio, 22 January 1935; Rochat, *Militari e politici*, p. 390. Rochat suggests that Badoglio may have magnified the difficulties, such as the need for massive amounts of wood to build the huts the force would need (in the event it used tents), as a means of himself taking over control of a war which De Bono was manifestly unqualified to direct: *ibid.*, pp. 121–2.

203 De Bono to ? Badoglio, 21 January 1935; *DDI* 7th series vol. XVI, no. 477, p. 501. ACS. N.2, De Bono to Badoglio, 22 January 1935 [quotation]. Carte Badoglio 49/6 scat. 3/n. 133.

204 AUSSME. Promemoria per S.E. il Capo del Governo: per l'Africa Orientale, 31 January 1935. Rep. H-9 racc. 11/ f. 2.

205 AUSSME. Promemoria: trasporti effettuati dai Ministeri dell'Aeronautica e delle Colonie per l'Africa Orientale, 31 January 1935. Rep. H-9 racc. 1/f. 2.

206 De Bono Diary, 13 February 1935: Rochat, *Military e politici*, p. 126.

207 Seduta del 5 febbraio 1935; Biagini and Gionfrida, *Lo stato maggiore generale*, pp. 338–42.
208 Seduta del 15 febbraio 1935; *ibid.*, pp. 353–5.
209 AMR. Pariani to Soddu, 10 February 1935; Pariani to Berti, 21 February 1935; Pariani to Baistrocchi, 27 February 1935 [quotation]. Quaderni Pariani III, IV, V.
210 Mussolini to De Bono, 13 February 1935; *cit.*, Fortunato Minniti, 'Oltre Adua. Lo sviluppo e la scelta della strategia operativa per la guerra contro l'Etiopia', *Società di storia militare* Quaderno 1993, p. 120.
211 Rochat, *Militari e politici*, pp. 342–4.
212 AUSSME. Ago to Baistrocchi, 6 February 1935; Bonzani to Baistrocchi, 6 February 1935; Grazioli to Baistrocchi, 7 February 1935; Amantea to Baistrocchi, 7 February 1935; Porrio to Baistrocchi, 8 February 1935 [Porrio put Zoppi first in his list]. Rep. H-5 racc. 54.
213 Seduta del 8 febbraio 1935; Biagini and Gionfrida, *Lo stato maggiore generale*, pp. 345–51.
214 Rodolfo Graziani, *Fronte Sud* (Milan: Mondadori, 1938), p. 31.
215 Baistrocchi to Graziani, 26 March 1935: Rochat, *Militari e politici*, pp. 413–4.
216 A contemporaneous estimate for Baistrocchi put the mobilisable Abyssinian force at between 500,000 and 680,000, one third of which could be mobilised on the northern and southern frontiers in 20 days and the whole in 60 days. AUSSME. 'Dati riassuntivi sulla situazione militare in genere dell'Etiopia', 5 March 1935. Rep. H-9 racc. 1/f. 2.
217 Badoglio to Mussolini, 6 March 1935: Rochat, *Militari e politici*, p. 396.
218 *Ibid.*, p. 404.
219 Mussolini to De Bono, 8 March 1935; Rochat, *Militari e politici*, pp. 407–8.
220 Mussolini's decision dramatically to increase the numbers of troops may have been influenced by the views of general Ezio Babbini, with whom he was in discussions and who, while pessimistic about some of the battle scenarios being touted about and the potential of air power necessarily to influence the ground combat, stressed Baratieri's mistake in attacking on 1 March 1896 without enough troops and suggested that six and not three white divisions were necessary. AUSSME. Babbini to Pariani, 6 February 1935. Rep. H-9 racc. 1/f. 2.
221 Badoglio to Mussolini, 12 March 1935; Rochat, *Militari e politici*, pp. 407–11.
222 AUSSME. Relazione sulla missione compiuta in Eritrea dal 9 al 16 marzo XIII [1935]. Rep. H-5 racc. 54.
223 AUSSME. Alla persona de S. E. il Capo del Governo: Africa Orientale–Competenze Comandi, 13 October 1935 [? April 1935]. Rep. L-13 racc. 69/C. 50. Rochat's dating of the memorandum to April 1935 must be correct; aside from the internal textual references which point to the earlier date, the original memorandum (which Rochat was apparently unable to consult), which is type-written, is dated and signed by a hand which is not Baistrocchi's: Rochat, *Military e politici*, pp. 129–31. The memorandum is accurately reproduced in Emilio Canevari, *La guerra italiana*, vol. I, pp. 400–2.
224 Mussolini to De Bono, 31 May 1935: Rochat, *Militari e politici*, p. 161.

225 Sedute del 8 & 9 maggio 1935; Biagini and Gionfrida, *Lo stato maggiore generale*, pp. 359–71.

226 Luigi Emilio Longo, *La campagna Italo-Etiopica*, vol. I, pp. 66–7; vol. II, p. 159.

227 ACS. N. 671, Programma di massima dei provvedimenti necessari per l'ulteriore sviluppo della organizzazione militare della Somalia, 31 January 1935, p. 20. Carte Graziani scat. 12.

228 ACS. N.1, Graziani to Frusci, 16 March 1935. Carte Graziani scat. 12.

229 ACS. T.2557 Mussolini to De Bono/Graziani, [arrived] 25 March 1935. Carte Graziani scat. 12.

230 ACS. N.3, Graziani to Frusci/De Bono, 20 March 1935. Carte Graziani scat. 12. Rochat, *Militari e politici*, p. 185.

231 Badoglio to Mussolini, 29 April 1935; Pariani to Baistrocchi, 15 June 1935. Rochat, *Militari e politici*, pp. 423–5, 427–8.

232 Rochat, *Militari e politici*, pp. 187–94.

233 ACS. Graziani to Lessona, 15 May 1935 [unsent]. Carte Graziani scat. 21.

234 ACS. Graziani to De Bono, 13 June 1935. Carte Graziani scat. 13.

235 De Bono to Graziani, 23 June 1935; Rochat, *Militari e politici*, pp. 447–8.

236 De Bono Diary, 28 July 1935; *cit.* Minniti, 'Oltre Adua', p. 128.

237 Badoglio to Mussolini, 9 July 1935; Rochat, *Militari e politici*, pp. 457–9.

238 Biastrocchi to Mussolini, 13 August 1935; Rochat, *Militari e politici*, pp. 468–9. Baistrocchi, like predecessors such as Gazzera but unlike Badoglio, under-rated or overlooked the role of air power as a factor in battle forty years after Adua.

239 ACS. Memoria segreta sull'organizzazione militare della Somalia, 11 July 1935, p. 2. Carte Graziani scat. 13.

240 *Ibid.*, p. 11.

241 ACS . Graziani to De Bono, 12 July 1935. Carte Badoglio 48/6 scat. 3/n. 189 all.

242 Baistrocchi to Graziani, 17 July 1935; Rochat, *Militari e politici*, p. 205. The terminology – *eventuale sbocco controffensivo* – is ambiguous, as '*eventuale*' means either 'possible', 'eventual' or 'future', tending towards the former.

243 Badoglio to Lessona, 1 August 1935; Rochat, *Militari e politici*, p. 466.

244 AUSMM. Processo verbale della riunione del 13 agosto 1935, p. 7. Direttive Generali DG 8/G1. How Valle calculated this figure is not known: on 30 June 1935 the air force's official strength was 1,506 aircraft, of which 537 were land fighters (plus 68 naval fighters) and 273 land bombers (plus 135 naval bombers), while a year later it possessed a total of 1,836 aircraft against a forecast twelve months previously of 2,593. ASAM, Relazione Io semestre 1 935 tabella 8; Relazioni Io semestre 1 936 tabella 8. Relazioni per il CSM Generale cart. 6, 7.

245 Processo verbale . . . 13 agosto, p. 13. *Loc. cit.*

246 Badoglio to Mussolini, 14 August 1935; Rochat, *Militari e politici*, p. 227.

247 AUSSME. N.3270, Baistrocchi to Comandanti delle divisioni dell'esercito mobilitate [e] delle divisioni Camicie Nere Mobilitate, 6 July 1935. Rep. L-13 racc. 69/c. 59.

248 AUSSME. Promemoria per S.E. il Capo del Governo: Misure in caso di ostilità inglese, 15 August 1935. Rep. H-9 racc. 1/t. 2.

249 AMR. Promemoria per S. E. Baistrocchi, 7 August 1935. Quaderni Pariani IX.

250 AMR. Pariani to Angioy, 13 August 1935; Pariani to Roatta, 25 September 1935; Pariani to Angioy, 30 September 1935; Pariani to Roatta, 17 October 1935. Quaderni Pariani IX, X.

251 Mussolini to De Bono, 26 June 1935; *cit.* Minniti, 'Oltre Adua', p. 132. Mussolini to De Bono, 21 August 1935; *DDI* 8th series vol. 1, no. 788, p. 806.

252 De Bono Diary, 3 September 1935; *cit.* Minniti, 'Oltre Adua', p. 133.

253 Mussolini to De Bono, 10 September 1935; *DDI* 8th series vol. II, no. 79, p. 69.

254 Badoglio to Mussolini, [?] September 1935; F. Rossi, *Mussolini e lo stato maggiore* (Rome: Tipografia Regionale, 1951), p. 26.

255 AUSSME. Baistrocchi to Badoglio, 27 September 1935 [underlining in original]. Rep. H-9 racc. 1/f. 2.

256 Carte Capponi. N.509, Indizi e voci concernante l'attuale situazione Italo–Inglese, 23 September 1935, p. 2. 'Londra – Embassy File'.

257 AUSSME. Badoglio to Baistrocchi, 29 September 1935. Rep. H-9 racc. 1/f. 2.

258 Mussolini to De Bono, 29 September 1935; *DDI* 8th series vol. II, no. 202, p. 183.

259 De Bono Diary, 30 September 1935; *cit.* Rochat, *Militari e politici*, p. 219 fn. 13.

260 AUSSME. Promemoria per S.E. il capo del Governo: Piano offensivo in A.O., 1 October 1935. Rep. L-13 racc. 69/C. 47.

261 'Bolletino del 18 aprile 1935': Ezio Cecchini, 'Organizzazione, preparazione e supporto logistico della campagna 1935–1936 in Africa Orientale', *Memorie Storiche Militari* 1979, p.31.

262 'Direttive per l'organizzazione del territorio conquistato in vista di un nuovo sbalzo offensivo nel territorio nemico', 8 October 1935; *cit.* Longo, *La campagna Italo–Etiopica* vol. I, p. 162.

263 Mori, *Mussolini e la conquista dell'Etiopia*, p. 163.

264 Suvich to Mussolini, 6 October 1935; *DDI* 8th series vol. II no. 265, pp. 250–1.

265 Mori, *Mussolini e la conquista dell'Etiopia*, pp. 126–7, 130–1.

266 Mussolini to Baistrocchi, Cavagnari, Valle & Dallolio, 19 October 1935; Longo, *La campagna italo-etiopica* vol. II, pp. 212–4.

267 Attolico to Mussolini, 7 October 1935; Attolico to Mussolini, 12 October 1935; Vernarecci di Fossombrone to Jacomini, 11 November 1935. *DDI* 8th series vol. II nos. 281, 317, 608, pp. 263–4, 294–5, 588–91.

268 Cerruti to Mussolini, 4 October 1935; Cerruti to Mussolini, 4 October 1935; Aloisi to Mussolini, 5 October 1935; Cerruti to Mussolini, 23 October 1935 & 5 November 1935; Colloquio Mussolini–Drummond, 5 November 1935. *DDI* 8th series vol. II nos. 239, 241, 252, 464, 562, pp. 226–7, 228, 236–7, 438, 538–40.

269 Suvich to Mussolini, 11 October 1935; *DDI* 8th series vol. II no. 316, p. 294.

270 Mussolini to De Bono, 20 October 1935; *DDI* 8th series vol. II no. 437, pp. 411–12.

271 Suvich to Aloisi, 28 October 1935; *DDI* 8th series vol. II no. 506, p. 473.

272 Cerruti to Mussolini, 5 October 1935; Cerruti to Mussolini 18 October 1935: *DDI* 8th series vol. II nos. 255, 400, pp. 239, 378–9. ASMAE: To.238041, Esteri to Marina (Gabinetto) etc., 23 October 1935. Affari Politici: Francia b.14/f. 2.

273 Mussolini to Cerruti, 26 October 1935; *DDI* 8th series vol. II no. 493, p. 461.

274 Grandi to Mussolini, 31 October 1935; *DDI* 8th series vol. II no. 526, pp. 502–4.

275 ASMAE. T.4252/1700, Attolico to Mussolini, 21 November 1935. Affari Politici: Francia b.16/f. 1–2.

276 'Ispezioni a comandi, truppe e servizi in Eritrea', 3 November 1935; Longo, *La campagna Italo-Etiopica* vol. II, pp. 245–66

277 Baistrocchi to Mussolini, 27 October 1935; Baistrocchi to Mussolini 28 October 1935: *ibid.* vol. II, pp. 267, 268–9.

278 De Bono to Mussolini, 17 November 1935; *ibid.* vol. II, pp. 300–1.

279 Cerruti to Mussolini, 11 December 1935; Colloquio Suvich–Chambrun, 12 December 1935; Suvich to Mussolini, 14 December 1935. *DDI* 8th series vol. II nos. 839, 842, 856, pp. 822–3, 824–6, 838–41.

280 'Inaugurazione di Pontinia', 18 December 1935; *OO* XXVII, pp. 202–3. Mori believes that the speech, news of which reached London by about 1, p.m., influenced Baldwin's decision later that day to ask for Hoare's resignation: Mori, *Mussolini e la conquista dell'Etiopia*, p. 223–4.

281 Grandi to Mussolini, 26 December 1935; *DDI* 8th series vol. II no. 918, pp. 905–10.

282 ASMAE. N.988S, Barbasetti to War Ministry, 21 December 1935; Affari Politici: Francia b.20/f. 1. The despatch has underlinings characteristic of Mussolini but does not have his '*visto*'.

283 Barbasetti to War Ministry, 26 December 1935; *DDI* 8th series vol. II no. 926 all., p. 919.

6 WARS, ARMS AND THE AXIS, 1936–1937

1 Cerruti to Ciano, 8 January 1937; *DDI* 8th series vol. VI no. 14, pp. 17–18.

2 Conversation with the Führer, 24 October 1936; M. Muggeridge (ed.), *Ciano's Diplomatic Papers* (London: Odhams, 1948), pp. 58–9.

3 Attolico to Ciano, 30 September 1936; *DDI* 8th series vol. V no. 134, pp. 144–5.

4 Mussolini to Grandi, 11 March 1936; Mussolini to Cerruti, 6 April 1936; Magistrati to Ciano, 2 December 1936. *DDI* 8th series vol. III nos. 435, 599, pp. 493, 661; vol. V no. 532, pp. 591–2.

5 R. H. Whealey, 'Mussolini's Ideological Diplomacy. An Unpublished Document', *Journal of Modern History* vol. 39 no. 4, December 1967, p. 435.

6 Hassell to Foreign Ministry, 22 February 1936. *DGFP* series C vol. IV no. 579, pp. 1172–7.

7 Attolico to Mussolini, 20 February 1936; Attolico to Mussolini, 26 February 1936. *DDI* 8th series vol. III nos. 261, 322, pp. 335–7, 383–5. For warnings that the question was 'on the table', see Cerruti to Mussolini, 15 January 1936; Attolico to Mussolini, 27 January 1936; Suvich to Mussolini, 29 January 1936; Cerruti to Mussolini, 4 February 1936; Attolico to Mussolini, 19 February 1936; *DDI* 8th series vol. III nos. 59, 124, 131, 172, 253, pp. 75–80, 159–60, 167–9, 209–11, 325–8.

8 Attolico to Mussolini, 17 March 1936; Cerruti to Mussolini, 7 March 1936. *DDI* 8th series vol. III nos. 479, 386, pp. 536–7, 447.

9 Attolico to Ciano, 18 November 1936; *DDI* 8th series vol. V no. 441, p. 491.

10 ASMAE. Appunto per il Duce [Ciano], 14 June 1937; n.2890/924, Attolico to Ciano, 16 June 1937. Affari Politici: Germania b.41/f. 3.

11 ASMAE. To.5626/1692, Attolico to Ciano, 9 December1936 Att: I problemi della politica interna della Germania (31 October 1936); Affari Politici: Germania b.32/f. 2. N.2940/946, Attolico to Ciano, 18 June 1937; Affari Politici: Germania b.37/f. 1. Blomberg's remark was underlined by Mussolini.

12 Marras to SIM, 2 December 1936; cit. Longo, *L'attività degli addetti militari italiani*, p. 273.

13 Attolico to Ciano, 13 December1936; Attolico to Ciano, 14 December 1936; *DDI* 8th series vol. V nos. 591, 592, pp. 662–3, 663.

14 Mallett, *Mussolini and the Origins of the Second World War*, pp. 108–9, 124–5.

15 Valle to Mussolini: Relazione sulla missione svolta in Germania dal 24 al 28.VI.XIV [1936]; *DDI* 8th series vol. V App. No. 1, pp. 785–9 [quo., p. 787].

16 ASMAE. N.3811/1310, Magistrati to War Ministry, 21 September 1936. Affari Politici: Germania b.33/f. 2. The passage quoted was underlined by Mussolini.

17 ASMAE. T.3449/1206, Magistrati to Ministry of Foreign Affairs, 26 August 1936; To.4243/1485, Attolico to Ministry of Foreign Affairs, 17 October 1936. Affari Politici: Germania b.33/f. 2.

18 Colonna to Ciano, 6 September 1936; *DDI* 8th series vol. V no. 22, pp. 18–19.

19 Attolico to Ciano, 15 September 1936; *DDI* 8th series vol. V no. 65, pp. 63–6.

20 ASMAE. Arone di Valentino to Ciano, 17 December 1936; *DDI* 8th series vol. V no. 619, pp. 695–6. N.3233/1271, Arone di Valentino to Ciano, 18 December 1936; Affari Politici: Germania b.35/f. 2. The latter despatch was read by Mussolini and the evidence underlined by him.

21 ASMAE. To.5215/1750, Attolico to Ciano, 23 December 1936; Affari Politici: Germania b.34/f. 1. The despatch was read by Mussolini and the passage on likely conflict underlined by him.

22 Dichiarazione Goering nell colloquio con Mussolini, 15 January 1937; Attolico to Ciano, 30 January 1937 att: Schmidt's notes of colloquio Mussolini–Goering 23 January 1937; Renzetti to Attolico, 22 March 1937. *DDI* 8th series vol. VI nos. 60, 109, 346, pp. 74, 133–4 [quo.], 418–9.

23 ASMAE. N.316, Attolico to Ciano, 8 December 1937. Ufficio Coordina-
    mento UC 3 #1119 b.2/ f. 3.
24 Bottai, *Diario*, 4 September 1937, 31 October 1937, p. 120.
25 UKNA. N.352, Japanese Ambassador Rome to Foreign Ministry Tokyo, 3
    December 1937. HW 12/222/070161.
26 Hassell to Foreign Ministry, 7 January 1936; *DGFP* series C vol. IV no. 485,
    pp. 975–6. Colloquio Suvich–von Hassell, 17 February 1936; *DDI* 8th series
    vol. III no. 241, p. 304.
27 HNA. Memo about talks with the Duce on June 12, 1936; Foreign Ministry
    Archives K. 100. See also Ciano to Attolico, 18 June 1936; *DDI* 8th series
    vol. IV no. 514, p. 574.
28 Colloquio Mussolini–von Hassell, 11 July 1936; DDI 8th series vol. IV no.
    503, pp. 564–5. ASMAE. N.2856/1020, Attolico to Foreign Ministry, 16 July
    1936. Affari Politici: Germania b.35/f. 3.
29 Dichiarazione Goering nel colloquio con Mussolini, 15 January 1937; *DDI*
    8th series vol. VI no. 60, pp. 74–5.
30 ASMAE. Relazione sui lavori della Commissione di coordinamento della
    economia italiana e germanica, 7 May 1937, p. 3. Affari Politici: Germania
    b.41/f. 1.
31 Hassell to Foreign Ministry, 18 February 1937; Memorandum by Neurath,
    4 May 1937; Hassell to Foreign Ministry, 25 May 1937; *DGFP* series C
    vol. VI nos. 216, 355, 385, pp. 457–61, 727–8, 790. Colloquio Mussolini –
    Ribbentrop, 6 November 1937; *DDI* 8th series vol. VIII no. 523, p. 670.
32 ASMAE. N.6/G, Ferreri to Marina, 8 January 1936; To.201401/17, Mosca
    to London Embassy, 14 January 1936; N.11/G, Ferreri to Marina, 10
    January 1936. Affari Politici: Francia b.20/f. 2, b.20/f. 1.
33 Cerruti to Mussolini, 13 January 1936; DDI 8th series vol. III no. 51,
    pp. 65–70. William I. Shorrock, *From Ally to Enemy*, pp.157–8, 171–2.
34 Cerruti to Mussolini, 21 March 1936 Grandi to Mussolini, 26 March 1936.
    DDI 8th series vol. III nos. 503, 529, pp. 568–9, 596–7.
35 ASMAE. Ferreri to Maristat, 24 April 1936. Affari Politici: Germania b.33/f.
    7.
36 ASMAE. N.564, Barbasetti di Prun to SIM, 20 April 1936. Affari Politici:
    Francia b.20/f. 1.
37 ASMAE. T.1029, Esteri to London Embassy, 4 March 1936; Affari Politici:
    Francia b.20/f. 1. Cerruti to Mussolini, 19 May 1936; Barbasetti to Cerruti,
    16 June 1936; Barbasetti to Badoglio, 14 September 1936; *DDI* 8th series vol.
    IV nos. 80, 294, pp. 86, 341–5; vol. V no. 63, pp. 61–2. The friendly noises
    were still being made as late as March 1938: Longo, *L'attività degli addetti
    militari italiani*, p. 209.
38 Mussolini to Grandi, 5 September 1936; *cit.* Mallett, Italian Naval Policy, pp.
    91–2.
39 ASMAE. N.398/S, Barbasetti to War Ministry, 30 July 1936. Affari Politici:
    Francia b.20/f. 1.
40 Shorrock, *From Ally to Enemy*, p. 190.
41 Colloquio Ciano–Neurath, 21 October 1936; *DDI* 8th series vol. V no. 256,
    p. 287. The English language version erroneously gives 'useless' for 'useful',

reversing the significance of the event: Muggeridge, ed., *Ciano's Diplomatic Papers*, p. 52.

42 Cerruti to Ciano, 9 December 1936, *DDI* 8th series vol. V no. 557, pp. 626–8. Both the quoted passages were underlined by Mussolini.

43 Cerruti to Ciano, 27 January 1937; Grandi to Ciano, 1 April 1937. *DDI* 8th series vol. VI nos. 92, 374, pp. 112–4, 453–4.

44 Shorrock, *From Ally to Enemy*, p. 205.

45 ASMAE. N.1230, Visconti Prasca to SIM, 11 August 1937, p. 8. Affari Politici: Francia b.26/f. 1.

46 ASMAE. N.1227, Visconti Prasca to SIM, 10 August 1937. Affari Politici: Francia b.26/f. 1.

47 ASMAE. T.14669, Foreign Ministry to London Embassy etc., 21 September 1937. Affari Politici: Francia b.27/f. 1–2.

48 ASMAE. Appunto per S.E. l'Ambasciatore [Magistrati], 19 October 1937. Affari Politici: Francia b.26/f. 1–4.

49 ASMAE. To.5502/1777, Attolico to Ministry of Foreign Affairs, 11 November 1937. Affari Politici: Francia b.26/f. 1–4.

50 Shorrock, *From Ally to Enemy*, p. 212.

51 Donosti [Luciolli], *Mussolini e l'Europa*, pp. 49–50.

52 Giordano Bruno Guerri, *Galeazzo Ciano una vita 1903/1944* (Milan: Bompiani, 1979), p. 229.

53 ASMAE. To.6454/128, Attolico to Ministry of Foreign Affairs, 30 January 1937. Affari Politici: Germania b.38/f. 2. See also Attolico to Mussolini, 27 January 1936; *DDI* 8th series vol. III no. 123, p. 158.

54 Attolico to Ciano, 30 January 1937 att: Schmidt's notes on colloquio Mussolini–Goering 23 January 1937; *DDI* 8th series vol. VI no. 109, p. 138.

55 Mallett, *Mussolini and the Origins of the Second World War*, p. 110; Guerri, *Galeazzo Ciano*, p. 254.

56 Colli [Roatta] to U[fficio] S[pagna], 9 February 1937. Ismael Saz and Javier Tusell, *Fascistas en España. La intervencion italiana en la Guerra Civil a traves de los telegramas de la "Missione Militare in Spagna" 15 Diciembre1936– 31 Marzo 1937* (Rome: Consejo Superior de Investigaciones Cientificas Escuela Espanola de Historia y Arqueologia en Roma, 1981) no. 204, p. 132.

57 Colli to US, 19 March 1937, 20 March 1937; *ibid.*, nos. 339, 345, pp. 179–80, 181–3 [quo., p. 182].

58 Quo. Guerri, *Ciano*, p. 256.

59 ASMAE. T.378, Grandi to Mussolini, 17 January 1936; Affari Politici: Francia b.20/f. 2. See also Grandi to Mussolini, 1 January 1936; Grandi to Mussolini, 7 January 1936; Grandi to Mussolini, 9 January 1936; Grandi to Mussolini, 23 January 1936. *DDI* 8th series vol. III nos. 2, 25, 33, 103, pp. 3–5, 31–3, 50–4, 134.

60 Carte Capponi. T.082, Grandi to Esteri, 21 January 1936. 'London Embassy 1935–6'.

61 Attolico to Mussolini, 16 January 1936; *DDI* 8th series vol. III no. 66, pp. 89–90.

62 Grandi to Mussolini, 18 March 1936; *DDI* 8th series vol. III no. 487, pp. 548–9.

63 Lamb, *Mussolini and the British*, p. 166.

64 Discorso di Milano, 1 November 1936; *OO* XXVIII, pp. 70–1.

65 Ciano to Attolico, 24 December 1936; *DDI* 8th series vol. V no. 647, p. 729. Later Attolico reminded Ciano that the Gentleman's Agreement was never considered as anything but an 'armistice': Attolico to Ciano, 25 February 1937; *DDI* 8th series vol. VI no. 210, p. 262.

66 Lamb, *Mussolini and the British*, p. 176.

67 AUSMM. Situazione politica ed apprestimenti militari, 17 April 1937. Direttive Generali DG 1/B1.

68 Egidio Ortona, *Diplomazia di Guerra: Diari 1937–1943* (Bologna: Il Mulino, 1993), p. 38 (6 July 1937).

69 William C. Mills, 'The Chamberlain–Grandi Conversations of July–August 1937 and the Appeasement of Italy', *International History Review* vol. 19 no. 3, August 1997, pp. 594–614.

70 William C. Mills, 'The Nyon Conference: Neville Chamberlain, Anthony Eden, and the Appeasement of Italy in 1937', *International History Review* vol. 15 no. 1, February 1993, pp. 1–22.

71 Conversation with the British Ambassador, 7 October 1936; *Ciano's Diplomatic Papers*, pp. 50–1.

72 Conversation with M. Stoyadinovich, Yugoslav Prime Minister, 11 December 1937; *ibid.*, p. 150.

73 Colloquio Mussolini–Goering, 15 January 1937: *DDI* 8th series vol. VI no. 60, p. 74.

74 Attolico to Ciano, 25 February 1937; *DDI* 8th series vol. VI no. 201, pp. 260–1.

75 Grandi to Mussolini, 8 February 1937; DDI 8th series vol. VI no. 144, p. 182. Grandi to Ciano 11 October 1937, *cit.* Mallett, *Mussolini and the Origins of the Second World War*, p. 149.

76 ASMAE. To. 5002/1644, Attolico to Ciano, 26 October 1937. Affari Politici: Germania b.41/f. 3.

77 AUSSME. To.382/162, Galli to Ministry of Foreign Affairs, 20 February 1936; cipher no. 983, Kiazim to High Command Istanbul, 24 December 1935. Rep. G–29 racc. 113/f. 15.

78 AUSSME. N.207, Mannerini to War Ministry, 9 March 1936; no. 382, Mannerini to War Ministry, 7 May 1936. Rep. G-29 racc. 113/f. 15. See also Longo, *L'attività degli addetti militari italiani*, pp. 535–7.

79 Carte Capponi. Intervista 14 April 1936. 'Interviste e colloqui'. See Suvich to Mussolini, 10 May 1936; Aloisi to Mussolini, 12 May 1936; *DDI* 8th series vol. IV nos. 5, 19, pp. 5–6, 16–17.

80 Carte Capponi: N.2268/588, Vitetti to Ministry of Foreign Affairs, 8 July 1936. 'Londra 1935–1937'. See also Cerruti to Mussolini, 21 April 1936; Galli to Mussolini, 29 May 1936, Galli to Mussolini, 29 May 1936; Galli to Ciano, 27 July 1936; *DDI* 8th series vol. III no. 723, pp. 767–8; vol. IV nos. 111,136, 600, pp. 129–35, 175–81, 667–8.

81 Galli to Ciano, 7 August 1936; *DDI* 8th series vol. IV no. 698, pp. 766–73.

82 Ciano to De Astis, 7 & 8 January 1937; Galli to Ciano, 20 March 1937; Galli to Ciano, 31 March 1937; *DDI* 8th series vol. VI nos. 19, 25, 308, 365, pp. 23, 30, 367–71, 437–9.

83 AUSSME. Studio N.3, Considerazioni circa l'approvigionamento di guerra dell'impero italiano in Africa, n.d. [after 30 June 1936]. Rep. F–9 racc. 7/f. 4.

84 AUSSME. Promemoria sui vari argomenti posti all'ordine della seduta del 24.2.1936 XIV del Consiglio dell'Esercito, 20 February 1936, p. 6. Rep. F-9 racc. 38/f. 1.

85 *Ibid.*, p. 8.

86 *Ibid.*, p. 10.

87 *Ibid.*, p.12.

88 AUSSME. Argomento XII: Politica in Albania – Relazione di S.E. il Ministro della Marina, February 1936, p. 4. Rep. F-9 racc. 40/ f. 1.

89 AUSSME. Argomento XII: Politica in Albania – Relazione del Ministero dell'Aeronautica, February 1936. Rep. F-9 racc. 40/f. 1.

90 AUSSME. Argomento VII: Nuovo programma di costruzioni del naviglio in tempo di guerra, February 1936. Rep. F-9 racc. 39/f. 1.

91 AUSSME. Ministero delle Communicazioni: Relazione per l'On. Commissione suprema di difesa – Trasporti dei rifornimenti della nazione in guerra, February 1936, pp. 4–5. Rep. F-9 racc. 39/f. 1.

92 *Ibid.*, pp. 9–11.

93 *Ibid.*, p. 21.

94 AUSSME. Argomento VI: Trasporti dei rifornimenti della nazione in guerra – Ente direttivo del traffico–Politica dei trasporti marittimi – Relazione di S.E. il Ministro della Marina, February 1936, p. 3. Rep. F-9 racc. 39/f. 1.

95 AUSSME. Commissione Suprema di Difesa: Verbale della XIII Sessione, seduta del 4 febbraio 1936, p. 25. Rep. F-9 racc. 38/f. 2.

96 *Ibid.*, seduta del 6 febbraio 1936, pp. 31–2.

97 *Ibid.*, pp. 38–41.

98 AUSSME. Preparazione militare terrestre dell'Albania, 15 July 1936. Rep. F-9 racc. 40/f. 1.

99 AMR. Pariani to colonel Pietradaprina, 15 April 1936; Riferimento al no. 35, 18 April 1936. Quaderni Pariani X, pp. 35, 38.

100 AUSSME. Attribuzioni del Capo di Stato Maggiore generale in guerra–Costituzione del suo Ufficio – Preparazione degli ufficiali per lo Stato maggiore generale, 31 December 1936. Rep. F-9 racc. 45/f. 1.

101 Ministero della Difesa, *L'esercito italiano tra la 1a e la 2a Guerra mondiale Novembre 1918–Giugno 1940*, p. 113.

102 AUSSME. Commissione Suprema di Difesa: Verbale della XIV Sessione, seduta del 2 febbraio 1937, pp. 12–21. [Mussolini's quo., p. 19.] Rep. F-9 racc. 42/f. 2.

103 *Ibid.*, seduta del 5 febbraio 1937, p. 30.

104 *Ibid.*, seduta del 8 febbraio 1937, pp. 48, 53.

105 *Ibid.*, seduta del 11 febbraio 1937, pp. 81–7. In 1935 Italy imported 827,828 tons of scrap iron and collected 485,507 tons; in 1936 the figures were respectively 348,339 tons and 632,913 tons, an overall reduction of 332,083 tons.

106 *Ibid.*, seduta del 10 febbraio 1937, pp. 60–2, 63–5.

107 Emilia Chiaravelli, *L'Opera della marina italiana nella guerra italo–etiopica* (Milan: Giuffrè, 1969), p. 24.

108 Tur, *Plancia ammiraglio*, pp. 172–3.

109 Bernotti, *Cinquant'anni*, p. 239.

110 Cit. Ferrante, *Il pensiero strategico navale in Italia*, p. 52.

111 Navy Ministry to Foreign Ministry, 14 August 1935; cit. Bernardi, *Il disarmo navale*, p. 617 fn. 51.

112 AUSMM. Direttive Conferenza Navale 1935, n.d., pp. 1–3. Cartelle Numerate b.2668.

113 AUSMM. Conversazione ammiragli Abrial–Decoux – Raineri-Biscia, 12 November 1935. Cartelle Numerate b.2668.

114 AUSMM. Pini to Cavagnari, 7 December 1935. Cartelle Numerate b.2668.

115 Bernardi, *Il disarmo navale*, pp. 628–39.

116 Grandi to Mussolini, 16 January 1935, 18 January 1935; *DDI* 8th series vol. III nos. 65, 82, pp. 87–8, 107–8.

117 Carte Capponi. Promemoria sulla conversazione svolta il pomeriggio del 12 febbraio 1936 tra l'ammiraglio Robert ed il governatore Carde e l'ammiraglio Raineri, il commandante Margottini ed il commandante Capponi. 'Conferenza Navale Londra 1935–6'.

118 AUSMM. Promemoria, n.d. [21 February 1936]. Cartelle Numerate b.2668.

119 Mussolini to Grandi, 22 February 1936; *DDI* 8th series vol. III no. 274, p. 346.

120 Carte Capponi. Promemoria sulla conversazione svolta il pomeriggio del 24 febbraio 1936 tra la delegazione del Regno Unito . . . e la delegazione Italiana. 'Conferenza Naval Londra 1935–6'.

121 Bernardi, *Il disarmo navale*, pp. 648–50.

122 AUSMM. Promemoria per S.E. il Capo del Governo: Linee fondamentali e principali caratteristiche del Trattato navale di Londra del 1936, 1 April 1936. Cartelle Numerate b.2668. The version published by Bernardi does not bear exact resemblance to this document: Bernardi, *Il disarmo navale*, p. 669.

123 Mazzetti, *La politica militare italiana*, pp. 188–90; Minitti, 'Il problema degli armamenti', pp. 42–4; Mallett, Italian Naval Policy, p. 75.

124 Peter Jackson, 'La perception des réarmaments allemand et italien et la politique navale de 1933–1939', *Révue Historique des Armées* no. 4, 2000, pp. 28–30; Reynolds M. Salerno, 'The French Navy and the Appeasement of Italy, 1937–9', *English Historical Review* vol. 112 no. 445, February 1997, pp. 70–4.

125 Carte Capponi. N.6 G.I/I, Situazione politica francese–Mutuo appoggio franco–inglese, 8 January 1936; N.11 G.3/3, Patto di mutua assistenza navale franco–inglese', 10 January 1936. 'Rapporti Parigi'.

126 Carte Capponi. Capponi to Ferreri, 8 January 1936; Ferreri to Capponi, 13 January 1936. 'Rapporti Parigi'.

127 Carte Capponi. N.58 G.I/I, Risposta francese al memorandum tedesco ed all'occupazione militare della zona renana. Reazioni nei riguardi del conflitto

italo–etiopico, 9 March 1936; N. 61 G.I/I, Note di politica estera, 11 March 1936. 'Rapporti Parigi'.

128 Carte Capponi. N. 122 G.3/3, Conversazioni tra Stati Maggiori francese–inglesie a Londra, 24 April 1934. 'Rapporti Parigi'.

129 Carte Capponi. N. 182 G.I/I, Manifestazione pro-Italia. Celebrazione del 14 luglio, 15 July 1936. 'Rapporti Parigi'.

130 AUSMM. Note su idee strategiche espresse in Francia, 22 February 1936. Direttive Generali DG 10/A10.

131 Carte Capponi. N.87/S, Intesa politico–militare franco–brittanico, 10 January 1936; N.90/S, Atteggiamento inglese questione AO–Apprestimenti bellici e navali, 14 January 1936. 'Ambasciata di Londra'.

132 Carte Capponi. Intervista con S.E. il Capo del Governo dalle ore 18,30 alle ore 18,50 circa [14 April 1936]. 'Interviste e colloqui'.

133 Carte Capponi. [Nota] 14 July 1936. 'Interviste e colloqui'.

134 Mallett, Italian Naval Policy, p. 84.

135 Alberto Santoni, 'La mancata risposta della Regia Marina alle teorie del Douhet: Analisi storica del problema della portaerei in Italia', in Aniello Gentile (ed.), *La figura e l'opera di Giulio Douhet* (Caserta: Società di storia patria di terra di lavoro, 1988), pp. 261–2.

136 AUSMM. Cavagnari to Valle, [–] February 1936. Direttive Generali DG 0/M10.

137 AUSMM. Ordine Operazione Op. N.A. no.1, 8 April 1936. Direttive Generali DG 1/D4.

138 AUSMM. Ordine generale di Operazione no. 1, 10 June 1936. Direttive Generali DG 10/B2.

139 AUSMM. N.1027, Preparazione segreta di basi clandestine per sommergibili in Oceano Indian, 7 May 1936; N.1420, Missione della nave 'Murena', 7 July 1936; N.3248, Missione della nave 'Murena', 13 July 1936. Direttive Generali DG 12/C2.

140 AUSMM. Isola Silhouette–proposta di acquisto, 8 April 1936. Cartelle Numerate b.1727.

141 AUSMM. Situazione delle forze, 22 September 1936. Direttive Generali DG 1/D5 bis.

142 AUSMM. Ipotesi di guerra, 13 December 1936. Direttive Generali DG 1/A1.

143 Carte Capponi. N.132/S, Atteggiamento inglese questione AO, 8 May 1935. 'Rapporti Londra'.

144 Carte Capponi. N.152/S, Esame del bilancio della Marina in luce di una speciale punto di vista, 3 July 1936. 'Rapporti Londra'.

145 AUSMM. Note sul 'Programma Navale', 22 January 1937. Direttive Generali DG 0/C0.

146 AUSMM. Programma 1938–1939, 18 May 1937. Direttive Generali DG 0/C0.

147 AUSMM. N.36, Fine periodo addestrativo Io novembre 1936–31 gennaio 1937; N.203, Fine 2o periodo addestrativo 31 gennaio–31 maggio 1937, 24 May 1937; N.854, Rapporto sul 3o periodo addestrativo–Io giugno–30 settembre 1937, 5 November 1937. Direttive Generali DG-5/A7/A0.

148 AUSMM. N.147, Rifornimento della Nazione in guerra, nell'ipotesi AB, 25 February 1937. Direttive Generali DG 5/C5.

149 AUSMM. Promemoria [24 March 1937]. Direttive Generali DG 1/A1.

150 AUSMM. Situazione politica ed apprestimenti militari, 17 April 1937. Direttive Generali DG 1/B1.

151 AUSMM. Studio circa la preparazione: Argomento 1o-Le forze navali, September 1937. Direttive Generali DG 0/A0.

152 AUSMM. Questioni mediterranee nei rapporti fra Italia e Gran Bretagna, 1 September 1937. Direttive Generali – Studi Politici P2/A8.

153 AUSMM. Considerazione del nostro problema strategico in base alla situazione politica del momento presente, 26 October 1937, pp. 1–4. Direttive Generali – Studi Politici P2/A8.

154 A handwritten addition raised a fourth issue: 'China and colonies(?)'. *Ibid.*, p. 4.

155 *Ibid.*, p. 8.

156 *Ibid.*

157 *Ibid.*, pp. 10–11.

158 AUSMM. Primo Studio per la redazione del documento di guerra N.8 (DG 8), October 1937. Direttive Generali DG 8/A0.

159 F. Bargoni, *L'impegno navale italiano durante la guerra civile spagnola* (Rome: Ufficio Storico della Marina Militare, 1992), pp. 134–5.

160 Mills, 'The Nyon Conference', pp. 1–22.

161 AUSMM. La conferenza mediterranea di Nyon, 12 September 1937. Direttive Generali – Studi Politici P1/A1.

162 AUSMM. Riassunto dell'attività svolta complessivamente dalla delegazione navale italiana a Parigi (25–30 settembre 1937). Direttive Generali – Studi Politici P1/A2.

163 AUSMM. N.3515, Bernotti to Marina: Missione a Biserta (30 Ottobre) in relazione agli accordi di NYON–Parigi, 31 October 1937, p. 5. Direttive Generali – Studi Politici P1/A3.

164 AUSMM. Manovre navali tedesche, September 1937. Cartelle Numerate b.2704/f. 2.

165 AUSMM. N.1876, Cavagnari to Badoglio: Progetti operativi, 18 November 1937. Cartelle Numerate b.2688.

166 AUSMM. N.3453, Badoglio to Valle, Cavagnari, Pariani, 29 November 1937. Direttive Generali DG 0/M1.

167 Ferrari, 'Dalla divisione ternaria alla binaria', pp. 52–5; *L'esercito italiano tra la 1a e la 2a guerra mondiale*, pp. 110–11.

168 Montanari, 'Il "Progetto A. O." e i suoi sviluppi', pp. 718–23. A month later SIM estimated that there were a maximum of 30,000 British and 13,000 Egyptian troops in Egypt, together with somewhere between 200 and 900 tanks and 829 land-based aircraft: Egitto e territori contermini all'Etiopia: Situazione militare all'1 maggio 1936, pp. 2, 6, 25. AUSSME Rep. H-3 racc. 40/f. 1.

169 Minitti, '"Il nemico vero"', pp. 594–6.

170 Seduta del 5 novembre 1936; Biagini and Gionfrida, *Lo stato maggiore generale*, pp. 373–4.

171 AMR. Pariani to genl. Rose, 18 November 1935. Quaderni Pariani XV, p. 37.
172 Seduta del 17 dicembre 1937; Biagini and Gionfrida, *Lo Stato Maggiore Generale*, pp. 378–82 [quo., p. 380].
173 AUSSME. N.9808, Graziani to Minister of Colonies, 22 December 1936. Rep. F-9 racc. 45/f. 6.
174 Baistrocchi to Mussolini, 28 January 1936; quo. De Biase, *Aquila d'Oro*, p. 398.
175 Sweet, *Iron Arm*, pp. 109–15, 123–4; Lucio Ceva and Andrea Curami, *La meccanizzazione dell'esercito fino al 1943* (Rome: Ufficio Storico dell Esercito, 1989) vol. I, p. 233.
176 AUSSME. Sintesi degli argomenti trattati da S.E. il Sottosegretario di Stato nella riunione del 4 luglio 1936. Rep. H-10 racc. 1/f. 5.
177 AUSSME. Riunione tenuta da S.E. il Sottosegretario di Stato il 24 luglio 1936. Rep. H-10 racc. 1/f. 10.
178 AMR. Pariani to gen. Bancale, 20 January 1936. Quaderni Pariani XI, p. 50.
179 AMR. Pariani to gen. Gambelli, 10 March 1936; Pariani to gen. Bancale, 1 April 1936. Quaderni Pariani X, pp. 19, 25.
180 AMR. Pariani to gen. Gambelli, 18 June 1936. Quaderni Pariani XI, p. 8.
181 AUSSME. E.Q.G.U.–Dichiarazioni riassuntive e conclusive di S.E. Baistrocchi, 30 March 1936, pp. 3, 10. Rep. L-13 racc. 69/c. 60.
182 *Ibid.*, p. 12.
183 AUSSME. Riunione tenuta da S.E. il Sottosegretario di Stato il 24 luglio 1936. Rep. H-10 racc. 1/10.
184 AUSSME. Promemoria per Il Duce: Progetto motorizzazione, 15 September 1936. Rep. L-13 racc. 69/C. 57. Mazzetti, *La politica militare italiana*, pp. 197–9.
185 AUSSME. Baistrocchi to Mussolini, 18 September 1936. Rep. L-13 racc. 69/b.35.
186 AMR. Pariani to Rosi, 14 November 1936. Quaderni Pariani XV, p. 23.
187 AMR. Pariani to Sorice, 11 November 1936. Quaderni Pariani XV, p. 14.
188 AUSSME. Promemoria per S.E. il Capo del Governo circa le Grandi Unità mobilitabili, 18 November 1936. Rep. H-9 racc. 1/c. 2.
189 Bottai, *Diario*, 31 October 1936, p. 114.
190 AMR. Pariani to Rosi, 9 February 1937. Quaderni Pariani XVII, pp. 35–7.
191 AUSSME. N.10 O.D.G.: Organizzazione delle terre italiane d'oltremare, January 1937, p. 7. Rep. F-9 racc. 45/f. 4.
192 AMR. Pariani to Rosi, 28 February 1937. Quaderni Pariani XVIII, p. 12. Sedute del 22 gennaio 1937, 26 febbraio 1937: Biagini and Gionfrida, *Lo Stato Maggiore Generale*, pp. 383–403.
193 ASAM. N.999, Situazione politica ed apprestimenti militari, 24 April 1937. OP1.4. The defence of Pantelleria was discussed by the chiefs of staff on 11 June 1937: Biagini and Gionfrida, *Lo Stato Maggiore Generale*, pp. 413–7.
194 Alberto Rovighi and Filippo Stefani, *La partecipazione italiana alla Guerra Civile Spagnola (1936–1939)* (Rome: Ufficio Storico dello Stato Maggiore

dell'Esercito, 1992–3), vol. I *Testo*, p. 314; Ceva and Curami, *La meccaniz-zazzione dell'esercito fino al 1943*, vol. I, pp. 201, 203, 206, 208.

195 AMR. Manovre Veneto Agosto 1937. Quaderni Pariani XXII, pp. 1–2. Sweet, *Iron Arm*, pp. 124–6, 128.

196 AMR. Pariani to Rosi, 3 November 1937; Pariani to Sorice, 8 November 1937. Quaderni Pariani XXI, pp. 24, 30. An 'autotransportable' division did not have its own trucks to move troops but did have motorised services (artillery etc.) instead of using horses.

197 Resoconto stenografico sulla riunione di generali del 22 Nov. 1937, presedi-uta dal Sottosegretario di Stato e Capo di Stato Maggiore dell'Esercito Gen.Pariani, relative a la costituzione della divisione binaria e ad altri argo-menti di carattere organico; *L'Esercito italiano tra la 1a e la 2a Guerra mondiale*, p. 244.

198 *Ibid.*, pp. 250–1.

199 AUSSME. Appunti presi alla riunione dei commandanti di G.U. tenuta da S. E. il Sottosegretario di Stato il giorno 23 novembre 1937, p. 4. Rep. H-10 racc. 1/ 2.

200 *Ibid.*, p. 6.

201 AUSSME. Appunti presi alla riunione dei commandanti di C.A. e Div. Tenuta da S.E. il Sottosegretario di Stato il giorno 24/XI/937, p. 3. Rep. H-10 racc. 1/ 2.

202 *Ibid.*, p. 7.

203 AMR. Pariani to Sorice, 30 December 1937. Quaderni Pariani XXIII, p. 23.

204 AUSSME. Relazione sui contatti avuti a Berlino giorni 25–28 febbraio 1936, p. 14. Rep. L-13 racc. 44/f. 4.

205 *Ibid.*, p. 9.

206 *Ibid.*, pp. 16–18, 20, 21.

207 *Ibid.*, p. 26.

208 AMR. Pariani to Pietracaprina, 3 April 1936. Quaderni Pariani XXII, p. 26.

209 AUSSME. Relazione sulle conversazioni a S.E., 25 May 1936. Rep. L-13 racc. 44/ f. 4.

210 AUSSME. Sintesi conversazioni 8 luglio 1936, p. 4. Rep. L-13 racc. 44/f. 4.

211 AUSSME. N.1224, Grandi manovre germaniche 1936 [Mancinelli], 28 September 1936, p. 9. Rep. L-10 racc. 8/c. 4.

212 AUSSME. N.1307, Impressioni della missione militare tedesca sulle grandi esercitazioni nel Veneto [Marras], 12 August 1937. Rep. H-3 racc. 11/f. varie II.

213 AUSSME. SIM Sezione 'Zuretti': Missione a Berlino 6–10 giugno 1937, 12 June 1937, pp. 3, 4. Rep. H-3 racc. 33/f. 7.

214 AUSSME. Visita Amico 'C' – 31 agosto–3 settembre 1937. Rep. H-3 racc. 33/f. 7.

215 AUSSME. N.8759, Pariani to Badoglio, 2 November 1936. Rep. H-6 racc. 12/f. I-6/0.

216 AUSSME. Piano 'Z': Direttive per l'impiego delle truppe, 21 April 1936, p. 3. Rep. H-6 racc. 8.

217 AUSSME. PR 9/N (Testo), 15 April 1937; PR 9/N Direttive per l'organizza-zione del servizio informazioni, 30 July 1937. Rep. H-6 racc. 10.

218 HNA. Diary of Events, 19 May 1936. Foreign Ministry Archives K. 100.

219 HNA. Diary of Events, 28 & 29 May, 4 & 8 June; Talk with Pariani on 8 June [1936]. Foreign Ministry Archives K. 100.
220 AMR. Pariani to Gorlier, 13 March 1936; Pariani to Perugi, 12 June 1936. Quaderni Pariani XII, p. 20; XIII, p. 5.
221 AUSSME. Situazione lavori ufficio [SIM]: Studi operativi, 28 May 1937. Rep. H-6 racc. 12/f. I-6.
222 AUSSME. N.836, Guillet to Pariani, 12 May 1936. Rep. H-6 racc. 9/f. J-6, 6.
223 AMR. Pariani to Gorlier, 20 May 1936. Quadeni Pariani XII, p. 48.
224 AUSSME. PR 10/a, 25 June 1936, p. 3. Rep. H-6 racc. 9/f. PR 10/a.
225 AUSSME. PR 10/a-Armata J, 29 July 1936. Rep. H-6 racc. 9/f. 1–7/1.
226 AUSSME. N.1580, Comando Designato d'Armata Bologna to Ministero della Guerra, 16 September 1936; PR 10a-Bologna, 1 October 1936. Rep. H-6 racc. 9/f. 1–7/1.
227 AUSSME. N. 8759, Pariani to Badoglio, 2 November 1936, p. 2. Rep. H-6 racc. 12/f. I–6/0.
228 AMR. Pariani to Gorlier, 5 February 1936. Quaderni Pariani XII, p. 13. See Minniti, 'Piano e ordinamento nella preparazione italiana alla guerra degli anni trenta', pp. 138, 140. Minniti perhaps under-rates the degree to which the new operational concepts drove the planning process; nor were Pariani's war plans very different from those that had traditionally been drawn up by the general staff.
229 AUSSME. N.8759, Pariani to Badoglio, 2 November 1936, p. 3. *Loc. cit.*
230 Seduta del 5 novembre 1936; Biagini and Gionfrida, *Lo Stato Maggiore Generale*, pp. 373–5 [quo., p. 375].
231 Seduta del 17 dicembre 1936; *ibid.*, pp. 377–82.
232 AUSSME. Comando del Corpo di Stato Maggiore: Situazione lavori d'ufficio, 28 May 1937. Rep. H-6 racc. 12/f. I–6/0.
233 AMR. Pariani to Rosi, 2 July 1937; Pariani to Soddu, 4 December 1937; Pariani to Rosi, 9 February 1937. Quaderni Pariani XIX, p. 22; XXII, p. 27, XVII, p. 35.
234 Seduta del 2 dicembre 1937; Biagini and Gionfrida, *Lo Stato Maggiore Generale*, pp. 420–3.
235 D'Avanzo, *Ali e poltrone*, pp. 205–7.
236 *Ibid.*, pp. 210, 223, 877–9; Pelliccia, *Valle*, p. 120.
237 D'Avanzo, *Ali e poltrone*, pp. 214–5, 222–3; Pelliccia, *Valle*, pp. 115, 117.
238 Alegi, 'Balbo e il riarmo clandestino tedesco', pp. 305–17.
239 AUSSME. N.35034, Valle to Badoglio: Relazione a S.E. il Capo del Governo sulla missione svolta in Germania dal 24 al 28.VI.XIV [1936], p. 5. Rep. L–8 racc. 11/1.
240 *Ibid.*, p. 10.
241 Quo. Botti and Cermelli, *La teoria della guerra aerea*, p. 554.
242 *Ibid.*, pp. 472–7.
243 'Unità di dottrina', *Rivista Aeronautica* May 1935; quo. *ibid.*, p. 482.
244 'I quattro compiti delle ali armate', *Rivista Aeronautica* December 1937; quo. *ibid.*, p. 499.
245 *Ibid.*, pp. 534–5.
246 D'Avanzo, *Ali e poltrone*, pp. 227–8.

247 Le forze armate della nazione: Discorso pronunciato al Senato, 30 March 1938. *OO* XXIX, p. 81.
248 Galeazzo Ciano, *Diario 1937–1943* (Milan: Rizzoli, 1980), p. 115.
249 ASAM. N.11246/S, Piano R 'B', 6 April 1936, pp. 3–4, 7. SIOS c. 296/f. 2.
250 ASAM. Pinna to Valle, 28 May 1936 [Valle's marginalia]. SIOS c. 296/f. 2.
251 ASAM. Valle to Cot, 19 June 1936. OP 1/b.4.
252 ASAM. N.13267, Piano R 'B', 18 August 1936. SIOS c. 296/f. 22/1.
253 ASAM. Scuola di Guerra Aerea II Corso Alti Studi Novembre 1936– Febbraio 1937. Manovra coi Quadri, [20 November 1936], p. 2. Fondo Esercitazioni b.8.
254 *Ibid.*, p. 3.
255 ASAM. N.10291, Valle to Badoglio, 28 January 1937. OP 1/b.4.
256 ASAM. N.2936S, Badoglio to Valle, 1 March 1937. OP 1/b.4.
257 ASAM. Piani di Radunata da mantenere in vigore, 20 February 1937. OP 1/b.4.
258 ASAM. Promemoria per S.E. il Capo di Stato Maggiore: Studio dei Piani di Radunata, 2 March 1937. OP 1/b.4.
259 ASAM. N.999, Valle to Pinna, 24 April 1937. OP 1/b.4.
260 ASAM. N.11860, Pinna to Valle, 10 June 1937. OP 1/b.4.
261 ASAM. N.21252, Tedeschini-Lalli to Ministero Aeronautica, 15 May 1937. OP 1/b.4.
262 ASAM. N.12012, Pinna to Army General Staff, 8 July 1937. OP 1/b.4.
263 ASAM. N.889, Cavagnari to Valle, 14 June 1937. OP 1/b.4.
264 ASAM. N.12985, Valle to Cavagnari, 27 August 1937. OP 1/b.4.
265 *Ibid.*
266 Pelliccia, *Valle*, p. 127.
267 Lucio Ceva, 'Influence de la guerre d'Espagne sur l'armement et les conceptions d'emploi de l'aviation de l'Italie fasciste', in *Adaptation de l'arme aérienne aux conflits contemporains et processus d'indépendance des armées de l'Air des origines à la fin de la Seconde Guerre mondiale* (Paris: Fondation pour les études de defense nationale, 1985), pp. 193–6.
268 'I quattro compiti delle ali armate', *Rivista Aeronautica* November 1937; quo. Botti and Cermelli, *La teoria della guerra aerea*, p. 531.
269 F. Raffaelli, 'Mezzi e metodi di guerra aerea nei cieli di Spagna', *Rivista Aeronautica* June 1938; quo. *ibid.*, p. 535.
270 *Ibid.*, p. 538.
271 G. Valle, 'La dottrina–lo spirito', *La Rassegna Italiana*, June 1939; quo. *ibid.*, p. 537.
272 Pelliccia, *Valle*, pp. 139–40. The aircraft concerned were the twin-engined Cant. Z 1011, Ca 135 and Ca 135 bis, the twin-engined Piaggio 32 and 32 bis, the S 85, the twin-engined Ba 88, and the triple-engined S 84 and S 84 bis.

7 THE YEAR OF TRUE 'REALISM', 1938

1 Burgwyn, *Italian Foreign Policy in the Inter-War period*, pp. 178–9, 181; G. Bruce Strang, *On the Fiery March: Mussolini prepares for war* (Westport, CT: Praeger, 2003), p.187; Mallett, *Mussolini and the Origins of the Second World War*, pp. 192–3.

2 Ciano, *Diario 1937–1943* 12 December1937, 1& 3 February 1938.

3 ASMAE. N.15 G.I/I, Naval Attaché Paris to Maristat, 9 January 1938. Ambasciata di Londra b.1036/f. 4.

4 ASMAE. N. 47: Conversazione con l'addetto militare britannico, colonello Beaumont Nesbitt, 20 January 1938. Ambasciata di Londra b.1036/f. 4.

5 Guerri, *Galeazzo Ciano*, pp. 297, 300–1.

6 Perth to Halifax, 10 March 1938; Perth to Halifax, 27 March 1938, Perth to Halifax, 2 April 1938, Perth to Halifax, 3 April 1938, Perth to Halifax, 14 April 1938, Perth to Halifax, 2 July 1938. *DBFP* series 2 vol. XIX nos. 627, 638, 649, 651, 658, 665, pp. 1021–31, 1060, 1074, 1076, 1082, 1132–3.

7 ASMAE. Grandi to Esteri, 9 April 1938; Grandi to Esteri [telephone], 9 April 1938. Ambasciata di Londra b.1007/f. 1.

8 UKNA. Japanese ambassador Rome to Foreign Ministry Tokyo, 18 May 1938. HW 12/226/071357.

9 Ciano to Attolico, 17 March 1938; *DDI* 8th series vol. VIII no. 351, p. 404.

10 HNA.N.239/154, Szabo to Hungarian Chief of Staff, 29 April 1938. Foreign Ministry Archive K.100.

11 AUSMM. Bollettino segreto No.774, 28 February 1938; Bollettino segreto No.776, 2 March 1938; Bollettino segreto No.784, 11 March 1938; Bollettino segreto No.795, 26 March 1938; Cartelle Numerate b.3276/f. 6. ASMAE. To.602063, Esteri to SIM etc., 2 April 1938. Ambasciata di Londra b.1036/f. 4.

12 AUSME. Z/3451, SIM to Ufficio Operazione, 12 March 1938. Rep. H-3 racc. 40/f. 4.

13 ASMAE. To.600385, Esteri to SIM etc., 21 January 1938. Ambasciata di Londra b.1036/f. 4.

14 ASMAE. Esteri to London Embassy etc., 19 January 1938. Ambasciata di Londra b.1036/f. 4. See also Boscarelli to Ciano, 5 March 1938; Indelli to Ciano, 8 March 1938. *DDI* 8th series vol. VIII nos. 266, 272, pp. 316–8, 323–4.

15 Ciano, *Diario 1937–1943* 26 January 1938.

16 Galli to Ciano, 12 May 1938; Galli to Ciano, 25 May 1938; Galli to Ciano, 6 July 1938; *DDI* 8th series vol. IX nos. 81, 162, [unnumbered], pp. 120–2, 215–20, 385-6 fn. 286. Salerno, The Mediterranean Triangle, pp. 226–7.

17 Drummond to Eden, 25 March 1937; *DBFP* 2nd series vol. XVIII no. 348, p. 530.

18 Ciano, *Diario 1937–1943* 23 & 24 April 1938. For his guest's account of the meeting, see R. J. Minney, *The Private Papers of Hore-Belisha* (London: Collins, 1960), pp. 114–117.

19 AUSSME. L'Egitto e gli accordi anglo-italiani: sviluppa delle forze armate egiziane, 16 July 1938. Rep. I-4 racc. 1.

20 Shorrock, *From Ally to Enemy*, pp. 214–6 [quo., p. 215].

21 AUSMM. N.45 G.5/6, Naval attaché Paris [Margottini] to Marina, 19 January 1938. Cartelle Numerate b.3272/f. 1.

22 UKNA. Japanese ambassador Rome to Foreign Ministry Tokyo, 18 May 1938. HW 12/226/071358.

23 'Il discorso di Genova: "Chi si ferma è perduto"', 14 May 1938. *OO* XXIX, pp. 99–102.

24 ASMAE. Promemoria per Sua Eccellenza l'Ambasciatore dell'Italia, 3, February 1938. Affari Politici: Germania b.45/f. 1. The memorandum was written by the air attaché, Gasperi.
25 Attolico to Esteri, 5 February 1938; *DDI* 8th series vol. VIII no. 99, pp. 112–4.
26 Attolico to Ciano, 21 February 1938; *DDI* 8th series vol. VIII no. 204, pp. 249–53.
27 AMR. Pariani to Sorice, 11 February 1938. Quaderni Pariani XXIV/23, p. 31.
28 Ciano, *Diario 1937–1943* 2 January, 11 & 13 February 1938; Appunto del Capo del Governo, 27 February 1938, *DDI* 8th series vol. VIII no. 235, pp. 281–2.
29 Plessen to German Foreign Ministry, 12 March 1938; *DGFP* series D vol. I no. 361, p. 583.
30 'L' "Anschluss" ', 16 March 1938. *OO* XXIX, pp. 67–71 [quo., p. 71].
31 Von Mackensen to German Foreign Ministry, 18 April 1938; *DGFP* series D vol. I no. 741, p. 1079.
32 Il discorso di Genova', 14 May 1938. *OO* XXIX, p. 99. Lamb's assertion that Mussolini was 'so angered by the Anschluss that he was ready to desert Hitler' and was as a result 'more anxious to reach agreement with Britain' over-states the case. Lamb, *Mussolini and the British*, pp. 207, 208.
33 Von Mackensen to Weizsacker, 20 April 1938; *DGFP* series D vol. I no. 745, p. 1083.
34 Attolico to Esteri, 16 June 1938; *DDI* 8th series vol. VIII no. 227, pp. 310–11.
35 ASMAE. N.571, Commercial Consul (Berlin) to Senator Giannini *et al.*, 12 February 1938. Affari Politici: Germania, b.41/f. 1.
36 ASAM. Ordine Generale per le Esercitazione Navale del 5 maggio 1938, pp. 7–9. Relazione per il C.S.M. Generale c. 10.
37 ASAM. Relazione sulla Manifestazione 'H' 8 maggio 1938. Fondo Esercitazioni b.9.
38 ASAM. Comando Divisione Aerea H: Relazione compilata dal Comandante 1a Divisione in base al questionario formulato dall'Ufficio di Stato Maggiore della Regia Aeronautica, n.d. Fondo Esercitazioni b.9.
39 Pelliccia, *Valle*, p. 131.
40 ASMAE. To.4893/392, Pittalis (Munich) to Esteri, 21 May 1938. Affari Politici: Germania b.46.
41 AUSSME. Notiziario No. 184: Visita del Führer, 15 May 1938. Rep. H-9 racc. 2/f. 2.
42 HNA. N.270/123, Szabo to Hungarian Chief of Staff, 10 May 1938. Foreign Ministry Archives K.100.
43 HNA. N.277/178, Szabo to Hungarian Chief of Staff, 12 May 1938. Foreign Ministry Archive K. 100.
44 Attolico to Ciano, 23 June 1938; *DDI* 8th series vol. X no. 253, pp. 342–6.
45 AUSSME. Collaborazione tecnica con la Germania, 8 July 1938; Rep. H-9 racc. 2/f. 3. War Ministry to Pariani, 8 July 1938; *DDI* 8th series vol. IX no. 296, p. 401. Ciano, *Diario 1937–1943* 27 June & 11 July 1938.

46 AUSSME. Promemoria per S.E. il Capo del Governo:Penetrazione germanica, 27 June 1938. Rep. H-9 racc. 2/f. 3.
47 AMR. Visita al Führer-Capisaldi, 11 July 1938. Quaderni Pariani XXVIII, pp. 8–9. See also Pariani to Mussolini, n.d.; *DDI* 8th series vol. IX no. 310, pp. 420–1.
48 Pariani to Ciano, 15 July 1938; *DDI* 8th series vol. IX no. 311, pp. 421–2.
49 Ciano to Grandi, 14 November 1938; *DDI* 8th series vol. X no. 398, pp. 428–30.
50 Ciano, *Diario 1937–1943*, 16 November 1938.
51 ASMAE. Appunto per il Duce, 2 December 1938. Affari Politici: Francia b. 33/f. 1-2.
52 Guariglia to Ciano, 14 December 1938; *DDI* 8th series vol. X no. 553, pp. 603–7.
53 Magistrati to Ciano, 11 October 1938; *DDI* 8th series vol. X no. 264, p. 266.
54 Marras to War Ministry, 22 September 1938; *DDI* 8th series vol. X no. 107, p. 103.
55 Attolico to Ciano, 15 November 1938; *DDI* 8th series vol. X no. 404, p. 436.
56 Mussolini to von Ribbentrop, 29 October 1938; *DDI* 8th series vol. X no. 349, pp. 360–1.
57 AMR. Pariani to Soddu, 19 November 1938. Quaderni Pariani XXXIII/32, p. 37.
58 Attolico to Ciano, 12 November 1938; Ciano to Pariani, 16 November 1938; Magistrati to Ciano, 17 December 1938. *DDI* 8th series vol. X nos. 392, 412, 567, pp. 417, 443, 618–9 [quo.].
59 AUSSME. Commissione suprema di difesa: Verbale della XV sessione, 1a seduta 3 February 1938, p. 18. Rep. F-9 racc. 46/f. 2.
60 *Ibid.* p. 24.
61 Ciano, *Diario 1937–1943*, 6 February 1938.
62 *Ibid.*, 3a seduta, 5 February 1938, p. 40.
63 *Ibid.*, p. 41.
64 *Ibid.*, p. 74. Summing up at the start of the next session on 7 February, Mussolini raised the 1939 figure to 250,000 tons on the basis of nothing at all.
65 *Ibid.*, 5a seduta 8 February 1938, pp. 80–5.
66 AUSSME. Organizzazione delle terre Italiane d'Oltremare: Relazione di S.E. il Ministro dell'Africa Italiana, n.d., p. 4. Rep. F-9 racc. 48/f. 4.
67 *Ibid.*, p. 11.
68 *Ibid.*, pp. 10–11.
69 AUSSME. Organizzazione delle terre italiane d'oltremare: relatore S.E. il Ministro dell'Aeronautica, n.d., p. 4. Rep. F-9 racc. 48/f. 4.
70 *Ibid.*, p. 7.
71 AUSSME. Organizzazione delle terre italiane d'oltremare: Relazione di S.E. il Ministro [della Marina], February 1938, p. 6. Rep. F-9 racc. 48/f. 4.
72 AUSSME. Organizzazione delle terre italiane d'oltremare:Relazione di S.E. il Sottosegretario di Stato per la Guerra, February 1938, p. 1. Rep. F-9 racc. 48/f. 4.

73 AUSSME. Commissione suprema di difesa, 5a seduta 8 February 1938, p. 86. *Loc. cit.*

74 *Ibid.*, p. 87.

75 AUSSME. La copertura alla frontiera libica occidentale, [February 1938], pp. 6–7, 10–11. Rep. F-9 racc. 48/f. 4.

76 AUSSME. Commissione suprema di difesa, 5a seduta 8 February 1938, p. 91. *Loc. cit.*.

77 *Ibid.*, 6a seduta 9 February, pp. 93–4.

78 AUSSME. Relazione per la Commissione suprema di difesa, January 1938, p. 7. Rep. F-9 racc. 49/ f. 3.

79 *Ibid.*, p. 9.

80 AUSSME. Commissione suprema di difesa, 6a seduta 9 February 1938, pp. 98–9. *Loc. cit.*

81 Ciano, *Diario 1937–1943* 3 March 1938.

82 AUSMM. N.579, Naval attaché London [Brivonesi] to Marina, 14 April 1938. Cartelle Numerate b.3249/f. 5.

83 ASMAE. Notiziario N. 7, Programma Britannica navale per il 1938, January 1938; Notiziario N. 86, Nuovi cannoni navale, June 1938; Notiziario N. 131, Rimodernamento della 'Queen Elizabeth', September 1938. Ambasciata di Londra b.1031/f. 2.

84 ASMAE. Crolla to Esteri, 3 March 1938; Ambasciata di Londra b. 1007/f. 1. AUSMM. T.8352, Esteri to Marina, 11 June 1938. Cartelle Numerate b.3249/f. 5.

85 AUSMM. N.003/S, Naval attaché Tokyo [Ghe] to Marina, 18 February 1938. Cartelle Numerate b.3249/f. 5.

86 AUSMM. Bollettino Segreto n. 809 Giappone, 12 April 1938. Cartelle Numerate b.3249/f. 5.

87 AUSMM. Bollettino segreto No.748, 28 January 1938. Cartelle Numerate b.3272/f. 1.

88 AUSMM. T.5702, Esteri to Marina, 23 April 1938; T.6203, Esteri to Marina, 2 May 1938; N.307 G.3/3, Naval attaché Paris [Margottini] to Maristat, 7 May 1938; T.6887, Esteri to Marina, 16 May 1938. Cartelle Numerate b.3249/f. 5.

89 Carte Capponi. 'Politica navale Britannica', 12 February 1938, pp. 1, 11, 14–16.

90 AUSMM. 'La politica navale nazionale', n.d. [c. 26 January 1938], pp. 1, 2. Direttive Generali DG A7/D4.

91 AUSMM. 'Studio circa la preparazione: Argomento 1o Le forze navali', January 1938, pp. 2–3, 5, 10. Direttive Generali DG 0/A7.

92 AUSMM. Cavagnari to Mussolini, 21 January 1938; N.5793, Commissariato generale per le fabbricazioni di Guerra to Ministero della Marina, 11 February 1938. Cartelle Numerate b.2703.

93 Robert Mallett, Italian Naval Policy, pp. 155–7, 317–8. Ristuccia demonstrates that Italy's shipbuilding capacity was starting to approach saturation: Cristiano Andrea Ristuccia, The Italian Economy under Fascism:1934–1943. The Rearmament Paradox, DPhil. University of Oxford 1998, pp. 233–4.

94 AUSMM. Ritardi nelle consegne dei materiali più importanti di competenza di Marinarmi per le unità navali in corso di contusione, 15 February 1938. Cartelle Numerate b.2703. Ristuccia suggests that the navy's belated recognition in 1940 that the 90 torpedoes a month available from 1940 were insufficient was most likely due to a revised conception of wartime consumption: Ristuccia, The Rearmament Paradox, pp. 262–3. The documents used here suggest that sheer lack of sufficient money to fund all the constituent elements of the programme played at least as large a role.

95 Ristuccia, The Rearmament Paradox, pp. 234–6.

96 AUSMM. Appunti presi alla riunione dei 13 gennaio 1938 XVIo presso S.E. il Ministro delle Finanze. Cartelle Numerate b.2703.

97 AUSMM. Guarneri to Cavagnari, 12 April 1938. b.2703.

98 Jackson, 'La perception des réarmaments allemand et italien', p. 31.

99 ASMAE. Notiziario N. 24, Programma navale francese, February 1938; Notiziario N. 101, Programma navale francese July 1938. Ambasciata di Londra b.1031/f. 2.

100 AUSMM. Attolico to Esteri, 17 June 1938. Cartelle Numerate b.3249/f. 5.

101 AUSMM. N.419, Somigli to Esteri, 25 June 1938. Cartelle Numerate b.3249/f. 5. The Italians calculated that Germany still had 35,812 'unused' tons and would get another 28,000 tons under the 35 per cent rule if England laid down two 40,000-ton battleships.

102 AUSMM. To.604368/35, Esteri to Berlin Embassy, 7 July 1938. Cartelle Numerate b.3249/f. 5.

103 AUSMM. Attività ufficio, 19 January 1938. Direttive Generali DG 15 A7/A0.

104 AUSMM. Nota verbale per S.E. il Sottocapo di stato maggiore, 22 January 1938. Direttive Generali DG 1/B1.

105 AUSMM. Questioni in sospeso con S.E. il Capo di stato maggiore generale, 31 January 1938. Direttive Generali DG 1/B1.

106 AUSMM.N.174, Rifornimento della nazione nell'ipotesi di conflitto Italia–Germania–Giappone contro l'Inghilterra–Francia–Russia, 18 January 1938, pp. 2–3, 6–7, 10. Direttive Generali DG 8/G5.

107 *Ibid.*, p. 6.

108 *Ibid.*, pp. 11–12.

109 *Ibid.*, p. 15 (underlining in original).

110 AUSMM. Pr.514, Sesta sessione della Sezione Alti Studi, 12 January 1938. Direttive Generali DG 15/A5/B1.

111 AUSMM. Promemoria per l'Ammiraglio capo reparto: Documenti di Guerra, 20 July 1938. Direttive Generali DG 1/A.

112 AUSMM. Documento di Guerra No.1, 1 July 1938, pp. 9–11, 13, 16, 18. Direttive Generali DG 1/A.

113 *Ibid.*, pp. 33–7. The latter idea at least was a contested one: this paragraph of the typescript bears the marginal annotation 'No'.

114 AUSMM. Estratto dal bollettino giornaliero del Reparto, 8 June 1938. Direttive Generali DG 15/E6/M2.

115 AUSMM. Esercitazione di mobilitazione di Guerra della marina francese (21–22–23 giugno 1938). Direttive Generali DG 10.

116 AMR. Pariani to Sorice, 16 March 1938. Quaderni Pariani XXVI, p. 2.

117 AMR. Pariani to Soddu, 1 May 1938. Quaderni Pariani XXVI, p. 40.

118 AMR. Pariani to Sorice, 26 March 1938. Quaderni Pariani XXVI, p. 6.

119 Canevari, *La Guerra italiana*, vol. I, pp. 567–8 fn. 2.

120 Pariani to Badoglio, 5 February 1938; *cit.*, Lucio Ceva, 'Un intervento di Badoglio e il mancato rinnovamento delle artiglierie italiane', *Il Risorgimento* anno XXVIII no.2, June 1976, p. 144.

121 AMR. Note, 29 March 1938; Pariani to Viscontini, 31 March 1938. Quaderni Pariani XXVI, pp. 13, 16.

122 Minniti, 'Il problema degli armamenti nella preparazione militare italiana, pp.111–4; Ristuccia, The Italian Economy under Fascism, pp. 143, 152, 155–6; Botti and Ilari, *Il pensiero militare italiano*, pp. 225–9; Ceva, 'Un intervento di Badoglio', p. 131.

123 Sweet, *Iron Arm*, pp. 135–42.

124 AMR. Pariani to Sorice, 26 March 1938; Pariani to Soddu, 3 April 1938; Pariani to Soddu, 21 April 1938. Quaderni Pariani XXVI, pp. 5, 19, 31.

125 Botti and Ilari, *Il pensiero militare italiano*, p. 205.

126 AUSSME. Pr.9172, Promemoria per il Comando designato dell'Armata del 'Po' relativo alla compilazione degli studi di radunata dell'Armata 'Po', 30 December 1938. Rep. M-3 racc. 126/f. 5.

127 AUSSME. Comando Designato d'Armata Torino: PR 12 Direttive Generali, 31 March 1938, pp. 1–2. Rep. H-6 racc. 13.

128 AUSSME. Comando Designato d'Armata Torino: PR 10 Direttive per la copertura, April 1938, pp. 1–4. Rep. H-6 racc. 10.

129 AUSSME. PR 12 Direttive per lo scacchiere alpino, 1 January 1938, pp. 2, 6, 7. Rep. H-6 racc. 16.

130 AUSSME. PR 12 Teatro d'operazioni nel Mediterraneo, 1 January 1938. Rep. H-6 racc. 14.

131 AUSMM. Pr.50, Esigenza 'T', 3 January 1938; Pr. 206, Pariani to Ministero della Marina, 14 January 1938. Direttive Generali DG 0/L6.

132 AUSSME. Telegramma inviato dall'Ambasciatore brittanico a Parigi al Foreign Office, 28 January 1938. Rep. H-9 racc. 2/f. 1.

133 AUSSME. N.Z/6403, Reparti francesi nel sud algerino e nel territorio del Ciad, 7 May 1938. Rep. H-3 racc. 1/f. A/1.

134 AUSSME. PR 12 Teatro d'operazioni dell'Africa settentrionale, 1 January 1938. Rep. H-6 racc. 14.

135 AMR. Pariani to Viscontini & Soddu, 10 January 1938. Quaderni Pariani XXIII, p. 48.

136 AMR. Pariani to Balbo [draft], 13 January 1938. Quaderni Pariani XXIV, pp. 4–5.

137 Ciano, *Diario 1937–1943*, 14 February 1938.

138 Von Mackensen to German Foreign Ministry, 18 July 1938; *DGFP* series D vol. I no. 792, p. 1152.

139 AUSMM. Pariani to Cavagnari, 7 May 1938. Direttive Generali DG-1/B1.

140 AUSMM. Esercitazioni anno XVI in Libia, 11–24 May 1938, pp. 20, 24–5, 26–8, 32–3. Cartelle Numerate b.2726/f. 2.

141 ASAM. Relazione sulla esercitazione di sbarco aereo svoltasi nelle manovre della Libia anno XVI, n.d., pp. 3, 5, 7. Fondo Esercitazioni b.10.
142 AMR. Riunione in Tripoli, 23-5-38; Pariani to Soddu, 31 May 1938. Quaderni Pariani XXVII, pp. 1, 4–7.
143 AUSSME. Problema operativo dell'Africa settentrionale-Memoria sulla possibilità e convenienza di una offensiva aereo-terrestre in Tunisia, June 1938, pp. 3–6, 7–8. Rep. N-11 racc. 4030/f. 9.
144 *Ibid.*, p. 8.
145 AMR. Pariani to Balbo, 10 June 1938. Quaderni Pariani XXVII, pp. 16–18.
146 HNA. N.112/65, Szabo to Hungarian Chief of Staff, 1 March 1938. Foreign Ministry Archive K. 100.
147 AMR. Pariani to Soddu, 3 April 1938. Quaderni Pariani XXVI, p. 20.
148 AUSSME. Il problema operativo alla frontiera nord in seguito all'Anschluss, 25 April 1938. Rep. H-6 racc. 13.
149 D'Avanzo, *Ali e poltrone*, pp. 213–5, 222–6.
150 Santoro. *L'Aeronautica italiana nella seconda Guerra mondiale* vol. I, pp. 15, 39.
151 Ceva, *Le forze armate*, p. 223.
152 Pelliccia, *Valle*, p. 137; D'Avanzo, *Ali e poltrone*, p. 250.
153 Pelliccia, *Valle*, p. 140.
154 Ristuccia, *The Rearmament Paradox*, pp. 183–5.
155 ASMAE. To.2428/733, Magistrati to Esteri, 12 April 1938, all: Promemoria per il R. Incaricato d'Affari [Liotta], 8 April 1938. Affari Politici: Germania b.49/f. 1. Liotta to Magistrati, 12 April 1938; *DDI* 8th series vol. VIII, p. 543 fn. 478/6.
156 Botti and Cermelli, *La teoria della guerra aerea*, pp. 530–2.
157 Mario Aimoni Cat, 'Il Concorso dell'Arma aerea alla conquista dell'Impero' in Tomaso Sillani, *Le forze armate dell'Italia fascista* (Rome: La Rassegna Italiana, 1939), p. 257.
158 Botti and Cermelli, *La teoria della guerra aerea*, p. 538.
159 Giuseppe Valle, 'La dottrina – lo spirito', in Sillani, *Le forze armate*, p. 270.
160 *Ibid.*, p. 272.
161 Santoro, *L'Aeronautica italiana*, vol. I, p. 14.
162 AUSSME. Missione a Berlino 27–31 marzo 1938. Rep. H-3 racc. 33/f. 7.
163 AUSSME. L/508, Materiale e munizioni da 100/17 e da 109/12, 28 January 1938; L/514, credito verso l'Austria per cessione materiali, 6 May 1938; N.39725, Sorice to Direzione Generale Artiglieria, 22 June 1938; German military attaché Rome to War Ministry, 24 October 1938. Rep. H-9 racc. 2.f. A-13.
164 AUSSME. Promemoria per S.E. il Capo del Governo: Situazione Cecoslovacchia, 6 April 1938. Rep. H-9 racc. 2/f. 3.
165 AUSSME. Per il Duce: Cecoslovakia, 3 May 1938. Rep. H-9 racc. 2/f. 2.
166 AUSSME. Cecoslovakia–Promemoria No. 9, 23 May 1938, No. 15, 27 May 1938, no. 17, 30 May 1938. Rep. H-9 racc. 2/f. 2.
167 AUSMM. N.346, Military Attaché Paris [Visconti Prasca] to SIM, 14 May 1938 [quo., pp. 4,7]. Cartelle Numerate b.2760/f. 1. AUSSME. Cecoslovakia–Promemoria No. 17, 30 May 1938. Rep. H-9 racc. 2/f. 3.

168 AUSSME. N/1025/A, Military Attaché Romania (Della Porta) to SIM, 22 March 1938. Rep. H-3 racc. 16/f. D; Mallett, *Mussolini and the Origins of the Second World* War, p. 181.

169 AUSSME. N.1246/A, Military Attaché Romania to SIM, 4 July 1938 all.: Relazione di S.E. il Sottosegretario all'Aeronautica italiana, S.E. il generale Valle, sulla visita effetuata in Romania, 10 June 1938, pp. 1, 2. Rep. H-3 racc. 16/f. D.

170 AUSSME. N. 1351/A, Military Attaché Romania to Aeronautica, 4 October 1938 [quo.]; N.1404/A, Military Attaché Romania to Aeronautica, 28 October 1938; N.5645, Military Attaché Romania to SIM, 4 December 1938; N.6485, Military Attaché Romania to SIM, 9 December 1938; T.6559, Della Porta to SIM, 24 December 1938. Rep. H-3 racc. 16/f. D.

171 AUSSME. N.5658, Military Attaché Bucharest Romania to SIM, 26 May 1938; N.7/2893, Informazione su URSS (Soddu), 26 May 1938; Promemoria per S.E. il Sottosegretario di stato-dichiarazione del sig. Moruzow direttore generale SIM rumeno, 30 June 1938. Rep. H-3 racc. 16/f. D.

172 AMR. Visita in Germania, 4–11 July 1938. Quaderni Pariani XXVIII.

173 AMR. Pariani to Sorice, 24 July 1938. Quaderni Pariani XXIX.

174 AUSSME. Situazione strategica dell'Italia, 21 June 1938, pp. 1–2. Rep. H-6 racc. 12.

175 *Ibid.*, [Studio Complemento] 24 June 1938 [p.1 – unnumbered].

176 *Ibid.*, [p.2].

177 AMR. Pariani to Soddu, 22 January 1937; Pariani to Viscontini and Soddu, 24 June 1938; Pariani to Viscontini, 24 June 1938; Piano V, 25 June 1938. Quaderni Pariani XXIV; XXVII..

178 HNA. N.312/199, Szabo to Hungarian chief of staff, 20 May 1938. Foreign Ministry Archive K. 100.

179 ASMAE. Pariani to Ciano, 30 July 1938. GAB 1174 (UC 58) b.3/f. 1.

180 AUSSME. Resoconto stenografico delle esposizioni fatte dagli addetti militari nei giorni 27–28–29 giugno 1938, pp. 19–20, 22–3, 24, 25, 40–1. Rep. L-10 racc. 8/c. 14.

181 *Ibid.*, p. 29.

182 *Ibid.*, p. 44.

183 AUSMM. Bollettino segreto No.871, 4 July 1938. Cartelle Numerate b.3276/f. 6.

184 *Ibid.*, p. 36.

185 Memorandum by the Foreign Minister, 4 August 1938: *DGFP* series D vol. II no. 334, pp. 533–4. Ciano, *Diario 1937–1943*, 20 August, 29 August, 17 September 1938.

186 AUSSME. N.1430, Badini to Ministero della Guerra, 27 August 1938. Rep. H-9 racc. 2/f. 2.

187 Strang, *On the Fiery March*, pp. 178–9; Mallett, *Mussolini and the Origins of the Second World War*, pp. 186–7, 190–1.

188 AMR. Pariani to Tripiccione, 10 September 1938. Quaderni Pariani XXIX.

189 AUSMM. N.560 G.I/I, Naval attaché Paris [Margottini] to Marina, 3 September 1938. Cartelle Numerate b.2760/f. 1.

190 AUSMM. N.588, Naval attaché Paris to Marina, 10 September 1938. Cartelle Numerate b.2760/f. 1. In the film to which Margottini took exception, 'Alerte en Mediterranée', English, French and German naval captains played leading parts but the Italian navy was nowhere to be seen.

191 Cernuschi, *Domenco Cavagnari*, pp. 149–50; Salerno, The Mediterranean Triangle, p. 229.

192 AUSMM. Studio preliminare per operazioni contro Francia-Inghilterra, 2 September 1938 [quo.p.5]. Direttive Generali DG 1 A/OA.

193 AUSMM. N.948, Ordine generale di operazione No. 7, 8 September 1938 [quo., p.2]; N.963, ordine generale di operazione No. 7, 10 September 1938. Direttive Generali DG1 A/A2.

194 AUSMM. Cavagnari to Lais, 10 September 1938. Direttive Generali DG 1/A.

195 Mallett, Italian Naval Policy, p. 167.

196 AUSMM. N.560 G.I/I, Naval attaché Paris to Marina, 3 September 1938, pp. 3–4. Cartelle Numerate b.2760/f. 1.

197 AUSMM. N.575 G.I/I, Naval attaché Paris to Marina, 7 September 1938. Cartelle Numerate b.2760/f. 1.

198 AUSMM. N.125/S., Military attaché Paris [Visconti Prasca] to Ministero della Guerra, 14 September 1938. Cartelle Numerate b.2760/f. 1.

199 HNA.N.671/443, Conversation with the Duce on 10 September, 1938. Foreign Ministry Archive K.100.

200 AUSSME. Promemoria per S.E. il Capo del Governo: Situazione politico–militare, 13, 14, 15, 17 September 1938. Rep. H-9 racc. 2/f. 2.

201 Von Mackensen to German Foreign Ministry, 15 September 1938: *DGFP* series D vol. II no. 494, p. 805.

202 AUSMM. Elenco dei provvedimenti sinora adottati dalla Regia Marina, 13 September 1938; Provvedimenti disposti per Lero-Tobruch e Bengasi, 15 September 1938. Direttive Generali DG 1/D5bis.

203 'Discorso di Trieste', 18 September 1938. *OO* XXIX, p. 146.

204 AUSSME. Promemoria per S.E. il Capo del Governo:Situazione politico-militare, 17, 20, 28, 29 September, 1 October 1938. Rep. H-9 racc. 2/f. 2.

205 AUSMM. N.757, Military attaché Paris to Ministero della Guerra, 20 September 1938 [quo.p.4]. Cartelle Numerate b.2760/f. 1.

206 AUSMM. N.608 G.I/I, Naval attaché Paris to Marina, 14 September 1938. Cartelle Numerate b.2760/f. 1.

207 AUSMM. N.635 G.I/I, Naval attaché Paris to Marina, 21 September 1938. Cartelle Numerate b.2760/f. 1.

208 AUSSME. Promemoria per S.E. il Capo del Governo: Situazione politico-militare, 18, 20, 21, 22 September 1938. Rep. H-9 racc. 2/f. 2.

209 AMR. Pariani to Soddu, 12 September 1938; Pariani to Soddu, 13 September 1938. Quaderni Pariani XXIX.

210 AMR. Pariani to Sorice, 14 September 1938; Pariani to Ollearo, 14 September 1938; Pariani to Ollearo, Soddu, Sorice, 14 September 1938. Quaderni Pariani XXIX.

211 AUSMM. Maristat: verbale della seduta del 24 settembre 1938. Direttive Generali DG 1/D2.

212 AUSSME. Promemoria per S.E. il Capo del Governo:Situazione politico–militare, 24, 25, 26 September 1938. Rep. H-9 racc.2/f. 2.

213 AUSMM. N.644 G.I/I, Naval attaché Paris to Marina, 24 September 1938. Cartelle Numerate b.2760/f. 1.

214 Ciano, *Diario 1937–1943*, 27 September 1938.

215 AMR. Pariani to Viscontini, 25 September 1938; Pariani to Viscontini, 26 September 1938; Riunione, 27 September 1938. Quaderni Pariani XXX.

216 AMR. Pariani to Mussolini, 27 September 1938. Quaderni Pariani XXX.

217 AMR. Relazione al Duce, 29 September 1938. Quaderni Pariani XXI.

218 AUSMM. N.652 G.I/I, Naval attaché Paris to Marina, 28 September 1938. Cartelle Numerate b.2760/f. 1.

219 AMR. Pariani to Viscontini, 2 October 1938. Quaderni Pariani XXXI.

220 ASMAE. To.8869/4976, Prunai to Esteri, 7 October 1938. Affari Politici: Francia b.34/f. 1–2.

221 AUSMM. N.685 G.I/I, Naval attaché Paris to Marina, 8 October 1938. Cartelle Numerate b.2760/f. 1.

222 AUSMM. N.1357, Naval attaché London [Brivonesi] to Marina, 7 October 1938. Cartelle Numerate b.2760/f. 1.

223 AUSMM.N.643 G.5/I, Naval attaché Paris to Marina, 24 September 1938. Cartelle Numerate b.2760/f. 1.

224 Ambassador in Italy to Foreign Ministry, 5 November 1938, 8 November 1938; *DGFP* series D vol. IV nos. 402, 406, pp. 521, 523–4.

225 AMR. Pariani to Sorice, 29 September 1938; Pariani to Viscontini, 30 September 1938. Quaderni Pariani XXXI.

226 AMR. Pariani to Sorice, Viscontini, Soddu, 16 October 1938. Quaderni Pariani XXXI.

227 AUSSME. [Note, headed Brennero], 9 October 1938; [Letter with no addressee or signature, headed Cosenza], 13 October 1938. Rep. H-5 racc.2(A)/f. 9. Both have passages underlined by Mussolini and are marked by him 'Pariani' – the second with three exclamation marks.

228 AUSSME. Promemoria per S.E. Il Capo del Governo: Inconvenienti in occasione dei recenti richiami, 26 October 1938. Rep. H-5 racc. 2(A)/f. 9.

229 AUSSME. Promemoria per S.E. il Capo del Governo: Svolgimento della mobilitazione parziale, 28 October 1938. Rep. H-5 racc. 2(A)/f. 9.

230 AMR. Riunione 24 November 1938. Quaderni Pariani XXXI.

231 AUSSME. Stralcio 'Notiziario mensile state esteri' del SIM–mese di Ottobre 1938, 5 December 1938. Rep. I-4 racc. 3/c. 5.

232 AUSSME. Stralcio 'Notiziario mensile stati esteri' del SIM–mese Ottobre, 2 December 1938. Rep. I-4 racc. 3/c. 5.

233 AUSSME. Stralcio 'Notiziario mensile stati esteri' del SIM–mese di ottobre 1938, 3 December 1938; Rep. I-4 racc. 3/c. 4. Notizie sulla Tunisia [SIM], 20 December 1938; Rep. H-3 racc. 40/f. 5.

234 AMR. Riunione Comandanti C. d'A., 3 October 1938. Quaderni Pariani XXXI, AUSSME. Riunione comandanti corpo d'armata [teoria bellica], 3 October 1938. Rep. H-10 racc. 1/f. 3.

235 AUSSME. Valorizzazione militare delle terre italiane d'oltremare, 12 November 1938, p. 1. [Emphasis in original.] Rep. F-9 racc.53/f. 1.

236 AUSSME. Relazione per la XVI sessione della Commissione suprema di difesa: parte militare – Appunti per S.E. il Sottosegretario [Ministero dell'Africa Italiana], December 1938, pp. 4-5. Rep. F-9 racc.53/f.1.

237 *Ibid.*, pp. 21, 24–5.

238 *Ibid.*, p. 42.

239 AUSMM. Considerazione del nostro problema strategico in base alla situazione politica del momento presente, 26 October 1938. Direttive Generali SP/P2/A8.

240 Mallett, *Italian Naval Policy*, pp. 176–7, 179.

241 AUSMM. N.211, Ordine del Giorno della XVIa Sessione della Commissione Suprema di Difesa – Febbraio 1939, 6 October 1938. Direttive Generali DG 0/N5.

242 AUSMM. Situazione schematica degli studi il 28 ottobre 1938, p. 7. Direttive Generali DG 15/A7.A0.

243 AUSMM. Studio generale per il trasporto di un corpo di spedizione in Africa settentrionale, November 1938, pp. 2–4. Direttive Generali DG 10/A2.

244 *Ibid.*, p. 12.

245 *Ibid.*, p. 15.

246 *Ibid.*, pp. 22–6.

247 AUSMM. Cavagnari to Mussolini, 2 October 1938. Cartelle Numerate b.3249/f. 5.

248 AUSMM. N.1474, Naval attaché Berlin [Pecori Giraldi] to Marina, 22 November 1938. Cartelle Numerate b.3249/f. 5.

249 AUSMM. N. 1590, Naval attaché Berlin to Marina, 16 December 1938. Cartelle Numerate b.3249/f. 5.

250 AUSMM. Promemoria per S.E. il Sottosegretario di Stato: Politica navale italo-tedesca, 18 December 1938. Cartelle Numerate b.3249/f. 5.

251 AUSMM. Promemoria circa le conversazioni svoltesi a Berlino il 6 e 7 gennaio 1939–XVIII fra i rappresentati della Marina italiana e quelli della Marina tedesca, 10 January 1939. Cartelle Numerate b.3249/f. 5.

252 AUSSME. Bollettino informazione della R. Marina del 19 dicembre [1938]. Rep. I-4 b.3/c. 4.

253 ASAM. N.1012, Valle to Pinna, 4 October 1938. OP 1 b.4.

254 ASAM. N.13878, Pinna to Valle, 5 November 1938. OP 1 b.4.

255 ASAM. Relazione sulla missione nel Reich effettuata dal 23 novembre al 3 dicembre 1938 [un-numbered]. Relazione per il C.S.M. Generale c. 10.

256 *Ibid.*

257 *Ibid.* This passage was underlined in red by Pricolo, who wrote on it in November 1970: 'It is the usual pious lies to justify our shortcomings.'

8 'SPEAK OF PEACE AND PREPARE FOR WAR', 1939–1940

1 UKNA. Relazione per il Gran Consiglio, [4 February 1939]. GFM 36/5/fr.000040.

2 *Ibid.* fr.000045.

3 Bottai, *Diario 1935–1944*, 21 March 1939, pp. 142–4.
4 'Alla vecchia guardia', 26 March 1939. *OO* XXIX, pp. 251–3.
5 ASMAE. To.00347/183, Attolico to Ciano, 11 January 1939. Affari Politici: Germania b.57/f. 1.
6 ASMAE. To.02524/761, Attolico to Ciano, 31 March 1939; To.4859/1458, Attolico to Ciano, 30 June 1939. Affari Politici: Germania b.57/f. 1.
7 ASMAE. N.1879/800, Rossi to Ciano, 16 May 1939. Affari Politici: Germania b.60.
8 ASMAE. Le trattative anglo–franco–sovietiche di Mosca (marzo–agosto 1939), n.d., pp. 1–2, 4. Affari Politici: Francia b.41/f. 1.
9 Mario Toscano, *The Origins of the Pact of Steel* (Baltimore MD: Johns Hopkins University Press, 1967), pp. 181, 244, 248–9, 252 [quo.].
10 Attolico to Ciano, 20 March 1939; *ibid.*, p. 183. ASMAE. To.02497/750, Magistrati to Ciano, 30 March 1939; Affari Politici: Germania, b.61.
11 ASMAE. To.02603/798, Attolico to Ciano, 2 April 1939. Affari Politici: Germania b.57/f. 1.
12 Attolico to Ciano, 18 April 1939, quo. Toscano, *Origins of the Pact of Steel*, p. 325 fn. 19.
13 Father Tacchi Venturi to Cardinal Maglione, 2 May 1939; *Records and Documents of the Holy See relating to the Second World War* vol. I: *The Holy See and the War in Europe, March 1939–August 1940* (London: Herder Publications, 1968), no. 18, p. 110. Toscano's suggestion that Italy's estimate of the possibility of localising a Polish–German war was one of three 'fundamental misunderstandings' at the Milan conference is thus open to question: Toscano, *Origins of the Pact of Steel*, p. 398.
14 Father Tacchi Venturi to Cardinal Maglione, 7 June 1939; *The Holy See and the War in Europe* I, no. 58, p. 161.
15 Shorrock, *From Ally to Enemy*, p. 246.
16 ASMAE. N.620/256, Rapporto per S.E. il Ministro degli Affari Esteri, 27 January 1939; Relazione per S.E. il Ministro degli Affari Esteri, 18 March 1939 and unheaded notes 21 March 1939; Suster to Ciano, 18 March 1939; Anfuso to Suster, 21 March 1939. Ufficio Coordinamento 61 #1177 b.2.
17 Strang, *On the Fiery March*, pp. 235, 240–1.
18 AUSSME. Promemoria per il Duce: Crisis europea–azioni svolta dai vari stati dal 31 marzo al 2 aprile '39, 5 April 1939. Rep. H-9 racc.3/f. 5.
19 ASMAE. N.2196/919, Guariglia to Ciano, 1 April 1939; Appunto per S.E. il Ministro, 18 May 1939; Anfuso to Suster, 22 May 1939; Dichiarazioni personali di S.E. il Ministro de Monzie, 26 May 1939. Ufficio Coordinamento UC 61 #1177, b.2.
20 ASMAE. N.3030/1296, Guariglia to Ciano, 10 May 1938; N.3178/1358, Guariglia to Ciano, 13 May 1938. Affari Politici: Germania, b.60. The cited remarks were underlined by Mussolini.
21 ASMAE. Promemoria 7 November 1939. Ufficio Coordinamento UC 61 #1177, b.2/f. 6.
22 Lamb, *Mussolini and the British*, p. 237.
23 Quo. Paul Stafford, 'The Chamberlain–Halifax visit to Rome: a reappraisal', *English Historical Review* vol. 98 no. 386, January 1983, p. 68.

24 UKNA. Shiratori to Foreign Ministry Tokyo, 8 January 1939. HW 12/235/073505.
25 AUSSME. Stralcio Notiziario mensile stati esteri del SIM, March 1939. Rep. I-4 racc. 3/c. 5.
26 Crolla to Ciano, 14 June 1939; Ciano to De Peppo, 15 June 1939; Guariglia to Ciano, 16 June 1939; Ciano to Grazzi, 17 June 1939. *DDI* 8th series vol. XII nos. 228, 235, 256, 262, pp. 197, 202–3, 218–20, 223.
27 AUSSME. Nuova base navale ed aerea inglese, 20 July 1939. Rep. I-4 racc. 3/c. 5.
28 Loraine to Ciano, 4 July 1939; Mussolini to Ciano, 7 July 1939. *DDI* 8th series vol. XII nos. 463, 505, pp. 349, 381–2.
29 Nello, *Un fedele disubbediente*, pp. 354–6; Strang, *On the Fiery March*, p. 273 fn. 124.
30 ASMAE. N.2797/75, Ciano to Attolico, 23 February 1939. Ufficio Coordinamento UC 4 #1120 b.3/f. 4.
31 The Military Attaché in Italy to the High Command of the Wehrmacht, 23 March 1939; *DGFP* series D vol. VI App. I no. II, p. 1109.
32 ASMAE. T.4339/111, Ciano to Attolico, 17 March 1939. Ufficio Coordinamento UC 6 #1122 b.5/f. 2.
33 Unsigned Memorandum [Record of the Keitel-Pariani conversation 4 April 1939]; *DGFP* series D vol. VI App. I n. III, p. 1111. This document must be misdated, as both German and Italian evidence speaks of conversations on 5–6 April: see Directive by the Chief of the High Command of the Wehrmacht, 17 April 1939, *DGFP* series D vol. VI App. I no. IV, p. 1112, and the evidence cited below in note 34.
34 Mario Toscano, 'Le conversazioni militari italo-tedesche alla vigilia della seconda guerra mondiale', *Rivista Storica Italiana* Anno LXIV fasc. 3, December 1952, p. 350; unsigned memorandum, *DGFP* series D vol. VI App. I no. III, p. 111.
35 Toscano, 'Le conversazioni militari italo–tedesche', pp. 351–2.
36 The Military Attaché in Italy to the High Command of the Wehrmacht, 24 April 1939; *DGFP* series D vol. VI App. I no. V, p. 1113.
37 AUSSME. Promemoria per il Duce: Collaborazione Italo–Germanica, 15 April 1939. Rep. H-9 racc. 3/f. 5.
38 The Naval Attaché in Italy to the High Command of the Navy, 13 May 1939; *DGFP* series D vol. VI App. I/VI, pp. 1114–5.
39 Tur, *Plancia Ammiraglio*, vol. III, p. 298.
40 AMR. Dal treno, 21 May 1939. Quaderni Pariani XXXXI.
41 Attolico to Ciano, 27 May 1939; *DDI* 8th series vol. XII no. 47, pp. 31–2.
42 Mussolini to Hitler, 30 May 1939 ['Memoriale Cavallero']; *DDI* 8th series vol. XII no. 59, pp. 49, 50.
43 Cavallero to Ciano, 6 June 1939; Cavallero to Ciano, 10 June 1939. *DDI* 8th series vol. XII nos. 134, 182, pp. 114–5, 161–2.
44 ASMAE. Appunto per S.E. il Ministro, 14 June 1939. Affari Politici: Germani b.41/f. 1.
45 Ciano to Attolico, 8 July 1939; Attolico to Ciano, 26 July 1939; Ciano to Magistrati, 27 July 1939. *DDI* 8th series vol. XII nos. 514, 679, 701, pp. 387, 512–3, 530.

46 Ciano, *Diario 1937–1943*, 26 August 1939.
47 AUSSME. Organizzazione delle terre italiane d'oltremare: Relazione di S.E. il Ministro dell'Africa Italiana, February 1939, pp. 1–3, 7–8, 11–12, 15, 31. Rep. F-9 racc. 53/f. 1.
48 AUSSME. Terre italiane d'oltremare: Libia II-Organizzazione militare di guerra e di pace, February 1939, pp. 5–7, 9–10, 13. Rep. F-9 racc. 53/f. 1.
49 AUSSME. Terre italiane d'oltremare: relazione di S.E. il Ministro della Marina, February 1939, pp. 3–5, 6, 11–12, 14. Rep. F-9 racc. 53/f. 1.
50 AUSSME. Terre italiane d'oltremare: Relazione di S.E. il Sottosegretario di Stato per la Guerra, 12 November 1938, pp. 3–4, 8–9. Rep. F-9 racc. 53/f. 1.
51 AUSSME. Terre italiane d'oltremare – Relatore: S.E. il Minstro dell'Aeronautica, February 1939, pp. 3–4. Rep. F-9 racc. 53/f. 1.
52 AUSSME. Commissione suprema di difesa:verbali della 1a seduta, 6 febbraio 1939, pp. 11–20 [quo., p. 19]. Rep. F-9 racc. 50/f. 2.
53 *Ibid.*, p. 23.
54 AUSSME. Promemoria per il Duce: Scorte di materie prime, 31 January 1939. Rep. H-9, racc. 3/f. 5.
55 Commissione suprema di difesa: verbali della 2a seduta, 7 febbraio, pp. 44, 45; 3a seduta, 8 febbraio, pp. 63–4, 65–6, 68–9; 4a seduta 9 febbraio, p. 78. *Loc. cit.*
56 AUSSME. Commissione suprema di difesa: verbali della 3a seduta , 8 February 1939, pp. 71–4. *Loc. cit.*
57 AUSSME. Promemoria sulla preparazione bellica della Libia occidentale, 16 June 1939; Rep. H-9 racc. 3/f. 5. N.807983, Elementi per la compilazione dell'ordine del giorno da presentare alla Commissione suprema di difesa–Febbraio 1940, 21 July 1939; Rep. F-9 racc. 57/f. 1.
58 Verbali della 4a seduta, 9 February 1939, pp. 86–8; verbali della 5a seduta, 11 February 1939, pp. 126–7. *Loc. cit.*
59 AUSSME. Mussolini to Balbo, 7 January 1939. Rep. N-11 c. 4031.
60 AMR. Riunione, 5 January 1939; Pariani to Viscontini, 5 January 1939; Riunione (Libia), 16 January 1939; Pariani to Soddu, 20 January 1939. Quaderni Pariani XXIV.
61 AUSSME. Z/3336, Stralcio: Promemoria per il Duce–Situazione militare Francia e Gran Bretagna al 22 febbraio 1939. Rep. H-3 racc. 43/f. 1. The memorandum carries a note by Pariani: 'The [enemy's] strength . . . has been over-estimated in order not to make a mistake by under-estimating it'.
62 Verbale della seduta del 26 gennaio 1939: Antonello Biagini and Fernando Frattolillo, eds., *Verbali delle riunioni tenute dal Capo di S. M. Generale* vol. I: (*1939–1940)* (Rome: Ufficio Storico dello Stato Maggiore dell'Esercito, 1982), p. 2.
63 AUSSME. Sintesi degli argomenti svolti durante le riunione tenuta il 4 febbraio1939 XVII alle LL. EE.I Comandanti di Corpo d'Armata. Rep. H-10 b.1.
64 AMR. Pariani to Badoglio: Operazioni Libia C, [4 February 1939]. Quaderni Pariani XXXVI.
65 AMR. Pariani to Soddu, 27 January 1939. Quaderni Pariani XXXVI.

66 AMR. Pariani to Basentini, 5 February 1939. Quaderni Pariani XXXVI.
67 AUSSME. Badoglio to Mussolini, 2 March 1939. Rep. I-4 racc. 6/c.13.
68 AUSSME. Badoglio to Musslini, 13 June 1939. Rep. I-4 racc. 6/c.13.
69 AUSSME. Promemoria per S.E. il Sottosegretario di Stato: Missione in O.M.S. dal 27 dicembre al 7 corrente, 11 January 1939, pp. 3–4. Rep. H-9 racc. 3/f. 5.
70 AUSSME. N.3023, Esercitazione armata del 'Po', February 1939; Rep. H-9 racc. 3/f. 5. AMR. Pariani to Soddu, 8 February 1939. Quaderni Pariani XXX.
71 AUSSME. Consiglio dell'esercito 8 May 1939 2: Provvedimenti e predisposizioni per la mobilitazione – Misure precauzionale del febbraio–marzo 1939, pp. 3–5. Rep. F-9 racc. 6/f. 3.
72 Mack Smith, *Mussolini's Roman Empire*, pp. 137–67.
73 AUSSME. Promemoria per il Duce: Munizionamento, 14 April 1939. Rep. H-9 racc. 3/f. 5.
74 AMR. Pariani to Viscontini, 25 April 1939. Quaderni Pariani XXXVIII.
75 AMR. Pariani to Sorice, 21 September 1939. Quaderni Pariani XXXVI.
76 AMR. Pariani to Soddu, 10 April 1939. Quaderni Pariani XXXVIII.
77 Cernuschi, *Cavagnari*, p. 179.
78 HNA. N. 528/1/39, Promemoria: About my conversation with Lt. Gen. Pariani, Secretary of War, on May 27, 1939. Foreign Ministry Archives K. 100.
79 Brian R. Sullivan, ' "Where one man, and only one man, led".' Italy's path from non-alignment to non-belligerency to war, 1937–1940', in Neville Wyllie, ed., *European Neutrals and Non-Belligerents during the Second World War* (Cambridge: Cambridge University Press, 2002), pp. 131–5.
80 AUSSME. Attuazione accordi militari franco–inglesi, 17 March 1939. Rep. H-3 racc. 35/f. 2.
81 AUSSME. FRANCIA–Situazione politico–militare al 18 aprile [1939]. Rep. H-3 racc. 20/f. 1. At the foot of this memorandum, Badoglio scrawled 'Goodbye Libya!'
82 AUSSME. FRANCIA–Situazione politico–militare al 20 aprile [1939]; Crisi europea: situazione al 20 aprile 1939. Rep. H-3 racc. 20/f. 1.
83 AUSSME. FRANCIA–Situazione politico–militare al 23 aprile 1939; Crisi europea–situazione al 24 aprile 1939; Crisi europea–situazione al 25 aprile 1939; Crisi europea–situazione al 27 aprile 1939[quo.]. Rep. H-3 racc. 20/f. 1.
84 AUSSME. Crisi europea–situazione al 28 aprile 1939. Rep. H-3 racc. 20/f. 1.
85 AUSSME. FRANCIA–Riepilogo sentimentale dell'attività militare francese (dal 21 al 28 aprile), 29 April 1939. Rep. H-3 racc. 20/f. 1.
86 AUSSME. Consiglio dell'esercito, 8 maggio 1939 I: Nuovo ordinamento dell'esercito e principali provvedimenti nel campo organico, pp. 5–7. Rep. F-9 racc. 6/f. 3.
87 *Ibid.* II: Provvedimenti e predisposizioni per la mobilitazione, pp. 1–2.
88 AUSSME. Verbale della seduta del Consiglio dell'esercito tenutasi l'8 maggio 1939 a Palazzo Venezia, p. 2. Rep. F-9 racc. 6.

89 *Ibid*, p. 3.
90 AUSSME. Consiglio dell'esercito, 9 maggio 1939, IV: Potenziamento dell'esercito. Rep. F-9, racc. 6/f. 3.
91 AMR. Riunione motorizzazione, 29 March 1939; Riunione motosparo, 21 August 1939. Quaderni Pariani XXXVIII, XXXXII.
92 AMR. La Guerra: Appunti per il Duce, n.d. [?11–20 May 1939]. Quaderni Pariani XXXX.
93 AMR. Discorso alla Camera, 10 May 1939. Quaderni Pariani XXXXII.
94 Ciano, *Diario 1937–1943*, 2 May 1939.
95 AUSMM. Studio sulla preparazione: promemoria sul programma anno XVII e seguenti, January 1939, pp. 1–4. Direttive Generali DG 04/A1.
96 *Ibid.*, pp. 7–13, 14; Programma navali per gli anni XVII, XVIII, XIX–Criteri informativi, 14 January 1939, *loc. cit.* As well as being desperately short of coal, iron and steel in the spring of 1939, Italy was carrying a deficit of more than 8,000,000,000 lire on the 1938/9 budget: Mallett, Italian Naval Policy and Planning for War, p. 327.
97 AUSMM. N.485 UT, Programma di costruzioni 1939, 11 April 1939. Cartelle Numerate b.3184/f. 7.
98 AUSMM. N.490 UT, Trattato Navale di Londra 1936–Informazioni relative al programma navale 1939. Cartelle Numerate b.3184/f. 7.
99 AUSSME. Brivonesi to Galati, 1 February 1939. Rep. I-4 racc. 3/c. 5.
100 AUSSME. Dall'Bollettino Informazione dell'Ufficio di Stato Maggiore della R. Marina, 23 February 1939; Rep. I-4 racc. 6/c. 10. Stralcio Notiziario mensile stati esteri del SIM, April 1939; Rep. I-4 racc. 3/c. 5.
101 Riunione di mercoledi 10 maggio 1939: Cernuschi, *Domenico Cavagnari*, pp. 288–94.
102 Riunione al Senato (29 maggio 1939): *ibid.*, pp. 295–300 [quo., p. 300].
103 AUSMM. Trasporto in Libia dei complementi mobilitazioni per i Corpi di Armata XXo e XXIo e per la Regia Aeronautica, 18 January 1939. Direttive Generali DG 10/A2.
104 AUSMM. Promemoria di servizio per il Capo Uff. Piani–Uff. S. M.–R. Marina, 2 February 1939; N.216 bis, Schema di trasporto di un corpo di spedizione in Africa Settentrionale, 28 February 1939. Direttive Generali DG 10/A2.
105 AUSMM. Schema di trasporto di un Corpo di spedizione in A.S., con modalità marittima di Guerra, 10 March 1939; N.643, Trasporto Corpo di spedizione in Africa Settentrionale, 21 March 1939. Direttive Generali DG 10/A2.
106 Notes for Wehrmacht Discussions with Italy, 26 November 1938; *DGFP* series D vol. IV no. 412 enc., pp. 530–1.
107 AUSSME. Notizie di politica navale, 13 January 1939. Rep. I-4 racc. 3/c.5.
108 AUSMM. Salza to Cavagnari, 24 April 1939. Cartelle Numerate b.2741.
109 AUSMM. NG 1322, Lowisch to Cavagnari, 27 May 1939. Cartelle Numerate b.2741.
110 AUSMM. N.988/S, Visita del Contrammiraglio tedesco del G.N. ZIEGER, 22 June 1939. Cartelle Numerate b.2741.

111 AUSMM. Aspetto navale connesso al recente patto di Milano, 10 May 1939. Cartelle Numerate b.3277/f. 9.

112 AUSMM. N.19, Margottını to Maristat, 10 January 1939. Cartelle Numerate b. 3272/f. 4.

113 Toscano, 'Le conversazioni militari talo-tedesche', pp. 366–7.

114 Record of the Conversations at Friedrichshafen on June 20–21, 1939; *DGFP* series D vol. VI App. I/XII, p. 1121.

115 Toscano, 'Le conversazioni militari italo–tedesche', pp. 368–71.

116 *Ibid.*, p. 377.

117 Conversation between the Italian admirals Sansonetti and De Courten and rear-admiral Schniewind and captain Fricke, 21 June 1939; *DGFP* series D vol. VI App. I/XIII, pp. 1124, 1125.

118 AUSMM. Nuovi aspetti della situazione Mediterranean rispetto alla situazione del settembre 1938, 18 May 1939. Direttive Generali DG 0/A4.

119 AUSMM. Bollettino segreto N.1071–Turchia, 10 March 1939; Bollettino Giornaliero N.1195–Turchia, 21 August 1939. Cartelle Numerate b.3276/f. 6.

120 AUSMM. Necessità di accelerare l'approntamento dei bacini adatti per le nuove corazzate da 35.000 tonn. in corso di costruzione. 1 July 1939: Direttive Generali DG 0/C0. Cavagnari to Cobolli Gigli, 17 July 1939: Direttive Generali DG 2/A7.

121 AUSMM. Necessità di iniziare l'esecuzione del programma navale anno XVII e di accelerarlo, in relazione alla importanza della nostra azione in oceano Indiano, 1 July 1939. Direttive Generali DG 0/A2.

122 AUSMM Necessità di accelerare l'esecuzione delle nostre nuove construzioni navali in relazione alla influenza di esse sullo schieramento e sulla situazione delle forze avversarie in Mediterraneo, 1 July 1939. Direttive Generali DG 0/A2.

123 Santoro, *L'aeronautica italiana*, vol. I, pp. 29–31, 46, 49–50; Ristuccia, The Italian Economy under Fascism, pp. 181–2, 200.

124 AUSMM. N.11903, Operazioni aeree iniziali interessante la guerra marittima, 6 June 1939. Direttive Generali DG 0/M1.

125 ASAM. Manovre Aereo-Navali luglio 1939. Tema Generale. Direttive particolari per i Comandi di Partito Forze aeree a disposizione dei Partiti, n.d., pp. 1–2. Fondo Esercitazioni b. 11.

126 ASAM. Manovre coi quadri Anno 1939, n.d., pp. 1–3. Fondo Esercitazioni b. 11.

127 ASAM. Manovre coi quadri Anno XVII – Discussione finale, n.d., pp. 718–9, 756–64. Fondo Esercitazioni b.11.

128 ASAM. Grandi Esercitazioni della Armata del Po – Anno XVII: Intervento delle Forze Aeree, n.d. [1939], p. 3. Fondo Esercitazioni b.11.

129 The Naval Attaché in Italy to the High Command of the Navy, 1 June 1939; *DGFP* series D vol. VI. App. I/IX, pp. 1117–9.

130 Memorandum by the Officer representing the OKM with the Operations Staff of the Luftwaffe, 12 June 1939; *ibid.* App. I/X, p. 1119.

131 Relazione sul viaggio in Germania, 24–28 June XVII: Lucio Ceva, 'Altre notizie sulle conversazioni militari italo–tedesche alla vigilia della seconda

guerra mondiale (aprile–giugno 1939)', *Il Risorgimento* Anno XXX no. 3, October 1978, pp. 175–8.

132 AUSSME. N.47/A-4, Considerazioni militari sulla situazione, 18 August 1939. Rep. H-9 racc. 3/f. 3. The report was passed by Pariani to Mussolini.

133 AUSSME. N.4625, Badoglio to Valle, Cavagnari and Pariani: Direttive di carattere operativo in dipendenza della situazione internazionale, 17 August 1939. Rep. H-5 c.2(b)/12.

134 HNA. Conversation with General Pariani from 1800 on Aug. 3 [1939]. Foreign Ministry Archives K. 100.

135 AUSSME. Sintesi delle direttive verbali impartite da S.E. il sotto capo op., 9 August 1939. Rep. H-6 racc. 15.

136 AUSSME. Preparazione militare jugoslava alla frontiera albanese, 20 April 1939. Rep. H-6 racc. 15.

137 AUSSME. Armata del Po: Direzione grandi esercitazioni anno XVII, 30 July 1939, pp. 1,8. Rep. H-6 racc. 15.

138 AMR. Pariani to Soddu, 17 August 1939; Riunione, 22 August 1939. Quaderni Pariani XXXXII. AUSSME. Operazion offensive E.J., August 1939. Rep. H-6 racc. 15.

139 AUSSME. Memoria relativa al piano operativo 'E.J', 24 August 1939, p. 6. Rep. H-6 racc. 15.

140 AMR. Piano operativo Grecia, 22 August 1939. Quaderni Pariani XXXXII. The Albanian Command left the meeting envisaging a slightly different force structure: one armoured division, three auto transportable divisions, eleven infantry divisions, one alpini division and two blackshirt divisions. AUSSME. N.6667, Grandi unità di rinforzo, 31 August 1939. Rep. H-6 racc. 15.

141 AUSSME.N.72349: Piano operativo italiano in caso di conflagrazione europea, 24 August 1939. Rep. H-5 c. 2(a)/1.

142 AUSSME. Promemoria per il Duce: Chiamata del 1913, 23 August 1939; Rep. H-5 c. 2(a)/12. AMR. Pariani to Bancale, 25 August 1939; Quaderni Pariani, XXXXIII.

143 AUSSME. Dati relativi alla forza dell'esercito, 16 August 1939. Rep. H-5 c. 2(a)/2.

144 AUSMM. N.72118, Situazione dell'esercito, 23 August 1939; N.73545, Sintesi dei principali provvedimenti attuati, in rapporto alla situazione internazionale, a tutto il 26 agosto 1939, 27 August 1939. Direttive Generale DG 0/L7. De Felice contends that the recall of the reserve classes was part of a 'bluff' by Mussolini to secure another Munich conference and some kind of settlement of the Polish crisis which would satisfy Germany: Renzo De Felice, *Mussolini il duce* II: *Lo stato totalitario 1936–1940* (Turin: Einaudi, 1981), pp. 662–6.

145 AUSSMM. Esame del problema strategico in caso di conflitto, nella attuale situazione politica, 20 August 1939. Direttive Generali DG 0/A2.

146 Giovanni Ansaldo, *Il giornalista di Ciano: Diari 1932–1943* (Bologna: Il Mulino, 2000), p. 196; *cit.* Cernuschi, *Cavagnari*, p. 181.

147 AUSSME. Comunicazione del Capo di S.M. dell'esercito francese circa misure militari alla frontiera franco–italiana, 23 August 1939. Rep. H-9 racc. 3/f. 5.

148 AUSSME. N.4672, Direttive per la preparazione bellica delle terre Italiane di oltremare, 27 August 1939. Rep. H-3 c. 2(b)/12.

149 AUSSME. N.4691, Direttive di carattere operativo per le terre Italiane di oltremare in dipendenza dell'attuale situazione internazionale, 29 August 1939. Rep. H-3 c.2(b)/12.

150 AMR. Pariani to Bancale, 30 August 1939. Quaderni Pariani XXXXIII.

151 AUSMM. N.4707, Difesa contraerei aeroporti e objective di interesse aeronautico, 31 August 1939. Direttive Generali DG 0/12.

152 AUSMM. N.4713, Studi di carattere operativo in dipendenza dell'attuale situazione internazionale, 1 September 1939. Direttive Generali DG 0/12.

153 AUSMM. N.284, Piano B=Obbiettivi, 6 September 1939. Direttive Generali DG 0/M10.

154 AUSMM. N.26184, Cooperazione Armero[sic]-Navale, 8 September 1939. Direttive Generali DG 0/M1.

155 AUSMM. N.27864, Aviazione per la Marina, 13 September 1939. Direttive Generali DG 0/M1.

156 AUSMM. N.038808, Aviazione da ricognizione per la R. Marina, 16 November 1939. Direttive Generali DG 0/M1.

157 AUSMM. N.18486, Aviazione da ricognizione per la R. Marina, 6 December 1939. Direttive Generali DG 0/M1.

158 AUSMM. N.2812, Aviazione da ricognizione per la R. Marina, 22 December 1939; N.2814, Aviazione da ricognizione per la R. Marina, 22 December 1939. Direttive Generali DG 0/M1.

159 AUSMM. N.5608, Aviazione da ricognizione per la R. Marina, 2 January 1940. Direttive Generali DG 0/M1.

160 AUSMM. N.28790, Concorso dell'aviazione da caccia alla difesa delle basi navali, 18 September 1939. Direttive Generali DG 0/M1.

161 AUSSME. Riunione Soddu–Bancale, 8 September 1939. Rep. H-6 racc 15.

162 AUSSME. Nuova ripartizione delle G.U. nei vari scacchieri, 9 September 1939. Rep. H-6 racc. 15. Pariani scrawled on the memorandum 'But are there not already orders for the study of the breakthrough? Was not the normal plan against Yugoslavia based on breakthrough?'

163 AUSSME. Colloqui confidenziali con addetti militari esteri. Con addetto Greco, Col. di S.M. ASSIMACOPOULOS, 26 September 1939. Rep. H-9 racc. 4/f. 1.

164 AUSSME. Riunione, 15 September 1939. Rep. H-5 racc. 15.

165 AUSSME. Sintesi degli argomenti trattati nella riunione del 29 settembre 1939 – XVII in Roma da S.E. il Capo di S.M. dell'esercito. Rep. M-3 racc.126/f. 5.

166 AUSSME. PR. 12 Frontiera orientale, 1 November 1939. Rep. H-6 racc. 19. The section noting the possibility of using German territory as a starting point for operations is marked with an ink cross.

167 AUSSME. Ammutinamenti reparti esercito jugoslavo e situazione morale complessiva, 18 October 1939. Rep. H-9 racc. 4/f. 1.

168 AUSSME. T.261/A, Roatta to SIM, 16 September 1939; T. Sorice to Roatta, n.d. Rep. H-9 racc. 3/f. 5.

169 AUSSME. Colloquio a Monaco di Baviera tra il capo di Servizio informazioni tedesco e i capi del SIM e del SIS, 17 September 1939; att. Appunti sulla situazione politica, 16 September 1939. Rep. H-9 racc. 4/f. 1.

170 AUSSME. Colloqui confidenziali con addetti militari esteri. Con adetto ungherese, col. SZABO', 30 September 1939; Con adetto jugoslavo, magg. TROJANOVIC, 30 September 1939; Con adetto rumeno, ten. col. PETRESCO, 3 October 1939. Rep. H-9 racc.4/f. 1.

171 AUSSME. Teatri d'operazione non interessante direttamente l'Italia N. 50, 14 October 1939; Teatri d'operazioni non interessante direttamente l'Italia N.53, 17 October 1939. Rep. H-3 racc.32/f. 2.

172 AUSSME. Teatri d'operazione non interessanti direttamente l'Italia N.57, 21 October 1939. Rep. H-3 racc. 32/f. 1.

173 AUSSME. Colloqui col capo del Servizio Informazione Militare ungherese, 7 October 1939. Rep. H-9 racc. 4/f. 1.

174 AUSSME. Promemoria per il Duce, 4 November 1939; att. Promemoria 29 October 1939. Rep. H-9 racc. 5/f. 1.

175 Ciano, *Diario 1937–1943*, 5, 10 & 18 September 1939.

176 Dorello Ferrari, 'La mobilitazione dell'esercito nella seconda guerra mondiale', *Storia Contemporanea* anno XIII no. 6, December 1992, pp.1011–3, 1027; Montanari, *L'esercito italiano alla vigilia*, pp. 509–14.

177 AUSSME. Balbo to Pariani, 10 September 1939. Rep. N-11 c. 4031. See also SIM report cited in Ferrari, 'La mobilitazione dell'esercito', p. 1014.

178 AUSSME. Alcuni dati di capacità produttiva industriale nel settore armi e munizioni, August 1939; Rep. H-1 racc. 7/f. 2. Sintesi rapporto Duce (Sorice), 20 September 1939; Rep. H-9 racc. 3/f. 5.

179 AUSSME. Produzione mensile attuale e prossima delle armi di fanteria, 28 September 1939. Rep. H-5 racc. 2(a)/2.

180 Ferrari, 'La mobilitazione dell'esercito', p. 1015; Ciano, *Diario 1937–1943*, 24 September & 16 October 1939.

181 AUSMM. Necessità di iniziare l'esecuzione di una parte del programma navale–A.XVII, 12 October 1939; Unità per la posa di mine in sbarramenti offensivi, November 1939. Direttive Generali DG 0/A2.

182 AUSSME. N.912/P, SIM to Pariani, 14 September 1939. Rep. H-9 racc. 4/f. 1. The intercepted message reporting the conversation was sent by the American naval attaché to United States Naval Intelligence.

183 AUSSME. Riunione, 30 October 1939. Rep. H-10 racc. 1.

184 Pariani to Badoglio, 2 November 1939: Montanari, *Vigilia* , pp. 368.

185 Badoglio to Mussolini, 1 November 1939: Antonello Biagini and Fernando Frattolillo, eds., *Diario storico del Comando supremo* vol. I: *11.6.1940–31.8.1940–Tomo II* (Rome: Stato Maggiore dell'Esercito Ufficio Storico, 1986), pp. 157–8.

186 AUSSME. Specchio esistenza e deficienza nuove armi alla data del 1-XI-39. Rep. H-5 racc. 2(a)/2.

187 AUSSME. Promemoria per S.E. il Capo di Stato maggiore generale: dati sintetici relativi ell'efficienza della R. Marina al 25 ottobre c.a. ed a quella che si presume raggiungibile al 1o maggio 1940. Rep. H-5 racc. 2(b). The navy had raised its estimate of annual fuel requirements in war from 2,000,000 tons

in August to 3,600,000 tons, partly to take account of the four battleships due to come into service in 1940.

188 AUSSME. Promemoria per S.E. il Capo di S.M. generale: Carburanti per l'Aeronautica Italiana, 25 October 1939; Carburanti per l'Aeronautica Italiana, 31 October 1939; Efficienza bellica della R. Aeronautica alle date del 15 ottobre 1939 e del 1o maggio 1940, 31 October 1939. Rep H-5 racc. 2(b).

189 Ciano, *Diario 1937–1943*, 7 & 8 November 1939.

190 AUSSME. Sintesi operativa, 2 November 1939. Rep. H-5 racc. 46.

191 AUSSME. Argomenti da trattare alla riunione dei capi di S.M. del 16 novembre [1939]. Rep. H-10 b.1.

192 Verbale della seduta del 18 novembre 1939: [Carlo Mazzaccara and Antonello Biagini, eds.], *Verbali delle riunioni tenute dal Capo di S.M. Generale* (Rome: Ufficio Storico dello Stato Maggiore dell'Esercito, 1983), vol. I, p. 18.

193 AUSSME. Carboni to Cavallero, 21 November 1939: encl. La campagna polacca secondo la propaganda germanica. Re. H-5 racc. 2(a)/2.

194 AUSSME. Principali attività del 1940 per l'efficienza dell'esercito, 16 December 1939. Rep. H-9 racc. 5/f. 1.

195 AUSSME. Stato di efficienza dell'esercito alla data del 27 novembre 1939/XVIII per le sole unità di costituzione immediate ossia: 71 divisioni, truppe e servizi di corpo d'armata e di armata, 29 November 1939. Rep. H-5 c. 2(a)/1.

196 AUSSME. Note, 13 December 1939. Rep. H-5 c.2(b)/17.

197 AUSSME. Fabbisogno approssimato di materie prime più importante per il complemento di un complesso di 60 divisioni, 15 December 1939; Fabbisogno approssimato di materie prime più importante per l'alimentazione di un complesso di 60 divisioni nel 1o anno di Guerra, 15 December 1939; Rep. H-1 racc. 7/c. 11. N.53685, Programmi e materie prime, 27 December 1939; Rep. H-1 racc. 7/c. 8. N.3015, GITAR to War Ministry, 31 October 1939; Rep. H-3 racc. 20/f. 10. FIAT was also in the process of trying to sell forty Cr 42 fighters to Belgium.

198 AUSSME. Nota sull'efficienza dell'Esercito (Elementi per il colloquio con S.E. Ciano), 10 January 1940. Rep. H-1 racc.8/c.2.

199 Ciano, *Diario 1937–1943*, 10 January 1940.

200 AUSSME. Programma nuove artiglierie, 22 December 1939. Rep. H-9 racc. 5/f. 1. The memorandum has the annotation 'Favorevole M'.

201 AUSSME. Promemoria per il Duce: Efficienza dell'esercito, 7 February 1940. Rep. H-9 racc. 7/f. 1.

202 AUSSME. Verbale della riunione del 21 febbraio 1940, p. 6. Rep. H-10 racc. 1/f. 5.

203 AUSSME. Lavori di fortificazioni eseguiti dalla Germania alla frontiera italiana, 13 January 1940; Rep. H-9 racc. 6. Dati sommari circa sistemazione difensiva frontiera nord, 27 February 1940; Rep. H-9 racc. 7/f. 1.

204 AUSSME. Verbale della riunione del 21 febbraio 1940, pp. 1–3. Rep. H-10 racc. 1/f. 5.

205 *Ibid.*, p. 8.

206 AUSSME. Forza alle armi, 22 March 1940. Rep. H-9 racc.7/f. 1. The numbers included 67,000 men from the class of 1916, whom it was proposed to release, 170,000 men from the class of 1917 who had been recalled, and 642,000 men of the classes of 1918, 1919 and 1920.

207 AUSSME. Costituzione delle FF. NN. nel 1940, 2 January 1940. Direttive Generale DG 0/A2.

208 AUSSME. Situazione dei CC.TT., 4 January 1940; Situazione attuale del naviglio sottile, 4 January 1940. Direttive Generali DG 0/A2.

209 AUSMM. Deficienze di naviglio sottile, 22 February 1940. Direttive Generali DG 0/A2.

210 AUSMM. Entità delle FF. NN. delle potenze minori nel Levante, 15 February 1940 (and marginalia). Direttive Generali DG 0/A2.

211 AUSMM. Resoconto sommario del tema di strategia della 9a sessione della S.A.S., January 1940. Direttive Generali DG 15/A5/B3.

212 AUSMM. N.12709/10, Esplorazioni sulle basi, 24 May 1940. Direttive Generali DG 0/M1.

213 AUSSME. Collaborazione tecnica con la Germania, 22 January 1940. Rep. H-9 racc.6.

214 AUSSME. Comunicazioni dell'addetto militare germanico, 3 aprile 1940. Rep. H-9 racc. 8/ f. 1.

215 AUSSME. BN.5281, Badoglio to Mussolini, 1 April 1940; Rep. I-4 racc. 6/c. 3. Also n. 5318, Badoglio to Mussolini, 15 April 1940: Emilio Faldella, *L'Italia nella seconda guerra mondiale-revisione di giudizi* (Bologna: Capelli, 1960), p. 89.

216 Faldella, *L'Italia e la seconda Guerra mondiale*, pp. 88–9.

217 AUSSME. Collaborazione italo–germanica, 3 May 1940. Rep. H-9 racc. 8/f. 1.

218 ASMAE. Cavallero to Ciano, 28 October 1939; [Cavallero to Ciano] Possibili direttrici dell'azione militare tedesca, n.d. GAB 385 #702 b.184.

219 ASMAE. To.608557, Gallina to SIM, 22 November 1939. Affari Politici: Germania b.58.

220 Attolico to Ciano, 4 December 1939; *DDI* 9th series vol. II no. 452, p. 356.

221 UKNA. Conversazione con questo Capo di Gabinetto, 30 March 1940. GFM 36/10/fr.000812-3.

222 AUSSME. Relazione di S.E. il Ministro della Marina: Scorte, February 1940, pp. 3–4. Rep. F-9 racc. 60/f. 1.

223 AUSSME. Relazione di S.E. il Sottosegretario di Guerra: Scorte, February 1940, pp. 4, 5. Rep. F-9 racc. 60/f. 1.

224 AUSSME. Commissione Suprema di Difesa Verbali della XVII Sessione (8–14 febbraio 1940), 1a seduta 8 February 1940, pp. 9–15. Rep. F-9 racc. 57/f. 2.

225 *Ibid.*, p. 25.

226 2a seduta, 9 February 1940, pp. 37–40. *Loc. cit.*

227 3a seduta, 10 February 1940, p. 52.

228 *Ibid.*, pp. 59, 69.

229 *Ibid.*, p. 75.

230 *Ibid*, p. 77.

231 *Ibid.*, p. 79. See also Pietro Badoglio, *Italy in the Second World War* (Oxford: Oxford University Press, 1948), p. 12.

232 Ciano, *Diario 1937–1943* 12 February 1940.

233 Commissione suprema di difesa, 4a seduta 12 February, p. 101. *Loc. cit.*

234 AUSSME. Terre italiane d'oltremare: Relazione di S.E. il Ministro della Marina, February 1940, pp. 5, 12–13. Rep. F-9 racc. 62/f. 1.

235 AUSSME. Terre italiane d'oltremare: preparazione bellica in Africa settentrionale, January 1940, pp. 6–9, 11–14, 18–19, 29 [quo.]. Rep. F-9 racc. 62/f. 1.

236 5a seduta, 13 February 1940, p. 116.

237 *Ibid.*, pp. 117–8.

238 6a seduta, 14 February 1940, p. 132.

239 Bottai, *Diario 1935–1944*, 21 January 1940, p. 174.

240 Commissione suprema di difesa, 6a seduta, pp. 132–5.

241 Bottai, *Diario 1935–1944* , 14 February 1940, p. 176.

242 UKNA. Unheaded memorandum for the king, 31 March 1940. GFM 36/7/fr.000314–28. Also *OO* XXIX, pp. 364–7.

243 UKNA. Invio in Germania di un contingente italiano (Convenzione militare della triplice alleanza), 3 April 1940. GFM 36/10/000833–4

244 AUSSME. Invio di truppe in Germania, 3 June 1940. Rep. H-9 racc. 8/f. 1.

245 Seduta del 9 aprile 1940: *Verbali delle riunioni tenute dal Capo di S.M. generale*, vol. I, p. 33. Faldella gives the formula 'offensive hypotheses' which is strictly inaccurate but undoubtedly was what Graziani meant: Faldella, *L' Italia e la seconda Guerra mondiale*, p. 81

246 *Ibid.*, pp. 38, 41–2.

247 Cernuschi, *Domenico Cavagnari*, p. 206.

248 AUSSME. Sintesi riunione al gabinetto dei capi di S.M. dei C. d'A., 10 April 1940. Rep. H-5 c.2(a)/1.

249 AUSSME. Completamento programma nuove artiglierie, 20 April 1940. Rep. H-9 racc. 8/f. 1.

250 AUSSME. Visita alla frontiera occidentale, 24 April 1940; Visita alla frontiere settentrionale, 1 May 1940. Rep. H-9 racc. 2/f. 3, racc.8/f. 1.

251 AUSMM. Ripercussioni delle operazioni tedesche in Norvegia e Danimarca sulla situazione geografica–strategica marittima, 11 April 1940. Direttive Generali DG 0/A4.

252 AUSMM. Previsioni circa la dislocazione delle unità maggiori anglo–francesi nel corso del 1940, 15 April 1940. Direttive Generali DG 0/A4.

253 Promemoria consegnata al Capo del Governo dal C.S.M. della Marina (14 aprile 1940): Cernuschi, *Domenico Cavagnari*, pp. 301–2.

254 Ciano, *Diario 1937–1943*, 11 April 1940.

255 Seduta del 6 maggio 1940: *Verbali delle riunioni tenute dal Capo di S.M. generale* vol. I, pp. 43–7.

256 Ciano, *Diario 1937–1943*, 9 & 10 May 1940.

257 De Felice, *Mussolini il duce* II, p. 804.

258 Quirino Armellini, *Diario di Guerra. Nove mesi al comando supremo* (Milan: Garzanti, 1946), p. 3 (11 May 1940).

259 Bottai, *Diario 1935–1944*, 25 May 1940, pp. 191–2.

260 Franco Badini, *Vita e morte segreta di Mussolini* (Verona: Mondadori, 1978), pp. 134–5; *cit.* Cernuschi, *Domenico Cavagnari*, p. 214 fn. 4.

261 AUSSME. Comando supremo delle forze armate, 19 April 1940; Organizzazione del comando supremo e degli alti comandi in Germania, Inghilterra e Francia, 10 May 1940. Rep. H-9 racc. 2/f. 2, racc. 8/f. 1.

262 Ciano, *Diario 1937–1943*, 29 May 1940.

263 AUSSME. N/01/200.741, Balbo to Mussolini, 11 May 1940. Rep. H-9 racc. 6/IT 5728.

264 AUSSME. Pezzi anticarro per la Libia, 11 May 1940. Rep. H-9 racc. 8/f. 1.

265 AUSSME. Richieste di materiali per A.S., 13 May 1940; att. Possibilità circa invii materiali richiesti Libia, n.d.. Rep. H-9 racc. 8/f. 1.

266 AUSSME. Approntamento dell'esercito, 13 May 1940. Rep. H-9 racc. 6.

267 AUSSME. Cessione di materiali bellici da parte della Germania, 18 May 1940. Rep. H-9 racc. 8/f. 1.

268 AUSSME. Efficienza dell'esercito, 25 May 1940, p. 3. Rep. H-9 racc. 6/f. 2.

269 *Ibid.*, p. 4.

270 AUSMM. N.04172/308, Provvedimenti adottati per il graduale appuntamento dell'Esercito, 27 May 1940. Direttive Generali DG 0/L7.

271 UKNA. Verbale della riunione tenuta nella stanza del Duce a Palazzo Venezia il 29 Maggio 1940. GFM 36/10/fr.00758–66. Also *OO* XXIX, pp. 396–9.

272 Seduta del 30 maggio 1940: *Verbali delle riunioni tenute dal Capo di SM generale* vol. I, pp. 48–53.

273 Armellini, *Diario di Guerra,*, pp. 12–13 (30 May 1940).

274 UKNA. N.5226, Situazione politico–militare, 1 June 1940. GFM 36/7/fr.000367/1-2.

275 AUSMM. Cavagnari to Ministero della Guerra, 28 May 1940. Comando Supremo b.A/1/sf. 1.

276 Sonia Moore (Helphand), I Dared To Love, A Russian Memoir 1917–1940 unpubl. mss. 1994, pp. 393 [citing Leon Helphand's diary 1 June 1940]. I am grateful to Dr Brian Sullivan for this source.

277 AUSMM. Nostro contegno contro la Francia all'apertura delle ostilità, 7 June 1940; . Badoglio to Pricolo, Gaziani, Cavagnari, 7 June 1940. Comando Supremo b.B/1, b.C/3.

278 Seduta del 5 giugno 1940: *Verbali delle riunioni tenute dal capo di S.M. generale* vol. I, p. 58.

CONCLUSION

1 Bottai, *Diario 1935–1944*, 24 November, 7 & 8 December, 9 December, 29 December 1935. Ciano's *Diario* has little to say about his activities in this regard.

2 'Sintesi del Regime', 18 March 1934; 'Allarmi', 14 May 1936. *OO* XXVI, pp. 190–1, XXVIII, p. 3.

3 Mussolini to Oviglio, 5 September 1924; quo. Renzo De Felice, *Mussolini l'alleato* vol. I: *L'Italia in Guerra 1940–1943* (Turin: Einaudi, 1990), p. 77.

4 For example, Mussolini to the Service Ministries, 27 March 1937; AUSMM, Cartelle Numerate b.2724/f. 3.

5 HNA. [Un-numbered] Szabo to Hungarian Chief of Staff, 19 April 1940. Foreign Ministry Archives K. 100.
6 Burgwyn, *Italian Foreign Policy in the Inter-War Period*, p. 35.
7 AUSMM. Appunti spedizioni in Tunisia, June 1924. Direttive Generali DG 10/A4.
8 Minniti, *Fino alla guerra*, pp. 17–18, 20–1.
9 *Contra* Minniti, *Fino alla Guerra*, pp. 225–6, 232.
10 Armellini, *Diario di Guerra*, p. 23 (9 June 1940).

Appendix 1: Ministers and Heads of the Armed Forces

MINISTERS OF WAR

Gen. Armando DIAZ	21 October 1922–30 April 1924
Lt. Gen. Antonino DI GIORGIO	30 April 1924–4 April 1925
Benito MUSSOLINI (acting)	4 April 1925–3 January 1926
Benito MUSSOLINI	3 January 1926–12 September 1929
Gen. Pietro GAZZERA	12 September 1929–22 July 1933
Benito MUSSOLINI	22 July 1933–25 July 1943

UNDER-SECRETARIES OF STATE FOR WAR

Gen. Ambrogio CLERICI	4 April 1925–4 May 1925
Lt. Gen. Ugo CAVALLERO	4 May 1925–24 November 1928
Gen. Pietro GAZZERA	24 November 1928–12 September 1929
Gen. Federico BAISTROCCHI	22 July 1933–7 October 1936
Gen. Alberto PARIANI	7 October 1936–31 October 1939
Gen. Ubaldo SODDU	31 October 1939–30 November 1940

CHIEFS OF THE ARMY GENERAL STAFF

Lt. Gen. Giuseppe VACCARI	3 February 1921–11 April 1923
Lt. Gen. Giuseppe FERRARI	11 April 1923–4 May 1925
Gen. Pietro BADOGLIO	4 May 1925–1 February 1927
Gen. Giuseppe FERRARI	1 February 1927–23 February 1928
Gen. Nicola GUALTIERI	29 July 1928–4 February 1929
Gen. Alberto BONZANI	4 February 1929–1 October 1934
Gen. Federico BAISTROCCHI	1 October 1934–7 October 1936
Gen. Alberto PARIANI	7 October 1936–3 November 1939
Marshal Rodolfo GRAZIANI	3 November 1939–24 March 1941

MINISTERS OF THE NAVY

Grand Admiral Paolo THAON DI REVEL	30 October 1922–9 May 1925
Benito MUSSOLINI	10 May 1925–14 September 1929
Adm. Giuseppe SIRIANNI	15 September 1929–7 November 1933
Benito MUSSOLINI	8 November 1933–25 July 1943

UNDER-SECRETARIES OF STATE FOR THE NAVY

Adm. Giuseppe SIRIANNI	14 May 1925–12 September 1929
Adm. Domenco CAVAGNARI	7 November 1933–11 December 1940

CHIEFS OF THE NAVY GENERAL STAFF

Vice-Adm. Giuseppe DE LORENZI	11 February 1921–16 November 1922
Rear-Adm. Gino DUCCI	9 May 1923–14 May 1925
Vice-Adm. Alfredo ACTON	15 May 1925–30 December 1927
Adm. Ernesto BURZAGLI	21 December 1927–16 August 1931
Adm. Gino DUCCI	17 August 1931–31 May 1934
Adm. Domenico CAVAGNARI	1 June 1934–8 December 1940

HIGH COMMISSIONERS AND MINISTERS FOR THE AIR FORCE

Benito MUSSOLINI (High Commissioner)	24 January 1923–29 August 1925
Benito MUSSOLINI	30 August 1925–11 September 1929
Marshal Italo BALBO	12 September 1929–6 November 1933
Benito MUSSOLINI	7 November 1933–25 July 1943

UNDER-SECRETARIES OF STATE FOR AIR

Aldo FINZI (Vice-commissioner)	24 January 1923–17 June 1924
Gen. Alberto BONZANI (Vice-commissioner with the rank of under-secretary of State)	10 July 1924–6 November 1926
Italo BALBO	6 November 1926–11 September 1929
Gen. Giuseppe VALLE	6 November 1933–31 October 1939
Gen. Francesco PRICOLO	31 October 1939–15 November 1941

CHIEFS OF THE AIR FORCE GENERAL STAFF

Gen. Pier Ruggiero PICCIO	1 January 1926–6 February 1927
Gen. Armando ARMANI	10 February 1927–13 October 1928
Gen. Giuseppe VALLE	22 February 1930–10 November 1933
Gen. Antonio BOSIO	22 November 1933–22 March 1934
Gen. Giuseppe VALLE	22 March 1934–10 November 1939
Gen. Francesco PRICOLO	10 November 1939–15 November 1941

CHIEF OF THE ARMED FORCES' GENERAL STAFF

Marshal Pietro BADOGLIO	4 May 1925–4 December 1940

Appendix 2: *Italian military expenditure 1934–41 (in millions of lire)*

Fiscal year	Army	Navy	Air Force	Total armed forces	Total state
1934–5	3,036	1,360	896	5,292	22,000
1935–6	7,472	2,927	2,339	12,738	67,000
1936–7	9,460	3,491	3,728	16,679	48,000
1937–8	6,250	3,041	4,086	13,377	40,630
1938–9	7,146	4,102	4,490	15,738	43,232
1939–40	15,350	6,393	7,228	28,971	70,652

Source: Cristiano Andrea Ristuccia, *The Italian economy under fascism: 1934–1943. The rearmament paradox*, DPhil. University of Oxford 1998, p. 51.

Appendix 3: *Strength of the Regia Aeronautica 1931–9*

	1931	1932	1933	1934	1935	1936	1937	1938	1939
Land fighters	318	463	508	569	537	727	701	475	601
Sea fighters	35	100	92	102	68	72	80	23	35
Land bombers	218	379	370	347	273	473	691	614	740
Sea bombers	91	148	163	132	135	81	65	56	66
Land–Air reconnaissance	310	406	390	323	282	239	400	354	346
Sea reconnaissance	144	173	188	207	159	194	214	186	184
Transport							34	35	
Ship-board aircraft	26	33	51	65	52	50	61	75	84
TOTAL	1142	1702	1762	1745	1506	1836	2246	1818	2056

Source: ASAM. Relazioni per il Capo di stato maggiore generale, cartella 6
(All figures are for 30 June each year).

Bibliography

ARCHIVES

ARCHIVIO CENTRALE DI STATO

Carteggi di personalità:
  Pietro Badoglio
  Emilio de Bono
  Rodolfo Graziani
Ministero dell'Aeronautica, Gabinetto
Ministero della Marina, Gabinetto (Archivio Segreto) 1934–1950
Presidenza del Consiglio dei Ministri
Segretario Particolare del Duce – Carteggio Riservato

ARCHIVIO DELL'UFFICIO STORICO DELLO STATO MAGGIORE DELL'ESERCITO

F-9	Commissione di Difesa–Consiglio dell'Esercito
F-18	Oltre Mare Spagna–Gabinetto
G-29	Addetti Militari
H-1	Ministero della Guerra–Gabinetto
H-3	SIM–Notiziari stati esteri–Bolettini
H-5	Stato Maggiore del Regio Esercito–'RR'
H-6	Piani operativi
H-9	Carteggio del Capo del Governo
H-10	Verbali riunioni: SSS alla Guerra-Comando Supremo–Capo SMG–Capo SMRE–Capo del Governo
I-3	Carteggio Comando Supremo e Stato Maggiore Generale–2a Guerra Mondiale
I-4	Carteggio Stato Maggiore Generale–Comando Supremo
L-3	Studi Particolari
L-8	Libia: Diari, memorie, sussidiario
L-10	Stato Maggiore del Regio Esercito–Vari uffici
L-13	Fondi:
	Carteggio Baistrocchi
	Carteggio Bonzani
	Carteggio Gazzera
	Carteggio Marras
L-14	Carteggio sussidario Stato Maggiore del Regio Esercito
M-3	Documenti Forze Armate Italiane restituiti dagli USA (già in mano tedesca)
N-11	Diari Storici 2a Guerra Mondiale

ARCHIVIO DELL'UFFICIO STORICO DELLA MARINA MILITARE

Cartelle Numerate
Comando Supremo
Consiglio Superiore della Marina
Direttive Generali

ARCHIVIO DELL'UFFICIO STORICO DELL'AERONAUTICA MILITARE

Cartelle numerate
Fondi Esercitazioni
Relazioni per il Capo di Stato Maggiore Generale
SIOS

ARCHIVIO STORICO DEL MINISTERO DEGLI AFFARI ESTERI

Affari Politici: Francia
Affari Politici: Germania
Affari Politici: Gran Bretagna
Affari Politici: Jugoslavia
Ambasciata di Londra
Gabinetto del Ministro 1923–1929
Gabinetto del Ministro 1930–1943
Ufficio di coordinamento del Gabinetto 1936–1943

ARCHIVIO DEL MUSEI DEL RISORGIMENTO E DI STORIA
CONTEMPORANEA, COMUNE DI MILANO

Quaderni Pariani

MUSEO DEL RISORGIMENTO E DELLA RESISTENZA, COMUNE DI
VICENZA

Archivio Maresciallo d'Italia Guglielmo Pecori Giraldi

ARCHIVIO CAPPONI

Carte dell'Ammiraglio Conte Ferrante Capponi

SERVICE HISTORIQUE DE L'ARMÉE DE TERRE

Catoire Journal

HUNGARIAN NATIONAL ARCHIVES

Szabo papers, Foreign Ministry papers K. 100

UNITED KINGDOM NATIONAL ARCHIVES

F.O. 371
GFM 36
HW 12

PUBLISHED DOCUMENTS

Ciano's Diplomatic Papers, ed. Malcolm Muggeridge, London: Odhams, 1948.
Documents on British Foreign Policy series 2, London: His Majesty's Stationery Office, 1946–
Documents on British Foreign Policy series 3, London: His Majesty's Stationery Office, 1949–
Documents on German Foreign Policy series C, London: Her Majesty's Stationery Office, 1957–
Documents on German Foreign Policy series D, London: His Majesty's Stationery Office, 1949–
I Documenti Diplomatici Italiani 7th series 1922–1935, Rome: Libreria dello Stato 1953–
I Documenti Diplomatici Italiani 8th series 1935–1939, Rome: Libreria dello Stato, 1991–
I Documenti Diplomatici Italiani 9th series 1939–1943, Rome: Libreria dello Stato 1954–
Opera Omnia di Benito Mussolini, ed. Edoardo and Duilio Susmel, Florence: La Fenice, 1951/1983.
Records and Documents of the Holy See relating to the Second World War, vol. I: *The Holy See and the War in Europe, March 1939–August 1940*, London: Herder Publications, 1968.

BOOKS

Aloisi, Pompeo *Journal (25 Juillet 1932–14 Juin 1936)*, Paris: Plon, 1957.
Alvaro, Corrado *Quasi una vita. Saggi*, Milan: Mursia, 1974.
Anfuso, Filippo *Roma Berlino Salò (1936–1945)*, Milan: Garzanti, 1950.
    I capi di S M dell'esercito: Alberto Bonzani, Rome: Comando del Carpo di Stato Maggiore dell'Esercito, n.d. [1938].
Anon. *L'esercito italiano tra la 1a e la 2a guerra mondiale novembre 1918 – giugno 1940*, Rome: Ufficio Storico dello Stato Maggiore dell'Esercito, 1954.
Argiolas, Tommaso *Corfù 1923*, Rome: Giovanni Volpe, 1973.
Armellini, Quirino *Diario di Guerra. Nove mesi al comando supremo*, Milan: Garzanti, 1956.
Badini, Franco *Vita e morte segreta di Mussolini*, Verona: Mondadori, 1978.
Badoglio, Pietro *La guerra d'Etiopia*, Milan: Mondadori, 1936.
    Italy in the Second World War, Oxford: Oxford University Press, 1948.
Baer, George W. *The Coming of the Italo–Ethiopian War*, Cambridge MA: Harvard University Press, 1967.

Test case. Italy, Ethiopia and the League of Nations, Stanford: Hoover Institute, 1976.

Baldini, Alberto *Elementi di cultura militare per il cittadino italiano*, Rome: Nazione militare, anno XIII [1934–5].

Bargoni, F. *L'impegno navale italiano durante la Guerra civile spagnola*, Rome: Ufficio Storico della Marina, 1992.

Bernardi, Giovanni *Il disarmo navale fra le due guerre mondiali (1919–1939)*, Rome: Ufficio Storico della Marina Militare, 1975.

Bernotti, Romeo *Fondamenti di tattica navale*, Livorno: Raffaele Giusti, 1920.

Cinquant'anni nella marina militare, Milan: Mursia, 1971.

Biagini, Antonello & Fernando Frattolillo, eds., *Diario storico del Comando Supremo* vol. I (*11.6.1940–31.8.1940*), Rome: Ufficio Storico dello Stato Maggiore dell'Esercito, 1986.

Biagini, Antonello and Alessandro Gionfrida *Lo Stato Maggiore Generale tra le due guerre (Verbali delle riunioni presediute da Badoglio dal 1925 al 1937)*, Rome: Stato Maggiore dell'Esercito Ufficio Storico, 1997.

Bonamico, Domenico *Mahan e Caldwell*, Rome: Edizioni Roma, 1938.

Bosworth, R. J. B. *Mussolini*, London: Arnold, 2002.

Bottai, Giuseppe *Diario 1935–1944*, Milan: Rizzoli, 2001.

Botti, Ferrucio and Virgilio Ilari *Il pensiero militare italiano dal primo al secondo dopoguerra*, Rome: Ufficio Storico dello Stato Maggiore dell'Esercito, 1985.

Botti, Ferrucio & Mario Cermelli *La teoria della guerra aerea in Italia dalle origini alla seconda guerra mondiale (1884–1939)*, Rome: Ufficio Storico dell'Aeronautica Militare, 1989.

Brivonesi, Bruno *Mare e cielo. Ricordi e nostalgie di un pioniere dell'aeronautica*, Rome: Ufficio Storico dell'Aeronautica, 1968.

Buckley, Thomas H. *The United States and the Washington Conference 1921–1922*, Knoxville TN: University of Tennessee Press, 1970.

Burgwyn, H. James *Il revisionismo fascista: la sfida di Mussolini alle grandi potenze nei Balcani e sul Danubio 1925–1933*, Milan: Feltrinelli, 1979.

Italian Foreign Policy in the Interwar period, 1918–1940, Westport CT: Praeger, 1997.

Busch, Briton Cooper *Mudros to Lausanne: Britain's Frontier in West Asia, 1918–1923*, Albany NY: State University of New York Press, 1976.

Cabiati, Aldo *La Guerra lampo: Polonia–Norvegia–Francia*, Milan: Corbaccio, anno XIX [1940].

Cadoma, Luigi *Lettere famigliari (1915–1918)*, Milan: Mondadori, 1967.

Canevari, Emilio *Graziani mi ha detto*, Rome: Magi-Spinetti, 1947.

La guerra italiana: Retroscena della disfatta, Rome: Tosi, 1948.

Canosa, Romano *Graziani. Il Maresciallo d'Italia dalla guerra d'Etiopia alla Repubblica di Salò*, Milan: Mondadori, 2005.

Cantalupo, Roberto *Fu la Spagna. Ambasciata presso Franco. Aprile 1937*, Milan: Mondadori, 1948.

Cappa, Alberto *La guerra totale e la sua condotta*, Milan: Fratelli Bocca, 1940.

Carboni, Giacomo *Memorie segrete 1935–1948 'Piu che il dovere'*, Florence: Parenti, 1955.

Caroli, Giuliano *Rapporti militari fra Italia e Romania dal 1918 al 1945*, Rome: Ufficio Storico dello Stato Maggiore dell'Esercito, 2000.

Cassels, Alan *Mussolini's Early Diplomacy*, Princeton NJ: Princeton University Press, 1970.

Cavallero, Carlo *Il dramma del Maresciallo Cavallero*, Milan: Mondadori, 1952.

Caviglia, Enrico *Diario 1925–1945*, Rome: Gherardo Casini, 1952.

Cernuschi, Enrico *Domenico Cavagnari: Storia di un Ammiraglio*, Rome: Rivista Marittima, 2001.

Cervone, Pier Paolo *Enrico Caviglia l'anti Badoglio*, Milan: Mursia, 1997.

Ceva, Lucio *Le forze armate*, Turin: UTET, 1981.

Ceva, Lucio & Andrea Curami *La meccanizzazione dell'esercito fino al 1943*, Rome Ufficio Storico dell'Esercito, 1989.

Charles-Roux, F. *Souvenirs diplomatiques. Une grande ambassade à Rome 1919–1925*, Paris: Fayard, 1961.

Chiaravelli, Emilia *L'Opera della marina italiana nella guerra italo–etiopica*, Milan: Giuffrè, 1969.

Ciano, Galeazzo *Diario 1937–1943*, Milan: Rizzoli, 1980.

Clarke, J. Calvitt III *Russia and Italy against Hitler: The Bolshevik–Fascist Rapprochement of the 1930s*, Westport CT: Greenwood, 1991.

Colliva, Giuliano *Uomini e aerei nella storia dell'aeronautica militare italiana*, Milan: Bramante, 1973.

Costa, Giuseppe *La nostra flotta militare* (Torino: Lattes, 1912).

Cova, Alessandro *Graziani–Un generale per il regime* Rome: Newton Compton, 1987.

Coverdale, John F. *Italian Intervention in the Spanish Civil War*, Princeton, NJ: Princeton University Press, 1975.

D'Avanzo, Giuseppe *Ali e poltrone*, Rome: Ciarrapico, 1976.

De Biase, Carlo *L'Aquila d'Oro. Storia dello Stato Maggiore Italiano (1861–1945)* Milan: Edizioni Borghesi, 1969/70.

De Felice, Renzo *Mussolini il fascista. La conquista del potere, 1921–1925*, Turin: Einaudi, 1966.

Mussolini il fascista. L'organizzazione dello Stato fascista 1925–1929, Turin: Einaudi, 1968.

Mussolini il duce. Gli anni del consenso,1929–1936, Turin: Einaudi, 1974.

Mussolini e Hitler: I rapporti segreti 1922–1933, Florence: Le Monnier, 1975.

Mussolini il duce. Lo stato totalitario,1936–1940, Turin: Einaudi, 1981.

Mussolini l'alleato. L'Italia in guerra 1940–1943 1: *Dalla guerra 'breve' alla guerra lunga*, Turin: Einaudi, 1990.

Del Boca, Angelo *Gli Italiani in Africa Orientale: La conquista dell'Impero*, Bari: Laterza, 1979.

Le guerre coloniali del Fascismo, Bari: Laterza, 1991.

di Giamberardino, Oscar *L'Ammiraglio Millo dall'impresa dei Dardanelli alla passione dalmatica*, Livorno: Società editrice tirrena, 1950.

Di Risio, Carlo *Tempesta sul ponte di volo*, Rome: Adnkronos Libri, 1987.

Dodd, William E. jr. & Martha Dodd, eds. *Ambassador Dodd's Diary 1933–1938*, New York: Harcourt, Brace, 1941.

Donolo, Vice-admiral Luigi and James J. Tritten *The History of Italian Naval Doctrine*, United States Naval Doctrine Command 3-00-009, 1995.

Donosti, Mario [Mario Luciolli] *Mussolini e l'Europa: la politica estera fascista*, Rome: Edizione Leonardo, 1945.

Douhet, Giulio *Le profezie di Cassandra*, Genoa: Lang & Pagano, 1931.

La guerra integrale, Rome: Franco Campitelli, 1936.

Faldella, Emilio *L'Italia nella seconda Guerra mondiale–revisione di giudizi*, Bologna: Capelli, 1960.

Falessi, Cesare *Balbo Aviatore*, Milan: Mondadori, 1983.

Farrell, Nicholas *Mussolini: A New Life*, Weidenfeld & Nicolson, 2003.

Favagrossa, Carlo *Perchè perdemmo la guerra: Mussolini e la produzione bellica*, Milan: Rizzoli, 1947.

Federzoni, Luigi *1927: Diario di un ministro del fascismo*, Florence: Passigli, 1993.

Ferrante, Ezio *Il Grande Ammiraglio Paolo Thaon di Revel* (Rome: Rivista Marittima, 1989).

Il pensiero strategico navale in Italia, Rome: Rivista Marittima, 1998.

Ferrari, Paolo, ed., *La grande guerra aerea 1915–1918: Battaglie – industrie – bombardamenti – assi – aeroporti*, Valdagano: Gino Rossato, 1994.

Fioravanzo, Giuseppe *A History of Naval Tactical Thought*, Annapolis MD: Naval Institute Press, 1979.

Fucci, Franco *Emilio De Bono: Il maresciallo fucilato*, Milan: Mursia, 1989.

Gabriele, Mariano and Giuliano Friz *La politica navale italiana dal 1885 al 1915* (Rome: Ufficio Storico della Marina, 1982).

Gallinari, Vicenzo *L'esercito italiano nel primo dopoguerra 1918–1920*, Rome: Ufficio Storico dello Stato Maggiore dell'Esercito, 1980.

Garzke, William H. Jr., and Robert O. Dulin Jr. *Battleships: Axis and Neutral Battleships in World War II*, Annapolis MD: Naval Institute Press, 1985.

Gooch, John *Army, State and Society in Italy, 1870–1915*, London: Macmillan, 1989.

Grandi, Dino *La politica estera dell'Italia dal 1929 al 1932*, Rome: Bonacci, 1985.

Graziani, Rodolfo *Il fronte sud*, Milan: Mondadori, 1938.

Ho difeso la patria, Milan: Garzanti, 1948.

Guariglia, Raffaele *Ricordi 1922–1946*, Naples: Edizioni Scientifiche Italiane, 1950.

Guerri, Giordano Bruno *Galeazzo Ciano una vita 1903/1944*, Milan: Bompiani, 1979.

Guspini, Ugo *L'orecchio del regime: le intercettazioni telephoniche al tempo del fascismo*, Milan: Mursia, 1973.

Halpern, Paul G. *The Mediterranean Naval Situation 1908–1914*, Cambridge MA: Harvard University Press 1971.

The Naval War in the Mediterranean 1914–1918, London: Allen & Unwin, 1987.

Ilari, Virgilio *Storia del servizio militare in Italia: 'Nazione militare' e 'Fronte del Lavoro' (1919–1943)*, Rome: Centro Militare di Studi Storici, 1990.

Ilari, Virgilio and Antonio Sema *Marte in Orbace: Guerra, esercito e milizia nella concezione fascista della Nazione*, Ancona: Nuove Ricerche, 1988.

Knox, MacGregor *Mussolini Unleashed, 1939–1941. Politics and Strategy in Fascist Italy's Last War*, Cambridge: Cambridge University Press, 1982.

Common Destiny: Dictatorship, Foreign Policy and War in Fascist Italy and Nazi Germany, Cambridge: Cambridge University Press, 2000.

Krop, Pascal *Les Secrets de l'espionnage français de 1870 à nos jours*, Paris: J. Clattes, 1994.

Labanca, Nicola *Caporetto: storia di un disfatta*, Florence: Giunti, 1997.

Lamb, Richard *Mussolini and the British*, London: John Murray, 1997.

Longo, Luigi Emilio *Francesco Saverio Grazioli*, Rome: Ufficio Storico dello Stato Maggiore dell'Esercito, 1989.

L'attività degli addetti militari italiani all'estero fra le due guerre mondiali (1919–1939), Rome: Ufficio Storico dello Stato Maggiore dell'Esercito, 1999.

La campagna Italo–Etiopica (1935–1936), Rome: Ufficio Storico dello Stato Maggiore dell'Esercito, 2005.

Lowe, C. J. & F. Marzari *Italian Foreign Policy 1870–1940*, London: Routledge & Kegan Paul, 1975.

Mack Smith, Denis *Mussolini's Roman Empire*, Harmondsworth: Penguin, 1977.

Mussolini, London: Weidenfeld & Nicolson, 1981.

Magistrati, Massimo *L'Italia a Berlino (1937–1939)*, Milan: Mondadori, 1956.

Mallett, Robert *The Italian Navy and Fascist Expansionism 1935–1940*, London: Cass, 1998.

Mussolini and the Origins of the Second World War, 1933–1940, Basingstoke: Palgrave Macmillan, 2003.

Mayda, Giuseppe *Graziani, l'Africano. Da Neghelli a Salò* Florence: La Nuova Italia, 1992.

Mazzaccara, Carlo and Antonello Biagini, eds., *Verbali delle riunioni tenute dal Capo di S. M. generale* vol. I, Rome: Ufficio Storico dello stato Maggiore dell'Esercito, 1983.

Mazzetti, Massimo *La politica militare italiana fra le due guerre mondiali (1918–1940)*, Salerno: Edizioni Beta, 1974.

Milza, Pierre *Mussolini*, Rome: Carocci, 2000.

Minniti, Fortunato *Fino alla guerra. Strategie e conflitto nella politica di potenza di Mussolini*, Naples: Edizioni Scientifiche Italiane, 2000.

Mockler, Anthony *Haile Selassie's War*, Oxford: Oxford University Press, 1984.

Montanari, Mario *L'esercito italiano alla vigilia della 2a guerra mondiale*, Rome: Ufficio Storico dello Stato Maggiore dell'Esercito, 1982.

Mori, Renato *Mussolini e la conquista dell'Etiopia*, Florence: Le Monnier, 1978.

Moseley, Ray *Mussolini's Shadow: The Double Life of Count Galeazzo Ciano*, New Haven CT: Yale University Press, 1999.

Nello, Paulo *Dino Grandi. La formazione di un leader*, Bologna: Il Mulino, 1987.

Un fedele disubbidiente. Dino Grandi da Palazzo Chigi al 25 luglio, Bologna: Il Mulino, 1993.

O'Brien, Paul *Mussolini in the First World War: The Journalist, the Soldier, the Fascist*, Oxford: Berg, 2004.

Ojetti, Ugo *I taccuini 1914–1943*, Florence: Sansoni, 1954.

Ortona, Egidio *Diplomazia di Guerra: Diari 1937–1943*, Bologna: Il Mulino, 1993.

Pedriali, Ferdinando *Guerra di Spagna e aviazione italiana,* Pinerolo: Società Storica Pinerolese, 1989.

Pedroncini, Guy, ed., *Histoire militaire de la France* vol. III: *De 1871 à 1940*, Paris: Presses Universitaires de France, 1992.

Pelagalli, Sergio *Il generale Efisio Marras addetto militare a Berlino (1936–1943)*, Rome: Ufficio Storico dello Stato Maggiore dell'Esercito, 1994.

Pelegrini, Ernesto *Umberto Pugliese*, Rome: Ufficio Storico della Marina Militare, 1999.

Pelliccia, Antonio *La Regia Aeronautica. Dalle origini alla 2a Guerra mondiale*, Rome: Ufficio Storico dell'Aeronautica Militare, 1996.

    Il Maresciallo dell'aria Italo Balbo, Rome: Ufficio Storico dell'Aeronautica Militare, 1998.

    Giuseppe Valle. Una difficile eredità, Rome: Ufficio Storico dell'Aeronautica Militare, 1999.

Petersen, Jens *Hitler e Mussolini. La difficile alleanza*, Bari: Laterza, 1973.

Pieri, Piero and Giorgio Rochat *Badoglio*, Turin: UTET, 1974.

Pieropan, Gianni *Il generale Giuseppe Vaccari (1866–1937)*, Vicenza: Comune Montebello Vicentino, 1989.

Pini, Giorgio *Vita di Umberto Cagni*, Milan: Mondadori, 1937.

Po, Guido *La guerra marittima dell'Italia*, Milano: Corbaccio, 1934.

Quartararo, Rosaria *Roma fra Londra e Berlino. La politica estera fascista dal 1930 al 1940*, Rome: Bonacci, 1980.

    Italia–URSS 1917–1941. I rapporti politici, Naples: Edizioni Scientifiche Italiane, 1997.

Repaci, Antonino *La Marcia su Roma*, Venice: Marsilio, 1990.

Roatta, Mario *Otto milioni di baionetti. L'esercito italiano in guerra dal 1940 al 1944*, Milan: Mondadori, 1946.

Robertson, Esmonde M. *Mussolini as Empire-Builder: Europe and Africa 1932–36*, London: Macmillan, 1977.

Rocca, Gianni *I disperati. La tragedia dell'Aeronautica italiana nella seconda guerra mondiale*, Milan: Mondadori, 1993.

Rochat, Giorgio *L'esercito italiano da Vittorio Veneto a Mussolini*, Bari: Laterza, 1967.

    Militari e politici nella preparazione della campagna d'Etiopia. Studi e documenti, Milan: Franco Angeli, 1971.

    Italo Balbo aviatore e ministro dell'Aeronautica 1926–1933, Ferrara: Bovolenta, 1979.

    Italo Balbo, Turin: UTET, 1986.

    Guerre italiane in Libia e in Etiopia: Studi militari 1921–1939, Treviso: Pagus, 1991.

    Ufficiali e soldati. L'esercito italiano dalla prima alla seconda Guerra mondiale, Udine: Gaspari, 2000.

Rochat, Giorgio and Giulio Massobrio *Breve storia dell'esercito italiano dal 1861 al 1943*, Turin: Einaudi, 1978.

Rossi, F. *Mussolini e lo stato maggiore*, Rome: Tipografia Regionale, 1951.

Rovighi, Alberto and Filippo Stefani *La partecipazione italiana alla Guerra Civile Spagnola (1936–1939)*, Rome: Ufficio Storico dello Stato Maggiore dell'Esercito, 1992–3.

Rumi, Giorgio *Alle origini della politica estera fascista (1918–1923)*, Bari: Laterza, 1968.

Sadkovich, James J. *The Italian Navy in World War II*, Westport CT: Greenwood Press, 1994.

Santoro, Giuseppe *L'aeronautica italiana nella seconda guerra mondiale*, Milan–Rome: ESSE, 1950–7.

Saz, Ismael & Javier Tusell *Fascistas en España. La intervenciòn italiana en la Guerra Civil a travès de los telegramas de la 'Missione Militare in Spagna' 15 Diciembre*

1936–31 Marzo 1937, Rome: Consejo Superior de Investigaciones Cientificas Escuela Espanol de Historia y Arquelogia, Rome, 1981.

Sbacchi, Alberto *Legacy of Bitterness: Ethiopia and Fascist Italy, 1935–1941*, Lawrenceville NJ: Red Sea Press, 1997.

Schmitz, David F. *The United States and Fascist Italy 1922–1940*, Chapel Hill NC: University of North Carolina Press, 1988.

Segrè, Claudio *Italo Balbo: A Fascist Life*, Berkeley CA: University of California Press, 1987.

Seton Watson, Christopher *Italy from Liberalism to Fascism, 1870–1925*, London: Methuen, 1967.

Shorrock, William I. *From Ally to Enemy: The Enigma of Fascist Italy in French Diplomacy, 1920–1940*, Kent OH: Kent State University Press, 1988.

SIFAR *Il servizio informazioni militare italiano dalla sua costituzione alla fine della seconda guerra mondiale*, Rome: Stato Maggiore della Difesa, 1957.

Sillani, Tomaso *Le forze armate dell'Italia fascista*, Rome: La Rassegna Italiana, 1939.

Sondhaus, Lawrence *The Naval Policy of Asustria–Hungary 1867–1918*, West Lafayette IA: Purdue University Press, 1994.

Stefani, Filippo *La storia della dottrina e degli ordinamenti dell'esercito italiano: Da Vittorio Veneto alla 2a Guerra mondiale*, Rome: Ufficio Storico dello Stato Maggiore dell'Esercito, 1985.

Strang, G. Bruce *On the Fiery March: Mussolini prepares for war*, Westport CT: Praeger, 2003.

Suvich, Fulvio *Memorie 1932–1936*, Milan: Rizzoli, 1984.

Sweet, J. J. T. *Iron Arm: The Mechanization of Mussolini's Army 1920–1940*, Westport CT: Greenwood Press, 1980.

Theodoli, Alberto *A cavallo di due secoli*, Rome: La Navicella, 1950.

Toscano, Mario *Pagine di storia diplomatica contemporanea* II: *Origini e vicende della seconda Guerra mondiale*, Milan, Giuffre, 1963.

The Origins of the Pact of Steel, Baltimore MD: Johns Hopkins University Press, 1967.

Tur, Vittorio *Plancia Ammiraglio*, Rome: Canesi, 1963.

Valle, Giuseppe *Uomini nei cieli*, Rome: Centro Editoriale Nazionale, 1958.

Venè, Gian Franco *Cronaca e storia della Marcia su Roma*, Venice: Marsilio, 1990.

Visconti Prasca, Sebastiano *La guerra decisiva*, Milan: Grossi, 1934.

Waley, Daniel P. *British Public Opinion and the Abyssinian War, 1935–6*, London: Temple Smith, 1975.

ARTICLES AND CHAPTERS

Alegi, Gregory 'Sette anni di politica aeronautica', in Carlo Maria Santoro, ed., *Italo Balbo: Aviazione e potere aereo*, Rome: Aeronautica Militare, 1998, pp. 137–67.

Apostolo, Giorgio & Andrea Curami 'The Italian Air Force from 1919 to 1923', in *Adaptation de l'arme aérienne aux conflits contemporains et processus d'indépendence des armées de l'Air des origines à la fin de la Seconde Guerre mondiale*, Paris: Fondation pour les études de défense nationale, 1985, pp. 257–67.

Askew, William C. 'Italian intervention in Spain: The agreements of March 31, 1934 with the Spanish Monarchist Parties', *Journal of Modern History* vol. 24 no. 2, June 1952, pp. 181–3.

Atkinson, David 'Geopolitics, cartography and geographical knowledge: envisioning Africa from Fascist Italy', in Morag Bell, Robin Butlin and Michael Heffernan, *Geography and Imperialism 1820–1940*, Manchester: Manchester University Press, 1995, pp. 265–97.

Azzi, Stephen Corrado 'The Historiography of Fascist Foreign Policy', *Historical Journal* vol. 36 no. 1, March 1993, pp. 187–203.

Barlas, Dilek 'Friends or Foes? Diplomatic Relations between Italy and Turkey, 1923–36', *International Journal of Middle East Studies* vol. 36, 2004, pp. 231–52.

Blatt, Joel 'The Parity that meant Superiority: French naval policy towards Italy at the Washington Conference, 1921–22, and Interwar French Foreign Policy', *French Historical Studies* vol. 12 no. 2, Fall 1981, pp. 223–48.

'France and the Washington Conference' *Diplomacy & Statecraft* vol. 4 no. 3, November 1993, 192–219.

Botti, Ferrucio 'La strategia marittima negli anni venti', *Bollettino d'Archivio dell'Ufficio Storico della Marina Militare* anno II no. 3, September 1988, pp. 241–57.

Cassels, Alan 'Mussolini and German Nationalism, 1922–25', *Journal of Modern History* vol. 35 no. 2, June 1963, pp. 137–57.

'Was there a Fascist Foreign Policy? Tradition and Novelty', *International History Review* vol. 5. no. 2, May 1983, pp. 255–68.

'Reluctant Neutral: Italy and the Strategic Balance in 1939', in B. J. C. McKercher & Roch Legault, eds., *Military Planning and the Origins of the Second World War in Europe*, Westport CT: Praeger, 2000, pp. 37–58.

Cecchini, Ezio 'Organizzazione, preparazione e supporto logistico della campagna 1935–1936 in Africa Orientale', *Memorie Storiche Militari* 1979, pp. 9–38.

Ceva, Lucio 'L'alto comando da Badoglio a Cavallero (1925–1941', *Il Movimento di Liberazione in Italia* no. 110, January–March 1975, pp. 41–77.

'Un intervento di Badoglio e il mancato rinnovamento delle artiglierie italiane', *Il Risorgimento* anno XXVIII no. 2, June 1976, pp. 117–72.

'Altre notizie sulle conversazioni militari italo-tedesche alla vigilia della seconda guerra mondiale (aprile–giugno 1939)', *Il Risorgimento* Anno XXX no. 3, October 1978, pp. 151–82.

'Appunti per una storia dello Stato Maggiore Generale fino alla vigilia della "non belligeranza" (giugno 1925–luglio 1939)', *Storia Contemporanea* vol. 10 no. 2, April 1979, pp. 207–52.

'Aspetti politici e juridici dell'Alto Comando militare in Italia (1848–1941)', *Il Politico* anno XLIX no. 1, 1984, pp. 81–120.

'Influence de la guerre d'Espagne sur l'armement et les conceptions d'emploi de l'aviation de l'Italie fasciste', in *Adaptation de l'arme aérienne aux conflits contemporains et processus d'indépendence des armées de l'Air des origines à la fin de la Seconde Guerre mondiale*, Paris: Fondation pour les études de défense nationale, 1985, pp. 191–9.

'1927. Una riunione fra Mussolini e i vertici militari', *Il Politico* anno L no. 2, 1985, pp. 329–37.

'L'evoluzione dei materiali bellici in Italia', in Ennio Di Nolfo, Romain H. Rainero and Brunello Vigezzi, eds., *L'Italia e la politica di potenza in Europe (1938–40)*, Milan: Marzorati Editore, 1985, pp. 343–90.

'Ripensare Guadalajara', *Italia Contemporanea*, no.192, September 1993, pp. 473–86.

'L'ultima vittoria del fascismo. Spagna 1938–1939', *Italia Contemporanea*, no. 196, September 1994, pp. 519–35.

'Pianificazione militare e politica estera dell'Italia fascista 1923–1940', *Italia Contemporanea* no. 219, June 2000, pp. 281–92.

'The Strategy of Fascist Italy: A Premise", *Totalitarian Movements and Political Religions*, vol. 2 no. 3, Winter 2001, pp. 41–54.

Clidiakis, Harry 'Neutrality and War in Italian Policy, 1939–1940', *Journal of Contemporary History* vol. 9 no. 3, July 1974, pp. 171–90.

Crozier, Andrew J. 'Philippe Berthelot and the Rome Agreement of January 1935', *Historical Journal* vol. 26 no. 2, June 1983, pp. 413–22.

Curami, Andrea & Giorgio Apostolo 'The Italian Aviation from 1923 to 1933', in *Adaptation de l'arme aérienne aux conflits contemporains et processus d'indépendence des armées de l'Air des origines à la fin de la Seconde Guerre mondiale*, Paris: Fondation pour les études de défense nationale, 1985, pp. 269–79.

Edwards, P.G. 'Britain, Mussolini and the Locarno–Geneva System', *European Studies review* vol. 10 no. 1, January 1986, pp. 1–16.

Ferrari, Dorello 'Dalla divisione ternaria alla binaria: una pagina di storia dell'esercito italiano', *Memorie Storiche Militari* 1982, pp. 49–78.

'La mobilitazione dell'esercito nella seconda Guerra mondiale', *Storia Contemporanea*, anno XIII no. 6, December 1992, pp. 1001–46.

Gilbert, Felix 'Ciano and his Ambassadors' in Gordon A. Craig and Felix Gilbert, eds., *The Diplomats 1919–1939*, New York: Athenaeum, 1967, vol. 2 pp. 512–54.

Heiberg, Morten 'Nuove considerazioni sulla Guerra di Spagna: la storia segreta dell'intervento militare italiano', in Robert Mallett & Morten Heiberg, eds., *Pensiero ed azione totalitaria tra le due guerre mondiali: Atti del Seminario Internazionale di Orte del 5 febbraio 2000*, Orte: Centro Falisco di studi storici, 2000, pp. 45–62.

Hughes, H. Stuart 'The Early Diplomacy of Italian Fascism', in Gordon A. Craig and Felix Gilbert, eds., *The Diplomats 1919–1939*, New York: Athenaeum, 1967, vol. 1 pp. 210–33.

Jackson, Peter 'La perception des réarmaments allemand et italien et la politique navale de 1933–1939', *Révue Historique des Armées* no. 4, 2000, pp. 23–32.

Knox, MacGregor 'Conquest, Foreign and Domestic, in Fascist Italy and Nazi Germany', *Journal of Modern History* vol. 56 no. 1, March 1984, pp. 1–57.

'Fascist Italy assesses its enemies' in Ernest R. May, ed., *Knowing One's Enemies: Intelligence Assessment before the Two World Wars* Princeton NJ: Princeton University Press, 1984, pp. 347–72.

'The Sources of Italy's Defeat in 1940: Bluff or Institutionalized Incompetence?', in Carol Fink, Isobel V. Hull and MacGregor Knox, eds., *German*

Nationalism and the European Response, 1890–1945, Norman OK: University of Oklahoma Press, 1985, pp. 247–66.

'I testi "aggiustati" dei discorsi segreti di Grandi', *Passato e Presente* vol. 13, January–April 1987, pp. 97–117.

'The Italian Armed Forces, 1940–3' in Allan R. Millett and Williamson Murray, eds., *Military Effectiveness* vol III: *The Second World War,* Boston: Allen & Unwin, 1988, pp. 136–79.

'The Fascist Regime, its Foreign Policy and its Wars: An "Anti-Anti-Fascist" Orthodoxy?', *Contemporary European History* vol. 4 part 3, November 1995, pp. 347–65.

Mack Smith, Denis *Mussolini as Military Leader,* The University of Reading Stenton Lecture, 1973.

'Mussolini: reservations about Renzo De Felice's Biography', *Modern Italy* vol. 5 no. 2, 2000, pp. 193–210.

Mallett, Robert 'The Anglo–Italian Trade War Negotiations, Contraband Control and the Failure to Appease Mussolini, 1939–1940', *Diplomacy & Statecraft* vol. 8 no. 1, March 1997, pp. 137–67.

'The Italian Naval High Command and the Mediterranean Naval Crisis, January–October 1935', *Journal of Strategic Studies* vol. 22 no. 4, December 1999, pp. 77–102.

'Fascist Foreign Policy and Official Italian Views of Anthony Eden in the 1930s', *Historical Journal* vol. 43 no. 1, March 2000, pp. 157–87.

Marder, Arthur J. 'The Royal Navy and the Ethiopian Crisis of 1935–36', *American Historical Review* vol. 75 no. 5, 1970, pp. 1327–56.

Marks, Sally 'Mussolini and Locarno: Fascist Foreign Policy in Microcosm', *Journal of Contemporary History* vol. 14 no. 3, July 1979, pp. 423–39.

Marzari, Frank 'Projects for an Italian–led Balkan Bloc of Neutrals September–December 1939', *Historical Journal* vol. 13 no. 4, December 1970, pp. 767–88.

Michaelis, Meir 'Italy's Mediterranean Strategy, 1935–39', in Michael J. Cohen and Martin Kolinsky, eds., *Britain and the Middle East in the 1930s: Security problems 1935–1939,* London: Macmillan, 1992, pp. 41–60.

Mills, William C. 'The Nyon Conference: Neville Chamberlain, Anthony Eden, and the Appeasement of Italy in 1937', *International History Review* vol. 15 no. 1, February 1993, pp. 1–22.

'The Chamberlain–Grandi Conversations of July–August 1937 and the Appeasement of Italy', *International History Review* vol. 19 no. 3, August 1997, pp. 595–619.

'Sir Joseph Ball, Adrian Dingli and Neville Chamberlain's "Secret Channel" to Italy 1937–1940', *International History Review* vol. 24 no. 2, June 1997, pp. 253–317.

Minniti, Fortunato 'Il problema degli armamenti nella preparazione militare italiana dal 1935 al 1943', *Storia Contemporanea* anno X no. 1, February 1978, pp. 5–61.

'Profilo dell'iniziativa strategica italiana dalla "non belligeranza" alla "guerra parallela" ', *Storia Contemporanea* anno XVIII no. 6, December 1987, pp. 1113–95.

'Piano e ordinamento nella preparazione italiana alla guerra negli anni trenta', *Dimensioni e problemi della ricerca storica* 1, 1990, pp. 119–60.

'Oltre Adua. Lo sviluppo e la scelta della strategia operativa per la guerra contro l'Etiopia', *Società di storia militare* Quaderno 1993, pp. 85–142.

'"Il nemico vero". Gli obbiettivi dei piani di operazione contro la Gran Bretagna nel contesto etiopico (maggio 1935–maggio 1936)', *Storia Contemporanea* anno XXVI no. 4, August 1995, pp. 575–602.

'L'ipotesi più sfavorevole. Una pianificazione operativa italiana tra strategia militare e politica estera (1927–1933)', *Nuova Rivista Storica* anno LXXIX fasc. III, September–December 1995, pp. 613–50.

Montanari, Mario 'Il progetto Africa Orientale e i suoi sviluppi', *Studi storico militari* 1987, pp. 705–32.

Morewood, Steven 'The Chiefs of Staff, the "men on the spot" and the Italo-Abyssinian emergency, 1935–36', in Dick Richardson and Glyn Stone, eds., *Decisions and Diplomacy: Essays in Twentieth-century International History*, London: Routledge, 1995, pp. 83–107.

Painter, Borden W. jr. 'Renzo De Felice and the Historiography of Italian Fascism', *American Historical Review* vol. 95 no. 2, April 1990, pp. 391–405.

Paoletti, Ciro 'Le risorse materiali della Regia Aeronautica nel 1929', *Rivista Italiana Difesa* no. 4, April 2005, pp. 90–7.

Pelagalli, Sergio 'Il generale Pietro Gazzera al ministero della Guerra (1928–1933)', *Storia Contemporanea* anno XX no. 6, December 1989, pp. 1007–58.

Pelliccia, Antonio 'L'aviazione navale in Italia', unpubl. mss., *Italo Balbo Aviatore: Convegno internazionale del centenario (1896–1996)*, Rome 7–8 November 1996.

Polastro, Walter 'La marina militare italiana nel primo dopoguerra (1918–1925)', *Il Risorgimento* anno XIX no. 3, September 1977, pp. 127–70.

Preston, Paul 'Mussolini's Spanish Adventure: From Limited Risk to War', in Paul Preston and Ann L. Mackenzie, eds., *The Republic besieged: civil war in Spain, 1936–1939*, Edinburgh: Edinburgh University Press, 1996, pp. 21–51.

Quartararo, Rosaria 'Inghilterra e Italia dal Patto di Pasqua a Monaco (con un'appendice sul "canale segreto" italo-inglese)', *Storia Contemporanea* anno VII no. 4, August 1976, pp. 607–716.

'Imperial defence in the Mediterranean on the Eve of the Ethiopian Crisis, July–October 1935', *Historical Journal* vol. 20 no. 1, March 1977, pp. 185–220.

'L'Italia e lo Yemen. Uno studio sulla politica di espansione italiana nel Mar Rosso (1923–1937)', *Storia Contemporanea* anno X no. 4/5, October 1979, pp. 811–71.

Reti, Gyorgy 'Le relazioni ungaro–italiane dall'Anschluss all'occupazione della Rutenia subcarpatia (1938–39)', *Il Politico* anno LII no. 4, December 1987, pp. 577–619.

'L'Asse Berlino–Roma e l'annessione dell'Austria alla luce dei rapporti diplomatici fra Italia ed Ungheria', *Storia delle relazioni internazionali* anno VII no. 1, 1991, pp. 141–61.

Richardson, Charles O. 'The Rome Accords of January 1935 and the Coming of the Italo–Abyssinian War', *The Historian* vol. 41 no. 1, November 1978, pp. 41–58.

Robertson, Esmonde 'Hitler and Sanctions: Mussolini and the Rhineland', *European Studies Review* vol. 7 no. 4, October 1977, pp. 409–35.

Rochat, Giorgio 'Mussolini, chef de guerre (1940–1943), *Révue d'histoire de la deuxième guerre mondiale* no. 100, October 1975, pp. 43–66.

'Douhet and the Italian military Thought 1919–1930', *Adaptation de l'arme aérienne aux conflits contemporains et processus d'indépendence des armées de l'Air des origines à la fin de la Seconde Guerre mondiale*, Paris: Fondation pour les études de défense nationale, 1985, 19–30.

'L'impego dei gas nella Guerra d'Etiopia 1935–36', *Rivista di storia contemporanea* no. 1, 1988, pp. 74–109.

'L'aeronautica italiana nella guerra d'Etiopia (1935–36)', *Studi Piacentini*, vol. 7, September 1990, pp. 97–124.

'Qualche dato sugli ufficiali di complemento dell'esercito nel 1940', *Ricerche storiche* anno XXIII no. 3, September–December 1993, pp. 607–35.

'Il fascismo e la preparazione militare al conflitto mondiale' in Angelo Del Boca, Massimo Legnami & Mario G. Rossi, eds., *Il regime fascista: storia e storiografia*, Bari: Laterza, 1995, pp. 151–65.

'Monarchia e militari dal fascismo alla repubblica', *Rivista di storia contemporanea*, no. 4, 1994–5, pp. 470–83.

'L'esercito di Mussolini visto dalla Francia', *Storia e memoria* no. 2, December 2003, pp. 28–43.

'Esercito di massa e società dalla I alla II Guerra mondiale' in Gianfranco Pasquino and Franco Zannino, *Il potere militare nelle società contemporanee*, Bologna: Il Mulino, n.d., pp. 233–54.

Sadkovich, James J. 'The Development of the Italian Air Force Prior to World War II', *Military Affairs*, July 1987, pp. 128–36.

'The Indispensable Navy: Italy as a Great Power, 1911–43', in N. A. M. Rodger, ed., *Naval Power in the Twentieth century*, Annapolis MD: Naval Institute Press, 1996, pp. 66–76.

Salerno, Reynolds M. 'The French Navy and the Appeasement of Italy, 1937–9', *English Historical Review* vol. 112 no. 445, February 1997, pp. 66–104.

Santoni, Alberto 'La mancata risposta della Regia Marina alle teorie del Douhet: Analisi storica delproblema della portaerei in Italia' in Aniello Gentile, ed., *La figura e l'opera di Giulio Douhet* (Caserta: Società di storia patria di terra di lavoro, 1998), 257–69.

Segrè, Claudio, 'Douhet in Italy: Prophet Without Honor?', *Aerospace Historian* June 1979, pp. 69–80.

Sema, Antonio 'La cultura dell'esercito' in AA.VV., *Cultura e societa' negli anni del Fascismo*, Milan: Cordani Editori, 1987, pp. 91–116.

Seton-Watson, Christopher 'The Anglo–Italian Gentleman's Agreement of 1937 and its Aftermath', in Wolfgang J. Mommsen and Lothar Kettenacker, eds., *The Fascist challenge and the policy of appeasement*, London: Allen & Unwin, 1983, pp. 267–83.

Shorrock, William I. 'France, Italy, and the Eastern Mediterranean in the 1920s', *International History Review* vol. 8 no. 1, February 1986, pp. 70–82.

Sirianni, Giuseppe 'Appunti sulla costituzione degli organi di comando in guerra', *Nuova Antologia* December 1933, pp. 526–33.

Smyth, Denis 'Duce Diplomatico', *Historical Journal* vol. 21 no. 4, December 1978, pp. 981–1000.

Stafford, Paul 'The French Government and the Danzig Crisis: The Italian Dimension', *International History Review* vol. 6 no. 1, February 1984, pp. 48–87.

'The Chamberlain–Halifax visit to Rome: a reappraisal', *English Historical Review* vol. 98 no. 386, January 1983, pp. 61–100.

Strang, G. Bruce 'War and Peace: Mussolini's Road to Munich', *Diplomacy & Statecraft* vol. 10 nos. 2/3, July/November 1999, pp. 160–90.

'Imperial Dreams: The Mussolini–Laval Accords of January 1935', *Historical Journal* vol. 44 no. 3, September 2001, pp. 799–809.

Sullivan, Brian R. 'The Italian Armed Forces 1918–1940', in Allan R. Millett and Williamson Murray, eds., *Military Effectiveness* vol. II: *The Interwar Period*, Boston: Allen & Unwin, 1988, pp. 169–217.

'A Fleet in Being: The Rise and Fall of Italian Sea Power, 1861–1943', *International History Review* vol. 10 no. 1, February 1988, pp. 106–24.

'The Impatient Cat: Assessments of Military Power in Fascist Italy, 1936–1940', in Williamson Murray and Allan R. Millett, eds., *Calculations: Net Assessment and the Coming of World War II*, New York: Free Press, 1992, pp. 97–135.

'Italian Naval Power and the Washington Disarmament Conference of 1921–1922', *Diplomacy & Statecraft* vol. 4 no. 3, November 1993, pp. 220–48.

'The Italian–Ethiopian War, October 1935–November 1941: Causes, Conduct and Consequences', in A. Hamish Ion and E. J. Etherington, eds., *Great Powers and Little Wars: The Limits of Power*, Westport CT: Praeger, 1993, pp. 167–201.

'The Primacy of Politics: Civil–Military Relations and Italian Junior Officers, 1918–1940', in Elliott V. Converse III, ed., *Forging the Sword: Selecting, Educating, and Training Cadets and Junior Officers in the Modern World*, Chicago: Imprint Publications, 1998, pp. 65–81.

'From Little Brother to Senior Partner: Fascist Italian Perceptions of the Nazis and of Hitler's Regime, 1930–1936', *Intelligence & National Security* vol. 13 no. 1, spring 1998, pp. 85–108.

' "Where One Man, and One Man Only, Led." Italy's Path from Non-alignment to Non-belligerency to War, 1937–1940', in Neville Wyllie, ed., *European Neutrals and Non-Belligerents during the Second World War*, Cambridge: Cambridge University Press, 2002, pp. 119–49.

'Downfall of the Regia Aeronautica, 1933–1943', in Robin Higham and Stephen J. Harris, eds., *Why Air Forces Fail*, Lexington KY: University Press of Kentucky, 2006, pp. 135–76.

Toscano, Mario 'Le conversazioni militari italo–tedesche alla vigilia della seconda guerra mondiale', *Rivista Storica Italiana* Anno LXIV fasc. 3, December 1952, pp. 336–82.

'Eden's Mission to Rome on the Eve of the Italo–Ethiopian Conflict', in A. O. Sarkissian, ed., *Studies in Diplomatic History and Historiography in Honour of G. P. Gooch*, London: Longmans, 1961, pp. 126–52.

Watt, D.C. 'An Earlier Model for the Pact of Steel: Draft Treaties exchanged between Germany and Italy During Hitler's Visit to Rome in May 1938', *International Affairs* vol. 33 no. 2, April 1957, pp. 185–97.

'The Rome–Berlin Axis, 1936–1940: Myth and Reality', *Review of Politics* no. 22, October 1960, pp. 519–43.

Whealey, Robert H. 'Mussolini's Ideological Diplomacy: An Unpublished Document', *Journal of Modern History* vol. 39 no. 4, December 1967, pp. 432–7

UNPUBLISHED MANUSCRIPTS AND DISSERTATIONS

Budden, Michael 'British policy towards Fascist Italy in the early stages of the Second World War', PhD University of London, 1997.

Capelluti, Frank J. 'The Life and Thought of Giulio Douhet', PhD, Rutgers University 1967.

Mallett, Robert 'Italian Naval Policy and Planning for War Against Great Britain, 1935–1940', PhD University of Leeds, 1996.

Moore [Helphand], 'Sonia I Dared to Love, A Russian Memoir 1917–1940'. Unpublished Manuscript, 1994.

Ristuccia, Cristiano Andrea 'The Italian Economy under Fascism: The Rearmament Paradox', DPhil. University of Oxford, 1998.

Soddu, Ubaldo 'Memorie e riflessione di un Generale (1933–1941)' 1948.

Salerno, Reynolds M. 'The Mediterranean Triangle: Britain, France, Italy and the Origins of the Second World War, 1935–40', PhD Yale University, 1997.

Sullivan, Brian R. 'A Thirst for Glory: Mussolini, the Italian Military and the Fascist Regime, 1922–1936', PhD Columbia University, 1984.

Index